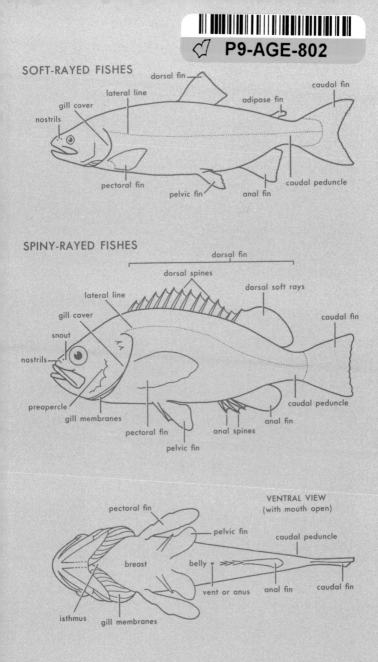

SOFT-RAYED FISHES

dorsal fin
lateral line
adipose fin
caudal fin
gill cover
nostrils
pectoral fin
pelvic fin
anal fin
caudal peduncle

SPINY-RAYED FISHES

dorsal fin
dorsal spines
dorsal soft rays
lateral line
gill cover
caudal fin
snout
nostrils
preopercle
gill membranes
pectoral fin
pelvic fin
anal spines
anal fin
caudal peduncle

VENTRAL VIEW
(with mouth open)

pectoral fin
pelvic fin
caudal peduncle
breast
belly
vent or anus
anal fin
caudal fin
isthmus
gill membranes

THE PETERSON FIELD GUIDE SERIES
Edited by Roger Tory Peterson

1. Birds — *R. T. Peterson*
2. Western Birds — *R. T. Peterson*
3. Shells of the Atlantic and Gulf Coasts and the West Indies — *Morris*
4. Butterflies — *Klots*
5. Mammals — *Burt and Grossenheider*
6. Pacific Coast Shells (including shells of Hawaii and the Gulf of California) — *Morris*
7. Rocks and Minerals — *Pough*
8. Birds of Britain and Europe — *R. T. Peterson, Mountfort, and Hollom*
9. Animal Tracks — *Murie*
10. Ferns and Their Related Families of Northeastern and Central North America — *Cobb*
11. Trees and Shrubs (Northeastern and Central North America) — *Petrides*
12. Reptiles and Amphibians of Eastern and Central North America — *Conant*
13. Birds of Texas and Adjacent States — *R. T. Peterson*
14. Rocky Mountain Wildflowers — *J. J. Craighead, F. C. Craighead, Jr., and Davis*
15. Stars and Planets — *Menzel*
16. Western Reptiles and Amphibians — *Stebbins*
17. Wildflowers of Northeastern and North-central North America — *R. T. Peterson and McKenny*
18. Mammals of Britain and Europe — *van den Brink*
19. Insects of America North of Mexico — *Borror and White*
20. Mexican Birds — *R. T. Peterson and Chalif*
21. Birds' Nests (found east of Mississippi River) — *Harrison*
22. Pacific States Wildflowers — *Niehaus and Ripper*
23. Edible Wild Plants of Eastern and Central North America — *L. Peterson*
24. Atlantic Seashore — *Gosner*
25. Western Birds' Nests — *Harrison*
26. Atmosphere — *Schaefer and Day*
27. Coral Reefs of the Caribbean and Florida — *Kaplan*
28. Pacific Coast Fishes — *Eschmeyer and Herald*

With best wishes

Bill Enrhmeyer

May 11, 1984

THE PETERSON FIELD GUIDE SERIES

A Field Guide to
Pacific Coast Fishes
of North America
from the Gulf of Alaska to Baja California

William N. Eschmeyer
Director of Research, and Curator
Department of Ichthyology
California Academy of Sciences

Earl S. Herald
Former Associate Director
Steinhart Aquarium
California Academy of Sciences

Illustrations by
Howard Hammann

Katherine P. Smith
Associate Illustrator

Sponsored by the National Audubon Society,
the National Wildlife Federation,
and the Sport Fishing Institute

HOUGHTON MIFFLIN COMPANY BOSTON
1983

For
Lisa, David, and Lanea Eschmeyer
and
Olivia W. Herald

Copyright © 1983 by William N. Eschmeyer, Olivia Walker Herald,
Howard Hammann, and Jon Gnagy

Library of Congress Cataloging in Publication Data

Eschmeyer, William N.
A field guide to Pacific Coast fishes
of North America.

(The Peterson field guide series)
Bibliography: p.
Includes index.
1. Fishes—Pacific Coast (North America)—Identifica-
tion. I. Herald, Earl Stannard. II. Title.
III. Series.
QL623.4.E83 1983   597.0979   82-11989
ISBN 0-395-26873-7
ISBN 0-395-33188-9 (pbk.)

Printed in the United States of America

M 10 9 8 7 6 5 4 3 2 1

Editor's Note

The gestation period of a *Field Guide* is long. Quite a number of years may elapse between the signing of the contract and publication of the finished book. This *Field Guide to Pacific Coast Fishes* had its seminal beginnings in 1945 when Earl Herald, then a young captain in the U.S. Air Corps, and I talked about such a book while we were assigned to the same project at the Air Force Base in Orlando, Florida.

During the latter months of World War II the Air Corps had assumed the responsibility of spraying some of the islands of the Pacific World with DDT, as a hedge against malaria. Some of the biologists in the armed services had their reservations about this new "wonder" chemical and, to its credit, the Air Corps launched the first scientific investigation into the possible side-effects on wildlife. Selected areas in central Florida were sprayed. Earl Herald monitored the fish and "herptiles," Captain Alexander Klots (who later authored the *Field Guide to the Butterflies*) assayed the impact on insects, while I made repeated censuses of the birds.

Herald, a superb swimmer and diver who knew fishes in their own environment, felt that the time was right for a *Field Guide to the Fishes* patterned after my *Field Guide to the Birds*. However, it was not until 1963 that he signed the contract and started work on this book. As Associate Director of the Steinhart Aquarium of the California Academy of Sciences in San Francisco, he had already built a formidable reputation as an ichthyologist, with many publications to his credit.

Scarcely ten years later, in 1973, his life was cut short by an unfortunate diving accident, and the task of carrying the project forward to its completion fell to his protégé, William Eschmeyer of the Academy's Department of Ichthyology. Only 9 of the plates (8 by Jon Gnagy) had been completed, and there were still 39 to go, as well as the bulk of the text. Dr. Eschmeyer (who by this time was moving up through the ranks to become the Academy's Director of Research) proved to be a highly organized and indefatigable worker, as did Howard Hammann, the artist, and Katherine Smith, his associate. Anyone who has written or illustrated a Field Guide knows that it is like serving a prison sentence — except that time is seldom shortened for good behavior.

This is the first comprehensive guide to the marine fishes found along our Pacific Coast. The fisherman, the scuba diver, the snorkeler, the underwater photographer, the marine biologist, and even the stroller on the beach will find this book a mine of information. Even the armchair naturalist, thumbing through the plates, will be fascinated by the visual feast of fishes that live out their lives in the waters off the west coast.

As Dr. Eschmeyer points out, a large number of the fishes portrayed in the color plates had not been figured before in color, mainly because most fishes lose their colors soon after they are taken from the water. Modern photographic techniques have made it possible for transitory colors to be recorded for later reference by the artist.

The observer with an ecological or environmental point of view will find a great deal of food for thought in this Field Guide. Predator-prey relationships, survival techniques, food chains, population dynamics, camouflage, symbiosis, etc., can be observed in infinite variety among the fishes.

The observation of life beneath the waves may be a recreation or a science. It can also satisfy the esthetic sense. The quality of light beneath the surface of the sea is ever-changing, engaging the eye with forms and colors that stir the imagination.

The problems of survival of the marine mammals — the whales, porpoises and seals — are easily dramatized, and a number of conservation organizations have arisen to publicize their plight. But the fishes which share the same marine waters are no less important in an evolutionary and ecological sense, and they are no less vulnerable. To those who know how to look for them, they send out signals when the sea is abused by pollution, exploitation, overfishing, or some other form of neglect. Inevitably the observant fisherman or the inquiring snorkeler becomes a monitor of the marine environment.

Roger Tory Peterson

Acknowledgments

Dr. Earl S. Herald began this guide in 1963. He was well known as the author of a very successful book, *Living Fishes of the World,* and as the TV host of "Science in Action." In addition, he was an innovative aquarium director and my first boss after graduate school. He died in a diving accident in 1973, and Houghton Mifflin Company asked me to suggest ichthyologists who I felt could complete the guide; I included my name among them, although with some hesitation. The company offered me a contract, and so began my participation in this exciting project. I am especially grateful to Mrs. Herald for her encouragement and for her assistance in providing Dr. Herald's materials and notes. Also, I want to acknowledge all who assisted Dr. Herald, especially those whose names are unavailable to me.

Preparation of a book like this one requires the cooperation of many people, and I am grateful for the generous support received from many individuals and institutions.

Perhaps only 30% of the fishes illustrated in color in this guide have been shown in color before. Since fishes lose their color when preserved, providing the illustrators with color photographs or slides or with live or recently captured specimens was a real challenge. Specimens of many of the shallow-water species were collected especially for this guide. The rarer species and deepsea fishes posed more of a problem. Through the thoughtfulness and consideration of colleagues, I was able to obtain the necessary color references.

I am grateful to the following people who gave me color slides or prints of fresh specimens, or who helped me find other sources for the color artwork: Gerald R. Allen, M. Eric Anderson, Herbert R. Axelrod, David W. Behrens, Frederick H. Berry, John C. Bleck, Michael O. Boorstein, Margaret G. Bradbury, Warren E. Burgess, Gregor M. Cailliet, Alfred D. Castro, Lo-chai Chen, Brent Cooke, Joseph Copp, Jeanne Davis, Lynn G. Dunne, John E. Fitch, W. I. Follett, Tony Frega, Warren C. Freihofer, Lloyd F. Gomez, Daniel W. Gotshall, David W. Greenfield, Gary Grossman, Leon E. Hallacher, Robert L. Hassur, Fred W. Herms, Jr., Edmund S. Hobson, Michael H. Horn, Tomio Iwamoto, Edwin Janss, Jr., Susan Jewett, Laurence L. Laurent, Robert J. Lavenberg, Robert N. Lea, Bruce M. Leaman, Milton Love, Kenneth E. Lucas, John E. McCosker, Jeffery W. Meyer, Geoffrey H. Moser, Alex E. Peden, David C. Powell, Jay C. Quast, Richard H. Rosenblatt,

Walter Schneebeli, Jack Schott, Jeffrey A. Seigel, David L. Stein, Tom Tucker, S. Jergen Westrheim, and the staff of Steinhart Aquarium.

Photographs or slides were loaned by the following institutions: Steinhart Aquarium and the Picture Collection of the California Academy of Sciences, the British Columbia Provincial Museum, T.F.H. Publications, Scripps Institution of Oceanography, California State University (Fullerton), California Department of Fish and Game, and the U.S. National Museum of Natural History.

I was able to study and photograph deepsea fishes during cruises sponsored by Oregon State University and the National Marine Fisheries Service laboratories in Seattle, Washington, and Tiburon, California. My participation in these cruises was made possible by Donald R. Gunderson, David L. Stein, William G. Pearcy, and Susumu Kato. Tomio Iwamoto made a special effort to save and photograph specimens during other cruises conducted by these organizations and by the Fisheries Research Board of Canada. Some of my field study resulted from research sponsored by a grant from the National Science Foundation (NSF 34213).

Eight of the plates (1–5, 29, 32, 33) were prepared by Jon Gnagy and one (19) by Howard Hammann under the direction of Dr. Herald. The other 39 were prepared by Howard Hammann and Katherine P. Smith under my supervision. Nearly all of the text figures were drawn by Beth A. Meinhard; Leonard J. V. Compagno assisted with the text figures of sharks and rays, helped modify plates 1–5, and prepared the initial outlines for the teeth shown in Figure 3.

What we know about fishes is based in large part on careful study by specialists. Researchers report their findings in scientific journals, and this knowledge is continually being updated and expanded. It is impossible to cite the hundreds of publications that were used in the preparation of this Field Guide, but I would like to single out these authors, whose works were particularly helpful: James E. Böhlke, Rolf L. Bolin, Lo-chai Chen, Norma Chirichigno, Leonard J. V. Compagno, Lillian J. Dempster, John E. Fitch, W. I. Follett, John L. Hart, Edmund S. Hobson, Carl L. Hubbs, Robert J. Lavenberg, Robert N. Lea, Daniel J. Miller, George S. Myers, Joseph S. Nelson, Alex E. Peden, John E. Randall, Richard H. Rosenblatt, Donald A. Thomson, Lionel A. Walford, Boyd W. Walker, Norman J. Wilimovsky, S. Jergen Westrheim, Alwyne C. Wheeler. The series, "FAO Species Identification Sheets for Fishery Purposes" (published by the Food and Agriculture Organization of the United Nations), was a valuable source of information on fish families. The following colleagues generously agreed to review portions of the manuscript within their areas of special expertise: Leonard J. V. Compagno extensively rewrote the section on sharks and rays, including much new information from his current studies. Kevin M. Howe strongly edited the section on sculpins and poachers. Comments and corrections on specific families or orders were provided by: Gerald R. Allen (damselfishes), M. Eric Anderson (zoarcids), Jonathan N. Baskin (catfishes), Frederick H. Berry (jacks), Carl E. Bond (snailfishes), Margaret G. Bradbury (batfishes), John C. Briggs (clingfishes), Warren E. Burgess (butterflyfishes), Labbish N. Chao (croakers), Lo-chai Chen (rockfishes), Daniel M. Cohen (argentines, cods, cusk-eels), Bruce B. Collette (atheriniforms, tunas, mackerels, and allies), James K. Dooley (tilefishes), Thomas H. Fraser (cardinalfishes), Ronald A. Fritzsche (pipefishes), Martin F. Gomon (wrasses), Richard L. Haedrich (veilfins, lancetfishes, squaretails, flotsamfishes, butterfishes, medusafishes), Robert L. Hassur (surfperches), Michael Hearne (smelts), Walter Ivantsoff (silversides), Tomio Iwamoto (grenadiers), Douglas F. Markle (slickheads, tubeshoulders), John E. McCosker (eels), Douglas Nelson (some sculpins), Theodore W. Pietsch (lophiiforms), William J. Richards (triglids), Joseph L. Russo (trichiurids, gempylids), David G. Smith (eels), William F. Smith-Vaniz (jacks), Victor G. Springer (blennies), John S. Stephens, Jr. (pikeblennies, blennies), Camm C. Swift (gobies), James C. Tyler (tetraodontiforms), Vadim Vladykov (lampreys).

Two experts generously reviewed the entire scientific text: John E. Fitch, former Research Director of the California Department of Fish and Game, concentrated on southern species; and Alex Peden, of the British Columbia Provincial Museum, critiqued the northern species. Both caught many errors and provided me with new "field characters" for identification and with information prior to its publication.

Others who do not fit into the above categories but who provided assistance include: Melissa A. Barbour, George C. Blasiola, Ray Brian, Freedom Child, Stephen B. Craig, William A. Dickman, F. Edward Ely, Gail Freihofer, Maurice C. Giles, James E. Gordon, Karren Hakanson, Randy Johnson, Leroy Joseph, David G. Kavanaugh, Diane L. Koepke, Johan Kooy, Gary Lam, Wayne A. Laroche, Susan Gray Marelli, Edward E. Miller, James Moberly, Robert Mohnhaup, Laurie Podshadley, Stuart G. Poss, Betty Powell, Sally Richardson, Tyson R. Roberts, William F. Rohrs, William C. Ruark, Kate Sholly, Pearl M. Sonoda, John Taylor, Margaret N. Tieger, Norman E. Weiss, and Francisca Velikoselsky.

The editors of Houghton Mifflin Company spent hundreds of hours helping with preparation of this guide. I am grateful for the assistance provided by Helen Phillips during the early stages, and thereafter to James Thompson, Lisa Gray Fisher, Peggy Burlet, Harry Foster, and Barbara Stratton. It was my pleasure (and an education) to work with all these people, and especially with Barbara Stratton, who was responsible for the final editing.

I am grateful to George E. Lindsay, Director, and to the Board of Trustees for permission to prepare this book at the California Academy of Sciences and for providing space to the illustrators.

I am indebted to Roger Tory Peterson for making this guide possible, and to other staff members of the Trade Division of Houghton Mifflin Company, including Paul Brooks, Austin Olney, Morton H. Baker, Stephen Pekich, Carol Goldenberg, Cope Cumpston, and Richard Tonachel.

Much of the format for this guide was established in collaboration with the authors of two other Peterson Field Guides in progress on fishes, and I thank C. Richard Robins and Carleton Ray and Reeve M. Bailey for their help in this phase.

It was my sincere pleasure to work with the talented illustrators Howard Hammann, Katherine P. Smith, and Beth A. Meinhard for a period of about 5 years. I also thank Lydia R. Eschmeyer and my children for their patience during preparation of this guide.

Finally, I thank my colleague Lillian J. Dempster for her assistance in all phases of the preparation of this book. This began with listing the species to be included, making plate layouts, and locating literature sources. She also provided advice on scientific and common names, kept track of new and pertinent literature, and served as proofreader, grammarian, translator, and friend.

William N. Eschmeyer
San Francisco

Contents

PLATES

(Grouped after p. 160)

A Field Guide to
Pacific Coast Fishes
of North America

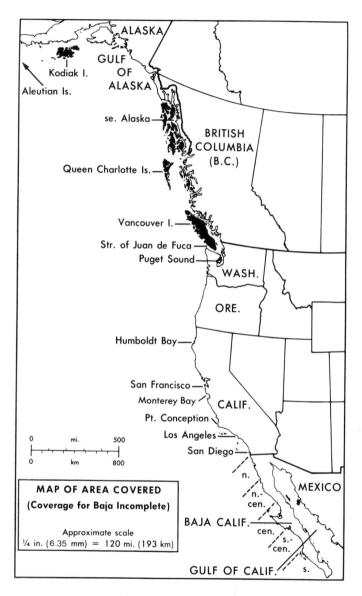

Map of Area Covered

1

About This Book

Whether you like to fish, dive, snorkel, or just enjoy an occasional stroll along the beach, at one time or another you no doubt have come across an unfamiliar fish and wondered what it was. Or you may have needed to identify a fish to comply with fishing regulations. Unfortunately, no comprehensive guide has been available to identify the marine fishes commonly encountered off the Pacific Coast of North America. *A Field Guide to Pacific Coast Fishes* is designed to fill that gap.

With a little practice in using this guide, you can easily learn to identify almost all of the common fish species in our area, and most of the uncommon ones. In fact, over 500 species are illustrated in the guide. This *Field Guide* is designed to lead you to a quick, reliable identification of all but the most challenging species. As in other Peterson Field Guides, the distinctive features of each species are highlighted on the plates (where you begin the identification process, at the center of the book) and in the text; these key features can be readily observed in fresh-caught specimens. Few specialists can remember all the species in their area; they too often begin by looking at pictures.

Since this Field Guide is for nonspecialists, technical jargon has been kept to a minimum. In the few instances where it is necessary to compare technical features (such as scale patterns) in order to distinguish between highly similar species, text illustrations have been added to make this easier. Technical terms that could not be avoided are defined in the text and/or in the Glossary, which begins on p. 305. Above all, this guide is designed for use in the field, so we hope it will find its place in your diving-gear bag, tackle box, boat, or in your pocket whenever you go near the ocean.

Area Covered. This *Field Guide* describes the fishes occurring in the marine coastal waters of the Pacific Coast of North America from the Gulf of Alaska to Baja California (see map, opposite). The species we describe do not restrict their range to that area, however; in fact, many of the species treated in this guide reach the Aleutian Islands, Bering Sea, Mexican waters, and some occur nearly worldwide. Within our primary area, all species found in depths shallower than about 650 feet (200 meters) are described in detail in their own species accounts. In addition, many deepsea fishes are included in separate accounts, in notes under other species, as family representatives, or in family accounts.

1

How to Use this Book. The key to making species identifications is to locate on a plate an illustrated specimen that closely matches your specimen. The human brain is a wonderful computer, and can quickly analyze differences between species in such important features as body shape, fin placement, and color differences. Suggestions to aid you in this visual comparison are provided on the page preceding the plates.

The major groups of fishes are arranged in this guide more or less in the order in which researchers classify them, with the exception of Plates 46–48, which show oceanic and deepsea fishes. With experience in using the guide, you will learn, for example, that sharks are on the first few plates, surfperches near the middle, and flatfishes (flounders, etc). toward the end. A short-cut index to plates showing common fish groups appears on the page preceding the first plate.

Once you have found an illustration that looks like your specimen, compare the diagnostic features highlighted by arrows on the plate and see if the brief description of that species on the legend page applies. Confirmation of your identification is important, so do not stop here. The legend will direct you to the text page where the species is described in more detail. Check each feature discussed in the species account and note whether the range given for the species includes the location where your specimen was captured. Read the information under **Similar species** carefully, to rule out look-alikes. This approach should lead you to the correct identification of nearly all shallow-water species and of the high-seas (oceanic) and deepsea species you are most likely to encounter. If you are still unsure of your identification, go back to the plates and try again.

The illustrations on the front and rear endpapers (inside the cover) show the general features of different major groups of fishes, and serve as a visual glossary for the rather limited number of anatomical terms you should learn. The Glossary (p. 305) further explains these and other unfamiliar terms.

Names. Most common and scientific names of species in this book correspond to those published in 1980 in the American Fisheries Society's *A List of Common and Scientific Names of Fishes from the United States and Canada,* known as the AFS List. Common names frequently vary with geographical region. Through the AFS List, the American Fisheries Society and the American Society of Ichthyologists and Herpetologists provide each species with an official, or primary, common name. This facilitates communication, not only between the food-processing industry and state and federal agencies, but among commercial and sport fishermen, consumers, writers, teachers, students, and scientists. The alternate common names of a few Pacific Coast fishes are so well-known that we have included them in the species headings — for example, the Sockeye or Red Salmon, *Oncorhynchus nerka.* Other alternate common names are mentioned under **Remarks** in species accounts, and are cross-referenced in the Index (pp. 313–336).

Scientific names are composed of two Latinized words, which are italicized. For example, the Sockeye Salmon is *Oncorhynchus nerka*. The first word is the name of the genus, and it always begins with a capital letter. One or more species may be included in that genus and will have *Oncorhynchus* as the first part of their name; in fact, all Pacific salmons belong to this genus. The second word, *nerka,* refers only to this one species of *Oncorhynchus*. Although scientific names are difficult to pronounce and are subject to change as zoologists' ideas of classification change, the scientific name for each species is a code word understood worldwide by all zoologists. The classification of birds and mammals is better known, so their scientific names are fairly stable. However, new fish species continue to be discovered and must be provided with a scientific name. Also, studies often reveal that two or more named species from different areas are actually the same species; in these cases the oldest scientific name has priority.

Genera are grouped into families (with names that end in "idae") and families are grouped into orders (with names ending in "iformes"). The names we use for families and orders follow the AFS List, except where more recent information is available in the technical literature or where we favor an alternate classification in current use.

Illustrations. We have portrayed fishes on the plates as they might look when alive or just captured. Those in color have been rendered from fresh-caught specimens, from photographs of fresh or live fishes, or from fishes kept in aquariums.

As you study the plates, keep in mind that, since each fish is shown from the side, only 1 pectoral and 1 pelvic fin will be visible. These fins actually come in pairs, but are usually discussed in the singular in species accounts and legends, to simplify comparisons between species.

A large species is usually shown larger than another, smaller species on the same plate but the fishes in this guide are not drawn to scale. The maximum size for each species or group of fishes is given on the legend page. Most of the original outline drawings were made from preserved specimens; in cases where they were adapted from illustrations in the technical literature, each one was compared with preserved specimens in the California Academy of Sciences fish collection. Certain technical features (such as body scales and finer details of fin rays) could not be shown, because their inclusion at the small size necessary for this book would have detracted from the overall fresh-specimen look we wanted to convey.

Over 498 specimens, representing 475 species, are shown in the 48 plates. Twenty-two of the plates are in color. Forty-four numbered line drawings are scattered throughout the text. The ones on legend pages clarify anatomical details that cannot be seen on the plates and, in some cases, illustrate rarer species that are not shown on the plates.

Size. Fishes do not grow to a set maximum size — they keep growing as long as they live, but at a slower rate as they get older. For each species we give the maximum length known — as measured from the tip of the snout (most anterior point) to the end of the caudal fin. (If the caudal fin is forked, the upper and lower lobes are pushed together slightly to achieve a maximum length.) In addition to the maximum length, sometimes we give the *usual* length of adults. Weights are given for some large species and for many sport fishes.

Measurements. Conversion to the metric system of weights and measures has already begun in the United States, but to many of us inches, feet, and pounds remain much more familiar than millimeters (mm), centimeters (cm), meters (m), and kilograms (kg). Measurements in this guide are therefore given in both kinds of units. Fishes that grow very large cannot be accurately measured to the nearest millimeter or quarter-inch or weighed to the nearest quarter-pound. Therefore, for larger fishes, lengths are rounded off to the nearest centimeter — except for a few huge fishes whose lengths are given in meters. For fishes under 10 centimeters, lengths are given to the nearest tenth of a centimeter. A rule comparing metric and U.S. units appears below and on the back cover, but a measuring tape of greater length is desirable for recording lengths of most fishes.

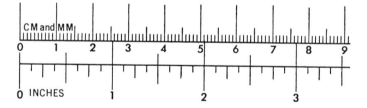

Depths of capture are variously reported in the technical literature in feet, fathoms, and meters. In this guide we use only feet and meters, and use tenth of a meter units for depths under 10 meters.

Measurements of parts of fishes are occasionally required to separate closely related species. These measurements are made on a straight line. For example, the length of the spinous dorsal fin is measured from the base of the first spine to the base of the last spine — in a straight line, not following the curvature of the body. More commonly, a comparison of two parts is used, and for this we employ the "goes into" method used by researchers. One need only "step off" (estimate) the number of times part one goes into part two, without actually measuring each part, such as "the eye diameter goes into the snout length about 2–2½ times."

Color. Although color and color pattern generally are very useful in identification of fishes, some variation among individuals of the same species is common. Radical differences in color between individual specimens of the same species are rarer, and we note these as exceptions in the guide. Young sometimes differ from adults in coloration. Fewer species show color differences between the male and female or have special breeding colors. Both sexes are illustrated on the plates when they differ markedly in coloration. In some species, individuals may have one color pattern at night and another one by day. Albino fishes are very rare, but specimens lacking pigment on part of the body are occasionally encountered. One problem in identifying fish species is that color fades quickly in captured specimens, so identifications should be made soon after capture.

Sex Differences. Males and females may vary in features other than color. One sex, usually the female, may grow to a larger size. Although fertilization is external in most fish species, in some it is internal. The males of these species often have a special organ (penislike structure) for delivering the sperm. Depending on the species, it may be a small, almost imperceptible swelling or (in some male sculpins, for example) a long, readily apparent organ. Male sharks, skates, rays, and chimaeras have fleshy claspers that are used to hold the females and aid in sperm transfer. The internal sex organs in fishes are similar, so during nonbreeding periods it is difficult to determine the sex of a fish. Usually the developing eggs give the female's ovary a granular texture, whereas the sperm in male testes is nongranular, white, and mushy. Occasionally females and males differ in other features. The anal fin may be modified or the pelvic fins may be longer in one sex, or there may be sex-linked differences in mouth parts or body shape (for example, male spawning salmons develop a hooked upper jaw).

Range. Most fish species have a restricted geographic range, but some species occur nearly worldwide. We give the total range of a species in this book, but this is usually larger than the normal range for the species. Stragglers artificially expand the normal distribution, especially in years with unusually high or low water temperatures, since each species can survive only in a certain temperature range. However, since the distributions of some species are not well-known, range extensions should be expected. These extensions should be brought to the attention of an ichthyologist at a natural history museum or to the appropriate personnel in state fish and game agencies or at public aquariums. Researchers will want to see the specimen if possible and will ask you for information on where, how, and when the capture was made.

Habitat. The habitat requirements for most species are rather precise. For example, some species occur only in rocky-bottom habitats and do not venture into other areas. Some species inhabit bays; others are found only along exposed rocky coasts or in tidepools. Still others spend their entire lives solely in or near kelp beds. Some species are territorial, and often defend a home crevice or hole; individuals of these species may spend most of their lives within a few hundred feet of their home base. The larvae of most marine species are planktonic. They ordinarily live in surface waters and move into the adult habitat as juveniles.

Activity Patterns. Fishes typically are active during the day and rest at night, but some are nocturnal. The foraging areas of a species may be different from its resting areas. For example, some fishes feed well above the bottom but retreat to the bottom at night. Many deepsea fishes migrate to surface or near-surface waters at night. Not surprisingly, the activity of tidepool and inshore fishes often is related to the tide cycle.

In some species, breeding is linked to major changes in activity patterns and distribution. For example, one or both sexes may guard the nest of eggs and stop eating during this period. The breeding site may also be located in an area that is not inhabited by that species at other times of the year. Anadromous species, such as salmons, make long migrations to fresh water to spawn. We often provide some information on habits and activity patterns in the accounts of families and species, but the format of a *Field Guide* limits the amount of natural history information we can include.

2

Collecting and Observing Fishes

As you become more interested in identifying fishes, you will probably want to catch a wider variety of species. If you are an experienced fisherman, you already know that you can catch more kinds of fishes by using a variety of baits or hooks and by fishing in different habitats. Some states allow the use of nets, traps, and similar gear; check your state's regulations for details. Certain fishes can be attracted to a light suspended over the side of a boat at night and captured with a dipnet. Another way to increase the number of species you can identify is to ask nearby fishermen if you can examine their catch. You can also learn to recognize fishes by making periodic visits to fresh fish markets or the grocery store. Public aquariums on the Pacific Coast also have excellent displays of native fishes. Consider yet another source: when you clean your catch, slit open the stomach and examine its contents. If your fish is a large predator, identifiable fishes will often be found. This will not only add to your understanding of the feeding habits of the species you catch but also to the list of Pacific Coast fishes you can identify.

Preserving Specimens. Colors of fishes fade rapidly after death, but you can slow down this process by keeping specimens out of sunlight and, if possible, on ice. They may be gutted and frozen, then thawed for later study. Unfortunately, there are no good color preservatives available. If you want to take an unusual specimen to a specialist for identification, freeze it and take it while it is still frozen. Scientists usually preserve specimens in a solution of 10% Formalin diluted from full strength Formalin (45–50% formaldehyde gas dissolved in water). This method can be used by serious collectors. Transfer the specimens to alcohol (45–50% isopropyl or 75% ethyl) after a few weeks. Labels for your specimens should be on high quality (rag) paper and capture data should be recorded in waterproof ink or typed (with a carbon ribbon).

Diving and Snorkeling. Interest in scuba diving and snorkeling has increased dramatically in recent years. Now many people can explore an underwater world that just two decades ago was unknown except to a few researchers and professional divers. The following suggestions may help you observe more underwater: Stay in one place for a length of time instead of swimming constantly over the bottom. Avoid making rapid movements, which will startle fishes and send them into hiding or chase them away; move in a casual, slow way. Since the color patterns of many fishes match their surroundings, examine the bottom carefully, or you will miss these cryptic animals. Do not forget to look into crevices, because many fishes live there. Bring an underwater slate along on your dives so you can record your observations. (You can make a slate by sanding a piece of white Plexiglass.) An ordinary pencil will write well on this surface, above or below water, and household scouring powder can be used to clean your slate.

Keeping a Journal. You will find that keeping a record of your catches and identifications will help you learn more about fishes and improve your fishing. Using waterproof ink in a sturdy field notebook, record the location, date, time of day, weather, depths fished, bait used, and species captured. Cloth fishing line with long and short bars marked (in waterproof black ink) at intervals of 10 or 25 feet (or every 5 or 10 meters) can be used to determine depths when fishing — just drop the line vertically in the water. Captains of party boats can provide you with bottom depths from their depth sounders. The length of the specimens you catch should also be entered in your journal. You can add notes on stomach contents, color, sex, and variations in features, including difficulties encountered in making identifications. If you usually fish in only a few areas, you can purchase navigation charts for those areas and annotate them, numbering your collection sites on the chart. As your journal grows, you will find it useful to cross-index it by species (so you can refer quickly to your notes on previously captured specimens). A scuba diver's field notebook will be similar, but will probably include many more observations on natural history and fish behavior.

Fish Photography. A photograph of each species you collect and identify is useful for identification and will add to your enjoyment and understanding of fishes. Photographs record colors that fade rapidly after death. They should be taken soon after capture, while the specimens are fresh and flexible. For typical fishes photograph the entire specimen from the side. Lay the pectoral fin back against the body, erect the dorsal, anal and pelvic fins, and spread the caudal fin. Sharks require, in addition, a view of the head from above and below, especially if a specialist will be consulted to confirm your identification. Photographing small specimens often requires special lenses and lighting.

Typical small fishes can be prepared for photographing in the following way. Lay the specimen on its side in a wax-bottomed pan (without liquid), which you can make by using paraffin (or just use Styrofoam or cardboard on the bottom). Refer to Fig. 1 (p. 9) to see how to pin the fins in an erect position, using noncorrosive pins (such as dressmakers' straight pins). Use a fine-bristle brush or an eyedropper to "paint" the fins with full-strength Formalin (available from pharmacies). Remove the pins after about 5 minutes and

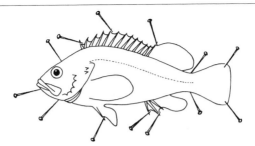

Fig. 1 A pinned-out specimen

the fins will remain erect. Then transfer your specimen to a suitable background. Specimens may be tamped dry with a paper towel to remove any liquid, which will cause glare and surface reflections; also avoid glare from direct sunlight. Place a ruler or some other object of known dimensions next to the fish so that the length of the specimen can be calculated from the slide or print. Then photograph the specimen.

Keep a record of the specimen and the frame numbers when taking photographs, or if you keep a journal, include notes on photographs taken. Write your identification and the circumstances of capture (place, date, etc.) on the slideholder or reverse of the print. As your collection grows you can arrange the photographs in an order that corresponds to the order of families or plates in this guide. (For more information on photographing fishes, consult the articles by J. E. Randall and by A. R. Emery and R. Winterbottom listed in our *References* section — p. 311).

Underwater photography of fishes is an exciting hobby but space does not allow us to discuss it in detail here. Special cameras, lenses, and housings for regular cameras are available for scuba divers and snorkelers who are interested in underwater photography. For more information, check with your local camera and dive shops.

Conservation. There are a number of endangered freshwater fish species in North America, and nearly all of them owe their precarious status to deteriorating water quality and other habitat modification or destruction by man. Fortunately, at present there are no known endangered marine species along our Pacific Coast, although in some areas, such as bays, habitat modification has caused changes in the species present. In a few cases, overfishing or heavy spearfishing has reduced population levels of certain species. Fishing regulations are designed to keep fish populations at adequate levels but at the same time to permit recreational and commercial fishing. Each state or province in our area has specific fishing regulations, and these should be consulted.

3

Jawless Fishes:
Hagfishes and Lampreys

These strange fishes are the only living representatives of the most
primitive vertebrates (Class Agnatha). They are *eel-like,* with a
long cylindrical body, but differ from eels and other fishes in a
number of major features. They have 1 or 5–16 *porelike* gill openings on each side. Hagfishes and lampreys *lack jaws, pelvic and
pectoral fins, and scales.* The body is supported, not by bone, but
by cartilage, fibrous material, and an unsegmented notochord.
About 65 species, classified in 2 orders: 1 family of hagfishes (Order
Myxiniformes) and 3 families of lampreys (Order Petromyzonti-
formes).

Order Myxiniformes
Hagfishes: Family Myxinidae

This order consists of only 1 family, the hagfishes. They are *slimy,
eel-like* fishes with 1 or 5–16 porelike gill openings, and a sucking,
funnel-like mouth surrounded by *barbels* (Fig. 20 opp. Pl.1). Hagfishes have no pectoral or pelvic fins. They live on mud bottoms of
cold seas; those at low latitudes occur in deep water — to 3500 ft.
(1067 m). Hagfishes are scavengers, occasionally seen feeding on
trawl catches or crawling out of specimens captured by longlines,
gill nets, or traps. They enter the mouth or anus of dead or confined fishes (such as ones in fish traps) and eat them from the
inside out, leaving only a "bag of bones" behind. Researchers have
caught them, using baited cans with openings just large enough for
a hagfish to enter. Known also as "slime eels" because they can
secrete bucketfuls of slime (mucus) when captured. Deposit sau-
sage-shaped egg cases on the bottom; no free larval stage. About 25
species, 5 in our area. **Note:** Besides the 2 species treated below, 3
others occur in very deep water off s. Calif.: (1) White-edged Hagfish, *Eptatretus* species, (2) Whiteface Hagfish, *Myxine circifrons,*
and (3) Bathybial Hagfish, *Myxine* species.

BLACK HAGFISH *Eptatretus deani*   **Not shown**
Identification: Similar to Pacific Hagfish but the 10–12 gill open-

ings are farther forward. Purplish black; edge of fin around rear of body sometimes pale. To 25 in. (64 cm).
Range: Se. Alaska to cen. Baja. **Habitat:** Mud bottom in deep water at 510–3800 ft. (155–1158 m); shallowest at high latitudes.
Similar species: See Pacific Hagfish (below).

PACIFIC HAGFISH
Eptatretus stoutii   **Pl. 1**
Identification: *Eel-like,* cylindrical, with *10–14 porelike gill openings. Eye not visible.* Fleshy *barbels* surround suckerlike mouth (Fig. 20 opp. Pl. 1). No pectoral or pelvic fins. Brown, tan, or gray above; lighter below. To 25 in. (64 cm).
Range: Se. Alaska to cen. Baja. **Habitat:** On or near bottom at 60–3096 ft. (18–944 m).
Remarks: Common, but rarely seen except by researchers. Horny plates on roof of mouth and on tongue rasp into the body of other fishes. Egg case (Fig. 20 opp. Pl. 1) about $1\frac{1}{4}$ x $\frac{3}{8}$ in. (3.3 x 1 cm), excluding threadlike tendrils.
Similar species: (1) Black Hagfish (above) is purplish black, has shorter head — 1st gill opening about $\frac{1}{6}$ of the way from mouth to end of tail (about $\frac{1}{4}$ in Pacific Hagfish). (2) See Note under Hagfishes (p. 10).

Order Petromyzontiformes

Jawless, eel-like vertebrates. 2 families (4 species) in the S. Hemisphere; 1 family (about 35 species) in the N. Hemisphere.

Lampreys: Family Petromyzontidae

Cylindrical, jawless, specialized vertebrates with a disk-shaped, *funnel-like mouth* armed with *horny teeth* (Fig. 21 opp. Pl. 1). No barbels. *7 porelike gill openings.* All lampreys hatch in fresh water and spend their early life as wormlike larvae (ammocoetes) in bottom sediment of rivers. After several years they undergo a radical change (transformation) to adulthood. At this stage, parasitic species develop rasplike teeth and a modified digestive tract. Nonparasitic species develop similar teeth but the digestive tract degenerates, and feeding and growth stop. Parasitic species feed by attaching themselves to other fishes and withdrawing blood (aided by an anticoagulant in their saliva) or consuming hunks of the host's flesh. Adults of several parasitic species move to the sea but must return to fresh water to spawn (anadromous movement). Some anadromous species grow to over $2\frac{1}{2}$ ft. (76 cm); nonparasitic freshwater species rarely exceed 1 ft. (30 cm). Lampreys occur throughout the N. Hemisphere. About 35 species, most in fresh water; 2 species (parasitic and anadromous) in our area.

RIVER LAMPREY *Lampetra ayresii*   **Not shown**
Identification: Similar to Pacific Lamprey but suckerlike mouth
has *3* lateral teeth and *2* supraoral teeth (Fig. 21 opp. Pl. 1). Metallic blue-black above, silvery on side, pale below. To 1 ft. (30 cm).
Range: Se. Alaska to San Francisco Bay. **Habitat:** Young in fresh
water; adults move to sea, return to fresh water to spawn.
Remarks: Parasitic and anadromous; when in sea, apparently
near shore. Feeds by ripping hunks of flesh from other fishes (especially herrings and salmons).
Similar species: See Pacific Lamprey (below).

PACIFIC LAMPREY *Lampetra tridentata*   **Pl. 1**
Identification: Eel-like, with a row of *7 porelike gill openings.* No
jaws; *mouth suckerlike,* with 4 lateral and 3 supraoral teeth (Fig.
21 opp. Pl. 1). Brown to bluish black above; paler below. To $2\frac{1}{2}$ ft.
(76 cm).
Range: Japan and Bering Sea to n.-cen. Baja. **Habitat:** Adults
usually in ocean; enter freshwater streams and lakes in spring and
summer to spawn. Young remain in gravel of stream bottom for
several years before migrating to ocean. Widespread in ocean,
often well offshore; near surface to 820 ft. (250 m).
Remarks: Attaches itself primarily to other fishes, from which it
draws blood and body fluids as food. Occasionally caught in trawls.
Eaten by sperm whales, harbor and fur seals. Scars from lamprey wounds are occasionally seen on such fishes as salmons,
Walleye Pollock, and Pacific Hake. Typical range of this lamprey,
including spawning area, is western N. America; adults captured in
the Bering Sea and Japan probably migrated or were carried there
by other fishes or whales.
Similar species: (1) River Lamprey (above) has 3 lateral and 2
supraoral teeth. (2) In eels and eel-like *jawed* fishes, mouth not
funnel-like; only 1 gill opening.

4

Cartilaginous Fishes:
Sharks, Rays, and Chimaeras

As the name implies, cartilaginous fishes, unlike bony fishes (Chapter 5), have a skeleton of cartilage, which is usually calcified but is not true bone. Their fins contain cartilaginous rodlike supports (ceratotrichia) — not bony spines or soft rays, as in bony fishes. (A spine is present at the front of each dorsal fin in some cartilaginous fishes.)

Cartilaginous fishes are divided into 2 groups: (1) sharks and rays (Subclass Elasmobranchi) and (2) chimaeras (Subclass Holocephali). Scales of most sharks and rays are small and toothlike (dermal denticles or placoid scales); they rarely overlap. Chimaeras (except the young of some species) are naked (unscaled). Sharks and rays have 5–7 gill slits on each side; chimaeras have 1. All male cartilaginous fishes have an elongate fleshy copulatory organ (clasper) at each pelvic fin. Male chimaeras also have a second pair of claspers (in front of the pelvic fins) and a strange clublike appendage on the forehead. Fertilization is internal. Oviparous species lay egg cases (Fig. 2); ovoviviparous species keep their eggs in the oviduct until the young hatch; still other species are viviparous and bear live young (which are nourished by a placentalike structure in the oviduct until birth).

Sharks and rays are predominantly marine; however, a few species enter fresh water, and a few live only in fresh water. The approximately 800 species are classified by some researchers into as many as 18 orders and 29 families. For identification purposes we treat them in 3 groups: (1) Typical sharks (p. 15) have a "shark" shape and gill slits on the side of the head. (2) Angel sharks (p. 44) are shaped much like rays, but their gill slits are partly on the side of the head and their large pectoral fins are not attached to the head. (3) Rays (p. 45) have a flattened head and body, with gill slits on the underside; the pectoral fins extend forward and are attached to the head, so that the head and body form a disk.

The approximately 35 species of chimaeras are marine, mostly in deep water, and are classified in 3 families (p. 59).

Egg cases (Mermaid's Purses) are found on
beaches, in adults, in trawl catches, etc.

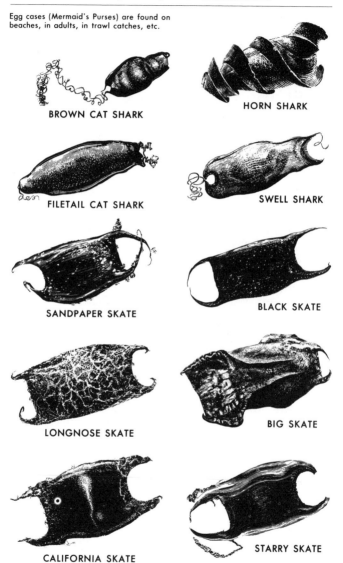

BROWN CAT SHARK

HORN SHARK

FILETAIL CAT SHARK

SWELL SHARK

SANDPAPER SKATE

BLACK SKATE

LONGNOSE SKATE

BIG SKATE

CALIFORNIA SKATE

STARRY SKATE

Fig. 2 Egg cases of certain sharks and skates

TYPICAL SHARKS

All but a few sharks are in this group. Most have a "shark" shape and a large mouth, usually on the underside of the head. Most have 5 gill slits on the side of the head, in front of or slightly above the pectoral fin; some have 6 or 7. Usually 1 anal and 2 dorsal fins, but sometimes no anal or only 1 dorsal fin. The skin is usually covered with denticles, giving it a sandpaperlike texture. The upper lobe of the caudal fin is usually longer than the lower lobe, and the vertebral column continues into the upper lobe, making the fin heterocercal. Most species are of moderate size but some are huge: the Basking Shark at 45 ft. (14 m) and the Whale Shark at over 60 ft. (18 m) are the largest fishes. Other species are very small — under 1 ft. (30 cm). Most sharks have sharp teeth (Fig. 3); all are predators, but the largest ones feed primarily on tiny plankton strained from the water. Some swim constantly; many rest on the bottom or in caves. Sharks are found in all oceans; many species occur in warm shallow water, but some are found only in the deep sea. In the tropics a few enter fresh water. The approximately 300 species are classified in 6 orders; about 35 species in our area.

Although the general conception of a shark is one of a huge ferocious man-eater, most do not fit this image. About 25 species are known to attack man; another 40 or so are potentially dangerous but no attacks by them have been recorded. The others are too small, too weakly armed, or live too deep. All large sharks, however, should be considered potentially dangerous to swimmers and divers and should not be molested or provoked.

Order Hexanchiformes

Mainly large deepwater sharks with 1 dorsal fin and 6–7 gill slits. Thought by many researchers to be the most primitive living sharks. 2–3 small families belong in this order; frill sharks and cow sharks occur in our area. Number of species uncertain (5 or more); 3 in our area.

Frill Sharks: Family Chlamydoselachidae

FRILL SHARK *Chlamydoselachus anguineus*   **Fig. 4, p. 21**
Identification: Elongate, with a *snakelike head* and *mouth* and *6 gill slits with wrinkled ("frilled") covers* (note collarlike cover at front, which connects 1st pair of gill slits). Only 1 dorsal fin (2 in most sharks). Lateral line an open canal. Mouth near front of snout. Teeth *3-cusped* (Fig. 3, no. 1; p. 16), *in prominent rows across jaws*. Brown to purplish black above; lighter below. To 6½ ft. (2 m). *(continued on p. 19)*

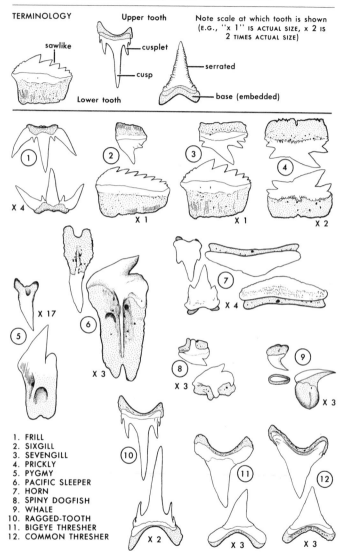

TERMINOLOGY

Upper tooth

Note scale at which tooth is shown (E.G., "x 1" IS ACTUAL SIZE, x 2 IS 2 TIMES ACTUAL SIZE)

sawlike

cusplet

cusp

Lower tooth

serrated

base (embedded)

1. FRILL
2. SIXGILL
3. SEVENGILL
4. PRICKLY
5. PYGMY
6. PACIFIC SLEEPER
7. HORN
8. SPINY DOGFISH
9. WHALE
10. RAGGED-TOOTH
11. BIGEYE THRESHER
12. COMMON THRESHER

Fig. 3 Teeth of sharks

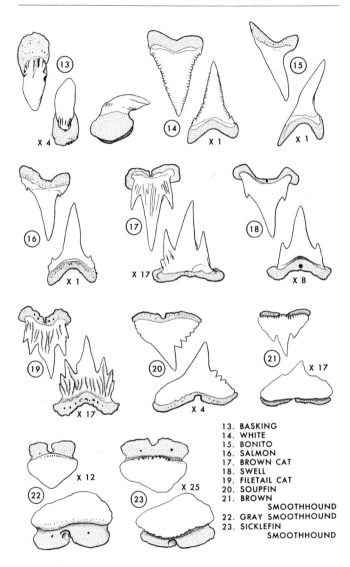

13. BASKING
14. WHITE
15. BONITO
16. SALMON
17. BROWN CAT
18. SWELL
19. FILETAIL CAT
20. SOUPFIN
21. BROWN
          SMOOTHHOUND
22. GRAY SMOOTHHOUND
23. SICKLEFIN
          SMOOTHHOUND

Fig. 3 Teeth of sharks (continued)

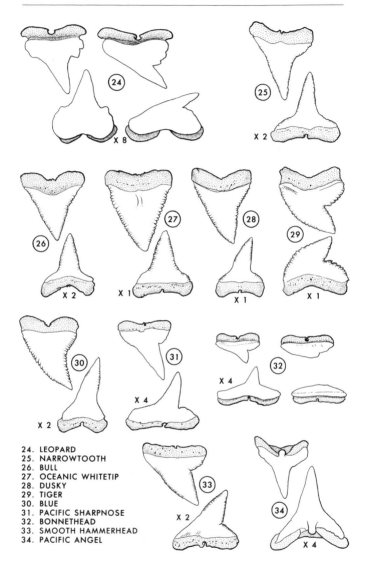

24. LEOPARD
25. NARROWTOOTH
26. BULL
27. OCEANIC WHITETIP
28. DUSKY
29. TIGER
30. BLUE
31. PACIFIC SHARPNOSE
32. BONNETHEAD
33. SMOOTH HAMMERHEAD
34. PACIFIC ANGEL

Fig. 3 Teeth of sharks (continued)

Range: E. Atlantic, s. Indian Ocean, New Zealand, Australia, Japan, and e. Pacific; 1 captured in a gill net near surface off Pt. Arguello (s. Calif.), another off Baja. **Habitat:** Usually in deep water — 400-4400 ft. (122-1340 m) or more — but occasionally at surface.

Remarks: One species in the family. Feeding habits virtually unknown; fish remains found in stomach of some specimens. Ovoviviparous, with huge eggs — about 4 in. (10 cm). 6-12 pups per litter; newborn about 2 ft. (61 cm).

Similar species: Cow sharks (below) that have 6 gill slits lack frilled covers, have mouth on underside of head, and different teeth.

Cow Sharks: Family Hexanchidae

This family and the frill sharks (above) are our only sharks with *1 dorsal fin* and *6-7 (not 5) gill slits.* Teeth in upper jaw pointed and small; ones in lower jaw *sawtoothlike.* Cow sharks are moderate to large. They live on or near the bottom in temperate and tropical seas, usually in deep water (but in high latitudes often enter bays). They are ovoviviparous. The family name refers to the heavy bulky body of these sharks. 3 or more species, 2 in our area.

SIXGILL SHARK *Hexanchus griseus*   **Pl. 1**
Identification: Unspotted, with *6 gill slits, 1 dorsal fin,* mouth on underside of head. Lower teeth *sawtoothlike* (Fig. 3, no. 2; p. 16). Dark brown or gray to black above; usually slightly lighter below. Most have a lighter streak along side. Eye greenish. Largest recorded specimen 15½ ft. (4.7 m), 1300 lb. (590 kg).
Range: Temperate seas worldwide; Aleutian Is. to n. Baja.
Habitat: In our area young in deeper parts of bays, adults probably in deep water. Captured elsewhere below 300 ft. (91 m); 1 taken off Portugal at 6133 ft. (1869 m).
Remarks: Eats fishes and crustaceans. May snap when caught, but none involved in unprovoked attacks. Litters large (22-108); newborn 2-3 ft. (61-91 cm).
Similar species: (1) Sevengill Shark (below) has 7 gill slits; body spotted. (2) Other similar sharks (except the Frill Shark) have 5 gill slits. (3) Frill Shark (p. 15) has different head shape with mouth at front and different teeth, frilled gill slits.

SEVENGILL SHARK *Notorynchus cepedianus*   **Pl. 1**
Identification: Our only shark with *7 gill slits. 1 dorsal fin.* Sandy gray to reddish above; paler below, with *scattered black spots.* Lower teeth *sawtoothlike* (Fig. 3, no. 3; p. 16). Males to at least 6⅚ ft. (2.1 m), 80 lb. (36 kg); females to 9 ft. (2.7 m), 326 lb. (148 kg).
Range: Temperate waters of S. Atlantic, Pacific, and Indian

Ocean; n. B.C. to Gulf of Calif., but most common off cen. Calif.; also Chile. **Habitat:** Often in shallow bays from B.C. to cen. Calif.; deeper off s. Calif.

Remarks: Eats fishes (including small sharks and Bat Rays) and sometimes carrion. Can be aggressive and dangerous when provoked or captured; no unprovoked attacks on humans recorded. Some researchers treat specimens from our area as a separate species, *Notorynchus maculatus*.

Similar species: (1) Sixgill Shark (p. 19) and (2) Frill Shark (p. 15) have 6 gill slits; other sharks in our area have 5.

Order Squaliformes

A large group of mainly small temperate-water and deepwater sharks. *No anal fin,* 2 dorsal fins. Snout long; mouth usually small, on underside of head; teeth often sharp and cutting. 2 families (but classifications differ); both in our area. About 65–75 species, 5 in our area.

Bramble Sharks: Family Echinorhinidae

These large sharks differ from the related dogfish sharks (see p. 22) in having most of the 1st dorsal fin *over* the pelvic fin. Denticles on body and head conical or platelike, with strong ridges. Spiracles small. Bramble sharks are not well known but occur virtually worldwide in temperate and tropical seas. Found in deep water — to at least 3000 ft. (914 m) — on outer continental shelves, upper continental slopes, and in submarine canyons. They feed on other sharks, bony fishes, cephalopods, and crustaceans. Ovoviviparous. 2 species, 1 in our area.

PRICKLY SHARK *Echinorhinus cookei*   **Fig. 4, p. 21**
Identification: Heavy-bodied, *dark brown* or grayish to black, with bristlelike denticles. *No anal fin.* 2 dorsal fins, *far back; 1st over large pelvic fin.* No spine at front of either dorsal fin. Teeth in both jaws flat and cutting, with 1–5 cusps (Fig. 3, no. 4; p. 16). In our area to 8 ft. (2.4 m); largest known 13 ft. (4 m).
Range: Off cen. Calif. to Baja and Gulf of Calif.; also Peru, Hawaii, and New Zealand. **Habitat:** Bottom-dwelling, in our area at 60–919 ft. (18–280 m).
Remarks: Most specimens seen in our area are immature; adults probably occur in deep water. Eats fishes (including other sharks) and octopuses.
Similar species: In dogfish sharks (p. 22), entire 1st dorsal fin is in front of the pelvic fin, and there is often a spine at the front of each dorsal fin.

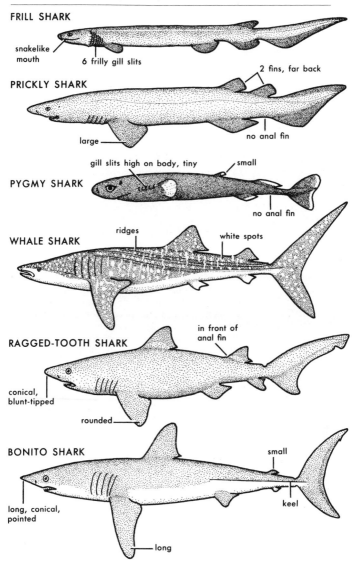

FRILL SHARK
snakelike mouth
6 frilly gill slits

PRICKLY SHARK
2 fins, far back
large
no anal fin

PYGMY SHARK
gill slits high on body, tiny
small
no anal fin

WHALE SHARK
ridges
white spots

RAGGED-TOOTH SHARK
in front of anal fin
conical, blunt-tipped
rounded

BONITO SHARK
small
long, conical, pointed
keel
long

Fig. 4 Some rare and uncommon sharks

Dogfish Sharks: Family Squalidae

A large group of sharks, mostly small in size. Like the Prickly Shark, they have *no anal fin;* but the entire 1st dorsal fin is *in front of* the pelvic fin, a *spine* is usually *at the front* of each dorsal fin, the denticles are smaller, and the spiracles are much larger. The largest dogfish sharks (sleeper sharks) grow to 13–21 ft. (4–6.4 m), but most are under 5 ft. (1.5 m). Some, at less than 6 in. (15 cm), are the smallest sharks known.

Dogfish sharks are found mostly in deep water on outer continental shelves, upper continental slopes, and insular slopes. They have been caught as deep as 9000 ft. (2743 m) and probably occur in deeper water. In tropical waters some species are pelagic but none regularly occur inshore. Sleeper sharks (*Somniosus* species) are the only sharks normally found in the arctic and subarctic. Dogfish sharks mainly eat fishes, crustaceans, and cephalopods; larger sleeper sharks also eat seals. Some dogfish sharks have light-producing skin organs. Ovoviviparous. About 65–70 species, 4 in our area.

PYGMY SHARK *Euprotomicrus bispinatus*   **Fig. 4, p. 21**
Identification: *Tiny; brown or black,* with *small white-edged fins.* Torpedo-shaped; snout long, bulbous. *Gill slits tiny, high on body.* 1st dorsal fin much *smaller* than 2nd; neither has a spine. 1st dorsal fin closer to pelvic fin than to pectoral fin. *No anal fin.* Teeth sharp-edged (Fig. 3, no. 5; p. 16); upper ones tiny, spikelike; lower ones large, wide, flat. Tiny light organs that look like black dots cover the ventral surface. Our *smallest* shark, one of the smallest known. Males to about $8\frac{3}{4}$ in. (22 cm), females to about $10\frac{1}{2}$ in. (27 cm).
Range: Widespread in S. Atlantic, s. Indian Ocean, and Pacific; rare off Calif., well offshore. **Habitat:** Open sea or near islands; surface possibly to ocean floor. Probably migrates near surface at night.
Remarks: Eats small pelagic fishes, squids, and crustaceans.
Similar species: Pacific Black Dogfish (see Note under Spiny Dogfish, p. 23) has a spine at front of each dorsal fin.

PACIFIC SLEEPER SHARK *Somniosus pacificus*   **Pl. 1**
Identification: *Large,* heavy body. 2 small dorsal fins of same size, 1st about midway between pectoral and pelvic fins; no spine at front of either dorsal fin. *No anal fin.* Eye small. Snout long, rounded. Flaccid when out of water. Upper teeth narrow, thornlike; lower teeth *flat,* sharp-edged (Fig. 3, no. 6; p. 16). Blackish brown to slate-green or light gray. Largest captured $14\frac{5}{12}$ ft. (4.4 m); reported to 23 ft. (7 m).
Range: Japan and Bering Sea to Alaska and to Baja. **Habitat:** On

or near bottom, but sometimes at surface or even intertidal. In shallow waters in north but deep-living from Calif. southward — at 780-6562 ft. (238-2000 m).

Remarks: Sluggish but voracious; eats fishes, seals, cephalopods, mollusks, and carrion. In cen. Calif. commonly enters Sablefish traps. Not known to be dangerous to humans. To several hundred large yolky eggs in females (embryos unknown); smallest specimen 31 in. (79 cm).

Similar species: (1) Spiny Dogfish is smaller, with a spine at front of each dorsal fin. (2) Other large sharks have an *anal fin.*

SPINY DOGFISH *Squalus acanthias*   **Pl. 2**
Identification: *Spine at front of each dorsal fin, no anal fin.* Snout long, flattened, pointed. Teeth in both jaws are flat with sharp edges (Fig. 3, no. 8; p. 16), forming a continuous cutting edge. Gray to light brown above; white below. White spots on side (except in some adults). To $5\frac{1}{4}$ ft. (160 cm), but most adults 2-4 ft. (61-122 cm); larger in northern part of range.

Range: All temperate and northern seas, but not in tropics; Alaska to cen. Baja. **Habitat:** Coastal. Very common in shallow bays from Alaska to cen. Calif.; in south apparently deeper.

Remarks: Probably the most common small shark in our area. Strong swimmer, voracious predator — eats fishes and invertebrates. A schooling species with inshore and migratory offshore populations; 1 tagged in Wash. was captured off Japan $7\frac{1}{2}$ years later. Ovoviviparous — up to 20 young per litter; gestation 22-24 months. Long-lived (to 40 years in northern waters); males mature at 13 years, females at 23 years. An excellent food fish when fresh. Formerly important for vitamin A in its liver oil. Often used for classroom dissection. *Caution:* can stab its captor with mildly toxic fin spines or inflict severe bites.

Similar species: (1) Most other typical sharks have an anal fin. (2) Pygmy, (3) Pacific Sleeper, and (4) Prickly Sharks (above) have no anal fin but lack a spine at front of either dorsal fin. (5) Horn Shark (p. 24) has a spine at front of each dorsal fin, but is dark-spotted and has a blunt head. **Note:** The Pacific Black Dogfish, *Centroscyllium nigrum,* has been captured off s. Calif. in Sablefish traps set at 2400-3840 ft. (732-1170 m). Like the Spiny Dogfish, it has a spine at front of each dorsal fin, but is black or dark gray with white-edged fins, has a short broad rounded snout, and 3- to 5-cusped bristlelike teeth in both jaws. To about 20 in. (51 cm). S. Calif. to Chile; also Cocos I., Galapagos Is., and Hawaii.

Order Heterodontiformes

Bullhead Sharks: Family Heterodontidae

These are the only sharks that have 2 dorsal fins (each with a *spine* at front) *and* an anal fin. Head broad, blunt. *Mouth small,* near tip of snout, well in front of eyes. A deep groove from nostril to mouth. Crushing teeth in back of mouth low and cuspless; front teeth have high cusps. No other sharks deposit eggs in hand-grenade-shaped capsules with spiral flanges (see Horn Shark egg case in Fig. 2, p. 14). Small — 2-5 ft. (61–152 cm) — bottom-dwellers of warm-temperate and tropical continental waters; mostly inshore, to at least 900 ft. (274 m).

Bullhead sharks are found in the e. Pacific from California to Peru, including the Galapagos Is.; in the w. Pacific from Japan to Australia; also off S. Africa. These harmless sharks eat mollusks, crabs, sea urchins, and small fishes. Only 1 family in the order; 8 species, 1 in our area.

HORN SHARK *Heterodontus francisci*   **Pl. 1**
Identification: A distinctive *spotted shark* with *an anal fin* and a strong *spine at front of each dorsal fin.* Note *piglike* snout and raised *ridge* above eye. Front teeth high-cusped, rear teeth low (Fig. 3, no. 7; p. 16). Tan to dark brown or grayish above; pale yellowish below. Usually has black spots; many young also have white spots. To 38 in. (96 cm), but most adults 2-3 ft. (61–91 cm).
Range: Cen. Calif. to Gulf of Calif.; rare north of s. Calif.
Habitat: Prefers rocky areas, in crevices and caves; also sandy patches and kelp beds. Intertidal and to 492 ft. (150 m), most common at 8–35 ft. (2.4–11 m).
Remarks: Sluggish, solitary; more active at night. Can clamber on bottom with flexible pectoral and pelvic fins. Eats crabs and small fishes. Mates Dec.–Jan.; lays large — to 5 in. (13 cm) — egg cases with spiral flanges (Fig. 2, p. 14) in Feb.–April; incubation 7-9 months. Harmless, but will nip if provoked.
Similar species: (1) No other typical shark has a spine at front of each dorsal fin *and* an anal fin. (2) Spiny Dogfish (p. 23) and (3) Pacific Black Dogfish (see Note under Spiny Dogfish) are our only other sharks with a spine at front of each dorsal fin.

Order Orectolobiformes

A moderately large, diverse, mainly tropical group of small to large sharks. Snout short; mouth well in front of eyes, near tip of snout. A deep groove from nostril to mouth. No spine at front of either dorsal fin. Except for the species in our area, these are mainly bottom-living inshore sharks. Most varied in Australia, but several occur in the Indian Ocean and tropical Pacific from S. Africa and the Red Sea to Japan and the cen. Pacific; 2 species in the Atlantic and e. Pacific. Many species lay eggs in oval cases, but some are ovoviviparous. 2–8 families (depending on classification used); about 30 species; 1 in our area.

Whale Sharks: Family Rhincodontidae

WHALE SHARK *Rhincodon typus*   **Fig. 4, p. 21**
Identification: *Huge,* with *pale spots and bars; 3 ridges* on back. Head broad, flat, with a wide mouth near tip of snout. 1st dorsal and pectoral fins large. *Long gill slits. Teeth tiny, hooked* (Fig. 3, no. 9; p. 16); adults have over 300 rows in an unbroken series across jaw; young have fewer rows (but over 100). Dark gray to reddish or greenish brown above; white or yellow below. *White* or yellow *spots* and bars. *The largest fish* — to 60 ft. (18 m), possibly to 70 ft. (21 m). A 38-ft. (12-m) specimen weighed 13 tons (11.8 mt). Young as small as 2–3 ft. (61–91 cm).
Range: Circumtropical in warm seas; a few sightings off s. Calif. Uncommon off s. Baja and s. Gulf of Calif., common off Galapagos Is.
Habitat: Near surface and usually near coasts. Often in schools.
Remarks: One species in the family. Generally harmless and slow; has been filmed, even ridden by divers, but has deliberately rammed fishing boats in Indian Ocean. Eats small crustaceans, fishes, and squids that it strains from the water. Often seen feeding in vertical position with head at surface — lowers itself to funnel water and food into mouth and then raises head above surface to allow water to drain from gill slits. Lays eggs in football-sized cases. Some researchers spell the family and genus names differently: Rhiniodontidae and *Rhiniodon.*
Similar species: (1) Basking Shark (p. 28) is also huge, but lacks spots and has even longer gill slits, extending to top and bottom of head. (2) Other sharks have a different color pattern and smaller gill slits.

Order Lamniformes

In this group and the Carcharhiniformes (p. 30) the snout is elongate and the mouth is on underside of head. No deep groove between the nostril and mouth. 2 dorsal fins, without a spine at the front. Anal fin present. Unlike Carcharhiniformes, Lamniformes have no lower nictitating membrane (see Fig. 5, p. 31). Upper front teeth separated from side teeth by either a toothless gap or by 1–6 smaller teeth; front teeth are the largest. The order is small but diverse and is found worldwide in a variety of habitats. 7 families (5 in the e. Pacific), 4 in our area. About 14 species, 7 in our area.

Sand Tiger Sharks: Family Odontaspididae

Large, heavy-bodied sharks with 2 dorsal fins about equal in size, and a deep upper precaudal pit. No keel on caudal peduncle. Lower lobe of caudal fin very short. Gill slits moderately long, entirely *in front of* pectoral fin. No nictitating membrane. Teeth slender, with 1 long cusp and usually 1 or more small sharp cusplets.

These are sluggish coastal sharks, found inshore and to 450 ft. (137 m). Worldwide in temperate and tropical waters. Solitary or in large schools. They eat a wide variety of fishes; also squids, crabs, and lobsters. Ovoviviparous. Newborn of 1 species are large — $3\frac{1}{4}$ ft. (99 cm) — having fed in the uterus on eggs from the ovaries (uterine cannibalism). 1 species (not found in our area) has attacked swimmers. The family was formerly called Carchariidae. 2-4 species, 1 in our area.

RAGGED-TOOTH SHARK   Fig. 4, p. 21
Odontaspis ferox

Identification: *Rare.* Bulky, with a *long bluntly conical snout.* 2 dorsal fins about same size, no spine at front. A deep upper precaudal pit. Teeth have a fanglike cusp, usually with 2 cusplets on either side of it (Fig. 3, no. 10; p. 16). Dark gray above; whitish below. Our specimens are blotched or have no markings; some European ones may have red spots. In our area to $12\frac{1}{6}$ ft. (3.7 m); elsewhere to $13\frac{1}{12}$ ft. (4 m).

Range: Usually temperate waters; Japan, Hawaii, Australia, New Zealand, S. Africa, ne. Atlantic, and Mediterranean; rare off s. Calif., also in Gulf of Calif. **Habitat:** Off s. Calif. at 42–510 ft. (13–155 m); elsewhere at 262–450 ft. (80–137 m).

Remarks: A rare fish-eating shark; not known to be dangerous. **Similar species:** (1) Mackerel sharks (p. 28) have a strong keel on the caudal peduncle and a crescent-shaped caudal fin, with the upper lobe not markedly longer than the lower lobe. (2) Requiem sharks (p. 36) have a nictitating membrane, and their last 1 or 2 gill slits are above (not in front of) the base of the pectoral fin.

Thresher Sharks: Family Alopiidae

Large, heavy-bodied sharks with a *huge caudal fin* — upper lobe about as long as the rest of the body, lower lobe short. Upper and lower precaudal pits. No keel on caudal peduncle. Anal and 2nd dorsal fins tiny. Teeth sharp-edged. Worldwide in temperate and tropical seas; coastal, epipelagic, and deepwater; found from surface to at least 1558 ft. (475 m). Thresher sharks eat fishes, squids, and pelagic crustaceans. Ovoviviparous. Probably harmless; not reported to attack humans. 3 or more species, 2 in our area.

BIGEYE THRESHER Fig. 22 opp. Pl. 2
Alopias superciliosus
Identification: *Caudal fin huge. Eye large,* extends to top of head
(permits vision overhead). *Horizontal groove* on side from above
eye almost to midbody. 9-12 teeth (Fig. 3, no. 11; p. 16) on each
side of both jaws. Dark gray above; paler gray or cream below.
Rear edge of 1st dorsal, pectoral, and pelvic fins dusky. Largest
specimen in our area was a 12⅓-ft. (3.8-m) male; elsewhere to
about 14-15 ft. (4.3-4.6 m).
Range: Atlantic, Indian Ocean, and cen. and w. Pacific; Calif. to
Gulf of Calif. **Habitat:** In our area gill-netted from surface to near
bottom at 360-600 ft. (110-183 m); elsewhere inshore, epipelagic,
and near bottom in deep water; surface to at least 1558 ft. (475 m).
Rare.
Remarks: Eats fishes and squids.
Similar species: (1) Common Thresher (below) has a smaller eye
(not extending to top of head), no groove on side; smaller but more
numerous teeth (14-30 on each side). (2) See Note under Common
Thresher.

COMMON THRESHER Pl. 2
Alopias vulpinus
Identification: Similar to Bigeye Thresher but has *smaller eye,
no groove on side,* 1st dorsal fin farther forward (Fig. 22 opp. Pl. 2).
Teeth triangular (Fig. 3, no. 12; p. 16). Brown, gray, blue-gray, or
blackish above; sometimes silvery, bluish, or golden on side; abruptly white below. White on belly extends to side and *over* pectoral fin base. Dorsal, pectoral, and pelvic fins blackish; caudal, pectoral, and pelvic fins sometimes have white dot at tip. Our largest
specimen — about 18 ft. (5.5 m) — was a pregnant female from
Calif.; elsewhere to at least 20 ft. (6.1 m).
Range: Apparently worldwide in all warm seas; Goose Bay (B.C.)
to Chile. **Habitat:** Offshore and near surface; young often inshore,
off beaches, and in shallow bays. In Indian Ocean occurs at depths
to at least 869 ft. (265 m).
Remarks: Eats fishes, squids, and other pelagic organisms. Uses
long caudal fin to bunch up and even stun schooling prey.
Ovoviviparous — litters of 2-6, nourished by uterine cannibalism.
Excellent food fish, sought by sport fishermen.
Similar species: See Bigeye Thresher (above). **Note:** The Pelagic
Thresher, *Alopias pelagicus* (Fig. 22 opp. Pl. 2), occurs off Mexico
and the Galapagos Is. and in w. and cen. Pacific and Indian
Oceans. In the e. Pacific it is poorly known and may be misidentified
as the Common Thresher. As in the Common Thresher, no groove
on side, but white on its underside does *not* extend over pectoral fin
base. Snout more elongate, head narrower, and *pectoral fin* nearly
straight and *broad* at tip (in Common Thresher more curved with
narrower tip).

Basking Sharks: Family Cetorhinidae

BASKING SHARK *Cetorhinus maximus*   **Pl. 2**
Identification: *Huge,* spindle-shaped body with a big mouth;
only the Whale Shark is larger. Caudal fin crescent-shaped, with a
longer lower lobe than in most sharks. Upper and lower precaudal
pits, a *strong caudal keel. Gill slits huge,* in front of pectoral fin,
extending to top and bottom of head. Head conical in adults, upturned and hooked in young; snout long. Teeth tiny, with curved
cusps (Fig. 3, no. 13, p. 17); adults have over 200 rows in each jaw.
Also have hundreds of rows of very long horny gill rakers (these are
shed periodically, all can be absent at the same time). Body grayish brown, slate, bluish gray, or black; lighter or grading to white
below. Sometimes has white patches and bars on snout and belly.
Said to reach 40–45 ft. (12.2–13.7 m), but most adults are under
32 ft. (9.8 m). Smallest in our area was 5.5 ft. (1.7 m). A 30-ft.
9.1-m) specimen weighed 8600 lb. (3900 kg).
Range: Worldwide in cold seas; few records from tropics; Aleutian
Is. and Gulf of Alaska to Gulf of Calif.; also Chile. **Habitat:**
Coastal and pelagic, often near surface, occasionally inshore and in
shallow bays. As in Atlantic, may migrate seasonally to deep
water.
Remarks: One species in the family. Harmless, but occasionally
aggressive when provoked. Divers have filmed it feeding: swims
slowly in a circle with its huge mouth open, straining small pelagic
animals with its numerous long gill rakers. Often breaks surface
with its broad triangular dorsal fin and tip of its caudal fin. Can
jump out of water. In our area may migrate south in winter and
north in summer. Often in schools or pairs. Pregnant females and
newborns rarely captured. Supports a small irregular fishery for
liver oil and fish meal; caught with harpoons from small boats.
Similar species. (1) Mackerel sharks (below) have larger teeth,
smaller gill slits, no gill rakers. (2) See Whale Shark (p. 25).

Mackerel Sharks: Family Lamnidae

Large heavy sharks with a streamlined, spindle-shaped body. Caudal fin crescent-shaped, nearly symmetrical — lower lobe slightly
shorter than upper lobe. 1st dorsal and pectoral fins large; anal and
2nd dorsal fins very small. Gill slits *long,* in front of pectoral fin,
but do not extend to top and bottom of head. Upper and lower
precaudal pits; a strong *keel* on caudal peduncle. Teeth few, large;
except a small tooth between front and side teeth of each upper
jaw.

Mackerel sharks are found worldwide in cold to tropical seas;
inshore, pelagic, or in deeper water — at depths up to 4200 ft.

(1280 m). These sharks eat a wide variety of fishes, sea mammals, sea turtles, marine birds, and squids. They are ovoviviparous, with small litters; the young are nourished by uterine cannibalism in some (probably all) species. These are fast-swimming, dangerous sharks. Like tunas they are partly warm-blooded; special vascular network keeps the heavy trunk muscles warmer than the water for greater muscle power and efficiency. 5 species, 3 in our area.

WHITE SHARK *Carcharodon carcharias* **Pl. 2**
Identification: Large, stout-bodied, with a large *caudal keel.* 1st dorsal fin begins over rear of pectoral fin; 2nd dorsal fin begins in front of anal fin. *Teeth huge, triangular,* with serrated edges (Fig. 3, no. 14; p. 17). Blackish or brownish to slaty blue or light gray above; lighter on side; white below. Often has a black spot at pectoral fin base and sometimes one on underside of pectoral fin near tip. To 25–30 ft. (7.6–9.1 m); our largest about 20 ft. (6.1 m); a female, 16⅔ ft. (5.1 m), weighed 2820 lb. (1279 kg).
Range: Worldwide in cool-temperate and tropical seas; Gulf of Alaska to Gulf of Calif.; also Panama to Chile. Probably prefers temperate waters. **Habitat:** Offshore and coastal; often near islands and seal and sea lion rookeries, off beaches, and inside shallow bays. Also in deep water; 1 taken off Cuba at 4200 ft. (1280 m).
Remarks: Also known as Great White Shark and Maneater Shark. *Our most dangerous shark,* implicated in many attacks on swimmers, divers, and boats. Fewer than 10 (usually fewer than 5) attacks a year off our coast. Usually inflicts only one nonfatal bite, suggesting that the shark confuses humans (especially in wet suits) with marine mammals or that the attacks are for territorial defense. Bites whales; sometimes kills but does not eat sea otters. In our area feeds on many kinds of fishes (including other sharks), seals, sea lions, and occasionally shellfish; also on sea birds and turtles elsewhere. Migration pattern and pupping grounds unknown; pregnant females extremely rare. Good eating when under 8 ft. (2.4 m). Specimens under 7 ft. (2.1 m) have cusplets on teeth; one at 4⁷⁄₁₂ ft. (1.4 m) had smooth-edged lower teeth. Fossilized teeth are well-known from several related species that became extinct millions of years ago. The largest fossilized teeth are 6 in. (15 cm) long; comparing these teeth with those of the White Shark suggests that the largest extinct relative (*Carcharodon megalodon*) grew to at least 45–50 ft. (14–15 m).
Similar species: (1) Snout of Bonito Shark (below) is acutely conical, 1st dorsal fin begins over or behind rear corner of pectoral fin; body usually slender; deep blue. (2) Salmon Shark (p. 30) has a small secondary caudal keel under the rear of the main one; 2nd dorsal fin above anal fin. (3) See Basking Shark (p. 28).

BONITO SHARK *Isurus oxyrinchus* **Fig. 4, p. 21**
Identification: *Snout long, acutely conical, pointed.* 1st dorsal fin

begins over or slightly behind rear corner of *long* pectoral fin. 2nd dorsal fin *small,* begins slightly ahead of anal fin. A strong *keel* on caudal peduncle but no secondary keel. Teeth have an extremely long, pointed, curved cusp but no cusplets (Fig. 3, no. 15; p. 17). Deep *blue above* and on side (fades to dark gray after death); white below. Has a black spot at pectoral fin base. Our largest was a female from s. Calif. $11\frac{5}{12}$ ft. (3.5 m), 1030 lb. (467 kg); largest known $12\frac{1}{2}$ ft. (3.8 m), 1102 lb. (500 kg). Most in our area less than 7–8 ft. (2.1–2.4 m).

Range: Probably worldwide in warm seas; Ore. to Gulf of Calif., but rare north of s. Calif.; also Ecuador to Chile. **Habitat:** Epipelagic and coastal, tropical; comes close to shore.

Remarks: Also known as the Shortfin Mako. Probably the fastest-swimming shark, capable of billfishlike leaps. Sought by sport fishermen — good eating but extremely active and aggressive when captured; should be treated with extreme caution. A dangerous species implicated in several attacks on humans and boats elsewhere. Eats schooling fishes (such as sardines and mackerels), Swordfish, Blue Shark, and squids.

Similar species: (1) Salmon Shark (below) is usually blotched and stouter; has a bluntly conical snout and small, straight, short-cusped teeth with cusplets. See (2) White Shark (above), (3) Basking Shark (p. 28), and (4) Blue Shark (p. 41).

SALMON SHARK *Lamna ditropis*   **Pl. 2**
Identification: Stout, with bluntly conical snout. *Secondary keel below* rear of *main caudal keel.* 1st dorsal fin begins far forward (over rear of pectoral fin base). 2nd dorsal fin small, above anal fin. Teeth large (Fig. 3, no. 16; p. 17); cusps short, nearly straight, cusplets stout except in very small individuals. Dark bluish gray, gray-black, or mottled gray above; white below. Has a black spot at pectoral fin base; adults have dark gray or black blotches on lower surface. To 10 ft. (3 m).

Range: Japan to Bering Sea; Gulf of Alaska to cen. Baja.
Habitat: Epipelagic, inshore and offshore; caught just off beaches in Calif. Subarctic to cold-temperate waters, abundant in Gulf of Alaska and off B.C.
Remarks: Also known as Mackerel Shark. Eats salmons, Tomcod, sculpins, and probably many other fishes. Damages commercial fishing gear, but seldom (if ever) attacks people or boats. 1 female had a litter of 4.
Similar species: See (1) White Shark (p. 29), (2) Bonito Shark (above), and (3) Basking Shark (p. 28).

Order Carcharhiniformes

Nearly half of our sharks belong to this order, which includes about 60% of all shark species. These sharks have a *long snout* and

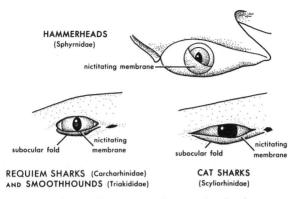

HAMMERHEADS
(Sphyrnidae)

nictitating membrane

nictitating
membrane

subocular fold

REQUIEM SHARKS (Carcharhinidae)
AND SMOOTHHOUNDS (Triakididae)

nictitating
membrane

subocular fold

CAT SHARKS
(Scyliorhinidae)

Fig. 5 Nictitating membranes in sharks

a *long mouth* (reaching the eye) on the underside of the head. *No* deep *groove* between the nostril and the mouth. *No spine* at front of either dorsal fin. *Nictitating membranes* (Fig. 5) present; lower one movable (also upper one in many species). No gap or small teeth between front and side teeth. Side teeth usually largest, except in smoothhounds (p. 33), in which largest teeth are at front of lower jaw. Most occur in tropical and warm-temperate waters but several inhabit cooler seas. 8 families, 4 in our area; about 190 species; 18–19 in our area.

Cat Sharks: Family Scyliorhinidae

Small sharks, mostly 12–39 in. (30–99 cm). 2 dorsal fins, *far back;* 1st begins over or behind front of pelvic fin. Head flat, with long slitlike or *catlike eyes* on top; eye can be closed by a nictitating membrane (Fig. 5). Large spiracles. No precaudal pit. No groove between nostril and mouth. Caudal fin nearly horizontal, lower lobe not expanded. Teeth very small, with needlelike cusp, usually with cusplets. *Several rows* of functional teeth in each jaw (not just the outside row).

Cat sharks are mainly bottom-dwelling sharks of tropical and warm-temperate waters, which are found from inshore to deep water on upper continental and insular slopes; but several species occur in cooler seas, especially in deep water. Deepwater cat sharks tend to be black but those at moderate depths often have complex patterns of dark and light colors. They feed on bony fishes, other small elasmobranchs, crustaceans, cephalopods, bivalves, and echinoderms. Most lay eggs but a few are ovoviviparous. Egg cases are brownish or amber — more elongate and spindle-shaped than skates' egg cases (Fig. 2, p. 14). Probably the largest family of sharks, with more than 85 species, 4 in our area.

BROWN CAT SHARK *Apristurus brunneus*   **Pl. 1**
Identification: Small, with a very long *shovel-like snout;* long *labial groove* (Fig. 6). Gill slits small. 2 dorsal fins, *far back* on body; 1st slightly smaller than 2nd. Teeth tiny (Fig. 3, no. 17; p. 17). Light to dark brown or brownish black. To $2\frac{1}{4}$ ft. (69 cm).
Range: Se. Alaska to n. Baja. **Habitat:** Deep water, sometimes well off bottom; to 3900 ft. (1189 m). More common and shallower from n. Calif. northward.
Remarks: Taken in trawls, Sablefish traps, and on longlines. Egg case (Fig. 2, p. 14) light brown, nearly rectangular, about 2 x $\frac{3}{4}$ in. (5.1 x 1.9 cm), with long tendrils.
Similar species: Filetail Cat Shark (p. 33) has a shorter snout and labial groove and a row of enlarged denticles on upper edge of caudal fin. **Note:** (1) The Longnose Cat Shark, *Apristurus kampae* (a rare species), has been caught in very deep water — at about 3000-6000 ft. (914–1829 m) — off cen. and s. Calif. and in the Gulf of Calif. Similar to Brown Cat Shark, but gill slits *longer* (Fig. 7), head broader; black. To 19 in. (48 cm). (2) The White-edged Cat Shark, *Apristurus* species, is known from one specimen from very deep water off cen. Calif. but has not been formally described or named.

SWELL SHARK *Cephaloscyllium ventriosum*   **Pl. 1**
Identification: Yellow-brown to creamy, with black or brownish *spots and saddles,* also white spots. When disturbed or caught may *inflate its stomach* with water or air. 1st dorsal fin much larger than 2nd. Gill slits small. To about $3\frac{1}{4}$ ft. (1 m).
Range: Monterey Bay to Acapulco (Mex.); also Chile. Common in s. Calif. but rare northward. **Habitat:** Rocky areas along coast or around offshore islands at 15-120 ft. (4.6–37 m); also deep water — to 1500 ft. (457 m). Common in or near kelp beds, usually rests on bottom.
Remarks: Harmless. Sluggish, crevice-dwelling, nocturnal. When inflated can wedge itself into crevices. Often seen singly, sometimes

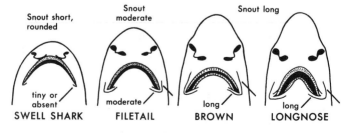

Fig. 6 Cat sharks — underside of head

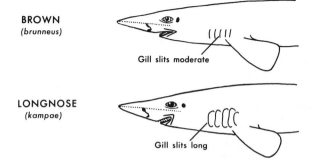

Fig. 7 Brown and Longnose Cat Sharks (comparison)

in groups. Enters lobster traps. Eats fishes and crustaceans. Egg case (Fig. 2, p. 14) large — 4 x 1¼ in. (10 x 3.2 cm) — and amber. Young — 5–6 in. (13–15 cm) — hatch after about 7½ months in the water.
Similar species: See Leopard Shark (p. 35).

FILETAIL CAT SHARK *Parmaturus xaniurus* **Pl. 1**
Identification: Note row of enlarged pointed *denticles on upper edge of caudal fin* (this area rough to touch). Has a moderate *labial groove* (Fig. 6, p. 32). Dorsal fins about same size. Gill slits small. Teeth often have cusplets (Fig. 3, no. 19; p. 17). Gray-brown to brownish black above; paler below. Occasionally has small white spots. Fins dusky, sometimes white-edged. To 2 ft. (61 cm).
Range: Bodega Bay (n. Calif.) to Baja and Gulf of Calif. **Habitat:** Deep water — about 300–4100 ft. (91–1250 m). Young sometimes well off bottom.
Remarks: Egg case has long tendrils (Fig. 2, p. 14); about 3¼ x 1¼ in. (8.3 x 3.2 cm). Another species in this genus may occur in our waters; it is unstudied and unnamed.
Similar species: (1) Brown Cat Shark (p. 32) has a longer snout and labial groove, lacks enlarged denticles on upper edge of caudal fin. (2) See Note under Brown Cat Shark.

Smoothhounds: Family Triakididae

Small to moderately large sharks with 1st dorsal fin ahead of the pelvic fin. *Eye elongated horizontally,* on top or side of head, with a *nictitating membrane* (Fig. 5, p. 31). Spiracles small but prominent. Teeth small, varying from sharp-edged and cusped (with cusplets) to blunt. 2nd dorsal fin larger than anal fin except in Soupfin Shark. To 1–7 ft. (30–213 cm). Unlike requiem sharks

(Family Carcharhinidae, p. 36), smoothhounds have no precaudal pit and their intestinal valve is spiral-shaped (not scroll-shaped).

These sharks occur in all temperate and tropical seas; mainly continental, inshore and near shore; common in shallow bays, but at least 1 (not in our area) lives in deep water — to 1620 ft. (494 m). They eat a variety of fishes and invertebrates; many prey heavily on shrimps and crabs. All probably are ovoviviparous or viviparous. About 40–45 species, 5 in our area.

SOUPFIN SHARK *Galeorhinus galeus* **Pl. 3**
Identification: Snout *long, pointed.* Eye oval. 2nd dorsal fin nearly over anal fin and about same size. Mouth (seen from bottom) broadly arched. Labial groove *long* but does not extend to front of mouth. *Terminal lobe* of caudal fin *extremely large,* about $\frac{1}{2}$ the length of upper lobe. Teeth triangular, sharp-edged, with cusplets (Fig. 3, no. 20; p. 17). Bluish to dusky gray above; white below. Young under 2 ft. (61 cm) have striking white edge on pectoral fin; both dorsal fins black-tipped, with a white spot; caudal fin black-tipped. Males to 6 ft. (1.8 m), 60 lb. (27 kg); females to $6\frac{1}{2}$ ft. (2 m), 100 lb. (45 kg).
Range: Temperate waters, nearly worldwide; northern B.C. to cen. Baja; also Peru and Chile. **Habitat:** Offshore, also coastal and in bays; muddy shallows and to 1350 ft. (411 m). Females usually at less than 180 ft. (55 m), males deeper.
Remarks: Schooling, abundant, wide-ranging, 1 tagged specimen migrated 1000 mi. (1609 km) in 22 months from s. Calif. to B.C. In Australia a tagged specimen was at liberty for 25 years. In Calif. males more common in north, females in south. Eats many kinds of fishes and squids. Ovoviviparous, with litters of 6–52 (avg. 35). Newborn about 14 in. (36 cm). From 1937 to 1946 the Soupfin Shark was intensively fished for the vitamin A in its liver oil; now taken for human consumption. Some researchers treat specimens from our area as a separate species, *Galeorhinus zyopterus.*
Similar species: (1) Requiem sharks (p. 36) have precaudal pits, caudal fin with much shorter terminal lobe and longer lower lobe. (2) See other smoothhounds (below).

GRAY SMOOTHHOUND **Fig. 24 opp. Pl. 3**
Mustelus californicus
Identification: Teeth *blunt* (Fig. 3, no. 22, p. 17). 1st dorsal fin begins *behind* the pectoral fin, rear edge slopes down at an angle. Rear edge of dorsal fins *not frayed.* Lower lobe of caudal fin *not elongate.* Gray or gray-brown above; white below. To $5\frac{1}{3}$ ft. (1.6 m) but usually under 4 ft. (1.2 m); males smaller than females.
Range: Cape Mendocino (n. Calif.) to Mazatlan (Mex.). **Habitat:** Mainly inshore; often at less than 12 ft. (3.7 m) but caught at 150 ft. (46 m). Abundant from s. Calif. southward, uncommon north of Pt. Conception.
Remarks: Viviparous. Usually seen alone or in schools of Leopard

Sharks. Wary when approached by divers. Eats crabs, shrimps, and small fishes.

Similar species: (1) Brown Smoothhound (below) has cusps on teeth; 1st dorsal fin begins over pectoral fin; rear edge of dorsal fins *frayed*. (2) In Sicklefin Smoothhound (below) 1st dorsal fin begins over pectoral fin; rear edge of 1st dorsal fin vertical; lower lobe of caudal fin pointed and *elongate* in specimens over 1 ft. (30 cm). (3) See Soupfin Shark (p. 34).

BROWN SMOOTHHOUND *Mustelus henlei*   Pl. 3

Identification: Rear of dorsal fins *frayed* (Fig. 23 opp. Pl. 3). 1st dorsal fin begins over pectoral fin, rear edge slants *downward*. Lower lobe of caudal fin *not* elongate. Teeth pointed, with cusps (Fig. 3, no. 21; p. 17). Usually iridescent bronze (but occasionally gray) above; white below. To 37 in. (94 cm).

Range: Coos Bay (Ore.) to Gulf of Calif.; also Ecuador and Peru.

Habitat: Common in shallow bays from San Francisco northward. Inshore to at least 656 ft. (200 m).

Remarks: Eats mainly crabs and shrimps; also small fishes, clamworms, and sea squirts. Viviparous. Newborn about $7\frac{1}{2}$ in. (19 cm).

Similar species: (1) Sicklefin Smoothhound (below) has blunt teeth and 1st dorsal fin with vertical rear edge, dorsal fins not frayed; lower lobe of caudal fin elongate, pointed, in specimens over 1 ft. (30 cm). See (2) Gray Smoothhound and (3) Soupfin Shark (p. 34).

SICKLEFIN SMOOTHHOUND   Fig. 23 opp. Pl. 3
Mustelus lunulatus

Identification: Teeth *blunt* (Fig. 3, no. 23; p. 17), sometimes with a low, sharp cusp. 1st dorsal fin begins *over* pectoral fin, rear edge *abruptly vertical* from apex. Dorsal fins *not frayed*. Lower lobe of caudal fin *elongate;* in specimens over 1 ft. (30 cm) *pointed and hooked*. Gray or brown above; white below. Females to $5\frac{2}{3}$ ft. (1.7 m); males smaller — $3\frac{7}{12}$ ft. (1.1 m) or more.

Range: San Diego to Peru. **Habitat:** Inshore.

Remarks: Least cold-tolerant of our smoothhounds; relatively rare in our area, but occasionally abundant around San Diego. Viviparous.

Similar species: (1) Pacific Sharpnose Shark (p. 41) has sharp-edged, compressed teeth; 2nd dorsal fin smaller than anal fin; precaudal pits. See (2) Soupfin Shark and (3) Gray and (4) Brown Smoothhounds (above).

LEOPARD SHARK *Triakis semifasciata*   Pl. 2

Identification: Grayish with bronze tinge above; white below. Note *broad black bars, saddles,* and *spots* on back and side; saddles solid in young, with light centers in adults. Adults have more spots. Snout short, bluntly rounded. Eye on top of head. Anal fin much smaller than 2nd dorsal fin. Terminal lobe of caudal fin long, but less than $\frac{1}{2}$ the length of upper lobe. Mouth (from below) broadly arched; teeth sharp-edged (Fig. 3, no. 24; p. 18), with cusplets (except in a few adults). Males to 5 ft. (1.5 m); females to 7 ft. (2.1 m), 70 lb. (32 kg).

Range: Ore. to Baja and n. Gulf of Calif. **Habitat:** Temperate coastal waters, mainly inshore. Prefers sandy and rock-strewn flat bottom near rocky reefs. Very common in n. Calif. bays. Usually at less than 12 ft. (3.7 m), but sometimes to 300 ft. (91 m).

Remarks: Strong-swimming, nomadic, schooling (often with other smoothhounds). Schools may visit areas briefly, then depart. Occasionally rests on bottom. Generally timid around divers; not considered dangerous. Eats a variety of fishes and invertebrates. Ovoviviparous, with litters of 4–29. Good eating.

Similar species: See (1) Swell Shark (p. 32) and (2) Tiger Shark (p. 40).

Requiem Sharks: Family Carcharhinidae

A diverse family of small to large sharks. In our species 1st dorsal fin base ahead of pelvic fin base. *Eye round or vertically oval,* with a nictitating membrane (Fig. 5, p. 31). Spiracles not present in our species (except Tiger Shark); very small if present in species from other areas. Lower lobe of caudal fin large. Teeth small to very large, sharp-edged, often very flat, and usually serrated. Requiem sharks, unlike their smoothhound relatives (above), have *precaudal pits* and a scroll-shaped intestinal valve.

These sharks are the dominant sharks of the tropics, occurring on continental shelves, around islands, and on the high seas. The Blue Shark and a few other species sometimes are found in cold water; some (especially the Bull Shark) enter fresh water. Requiem sharks eat a variety of marine vertebrates, also some invertebrates. Many species are big, large-toothed, and dangerous — a majority of the sharks known to attack humans are in this family. All are viviparous except the ovoviviparous Tiger Shark. About 50 species, 6–7 in our area. Rare species in our area are shown in Fig. 8.

Over half the requiem sharks belong to the genus *Carcharhinus,* commonly known as gray sharks. They are difficult to identify. The upper teeth are narrow-cusped to broadly triangular, and serrated; most of the lower teeth have a vertical cusp. The labial groove is very short, hardly visible when mouth is closed (Fig. 9, p. 40). No spiracles. 1st dorsal fin closer to pectoral fin than to pelvic fin or about equidistant from both. No keel on caudal peduncle. Gray sharks are gray or brown (not blue), often with dusky, black, or white fin markings. About 32 species, 4 in our area. 7–8 other species in the e. Pacific range northward to the Pacific coast of Baja; because they are active and highly mobile, they can be expected to reach s. Calif. as summer accidentals during "warmwater" years (see Note under Narrowtooth Shark, p. 38).

Note relative position of fins

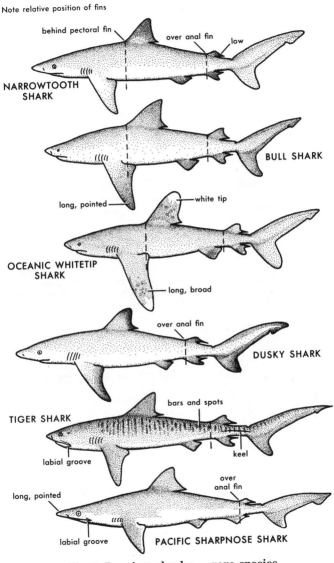

NARROWTOOTH SHARK — behind pectoral fin, over anal fin, low

BULL SHARK

OCEANIC WHITETIP SHARK — long, pointed, white tip, long, broad

DUSKY SHARK — over anal fin

TIGER SHARK — labial groove, bars and spots, keel

PACIFIC SHARPNOSE SHARK — long, pointed, labial groove, over anal fin

Fig. 8 Requiem sharks — rare species

NARROWTOOTH SHARK   Fig. 8, p. 37
Carcharhinus brachyurus
Identification: Upper teeth narrow-cusped (Fig. 3, no. 25; p. 18).
1st dorsal fin small, tip rounded; begins behind pectoral fin. 2nd
dorsal fin *low,* over anal fin, nearly triangular. Pectoral fin pointed.
Most *lack a middorsal ridge,* but some have a weak one. Usually
dark gray-brown above; white below. Tip of pectoral fin dusky or
blackish. Males to $8^{11}/_{12}$ ft. (2.7 m); females to $9^{1}/_{2}$ ft. (2.9 m).
Range: S. Atlantic, w. Indian Ocean, Pacific; s. Calif. to Gulf of
Calif., also Peru. Rare — occasional summer migrant in our area.
Habitat: Inshore, continental. Prefers warm-temperate waters,
rarer in tropics.
Remarks: Mainly eats fishes (usually bottom-living ones); also
cephalopods. Has attacked people outside our area. Newborn 12–
16 in. (30–41 cm).
Similar species: (1) Dusky Shark (p. 39) has broadly triangular
upper teeth and a middorsal ridge. (2) Bull Shark (below) has
broadly triangular upper teeth; a larger 1st dorsal fin, farther forward; a larger, higher 2nd dorsal fin; body usually much stouter,
with a heavier head. (3) Oceanic Whitetip Shark (p. 39) has
broadly triangular upper teeth; large, very rounded 1st dorsal and
pectoral fins; high 2nd dorsal fin. **Note:** Other gray sharks
(*Carcharhinus* species) and a species of a related genus (*Negaprion*)
have *no middorsal ridge* and have narrow-cusped teeth; they
reach s. Baja and should be expected off s. Calif. in "warm-water"
years: (1) Blacktip Shark or Volador, *Carcharhinus limbatus,* has
a narrower, more pointed snout; straighter, more erect, upper teeth
with higher cusps; a larger 1st dorsal fin, which begins over rear
corner of pectoral fin; fins have more prominent black tips. (2) In
Smalltail Shark or Cuero Duro, *C. porosus,* the 2nd dorsal fin begins well behind the front of the anal fin (in other species usually
about opposite or in front of anal fin). (3) Pico Blanco, *C. velox,*
has an extremely narrow snout; with large, close-set nostrils (separated by less than twice their width; in other species over 3 times
width). (4) Lemon Shark, *Negaprion brevirostris,* has a short
blunt snout; both dorsal fins about same size (2nd much smaller
than 1st in *Carcharhinus* species). (5) See Silvertip Shark under
Oceanic Whitetip Shark (p. 39).

BULL SHARK   Fig. 8, p. 37
Carcharhinus leucas
Identification: Upper teeth broadly triangular (Fig. 3, no. 26; p.
18). 1st dorsal fin large, with *pointed tip;* begins about over rear
corner of pectoral fin. 2nd dorsal fin high, rear edge vertical from
apex. Pectoral fin *long, pointed. No* middorsal ridge. Snout shorter
(Fig. 9, p. 40), body heavier, and head and jaws more massive than
in related species. Gray above; white below. Fin tips dusky. To at
least $9^{5}/_{6}$ ft. (3 m) — probably to 11 ft. (3.4 m).
Range: Widespread in all warm seas; possibly s. Calif.; s. Baja to

Peru. Also in many tropical rivers and lakes with sea outlets; sometimes over 2000 mi. (3219 km) inland. **Habitat:** An inshore species able to tolerate a range of salinity; often enters fresh water and bays of high salinity; often in bays, estuaries, and near river mouths.

Remarks: Also known as the Gambuso. Eats fishes (often other sharks and rays), other marine vertebrates, crustaceans, mollusks, and carrion. Particularly *dangerous* — several attacks on humans recorded. Occurrence in our area uncertain.

Similar species: (1) Dusky Shark (below) is usually more slender, has a middorsal ridge; 2nd dorsal fin low. (2) Oceanic Whitetip Shark (below) has white-tipped fins. See (3) Narrowtooth Shark (p. 38).

OCEANIC WHITETIP SHARK   Fig. 8, p. 37
Carcharhinus longimanus

Identification: Upper teeth broadly triangular, edges serrated (Fig. 3, no. 27; p. 18). 1st dorsal fin *large* with broadly *rounded* tip; begins between rear of pectoral fin base and rear corner of pectoral fin. 2nd dorsal fin high, rear edge vertical from apex. Pectoral fin *long,* tip *broadly rounded.* Usually a middorsal ridge. Dark gray with bronze tinge above; white below. Individuals over about $4\frac{1}{3}$ ft. (1.3 m) have *white tips* on 1st dorsal, pectoral, caudal, and pelvic fins; dark or black blotches on pelvic fin, anal fin, and caudal peduncle. Males to at least 8 ft. (2.4 m), females to at least $8\frac{11}{12}$ ft. (2.7 m); reported to $11\frac{5}{12}$ ft. (3.5 m).

Range: Circumtropical and epipelagic, reaching tropical e. Pacific offshore. 1 captured near Cortez Bank (s. Calif.). **Habitat:** Oceanic, usually well offshore but approaches shore where continental shelf is narrow. Often at or near surface, but to at least 500 ft. (152 m). Common offshore.

Remarks: Active but slow swimmer. Eats fishes, squids and other pelagic mollusks, and carrion. Newborn about 2 ft. (61 cm). Definitely *dangerous,* with several known attacks outside our area. Sometimes called *Carcharhinus maou.*

Similar species: (1) Dusky Shark (below) has pointed pectoral fin, smaller dorsal fins; *no white tips* on fins. See (2) Narrowtooth Shark and (3) Bull Shark (p. 38). **Note:** The Silvertip Shark, *Carcharhinus albimarginatus,* an insular and continental species of the Pacific and Indian Ocean, reaches s. Baja from the south. It has a long, *pointed* pectoral fin, usually has a middorsal ridge, and tips of its 1st dorsal fin and caudal fin are white.

DUSKY SHARK *Carcharhinus obscurus*   Fig. 8, p. 37
Identification: *Has* a middorsal ridge. Upper teeth broadly triangular (Fig. 3, no. 28; p. 18). 1st dorsal fin with rounded tip; begins about over rear corner of pectoral fin. 2nd dorsal fin low, *over anal fin,* with rear edge sloping obliquely from apex. Pectoral fin has an angular tip. Gray above; white below. Fins dusky or black-tipped

in specimens less than about 3¼ ft. (1 m). Males to at least 11⅙ ft. (3.4 m), females to 12¹⁄₁₂ ft. (3.7 m).

Range: Wide-ranging in Atlantic, w. Indian Ocean, and off Australia; Redondo Beach (s. Calif.) to Gulf of Calif. **Habitat:** Warm water; offshore along outer continental shelf, also inshore.

Remarks: Also known as Bay Shark. Eats fishes (including small sharks and rays), occasionally squids and other invertebrates, and carrion. Newborn 28–29 in. (71–74 cm). Dangerous, but no attacks recorded in our area.

Similar species: See (1) Narrowtooth and (2) Bull Sharks (p. 38), and (3) Oceanic Whitetip Shark (p. 39). **Note:** 3 other species of *Carcharhinus* with a middorsal ridge reach s. Baja: (1) Silky Shark, *Carcharhinus falciformis,* is epipelagic. Its upper teeth are narrow-cusped, with strong, low cusplets on both sides. 1st dorsal fin begins behind the pectoral fin. (2) Galapagos Shark, *C. galapagensis,* is insular and coastal. Its 1st dorsal fin is higher, more erect, pointed; 2nd dorsal fin higher, with rear edge almost vertical from apex. (3) Bignose Shark, *C. altimus,* has a longer snout with a distinct fingerlike lobe on nostril (hardly developed in Dusky Shark). Its 1st dorsal fin is larger, more angular, and begins over rear of pectoral fin base.

TIGER SHARK *Galeocerdo cuvier*   **Fig. 8, p. 37**
Identification: Large, with dusky gray-black to black *bars and spots* (prominent in young but fade — sometimes lost by adulthood). Snout broad, blunt, extremely short; upper labial groove *long* (Fig. 9). Spiracle prominent. Teeth in both jaws large, serrated, with oblique cusp and heavy cusplets (Fig. 3, no. 29; p. 18). A low *keel* on caudal peduncle. Our largest specimen was 9 ft. (2.7 m), but giants elsewhere reach 18–24 ft. (5.5-7.3 m) — largest weighed about 6800 lb. (3084 kg).

Range: Worldwide in warm seas; s. Calif. to Peru, including offshore islands. **Habitat:** Coastal to well offshore but not usually

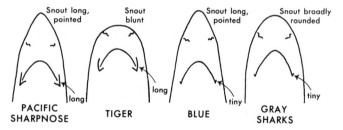

Fig. 9 Requiem sharks — underside of head

oceanic; also in shallow bays, estuaries, and river mouths. Abundant in tropics, sometimes moves into cooler waters.
Remarks: Eats almost all vertebrates, also lobsters, squids, and garbage. One of the most *dangerous* sharks, but rare or accidental in our area. Litters of 10–82. Newborn 18–19 in. (46–48 cm). Species name sometimes spelled *cuvieri*.
Similar species: (1) Gray sharks (*Carcharhinus* species, pp. 38–40) have a short labial groove, no spiracle, no caudal keel, and no bars or spots. (2) See Leopard Shark (p. 35).

BLUE SHARK   Pl. 2
Prionace glauca
Identification: Large, slender, graceful. Brilliant *dark blue above;* lighter iridescent blue on side; white below. Snout *long, narrow, pointed* (Fig. 9). No spiracle. A low keel on caudal peduncle (more easily felt than seen). Pectoral fin *long.* Base of 1st dorsal fin usually closer to pelvic fin than to pectoral fin. Except in newborns, teeth large, curved, serrated, without heavy cusplets (Fig. 3, no. 30; p. 18). To about $12\frac{1}{2}$ ft. (3.8 m) but most in our area under 6 ft. (1.8 m).
Range: Worldwide in warm seas; Gulf of Alaska to Chile. The only species in the family that is common and widespread in our area. More cold-tolerant than others in family; prefers waters between 45°–69°F (7°–21°C). Seasonal in parts of range, migrates northward in summer. **Habitat:** Primarily offshore and epipelagic, but comes close inshore (especially at night). Usually at or near surface; deeper in tropics.
Remarks: Active surface swimmer. Eats almost anything, including garbage and carrion, but prefers fishes and squids. A *dangerous* shark implicated in attacks in our area and elsewhere. Sometimes harasses divers in our area. Caught and eaten by humans but will snap and thrash when boated. Litters of 4–82. Newborn about 19 in. (48 cm).
Similar species: (1) Gray sharks (*Carcharhinus* species, pp. 38–40) are gray or brownish, with 1st dorsal fin closer to pectoral fin than to pelvic fin or equidistant between; no caudal keel; usually a stouter body. (2) Bonito Shark (p. 29) has an acutely pointed snout, longer gill slits, smooth teeth, a strong wide caudal keel, a crescent-shaped caudal fin, and a heavier, more spindle-shaped body.

PACIFIC SHARPNOSE SHARK   Fig. 8, p. 37
Rhizoprionodon longurio
Identification: Small, with *small fins* (except 1st dorsal) and a *long snout.* The only species in the family in our area in which the *2nd dorsal fin* begins well *behind front of anal fin.* 1st dorsal fin closer to pectoral fin than to pelvic fin. A *long* prominent *labial groove* (Fig. 9). No spiracle. Teeth small, oblique-cusped, smooth-edged or (upper teeth of adults) finely serrated (Fig. 3, no. 31;

p. 18). Brown or grayish above; white below. To at least $3^{7}/_{12}$ ft. (1.1 m), may reach 5 ft. (1.5 m).

Range: S. Calif. to Peru. Marginal in our area; a few records from s. Calif. Common off s. Baja, in Gulf of Calif., and southward.

Habitat: Inshore, coastal.

Remarks: Newborn about 13 in. (33 cm).

Similar species: In Smalltail Shark (see Note under Narrowtooth Shark, p. 38) location of 2nd dorsal fin is similar, but labial groove is short, serrations on upper teeth are stronger, and lower teeth have a more vertical cusp.

Hammerhead Sharks: Family Sphyrnidae

Closely related to and probably descended from requiem sharks (p. 36), but the *head is expanded* on each side. The eye is circular or vertically oval, with a nictitating membrane (Fig. 5, p. 31). No spiracle. 2nd dorsal fin same size as or smaller than anal fin. Lower lobe of caudal fin large. Teeth in both jaws small to large, sharp-edged or flat, smooth or serrated, with oblique (not vertical) cusp. A precaudal pit. Intestinal valve scroll-shaped.

Hammerheads are found worldwide in warm seas. They are very common in the tropics, on continental shelves, around islands, and well offshore, but none are truly epipelagic. Most are primarily

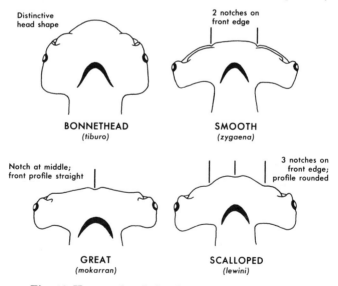

Fig. 10 Hammerhead sharks — underside of head

fish-eaters, but the Bonnethead mainly eats crustaceans. Five species are small — under 6 ft. (1.8 m) — and probably harmless, but the other 4 are large and presumed dangerous. Probably all are viviparous. 9 species, 3 in our area.

BONNETHEAD *Sphyrna tiburo*   **Fig. 10, p. 42**
Identification: A small hammerhead, with a narrow *spade-shaped head* (Fig. 10). Front teeth cusped; rear teeth *molarlike,* used for crushing (Fig. 3, no. 32; p. 18). Gray or grayish brown above; grayish or white below. Often has scattered black dots on side. To 4½ ft. (1.4 m), may reach 6 ft. (1.8 m).
Range: San Diego to Peru; also w. Atlantic. Common from Gulf of Calif. southward, rare in our area. **Habitat:** Inshore; bays and estuaries.
Remarks: Harmless, small, active. Eats crabs, shrimps, and other crustaceans; octopuses and other mollusks; and small fishes. Litters of 4–12. Newborn about 1 ft. (30 cm).
Similar species: See Smooth Hammerhead (below).

SMOOTH HAMMERHEAD *Sphyrna zygaena*   **Pl. 3**
Identification: Large; head shaped like a broad *2-bladed ax,* notched at front (but not at midline) into 3 lobes (Fig. 10, p. 42). Teeth stout-cusped (Fig. 3, no. 33; p. 18). Dark gray, brownish, or greenish gray above; lighter on side; white or whitish gray below. Fins have dusky edges and tip; sometimes black on pectoral fin. To about 13 ft. (4 m); at 12½ ft. (3.8 m) about 900 lb. (408 kg).
Range: Widespread in all warm-temperate to subtropical seas; rare or absent in tropics; cen. Calif. to Gulf of Calif.; also Panama to Chile. **Habitat:** Coastal, usually well offshore but sometimes inshore.
Remarks: Strong swimmer, active, and dangerous, but uncommon in our area. Most abundant off s. Calif. in warm summers. Eats many kinds of fishes (commonly other sharks and stingrays), cephalopods, and crustaceans. Newborn about 2 ft. (61 cm).
Similar species: Head of Bonnethead (above) not as broad, spade-shaped. **Note:** (1) Scalloped Hammerhead, *Sphyrna lewini,* is a cosmopolitan tropical species known in our area from 1 confirmed capture off Santa Barbara (s. Calif.). Teeth, pelvic fin edges, and 2nd dorsal fin are like Smooth Hammerhead's, but head has 3 notches, including 1 at the midline (Fig. 10, p. 42), and rear tip of 2nd dorsal fin is almost opposite the precaudal pit (well ahead of pit in Smooth Hammerhead). (2) Great Hammerhead, *S. mokarran,* is another wide-ranging tropical hammerhead that reaches s. Baja and may enter our area in exceptionally warm summers. Teeth strongly serrated; pelvic fin has deeply concave rear edge (nearly straight in Smooth Hammerhead); 2nd dorsal fin high, with free rear lobe as long as fin is high (length about twice height of fin in Smooth Hammerhead).

ANGEL SHARKS
Order Squatiniformes
Family Squatinidae

Angel sharks are an archaic, highly specialized group with uncertain relationships to other living elasmobranchs. They have some features in common with typical sharks (p. 15) and rays (p. 45). The head and body are *flattened.* Eyes and large spiracles on top. Snout very short; nostrils at front, with prominent skin flaps. Mouth wide, at front of snout; teeth single-cusped. Five gill slits on each side at *rear of head,* extending to *underside* (Fig. 24 opp. Pl. 3). Pectoral fins very large, each with a *free triangular lobe* extending forward along the head (not attached to head as in rays). *2 dorsal fins, far back* on body behind pelvic fins. *No* anal fin. A *large* caudal fin, with lower lobe larger than upper lobe.

These small to medium-sized sharks — 3–8 ft. (0.9–2.4 m) — occur virtually worldwide in shallow warm continental waters, often in sandy areas on the bottom. Ovoviviparous. They eat fishes and bottom invertebrates. 1 family in the order; 10–12 species, 1 in our area.

PACIFIC ANGEL SHARK *Squatina californica*   **Pl. 3**
Identification: Body flattened as in rays, but expanded pectoral fins are not attached to head and *gill slits* are *in a notch* at rear of head (Fig. 24 opp. Pl. 3). Resembles guitarfishes (p. 45) but front end is blunt and mouth is at *front.* A few denticles on undersurface; uppersurface has denticles, those in a middorsal row are enlarged. Teeth sharp, single-cusped (Fig. 3, no. 34; p. 18). Reddish or grayish brown to dark brown or blackish, usually with dark spots; white below. To 5 ft. (1.5 m), 60 lb. (27 kg).
Range: S. Alaska to Baja and Gulf of Calif.; rare north of Calif.; also Peru to s. Chile. **Habitat:** Offshore and in shallow bays; often on sand or mud bottom, near kelp or rocks, or canyons. Mostly at 10–150 ft. (3–46 m), but in Gulf of Calif. to 600 ft. (183 m).
Remarks: Eats fishes. Its powerful jaws can be quickly protruded to capture prey and are potentially dangerous to fishermen and divers.
Similar species: In rays (below) pectoral fins are completely joined to head, forming a disk; gill openings are on undersurface of disk.

RAYS

Rays are *flattened,* like angel sharks (p. 44) but unlike typical sharks (p. 15). The pectoral fins are enlarged and expanded forward; they attach to the head and form a flat *disk* with the head and body. The *gill slits* are on the *undersurface.* The *spiracles* are *large* and on the uppersurface. Rays take in water for respiration through the spiracles instead of the mouth; this allows them to rest on, or partially bury themselves in, the bottom. The mouth is on the undersurface in most rays but at the front end in some. *No anal fin.* Some have no dorsal fin, others 1 or 2; if present usually far back, on the tail. Usually a small caudal fin. Denticles (small prickles) vary: some rays are covered with them, others are naked or have only patches of denticles; many have a median (middorsal) row of enlarged denticles (spines) down the back and tail. In stingrays and their relatives (p. 54) some tail denticles are modified into long barbed spines — these and the spines at the front of the dorsal fins in some rays are commonly called stings; they can cause severe wounds. Electric rays can jolt would-be predators (and humans) with an electric shock.

Most rays are marine, but some enter fresh water and a few live exclusively in fresh water. Nearly all rays live on the bottom, but a few (manta rays and relatives) are pelagic. Rays are found from close inshore to offshore waters over 1 mile (1609 m) deep. As a group they have been very successful in colonizing the deep sea. Some have teeth fused into crushing plates; most eat invertebrates, a few strain plankton. Skates lay eggs, but other rays are ovoviviparous. 4–5 orders; about 20 families, 8 in our area; 425–440 species, at least 23 in our area.

Order Rhinobatiformes

The most primitive rays, with a long, *thick* broad-based tail, and 2 large dorsal fins well ahead of a *large* caudal fin. Disk relatively narrow. Teeth small and blunt, used for crushing. No long stings on tail, no electric organs. Body covered with denticles, usually with 1 or more rows of spines on back or on back and tail. Most are ovoviviparous, but at least 1 species may lay eggs. 3–4 families, 2 in our area; 47–50 species, 3 in our area.

Guitarfishes: Family Rhinobatidae

Flattened rays with 2 dorsal fins, a *thick tail,* and a *caudal fin.* Our guitarfishes differ from the closely related thornbacks (p. 46) in having 1 middorsal row of spines and an angular (not rounded) snout. To about 6 ft. (1.8 m). Guitarfishes live on or near the bottom in all warm-temperate to tropical seas; mostly inshore, but caught at depths up to 1200 ft. (366 m). About 38 species, 2 in our area.

SHOVELNOSE GUITARFISH   Pl. 3
Rhinobatos productus
Identification: No dark bars. Snout *long, pointed.* Disk longer than it is wide. 1 row of spines on back and tail. Sandy brown above; white below. Females to 5½ ft. (1.7 m), 40½ lb. (18.4 kg); males smaller.
Range: San Francisco to Gulf of Calif., rare north of Monterey Bay. **Habitat:** Sand or mud-sand bottom in shallow coastal waters, bays, sloughs, and estuaries. To 50 ft. (15 m).
Remarks: Eats crabs, worms, clams, and small fishes. Nomadic, gregarious, often extremely abundant. Burrows in sand when resting. Normally harmless, but one male that was following a female Shovelnose Guitarfish nipped a diver. Flesh along back good eating. Up to 28 per litter. Newborn 6 in. (15 cm).
Similar species: (1) Banded Guitarfish (below) has a broader snout, dark *bars* on back. (2) Thornback (p. 47) has 3 rows of spines on its back and tail and a *rounded* snout.

BANDED GUITARFISH   Pl. 3
Zapteryx exasperata
Identification: Differs from Shovelnose Guitarfish in having *dark bars* on back, a broad snout and disk (disk about as wide as long). 1 row of spines on back and tail. Brownish to dark gray with blackish bars above; white spots below (but black spots near edge). To 3 ft. (91 cm).
Range: S. Calif. to Panama. Rare in our area, common in Gulf of Calif. **Habitat:** Prefers rocky areas, especially crevices and caves. Tidepools and to 70 ft. (21 m).
Remarks: Often rests in rocky crevices, but seldom buries itself in sand.
Similar species: (1) See Shovelnose Guitarfish (above). (2) Thornback (p. 47) has no dark bars, a broadly rounded snout, and *3 rows* of enlarged spines on its back and tail.

Thornbacks: Family Platyrhinidae

Shape, tail, and caudal fin similar to those of guitarfishes but snout more rounded. 1 or 3 rows of large hooked spines on back and tail. Most 2–3 ft. (30–61 cm). Found in warm-temperate and tropical continental shelf waters of e. Pacific, and off Japan, China, India, and w. Africa. Habits similar to those of guitarfishes. 1 species may lay skatelike egg cases, but the others (including ours) are ovoviviparous. About 5 species, 1 in our area.

THORNBACK *Platyrhinoidis triseriata*   **Pl. 3**
Identification: Large rounded disk; long *stout* tail with *2 large dorsal fins* and a caudal fin. *3 rows of enlarged hooked spines* on back and tail. Brown, gray-brown, or olive-brown above; white or cream below. To 3 ft. (91 cm).
Range: San Francisco to Baja; rare north of Monterey Bay.
Habitat: Fine sand to mud bottom, often near kelp beds, off beaches; to 150 ft. (46 m); sometimes abundant on mud flats of coastal bays. Often buries itself in bottom sediments.
Remarks: Eats small sand-dwelling crustaceans, worms, and mollusks.
Similar species: (1) Skates (below) have a slender tail with small dorsal fins near its tip and a smaller caudal fin. (2) Pacific Electric Ray (p. 53) has a short tail; a short, broad, symmetrical caudal fin; spots on uppersurface; smooth skin. (3) Shovelnose Guitarfish (p. 46) has 1 row of enlarged spines.

Order Rajiformes

The largest group of rays, including almost half the species. They have a slender flattened tail, usually with 2 dorsal fins (a few species outside our area have 1 or none), far back on the tail, a small or rudimentary caudal fin, and no stings. Disk large, usually rhomboidal (occasionally circular). Teeth small, blunt or pointed, used for holding and crushing. Usually have denticles or spines on some part of the head, body, or tail. *Adult males have rows of hooked spines near lateral edges of disk (alar) and near front edge of disk (malar).* Worldwide, but most common in cold waters, including the deep sea. Many have small elongate organs in the tail that generate low-voltage electric currents. This order includes the skates, which are our only egg-laying rays — see egg cases in Fig. 2 (p. 14). 3-5 families, of which only the true *skates* (Family Rajidae) reach our area. About 190 species, at least 11 in our area.

Skates: Family Rajidae

The largest family of cartilaginous fishes. This subgroup of rays usually has denticles and large spines on the disk and tail (in some only on tail), 2 dorsal fins (1 New Zealand species has only 1), and a small or rudimentary caudal fin. Largest to about 8 ft. (2.4 m), but some mature below 1 ft. (30 cm). Common in Arctic, subantarctic, and cold-temperate seas. In warm-temperate and tropical seas they occur in deep waters; some at very great depths — to 9528 ft. (2904 m). They move by undulating the edges of their disk (pectoral fins). Usually feed on bottom invertebrates and fishes. At least 177 species, 11 or more in our area.

Our skates (Fig. 11) are grouped into 2 genera: softnosed

See inside of front cover for terminology

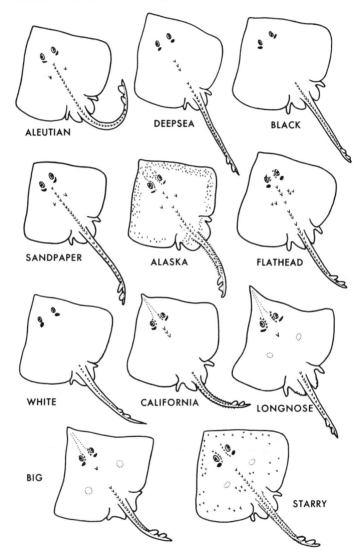

Fig. 11 Skates — body shape and spination

(*Bathyraja* species) and hardnosed (*Raja* species). (1) In softnosed skates the rostral (snout) cartilage is slender, and the snout is soft, flabby, and flexible. Cartilaginous supports of the pectoral fins reach the tip of the snout. Most of our softnosed skates are deepwater or Alaska and Bering Sea species, several of which are poorly known. (2) Hardnosed skates have a thick, stiff rostral cartilage that reinforces the snout and makes it rigid (but somewhat flexible in the Deepsea Skate). Cartilaginous supports of the pectoral fins end well behind the snout tip. Hardnosed skates are common inshore, but some also occur in deep water.

ALEUTIAN SKATE *Bathyraja aleutica* **Fig. 11, p. 48**
Identification: *Shoulder* (*scapular*) *spines* but no eye (orbital) spines, and no coarse spines on snout or disk, but 1 row of *middorsal spines* from nape to dorsal fin (usually continuous, but sometimes a space at rear of disk). Small denticles cover uppersurface, undersurface largely smooth. Softnosed — snout long, broadly triangular. Space between eyes deeply concave. Tail (anus to tip) longer than disk. Dark brown to olive above; white below. To 4–5 ft. (1.2–1.5 m) long, $2\frac{1}{2}$–3 ft. (76–91 cm) wide.
Range: N. Japan to Aleutian Is. and se. Alaska. Common in Gulf of Alaska. **Habitat:** On bottom, at 300–720 ft. (91–219 m) off Alaska, 984–2296 ft. (300–700 m) off Japan.
Remarks: Egg case prickly, with long horns; moderately large — $4\frac{3}{4}$–$5\frac{1}{2}$ in. (12–14 cm) long.
Similar species: See Fig. 11. (1) Longnose Skate (p. 52) is hardnosed, with an acutely *pointed snout;* front edge of disk *curves inward* (concave); orbital but no scapular spines. (2) Big Skate (p. 51) is hardnosed, with a short snout and shallowly notched pelvic fins; different color. (3) Sandpaper Skate (p. 50) has a short snout, area between eyes flat or slightly concave, coarser denticles on uppersurface. (4) Alaska Skate (p. 50) has a short snout, coarse denticles and spines on uppersurface, orbital spines, 2 white spots on disk; tail (anus to tip) shorter than disk (except in young). (5) Flathead Skate (see Fig. 11 and Note under Sandpaper Skate) has orbital spines, flat space between eyes. **Note:** (1) The poorly known Bering Skate, *Bathyraja interrupta,* has been recorded only in deep waters of the Bering Sea. Resembles the Aleutian and Alaska Skates, but has 4 middorsal spines on back, separated from row on tail. (2) The rare Deepsea Skate, *B. abyssicola* (Fig. 11, p. 48), is known from scattered reports from Queen Charlotte Is. to n. Baja at about 4200–9528 ft. (1280–2904 m). It has a long, broadly triangular snout like the Aleutian Skate, but it lacks scapular spines; *both* surfaces of disk covered with minute denticles (some small individuals have smooth areas), disk very narrow (about as wide as it is long — narrower than in our other skates), and both disk surfaces the *same* color (gray, brown, or whitish) except in some individuals with white blotches below. To at least $4\frac{1}{2}$ ft. (137 cm).

SANDPAPER SKATE   Fig. 11, p. 48; Pl. 4
Bathyraja kincaidii

Identification: Scapular spines but no orbital ones; middorsal spines continuous from nape to 1st dorsal fin or isolated groups at nape, midback, and on tail. Uppersurface covered with moderately coarse denticles, undersurface nearly smooth. Softnosed — snout short, broadly rounded, triangular. Tail (anus to tip) slightly longer than disk. Space between eyes flat or slightly concave. Dark brown to blackish above (young sometimes have darker spots); white below. Usually 2 white spots on side of tail. To $2\frac{5}{6}$ ft. (86 cm).

Range: Alaska to Cortez Bank (s. Calif.). **Habitat:** On bottom at 180–4500 ft. (55–1372 m).

Remarks: Egg case rough, with strong side keels and long horns (Fig. 2, p. 14); small — about $2\frac{1}{4}$ x $1\frac{3}{4}$ in. (5.7 x 4.4 cm).

Similar species: See also Fig. 11 (p. 48). (1) Alaska Skate (below) has concave space between eyes, orbital spines, 2 white eyespots on the disk; tail (anus to tip) shorter than disk (except in young). (2) White Skate (see Note under Black Skate) and (3) Black Skate (p. 51) have no large disk spines (except alar spines of adult males). (4) Starry Skate (p. 53) is hardnosed; has orbital but usually no scapular spines. (5) See Aleutian Skate (p. 49). **Note:** The rare Flathead Skate, *Bathyraja rosispinis* (Fig. 11), has been recorded in the Bering Sea; also 1 deep record off Ore. Like the Sandpaper Skate, it has scapular spines, 1 row of middorsal spines, coarse denticles on uppersurface, a broadly triangular snout, and a flat space between the eyes. It differs in having orbital spines and a longer snout.

ALASKA SKATE   Fig. 11, p. 48
Bathyraja parmifera

Identification: Scapular and orbital spines, middorsal spines continuous from nape to 1st dorsal fin, coarse denticles on uppersurface but undersurface largely smooth. Softnosed — snout short, blunt, broadly triangular. Tail stout, shorter than disk. Space between eyes strongly concave. Dark brown with dark spots and 2 prominent white eyespots above; white below, with dark blotches on tail. To 2–3 ft. (61–91 cm).

Range: Bering Sea to se. Alaska. **Habitat:** On bottom at 96–1206 ft. (29–368 m); common in Gulf of Alaska.

Remarks: Egg case unknown.

Similar species: (1) Flathead Skate (see Note under Sandpaper Skate) has orbital spines but a flat space between the eyes. (2) White Skate (see Note under Black Skate) and (3) Black Skate (below) have no large disk spines (except alar spines of adult males). (4) Starry Skate (p. 53) is hardnosed; has no eyespots and a shorter, blunter snout. See (5) Sandpaper Skate (above) and (6) Aleutian Skate (p. 49).

BLACK SKATE *Bathyraja trachura*   **Fig. 11, p. 48; Pl. 4**
Identification: No large disk spines (except alar spines of adult males). Scattered small denticles on front uppersurface, undersurface smooth. Softnosed — snout short, broadly triangular. Black to dark slate-gray or brown on *both* surfaces, but sometimes slightly lighter below. To 35 in. (89 cm) long, 22 in. (56 cm) wide.
Range: Bering Sea to n. Baja. **Habitat:** Usually on bottom in deep water — 2400–6540 ft. (732–1993 m).
Remarks: Egg case smooth, with long slender horns (Fig. 2, p. 14); moderately large — about $4\frac{3}{4}$ x 3 in. (12 x 8 cm). Also known as the Roughtail Skate.
Similar species: (1) California Skate (p. 52) and (2) Starry Skate (p. 53) are hardnosed, have large spines on back; pale undersurface. See (3) Sandpaper Skate and (4) Alaska Skate (p. 50).
Note: (1) White Skate, *Bathyraja spinosissima* (Fig. 11), known from Ore. and Calif. at 4200–6000 ft. (1280–1829 m), also lacks large disk spines (except alar spines of adult males), but it is pale gray *both* above and below, with small denticles on *both surfaces*. Also has a wide gap between 2nd dorsal fin and caudal fin (narrow in other skates in our area). (2) A softnosed skate, *Bathyraja* species, in deep water — 8202 ft. (2500 m) — off Wash. also has no large spines (only small denticles) on the uppersurface and no denticles on the undersurface. Unlike the Black Skate, it is light-spotted and brown above, with a white area on the underside of the head, gills, abdomen, and tail and a somewhat longer snout.

BIG SKATE *Raja binoculata*   **Fig. 11, p. 48; Pl. 4**
Identification: Our *largest* skate. Our only skate with a weak notch in rear edge of each pelvic fin. Orbital spines (in large specimens buried in skin), no scapular spines. Usually 1 spine at midback, followed by a middorsal row of spines over pelvic fins and on tail (sometimes no row over pelvic fins); uppersurface otherwise lacks large spines (except alar and malar spines of adult males), but large adults have small denticles. Undersurface nearly smooth. *Snout long,* bluntly pointed, broadly triangular. Gray, brown, reddish brown, olive-brown, or blackish, often with rosettes of white spots, darker mottling, and 2 prominent eyespots above; whitish, sometimes with dark spots or blotches, below. To 8 ft. (2.4 m) but rarely over 6 ft. (1.8 m); 200 lb. (91 kg) at 6 ft. (1.8 m).
Range: Bering Sea and se. Alaska to cen. Baja; rare south of Pt. Conception. **Habitat:** Common at moderate depths — 10–360 ft. (3–110 m).
Remarks: Commercially important — sides of disk are eaten. Feeds on crustaceans and fishes. Egg case large — nearly 1 ft. (30 cm) long — with 2 curved ridges on upper surface, 2 keels on each side, and short horns (Fig. 2, p. 14). 1–7 (avg. 3–4) embryos per case; only 1 per case for other skates in our area.
Similar species: (1) California Skate (p. 52) has an acutely

pointed snout, deeply notched pelvic fins. (2) Longnose Skate
(below) has a longer, more pointed snout; front edge of disk deeply
concave (nearly straight in Big Skate). (3) Deepsea Skate (see Note
under Aleutian Skate, p. 49) has deeply notched pelvic fins, no
orbital spines; minute denticles on *both* of its surfaces; is softnosed; and brown, gray, or whitish on both surfaces. (4) See Aleutian Skate (p. 49). **Note:** A large — 37 in. (94 cm) — hardnosed
skate, *Raja* species, is known from very deep water — 5248 ft.
(1600 m) — off B.C. and Ore. It has a long, broadly pointed snout
like the Big Skate, but has deeply notched pelvic fins, 3 strong
orbital spines at each eye, a wider mouth, no spots on the uppersurface, and a thicker disk. Most likely the adult of *Raja badia,*
known from young taken in the Gulf of Calif. and the Gulf of
Panama.

CALIFORNIA SKATE *Raja inornata*   **Fig. 11, p. 48; Pl. 4**
Identification: A *moderately long,* acutely *pointed snout.* Front
edge of disk slightly concave. Pelvic fins deeply notched. No orbital
or scapular spines. Middorsal spines on tail, sometimes over pelvic
fins and at midback; disk otherwise smooth except for scattered
small denticles and alar and malar spines of adult males. Undersurface smooth. Olive-brown above, sometimes with dark mottling
and occasionally 2 dark rings or eyespots; tan below. To $2\frac{1}{2}$ ft.
(76 cm).
Range: Str. of Juan de Fuca to cen. Baja. **Habitat:** Common
inshore and in shallow bays, sometimes in deep water; 60 ft. (18 m)
or less to 2200 ft. (671 m).
Remarks: Important commercially in Calif. Egg case smooth,
with long horns (Fig. 2, p. 14); $2\frac{4}{5}$-$3\frac{1}{2}$ in. x $2\frac{2}{5}$-$3\frac{1}{5}$ in. (7-9 cm x
6-8 cm).
Similar species: (1) Starry Skate (p. 53) has a *blunt* snout; front
edge of disk more convex, uppersurface rough. (2) Longnose Skate
(below) has a longer snout; front edge of disk *curves inward.* See
(3) Black Skate and (4) Big Skate (p. 51).

LONGNOSE SKATE *Raja rhina*   **Fig. 11, p. 48; Pl. 4**
Identification: Note the *extremely long, acutely pointed snout.*
Front edge of disk *curves inward* (concave). Pelvic fins deeply
notched. Orbital spines; middorsal spines on tail. Undersurface
mostly smooth (except snout and front edge of disk in large individuals). Dark brown above, with 2 dark eyespots; sometimes has
faint light and dark spots. Bluish, gray, black, or light brown
below, with dark spots or blotches. To about $4\frac{1}{2}$ ft. (137 cm), males
smaller.
Range: Se. Alaska to cen. Baja. **Habitat:** On bottom at 180-
2040 ft. (55-622 m).
Remarks: Important commercially in Calif. Egg case rough, with
loose covering of fibers, short horns (Fig. 2, p. 14); $3\frac{3}{4}$-5 in. x $2\frac{1}{4}$-3 in.
(9.5-13 cm x 5.7-7.6 cm).
Similar species: Deepsea Skate (see Note under Aleutian Skate,

p. 49) also has a long snout and deeply notched pelvic fins, but lacks orbital spines; snout flabby, more broadly pointed; *both* surfaces densely covered with small denticles, at least in specimens over 1½–2 ft. (46–61 cm).

STARRY SKATE *Raja stellulata*   **Fig. 11, p. 48; Pl. 4**
Identification: Our *spiniest* hardnosed skate; uppersurface *and* much of *undersurface* covered with *prickly denticles.* Large middorsal spines on back and tail (continuous or grouped). Orbital spines, usually no scapular spines. Snout very *short,* bluntly pointed, broadly angular. Pelvic fins deeply notched. Brown or gray-brown above, often spotted; white below. Often 2 eyespots with yellow center and brownish ring. To about 2½ ft. (76 cm).
Range: Bering Sea to n. Baja. **Habitat:** On bottom at 60–2400 ft. (18–732 m).
Remarks: Egg case striated, with long horns (Fig. 2, p. 14); 2¾–3¼ in. x 2½–2¾ in. (7–8.2 cm x 6.4–7 cm).
Similar species: See Fig. 11 (p. 48) and characteristics of *Raja* species (under Family Rajidae, p. 49). See (1) Sandpaper and (2) Alaska Skates (p. 50), (3) Black Skate (p. 51), and (4) California Skate (p. 52).

Order Torpediniformes

These rays have an *oval disk,* a *short stout tail,* a *large caudal fin,* and 1 or 2 dorsal fins, or none at all. Both disk surfaces *smooth,* without prickly denticles. Teeth small, pointed. The large kidney-shaped electric organ at the base of each pectoral fin is often visible through the skin as a honeycombed or reticulated (netlike) oval area. Worldwide in cool-temperate to tropical waters, but mostly in the tropics. Most live on mud or sand bottoms at moderate depths, but some occur in deep water — to 3510 ft. (1070 m). They eat crustaceans, worms, other invertebrates, and fishes. All are ovoviviparous. 4 families — 2 in the e. Pacific, 1 in our area. About 40 species, 1 in our area.

Electric Rays: Family Torpedinidae

Disk oval; a large symmetrical caudal fin. Mouth wide, arched — not tubelike. Worldwide in tropical and temperate seas. These rays can capture relatively large prey fishes. Their powerful electric current can stun prey and fend off enemies (including humans who handle them). They swim the way sharks do, by moving the tail — not undulating the disk. They are sometimes called torpedo rays. 11–14 species, 1 in our area.

PACIFIC ELECTRIC RAY *Torpedo californica*   **Pl. 4**
Identification: Disk nearly *round, thick, flabby.* Skin smooth. Tail short, stocky, with 2 dorsal fins and a *large caudal fin.* Dark

gray, bluish, or brownish gray above; often with small, irregular black spots. White to slate-gray below. Females reach over $4\frac{1}{2}$ ft. (137 cm), 90 lb. (41 kg); males grow to 3 ft. (91 cm).
Range: Northern B.C. to cen. Baja. Electric rays off Peru, Chile, and Japan may belong to this species. **Habitat:** Common on fine sand bottoms, buried in sand, or swimming just above it; often around rocks and in kelp beds; at 10–900 ft. (3–274 m).
Remarks: Eats herrings, halibuts, and other fishes. In s. Calif. moves inshore and feeds at night in rocky areas. Sometimes aggressive toward divers (swims at them with mouth open) when disturbed or provoked, but apparently no human has been injured by the electric shock.

Order Myliobatidiformes

Almost all of these rays have 1 or more long barbed *stings* on the tail. The tail is long and *whiplike,* without a caudal fin (except in Round Stingray, which has a short stout tail and a small caudal fin). 1 or no dorsal fin. Body smooth or covered with denticles and large spines. No electric organs. They give birth to live young — embryos are nourished by a milky substance secreted from hairlike processes (trophonemata) that line the walls of the female's uterus. Mainly a tropical group, relatively few species in temperate seas. 6–8 families, 4 in our area. About 150 species, 8 in our area.

Stingrays: Family Dasyatididae

These rays have a flat head, merged with the disk. The disk is rhomboidal to nearly circular in outline, and stingrays move by undulating the disk edges. No dorsal fin and usually no caudal fin. All but 1 tropical species have 1 or 2 large *stings* well back on the tail, which is *long and slender* (except in Round Stingray, which has a short tail and a small caudal fin). When disturbed, a stingray can whip its tail upward and sideways and drive the sting into a victim, injecting venom produced in a gland at the base of the sting. Stings may serve as a weapon against predators (especially sharks). Stingray wounds have been fatal to humans, but apparently not in our area. Teeth small, blunt or pointed, in bands, used for crushing — mollusks form a part of the diet in many stingrays. Ovoviviparous.

  Stingrays occur worldwide, mostly in warm coastal waters (some off oceanic islands, a few in deep water, 1 pelagic). Several species are common in tropical rivers and lakes. About 100 species, 3 in our area.

DIAMOND STINGRAY *Dasyatis brevis*   **Pl. 5**
Identification: Large. *Diamond-shaped disk,* angular in front. The *whiplike tail* is longer than the disk, with a long *sting* closer to

base of tail than tip. Brown or blackish above; white below. To at least 6 ft. (183 cm) long; to 4 ft. (122 cm) wide; males smaller.
Range: Possibly B.C.; s. Calif. to Peru. Rare in our area, common in Gulf of Calif. **Habitat:** Sandy areas; often around rocks and kelp beds; shore to 55 ft. (17 m).
Remarks: Its size and long sting make this ray potentially more dangerous than the Round Stingray (below). Has probably caused at least 1 death in Gulf of Calif. Specimens from our area sometimes called *Dasyatis dipterura*.
Similar species: (1) Pelagic Stingray's disk is rounded in front (below and Fig. 25 opp. Pl. 5); both surfaces purplish. (2) Round Stingray (below) is smaller, with a round disk; has a thick short tail with a caudal fin. (3) California Butterfly Ray (p. 56) has a much wider disk, shorter tail.

PELAGIC STINGRAY   Fig. 25 opp. Pl. 5
Dasyatis violacea
Identification: Dark purplish above; purplish to lead-gray below. Disk diamond-shaped, but broadly *rounded* in front. Tail longer than disk; with a *long sting*. No caudal fin. To $5\frac{1}{3}$ ft. (163 cm).
Range: Pacific, Atlantic, and Mediterranean; B.C., s. Calif., Baja, and Galapagos Is. Rare in our area; B.C. record doubtful.
Habitat: The only normally pelagic stingray. Found in warm-temperate and tropical seas, deep ocean and inshore in open bays. In the Atlantic most caught at 120–780 ft. (37–238 m) over deep water.
Remarks: Feeds on small pelagic fishes, squids, and shrimps. Often captured on longlines.
Similar species: (1) Diamond Stingray (above) is more angular in front. (2) Round Stingray (below) has a round disk; tail short and stout, with a caudal fin. (3) In California Butterfly Ray (p. 56) disk is wider, triangular in front; tail short, with a tiny sting.

ROUND STINGRAY *Urolophus halleri*   Pl. 5
Identification: Small, with a nearly round disk. *Tail stout, shorter than disk,* with a long *sting* and a *caudal fin.* Brownish or gray-brown above, usually with yellow spots or reticulations; white to yellowish below. To 22 in. (56 cm).
Range: Eureka (n. Calif.) to Panama. **Habitat:** Sand or mud bottom off beaches and in bays and sloughs; at 3–70 ft. (0.9–21 m).
Remarks: Our most common stingray. Causes injuries to many swimmers each year. Large numbers congregate just off beaches and will sting when stepped on; wounds apparently nonfatal. Feeds on benthic invertebrates and small fishes. Mature females usually occur deeper than males; in s. Calif. move inshore in June to mate and again in Sept. to bear 1–6 young. Some researchers place round stingrays in their own family (Urolophidae).
Similar species: (1) Diamond Stingray (p. 54) and (2) Pelagic Stingray (above) have a whiplike tail and no caudal fin.

Butterfly Rays: Family Gymnuridae

The disk of these extremely flattened rays is shaped like a broad rounded *diamond,* twice as wide as it is long. Tail slender and *whiplike,* much shorter than disk, with *no caudal fin.* Our species usually has a *small sting* and no dorsal fin; others lack the sting or have a small dorsal fin. Mouth small, with many tiny pointed teeth. Largest at least 7 ft. (2.1 m) *wide;* unconfirmed reports of disks about 13 ft. (4 m) wide.

Butterfly rays are essentially tropical; found in all warm seas, rarer in temperate waters. These rays prefer coastal waters; often in shallow bays, estuaries, and river mouths. They eat small fishes, clams, and crustaceans. They swim the way stingrays do, by undulating the edges of their disk. About 11 species, 1 in our area.

CALIFORNIA BUTTERFLY RAY   Pl. 5
Gymnura marmorata
Identification: Note the *diamond-shaped disk,* which is almost *twice as wide* as it is *long. Tail short, slender,* usually with a *small sting* at its base. Usually brownish above, sometimes mottled with small brown or blackish close-set spots; white below. Possibly to 5 ft. (1.5 m) wide.
Range: Pt. Conception to Peru. **Habitat:** Warm-temperate to tropical shallow bays and beaches.
Similar species: (1) Skates (p. 47) and (2) stingrays (p. 54) have a narrower disk (width less than $1\frac{1}{2}$ times the length).

Eagle Rays: Family Myliobatididae

In these rays and the mantas (which are related) the head is sharply distinct from the disk; but in eagle rays it is *massive* and elevated well *above the disk. Snout* thick and *spadelike.* Mouth small and transverse. Tail *whiplike* and very long (longer than disk), with *no caudal fin.* Large dorsal fin at base of tail, with a *sting* close behind it (sting absent in some species). The pectoral fins that form the sides of the disk in eagle rays and mantas are narrow and pointed near the tip; they are used for flapping, "bird-like flight" through the water (unlike the undulating movement of skates, stingrays, and butterfly rays).

Eagle rays have massive jaws with large *platelike teeth,* which are arranged in a central wide row and usually 3 narrow rows on each side (1 genus has only a central row). These rays smash and grind hard-shelled mollusks and crustaceans, but also eat softer prey, including worms. Apparently the muscular snout is used to root out prey. Some species reach a width of at least $7\frac{3}{4}$ ft. (2.4 m), possibly 10 ft. (3 m).

Eagle rays occur worldwide in tropical and temperate shallow seas. Some are extremely common in shallow bays and estuaries. Approximately 20 species, 1 in our area.

BAT RAY   **Pl. 5**
Myliobatis californica
Identification: Note the raised *massive head.* A dorsal fin at the base of a long *whiplike tail* with *sting* just behind it. Jaws heavy, with *platelike teeth.* Dark brown, olive, blackish brown, or blackish above; white below. To about 6 ft. (1.8 m) wide.
Range: Ore. to Gulf of Calif. **Habitat:** Very common in sandy and muddy bays and sloughs, also on rocky bottom and in kelp beds; sometimes buries itself in sand. Intertidal and to 150 ft. (46 m).
Remarks: Found singly or in groups. Should be handled with care because of its sting and powerful crushing jaws. Eats clams, abalones, oysters, marine snails, worms, shrimps, and crabs. Digs up food with disk edges and snout, and will even bite off overhanging ledges to get at food. Apparently mates in summer; litters of fewer than 10 are born the following summer.
Similar species: (1) Mantas (below) have a pair of hornlike head flaps and small hooked teeth. (2) Stingrays (p. 54) have a flat head (not raised above disk), small teeth, and no dorsal fin. **Note:** 2 other e. Pacific eagle rays (both with a narrower, longer snout) occasionally reach s. Baja. (1) Longnose Eagle Ray, *Myliobatis longirostris,* has a flatter head and bowed (convex) tooth plates (flat or slightly concave in Bat Ray); (2) the Striped Eagle Ray, *Pteromylaeus asperrimus,* has transverse stripes on uppersurface. (3) A common species occurring from Baja south, the Gabilan, *Rhinoptera steindachneri,* belongs to a related family, the cownose rays (Family Rhinopteridae). Cownose rays, unlike eagle rays, have a double-lobed snout.

Mantas: Family Mobulidae

These are large rays with a unique pair of *hornlike flaps on* the *head* (see Fig. 26 opp. Pl. 5). A prominent dorsal fin at base of a long whiplike tail; no caudal fin. Sometimes a small sting is present, just behind dorsal fin. Mouth large, slotlike, and transverse; teeth numerous, very small, hooked. Some mantas are gigantic — 18–23 ft. (5.5–7 m) wide.
   Mantas occur in all warm-temperate to tropical seas. They are active swimmers that "fly" through the water the way eagle rays do. They feed mostly on pelagic crustaceans and small schooling fishes, which they "herd" into the mouth with the head flaps and strain from the water with complex filter plates at the gills. They are called devil rays in some areas. 10–14 species, all poorly known; names of the 3 in our area are provisional.

MANTA *Manta birostris*   **Pl. 5**
Identification: Large, with a pair of *hornlike flaps* on a *large head.* Pectoral fins *long and pointed.* Usually no sting. Mouth at front; teeth only in lower jaw. Black to dark brown above; white below. Often has white patches on head. In our area to at least

18½ ft. (5.6 m) wide, 2310 lb. (1048 kg); in Atlantic to 22 ft. (6.7 m) wide, over 1.6 tons (1.4 mt).

Range: Atlantic, possibly all warm seas; s. Calif. to Peru, and offshore islands. Uncommon or rare; may move into our area with influxes of warm water. **Habitat:** Pelagic near surface. In our area frequents coasts; elsewhere sometimes far from land. Often swims at or near surface; can leap or somersault out of water.

Remarks: Eats small fishes and planktonic crustaceans. The population in the e. Pacific, formerly called *Manta hamiltoni,* apparently is the same species as the one in the Atlantic; *Manta* species from the Indian Ocean and cen. Pacific also may be identical.

Similar species: In (1) Spinetail and (2) Smoothtail Mobulas (below) mouth is on the *underside* of head, which is narrower (Fig. 26 opp. Pl. 5); teeth in both jaws.

SPINETAIL MOBULA *Mobula japanica*   **Fig. 26 opp. Pl. 5**
Identification: Mouth on underside of head (Fig. 26); teeth in *both* jaws, in rows extending to corners of mouth. A small sting at base of whiplike tail. Black above; white below. To at least 7 ft. (2.1 m) wide, 253 lb. (115 kg).
Range: N. Pacific; s. Calif. (off Santa Cruz I.). **Habitat:** Pelagic; near surface on high seas.
Similar species: (1) Smoothtail Mobula (below) has no sting, and a space between rows of teeth and mouth corners. (2) See Manta (above).

SMOOTHTAIL MOBULA *Mobula lucasana*   **Not shown**
Identification: Like Spinetail Mobula but no sting on the whiplike tail. Black or gray-black above; whitish below. To 7⅓ ft. (2.2 m) wide.
Range: S. Calif. to Costa Rica; may also occur off Senegambia (formerly Senegal), Africa. **Habitat:** Coastal and offshore.
Remarks: Makes spectacular leaps out of the water. A poorly known stingless mobula, *Mobula tarapacana,* occurs off Chile and might be the same species.
Similar species: See (1) Manta (p. 57) and (2) Spinetail Mobula (above).

CHIMAERAS: Subclass Holocephali
Order Chimaeriformes

An ancient group of cartilaginous fishes. Their gills are covered by a flap, resulting in 1 external opening on each side. The body tapers to a slender tail. 2 dorsal fins — 1st with a spine; 2nd spineless, long, and low. 2 pairs of upper and 1 pair of lower tooth plates; the teeth project from the mouth like rat incisors. Lateral line conspicuous. Skin slippery, unscaled (small denticles on back in some species, but not in ours). Male has a knockerlike clasping organ on forehead, 2 hooked clasping organs before the pelvic fins, and — as in other male cartilaginous fishes — a clasper (copulatory organ) covered by small hooked denticles at each pelvic fin. Chimaeras are found nearly worldwide. Many live at very great or moderate depths; a few occur in shallow water at high latitudes. 3 families, 2 in our area; about 35 species, 3 in our area.

Chimaeras: Family Chimaeridae

These have a short, blunt, rounded snout. Largest to 5 ft. (1.5 m). The family is nearly worldwide in all seas. They are found from near shore to offshore at depths up to 7741 ft. (2359 m); most occur in deep water. They feed on invertebrates and fishes and are feeble swimmers. They lay eggs in elongate, spindle-shaped cases. About 25 species, 2 in our area.

SPOTTED RATFISH *Hydrolagus colliei*   **Pl. 6**
Identification: Unmistakable — large *rabbitlike head,* long tapering body. Prominent lateral line canals on unscaled *slippery skin.* Large *spine* at front of short 1st dorsal fin. Male has clublike appendage on forehead. Eye green. Pectoral fin *large,* triangular, with a fleshy base. Silvery or brownish, often with iridescent shadings of gold, green, and blue; has *white spots* on back. Caudal and dorsal fins dark-edged. To 38 in. (96 cm).
Range: Se. Alaska to Baja and n. Gulf of Calif.; common off B.C. to n. Calif. **Habitat:** Near bottom; close inshore from Wash. northward, deeper southward — to 2995 ft. (913 m).
Remarks: Eats clams, crustaceans, and fishes. Lays 5-in. (13-cm) brown egg cases (Fig. 27 opp. Pl. 6) on bottom, usually in spring and summer. Dorsal fin spine is venomous and can cause a painful, though not fatal, wound. Liver yields excellent machine oil.
Similar species: (1) A Black Ratfish, *Hydrolagus* species (not shown), was taken in a Sablefish trap at 4597 ft. (1401 m) off s. Calif. in 1978; 2 specimens were collected earlier in the Gulf of Calif. It is blue-black, without spots, and its 2nd dorsal fin is unnotched (deeply notched in the Spotted Ratfish). It may be a new species. (2) A specimen of the Longnose Chimaera, *Harriotta raleighana* (not shown), was recently caught in a Sablefish trap set in very deep water off s. Calif. Previously it was known from waters off s.-cen. Baja and from egg cases collected off s. Calif. It was also photographed in the Gulf of Calif. It belongs to another family (Rhinochimaeridae) that differs in having a *long, spearlike snout.*

5

Bony Fishes: Class Osteichthyes

This class includes all fishes except jawless ones (Chapter 3) and jawed cartilaginous fishes (Chapter 4). Bony fishes have jaws and, except in some fishes with reduced ossification, a bony skeleton. There is a single gill opening on each side (but sometimes the openings are united under the head). Scales are usually thin and overlapping, but some groups have none. The soft fin rays are striated (see rear endpapers), and, in cross-section, consist of 2 halves. Bony fishes vary greatly in shapes and sizes. They occur in virtually all waters of the world, from altitudes of over 3 mi. (4828 m) to the deepest ocean trenches nearly 7 mi. (11,265 m) below sea level. About 38 orders and 425 families, but classifications vary. About 25,000 species, of which about 10,000 (40%) occur in fresh water, the remainder in the sea.

Order Acipenseriformes

A primitive group composed of sturgeons (Family Acipenseridae) and paddlefishes (Family Polyodontidae). The skeleton is mostly cartilaginous, and the backbone curves upward into the caudal fin, making it heterocercal, as in sharks. Upper lobe of caudal fin longer than lower lobe. Mouth on underside of head. The 2 species of paddlefishes are restricted to fresh water; they have a flattened, paddlelike snout and virtually no scales. Sturgeons occur mostly in fresh water, but some are found in the ocean.

Sturgeons: Family Acipenseridae

Large, bottom-living, primitive fishes. Five rows of scutes (large bony plates) on body: 1 on back, 1 at middle of each side, and 1 on each side of belly). Scutes better developed in young, virtually disappear in very old individuals. Skin between scute rows usually rough. Head bony. Snout long, with row of 4 barbels in front of mouth. Mouth ventral, protrusible; no teeth in adults. Sometimes a spiracle above and behind eye. 1 dorsal fin, far back. Caudal fin heterocercal, with upper lobe longer than lower lobe. Adults 3–20 ft. (91–610 cm) or more, to 3200 lb. (1451 kg).

Sturgeons are found in North America and Eurasia. All of these fishes spawn in fresh water, but several species are anadromous, spending much of their life in the sea but moving to fresh water to spawn. In salt water most are found in bays and estuaries. Sturgeons feed primarily on bottom organisms such as worms, mollusks, and crustaceans, which they slurp up with their protrusible mouth. Populations have decreased in N. America, where they are now of limited sport and commercial importance; valuable elsewhere for caviar, meat, and other products. About 25 species, 2 in our area.

GREEN STURGEON *Acipenser medirostris*   **Pl. 6**
Identification: *23–30 bony scutes* in the midside row. 1–2 middorsal scutes *after* the *dorsal fin*. 4 *barbels,* usually *closer to mouth* than to snout tip. Young have a shovel-like snout. Grayish white to olive-green; some northern fish have stripes on belly and lower side. To 7 ft. (213 cm), 350 lb. (159 kg).
Range: Japan to n. Baja. **Habitat:** Often in brackish water; more common in ocean than White Sturgeon. Bottom-grubbing.
Similar species: See White Sturgeon (below).

WHITE STURGEON *Acipenser transmontanus*   **Pl. 6**
Identification: Similar to Green Sturgeon, but *38–48 bony scutes* in the midside row. No middorsal scute after the dorsal fin. 4 *barbels, closer to tip of snout* than to mouth. Grayish white. Formerly to 20 ft. (6.1 m), 1800 lb. (816 kg), but maximum today about 10 ft. (3 m), 400 lb. (181 kg).
Range: Alaska to n. Baja. **Habitat:** Mainly in fresh water; occasionally moves to ocean. Common in large rivers.
Remarks: Spawns in spring in fresh water. Does not mature until at least 11 years old. Important commercially for flesh and eggs (caviar), but less so since early 1900s. Gas-bladder linings were used to make gelatin (isinglass) until late 1800s.
Similar species: See Green Sturgeon (above).

Order Elopiformes

A small order including tarpons, bonefishes, and relatives. These fishes have *no fin spines, 1 dorsal fin,* abdominal pelvic fins (at midbelly), and *cycloid* scales. Most are *silvery.* As in eels, the larvae are ribbonlike (leptocephalous, see Fig. 12, p. 63). They differ from herrings and their relatives (Order Clupeiformes, p. 70) and from salmons and salmonlike fishes (Order Salmoniformes, p. 75) in a number of internal features and in having leptocephalous larvae. Herrings (except one African species) lack a lateral line, and Salmoniformes usually have an adipose fin (on the back ahead of the caudal fin). Worldwide, mostly in shallow tropical and temperate coastal seas but sometimes in rivers. 2–3 families; about 12 species, 2 in our area.

Tarpons: Family Elopidae

Large-mouthed, slender, mostly *silvery*. Pectoral fin *low* on body.
1 dorsal fin, nearly over pelvic fin; no fin spines. *No* adipose fin.
Caudal fin large and strongly *forked*. An elongate *bony plate*
(gular plate) at midline of chin. Numerous (up to 30 or more)
branchiostegal rays (bony splints on underside of head, which support the gill membranes). Scales small, *cycloid*. A lateral line. Most
are 1–3 ft. (30–91 cm). Adults feed mainly on crustaceans and
small fishes. Tarpons and their relatives occur in shallow warm
seas and in estuaries; sometimes in fresh water. About 7 species,
1 in our area.

MACHETE *Elops affinis*   **Pl. 6**
Identification: Slender, *silvery, large-mouthed. 1* dorsal fin with
only soft rays, pelvic fin *abdominal;* no scutes on belly. Caudal fin
long, deeply *forked.* Bluish above; silvery below. To 3 ft. (91 cm).
Range: Mandalay Beach (s. Calif.) to Peru; rare north of s. Baja.
Habitat: Shallow inshore areas, in schools.
Similar species: (1) Bonefish (below) has smaller mouth, jaw
does not reach eye. (2) In anchovies (p. 73 and Pl. 7) jaw extends
well past eye but snout projects beyond mouth, *no* lateral line.
(3) Our herrings (p. 70 and Pl. 7) are usually smaller and more
compressed; most have sawtoothed scales on belly, no lateral line.

Bonefishes: Family Albulidae

Medium-sized, mostly silvery. *Snout conical,* cartilaginous; *projects* beyond lower jaw. Mouth fairly small, almost horizontal. A
lateral line. Pectoral fin low on body; pelvic fin far back; no fin
spines. To about $3\frac{1}{2}$ ft. (107 cm). Probably as many as 4 species,
1 in our area.

BONEFISH *Albula vulpes*   **Pl. 6**
Identification: Snout *cartilaginous, conical;* mouth *small.* 1 dorsal fin, at midback over pelvic fin. Mostly silvery. Back bluish or
greenish with faint dusky stripes and bars (more pronounced in
young), which fade quickly at death. Base of some fins often yellowish. To about $1\frac{1}{2}$ ft. (46 cm) in e. Pacific, to over 3 ft. (91 cm)
elsewhere.
Range: Virtually all warm seas; San Francisco to Peru; uncommon north of Baja. **Habitat:** Inshore, including bays and estuaries. Often seen with tail out of water while it grubs for worms,
crustaceans, and mollusks on sand and mud flats.
Remarks: Highly prized as a sport fish, but incidental in our area.
Flesh tasty but has many small bones. Some populations might be
different species.

Similar species: (1) Jaw of Machete (p. 62) extends well past eye; 12–16 anal fin rays (8–10 in Bonefish). (2) Our herrings (Pl. 7) lack a lateral line; many have sawtoothed scales on belly, different snout, are more compressed. (3) In anchovies (Pl. 7) jaw extends well past eye. **Note:** The Milkfish, *Chanos chanos* (Order Gonorhynchiformes, Family Chanidae), occasionally strays to s. Calif. Like the Bonefish, it is silvery, with a small mouth, large forked caudal fin, no adipose fin, similar fin location. It is larger — to 5 ft. (152 cm) — with a shorter snout. Mouth when viewed from front is like a broad inverted V (not horizontal and not below a conical snout as in Bonefish). Widespread in Pacific and Indian Ocean; mostly oceanic.

Order Anguilliformes

A large order of *true eels,* including typical eels (Suborder Anguilloidei) and gulper eels (Suborder Saccopharyngoidei). Snakelike elongate body. No fin spines. *No* pelvic fins; often no pectoral fins. Most have no distinct caudal fin. Gill opening small. Most *lack* scales. All apparently have a strange transparent, ribbonlike larval stage called a *leptocephalus* (Fig. 12). Except for 1 family of freshwater eels, all are marine. They occur in a variety of habitats from inshore to the deep sea; some bury themselves in the bottom, many live on coral reefs, others on or off the bottom at great depths. Most occur in tropical and subtropical waters. About 20 families, 450 species.

Besides the 4 shallow-water families described in detail below, 8 rare deepwater families occur in the Pacific off N. America. It is unlikely that these eels would be seen or captured except by researchers using special trawls. These deepwater families are discussed briefly on pp. 66–69 and family representatives are shown in Fig. 13, p. 67. **Note:** In addition, leaflike leptocephali — to about 1 ft. (30 cm) — named the Leaflike Eel, *Thalassenchelys coheni,* have been taken in midwater trawls off our coast. Their bodies are about ⅓ as deep as they are long. These larvae contain developing eggs, so transformation to "adult" features may not even occur or the adult stage is short-lived. Researchers are still uncertain about family placement for this species.

Fig. 12 Eel larva (leptocephalus)

Morays: Family Muraenidae

Common, warm-water, rock- and reef-dwelling eels with a muscular, slightly compressed body. Head usually elevated behind eyes.
No pectoral fins (unlike most eels). Teeth well developed; usually
have canine teeth. Gill opening nearly *round*. No lateral line or
scales. Most have conspicuous pattern of blotches, spots, or bars.
Usually under 4 ft. (122 cm) but a few to 10 ft. (305 cm). Morays
are found in all warm seas, mostly in shallow tropical areas, among
coral and rocks; a few live in temperate waters. Some occur as deep
as 1640 ft. (500 m). Most are nocturnal and feed on fishes or any
dead organism. About 100 species, 1 in our area.

CALIFORNIA MORAY *Gymnothorax mordax*   **Pl. 6**
Identification: Our only shallow-water eel with *no pectoral fins*
(all eels lack pelvic fins). Somewhat compressed; head rises behind
eye. Dark brown to green, mottled. To 5 ft. (152 cm).
Range: Pt. Conception to s. Baja. **Habitat:** Common among
rocks; dwells in crevices or holes, usually with only head protruding. Shallow water and to 130 ft. (40 m), usually at 2–65 ft. (0.6–
20 m).
Remarks: Active mostly at night. Eats crustaceans, octopuses,
and small fishes. Handle with care — teeth can cause serious lacer-
ations. Sometimes bites skindivers without warning, but usually
bites only if prodded, speared, or captured; unlikely to leave its
hiding place to attack swimmers. Can be eaten; some morays in
other areas are occasionally poisonous. Leptocephali and young
virtually unknown. Long-lived — large specimens probably over
30 years old.

Conger Eels: Family Congridae

A large family of eels. Most have pectoral fins. Teeth stout; no long
canines. Eyes and lips well developed. Gill opening usually slitlike.
A lateral line but no scales. Most are gray or brown; dorsal and
anal fins sometimes have black edges. Most are active predators
that feed on other fishes and invertebrates. Common lengths are
1–3 ft. (30–91 cm), but some reach 9 ft. (2.7 m) or more. Worldwide
in tropical waters of all oceans, both shallow and deep. About 150
species, 1 in our area.

CATALINA CONGER *Gnathophis catalinensis*   **Pl. 6**
Identification: Brownish-gray, with a prominent pectoral fin.
Dorsal fin begins above rear of pectoral fin. Tail rounded, fin rays
at tip. A lateral line. To 16½ in. (42 cm).
Range: S. Calif. to Gulf of Calif. **Habitat:** Soft bottom. Burrows
tailfirst into loose sand. At 30–1200 ft. (9–366 m).

Similar species: (1) California Moray (above) is more compressed, has *no* pectoral fin. (2) In Pacific Worm Eel (below) dorsal fin begins well behind pectoral fin. In (3) Pacific Snake (below) and (4) Yellow Snake Eels (p. 66) end of tail is hard and pointed, with no fin rays. (5) See rare deepsea eels in Fig. 13, p. 67.

Snake Eels and Worm Eels:
Family Ophichthidae

Slender, nearly round eels. Many of these snakelike eels burrow tailfirst with a reinforced, pointed *spikelike tail.* Gill opening small, slitlike or round. A lateral line is present. Ours have pectoral fins. Posterior nostrils are uniquely in the mouth or just above the upper lip. Branchiostegal rays (gill supports) overlap at throat, unlike in most other eels. Many are mottled, barred, or spotted. To about 10 ft. (305 cm) but most 2–3 ft. (61–91 cm). Worldwide, mostly in tropical and subtropical seas, less common in temperate waters. They usually live on the bottom, some burrow; inshore to over 2461 ft. (750 m). Over 200 species; about 40 in the tropical e. Pacific, 3 or 4 reach Calif.

PACIFIC WORM EEL *Myrophis vafer* **Pl. 6**
Identification: Brownish, round, very elongate. Fin rays around tail tip. Dorsal fin begins *far behind* pectoral fin. To $18\frac{1}{4}$ in. (46 cm).
Range: San Pedro (s. Calif.) to Peru. **Habitat:** Tidepools, shallow areas, mostly on sand; to 36 ft. (11 m).
Remarks: Young are attracted to lights at sea surface.
Similar species: (1) California Moray (p. 64) has *no* pectoral fins. (2) In Catalina Conger (p. 64) dorsal fin begins *over* rear of *pectoral fin.* (3) Snake eels (below) have a spikelike tail, with no fin rays at tip.

PACIFIC SNAKE EEL *Ophichthus triserialis* **Pl. 6**
Identification: Snakelike. *Dark spots* on a tan body. End of tail *spikelike,* without fin rays. To $44\frac{1}{2}$ in. (113 cm).
Range: Off Klamath R. (n. Calif.) to Peru, including Gulf of Calif. and Galapagos Is. Rare north of Baja. Common on shrimp grounds from Gulf of Calif. southward. **Habitat:** Shallow bottom, to about 75 ft. (23 m); burrows in bottom.
Remarks: Sometimes caught on hook and line.
Similar species: (1) Yellow Snake Eel (p. 66) is not spotted. (2) Pacific Worm Eel (above) lacks spots; tail has fin rays at tip.
Note: Another spotted eel, the Tiger Snake Eel, *Myrichthys maculosus,* is known in our area from 2 doubtful records. Its spots are arranged more or less in 4 rows (not random). Occurs throughout the Pacific and Indian Oceans; e. Pacific population formerly called *Myrichthys tigrinus.*

YELLOW SNAKE EEL *Ophichthus zophochir*   **Pl. 6**
Identification: *Spikelike tail* with no fin rays (as in Pacific Snake
Eel) but *no spots*. Brown or maroon above; lighter below. To
$34\frac{1}{2}$ in. (88 cm).
Range: Eureka (n. Calif.) to Peru; uncommon north of Baja.
Habitat: Rocky and sandy areas, to 210 ft. (64 m).
Similar species: (1) Pacific Snake Eel (p. 65) is spotted. (2) Pacific Worm Eel (p. 65) has fin rays at tip of tail; dorsal fin begins
farther back.

Pike Congers: Family Muraenesocidae

A small family of elongate scaleless eels with large pectoral fins.
Body round in front, compressed toward rear. *Mouth large,* jaw
extends past eye; usually with prominent teeth. Fanglike teeth in
roof of mouth. Dorsal fin begins over or just before pectoral fin.
Gill opening large (for an eel), slitlike. Tail compressed, not threadlike, with tiny rayed fin at tip. Most are large — to 7 ft. (213 cm).
Pike congers occur in warm shallow waters, including estuaries
and fresh water. About 10 species; the species in our area is ques-
tionably placed in this family. **Family representative:** Twin-
pored Eel, *Xenomystax atrarius* (see pike congers in Fig. 13, p. 67).
To about 25 in. (64 cm). Off Vancouver I., the Gulf of Calif., and
Cen. America to Chile, at over 500 ft. (152 m).

Neck Eels: Family Derichthyidae

These eels have a short snout and a *narrow "neck."* Dorsal fin
begins well behind the head, anal fin begins after midbody. Large
pores around eye and on lower jaw. To $10\frac{1}{2}$ in. (27 cm). Worldwide
in tropical and temperate seas; midwater — at 1500–6000 ft. (457–
1829 m). 3 species, 1 in our area. **Family representative:** Neck
Eel, *Derichthys serpentinus* (see neck eels in Fig. 13, p. 67). To
$10\frac{1}{2}$ in. (27 cm). Worldwide in temperate seas, usually below
1500 ft. (457 m).

Duckbill Eels: Family Nettastomatidae

A small family of extremely elongate eels. Snout pointed, with an
expanded fleshy tip. Our species have *no pectoral fins.* Dorsal fin
begins about over the gill opening. Tail compressed, whiplike. Most
2–3 ft. (61–91 cm). These eels occur in deep midwater, mostly at
low latitudes. About 20 species, 3 in our area. **Family representative:** Dogface Witch Eel, *Facciolella gilberti* (see duckbill eels in
Fig. 13, p. 67). To 2 ft. (61 cm). Pt. Conception to Panama or farther south.

Note mouth shape and size, origin of dorsal
fin, presence or absence of pectoral fins

PIKE CONGERS
(Muraenesocidae)

NECK EELS
(Derichthyidae)

narrow 'neck'

DUCKBILL EELS
(Nettastomatidae)

SNIPE EELS
(Nemichthyidae)

SAWTOOTH EELS
(Serrivomeridae)

BOBTAIL EELS
(Cyematidae)

dartlike profile

eye

UMBRELLAMOUTH GULPERS
(Eurypharyngidae)

eye

WHIPTAIL GULPERS
(Saccopharyngidae)

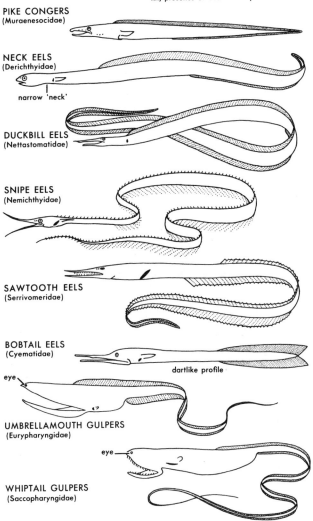

Fig. 13 Deepsea eel families

Snipe Eels: Family Nemichthyidae

Delicate deepsea eels with an extremely long tapering tail. *Long curved jaws* that do not close completely. No scales. Dorsal fin begins near head. Pectoral fins present. Teeth point inward in both jaws. Usually black or brownish. To over 4 ft. (122 cm). Snipe eels occur in all warm oceans, usually at great depths; some apparently worldwide.

These eels apparently orient themselves vertically in the water with the mouth pointing upward, and are thought to feed on pelagic crustaceans, capturing them by entangling the crustaceans' antennae in their jaws. Snout shorter in males than in females; sexes formerly considered different species in separate genera. Rarely seen; usually caught in midwater trawls in deep water; in s. Calif. also captured in Sablefish traps. About 9 species, 4 in our area. **Family representative:** Blackline Snipe Eel, *Avocettinops infans* (see snipe eels in Fig. 13, p. 67). To about 2 ft. (61 cm). Atlantic and Pacific.

Sawtooth Eels: Family Serrivomeridae

Silvery eels resembling snipe eels, but the dorsal fin begins *well behind* the head, above and behind the origin of the anal fin. 1 row of sawlike teeth in roof of mouth. To about 2½ ft. (76 cm). Usually in deep midwater, but may migrate to near surface. They occur in temperate and tropical latitudes of all oceans. About 10 species, 2 in our area. **Family representative:** Sawtooth Eel, *Serrivomer sector* (see sawtooth eels in Fig. 13, p. 67). To about 2½ ft. (76 cm). Pacific; cen. Calif. to Chile.

Bobtail Eels: Family Cyematidae

Peculiar long-jawed, blackish deepsea eels. Dorsal fin opposite anal fin; both begin at midbody and end in a way that creates a *dartlike profile*. Gill opening small, on underside. To about 6 in. (15 cm). Widely distributed in tropical and temperate latitudes of all oceans; in e. Pacific from Ore. to Panama. They occur in midwater, at depths below about 2000 ft. (610 m). Apparently only 1 species. **Family representative:** Bobtail Eel, *Cyema atrum* (see bobtail eels in Fig. 13, p. 67).

Whiptail Gulpers:
Family Saccopharyngidae

Peculiar delicate, black, scaleless eels with a *huge mouth*. Teeth curved and well developed but not fanglike. Dorsal fin begins well behind head. *Eye tiny, near snout tip.* Some have luminous grooves on body and tail. Stomach expandable, capable of holding large prey (thought to feed mostly on fishes). To about 6 ft. (183 cm), counting the extremely elongate tail, which is often broken during capture. Nearly worldwide in extremely deep midwater. Caught in midwater trawls, occasionally found dead at the surface. Species poorly known, at least 4; 1 has been taken off s. Calif. **Family representative:** *Saccopharynx* species (see whiptail gulpers in Fig. 13, p. 67). (**Note:** Small specimens of the bizarre Paddletail Onejaw, *Monognathus ahlstromi* — Family Monognathidae — are also known from off our coast. This species resembles whiptail gulpers in shape but has *no upper jaw,* front of *head rounded.*)

Umbrellamouth Gulpers:
Family Eurypharyngidae

Similar to whiptail gulpers, but mouth is even larger and the dorsal fin begins *over* the head. Teeth small. Gill opening and small pectoral fin low on side. *Eye tiny, at tip of snout.* Black. To 2½ ft. (76 cm). Probably nearly worldwide. Some are found as shallow as 1800 ft. (549 m), most at depths below 4000 ft. (1219 m). Apparently feeds mostly on crustaceans and fishes. Evidently only 1 species. **Family representative:** Umbrellamouth Gulper, *Eurypharynx pelecanoides* (see umbrellamouth gulpers in Fig. 13, p. 67).

Order Notacanthiformes

Deepsea eel-like fishes, including spiny eels and halosaurs. Unlike true eels, they have *fin spines and pelvic fins.* Elongate body tapers toward tail; no caudal fin (but sometimes broken tail regenerates with appearance of a caudal fin). Snout projects. Eye covered by transparent skin that is continuous with the skin on the head. Larvae leptocephalous, *huge* — to at least 6 ft. (183 cm). Unlike eel leptocephali, these have pelvic fins. Adults to at least 4–5 ft. (122–152 cm) but usually under 3 ft. (91 cm). They occur in all tropical and temperate seas. Most are found in the deep sea; all apparently live on or near the bottom. 3 families, 1 in our area; about 25 species, 2 in our area.

Spiny Eels: Family Notacanthidae

Eel-like fishes with a dorsal fin composed of short *isolated spines* not connected by membranes. Body compressed, tapers to a point. Mouth on underside of head; snout long. Pelvic fins present. Anal fin long, with spinous rays at front. To about 4 ft. (122 cm). Spiny eels are usually found deep in tropical and temperate seas; but a few occur as shallow as 420 ft. (128 m); mostly on the bottom. Nine species; 2 in our area, others reported from the Bering Sea. **Family representative:** Longnose Tapirfish, *Polyacanthonotus challengeri* (Fig. 14).

Fig. 14 Spiny Eel

Order Clupeiformes

A large order that includes herrings, anchovies, and their relatives. Most are compressed silvery fishes. No lateral line (except in 1 African species). 1 dorsal fin. Pelvic fins abdominal. No adipose fin, fin spines, or gular plate. Body often compressed; belly with a keel of modified scales (scutes). Most occur in schools. They support major fisheries — many are eaten by man; eggs of some are harvested; some are processed into oil, fertilizer, and fish meal. They are also eaten by larger fishes, aquatic mammals, and sea birds. Many species occur in fresh water, but most occur in shallow bays and shore waters of all tropical and temperate seas. 4–7 families (depending on classification used); 3 in our area. At least 300 species; 11 in our area.

Herrings: Family Clupeidae

Small, compressed silvery fishes. Belly of most sawtoothed, with a keel of *scutes.* They have *1 short dorsal fin* near the middle of the back, *no* adipose fin, and no fin spines. Pelvic fins *abdominal.* Caudal fin deeply *forked.* Scales *cycloid,* but head unscaled. Similar to anchovies (p. 73), but with a smaller mouth. Round herrings (p. 73) are more cigar-shaped, with a round smooth belly; pelvic fins completely behind the dorsal fin. Salmoniformes (p. 75) usually have an adipose fin; no scutes on belly. Most herrings are under 1 ft. (30 cm) but some reach 2½ ft. (76 cm).

Herrings are found in shallow waters of all seas, except in polar regions. Several subgroups occur in fresh water; some species are anadromous. Most herrings occur in schools. Many feed by straining minute organisms from the water with their long gill rakers, and some have a special pouch where they accumulate tiny food particles before swallowing them. A few "pick" small organisms from the water, and a few feed on fishes. About 200 species, 6 in our area.

AMERICAN SHAD   Pl. 7
Alosa sapidissima
Identification: Our *largest* herring. Body deep, compressed. Belly has sharp *keeled scutes* (Fig. 28 opp. Pl. 7). A row of *dark spots* on side. Dark blue above; silvery below. To 2½ ft. (76 cm).
Range: Introduced into Calif. from Atlantic in 1870s. Now from Kamchatka (USSR) to Alaska and to n. Baja. **Habitat:** Anadromous. In schools.
Remarks: Usually fished in fresh water in late spring and summer during spawning runs. Good game fish, especially when a flyrod is used. Delicious smoked. Usually feeds on minute organisms strained from the water.
Similar species: Pacific Sardine (p. 72) is our only other herring with a row of dark spots on the side, but its body is not as deep and its scutes are weaker.

PACIFIC HERRING *Clupea pallasii*   Pl. 7
Identification: Compressed, with *no black spots* on side; last dorsal fin ray *not elongate*. Pelvic fin under dorsal fin. Scutes on belly weak, not strongly keeled (Fig. 28 opp. Pl. 7). No striations on gill cover. Bluish green to olive above; silvery below. To 1½ ft. (46 cm).
Range: Korea and Japan to Arctic Alaska and to n. Baja; rare south of cen. Calif. **Habitat:** Frequently offshore, but usually inshore in harbors and large estuaries during spawning—in winter and/or spring (later in north). In schools.
Remarks: Each female can lay up to about 125,000 eggs; eggs are sticky and cling in masses to eelgrass, kelp, and fixed objects. In parts of our area eggs are harvested by hand and often exported to Japan. Fished commercially from San Francisco northward; usually marketed salted, cured, or fresh; in earlier times was a source for fish meal and oil; also used as bait. Some populations have decreased drastically. Considered by some researchers to be a Pacific population of the Atlantic Herring, *Clupea harengus,* not a separate species.
Similar species: (1) Pelvic fin of Pacific Round Herring (p. 73) is farther back, below rear of dorsal fin. (2) Pacific Sardine (p. 72) occasionally has no spots on side, but has *striations* on gill cover.

THREADFIN SHAD   Pl. 7
Dorosoma petenense
Identification: Small, compressed, silvery. *1 dark spot behind head. Last ray in dorsal fin* greatly *elongate* (threadlike). To about 9 in. (23 cm).
Range: Introduced into Calif. from Tenn. in 1953. Now occasionally in sea off Calif. and Ore. **Habitat:** Mostly in fresh water; taken in larger bays and harbors.
Similar species: (1) Middling Thread Herring (p. 72) has no large prominent dark spot. (2) Flatiron Herring (p. 72) has dark spot but last ray in dorsal fin is *not* elongate.

FLATIRON HERRING *Harengula thrissina*   **Pl. 7**
Identification: Small, deep-bodied, compressed. Eye large. A *black spot* behind head. Last ray in dorsal fin *not* elongate. *Strong scutes* on belly (as in American Shad, Fig. 28 opp. Pl. 7). Eye large. Bluish above; grading to silvery below. To $7\frac{1}{4}$ in. (18 cm).
Range: La Jolla (s. Calif.) to Peru; rare north of s. Baja. **Habitat:** Pelagic, near shore.
Similar species: In Threadfin Shad (p. 71) last ray in dorsal fin is *elongate.*

MIDDLING THREAD HERRING   **Not shown**
Opisthonema medirastre
Identification: Deep-bodied, strongly compressed. Last ray in dorsal fin greatly *elongate, threadlike.* No large dark spot behind head, but often has 1 or more rows of small spots or faint stripes on back. Silvery blue above; silvery below. To $10\frac{3}{4}$ in. (27 cm).
Range: Redondo Beach (s. Calif.) to Peru; common from s. Baja southward; stragglers reach s. Calif. **Habitat:** Pelagic, usually near shore in large schools.
Remarks: Sometimes used as bait for tunas.
Similar species: In Threadfin Shad (p. 71) last dorsal fin ray is elongate, but a black spot is present behind head. **Note:** The Deepbody Thread Herring, *Opisthonema libertate,* also has an elongate last dorsal fin ray, and it differs from the Middling Thread Herring only in technical features. Common from s. Baja southward, but specimens are occasionally caught off s. Calif. (may be releases from bait tanks of tuna boats); expect stragglers in warm-water years.

PACIFIC SARDINE *Sardinops sagax*   **Pl. 7**
Identification: Spindle-shaped, usually with *several dark spots* (number and arrangement vary) *on upper side.* Gill cover *striated.* Belly moderately compressed; with weakly keeled scutes (see Pacific Herring, Fig. 28 opp. Pl. 7). Pelvic fin under dorsal fin. Bluish to dark green above; silvery below. To $16\frac{1}{4}$ in. (41 cm) but usually less than 1 ft. (30 cm).
Range: Kamchatka (USSR) to se. Alaska and to Guaymas (Mex.); most common from Calif. southward. **Habitat:** Pelagic, usually near shore. In large schools.
Remarks: Formerly supported a major fishery off Calif. with peak yearly catches of over 1 billion lb. (454 million kg) in the 1930s, but stocks decreased in the late 1940s and early 1950s and the commercial fishery collapsed. Still important as food for predatory fishes and marine birds and mammals. Occasionally taken on small baited hook. Sometimes sold as bait. In Canada and Alaska known as Pilchard. Populations of herrings off Chile and Peru may belong to this species.
Similar species: (1) American Shad (p. 71) has a deeper body, stronger scutes, and usually more soft rays in anal fin (19–23, not

17–20). (2) In rare cases when Pacific Sardine has no spots, it might be confused with Pacific Herring (p. 71), which has no striations on the gill cover.

Round Herrings: Family Dussumieriidae

A small family of elongate, rounded, herringlike fishes. Belly *rounded,* not sawlike, with only 1 or 2 weak scutes at pelvic fin. No lateral line. Numerous (14–19) branchiostegal rays. Like herrings but unlike anchovies (see Pl. 7), they have a small mouth (jaw does not extend past eye). To about 14 in. (36 cm). Dwarf herrings — a tropical round-bellied group — are sometimes placed in this family, but they belong in the herring family (Clupeidae). Worldwide in warm seas. 2–4 species, limits poorly defined; 1 in our area.

PACIFIC ROUND HERRING   Pl. 7
Etrumeus acuminatus
Identification: Cylindrical. 1 dorsal fin, at midback. No large black spots but sometimes has row of specks on back. Last ray in dorsal fin not elongate. Belly rounded and smooth, with no scutes except for 1 obscure W-shaped scute at base of pelvic fin. Pelvic fin begins just below rear of or *behind* dorsal fin. No lateral line. Bluish above; silvery below. To 1 ft. (30 cm).
Range: Monterey Bay to Chile. **Habitat:** Pelagic, inshore; usually in large schools.
Remarks: Populations off Japan and in the Atlantic are sometimes considered part of this species; if they are the same species then the name *Etrumeus teres* would be used for all populations.
Similar species: (1) Our herrings (above) are more compressed, and the pelvic fins begin under the dorsal fin. (2) In anchovies (below) the jaw extends past the eye.

Anchovies: Family Engraulididae

Mostly silvery, small, compressed fishes with a *long snout* that overhangs a large mouth. Upper *jaw extends well past eye,* sometimes nearly to gill opening. Otherwise much like herrings in shape and fin location. 1 dorsal fin, no adipose fin. No fin spines or lateral line. Our species have no scutes on the belly. Many have a silvery side stripe. Most under 1 ft. (30 cm).

Anchovies are found in warm waters near shore in all oceans, usually in schools. Some enter rivers; a few occur in fresh water. They are important as food for predatory fishes and marine birds and mammals. Frequently used as bait, and in some areas harvested for food or processed into fish meal and oil. About 135 species, 4 in our area.

DEEPBODY ANCHOVY *Anchoa compressa* **Pl. 7**
Identification: Compressed, deep body. *29 or more rays in anal fin.* Brownish to green above; silvery below. Broad silver stripe on side. To 6½ in. (16 cm).
Range: Morro Bay (cen. Calif.) to n. Baja. **Habitat:** Common in bays and estuaries, often on outer coast; in schools.
Similar species: (1) Other anchovies have fewer than 27 anal fin rays. (2) Herrings (p. 70) and (3) Pacific Round Herring (p. 73) have a small mouth (upper jaw does not extend past eye). (4) Smelts (p. 80) have an adipose fin. (5) Silversides (p. 117) also have a silver stripe, but *2 dorsal fins* and a *small* mouth. (6) See Machete (p. 62).

SLOUGH ANCHOVY *Anchoa delicatissima* **Pl. 7**
Identification: *Small,* compressed, *23–26* anal fin rays. Greenish above; white below. A silver side stripe. To 3¾ in. (9.5 cm).
Range: Long Beach Harbor (s. Calif.) to s. Baja. **Habitat:** Bays and estuaries, sometimes on outer coast; usually in small schools.
Similar species: (1) Deepbody Anchovy (above) has silver on inside of gill cover (dusky in Slough Anchovy), and 29 or more anal fin rays. (2) See under Deepbody Anchovy (above).

ANCHOVETA *Cetengraulis mysticetus* **Not shown**
Identification: *Deep-bodied,* compressed. Gill membranes *joined* under head. Pelvic fin begins just slightly in front of dorsal fin. Greenish above; silvery below. To about 7 in. (18 cm).
Range: S. Calif. to Peru; rare north of s. Baja. **Habitat:** Mostly offshore, also bays and estuaries; in large schools.
Remarks: Only stragglers reach our area (may be releases from bait tanks of tuna boats).
Similar species: (1) Gill membranes are not joined in our other anchovies. (2) See under Deepbody Anchovy (above).

NORTHERN ANCHOVY *Engraulis mordax* **Pl. 7**
Identification: Our *most common* and *most northern anchovy.* Our only one that is *round* in cross section (not compressed). Anal fin begins below *rear* of dorsal fin. Blue to greenish above; silvery below. Adults have a faint silver side stripe. To over 9 in. (23 cm) but rarely over 7 in. (18 cm).
Range: Queen Charlotte Is. to tip of Baja. **Habitat:** Coastal, usually near shore; also to 720 ft. (219 m). Pelagic, usually in tightly packed schools.
Remarks: Important as food for other fishes and marine birds and mammals. Supports a bait fishery; most bait fishes sold as "anchovies" are this species. Also caught commercially for processing into fish meal and oil.
Similar species: (1) Other anchovies (above) are compressed and their anal fin begins under the middle of the dorsal fin. (2) See under Deepbody Anchovy (above). (3) See Pacific Round Herring (p. 73).

Order Salmoniformes

A large, diverse order including trouts, salmons, smelts, and their relatives. Most are elongate. A short dorsal fin near midbody. A small *adipose fin,* usually over the anal fin. Pectoral fin low on side. Pelvic fins abdominal. No fin spines. *Scales cycloid,* but head unscaled. 2 bones (maxillary and premaxillary) usually form the upper jaw. Photophores are present in many families. Found in all oceans and in fresh water; many marine species occur in deep water. Besides the 3 shallow-water families treated in detail below, 12 deepwater families off our coast are described on pp. 84–90; representative species of these families are shown in Fig. 15 (p. 86–87) or Pl. 48. About 25 families (depending on classification used), 15 or 16 in our area; over 500 species, at least 70 in our area.

Trouts and Salmons: Family Salmonidae

This well-known family includes two major groups: trouts, salmons, chars (Subfamily Salmoninae); and whitefishes (Subfamily Coregoninae). All have *small cycloid scales* and an *adipose fin;* the pelvic fins are *abdominal,* with a V-shaped *skin flap* at base. *No* fin spines — only soft rays. A *prominent* lateral line. Body usually *robust* (not compressed). These cold-water fishes are native to the N. Hemisphere, but some trouts and salmons have been introduced elsewhere.

Trouts, salmons, and chars have a square-cut caudal fin and strong jaw teeth; whitefishes have a forked caudal fin and weak jaw teeth. Most young whitefishes lack parr marks (dark bars on the side) characteristic of most young trouts, salmons, and chars (Fig. 29 opp Pl. 9). Whitefishes are entirely freshwater and thus are not treated further in this guide. Trouts and chars are primarily freshwater, but a few occur near shore in our area.

The 5 Pacific salmons are among our most familiar species. They are anadromous, spending from 1 to several years at sea (depending on the species), and often migrate hundreds or even thousands of miles before returning to spawn in the stream where they were born. Adult Pacific salmons (except for some yearling King Salmon males) die after spawning, but trouts, chars, and the Atlantic Salmon do not. Salmons spawn in bottom gravel of cold-water streams and lakes. Their large eggs — $\frac{1}{6}$–$\frac{1}{3}$ in. (4–8 mm) — are deposited in depressions or nests (redds). After fertilization, the eggs are covered with gravel. Several months are required for incubation and for the larvae to wiggle up through the gravel. The young of some salmons move to the ocean soon after emerging, but others may remain in fresh water for several years. Except for the Pink Salmon, young of our species have parr marks while in fresh water or when they just enter the sea. Young are difficult to identify; their appearance varies with size. The color patterns and characters shown in Fig. 29 (opp. Pl. 9) can be used to identify most young. Adults of the same species from different populations also may differ in coloration. About 70 species; 11 in the sea or in saltwater bays in our area.

PINK SALMON *Oncorhynchus gorbuscha*   **Pls. 8, 9**
Identification: Large *black*, mostly *oval spots* on *all* of *caudal fin* and *upper body*. In sea metallic blue or bluish green above; silvery below. At spawning, males develop a *humped back* and a hooked upper jaw (Pl. 9); back, side, and caudal fin usually reddish to yellowish. Females have no hump; jaw not markedly hooked, olive-green on side. Young lack parr marks (Fig. 29 opp. Pl. 9). To $2\frac{1}{2}$ ft. (76 cm), 12 lb. (5.4 kg) but usually 3–5 lb. (1.4–2.3 kg).
Range: Japan to the Arctic Ocean and south to n. Calif.; occasionally strays as far south as La Jolla (s. Calif.). Introduced in other areas, successfully in the upper Great Lakes. **Habitat:** Anadromous, in sea and coastal streams.
Remarks: Sometimes called the Humpback Salmon. Usually spawns near the sea in the fall; young emerge the following spring and soon move into the sea. Normally returns to spawn when 2 years old.
Similar species: (1) Coho Salmon (p. 77) lacks black spots on the lower half of the caudal fin. (2) Chinook Salmon (p. 77) has small *irregular* black spots. (3) Young Pink Salmon resemble smelts (p. 80 and Pl. 10), but snout is rounded in salmons and projects slightly beyond mouth.

CHUM SALMON *Oncorhynchus keta*   **Pls. 8, 9**
Identification: *Fine specks* on back, but *no black spots*. In sea metallic blue above; silvery below. Fins mostly dusky, edges of pelvic and anal fins usually pale in mature specimens (shown). At spawning, blackish or dark olive above; side with reddish or dusky irregular bars or blotches on dull greenish background; anal and pelvic fins white-tipped (especially in males); front teeth of males become more enlarged than in other salmons. To 40 in. (102 cm), 33 lb. (15 kg) but usually 10–15 lb. (4.5–6.8 kg).
Range: Japan to Arctic Alaska and to San Diego. **Habitat:** Anadromous, in sea and coastal streams.
Remarks: Called Dog Salmon in some areas. In our area spawns in streams that are close to the sea in late fall or in winter (in some areas even later). Young emerge in spring and early summer and move to the sea. Migrates extensively in the ocean. Matures and returns to home stream to spawn, usually after 3–5 years.
Similar species: (1) Sockeye Salmon (p. 77) has no white tips on fins and usually more than 30 gill rakers and rudiments on the first arch (16–18 in Chum Salmon; see rear endpapers). (2) Other salmons have black spots.

COHO or SILVER SALMON   Pls. 8, 9
Oncorhynchus kisutch

Identification: Black *spots* on *back* and on *upper part* of caudal fin. Gums *white* at base of teeth. In sea metallic blue above; silvery below. At spawning, males are dusky green on upper back and head, *bright red* on side, often blackish below; females bronze to *pinkish* red on side. To 38½ in. (98 cm), 31 lb. (14 kg) but usually 6–12 lb. (2.7–5.4 kg).

Range: Korea and Japan to Arctic Alaska and south to Baja. Rare in fresh water south of Santa Cruz (cen. Calif). **Habitat:** Anadromous, in sea and coastal streams.

Remarks: Known as the Silver Salmon, especially in Calif. Spawns in fall or winter. Young emerge in spring and usually remain in fresh water for 1 year. Matures in 2–4 years, most often in 3rd year.

Similar species: Chinook Salmon (below) has spots on all of caudal fin and gums black at base of teeth.

SOCKEYE or RED SALMON   Pls. 8, 9
Oncorhynchus nerka

Identification: Fine black specks but *no black spots* on back or caudal fin. 28–40 gill rakers and rudiments on 1st arch (see rear endpapers). In sea metallic blue-green above, silvery below. At spawning, males have a green head, bright red body, yellowish-green caudal fin, white lower jaw; females similar to males, but have green or yellow blotches in some populations. To 33 in. (84 cm), 15 lb. (6.8 kg) but usually 5–8 lb. (2.3–3.6 kg).

Range: N. Japan to Bering Sea and to Los Angeles. Rare in streams south of the Columbia R. system. **Habitat:** Anadromous, in sea and coastal streams.

Remarks: Sockeye Salmon is the official common name, but Red Salmon and Blueback Salmon widely used. Landlocked populations are common; those in Calif. are known as Kokanee Salmon. Spawns in summer, usually only in streams with lakes in their course; adults normally spend a short time in a lake and spawn at its edges, or above or just below it. Young usually emerge in spring and spend 1–3 years in the lake before moving to sea. Adults spend 1–4 years at sea; 2 years is common for B.C. stocks.

Similar species: Chum Salmon (p. 76) also lacks black spots, but has 18–26 gill rakers and rudiments on 1st arch.

CHINOOK or KING SALMON   Pls. 8, 9
Oncorhynchus tshawytscha

Identification: The *largest salmon;* specimens over 30 lb. (14 kg) are almost always this species. Upper back and *all* of caudal fin (and dorsal fin and adipose fin) have *irregular black spots*. Gums *black* at base of teeth. In sea bluish or greenish blue to gray or black above; silvery below. Maturing specimens very dark; smaller males often dull yellow; larger males often blotchy, dull red on

side. Females blackish. To 58 in. (147 cm); usually 10–15 lb. (4.5–6.8 kg), rarely over 50 lb. (23 kg); 1 specimen from Alaska reportedly weighed 135 lb. (61 kg).
Range: Japan to Bering Sea and to San Diego. Rare in fresh water south of the Sacramento-San Joaquin R. system (cen. Calif.).
Habitat: Anadromous, in sea and coastal streams.
Remarks: Official common name is Chinook Salmon, but in Calif. commonly called King Salmon; other names include Spring, Tyee, Blackmouth, and Quinnat Salmon. Record catch with sport gear weighed 92 lb. (41.7 kg). Most enter streams to spawn in fall but also in many rivers in spring. Spawns principally in large rivers, often near the sea but sometimes up to 600 mi. (966 km) inland. Young usually go to sea soon after hatching, but may remain in fresh water for 1 year. Most return to spawn after 4–5 years.
Similar species: (1) Sockeye (p. 77) and (2) Chum Salmons (p. 76) have *no* large black spots. (3) Coho Salmon (p. 77) has no black spots on *lower half* of caudal fin and has white gums near base of teeth. (4) Pink Salmon (p. 76) has large *oval* spots on upper back and caudal fin, and does not exceed $2\frac{1}{2}$ ft. (76 cm).

CUTTHROAT TROUT *Salmo clarkii*   Pl. 8
Identification: Usually a freshwater fish, but some populations are anadromous. In sea resembles the Rainbow Trout, but usually has a *red or orange "cutthroat" mark* on lower jaw. Body and fins (except pelvic fin) have *dark spots*. Inside of mouth white. Small *teeth on rear of tongue.* Bluish above; silvery below. In fresh water greenish above, lighter on side, silver below. Smaller in the sea — to about $2\frac{1}{2}$ ft. (76 cm), 17 lb. (8 kg) but usually 1–4 lb. (0.4–1.8 kg); freshwater specimens larger, record is 41 lb. (19 kg).
Range: In sea, from Gulf of Alaska to Eel R. (n. Calif.). **Habitat:** When in sea usually near rivers and estuaries; more common in fresh water.
Remarks: The anadromous Cutthroat Trout is often recognized as a subspecies, *Salmo clarkii clarkii,* with the common name Coast Cutthroat Trout, to distinguish it from strictly freshwater populations. Spawns in coastal streams in late winter or spring. Young move downstream when 2–4 years old and usually go to sea for a few months before returning to spawn in late fall or winter. Like other trouts (but unlike Pacific salmons) adults usually survive spawning.
Similar species: (1) Rainbow Trout (below) has no red "cutthroat" mark on lower jaw and no teeth on tongue. (2) Our salmons have 14 or more anal fin rays (Cutthroat Trout has 8–12) and no teeth on tongue. (3) See Note under Rainbow Trout (below).

RAINBOW TROUT or STEELHEAD   Pl. 8
Salmo gairdnerii
Identification: In sea bluish above; silvery below. Has *small black spots* on *back* and *most fins.* Sometimes a red to pink *side*

stripe. Head short; diameter of eye about equal to length of snout. Inside of mouth white. In fresh water back more greenish and side less silvery. To 45 in. (114 cm), over 40 lb. (18 kg) but usually less than 10 lb. (4.5 kg).
Range: Japan to Bering Sea and south to n. Baja; in sea only as far south as San Luis Obispo Co. (cen. Calif.). **Habitat:** Anadromous, in sea and coastal streams.
Remarks: A sea-run Rainbow Trout is called a "Steelhead." An important game fish. Spawns in coastal streams in fall or winter. Most young remain in fresh water 2–3 years, then move to sea for 2–3 years. Adults usually survive spawning. Can migrate extensively at sea.
Similar species: See (1) Cutthroat Trout (p. 78) and (2) Dolly Varden (below). (3) Salmons have 14 or more (not 9–12) anal fin rays. **Note:** Brown Trout, *Salmo trutta,* of European origin but introduced widely, occasionally enters the sea in our area. In sea resembles the Rainbow Trout but spots are less conspicuous, has no side stripe; it lacks the cutthroat mark of Cutthroat Trout. In fresh water Brown Trout has large dark spots on its head and upper body; spots on the side are surrounded by a pale halo. Sometimes has red spots.

DOLLY VARDEN *Salvelinus malma*   **Pl. 8**
Identification: A troutlike char, usually found in fresh water. In sea mostly dark blue above; silvery on side; silvery to white below (but sometimes pinkish on lower side). *Cream-colored* (not black) *spots* on most of body. Color varies more in fresh water, but usually bright yellow to red spots on back and side. To about 3 ft. (91 cm) but usually $1\frac{1}{2}$–2 ft. (46–61 cm); to 40 lb. (18 kg).
Range: Korea to Bering Sea and to Ore., with a freshwater population in Calif. (McCloud R. system) and in other western states. Most abundant in salt water in north, no records from sea south of Ore. **Habitat:** Anadromous, in sea and coastal streams.
Remarks: Many populations (some entirely freshwater) and possibly more than 1 species. Anadromous individuals may spend 2–3 years at sea, evidently near shore; migrate upstream usually in fall, spawn in spring.
Similar species: (1) Trouts and (2) salmons (above) lack pale spots, and salmons have 14 or more anal fin rays (8-11 in Dolly Varden). **Note:** (1) The Arctic Char, *Salvelinus alpinus,* a circumpolar anadromous or freshwater relative of the Dolly Varden, occurs in our area but only in Alaska. Similar to Dolly Varden at sea but has larger, pale to red spots and has more gill rakers (7–13 on upper part of 1st arch and 12–19 on lower part, not 3–9 and 8–14 — see rear endpapers). (2) The Bull Trout, *S. confluentus,* is primarily a freshwater species and is closely related to the Dolly Varden. It occurs from Alaska to Calif.; occasionally caught in bays, especially Puget Sound. Extremely difficult to distinguish

from Dolly Varden, but eye higher on head, and head slightly flatter and longer — distance from tip of snout to rear of gill cover divides into length of body from end of snout to base of tail 3.6–3.9 times (more than 4 times in Dolly Varden).

Smelts: Family Osmeridae

These slender, frail, *silvery,* shallow-water fishes are usually found in schools. Dorsal fin *short,* at midbody. Unlike herrings, smelts have *an adipose fin.* Scales are cycloid, but head is unscaled. Pelvic fins abdominal, with *no* skin flap at base. A lateral line is present, but often only on front of body. Smelts are usually dark above, silvery below; some have a silvery side stripe.

Smelts are found only in the Northern Hemisphere, in temperate to cold subarctic waters of the North Atlantic, Arctic, and North Pacific. Most smelts are marine, but a few species are anadromous or landlocked in freshwater. Some spawn on sandy beaches, usually in the surf; others spawn in fresh water. The Eulachon dies after spawning but the others do not. Smelts feed on small fishes and invertebrates. Some have a characteristic cucumberlike odor. At maturity, males of some species develop tubercles on the scales or a hairy ridge along the side, and their fins also change shape. Note that despite their names, the Jacksmelt and Topsmelt are silversides (Family Atherinidae, p. 117), not true smelts. Possibly 11 species, 8 in our area.

WHITEBAIT SMELT *Allosmerus elongatus*   **Pl. 10**
Identification: Look for the large *canine tooth* in roof of mouth, sometimes with a smaller tooth on either side (Fig. 30 opp. Pl. 10). Eye large. Greenish gray above, with a distinct silver side stripe. Adult males have a longer anal fin. To 7 in. (18 cm).
Range: Vancouver I. to San Francisco; San Pedro(?) (s. Calif.).
Habitat: Marine, nonanadromous, coastal. Often abundant in bays. In schools.
Remarks: Important as food for larger fishes. Spawns on subtidal sand banks.
Similar species: (1) Most other smelts have no enlarged teeth in roof of mouth, but Rainbow Smelt (p. 82) has two. (2) Silversides (p. 117) resemble smelts in size and coloration, but they have 2 *separate* dorsal fins, *no adipose fin,* and a *small mouth.* (3) Herrings (p. 70) have no adipose fin.

SURF SMELT *Hypomesus pretiosus*   **Pl. 10**
Identification: Mouth small, upper jaw ends *before* middle of eye. Pelvic fin usually begins under front of (not before) dorsal fin. Live specimens have a silvery side stripe, which darkens at death. Small pointed teeth, none enlarged. Blue-green above; silvery on side. Adult males more golden than females. To about 10 in. (25 cm).

Range: Prince William Sound (Gulf of Alaska) to Long Beach (s. Calif.). A subspecies, *Hypomesus pretiosus japonicus,* occurs from Korea to Alaska. **Habitat:** Marine, sometimes enters brackish water.

Remarks: One of the most frequently captured smelts; when spawning, often taken in surf with nets. Also caught commercially. Buries eggs on beaches — in coarse sand of surf zone on incoming tide. Spawns during daylight and is often called the Day Smelt, while Night Smelt (p. 82) spawns at night; often in the same area. **Similar species:** (1) Delta Smelt (below) has 10–12 pectoral fin rays (Surf Smelt 14-17). See (2) Whitebait Smelt (p. 80) and (3) Capelin (below).

DELTA SMELT *Hypomesus transpacificus* **Pl. 10**
Identification: Mouth small, upper jaw ends *before* middle of eye. Teeth small, *none* enlarged. 10–12 pectoral fin rays. Pelvic fin begins under front of dorsal fin. Mostly silvery, with a faint, speckled side stripe. To about 4½ in. (11 cm).
Range: Sacramento-San Joaquin R. system (cen. Calif.). A subspecies in Japan. **Habitat:** Brackish and fresh water.
Similar species: (1) Surf Smelt (p. 80) is the only other common small-mouthed smelt, but it is a wide-ranging marine species with 14–17 pectoral fin rays and a larger body — to 10 in. (25 cm). (2) Other smelts have a large mouth (upper jaw extends *past* middle of eye).

CAPELIN *Mallotus villosus* **Pl. 10**
Identification: A northern smelt with very *small scales* — more scale rows (170–220) cross lateral line than in other smelts. *Adipose fin rectangular,* with a very long base (longer than in our other marine smelts). 17–20 pectoral fin rays. Adult males have a prominent "hairy" band along side and long-based anal and pelvic fins. Olive-green above; silvery below. Usually has black dots on gill cover. In Pacific to about 8½ in. (22 cm).
Range: Circumpolar, in Arctic, N. Atlantic, and N. Pacific; Korea to Str. of Juan de Fuca. **Habitat:** Marine, oceanic; to 263 ft. (80 m). In schools.
Remarks: Comes inshore in large schools from April–Oct. to spawn on fine gravel or sand beaches; incubation 2–3 weeks. A common and important forage fish for other fishes; of limited commercial importance in our area.
Similar species: (1) Eulachon (p. 82) has *striated* gill cover (Fig. 30 opp. Pl. 10); 10–12 pectoral fin rays. (2) Rainbow Smelt (p. 82) has 11–14 pectoral fin rays, a larger mouth, and prominent *teeth* on tongue. (3) Night Smelt (p. 82) has a larger mouth, prominent *teeth* on tongue, larger scales in fewer rows (62–65) on side. (4) Longfin Smelt (p. 82) has 10–12 pectoral fin rays, *shorter*-based adipose fin, *canine teeth* on tongue.

RAINBOW SMELT *Osmerus mordax* **Pl. 10**
Identification: Mouth large, upper jaw reaches *rear* of eye. *2 large* canine *teeth* (and sometimes smaller ones) in roof of mouth; prominent *teeth* on tongue. Called Rainbow Smelt because of iridescent colors: olive-green above; silvery on side, usually with a conspicuous silver side stripe. Most have many dark specks on upper body. Rarely to 13 in. (33 cm), but in our area usually less than 8 in. (20 cm).
Range: N. Atlantic, Arctic, and N. Pacific; south to Vancouver (B.C.); rare south of Alaska. **Habitat:** Anadromous, or landlocked in fresh water.
Remarks: In our area life history poorly known; probably spawns in rivers above tidewater in spring, young move to sea.
Similar species: Most other smelts have a smaller mouth (upper jaw ends *before* middle of eye) and no enlarged teeth in roof of mouth — except Whitebait Smelt (p. 80), which has one.

NIGHT SMELT *Spirinchus starksi* **Pl. 10**
Identification: Mouth large, upper jaw extends to *rear* of eye. *Canine teeth* on tongue, but no enlarged teeth in roof of mouth. Brownish to greenish above, shading to silver on side and below. To 9 in. (23 cm).
Range: Se. Alaska to Pt. Arguello (cen. Calif.). **Habitat:** Marine.
Remarks: In our area life history poorly known, but spawns in surf at night. Captured when spawning, occasionally caught on hook and line; also fished commercially.
Similar species: See Longfin Smelt (below).

LONGFIN SMELT *Spirinchus thaleichthys* **Pl. 10**
Identification: *Mouth large,* upper jaw extends *to rear* of eye or beyond; chin projects in front. Jaw teeth small, none enlarged, but *canine teeth* on tongue. *Pectoral fin longer* than in any other smelt — almost reaches or extends past front of pelvic fin. Adult males have a larger, rounder anal fin and are usually darker than females. Greenish brown above; silvery below. No silver side stripe. To 6 in. (15 cm).
Range: Prince William Sound (Gulf of Alaska) to Monterey Bay. **Habitat:** Anadromous — ascends rivers in cooler months to spawn. In sea usually inshore. A few landlocked populations.
Similar species: (1) Most like the Night Smelt (above) but its pectoral fin ends well before front of pelvic fin. (2) Other smelts have a smaller mouth and/or enlarged teeth in roof of mouth, and (3) Eulachon (below) has a *striated* gill cover.

EULACHON *Thaleichthys pacificus* **Pl. 10**
Identification: Our only smelt with marked *striations on gill cover* (Fig. 30 opp. Pl. 10). 4–6 gill rakers on upper limb of 1st gill arch (see rear endpapers). Upper jaw extends to *rear* of eye. Usually no enlarged teeth. Adult males have a thickened ridge along side.

Bluish brown above with fine black speckling on back; shading to silver below. Caudal fin often *speckled.* To 10 in. (25 cm).
Range: Pribilof Is. (Bering Sea) and western coast of N. America south to Monterey Bay. **Habitat:** Anadromous; near shore and in coastal inlets and rivers. Young apparently deeper.
Remarks: From the Klamath R. (n. Calif.) northward moves into rivers to spawn in Mar.–May; dies after spawning. Young carried to sea by currents. Adults caught with dipnets during spawning runs; flesh rich and oily, excellent flavor. Source of food and cooking oil for Indians; they also dried specimens, inserted a wick, and used them as a torch, hence the alternate name Candlefish. An important food for other fishes and other marine animals.
Similar species: Other smelts have 8–14 gill rakers on upper part of 1st gill arch, no marked striations on gill cover.

Argentines: Family Argentinidae

These deepsea smeltlike fishes have 1 dorsal fin at midbody, usually an adipose fin, and a forked caudal fin. Pelvic fins abdominal, usually under dorsal fin; no skin flap at base of pelvic fin. Pectoral fin usually low on side. Eye large. Head usually pointed in front. Mouth small; jaws usually toothless, but teeth often present on tongue. Generally silvery; most have a silvery or brownish side stripe. These fishes are delicate and small — usually less than 8 in. (20 cm) but some grow to over 1 ft. (30 cm).

Argentines are found nearly worldwide in temperate and tropical waters. Some are bottom or near-bottom fishes — mostly at 300–1200 ft. (91–366 m). Others are pelagic near surface and at moderate depths. About 30 species (some poorly known), 4 in our area.

PACIFIC ARGENTINE *Argentina sialis*   **Pl. 10**
Identification: Resembles smelts but mouth *smaller,* eye larger, snout more *pointed.* Anal fin *far back,* under *adipose fin.* Body compressed. Mostly silvery; faint dark bars (fade soon after death). To 8½ in. (22 cm).
Range: Mouth of Columbia R. (Ore.) to s. Baja and Gulf of Calif.
Habitat: On or near bottom at 36–900 ft. (11–274 m).
Remarks: Most likely to be observed as stomach content of predatory fishes (especially rockfishes).
Similar species: (1) Smelts (above) have a larger mouth, upper jaw reaches at least to front of eye. (2) Deepsea smelts (p. 84) are mostly blackish; upper jaw reaches (or nearly reaches) front of eye. (3) Other fishes with an adipose fin (see especially Fig. 15, pp. 86–87) have a larger mouth or photophores (dotlike light organs). **Note:** 3 other argentines are pelagic in deep water off our coast: (1) Dusky Pencilsmelt, *Microstoma microstoma,* has no adipose fin and is more elongate; pelvic fin begins in front of dorsal

fin. (2) Stout Argentine, *Nansenia crassa,* has an adipose fin but is blackish. (3) Bluethroat Argentine, *N. candida* (see Argentinidae in Fig. 15, p. 86), also has an adipose fin and is silvery like the Pacific Argentine, but has fewer pectoral fin rays (about 11, not 15–18).

Deepsea Smelts: Family Bathylagidae

These small deepsea fishes are similar in appearance and fin location to argentines (above) and smelts (p. 80). Eye *large.* Mouth *small,* with weak teeth. No photophores. Scales large, cycloid, easily rubbed off. Most are blackish or gray but some are silvery. To about $7\frac{1}{2}$ in. (19 cm). Deepsea smelts occur in deep midwaters of all oceans. About 30 species (most poorly known), at least 5 in our area. **Family representative:** California Smoothtongue, *Leuroglossus stilbius* (see Bathylagidae in Fig. 15, p. 86), is most likely to be encountered. To 6 in. (15 cm). Abundant in midwater from near surface to 2264 ft. (690 m). Caught in midwater trawls. Oregon to Gulf of Calif. Other deepsea smelts in our area have a more rounded, shorter snout (not as long as eye diameter).

Spookfishes: Family Opisthoproctidae

These peculiar, delicate, deepsea fishes come in several shapes. In our species the eyes are *tubular* and point *upward.* 1 dorsal fin, far back; usually followed by an *adipose fin.* Pelvic fins *long,* often high up on side. Mouth small, with small teeth. Scales *large,* cycloid, easily rubbed off. Sometimes have light organs. To about 6 in. (15 cm) but most under 3 in. (7.6 cm). Spookfishes occur in all temperate and tropical seas, most at great depths in midwaters — usually deeper than 500 ft. (152 m). About 15 species (most poorly known), probably 4 in our area. **Family representatives:** (1) Brownsnout Spookfish, *Dolichopteryx longipes* (see Opisthoproctidae 1 in Fig. 15, p. 86). To 6 in. (15 cm). Apparently occurs worldwide in temperate and tropical waters at 500–1500 ft. (152–457 m). (2) Barreleye, *Macropinna microstoma* (see Opisthoproctidae 2 in Fig. 15, p. 86). To $1\frac{3}{4}$ in. (4.4 cm). A deep pelagic species; Bering Sea to Baja at about 325–2925 ft. (99–891 m).

Bristlemouths: Family Gonostomatidae

Some bristlemouths are very abundant, but they are rarely seen except by researchers. They are deepsea fishes, with a moderately long, compressed body, and often an adipose fin. *Photophores* present — those *along belly* usually are nearly evenly spaced in a *row.* No barbels. Eye large to small. Teeth small, none fanglike. Most bristlemouths are blackish (but much skin is commonly lost during capture); some nearly transparent. Scales (when present) are large, cycloid, easily rubbed off. Size varies — to about 14 in. (36 cm) but most under 3 in. (7.6 cm). Found in deep midwaters of all temperate and tropical seas. About 25 species, at least 6 in our area. Some species formerly included in this family are now placed in the next 2 families. The 3 families are not easily distinguished on the basis of external features. **Family representative:** Benttooth Bristlemouth, *Cyclothone acclinidens* (see Gonostomatidae in Fig. 15, p. 86). To $2\frac{4}{5}$ in. (7.1 cm). Worldwide in tropical and temperate seas at 180–3412 ft. (55–1040 m).

Hatchetfishes: Family Sternoptychidae

Hatchetfishes are small deepwater fishes, some of which resemble bristlemouths. Body usually deepest in front; strongly compressed and *hatchet-shaped* in some. Mouth *large,* points upward. *Photophores* often *large* — in rows or clumped in short series. Eye somewhat *tubular* in some. Usually an adipose fin, often with a long base. Most under 3 in. (7.6 cm). Hatchetfishes occur in the open sea, mostly in deep water in tropical and temperate seas. The marine species are not related to the freshwater "hatchetfishes" of fish hobbyists. About 40 species, 10 in our area. **Family representatives:** (1) Silver Hatchetfish, *Argyropelecus lychnus* (Pl. 48). To $2\frac{1}{3}$ in. (5.9 cm). E. Pacific; s. B.C. to Calif. and farther south; bathypelagic. (2) Bottlelights, *Danaphos oculatus* (see Sternoptychidae in Fig. 15, p. 86). To $2\frac{1}{4}$ in. (5.7 cm). Pacific and Indian Oceans at about 600–3000 ft. (183–914 m).

Lightfishes: Family Photichthyidae

These deepsea midwater fishes resemble some species of the 2 preceding families. They are elongate, and the mouth is large with no fangs. Eye moderate to large; tubular in some species. Photophores — ones on belly usually evenly spaced in rows. Usually an adipose fin. Scaled. Most are black, but much skin and scales are commonly rubbed off during capture. To about 13 in. (33 cm). Perhaps 25 species, at least 5 in our area. **Family representative:** Oceanic Lightfish, *Vinciguerria nimbaria* (see Photichthyidae in Fig. 15, p. 86). To about 2 in. (5.1 cm). All tropical and temperate seas; in our area from Calif. southward; deep-living.

Scaly Dragonfishes: Family Stomiatidae

These long, slender, compressed deepsea fishes have 5–6 rows of pigmented *hexagonal areas on the side,* each covered by a scale (as in the next family). Dorsal fin over anal fin, far back. No adipose fin. Mouth large; some teeth *fanglike.* A barbel at chin (apparently used as lure). Tiny photophores cover much of body; ones on belly are in 2 long rows on each side. Scales thin, usually lost during

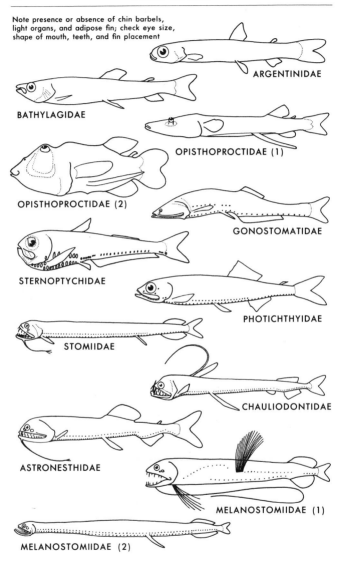

Note presence or absence of chin barbels,
light organs, and adipose fin; check eye size,
shape of mouth, teeth, and fin placement

ARGENTINIDAE

BATHYLAGIDAE

OPISTHOPROCTIDAE (1)

OPISTHOPROCTIDAE (2)

GONOSTOMATIDAE

STERNOPTYCHIDAE

PHOTICHTHYIDAE

STOMIIDAE

CHAULIODONTIDAE

ASTRONESTHIDAE

MELANOSTOMIIDAE (1)

MELANOSTOMIIDAE (2)

Fig. 15 Deepsea Salmoniform and Myctophiform families

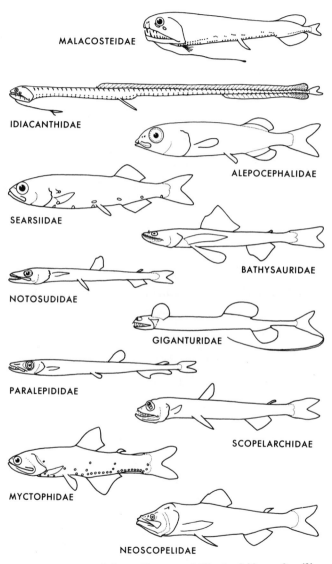

Fig. 15 Deepsea Salmoniform and Myctophiform families

capture. Blackish, iridescent. To about 16 in. (41 cm). They occur worldwide in tropical and temperate waters, usually at about 984–1640 ft. (300–500 m). About 10 species, 1 in our area. **Family representative:** Blackbelly Dragonfish, *Stomias atriventer* (see Stomiidae in Fig. 15, p. 86). To 10 in. (25 cm). Calif. to Mexico (possibly to Chile), usually at less than 1000 ft. (305 m).

Viperfishes: Family Chauliodontidae

Compressed deepsea fishes with pigmented hexagonal areas under scales (similar to those on scaly dragonfishes). The dorsal fin is *just behind the head;* 1st ray long, filamentous. Mouth *large,* with *huge fangs that protrude from the mouth.* Some species (but not ours) have a small chin barbel. Photophores — those on belly in rows. An adipose fin; also a similar fin or flap on belly before the anal fin. Most under 1 ft. (30 cm). Viperfishes occur in all oceans; they are usually pelagic, sometimes on or near bottom; usually at great depths but occasionally at less than 100 ft. (30 m). About 6 species, one in our area. **Family representative:** Pacific Viperfish, *Chauliodus macouni* (see Chauliodontidae in Fig. 15, p. 86). To 10 in. (25 cm). Gulf of Alaska to cen. Baja, from 250 ft. (76 m) possibly to 5000 ft. (1524 m).

Snaggletooths: Family Astronesthidae

Small fishes with rows of photophores on belly — most evenly spaced, in 2 rows. Dorsal fin begins near midbody, between pelvic and anal fins. Adipose fin; often a similar fin on belly before anal fin. A chin barbel. *No scales.* Teeth moderate to large, usually some fanglike. Most snaggletooths are fairly small — to about 6 in. (15 cm) — but some to 1 ft. (30 cm). Snaggletooths occur in temperate and especially tropical waters; most at 330–984 ft. (100–300 m), but some as deep as 9842 ft. (3000 m). About 25 species, 2 in our area. **Family representative:** Panama Snaggletooth, *Borostomias panamensis* (see Astronesthidae in Fig. 15, p. 86). To 1 ft. (30 cm). E. Pacific; Pt. Conception southward. Bathypelagic.

Scaleless Dragonfishes:
Family Melanostomiidae

A large family of slender deepsea fishes. Photophores, in rows on belly. Many have a very long *chin barbel.* Jaws large; usually some canine teeth. No *scales.* (Except for loosejaws — the next family — our other deepsea fishes with photophores have scales.) Dorsal fin *far back,* usually over anal fin. Some have no pectoral fins, usually no adipose fin. Mostly black. Most about 4–6 in. (10–15 cm), but some over 1 ft. (30 cm). Scaleless dragonfishes occur in temperate and tropical seas, usually at moderate depths. About 90 species, 7 in our area. **Family representatives:** (1) Highfin Dragonfish, *Bathophilus flemingi* (see Melanostomiidae 1 in Fig. 15, p. 86). To about 6½ in. (16 cm). B.C. to Baja. (2) Longfin Dragonfish, *Tactostoma macropus* (see Melanostomiidae 2 in Fig. 15, p. 86). To 13½ in. (34 cm). Gulf of Alaska to s. Calif.

Loosejaws: Family Malacosteidae

These fishes have *no skin between their lower jaws,* and hence no floor to the mouth, so their lower jaws are "loose" — the source of their name. Like scaleless dragonfishes and snaggletooths (above) they have an *elongate* body and *no scales.* Photophores on head and body, commonly in rows on belly. Dorsal fin far back, over anal fin. *No* adipose fin. Some species have no pectoral fins. Many have a *chin barbel.* Jaws very elongate; teeth well developed, some fanglike. Mostly black. Most are small — under 9 in. (23 cm). Loosejaws occur in all warm oceans; they are bathypelagic — to 4000 ft. (1219 m) — but are sometimes taken near the surface in midwater trawls. About 10 species, 2 in our area. **Family representative:** Shiny Loosejaw, *Aristostomias scintillans* (see Malacosteidae in Fig. 15, p. 87). To about 9 in. (23 cm) but usually under 6 in. (15 cm). Southern B.C. to cen. Baja.

Blackdragons: Family Idiacanthidae

A small group of *very elongate* deepsea fishes. *Dorsal and anal fins long,* extend nearly to caudal fin. *No adipose fin.* Adults have no pectoral fins; males also lack pelvic fins. Females have fanglike teeth, males have no jaw teeth. Females have a chin barbel (shown). *No scales.* Rows of *photophores* on belly. Males dark brown; females black. Males to about 3 in. (7.6 cm); females to 16 in. (41 cm). Deepsea fishes — near the surface to about 6562 ft. (2000 m). About 3 species, 1 in our area. **Family representative:** Pacific Blackdragon, *Idiacanthus antrostomus* (see Idiacanthidae in Fig. 15, p. 87). Calif. to tropical e. Pacific.

Slickheads: Family Alepocephalidae

Deepsea fishes usually characterized by an *unscaled ("slick") head* — hence the family name. Dorsal fin often over anal fin, both usually after the midbody. Scales are small to large, cycloid, but some species are unscaled. Skin slippery, flesh flabby. No adipose fin, fin spines, or barbels. Some have no teeth; others have small to large (fanglike) teeth. When light organs are present, they are under scales, or skin, or on stalks arranged irregularly or in complex patterns. Most are blackish. Usually to about 1 ft. (30 cm) but some reach 2 ft. (61 cm) or more. Some species probably school. Slickheads occur in all temperate and tropical seas; most below 1500 ft. (457 m), usually near or on bottom. About 75 species, 7 in our area. Slickheads are related to tubeshoulders (below); some researchers combine both families into one. **Family representative:** California Slickhead, *Alepocephalus tenebrosus* (see Alepocephalidae in Fig. 15, p. 87), is the most common species in our area. To 2 ft. (61 cm). Caught in trawls, traps, and on setlines. Bering Sea to at least Calif. Near and on bottom at 150–5000 ft. (46–1524 m).

Tubeshoulders: Family Searsiidae

Tubeshoulders resemble slickheads (above); sometimes the two families are combined. Body shape and fin location are very similar. Dorsal fin far back, over anal fin. Pelvic fins abdominal, about at midbody. *No* adipose fin. Scales cycloid. Teeth present on both jaws, but sometimes tiny. A *tubelike projection* is located just above the pectoral fin — this is the external opening of a sac (shoulder organ) that is thought to secrete a luminous mucus. This "tube" is also the source of the family's name. Some species have light organs, mostly on the belly but not tightly packed in a row. Most under 8 in. (20 cm). Adults normally seem to occur below 3000 ft. (914 m), young shallower. Unlikely to be seen except by researchers using midwater trawls. About 25 species (many poorly known), 6 in our area. **Family representative:** Shining Tubeshoulder, *Sagamichthys abei* (see Searsiidae in Fig. 15, p. 87), is the most common and most northern tubeshoulder in our area. To about 13 in. (33 cm). B.C. to Calif., also other areas of N. Pacific and se. Pacific.

Order Myctophiformes

A diverse group of mostly deepsea families — somewhat intermediate between the primitive lower fishes and the advanced fishes treated in subsequent orders. The order is not easily distinguished from the trouts and their allies (Order Salmoniformes) and from some higher fishes on the basis of external features, but each myctophiform family is distinctive. The maxillary bone does not border the mouth as it does in most salmoniform fishes and other lower fishes. They have no fin spines, only soft rays. Most species have an *adipose fin*. The pelvic fins are usually abdominal. When present, scales are *cycloid*. Many have *photophores*. Some researchers include other families in this order, or divide it into 2 or more orders. About 16–17 families, 7 in our area. Only a family representative is given for the deepsea families.

Lizardfishes: Family Synodontidae

Elongate *cylindrical* fishes with a *lizardlike head.* Mouth *large,* with many small, sharp teeth. Dorsal fin at about midbody. No spinous fin rays. An adipose fin (except in adults of 1 Australian species). Anal fin short, below adipose fin. Pelvic fins abdominal, but fairly far forward (ahead of dorsal fin), with 8-9 rays. Caudal fin forked. Most are brownish. To about 25 in. (64 cm).

Lizardfishes are found in warm shallow waters of all oceans, mostly on sand or mud bottoms. These fishes usually sit on the bottom; some species bury themselves in the sediment with only their eyes exposed. Young lizardfishes are nearly transparent, elongate, scaleless, with a row of black blotches under the skin on the belly. About 35 species, 1 in our area. **Note:** We include the deepsea lizardfishes (Family Bathysauridae) in this family although some researchers treat them as a separate family. The 3 species live deep — usually below 5400 ft. (1646 m). They are similar to lizardfishes, but the head is flattened and the teeth are curved and barbed. 1 species occurs in our area, off Oregon: the Highfin Lizardfish, *Bathysaurus mollis* (see Bathysauridae in Fig. 15, p. 87). To about 29 in. (74 cm). Atlantic and Pacific.

CALIFORNIA LIZARDFISH *Synodus lucioceps*   **Pl. 10**
Identification: Cylindrical, elongate. Head *small,* lizardlike. Snout nearly *triangular* when viewed from above. Jaw extends well past eye. Teeth *large,* caninelike. A small *adipose fin.* Pelvic fin begins before or under front of dorsal fin. Mostly brown above; lighter below. Pelvic fin yellowish. To about 25 in. (64 cm).
Range: San Francisco to Guaymas (Mex.). **Habitat:** On mud or sand bottom at 5-750 ft. (1.5-229 m) but usually at 60-150 ft. (18-46 m).
Remarks: Sometimes caught on baited hook, but not considered good eating. Not likely to be confused with any other species in our area. Young — less than 3 in. (7.6 cm) — are nearly transparent, with a row of large black spots under the skin on the belly.

Telescopefishes: Family Giganturidae

These rare, peculiar deepsea fishes have large *tubular eyes* that *point forward.* Mouth large, jaw extends past eye. Teeth numerous — movable, can be depressed backward. No scales or light organs. Pectoral fin high on side, above the gill opening. No pelvic fins. No adipose fin (at least in adults). Middle rays of lower lobe of caudal fin elongate. Mostly silvery. Telescopefishes occur in all warm oceans, probably at about 1640-3280 ft. (500-1000 m). About 5 species, 1 in our area. **Family representative:** Pacific

Telescopefish, *Rosaura lisae* (see Giganturidae in Fig. 15, p. 87). To about 8 in. (20 cm). Few specimens — so far only known to occur off s. Calif., n. Baja, north of Hawaii, and in S. Pacific. Bathypelagic.

Lancetfishes: Family Alepisauridae

A small family of elongate deepsea fishes with a long, high, *sail-like dorsal fin,* which begins behind the head and continues almost to the small *adipose fin.* A fleshy keel on the caudal peduncle. Mouth large, with small teeth in jaws but long, *daggerlike teeth in roof of mouth.* Body flaccid, scaleless; bones weak. Pectoral fins long, low on body. Pelvic fins abdominal, under middle of dorsal fin; with 8–10 rays. Lancetfishes are *large* predatory fishes, among the largest in the deep sea — to 6⅚ ft. (208 cm), 15 lb. (6.8 kg). They are wide-ranging in midwaters of the Atlantic and Pacific, occasionally near the surface. 2–3 species, 1 in our area.

LONGNOSE LANCETFISH *Alepisaurus ferox*   **Pl. 47**
Identification: A distinctive large deepsea fish with a long slender body and a large *sail-like dorsal fin.* Small *adipose fin.* Long, *daggerlike teeth in roof of mouth.* Mostly iridescent; fins brown to black. To 6⅚ ft. (208 cm).
Range: Almost worldwide in temperate and tropical seas; Unalaska I. (Alaska) to Chile. **Habitat:** Pelagic to bathypelagic — from near surface to 6000 ft. (1829 m).
Remarks: Not likely to be confused with any other species in our area. Rarely encountered; sometimes washes up on beaches or occasionally caught on halibut longlines or trolling gear. The delicate dorsal fin is usually damaged during capture. A voracious predator; digestion is apparently slow — unusual deepsea specimens have been found as stomach contents. Hermaphroditic; individuals bisexual.

Daggertooths: Family Anotopteridae

DAGGERTOOTH *Anotopterus pharao*   **Pl. 47**
Identification: Easily identified — slender, elongate, with *no dorsal fin.* A small *adipose fin.* A small projection at tip of lower jaw. Mouth large, with strong teeth; largest teeth fanglike, in a row on both sides of the mouth roof. Anal fin small, under adipose fin. Mostly iridescent to silver, but darker above and at rear. Caudal fin dark; pectoral fin rays black-tipped. Large — to about 4⅚ ft. (147 cm), 3⅜ lb. (1.6 kg).
Range: Japan to Bering Sea and to s. Calif., and offshore in the N. Pacific; also Atlantic and Antarctic, but evidently rare or absent in tropics. **Habitat:** Pelagic, in a wide range of depths in deep seas, sometimes near surface.

Remarks: Apparently 1 species in the family, but more specimens must be studied; captures should be reported to a natural history museum. A predator. Preyed on by other fishes (such as albacores) and whales. Sometimes caught by salmon trollers.

Pearleyes: Family Scopelarchidae

These rare deepsea fishes get their name from a unique glistening *white spot on the eye* (called a pearl organ). The *eyes* are *tubular* and somewhat telescopic — directed upward, or forward and upward. *Small dorsal fin* begins before midbody; a slender *adipose fin.* Cycloid scales on body and rear of head. Upper jaw extends beyond middle of eye; lower jaw curves upward. 2 rows of teeth in lower jaw; inner row larger, caninelike. No rows of photophores.

Adults are presumed to be mostly mesopelagic and bathypelagic — most live at about 1640–3280 ft. (500–1000 m), but some are found shallower and at night possibly range near the surface. Pearleyes are sometimes found in the stomach of such deep-feeding sportfishes as albacores and salmons, but are most likely to be seen only by researchers using midwater trawls in deep water. Worldwide in temperate, tropical, and Antarctic waters. Some grow to more than 9 in. (23 cm) but most are under 5 in. (13 cm). Hermaphroditic. 17 species, 5 in our area. **Family representative:** Northern Pearleye, *Benthalbella dentata* (see Scopelarchidae in Fig. 15, p. 87). To about $9\frac{1}{4}$ in. (24 cm). N. Pacific; Gulf of Alaska to Baja. Usually at 1640–3280 ft. (500–1000 m).

Barracudinas: Family Paralepididae

These elongate, slender, deepsea fishes have a compressed, *pointed* head. Mouth usually large, with sharp teeth but no long fangs. Dorsal fin *small,* located at about midbody. *Adipose fin* over rear of anal fin; a similar fin precedes anal fin in some species. Pelvic fins abdominal. Anal fin *longer* than dorsal fin; *far back,* near caudal fin. Anus well in front of anal fin, usually below or before tip of pelvic fin. Some species have no scales, except for lateral line; other species have cycloid scales. Either no light organs or 1 or 2 luminous ducts located in muscles of belly. Scaled species are usually silvery, unscaled ones nearly transparent. To 3 ft. (91 cm).

Barracudinas occur in all temperate and tropical seas, in midwater, occasionally at surface. Observers in diving saucers have reported that they swim vertically, with the head up. Whales and predatory fishes such as albacores and salmons feed on them. About 50 species, 6 or 7 in our area. **Family representative:** Slender Barracudina, *Lestidiops ringens* (see Paralepididae in Fig. 15, p. 87). An unscaled species. To about $8\frac{1}{4}$ in. (21 cm). B.C. to cen. Baja, from near surface to bathypelagic depths.

Paperbones: Family Notosudidae

A small family of elongate deepsea fishes that are similar in shape
and fin location to barracudinas (above). Eyes and mouth large;
teeth small, pointed. An adipose fin. No light organs. Scales relatively large, cycloid, easily rubbed off. 15–21 anal fin rays (20–24 in
barracudinas). To about 20 in. (51 cm). Worldwide in temperate
and tropical seas. Adults are probably bathypelagic, young shallower. May be found as stomach content of deep-feeding sportfishes, but most likely to be seen only by researchers using
midwater trawls. Number of species uncertain — about 6, including 1 in our area. **Family representative:** Scaly Paperbone,
Scopelosaurus harryi (see Notosudidae in Fig. 15, p. 87). To
$8\frac{1}{2}$ in. (22 cm). N. Pacific; off Japan, B.C., and s. Calif. at about
1640–2625 ft. (500–800 m).

Lanternfishes: Family Myctophidae

A large family of deepsea fishes. All species have *many small round
photophores* on head and body; most on ventral surface, in groups
and broken rows. *Snout blunt;* mouth fairly large, with small teeth.
Eye large. Dorsal fin near midbody; an adipose fin. Pelvic fins abdominal. Anal fin usually begins below dorsal fin. Scales large,
easily rubbed off. Brown to black, bluish black, or blackish silver.
These fishes are small — most about $2\frac{1}{2}$–4 in. (6.4–10 cm) but a
few reach 9–12 in. (23–30 cm).

Lanternfishes occur in all oceans. Nearly all of these are oceanic,
living at moderate to deep depths during the day and migrating to
or near surface at night. At night some species can be seen and
caught with a dipnet if a light is suspended from a drifting ves-
sel. Fed on by a variety of oceanic predators and may be
found as stomach content of such fishes as albacores and salmons.
Genera and species are identified on the basis of technical features,
especially the position and arrangement of photophores. About
250 species, about 35 in our area. **Family representatives:** (1)
Northern Lampfish, *Stenobrachius leucopsarus* (Pl. 48). To 5 in.
(13 cm). Japan to Bering Sea and to n. Baja. (2) Broadfin
Lampfish, *Lampanyctus ritteri* (see Myctophidae in Fig. 15, p. 87).
To $7\frac{1}{2}$ in. (19 cm). B.C. to Mexico. Bathypelagic.

Blackchins: Family Neoscopelidae

A small family of deepsea fishes that resemble lanternfishes but
have smaller eyes and fewer photophores (or none). Scales large,
easily rubbed off. Dorsal fin before midbody, not over anal fin. An
adipose fin. Mostly blackish. To about 1 ft. (30 cm). Blackchins

occur in midwater of all temperate and tropical seas at about 2296–6562 ft. (700–2000 m). About 6 species, 2 in our area. **Family representative:** Blackchin, *Scopelengys tristis* (see Neoscopelidae in Fig. 15, p. 87). To 8 in. (20 cm). Atlantic, Indian, and Pacific Oceans; s. Calif. to Chile in e. Pacific.

Order Cypriniformes

These fishes are found almost entirely in fresh water. The order, with many families and perhaps 3500 species, is included here only because the Common Carp sometimes occurs in brackish bays and estuaries in our area. With catfishes (Order Siluriformes) the cypriniforms form a larger group (Superorder Ostariophysi), which is characterized by a Weberian apparatus (a series of small bones connecting the gas bladder to the inner ear). The order includes the characins and minnows and their relatives, and is well represented on all continents except Australia and Antarctica.

Minnows and Carps: Family Cyprinidae

Minnows and their relatives (unlike nearly all other fishes in the Superorder Ostariophysi) lack jaw teeth and have 1–3 rows of *large* teeth in the *throat*. They *lack* an adipose fin. Other differences are primarily internal ones. Most are under 10 in. (25 cm), but some in Asia are quite large — to 9 ft. (274 cm). This family occurs in Africa, Europe, Asia, and N. America. A few species enter brackish water, but most are strictly freshwater fishes. Over 1500 species, including many in N. America; 1 sometimes enters brackish water in our area.

COMMON CARP   Pl. 6
Cyprinus carpio
Identification: Heavy body, with 1 dorsal fin, *no* adipose fin, a *forked* caudal fin, and *large cycloid* scales. 1st ray of dorsal fin is modified into a *serrated spine*. Mouth protrusible. No jaw teeth. Large specimens have 2 small *barbels* on each side (1 on upper lip, 1 at corner of mouth). Olive-green to brownish above; yellowish below. Anal fin and lower half of caudal fin sometimes reddish; often dark brown specks between scales. To several feet in fresh water, smaller in salt water.
Range: Originally Europe and Asia, now widely introduced elsewhere. **Habitat:** Mostly fresh water, but occasionally caught in sea off B.C. and in large bays such as San Francisco Bay.
Similar species: Most other fishes with a similar shape have several spines in the dorsal fin, rough (ctenoid) scales, or a rounded caudal fin.

Order Siluriformes

This order includes all catfishes. Some have no scales; others have overlapping bony plates on the body. Most have teeth in the mouth and an adipose fin. 1–4 pairs of *barbels* near the mouth. Most have a strong *spine* at front of dorsal and pectoral fins. About 30 families (4 with some marine species); 1 family in our area. Perhaps 2200 species, 1 in our area.

Sea Catfishes: Family Ariidae

A large family of fishes with a *typical catfish shape*. A strong spine at the front of the dorsal and pectoral fins. An adipose fin. Pelvic fins abdominal. Anal fin under adipose fin. Caudal fin strongly forked. Head bony, unscaled; no bony plates or scales on body. 1–3 (usually 3) pairs of *barbels near mouth*. Most sea catfishes are gray or blue to brown with a silvery sheen on back and side; paler or white below. Most grow to about $1\frac{1}{2}$ ft. (46 cm).

Sea catfishes occur in coastal marine, brackish, or fresh water in tropical regions. Most are marine, living along coasts, especially in or near rivers and estuaries. Some school or aggregate. Males of many species incubate the eggs in their mouth. About 75 species (many poorly known); 1 in our area.

CHIHUIL *Bagre panamensis*   **Pl. 6**
Identification: Typical *catfish shape*. Strong spine at front of dorsal and pectoral fins. Has an adipose fin. *Long barbel* at rear *corner of mouth,* 1 pair at chin. Gray above; white below. To 20 in. (51 cm).
Range: Off Santa Ana R. (s. Calif.) to Peru; rare north of s. Baja. Only 1 specimen recorded from Calif.; considered a stray from the south. **Habitat:** Inshore, usually on mud bottom.
Remarks: *Caution* — the spine at the front of the dorsal and pectoral fins is venomous and can cause a painful wound.

Order Gadiformes

This order includes cods and their relatives. Their dorsal and anal fins are *long* and often *separated* into 2 or 3 fins. No fin spines, except in most grenadiers, which have a spinelike 2nd ray (commonly serrated) in the dorsal fin. The pelvic fins are thoracic, sometimes reduced to filaments (1 genus of grenadiers has no pelvic fins). Scales usually cycloid (but prickly in some grenadiers). Many have a chin barbel. Caudal fin shape varies; slightly forked or square-cut in some, but greatly reduced or lost in those with the body tapered to a point. The order includes some tropical shore species but is most common in cold nearshore waters and the deep sea. Most live near the bottom. 1 group occurs in the Antarctic, and 1 or 2 species in fresh water. Many (such as the cods and haddocks) are of major commercial importance. 8 families, 5 in our area; about 480 species, about 18 in our area.

Cods: Family Gadidae

Elongate fishes with small cycloid scales. Our cods have *3 dorsal fins* and *2 anal fins;* some in other areas have 1 or 2 dorsal fins and 1 anal fin. No spinous fin rays. Many have a chin barbel. Pelvic fins thoracic, slightly ahead of pectoral fins. Caudal fin square-cut to slightly indented. Many are small — under 1 ft. (30 cm) — but some, such as the Atlantic Cod, reach 6 ft. (183 cm).

Cods occur primarily in cold waters, in all seas; only 2 species are found in fresh water. They usually live on or near the bottom. Large females of some species can contain a huge number of eggs — often over 1 million and sometimes over 15 million. About 75 species; 3 in our area.

PACIFIC COD   Pl. 11
Gadus macrocephalus
Identification: Body elongate, caudal fin square-cut. *3 dorsal fins.* Note the *chin barbel* (length about equal to eye diameter). *2 anal fins* — 1st begins below front of 2nd dorsal fin. Brown to gray above, with brown spots or pale areas on back and side; lighter below. Fins somewhat dusky; dorsal, caudal, and anal fins usually white-edged. To 45 in. (114 cm).
Range: Widely distributed in cooler regions of Pacific and adjacent seas; Japan to Bering Sea and to Santa Monica (s. Calif.), but rare south of n. Calif. **Habitat:** Usually near bottom; wide-ranging — 40–1800 ft. (12–549 m). Usually shallower in spring, deeper in fall.
Remarks: Of major commercial importance along the coast of N. Pacific; the most important trawl-caught bottom fish off B.C., where it is known as the Gray Cod. Marketed fresh and frozen, often as fish sticks.
Similar species: (1) Pacific Tomcod (p. 98) has smaller chin barbel (length equals about $\frac{1}{2}$ eye diameter); 1st anal fin begins under rear of 1st dorsal fin. (2) Walleye Pollock (p. 98) usually lacks chin barbel; lower jaw projects slightly. (3) In Pacific Hake (p. 99) 2nd dorsal and anal fins deeply *notched* (not separated into 2 fins), no chin barbel. (4) Moras (p. 99) in our area have a similar shape and a chin barbel, but only 2 dorsal fins. (5) Other similar fishes have spines in their 1st dorsal fin and only 1 or 2 dorsal fins.

PACIFIC TOMCOD *Microgadus proximus*   **Pl. 11**
Identification: *3 dorsal fins, 2 anal fins.* A short *chin barbel*
(length about $\frac{1}{2}$ eye diameter). 1st anal fin begins below rear of 1st
dorsal fin. Olive-green or brownish above; white below. Edge of fins
dusky. To 1 ft. (30 cm).
Range: Bering Sea to Pt. Sal (cen. Calif.). **Habitat:** On or near
bottom; adults at about 90–720 ft. (27–219 m), young shallower,
often near surface.
Remarks: Not abundant or large enough for commercial fishery,
but highly regarded for taste. Caught in trawls while fishing for
other species. Young often caught on hook and line. An important
prey species.
Similar species: (1) Pacific Cod (p. 97) is larger, usually with
spots and a longer chin barbel; 1st anal fin begins farther back
(below front of 2nd dorsal fin). (2) Walleye Pollock (below) usually
has no chin barbel, lower jaw projects slightly; also has more gill
rakers (34–40, not 22–28) on 1st arch. (3) See Pacific Hake (p. 99).

WALLEYE POLLOCK *Theragra chalcogramma*   **Pl. 11**
Identification: Similar to the 2 preceding cods, with *3 dorsal fins
and 2 anal fins.* Chin barbel tiny when present. Lower jaw projects
slightly beyond upper jaw. Olive-green to brown, often with faint
blotching or mottling above; silvery on side; whitish below. 1st
anal fin pale but other fins dusky. Young have 2–3 narrow yellowish stripes along side. To 3 ft. (91 cm).
Range: Coasts of N. Pacific, from Japan to Bering Sea and to
Carmel (cen. Calif.). **Habitat:** Usually offshore, mostly near bottom; surface to 1200 ft. (366 m).
Remarks: Also known as Pacific Pollock and Bigeye Pollock.
Occasionally caught on hook and line. Flesh is soft, little sought by
U.S. and Canadian fishermen, but is used as food for minks and
humans in other areas. Fed on by seals, porpoises, and predatory
fishes.
Similar species: (1) Pacific Tomcod (above) and (2) Pacific Cod
(p. 97) have a chin barbel; upper jaw projects slightly. (3) In Pacific Hake (p. 99) 2nd dorsal and anal fins are long and notched
(not separated into 2 fins); mouth larger, toothy. (4) See also under
Pacific Cod.

Hakes and Relatives: Family Merlucciidae

Hakes are usually placed in a separate family from the cods on the
basis of certain internal features, but researchers do not agree on
the groups that belong to this family. The one species in our area
belongs to Subfamily Merlucciinae; it resembles some cods very
closely but has a *V-shaped ridge* on the top of the head. Other
hakes are much like ours and are known from the N. Pacific, e.
Pacific, southern S. America, Africa, New Zealand, and nearly

throughout the Atlantic. Hakes occur at moderate depths, but are usually found in deeper waters at lower latitudes. They support commercial fisheries in cold-water areas. Other groups that are often included in this family have a pointed tail and resemble grenadiers (p. 100) more than hakes. About 12 species; 1 in our area.

PACIFIC HAKE
Pl. 11

Merluccius productus

Identification: Similar to cods, with an elongate body and square-cut caudal fin. *2nd dorsal fin and anal fin deeply notched* (not separated into 2 fins). *No* chin barbel. Lower jaw projects slightly. Sharp teeth. Scales tiny and cycloid, frequently rubbed off during capture. Body soft. Silvery, with black speckles on back. Inside of mouth black. To 3 ft. (91 cm).

Range: Coast of Asia to Alaska and to Magdalena Bay (s. Baja) and Gulf of Calif. **Habitat:** Common at moderate depths. Near bottom or higher in water column — to 3000 ft. (914 m) but usually shallower than 750 ft. (229 m). In schools.

Remarks: Occasionally caught while trolling for salmon. Hakes are usually not fished commercially in our area by Americans and Canadians because the flesh is soft, but the species is being increasingly harvested by foreign countries, to be frozen fresh or processed into fish meal. Important prey for sea lions and small cetaceans.

Similar species: (1) Our cods (above) have 3 dorsal fins and 2 anal fins. (2) Sablefish (p. 154) has short anal and 2nd dorsal fins; spines in 1st dorsal fin. (3) Moras (below) have a chin barbel.

Moras: Family Moridae

Externally these fishes vary widely, but they all have 2 extensions from the gas bladder that are attached to the rear of the skull. They have 1, 2, or (sometimes) 3 dorsal fins and 1 or 2 anal fins; many have a chin barbel. Found in all seas, usually in deep water. About 70 species. The two moras in our area have a short 1st dorsal fin followed by a long 2nd dorsal fin, a caudal fin, a long anal fin (slightly notched in 1 species), a chin barbel, *projecting snout,* and a shelflike ridge on the side of the snout. **Note:** The Arrowtail, *Melanonus zugmayeri* (not shown), belongs to yet another family of codlike fishes (Melanonidae) that might be confused with moras or cods. It is black and delicate, with a long 1st dorsal fin and a long 1st anal fin. The rear fins (2nd dorsal, caudal, and 2nd anal) join to form 1 pointed (arrow-shaped) fin at the tail, hence the species' name. No chin barbel. In our area this species is known from a few specimens collected by researchers using midwater trawls in deep water off B.C. and Calif.; it also occurs in other parts of the Pacific and in the Atlantic and Indian Oceans.

PACIFIC FLATNOSE *Antimora microlepis* **Pl. 48**
Identification: Deep-living. Snout flattened, *pointed,* with shelf-like ridge on side. Body elongate. 1st dorsal fin short, with *long, filamentous* 1st ray. 2nd dorsal fin *long.* Anal fin long, notched at middle. Look for the small chin barbel. Pelvic fin at *throat.* Blackish, or dark blue-gray to olive-green; edge of fins often darker. (Skin on body often rubbed off during capture by trawl.) To 29 $\frac{1}{2}$ in. (75 cm) and probably larger.
Range: N. Pacific in deep water; all along our coast. **Habitat:** Usually near bottom at about 1500-9500 ft. (457-2896 m).
Remarks: Caught in trawls, traps, and on set lines.
Similar species: (1) Hundred-fathom Mora (below) has a continuous (unnotched) anal fin that begins below 1st dorsal fin; snout rounded. (2) Our cods (p. 97) have *3* dorsal fins and a rounded snout; 1st anal fin begins at or before midbody. (3) Pacific Hake (p. 99) is silvery; lacks a chin barbel and shelflike ridge on its snout.

HUNDRED-FATHOM MORA **Not shown**
Physiculus rastrelliger
Identification: Similar to Pacific Flatnose (Pl. 48), but snout rounded. Anal fin unnotched, begins below 1st dorsal fin. Pelvic fin near throat. Has a chin barbel. Nearly uniform dusky to grayish olive. To 8 in. (20 cm).
Range: Eureka (n. Calif.) to Gulf of Panama. **Habitat:** Near bottom at about 420-1700 ft. (128-518 m).
Similar species: See (1) Pacific Flatnose (above) and (2) Arrowtail (see Note under Moras — p. 99).

Grenadiers: Family Macrouridae

Grenadiers, also known as rattails and whiptails, are the dominant fishes on continental slopes. These common deepsea fishes have a characteristic shape, with a large head and a long *tail that tapers to a point.* No caudal fin (except in 1 species). The pelvic fins are *forward* (thoracic). The 1st dorsal fin is *short,* with a tiny 1st ray and often with a long, spinelike 2nd ray (sometimes serrated or filamentous). The 2nd dorsal fin and anal fin are *very long,* with no spines. Skin *rough* — most have spiny scales (which are often lost during capture in trawls). Most species have a chin barbel. Many have a long snout, which projects over the mouth. Most are under 2 ft. (61 cm) but some reach over $4\frac{1}{2}$ ft. (137 cm).

Grenadiers occur worldwide from the Arctic to the Antarctic, but not in shallow water. Most species live near the bottom, but a few are pelagic. Some large grenadiers are eaten by humans and new fisheries are being developed, using trawls, traps, and deep setlines. About 300 species (many with a wide range), about 11 in our area.

Our grenadiers belong to 6 genera: (1) Midwater Grenadier, *Mesobius berryi,* lacks a chin barbel and is bathypelagic. (2) In *Coelorinchus* species the anus is at the front of the anal fin behind a large black naked area (the fossa, a light organ) and there is a *spiny ridge* on the side of the head. In (3) *Nezumia* species and (4) *Malacocephalus* species, the anus is far ahead of the anal fin, usually with a small black fossa in front. In addition, *Malacocephalus* species have large teeth in a single row in the lower jaw. In (5) *Coryphaenoides* species and (6) the Giant Grenadier, *Albatrossia pectoralis,* the anus is at the front of the anal fin; no black fossa. Unlike the *Coryphaenoides* species, the Giant Grenadier has a short pelvic fin (length less than half that of the head) and usually only 7 rays in pelvic fin. **Family representatives:** (1) Shoulder-spot Grenadier, *Coelorinchus scaphopsis* (Pl. 48), and (2) Pacific Grenadier, *Coryphaenoides acrolepis* (Pl. 48).

Order Ophidiiformes

A large group of deepsea fishes. Most are shaped like a letter opener, tapering toward the rear. Dorsal and anal fins *long;* join caudal fin or end just before it. Caudal fin rounded to elongate, sometimes filamentous, not forked. When present, pelvic fins are *under gill opening* or farther forward, *at throat,* with only 1 or 2 soft rays. Most species live in the deep sea, but some are found in other habitats, including shallow seas and fresh water. Some researchers place the eelpouts (Family Zoarcidae — p. 103) in this order. 3 families, 2 in our area. About 370 species, 8 in our area.

Cusk-Eels: Family Ophidiidae

Most cusk-eels are tapered, like a letter opener. The *long* dorsal and anal fins usually join the caudal fin to form a pointed tail; the caudal fin in some species is long and threadlike. Pelvic fins, when present, are far forward, on the underside of the head — roughly below the eye. Most about 1 ft. (30 cm), but some reach 3 ft. (91 cm) or more — a few to 5 ft. (152 cm).

Cusk-eels occur mostly in temperate and tropical seas, but a few are found in fresh water. Some cusk-eels are blind and live in freshwater caves or the deep sea. Many of the marine species live in the deep sea. About 190 species, 2 in shallow water in our area. **Note:** Besides the two species described below, 3 others (not shown) occur in very deep water off our coast: (1) The Threadfin Cusk-eel, *Dicrolene filamentosa,* has free, elongate lower pectoral fin rays and no separate caudal fin; pelvic fin at breast. (2) The Paperbone Cusk-eel, *Lamprogrammus niger,* has dorsal and anal fins that join the caudal fin; large lateral line scales; no pelvic fins. (3) The

Giant Cusk-eel, *Spectrunculus grandis,* also has dorsal and anal fins that join the caudal fin, pelvic fin at breast; but the lateral line is short, only on front of body.

SPOTTED CUSK-EEL *Chilara taylori*   **Pl. 20**
Identification: Note the *letter-opener* shape. Dorsal and anal fins join pointed caudal fin. Look for the *filamentous pelvic fin* far forward (*at the throat*), below the eye. Adults brown to cream, with dark spots on side and orange tinge near lips; young under 4 in. (10 cm) have no spots or orange near lips. To 14 in. (36 cm).
Range: N. Ore. to cen. Baja. **Habitat:** On sand bottom at 4–800 ft. (1.2–244 m) and deeper.
Remarks: Often burrows tailfirst in sand, lives in mucus-lined holes. Most active at night and on overcast days. Important food for sea lions and cormorants.
Similar species: (1) In Basketweave Cusk-eel (below) scales are arranged in a crisscross pattern; no spots. (2) See Note under cusk-eels (above) for other deepwater species. (3) In other fishes with the same shape the pelvic fins are farther back (not at the throat).

BASKETWEAVE CUSK-EEL *Ophidion scrippsae*   **Pl. 20**
Identification: Similar to Spotted Cusk-eel in shape and in having a *filamentous pelvic fin at the throat,* but scales are arranged in an unusual *crisscross pattern.* Brownish to olive above; paler brown below. No spots. To nearly 11 in. (28 cm).
Range: Pt. Arguello (n. Calif.) to Gulf of Calif. **Habitat:** Usually on sand bottom at 9–230 ft. (2.7–70 m).
Similar species: (1) Spotted Cusk-eel (above) usually spotted; no crisscross scale pattern. (2) Purple Brotula (p. 103), (3) eelpouts (Pl. 11 and p. 103), and (4) other fishes with this shape lack the crisscross scale pattern.

Livebearing Brotulas: Family Bythitidae

These fishes resemble cusk-eels but are ovoviviparous. The males have a copulatory organ (penis). When present, the *pelvic fins* are on the *breast* (thoracic) under the gill openings (as in some cusk-eels). In some species the dorsal and anal fins join the caudal fin to give the body a letter-opener shape, but in others the caudal fin is entirely separate. Scales present or absent. Many are about 6–12 in. (15–30 cm) but some are larger.

Habitat varies with species, from fresh water to extremely deep sea; most brotulas are found near shore or at moderate depths in oceans. About 150 species, 2 in our area in shallow water. **Note:** A third species, the Rubynose Brotula, *Cataetyx rubrirostris* (not shown), is known from off our coast at moderate depths — at about 1800 ft. (549 m) or more. Its dorsal and anal fins join the caudal fin; pelvic fin has *only 1 ray,* at throat. This brotula also has a spine on the gill cover, 1 lateral line, and a hooklike bone on the lower front edge of the eye socket. To about 5 in. (13 cm).

RED BROTULA *Brosmophycis marginata*   **Pl. 20**
Identification: An elongate fish with a *separate* caudal fin. Pelvic fin *filamentous,* with *2 rays,* at breast before pectoral fin. Mostly *red,* brownish red, or brown above; paler below. Fins usually reddish. To $1\frac{1}{2}$ ft. (46 cm).
Range: Se. Alaska to n. Baja. **Habitat:** Rocky areas, at 10–840 ft. (3–256 m) but usually deeper than 50 ft. (15 m). A secretive fish.
Similar species: (1) Purple Brotula (below) has 2 lateral lines and no separate caudal fin; slate gray to purplish black. In (2) Spotted and (3) Basketweave Cusk-eels (p. 102), pelvic fins are filamentous but at the *throat;* caudal fin not separate. (4) Eelpouts (Pl. 11 and below) in our area have small pelvic fins or no pelvic fins, and dorsal and anal fins join caudal fin.

PURPLE BROTULA *Oligopus diagrammus*   **Pl. 20**
Identification: Note *letter-opener shape;* dorsal and anal fins *join pointed* caudal fin. Pelvic fin *filamentous* and short, with *1 ray,* at the *breast. 2 lateral lines. Slate gray to purplish black.* To 8 in. (20 cm).
Range: San Clemente I. (s. Calif.) to Panama and Galapagos Is. **Habitat:** Rocky areas at 18–60 ft. (5.5–18 m). Hides during the day.
Similar species: (1) Red Brotula (above) has a *separate* caudal fin and a longer pelvic fin. (2) In Spotted and (3) Basketweave Cusk-eels (p. 102) pelvic fins are at the throat. (4) Eelpouts (Pl. 11 and below) have minute pelvic fins or no pelvic fins; their gill membranes are joined at the throat. (5) See Note under livebearing brotulas (p. 102).

Eelpouts: Family Zoarcidae

Like cusk-eels and some brotulas (above), eelpouts have an elongate, tapered body, with long dorsal and anal fins that extend around the pointed tail, creating a *letter-opener shape.* The head is relatively large, and the mouth is often big, with thick lips. Upper jaw usually *projects beyond* lower jaw. Pelvic fins, when present, are tiny and on the breast (thoracic), in front of the pectoral fins. Our eelpouts have no fin spines, but a few species elsewhere do have them. No scales or small cycloid ones, usually buried (embedded). Most eelpouts are under $1\frac{1}{2}$ ft. (46 cm).

Eelpouts occur worldwide in cold seas, including the Arctic and Antarctic Oceans. Some species are found in shallow temperate and polar seas, but most live on the bottom at moderate or great depths. Some live in midwater, as do the young of some bottom-living species, but those in the tropics are found only in deep water.

Eelpouts are thought by some researchers to be related to the blennylike fishes, but others consider them to be closer to the cusk-eels and livebearing brotulas, which they resemble at least superficially. Over 200 species (but most are poorly known); new ones are being discovered. About 35–40 species in our area (most in deep water). Occasionally caught in trawls and traps. The 11 species that are most likely to be found are described below; 6 of them are shown in Pl. 11. To confirm the identification of a specimen in our area as an eelpout, rule out the following look-alikes: cusk-eels (p. 101; Pl. 20), livebearing brotulas (p. 102; Pl. 20), the Arrowtail (see Note under Moras, p. 99), and grenadiers (p. 100; Pl. 48). See also true eels (p. 63; Pl. 6), graveldivers (p. 259; Pl. 42), gunnels (p. 255; Pl. 39), and the Wolf-eel (p. 257; Pl. 40).

TWOLINE EELPOUT *Bothrocara brunneum*　　　　**Not shown**
Identification: Large, deep body. Lateral line in *2 parts* (short segment on shoulder area, longer one at midbody). *No pelvic fins.* Gill opening large, extends far forward on the throat. Gill rakers short and blunt. Head pitted, especially below eye. Nearly uniform brown or gray; dorsal and anal fins darker at edge and somewhat transparent at base; fins at tip of tail black. To 26 in. (66 cm).
Range: Sea of Okhotsk (USSR) to Bering Sea and to n. Baja.
Habitat: Mud or sandy-mud bottom at 654–6000 ft. (199–1829 m), usually deeper than 1500 ft. (457 m).
Remarks: A fairly common eelpout — the largest one in our area. Caught in bottom trawls and Sablefish traps.
Similar species: Other look-alikes likely to be found in our area do not have a 2-part lateral line.

SNAKEHEAD EELPOUT　　　　　　　　**Not shown**
Embryx crotalinus
Identification: Large, with *fleshy lips. Large pores around mouth. No* teeth on roof of mouth. Scaled, including gill cover. Pelvic fins present. Pectoral fin rounded. Gill opening ends just below pectoral fin base. Brownish blue to violet. Dorsal, anal, and pectoral fins, and lower part of head black. To $17\frac{1}{4}$ in. (44 cm).
Range: Bering Sea to n. Baja. **Habitat:** Mud bottom at 657–6000 ft. (200–1829 m), usually deeper than 2000 ft. (610 m).
Similar species: (1) Other eelpouts described here have a notched pectoral fin, or teeth on roof of the mouth, or no scales on the gill cover, or no pelvic fins. (2) A few other poorly known deep-living eelpouts in our area (*Lycenchelys* species and two more *Embryx* species) are similar but are not treated in this guide.

PALLID EELPOUT *Lycodapus mandibularis*　　　**Not shown**
Identification: *No pelvic fins or scales.* Skin transparent, loose. Gill opening large — extends from above pectoral fin to far forward on the throat. Silvery white to translucent cream, often with

fine black specks. Dorsal and anal fins transparent at front, black at rear. Small — to about 8 in. (20 cm).
Range: Prince William Sound (Gulf of Alaska) to s. Calif.
Habitat: Midwater, from near surface at night to about 2625 ft. (800 m) during day; sometimes captured in bottom trawls but definitely a pelagic species.
Note: Several other deep-living *Lycodapus* species (not included in this guide) occur off our coast. Like the Pallid Eelpout, they have loose naked skin, no pelvic fins, a large gill opening, and a mouth at front of head (snout does not project noticeably beyond it).

SHORTFIN EELPOUT *Lycodes brevipes*   **Pl. 11**
Identification: Pelvic fin tiny (shorter than eye diameter). Pectoral fin rounded. Scales embedded. Brown above with *9–13 pale bars;* pale on side; belly blue-black. Top of head dusky. Dorsal and anal fins dark-edged. To $11\frac{3}{4}$ in. (30 cm).
Range: Sea of Okhotsk (USSR) to Bering Sea and to Ore.
Habitat: Sand or mud bottom at 90–2106 ft. (27–642 m).
Similar species: (1) Black Eelpout (below) has a *notched* pectoral fin. (2) See Wattled Eelpout (p. 106).

BIGFIN EELPOUT *Lycodes cortezianus*   **Pl. 11**
Identification: *Pectoral fin large, rounded.* No pelvic fins. *Black edge* on dorsal fin (sometimes only at front) and on fins at tail area. No teeth at *center* of roof of mouth, but teeth present at *sides* of roof of mouth. Brown to blue-black above; lighter below. Pectoral fin blue-black with a yellow edge, but sometimes entirely pale in small specimens. Peritoneum black. Large — to $19\frac{1}{2}$ in. (50 cm).
Range: Queen Charlotte Sound (B.C.) to San Diego. **Habitat:** Mud bottom at 240–2034 ft. (73–620 m). Common in trawl hauls, occasionally in Sablefish traps.
Remarks: Formerly placed in the genus *Aprodon.*
Similar species: (1) Blackbelly Eelpout (below) has similar pectoral fins and no pelvic fins, and black at front of dorsal fin, but belly usually black, fins near tail not black-edged. (2) See Snakehead Eelpout (p. 104).

BLACK EELPOUT *Lycodes diapterus*   **Pl. 11**
Identification: Pectoral fin *notched.* Pelvic fin small. Brownish or blue above, with *8–9 whitish V-shaped bars or irregular blotches on back* (less prominent in adults). Fins mostly black or bluish black, usually darker at edge. To 13 in. (33 cm).
Range: Japan to Bering Sea and to San Diego. **Habitat:** Mud bottom at 42–3456 ft. (13–1053 m).
Similar species: (1) Shortfin Eelpout (above) also has white bars on back, but pectoral fin is *rounded.* (2) See Wattled Eelpout (p. 106).

BLACKBELLY EELPOUT *Lycodes pacificus*   **Pl. 11**
Identification: A large eelpout with a small pelvic fin and large,

rounded pectoral fin. *Black at front of dorsal fin* and on *belly.*
Dorsal and anal fins black-edged near tail tip. Gray to reddish
brown, but young have pale bars on body. To 1½ ft. (46 cm).
Range: Gulf of Alaska to n. Baja. **Habitat:** Mud bottom at 30-
1308 ft. (9.1-399 m). Common in trawl hauls.
Remarks: Preyed on by Sablefish and certain rockfishes. For-
merly placed in the genus *Lycodopsis.*
Similar species: See preceding 3 eelpouts.

WATTLED EELPOUT *Lycodes palearis*   **Not shown**
Identification: A large eelpout. Pelvic fin small (in adults, fin
length equals eye diameter). Pectoral fin large, rounded. Dorsal
and anal fins have narrow dark edge. Light brown to blackish
above; paler below. Young have white bars on side — 2 bars before
front of dorsal fin. To 20 in. (51 cm).
Range: Bering Sea to Ore. **Habitat:** Mud or sand bottom at 180-
930 ft. (55-283 m).
Remarks: Close relatives of this eelpout occur from Japan to the
Bering Sea.
Similar species: (1) Young of Shortfin Eelpout (p. 105) also have
white bars on side, but only *1* bar before front of dorsal fin. (2)
Bigfin Eelpout (p. 105) has no teeth at center of roof of mouth
(unlike Wattled Eelpout). See (3) Black and (4) Blackbelly Eelpouts (p. 105).

BEARDED EELPOUT *Lyconema barbatum*   **Pl. 11**
Identification: Our only *dark-spotted* eelpout. *Cirri* on underside
of *lower jaw.* Pelvic fin small. Small — to 6¾ in. (17 cm).
Range: S. Ore. to n.-cen. Baja. **Habitat:** Mud or sandy-mud bottom at 270-1224 ft. (82-373 m).
Similar species: Spotted Cusk-eel (p. 102; Pl. 20) has no cirri on
lower jaw; pelvic fin long, filamentous.

PERSIMMON EELPOUT *Maynea californica*   **Pl. 11**
Identification: Our only *rose-red or persimmon-colored eelpout.*
No pelvic fins. Pectoral fin large, rounded, bright orange. To 8¾ in.
(22 cm).
Range: Monterey Bay to San Diego. **Habitat:** In dead bottom-
drifting kelp or eelgrass that accumulates in submarine canyons
and deep basins; at 239-1787 ft. (73-545 m) but usually at less than
659 ft. (201 m). Common in appropriate habitats.
Remarks: This species and its unusual habitat have been studied
by researchers who collect specimens by lowering a square lift net
containing seaweed. The fish are attracted to the seaweed and remain there while the net is lifted to the surface. They eat mostly
amphipod crustaceans.
Similar species: (1) Snakehead Eelpout (p. 104) is brownish blue
to violet, has pelvic fins; no teeth at center of roof of mouth (unlike
Persimmon Eelpout). (2) Other eelpouts described here have pelvic
fins or smaller pectoral fins; different color.

MIDWATER EELPOUT   **Fig. 31 opp. Pl. 11**
Melanostigma pammelas
Identification: Our only eelpout with a *blunt head* and a *small, round gill opening* above the pectoral fin. No pelvic fins. Head and belly black, rest of body dark brown; young mostly clear. Small — to 4¼ in. (11 cm).
Range: Queen Charlotte Is. to cen. Mex. **Habitat:** Pelagic in deep coastal waters at 314–3937 ft. (96–1200 m) or deeper.
Remarks: In our area this is 1 of 3 eelpouts known to live well off the bottom.
Similar species: Most of our other eelpouts have a large slitlike gill opening; head not as blunt. **Note:** Cuskpout, *Derepodichthys alepidotus,* occurs off our coast at depths greater than 3280 ft. (1000 m). It also has a blunt head and a small gill opening, but it has pelvic fins (at the throat). To about 6½ in. (16 cm).

Order Batrachoidiformes

Toadfishes: Family Batrachoididae

These fishes have a large flattened head and a tapered body. Many have fleshy skin flaps or barbels on the head. *1st dorsal fin small, with 2-4 spines,* followed by a *long,* soft-rayed 2nd dorsal fin that nearly reaches the caudal fin. Anal fin long, without spines, opposite 2nd dorsal fin. Pelvic fins at *throat* (ahead of pectoral fins). A strong *spine on gill cover.* Most species have no scales. One group, the midshipmen, are the only normally inshore fishes with rows of *photophores* (light organs).
   Most toadfishes are about 1 ft. (30 cm); a few reach 1½ ft. (46 cm). Toadfishes are sluggish inshore bottom-dwellers of tropical seas. A few species range into temperate waters or to moderate depths, and a few others enter brackish water or live in fresh water. In some species, the dorsal fin spines and spine on gill cover are venomous — stings are painful but not fatal. Most toadfishes can make croaking, grunting, or whistling sounds. Only 1 family in the order. About 50 species, 2 in our area.

SPECKLEFIN MIDSHIPMAN *Porichthys myriaster*   **Pl. 34**
Identification: *Rows of pearly dots* (photophores) on head and body. 1st dorsal fin tiny, with *2 spines;* 2nd dorsal fin long, soft-rayed. Anal fin long. Pelvic fin *under head. No scales.* Dorsal and pectoral fins *spotted.* Iridescent — purplish gray to brown above; yellowish below. To 20 in. (51 cm).
Range: Pt. Conception to s. Baja. **Habitat:** Rocky areas and soft bottom, common in bays. Usually rests on or buries itself in bottom. To about 400 ft. (122 m).
Remarks: Can make a humming or grunting sound. More active at night. Photophores can be made to glow in the laboratory.

Spawns in late spring or summer; female attaches eggs to underside of rock, male guards eggs and young. Occasionally caught on hook and line or speared by divers.
Similar species: Plainfin Midshipman (below) has no spots on dorsal or pectoral fins; different pattern of photophores on underside of head (Fig. 35 opp. Pl. 34).

PLAINFIN MIDSHIPMAN *Porichthys notatus*   **Pl. 34**
Identification: Similar to Specklefin Midshipman except fins are *unspotted,* and photophores on underside of head are arranged in a V (not in a U) — Fig. 35 opp. Pl. 34. Dark brown to olive or iridescent purple above; silvery on side; yellowish on belly. Some dusky blotches on back and side. To 15 in. (38 cm).
Range: Se. Alaska to Gulf of Calif. and possibly farther south.
Habitat: Usually mud or sand bottom; common in bays, especially during spawning. To 1200 ft. (366 m).
Remarks: Two populations; 1 from Ore. northward and the other from San Francisco southward — few specimens reported from area in-between. Important prey of seals and sea lions.
Similar species: See Specklefin Midshipman (above).

Order Gobiesociformes

Clingfishes: Family Gobiesocidae

Mostly small inshore fishes with a peculiar *adhesive* (sucking) *disk on the breast* (Fig. 33 opp. Pl. 21). Dorsal fin *opposite* anal fin, fairly *far back.* No fin spines. *No scales.* When viewed from above, many clingfishes look like tadpoles or frying pans: the head is large and flattened, the body tapers sharply behind. Most are less than 2½–3 in. (6.4–7.6 cm), a few reach 6 in. (15 cm), and 1 species grows to about 14 in. (36 cm).

Clingfishes occur in tropical and temperate waters of all oceans. A few freshwater species are found in fast-flowing streams of Central America, the Caribbean, and Cocos I. (southwest of Costa Rica). Many live in the intertidal surge zone, where they cling to rocks with the sucking disk. Some live on kelp, marine grasses, or between the spines of sea urchins.

Two other groups have a sucking disk on the breast: (1) Snailfishes (Family Liparididae — p. 190) have a similar disk (Fig. 33 opp. Pl. 21) but their dorsal fin begins just behind the head. (2) Gobies (Family Gobiidae — p. 260) have pelvic fins that join to form a suction cup (Fig. 32 opp. Pl 19); they have a spinous dorsal fin. Our clingfishes have either short dorsal and anal fins (with 8 or fewer rays) or longer fins. Species are usually identified on the basis of technical features, such as the number of fin rays, tooth shape, and disk details. Clingfishes may be seen by an observant diver or may be found in the stomach of predatory fishes; the Northern

Clingfish (below) can be found hiding under rocks in the intertidal zone as well as in the kelp canopy. Otherwise they are rarely seen by laymen. One family in the order. About 140 species, 7 in our area.

LINED CLINGFISH *Gobiesox eugrammus*   **Pl. 21**
Identification: Nearly translucent cream, with *orange* or *red marks*. Dorsal and caudal fins *black, with white edges*. Eye large — diameter about equal to distance between eyes. More than 10 rays in dorsal and anal fins. Small — to $2\frac{1}{4}$ in. (5.7 cm).
Range: Bird Rock (s. Calif.) to n. Baja and Guadalupe I. (off n.-cen. Baja). **Habitat:** Apparently lives near or under sea urchins at 30–270 ft. (9–82 m).
Similar species: (1) Northern and (2) Bearded Clingfishes (below) are similar in body shape and in number of dorsal and anal fin rays, but lack red or orange marks.

NORTHERN CLINGFISH *Gobiesox maeandricus*   **Pl. 21**
Identification: Robust, with a *large head and disk*. In our area, *any clingfish over 3 in.* (*7.6 cm*) is this species. Color varies; gray to brown or red, usually with a chainlike dark pattern. Dark lines radiate from eye. To $6\frac{1}{2}$ in. (16 cm).
Range: Se. Alaska to s. Calif., also off Baja (on drifting kelp); rare south of Pt. Conception. **Habitat:** Intertidal rocky areas among algae, and on kelp (often high in kelp canopy). At depths up to 26 ft. (7.9 m).
Remarks: Our *northernmost* clingfish — it and Kelp Clingfish are the only ones north of s. Calif.
Similar species: (1) Bearded Clingfish (below) is often spotted, and has prominent papillae on head (especially near mouth). (2) California Clingfish (below) is smaller, has fewer anal fin rays (9–10, not 11–13). (3) See Lined Clingfish (above).

BEARDED CLINGFISH *Gobiesox papillifer*   **Not shown**
Identification: *Numerous papillae on head* (especially near mouth). More than 9 dorsal and anal fin rays; 23–25 pectoral fin rays. Light brown to gray, often with dark spots. Small — to $2\frac{1}{4}$ in. (5.7 cm).
Range: San Pedro (s. Calif.) to Panama Bay; 1 record north of Baja. **Habitat:** Intertidal.
Similar species: (1) California Clingfish (below) has 18–21 pectoral fin rays, no papillae on head. See (2) Northern and (3) Lined Clingfishes (above).

CALIFORNIA CLINGFISH *Gobiesox rhessodon*   **Pl. 21**
Identification: Gray to brown with darker marks. More than 9 dorsal and anal fin rays. Small — to $2\frac{1}{2}$ in. (6.4 cm).
Range: Pismo Beach (cen. Calif.) to cen. Baja. **Habitat:** Intertidal and to 35 ft. (11 m).

Similar species: (1) See Lined, Northern, and Bearded Cling-fishes (p. 109). (2) Clingfishes of the genus *Rimicola* (below) have short dorsal and anal fins and a slender body.

SOUTHERN CLINGFISH *Rimicola dimorpha*   **Not shown**
Identification: *Tiny,* slender. Dorsal and anal fins short. 15–16 pectoral fin rays. Males have a *prominent* genital papilla (penislike structure) — length almost equal to depth of body at anal fin. Color when alive unknown. To 1¼ in. (3.2 cm).
Range: N. Channel Is. (s. Calif.) to cen. Baja. **Habitat:** Inshore (details poorly known).
Similar species: (1) Very similar to Kelp Clingfish (below), but male Kelp Clingfishes lack the greatly enlarged genital papilla. Female Kelp Clingfishes are virtually indistinguishable from fe-male Southern Clingfishes, but *any specimen from cen. Calif. northward* would be a Kelp Clingfish. (2) Slender Clingfish (below) has 17–19 pectoral fin rays. (3) The 4 *Gobiesox* species in our area (p. 109) have a broad head and long dorsal and anal fins, unlike the 3 *Rimicola* species.

SLENDER CLINGFISH *Rimicola eigenmanni*   **Pl. 21**
Identification: Slender, with a small disk and short dorsal and anal fins (with 5–8 rays). 17–19 pectoral fin rays. Color varies, matches surroundings: may be tan or green, or less commonly red, brown, or yellow; sometimes with a pale side stripe. To 2¼ in. (5.7 cm).
Range: Near San Pedro (s. Calif.) to s. Baja. **Habitat:** Intertidal and to 48 ft. (15 m).
Similar species: (1) Southern and (2) Kelp Clingfishes usually have fewer than 17 pectoral fin rays. (2) See under Southern Clingfish (above).

KELP CLINGFISH *Rimicola muscarum*   **Pl. 21**
Identification: A *northern* species — *any clingfish* caught *north of cen. Calif.* is this species *or* the Northern Clingfish (p. 109). Simi-lar to Southern and Slender Clingfishes (above) in body shape and fin location. Greenish to brown, sometimes with a reddish or orange side stripe. To 2¾ in. (7 cm).
Range: Queen Charlotte Is. to n. Baja. **Habitat:** Clings to strands of kelp (often high in kelp canopy) or eelgrass with its disk; moves to seek food or cover. Rarely in tidepools.
Similar species: See under Slender Clingfish (above).

Order Lophiiformes

These peculiar, mostly deepsea fishes, are unlikely to be seen ex-cept by researchers using midwater trawls. Their 1st dorsal fin spine is *well separated* from the rest of the dorsal fin and *modified into a "fishing pole"* (illicium), usually bearing a terminal "bait" or

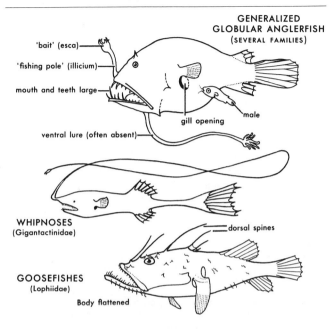

Fig. 16 Deepsea Lophiiform families

lure (esca) — see Fig. 16. Gill opening usually *small, far back* (below or behind the pectoral fin). Many species are *globular,* but some are strongly flattened. Usually no pelvic fins (when present, on breast). Pectoral fins fanlike, often on a "stalk" and appearing to have an "elbow." No scales, but some species have prickly or spiny skin. Most are small — under 1 ft. (30 cm) — but some reach 3½ ft. (107 cm). All are marine; most occur in very deep seas, but a few live in tropical and temperate waters near shore or at surface. Some have light organs (especially associated with the esca). In certain deepsea species males are dwarfed and attach themselves to females and live (parasitically) off their blood supply. About 16 families, 9 in our area; roughly 250 species, 16 in our area. Two families and 2 species are described below, but the 7 deepsea families (14 species) in our area are not treated in this guide, except for the family representatives shown in Fig. 16.

Frogfishes: Family Antennariidae

These sluggish globular fishes have prickly or warty skin. Their pectoral fins are armlike, with the gill opening near or just behind the "elbow." Most are under 3–4 in. (7.6–10 cm); some reach about 15 in. (38 cm). They occur in all shallow tropical seas; a few enter temperate waters. Most live on the bottom, but others occur among coral or in sargassum (seaweed) in the open ocean. Some can puff themselves up by filling the stomach with water or air. About 50 species, 1 in our area.

ROUGHJAW FROGFISH *Antennarius avalonis*   **Pl. 13**
Identification: A grotesque, globe-shaped fish with prickly skin. Look for the small gill opening *behind the armlike pectoral fin.* Small pelvic fin. Fleshy "lure" between eyes (can be wriggled to attract prey). Color varies: brown to gray, or orange, lemon, red, or black; usually with darker mottling. Dark lines radiate from pupil. To 13½ in. (34 cm).
Range: Santa Catalina I. (s. Calif.) to Peru. **Habitat:** Usually rocky areas; intertidal and to 360 ft. (110 m).
Similar species: Only a few fishes have a balloon-shaped body: (1) Globular anglerfishes (several families — Fig. 16, p. 111) are dark red-brown or black, have no pelvic fins, and live in the deep sea. (2) Snailfishes (p. 190) usually have a disk on the breast; gill opening in front of pectoral fin. (3) In sculpins, such as the Tadpole and Blob Sculpins (p. 180), gill opening is before the pectoral fin, which is not armlike.

Batfishes: Family Ogcocephalidae

These truly bizarre fishes are armored with spines or tubercles. The inshore species, at least, use their armlike pectoral fins and strutlike pelvic fins to "walk" on the bottom. Body very flat (less so in some deepwater species). In many species a beak projects from the snout. Mouth small. Peculiar dorsal fin spine modified into a short "fishing pole" with a fleshy "bait" or lure; when not in use, pole and lure are hidden in a cavity on the snout (see front view, Pl. 13). The lure may emit a chemical attractant — when presented with food in an aquarium, batfishes project the lure to attract prey. They eat small mollusks, clams, worms, and fishes. Most batfishes are under 6 in. (15 cm), the largest ones reach 15 in. (38 cm). Batfishes occur worldwide in tropical seas, a few in temperate waters. Usually on sand or mud bottom, in shallow and deep water. About 60 species, 1 in our area.

SPOTTED BATFISH *Zalieutes elater*   **Pl. 13**
Identification: Peculiar *flattened body,* with *armlike* pectoral fins. A small gill opening *behind* pectoral fin. Skin rough, covered with tubercles. Light brown or tan with darker brown spots. Usually *2 ocelli* on back. To 6 in. (15 cm).
Range: Pt. Conception to Peru; rare north of Baja. **Habitat:** Sand bottom at 60–372 ft. (18–113 m).

Remarks: Occasionally seen "walking" on bottom by divers, or found washed ashore. One of nature's oddities, frequently brought to natural history museums for identification.

Order Atheriniformes

These fishes vary in shape: many are elongate, most are slender. The *mouth* is *small.* In some species the snout extends into a beak. Dorsal and anal fins are usually opposite each other and far back, with only soft rays, but in a few species the soft dorsal fin is preceded by a small spinous dorsal fin. Pectoral fins frequently high up on side. Pelvic fins abdominal, usually with 6 soft rays. Lateral line often low on side. Scales cycloid. Most are silvery. Usually 1 ft. (30 cm) or less, some larger. Most inhabit tropical surface waters (fresh water as well as seas). There are no deepsea species in the order. Usually grouped into 16 families, 6 in our area. About 800 species, 13 in our area (but only 2 north of Calif.).

Flyingfishes: Family Exocoetidae

Distinguished by their long *winglike pectoral fins* (used for aerial gliding); some also have enlarged pelvic fins. Mouth *small;* no beak (except in young of some species). No fin spines. 1 dorsal fin, opposite the anal fin, far back. Caudal fin *forked;* lower lobe usually *longer* than upper lobe. Most under 1 ft. (30 cm), a few reach $1\frac{1}{2}$ ft. (46 cm). They do not flap their pectoral fins but glide with their fins outstretched. Flyingfishes are sold as bait for marlins and are also eaten by humans. At night they can be attracted with a light. They mainly eat small crustaceans.

Flyingfishes occur worldwide in warm seas. Usually found offshore at the surface; often congregate around islands. Some researchers combine the flyingfishes and halfbeaks (next family) into one family. About 50 species (as treated here), 3 in our area.

CALIFORNIA FLYINGFISH *Cypselurus californicus*   **Pl. 12**
Identification: Our only common flyingfish. Pectoral fin *long,* extends beyond rear of dorsal fin (when pressed against side of body). Snout *short* (length about equal to eye diameter). Blue-gray above; silvery below. Upper part of pectoral fin dark. To 19 in. (48 cm).
Range: Astoria (Ore.) to s. Baja; rare north of Pt. Conception.
Habitat: Oceanic; at surface.
Remarks: In summer easily observed from boats off s. Calif. This flyingfish supports a small summer gill-net fishery around islands off s. Calif.
Similar species: (1) In Sharpchin Flyingfish (p. 114) pectoral fin

is shorter — extends only to front of dorsal fin. (2) See Blotchwing Flyingfish (below).

BLOTCHWING FLYINGFISH   Not shown
Cypselurus hubbsi

Identification: Similar to California Flyingfish in shape and color, but has 40 or fewer scales between head and front of dorsal fin (California Flyingfish has about 50). Pectoral fin is darker at upper rear edge (not uniformly dusky). To 16 in. (41 cm).
Range: Worldwide in the tropics, occasionally as far north as Santa Catalina I. (s. Calif.). **Habitat:** Oceanic; at surface.
Similar species: See California Flyingfish (p. 113). **Note:** The Blackwing Flyingfish, *Hirundichthys rondeletii,* has been recorded just south of Calif. It resembles the Blotchwing Flyingfish but has 11–13 (not 8–10) anal fin rays and 16–18 (not 15–16) dorsal fin rays. 2nd ray in pectoral fin is unbranched (branched in Blotchwing and California Flyingfishes). About 30 scales between head and dorsal fin.

SHARPCHIN FLYINGFISH *Fodiator acutus*   Pl. 12
Identification: Note the relatively *short pectoral fin,* (for a flyingfish), which reaches only to front of dorsal fin. Snout length *greater than* eye diameter. Lower jaw extends *beyond* upper jaw (more so in young). Dorsal fin *high, rounded.* Dark blue above; silvery white below. To 9½ in. (24 cm).
Range: Worldwide in tropical seas; s. Calif. to Peru (including Galapagos Is.). **Habitat:** Mostly oceanic; at surface.
Remarks: Thought by some researchers to belong to the halfbeak family (Hemiramphidae — below).
Similar species: See (1) California (p. 113) and (2) Blotchwing Flyingfishes (above).

Halfbeaks: Family Hemiramphidae

Easily identified by their "half beak" — the *lower jaw* is *long; upper jaw much shorter.* Dorsal and anal fins far back. Pelvic fins abdominal, with 6 soft rays. Lateral line *low* on side (near ventral surface). Blue to green above; silvery white below. Most are under 1 ft. (30 cm), some reach 1½ ft. (46 cm). All but a few species live in warm seas, but some enter estuaries, and — in S. America and Asia — some live in fresh water. About 75 species, 4 reach s. Calif.

RIBBON HALFBEAK *Euleptorhamphus longirostris*   Pl. 12
Identification: *Lower jaw very long, upper jaw short.* Pectoral fin *long* (reaches well past eye if folded forward). Dorsal fin long (with 21 or more rays); opposite anal fin of same length. Greenish above; silvery below. To 1½ ft. (46 cm).
Range: Tropical Pacific and Indian Oceans; s. Calif. to Galapagos Is. **Habitat:** Usually oceanic but enters large open bays; at surface.

Remarks: Sometimes identified as *Euleptorhamphus viridis.*
Similar species: (1) Longfin Halfbeak (below) has a shorter anal
fin (begins below middle of dorsal fin). (2) In California and (3)
Silverstripe Halfbeaks (below) beak, pectoral fins, and dorsal fin
(with 16 or fewer rays) are all shorter. (4) *Both jaws* are long in
marine needlefishes (below).

LONGFIN HALFBEAK *Hemiramphus saltator*   **Not shown**
Identification: Similar to California Halfbeak (below) but anal
fin is *shorter,* begins below *middle* of dorsal fin. Usually 13–14
dorsal fin rays. 11–13 anal fin rays. Brownish above; silvery below.
To 18¾ in. (48 cm).
Range: S. Calif. to Ecuador (including Galapagos Is.); rare north
of Baja. **Habitat:** Oceanic; near surface.
Remarks: Used as bait by sport fishermen seeking billfishes — a
choice prey of billfishes.
Similar species: See Ribbon Halfbeak (above).

CALIFORNIA HALFBEAK *Hyporhamphus rosae*   **Pl. 12**
Identification: Pectoral in *short* (length about ½ the beak). Usually has 14–15 dorsal fin rays; 15–16 anal fin rays. Greenish above,
with a silver side stripe. Beak *red-tipped.* To 6 in. (15 cm).
Range: Santa Ana (s. Calif.) to Costa Rica. **Habitat:** Near shore,
frequently in coastal bays; at or near surface. Often in small
schools.
Similar species: (1) See Silverstripe Halfbeak (below). (2) Ribbon Halfbeak (p. 114) has a longer beak and pectoral fin. (3)
Longfin Halfbeak (above) has a short anal fin, which begins below
middle (not front) or dorsal fin.

SILVERSTRIPE HALFBEAK   **Not shown**
Hyporhamphus unifasciatus
Identification: Similar to California Halfbeak (above) in shape
and size of fins, but beak is usually shorter (head length goes into
beak length 0.8–1.3 times, not 1.1–1.6 times). Dorsal and anal fins
are covered with tiny scales (fins unscaled in California Halfbeak).
Greenish above; silvery below. To 10½ in. (27 cm).
Range: San Diego to Peru (including Galapagos Is.). **Habitat:**
Near shore, also well out to sea; at surface.
Similar species: See California Halfbeak (above).

Needlefishes: Family Belonidae

Needlefishes are often seen leaping or skittering at the surface.
They are easily recognized by the long, nearly round body and the
long, toothed jaws, which are drawn out into a *beak.* In marine
needlefishes *both jaws* are long, but in some freshwater species the
upper jaw is short (as in halfbeaks, above). 1 dorsal fin, nearly

opposite the anal fin, *far back*. Pelvic fins abdominal. Green to
blue above; silvery white below. Most under 2 ft. (61 cm), a few to
4 ft. (122 cm), one about 6 ft. (1.8 m). Needlefishes occur in all
tropical and warm-temperate seas; a few live in fresh water. Found
at or near surface, usually in schools near shore. Most feed on
fishes, which they catch sideways in their beaks. 31–32 species, 1 in
our area.

CALIFORNIA NEEDLEFISH   Pl. 12
Strongylura exilis
Identification: *Both jaws* are elongated into a *beak*. Dorsal and
anal fins *far back*. Jaw teeth sharp, usually greenish. Scales small,
cycloid. Greenish blue above; silvery below. To 3 ft. (91 cm).
Range: San Francisco to Peru (including Galapagos Is.); rare
north of Santa Barbara (s. Calif.). **Habitat:** Bays and harbors; at
or near surface. Usually in small schools.
Remarks: Occasionally caught on hook and line. Flesh often
greenish or bluish, turns white when cooked.
Similar species: (1) In our halfbeaks (p. 114) only the *lower* jaw
is elongated. (2) California Barracuda (p. 235; Pl. 35) has 2 dorsal
fins.

Sauries: Family Scomberesocidae

Elongate, slender fishes. The snout is *pointed,* drawn out into a
short beak in some species. Sauries have about 5–7 *finlets* (small
flaglike fins) behind the dorsal and anal fins, which are *far back*.
Pelvic fins abdominal. Lateral line *low* on body (near the ventral
surface). Scales cycloid. Usually green above, with a silver side
stripe; silvery below. Most under 1 ft. (30 cm), largest to 17 in.
(43 cm).
    Sauries are oceanic, near-surface fishes found mostly in temper-
ate waters of the Atlantic and Pacific. 4 species, 1 in our area.

PACIFIC SAURY *Cololabis saira*   Pl. 12
Identification: Body *elongate*. Note the *5–6 finlets* behind the
dorsal and anal fins, which are opposite each other and *far back*.
Lateral line *low* on side. Green to blue above; silvery on side. To
14 in. (36 cm).
Range: Throughout N. Pacific from Japan to Gulf of Alaska and
to Revilla Gigedo Is. (Mex.). **Habitat:** Generally offshore; usually
near surface; in schools.
Remarks: At night can be attracted with a light and captured
with a dipnet. Fished commerically in the w. Pacific and occasionally elsewhere. Flesh often greenish or bluish, turns white when
cooked. Fed on by predatory fishes, marine mammals, and sea
birds.
Similar species: (1) Needlefishes (above) and (2) halfbeaks

(p. 114) have no finlets. (3) Flyingfishes (p. 113) have longer pectoral fins, no finlets. (4) Silversides (below) have 2 dorsal fins, no finlets.

Killifishes: Family Cyprinodontidae

Small fishes with a *rounded* or truncate caudal fin and *1 spineless dorsal fin,* at midbody. The anal fin is usually opposite the dorsal fin. When present, pelvic fins are abdominal. *Mouth small, points upward* for feeding at surface, especially on insects and their larvae, although many killifishes feed throughout the water column. Most are under 4 in. (10 cm), a few reach 6 in. (15 cm). Especially during the breeding season, males tend to be more elaborately colored than females.

Killifishes are found in most tropical and warm-temperate fresh waters; all can tolerate some salinity, and a number live in the sea or move back and forth between fresh and salt water. In S. America and Africa some species live in ponds that periodically dry up; adults die, but the drought-resistant eggs survive. Many are important aquarium fishes, known as egg-laying topminnows. Over 400 species, 1 in the sea in our area.

CALIFORNIA KILLIFISH *Fundulus parvipinnis* **Pl. 12**
Identification: Mouth *small,* caudal fin slightly *rounded.* 1 dorsal fin, at midbody. Olive-green above; yellowish brown below. Usually short dark bars on the side, often a faint side stripe. Breeding males are dark brown to blackish. To 4¼ in. (11 cm).
Range: Morro Bay (cen. Calif.) to n. Baja; a subspecies farther south. **Habitat:** Common in bays and salt marshes near shore.
Remarks: Often used in laboratories for environmental studies.
Similar species: (1) Silversides (below) have a forked caudal fin and 2 dorsal fins. (2) Smelts (p. 80; Pl. 10) have an adipose fin; anal fin is opposite and behind dorsal fin; caudal fin is forked. **Note:** The Rainwater Killifish, *Lucania parva,* is a freshwater species that occasionally enters large brackish bays in our area, such as San Francisco Bay. It is not native; probably was introduced in our area as eggs attached to live oysters imported from the Atlantic states for culture. Resembles the California Killifish in shape and fin location, but it is smaller and lacks bars. To about 1¾ in. (4.4 cm).

Silversides: Family Atherinidae

Elongate fishes with *2 dorsal fins* (in our species the 1st fin is small). They are *silvery,* and most have a bright silver side stripe. Mouth usually small. *No lateral line.* Pelvic fins abdominal. Usually 2–6 in. (5–15 cm); a few (including our species) reach at least 1 ft. (30 cm).

Silversides are found worldwide in tropical and temperate seas. Many species are marine or estuarine; some silversides live in fresh water. Marine species occur inshore, usually in large schools. An important food source for other fishes; some are eaten by humans. They resemble true smelts (p. 80; Pl. 10), but smelts have an adipose fin and *only 1* dorsal fin. About 150 species, 3 in our area.

TOPSMELT *Atherinops affinis*   **Pl. 12**
Identification: *2 dorsal fins; 1st one small,* with *5-9 spines. 5-8 scales* between dorsal fins. No adipose fin. Anal fin begins *below* 1st dorsal fin. Mouth small, at tip of snout; can be protruded. Jaw teeth *forked,* in a *single* row (magnification needed). Green above, with a bright silver side stripe; silvery below. To 14$\frac{1}{2}$ in. (37 cm).
Range: Vancouver I. to Gulf of Calif. **Habitat:** Common in inshore waters (including bays, rocky areas, and kelp beds); in schools.
Remarks: Occasionally caught on hook and line, usually from piers; also fished commercially.
Similar species: (1) In Jacksmelt (below) anal fin begins noticeably *behind* (not directly below) 1st dorsal fin; 10-12 scales between dorsal fins; jaw teeth unforked, in several rows on each jaw. (2) California Grunion (below) has 7-9 scales between dorsal fins; no teeth or small, unforked jaw teeth. (3) Surf Smelt (p. 80) and other true smelts (p. 80; Pl. 10) have only 1 dorsal fin and an adipose fin.

JACKSMELT *Atherinopsis californiensis*   **Pl. 12**
Identification: Most silversides longer than 1 ft. (30 cm) are this species. Resembles Topsmelt but anal fin begins *behind* (not directly below) 1st dorsal fin. *10-12 scales* (hard to count) between the dorsal fins. Jaw teeth *unforked,* in several rows (magnification needed). Greenish blue above, with a silver side stripe; silvery below. To 17$\frac{1}{2}$ in. (44 cm).
Range: Yaquina Bay (Ore.) to s. Baja. **Habitat:** Inshore (including bays); in schools.
Remarks: Often caught on hook and line. Also fished commercially and sold fresh. An important source of food for other fishes.
Similar species: (1) In Topsmelt (above) anal fin begins *below* 1st dorsal fin; fewer scales (5-8) are present between dorsal fins; jaw teeth are forked and in 1 row. (2) California Grunion (below) is smaller; anal fin begins *below* 1st dorsal fin, and jaw teeth (when present) are minute.

CALIFORNIA GRUNION *Leuresthes tenuis*   **Pl. 12**
Identification: *Smaller* and more slender than our other silversides. Anal fin begins *below* 1st dorsal fin. *7-9 scales* (hard to count) between the dorsal fins. Jaw teeth *tiny or absent.* Mouth can be protruded (almost tubular when fully extended). Greenish

above, with a silver-blue side stripe; silvery below. Bluish blotch on cheek (yellowish in our other silversides). To $7\frac{1}{2}$ in. (19 cm).
Range: San Francisco to s. Baja; rare north of s. Calif. **Habitat:** Inshore and to 60 ft. (18 m).
Remarks: The California Grunion is well known for its unusual spawning habits: adults spawn at night, on sand beaches at high tides in the spring and summer (from 2–6 nights after the full moon and new moon). Eggs are buried in moist sand and hatch about 15 days later during the next series of high tides. Grunion hunting has become a famous sport in s. Calif., and licensed sport fishermen are permitted to catch adults by hand when they are on the beach.
Similar species: See (1) Jacksmelt and (2) Topsmelt (p. 118).

Order Lampriformes

Peculiar oceanic and deepsea fishes of various shapes and sizes (mostly *large;* some are huge). Many species are very elongate; in most body is compressed, often ribbonlike. Dorsal fin long, frequently highest in front. Usually no fin spines, but sometimes 1 or 2 at front of dorsal fin. When present, pelvic fins are thoracic. Scales small, cycloid (but many species have none). Mouth can be protruded. Many are silvery, with red fins. They are found worldwide; most species are apparently pelagic at moderate depths; occasionally caught near the surface or found washed ashore. 6 families (but others are sometimes placed in this order), 4 in our area. About 20 species, 6 in our area.

Opahs: Family Lampridae

OPAH *Lampris guttatus*   **Pl. 46**
Identification: Easily identified by the *oval* shape, *scarlet fins and mouth,* and silvery-blue *iridescent* body with *white spots.* Dorsal fin long, high in front. Pectoral fin points *upward.* Scales minute, cycloid. To $4\frac{1}{2}$ ft. (137 cm), 160 lb. (73 kg); reported to 6 ft. (183 cm), 500–600 lb. (227–272 kg).
Range: Worldwide in temperate and tropical seas; Japan to Gulf of Alaska and to Gulf of Calif. **Habitat:** Oceanic; apparently able to live at fairly great depths.
Remarks: The only species in the family. Also known as the Moonfish. An effective predator — eats a variety of fishes and invertebrates, including squids and crabs. Occasionally caught by salmon and Albacore fishermen; also caught on tuna longlines. Flesh is salmon-colored but darker over pectoral fin; dry but tasty, excellent when smoked.
Similar species: Ocean Sunfish (p. 300; Pl. 46) — our only other large oval species — has no pelvic fins or red pigment; its gill opening is tiny, and the rear end of the body is a different shape.

Crestfishes: Family Lophotidae

Elongate, silvery, ribbon-shaped fishes with *crimson fins* and a
protruding *forehead.* Crestfishes are rare, and the number of species is uncertain — perhaps 2. They are found in temperate oceanic
waters, evidently mostly at moderate depths. 1 in our area.

CRESTFISH *Lophotus lacepede*   **Pl. 46**
Identification: Rare and strange. Body elongate, *ribbonlike,* silvery; fins *crimson.* Note the peculiar head, with a protruding or
squarish forehead. Dorsal fin long, *crested* in front. Anal fin near
caudal fin; both *short.* No pelvic fins (except possibly in young).
Scales tiny, cycloid, easily rubbed off. To 40 in. (102 cm) in our
area; elsewhere a similar species or the same species reaches 6 ft.
(183 cm).
Range: Apparently nearly worldwide in warmer seas; s. Calif.
Habitat: Oceanic; probably at great depths.
Remarks: Also known as the Unicornfish. An internal sac produces "ink" that can be discharged from its vent (anus). A few
specimens have been caught on hook and line; some have been
found in stomachs of tunas, others floundering at the surface or in
the surf. Specimens from our area may be a different species; researchers would like additional specimens to clarify the taxonomy.
Species name sometimes spelled *lacepedei.*
Similar species: Ribbonfishes (below) lack an anal fin and the
high forehead.

Ribbonfishes: Family Trachipteridae

These rare fishes are usually *ribbonlike* and delicate, with a very
compressed body. Most are silvery, with red fins. The dorsal fin is
long, and extends from the head to the base of the caudal fin. *No
anal fin.* Caudal fin usually has no lower lobe, upper lobe often
points *upward.* Some species are large — to nearly 6 ft.
(183 cm) — and many undergo radical changes as they grow (for
example, they lose their pelvic fins or scales).
    Ribbonfishes are found in all oceans except the Antarctic Ocean.
Little is known about the habits of these fishes, but evidently they
are wide-ranging in oceanic waters and are able to live at great
depths. Many are captured rather frequently (especially at night
by commercial fishermen using enclosing nets); some are regurgi-
tated by captured Albacores or tunas. Others are found floundering near the surface, in the surf, or washed ashore. They have been
observed from deep-diving submersibles to orient themselves at a
45° angle with the head up and to move by undulating the dorsal
fin. Probably 7–10 species, 4 in our area.

WHIPTAIL RIBBONFISH *Desmodema lorum*   **Pl. 47**
Identification: This strange oceanic species has an *extremely elongate,* tapered body with a *filamentous* (whiplike) tail. Dorsal fin extends from head to tail. No anal fin. Caudal fin *tiny.* Young have a deeper body, shorter tail, and a fanlike pelvic fin that disappears with growth. Adults mostly silvery, unspotted; fins crimson, dorsal fin dark at rear. Large young have round dark spots. To about $3\frac{3}{4}$ ft. (114 cm).
Range: Probably only the N. Pacific; off cen. Calif. to s. Baja.
Habitat: Oceanic; young near surface, adults probably deeper (details unknown).
Similar species: (1) Scalloped Ribbonfish (p. 122) has a deeper body, with a wavy lateral line at rear. (2) Body of Tapertail Ribbonfish (below) tapers quickly from head to midbody but rear of body straplike (not tapered). (3) King-of-the-Salmon (below) usually has several dark blotches on its side, and its body is less tapered. (4) Crestfish (p. 120) has an anal fin and a high forehead. (5) Oarfish (p. 122) has a long, rodlike pelvic fin.

KING-OF-THE-SALMON *Trachipterus altivelis*   **Pl. 46**
Identification: Elongate, *ribbonlike. Long dorsal fin,* highest in front. Caudal fin points *upward.* No anal fin. Mouth fairly small, at end of a sloping snout. Eye large. Pelvic fin long in young, virtually absent in adults. *Silver,* with *crimson fins;* blackish above eye. Young have 3–5 dark blotches along side. To about 6 ft. (183 cm); larger specimens reported.
Range: Alaska to Chile. **Habitat:** Oceanic; depths uncertain, at least to 1640 ft. (500 m). Also found near surface, but large adults sometimes feed on bottom.
Remarks: The common name comes from an Indian legend, which describes this fish as the "King" that leads salmons back to rivers each year. Sometimes captured while trolling for salmon; also caught in nets, and occasionally found washed ashore.
Similar species: (1) In Scalloped Ribbonfish (p. 122) lateral line is wavy on rear of body, and profile tapers more quickly toward the rear. (2) In Whiptail Ribbonfish (above) body tapers quickly at middle, very thin thereafter. (3) In Tapertail Ribbonfish (below) rear $\frac{1}{3}$ of body is straplike.

TAPERTAIL RIBBONFISH *Trachipterus fukuzakii*   **Pl. 47**
Identification: Elongate, ribbonlike. *No* anal fin. Caudal fin *points upward.* Body *tapers sharply* at middle; last $\frac{1}{3}$ of body thin, *straplike. Silvery,* with dark blotches on side. Fins *red.* To just over $4\frac{2}{3}$ ft. (143 cm).
Range: Alamitos Bay (s. Calif.) to Chile. **Habitat:** Oceanic; at or near surface at night, deeper during the day.
Remarks: Only 1 specimen has been taken off Calif.
Similar species: See (1) Whiptail Ribbonfish and (2) King-of-the-Salmon (above).

SCALLOPED RIBBONFISH *Zu cristatus*   **Pl. 47**
Identification: Can be distinguished from other ribbonfishes
(above) by *wavy* lateral line on rear of its body. Body elongate,
compressed; tapers abruptly at midbody (less so in adults than in
young). Adults have *no* pelvic fin; no greatly elongate dorsal fin
rays, and a tiny caudal fin. Young (Pl. 47) — under about 1 ft.
(30 cm) — have a *scalloped* ventral profile between the pelvic fin
and anus, a *long* pelvic fin, *long* rays at front of dorsal fin, and a
large, *fanlike* caudal fin. (These features are transitional in inter-
mediate-sized specimens.) Silvery, with vague dark bars (more distinct in young). Fins mostly red, with some black patches; rear of
caudal fin black. To 40 in. (102 cm).
Range: Worldwide in warm seas; off Newport Beach (s. Calif.) to
Peru and Galapagos Is. **Habitat:** Oceanic; young shallow, adults
probably deep (details unknown).
Remarks: Rare — any capture should be brought to the attention of an ichthyologist.
Similar species: In the 3 other ribbonfishes (p. 121), the lateral
line is not wavy at rear of body.

Oarfishes: Family Regalecidae

OARFISH *Regalecus glesne*   **Pl. 46**
Identification: A spectacular *huge,* silvery fish with *red* fins. Dorsal fin bright crimson with long rays at front, forming a cockscomb
on head. Pelvic fin consists of only *1 ray;* it is *long* and often *expanded at tip* like an oar (hence the name). Elongate body tapers
to a small caudal fin, which can be tiny or even lost. No scales.
Silvery; banded or blotched with black. *To 35 ft.* (11 m), possibly
500 lb. (227 kg).
Range: Topanga Beach (s. Calif.) to Chile. The same species or a
similar one occurs nearly worldwide. **Habitat:** Oceanic, temperate
and tropical seas. Can live at great depths.
Remarks: Probably not the only species in the family, but so few
oarfishes are captured and changes with growth are so extensive
that no one is sure; ichthyologists would like more specimens to
study. Most likely to be found washed ashore. A deepsea "mon-
ster."
Similar species: Ribbonfishes (above) have no pelvic fins (in
adults); pelvic fins (when present) contain more than 1 ray.

Order Beryciformes and Relatives

An intermediate group between the "lower fishes" (with few, if
any, fin spines) and the "advanced," typically perchlike fishes
(with well-developed fin spines). The species are of various shapes
and sizes. In many species the dorsal and anal fins are opposite

each other and far back. Pelvic fins are abdominal or thoracic, with 1 spine and usually *more than 5 soft* rays. Most species are under 10 in. (25 cm). Many live in the deep sea; others are common in shallow tropical waters. Researchers do not agree on which families should be placed in this order, so classifications vary. Some place a few of these families in other orders (Cetomimiformes, Miripinniformes); we include them here for a total of about 17 families. No shallow-water fishes of this group reach our area; the 7 deepsea families that occur off our coast are described below, and family representatives are shown in Fig. 17 (p. 124).

Bigscales: Family Melamphaidae

Most of these small deepsea fishes are black or dark brown, with large, cycloid scales (often rubbed off during capture). Dorsal fin at midbody, usually with 1–3 weak spines at front. Anal fin short, nearly opposite or slightly to rear of dorsal fin. Pelvic fins thoracic (roughly below pectoral fins), with 1 spine and 6–8 soft rays. They usually have well-marked pores on head, and frequently ridges or crests. Most species reach 4–6 in. (10–15 cm). Bigscales are found in all oceans except the Arctic Ocean and Mediterranean Sea; most occur at tropical and warm-temperate latitudes. Adults are usually bathypelagic, young shallower. They are eaten by marine mammals and large fishes. About 35 species, 8 in our area (all with the same shape as the one illustrated; some have a larger or smaller eye or a longer dorsal fin). **Family representative:** Crested Bigscale, *Poromitra crassiceps* (see Melamphaidae in Fig. 17, p. 124). To about 6 in. (15 cm). In e. Pacific from Alaska to Chile.

Fangtooths: Family Anoplogastridae

Evidently there is only 1 species in the family. It is easily identified by its large, bony, sculptured head and large mouth with fanglike teeth. Body deepest toward the front. Black to dark brown. Found in midwaters of the Atlantic and Pacific; Ore. to Panama. Adults usually occur at depths below 2000 ft. (610 m). **Family representative:** Fangtooth, *Anoplogaster cornuta* (see Anoplogastridae in Fig. 17, p. 124). To about 6 in. (15 cm).

Spinyfins: Family Diretmidae

Oval to nearly circular, compressed fishes with large eyes. *No* lateral line. Dorsal and anal fins are fairly long, nearly opposite each other. Pelvic fins with 1 prickly spine, usually 6 soft rays. Caudal fin forked. Scales prickly. Adults blackish brown, young mostly silvery. Largest to 15¾ in. (40 cm). Oceanic; adults probably near bottom at moderate to great depths, young shallower. At least 2 species, 1 in our area. **Family representative:** Large Spinyfin,

Diretmus pauciradiatus (see Diretmidae in Fig. 17). To about 15¾ in. (40 cm). Nearly worldwide, mostly at tropical and warm-temperate latitudes. Known in our area from 1 specimen trawled off Wash. at about 650 ft. (198 m).

Whalefishes: Family Cetomimidae

These rare bathypelagic fishes have a *huge mouth* and *no scales*. They also have *no* pelvic fins (unlike the next 2 families). Dorsal and anal fins far back. No fin spines. Lateral line prominent. Eye small to tiny. *Reddish orange* to *brown*. To about 9 in. (23 cm). Whalefishes occur worldwide at low latitudes; probably at depths below 2000 ft. (610 m). About 10 species, 2 off Calif., another just south of Calif. **Family representative:** Pink Flabby Whalefish, *Cetostoma regani* (see Cetomimidae in Fig. 17). To 9 in. (23 cm). Atlantic and Pacific; off cen. Calif.

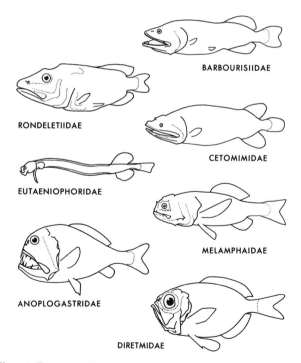

BARBOURISIIDAE

RONDELETIIDAE

CETOMIMIDAE

EUTAENIOPHORIDAE

MELAMPHAIDAE

ANOPLOGASTRIDAE

DIRETMIDAE

Fig. 17 Deepsea Beryciform and Cetomimiform families

Velvet Whalefishes:
Family Barbourisiidae

Extremely rare bathypelagic fishes. Apparently only 1 species in the family. Dorsal and anal fins far back, opposite each other. *No fin spines.* Pelvic fins abdominal. Skin loose but tough and furry — densely covered with tiny spines. (Whalefishes — above — and redmouth whalefishes — below — have smooth skin.) Lateral line a continuous row of pores in large scales. *Red.* To about 15 in. (38 cm). Worldwide at low latitudes. **Family representative:** Velvet Whalefish, *Barbourisia rufa* (see Barbourisiidae in Fig. 17, p. 124). 1 captured off n.-cen. Calif.

Redmouth Whalefishes:
Family Rondeletiidae

Rare bathypelagic fishes resembling those in the preceding 2 families. Head and mouth large. Dorsal and anal fins *far back,* opposite each other. *No fin spines.* Pectoral and pelvic fins small; pelvic fins abdominal. *No scales.* Lateral line a *series of pores* in *short vertical rows.* Orange-brown; mouth *reddish orange.* To about 6 in. (15 cm). Found in all tropical and temperate seas. Average depth about 3280 ft. (1000 m); caught as shallow as about 1150 ft. (350 m). 2 species, 1 in our area. **Family representative:** Armored Redmouth Whalefish, *Rondeletia loricata* (Rondeletiidae in Fig. 17, p. 124). To about 6 in. (15 cm). Worldwide in tropical to temperate seas; off s. Calif.

Ribbontails: Family Eutaeniophoridae

Little is known about these small, aberrant, rare oceanic fishes. They are very elongate, with the dorsal and anal fins far back, opposite each other. *No* scales. Pelvic fins long and narrow, below pectoral fins. In young an extremely long *ribbonlike streamer* projects from the caudal fin. Probably dusky when alive. To about $2\frac{1}{4}$ in. (5.7 cm), excluding caudal streamer. Ribbontails are found in tropical and warm-temperate seas; habitat poorly known. Probably 3 species, 1 in our area. **Family representative:** Festive Ribbontail, *Eutaeniophorus festivus* (Eutaeniophoridae in Fig. 17, p. 124). Atlantic and Pacific; off Calif.

Order Zeiformes

Mostly deepsea fishes. Spinous part of dorsal fin separated from soft-rayed part by a notch. Body generally deep and compressed. Pelvic fins thoracic or nearly so, with 1 spine and usually *more than 5* (5–9) soft rays. Scales often modified, scutelike. Mouth usually oblique, jaws protrusible. Young often look very different from adults. Many species are silvery. Most are about 6–12 in. (15–30 cm). Nearly worldwide; most on continental shelves. Young apparently are pelagic (some grow quite large); most adults are found near bottom at moderate to great depths. 6 families, 2 in our area. About 50 species (many poorly known), 2 in our area.

Oreos: Family Oreosomatidae

A poorly known family of deepsea and oceanic fishes. They are *deep-bodied,* with a *large eye* and *protrusible mouth.* Adults have mostly overlapping cycloid or ctenoid scales. Smaller, pelagic young (called pelagic prejuveniles) are oval in profile, with leathery skins and large hardened cones or scaled "hills" on the side. Some prejuveniles reach 4–5 in. (10–13 cm) or more before they lose the cones or "hills" and develop the adult shape and scalation. The prejuveniles were so different in their features that they were long thought to be separate species. Most adults are 8–12 in. (20–30 cm), some reach about 2 ft. (61 cm). Oreos occur nearly worldwide, but most live in the S. Hemisphere. Adults are found near bottom at moderate depths — about 500–2400 ft. (152–732 m). Probably 12 species, 1 in our area.

OXEYE OREO *Allocyttus folletti*   **Pl. 48**
Identification: Eye of adults *large.* Scales *granular* on the belly and between eye and dorsal fin; cycloid on side. Look for rows of spiny scales at base of dorsal and anal fins. Mouth protrusible. Adults dusky, unspotted. Young (Fig. 18) — to about 5 in. (13 cm) — are *ovoid,* with *dark spots,* leathery skin, small tuberclelike "cones" on lower side, and a row of enlarged platelike scales near pelvic fin. To 15 in. (38 cm).
Range: N. Pacific; Japan to Bering Sea and to s.-cen. Calif.
Habitat: Young oceanic; adults near bottom at about 1200–2400 ft. (366–732 m) and probably deeper.
Remarks: Adults are caught in bottom trawls, young in midwater trawls.

Fig. 18 Oxeye Oreo (young)

Similar species: Mirror Dory (below) has a smaller eye and large *scutes* at base of dorsal and anal fins.

Dories: Family Zeidae

Most dories resemble oreos (above) in having a *deep body* and a *protrusible mouth.* They have *large scutes* (modified scales) at the base of the dorsal and anal fins, also on belly and breast. Many are silvery. To about 1–2 ft. (30–61 cm). Dories are found in all oceans; adults usually on or near bottom in shallow to deep water. About 10 species, 1 in our area.

MIRROR DORY *Zenopsis nebulosa* **Pl. 48**
Identification: Look for large *platelike scutes* at base of dorsal and anal fins and on the belly and breast. Body deep, compressed. Mouth protrusible. Young have dorsal fin spines that extend into long *filaments* (shorter in adults), and a long pelvic fin. Mostly silvery, with some black (especially on top of head). To 19 in. (48 cm).
Range: Rare, but evidently widespread in temperate waters of N. and S. Pacific; off cen. and s. Calif. **Habitat:** Young probably pelagic; adults usually taken near bottom. Caught off Calif. at about 200–600 ft. (61–183 m), reported elsewhere at depths from about 100 ft. (30 m) to below 1000 ft. (305 m).
Remarks: Fished commercially off Australia and New Zealand.
Similar species: See Oxeye Oreo (p. 126).

Order Gasterosteiformes

These fishes have a *small mouth,* usually at the end of a *tubular snout.* Some species are armored with bony plates. When present, pelvic fins are abdominal or nearly thoracic. Most inhabit warm seas, but some, such as the sticklebacks, live in fresh water; a few pipefishes live in rivers. They are common in vegetated areas. Color and shape vary: many are elongate; most are under 8 in. (20 cm). Many eat small crustaceans. Pipefishes, seahorses, and snipefishes are sometimes placed in their own order (Syngnathiformes), but we include them here. 7–9 families, 4 in our area; about 200 species, 9 in our area.

Sticklebacks: Family Gasterosteidae

These are small fishes with 2–15 *isolated spines before the soft-rayed dorsal fin.* They usually have thin bony plates instead of scales on the side. Most are under 4 in. (10 cm). Sticklebacks occur in fresh and salt waters of the N. Hemisphere. About 8 species (but many subspecies or populations); 1 in the sea in our area.

THREESPINE STICKLEBACK
Pl. 13

Gasterosteus aculeatus

Identification: Easily recognized by the *3 isolated spines* (2 large, 1 small) *before* the soft-rayed *dorsal fin*. Thin *bony plates* on side (number varies). Caudal peduncle slender, keeled. Pelvic fin has *1 spine and 1 ray*. Olive or blackish above; silvery below. Breeding males have a reddish head and underparts. To 4 in. (10 cm).

Range: Korea to Bering Sea and Aleutian Is., and to n. Baja; in sea only as far south as Monterey Bay. Also in N. Atlantic.
Habitat: Fresh and salt water; usually near shore. In sea to about 90 ft. (27 m).
Remarks: Anadromous — spawns mostly in fresh water, where male builds a nest and guards the eggs. Eats small pelagic organisms (especially crustaceans), also small fishes. Eaten by fishes, seals, and sea birds.

Tubesnouts: Family Aulorhynchidae

These stickleback relatives are elongate, and have a *small mouth at* the *end of a long snout*. 24–26 short isolated dorsal fin spines precede a soft-rayed dorsal fin that is opposite the anal fin. Thin bony plates on side. To 7 in. (18 cm). Tubesnouts occur only in the N. Pacific. 2 species, 1 in our area.

TUBESNOUT *Aulorhynchus flavidus*
Pl. 13

Identification: Elongate. *Mouth small,* at end of *long snout.* About *25 isolated spines precede* the soft *dorsal fin.* Pelvic fin below pectoral fin. Anal fin opposite soft dorsal fin. Brownish above, with darker bars; white below. Silvery behind head; dark stripe on head, often extends onto body. To 7 in. (18 cm).

Range: Sitka (Alaska) to n. Baja. **Habitat:** In kelp beds, eelgrass, rocky areas, and over sand bottom. Usually near the surface in schools, also at depths up to 100 ft. (30 m); sometimes in dense schools well offshore.
Remarks: Builds a spawning nest (usually in kelp), which the male guards. Eats small pelagic organisms. An interesting aquarium pet.

Snipefishes: Family Macroramphosidae

Compressed, mostly silvery fishes that have a *small mouth* at the end of a *long snout,* and a short spinous dorsal fin with a *very long 2nd spine.* Most have thin bony plates on side. To about 1 ft. (30 cm). Snipefishes occur mostly in shallow tropical to warm-temperate seas; usually in schools. About 11 species, 1 in our area.

SLENDER SNIPEFISH *Macroramphosus gracilis*
Pl. 13

Identification: Note *tiny mouth* at end of *long tubular snout.* 2

dorsal fins — 1st one spinous, with a *very long 2nd spine.* Body compressed. Pelvic fin abdominal. Mostly silvery, often with a pink or greenish cast; back dark. To 6 in. (15 cm).
Range: Worldwide in warm seas; s. Calif. southward. **Habitat:** Wide-ranging; near surface to near bottom, sometimes in huge schools.
Similar species: Other species in our area whose mouth is small and at the end of a long tubular snout have a different shape and no elongate 2nd dorsal fin spine.

Pipefishes and Seahorses: Family Syngnathidae

These fishes are encased in *bony rings,* giving the body a segmented look. Mouth small, toothless, at end of *long snout.* 1 dorsal fin, at midbody. No pelvic fins. Pipefishes have a caudal fin but seahorses do not. Seahorses have a cocked head and a coiled tail. Gills are tufted. Males have a brood pouch on the abdomen and tail; female places eggs in pouch; male carries the eggs, which hatch in the pouch, and "gives birth" to the young. Many species are brownish; some are brightly colored. Adults from about 1 in. (2.5 cm) to about 1 ft. (30 cm); largest specimens reach about 21 in. (53 cm). Pipefishes and seahorses are found worldwide in temperate and tropical waters. Nearly all live in the sea, a few enter rivers; most are found in eelgrass or other vegetation in shallow water, a few live among corals. They are poor swimmers and mimic vegetation for cover.

   To identify pipefishes, the rings around the body (trunk) and tail must be counted. The ring bearing the pectoral fin is counted as the first trunk ring, and the anus is on the last trunk ring. The ring bearing the anal fin is usually the first tail ring; but if the anus and anal fin are on same ring, then that ring is the 1st tail ring and the preceding ring is the last trunk ring. Color is extremely variable and of little use in identification. Perhaps 175 species (about 25 are seahorses); 1 seahorse and 6 pipefishes in our area.

PACIFIC SEAHORSE *Hippocampus ingens*   **Pl. 13**
Identification: The only seahorse in our area. Body and tail covered with bony rings. Tail long, *coiled;* no caudal fin. 1 dorsal fin. Note the peculiar "horse-shaped" head, which is cocked at an angle to the body. Red, tan, yellow, or green, usually with white bands around body after every 6–7 rings. Some have white mottling. To 1 ft. (30 cm).
Range: San Diego to Peru (including Galapagos Is.); an old (doubtful) record from San Francisco Bay. **Habitat:** Usually offshore; most captured by dredging at 33 ft. (10 m) or deeper. Occasionally taken at surface.

SNUBNOSE PIPEFISH *Bryx arctus*   **Pl. 13**
Identification: Our only *short-nosed* pipefish. 14–16 (usually 15) trunk rings. 36–41 (usually 39–40) tail rings. 18–23 (usually 19) dorsal fin rays. Brown, olive, or blackish; sometimes a black spot between trunk rings; occasionally a narrow white ring after every 4–5 rings. To 4¾ in. (12 cm).
Range: Tomales Bay (n. Calif.) to Mazatlan (Mex.); throughout Gulf of Calif.; rare north of Santa Barbara (s. Calif.). **Habitat:** Along coast, usually in shallow bays and sloughs among eelgrass and other seaweeds. Also pelagic. Found at depths up to 60 ft. (18 m).
Remarks: Sometimes placed in the genus *Syngnathus*.
Similar species: Other pipefishes (below) in our area have a longer snout.

BARRED PIPEFISH *Syngnathus auliscus*   **Pl. 13**
Identification: Snout medium-sized. In adults trunk and tail rings have sharp edges. 14–16 (usually 15) trunk rings. 34–39 (usually 36–37) tail rings. 26–33 (usually 27–30) rays in dorsal fin. Green or brown; occasionally a narrow white ring after every 5–6 rings. To 7 in. (18 cm).
Range: Santa Barbara Channel (s. Calif.) to n. Peru. **Habitat:** Shallow bays and lagoons; in eelgrass.
Similar species: See under Bay Pipefish (p. 131).

KELP PIPEFISH *Syngnathus californiensis*   **Not shown**
Identification: Snout long, compressed. Usually more tail rings (46–52) than in our other pipefishes (except Barcheek Pipefish, below). 19–22 (usually 21) trunk rings. 46–52 (usually 48–49) total rings. 40–48 (usually 42–46) rays in dorsal fin. Greenish, yellowish, or brownish, with small dark speckles. To 19½ in. (50 cm).
Range: Bodega Bay (n. Calif.) to s. Baja. **Habitat:** Kelp beds, rarely in bays; to 48 ft. (15 m).
Similar species: See under Bay Pipefish (p. 131).

CHOCOLATE PIPEFISH   **Not shown**
Syngnathus euchrous
Identification: Snout long, round. 2 subspecies, counts in our area: 18–20 trunk rings; 42–49 (usually 45–46) tail rings; 61–68 total rings; 38–45 rays in dorsal fin. Greenish brown to reddish brown, with white blotches and bluish specks. Gill cover and streak behind eye bluish silver. Plates covering pouch brown. To 10 in. (25 cm).
Range: Redondo Beach (s. Calif.) to cen. Baja. **Habitat:** In eelgrass and in drifting algae; off rocky shores. Near shore to 36 ft. (11 m).
Remarks: Some specimens have been caught by dipnet under a light at night.
Similar species: See under Bay Pipefish (p. 131).

BARCHEEK PIPEFISH

Not shown

Syngnathus exilis

Identification: Snout long, compressed. 17–20 trunk rings. 43–50 (usually 45–47) tail rings. 63–68 total rings. 35–43 (usually 37–40) rays in dorsal fin. Greenish to reddish brown; usually a dark stripe behind lower part of eye. Light specks on top of head. To about 10 in. (25 cm).

Range: Half Moon Bay (cen. Calif.) to s.-cen. Baja and Guadalupe I. off n.-cen. Baja. **Habitat:** Sand beaches, often in drifting algae.

Similar species: See under Bay Pipefish (below).

BAY PIPEFISH

Pl. 13

Syngnathus leptorhynchus

Identification: Common. Snout *long,* round. 16–21 trunk rings. Northern population has 39–46 tail rings, 34–44 rays in dorsal fin; southern population has 36–43 tail rings; 28–38 rays in dorsal fin. 53–63 total rings. 28–43 dorsal fin rays. Gray to green (occasionally tan), often flecked with other colors. To 13 in. (33 cm), southern population only to 9½ in. (24 cm).

Range: Sitka (Alaska) to s. Baja; northern population from Alaska to Monterey Bay, southern population from Morro Bay southward. **Habitat:** Common in eelgrass of bays and sloughs.

Similar species: (1) Snubnose Pipefish (p. 130) has a short snout. The longer-snouted (2) Barred, (3) Kelp, (4) Chocolate, and (5) Barcheek Pipefishes (above) are similiar to the Bay Pipefish, but do not occur north of n. Calif. The snout is compressed in Bay and Barcheek Pipefishes, shorter and round in Chocolate and Kelp Pipefishes. Barred Pipefish has fewest trunk rings (only 14–16, not 17 or more). Kelp Pipefish occurs among giant kelp, rarely enters bays, and usually has more tail rings (average 48–49).

Order Scorpaeniformes

A large order known as the "mail-cheeked" fishes because of a bony connection (suborbital stay) under the cheek that connects bones under the eye (called suborbitals) with the front of the gill cover. Most species have a spiny head. Their shape varies; some are basslike. Most have rounded pectoral fins, and a square-cut or rounded caudal fin (rarely forked). Usually under 1 ft. (30 cm), some reach 3 ft. (91 cm) or more. Worldwide, but best represented in the N. Hemisphere. Nearly all families are marine. They occur inshore and to moderate depths offshore. About 20 families, 8–10 families in our area (depending on classification used). About 1000 species, over 230 in our area.

Scorpionfishes and Rockfishes:
Family Scorpaenidae

The largest family in our area, with about 65 species (including over 60 kinds of rockfishes). They have a suborbital stay (a bony connection under the cheek), and most have spines on the head. Red and brown are the predominant colors. Size varies: many species are 6–12 in. (15–30 cm); some reach at least 3 ft. (91 cm). The family is essentially marine, but a few species enter tropical rivers. The fin spines are venomous in most species, but only slightly so in most of ours. Fertilization is internal (apparently in all species). Some lay eggs (often in gelatinous masses); others (including all rockfishes) are ovoviviparous. About 400 species in 50 genera; over 100 species (including all but 4 of ours) belong to the genus *Sebastes,* commonly known as rockfishes or rockcods.

Rockfishes (*Sebastes* species) are basslike, with a more or less compressed body and large mouth. The head is usually spiny; nearly all species have 5 spines on the preopercle (rear cheek area). The dorsal fin is continuous, with 12–15 spines and 9–16 soft rays (last ray double), but is usually well notched just before the last spine. The anal fin has 3 spines and 5–9 soft rays (last ray double). Caudal fin rounded, or square cut to slightly forked; pectoral fins rounded or wedge-shaped.

In our area rockfishes are common in clean bays, along shore, in kelp beds, and offshore to about 1500 ft. (457 m); a few range deeper. Many live in rocky areas, others on soft bottom offshore. Rockfishes are major predators in our area. They are important as sport fishes and some are also fished commercially. Most adults are 1–2 ft. (30–61 cm), a few over 3 ft. (91 cm). **Caution:** the dorsal and anal fin spines are slightly venomous, sometimes producing irritation in the wound, so handle with care. At least 62 species in our area (about 35 more in the nw. Pacific, 2–3 off Peru and Chile, about 5 — known as redfishes — in the N. Atlantic, and 1 in the S. Atlantic). Species are most easily identified by color (see Pls. 23–28), so page and plate numbers are usually cross-referenced for similar species in the accounts below.

CALIFORNIA SCORPIONFISH *Scorpaena guttata*   **Pl. 23**
Identification: Stocky, with a large mouth, spiny head, and large fan-shaped pectoral fin. *12 spines,* 9–10 soft rays in dorsal fin. A row of *spines under eye* extends onto rear cheek area. Red to brown, with pale mottling (deeper-living specimens more red); dark spots on body and fins. To 17 in. (43 cm).
Range: Santa Cruz (cen. Calif.) to Gulf of Calif.; rare north of s. Calif. **Habitat:** Usually in rocky areas of bays and along shore, especially in caves and crevices; shallow water to about 600 ft. (183 m), but usually above 100 ft. (30 m).

Remarks: *Caution:* fin spines venomous; puncture wound can be extremely painful. Immerse wound in hot water; if severe, consult a doctor. Eggs are embedded in gelatinous walls, which form 2 free-floating, hollow, pear-shaped balloons that are attached at the smaller ends. An excellent food fish. Also known as the Sculpin (though not in the sculpin family).

Similar species: (1) Rainbow Scorpionfish (below) has 13 dorsal fin spines; color different. (2) Thornyheads (p. 152) usually have 15-16 dorsal fin spines, are mostly red, and live deeper. (3) Rockfishes (*Sebastes* species — below) have 1 or no spines (not a row) below the rear of the eye and different coloration. (4) The Cabezon (a sculpin — p. 182) has a skin flap on snout, 15-18 soft rays in dorsal fin, no scales, different head spination.

RAINBOW SCORPIONFISH *Scorpaenodes xyris*　　**Pl. 23**
Identification: Small — usually 3-5 in. *13 spines in dorsal fin. Row of spines under eye* extends onto rear cheek. Reddish brown to brown, with dark spots on body and fins. A large reddish to brown *spot on gill cover*. To 6 in. (15 cm).
Range: San Clemente I. and Santa Catalina I. (s. Calif.) to Peru, including Galapagos Is. **Habitat:** Usually in rocky areas; shallow water and to about 85 ft. (26 m).
Similar species: See California Scorpionfish (above).

ROUGHEYE ROCKFISH *Sebastes aleutianus*　　**Pl. 27**
Identification: 2-10 spines in a *rasplike ridge* just below front of eye. Red or reddish black, more pinkish below; some vague dusky blotches. Fins reddish, usually dark-edged. In large specimens mouth white to pink inside, with black blotches. Large — to 38 in. (96 cm).
Range: Aleutian Is. to San Diego. **Habitat:** Deep water; on bottom at 600-2400 ft. (183-732 m).
Similar species: Shortraker Rockfish (p. 135; Pl. 27) is similar but lacks rasplike ridge of spines. (2) Aurora Rockfish (p. 134; Pl. 28) has no dark blotches.

PACIFIC OCEAN PERCH *Sebastes alutus*　　**Pl. 28**
Identification: Light red above; whitish below. Usually has dark saddles along back; often a large olive-green area below soft dorsal fin. Note *protruding knob at tip of chin.* Head spines *weak.* To 20 in. (51 cm).
Range: Japan and Bering Sea to La Jolla (s. Calif.); common from Ore. northward. **Habitat:** Abundant offshore, trawled at 180-2100 ft. (55-640 m); adults usually below 400 ft. (122 m).
Remarks: Grows slowly; probably lives for 30 years. Most important commercial rockfish in the ne. Pacific; marketed as fillets.
Similar species: Several other reddish rockfishes usually have dark saddles on back — see Pl. 28: (1) Darkblotched Rockfish (p. 137) has 5 blackish patches on back, no protruding knob on chin, a

deeper body; (2) Halfbanded Rockfish (p. 150) has dark streaks between rays in caudal fin, 2 dark blotches on side, no prominent knob on chin; (3) In Sharpchin Rockfish (p. 152) 2nd spine in anal fin is longer than 3rd one (2nd spine shorter than 3rd one in Pacific Ocean Perch); (4) Stripetail Rockfish (p. 150) has dark streaks between caudal fin rays, no protruding knob on chin. (5) Yellowmouth Rockfish (p. 147; Pl. 27) has a smaller knob on chin, yellow and black blotches inside pinkish mouth.

KELP ROCKFISH *Sebastes atrovirens* **Pl. 26**
Identification: Olive-brown to gray brown, with darker brown mottling; sometimes pinkish below. To 16¾ in. (42 cm).
Range: Timber Cove (Sonoma Co., cen. Calif.) to cen. Baja.
Habitat: Usually on or near bottom in kelp beds or rocky areas; to 150 ft. (46 m), common at 30–40 ft. (9.1–12 m).
Remarks: Frequently caught on baited hook in kelp beds, and seen by divers "hanging" or resting on kelp.
Similar species: (1) Brown Rockfish (below; Pl. 26) has a dark blotch on gill cover. (2) Grass Rockfish (p. 147; Pl. 26) has stubby gill rakers (width roughly equals length).

BROWN ROCKFISH *Sebastes auriculatus* **Pl. 26**
Identification: Light brown, with darker brown mottling (especially blotches on back). Note *prominent dark brown blotch* on gill cover. Belly and base of pectoral fin usually pinkish. To 21½ in. (55 cm).
Range: Se. Alaska to cen. Baja. **Habitat:** Widely distributed in shallow water and bays; near shore and to 420 ft. (128 m).
Remarks: Commonly caught by sport fishermen in cen. Calif.
Similar species: Easily confused with 2 other mostly plain-colored (but not black) inshore species (both on Pl. 26): (1) Kelp (above) and (2) Grass Rockfishes (p. 147) have no dark blotch on gill cover; Grass Rockfish has stubby gill rakers.

AURORA ROCKFISH *Sebastes aurora* **Pl. 28**
Identification: Bright pinkish red or orangish red; mostly solid-colored. 24–28 gill rakers on 1st arch. Small toothed knob at tip of each upper jaw. 5–6 (usually 6) soft rays in anal fin (last one double, counted as 1). 2nd spine in anal fin long (length about 1½ times eye diameter). To 15½ in. (39 cm).
Range: Southern B.C. to cen. Baja. **Habitat:** Common offshore; trawled on soft bottom and caught in Sablefish traps at 600–2520 ft. (183–768 m).
Remarks: When trawled, scales usually rub off, leaving white pockets bordered by red.
Similar species: (1) Splitnose Rockfish (p. 138; Pl. 28) has a more prominent knob at tip of each upper jaw, a larger eye (diameter nearly equal to length of 2nd spine in anal fin), 32–37 gill rakers on 1st arch. (2) Rougheye Rockfish (p. 133; Pl. 27) has 2–10 spines on

rasplike ridge below front of eye; more gill rakers (29–34). See (3) Chameleon Rockfish (p. 146) and (4) Yellowmouth Rockfish (p. 147; Pl. 27).

REDBANDED ROCKFISH *Sebastes babcocki*   **Pl. 23**
Identification: Pinkish white, with *4 broad red bars* (blackish in smaller specimens). 2 oblique bars on head. Bar beginning at front of spinous dorsal fin slants down and *back* toward pectoral fin. To 25 in. (64 cm).
Range: Amchitka I. (Aleutian Is.) to San Diego; uncommon south of San Francisco. **Habitat:** Soft bottom at 300–1560 ft. (91–475 m).
Similar species: In Flag Rockfish (p. 149; Pl. 23) bar below front of dorsal fin more *vertical,* extends down onto gill cover; usually 17 pectoral fin rays (usually 19 in Redbanded Rockfish). Usually caught on hook and line (Redbanded Rockfish most often trawled).

SHORTRAKER ROCKFISH *Sebastes borealis*   **Pl. 27**
Identification: Large. Pink or orange-pink, with vague red to orange bars. Fins reddish; pelvic and pectoral fins sometimes black-edged. Mouth and gill chamber usually red, with black blotches. To 38 in. (96 cm).
Range: Se. Kamchatka (USSR) to Ft. Bragg (n. Calif.). **Habitat:** Little known; soft bottom near 1000 ft. (305 m).
Similar species: Rougheye Rockfish (p. 133; Pl. 27) has rasplike ridge of spines below front of eye.

SILVERGRAY ROCKFISH *Sebastes brevispinis*   **Pl. 24**
Identification: Mouth large; *chin projects* strongly. *Gray above; silver-gray on side; white below.* Anal, pelvic, and pectoral fins tinged with red or pink near base. Lips blackish. To 28 in. (71 cm).
Range: Bering Sea to Santa Barbara I. (s. Calif.). **Habitat:** Wide-ranging; 100–1200 ft. (30–366 m).
Remarks: Important commercially from se. Alaska to Ore.
Similar species: (1) Bocaccio (p. 145; Pl. 24) is usually reddish (not gray) on side; usually has more soft rays in anal fin (8–10, not 7–8) and fewer pectoral fin rays (15–16, not 16–18). (2) Other species with a projecting lower jaw have red or pink on the body.

GOPHER ROCKFISH *Sebastes carnatus*   **Pl. 24**
Identification: Stout body. *Brownish to olive,* mottled with pale areas; about 6 large *flesh-colored* to slightly whitish areas on back. To 15½ in. (39 cm).
Range: Eureka (n. Calif.) to cen. Baja. **Habitat:** Holes or crevices in rocky areas to 180 ft. (55 m); more common below 50 ft. (15 m). Territorial.
Similar species: (1) Black-and-Yellow Rockfish (p. 136; Pl. 24) has bright *yellow* (not flesh-colored) areas on back and dorsal fin. (2) A number of predominantly *reddish* rockfishes have about 5 *whitish* areas along the back (see Pl. 25).

COPPER ROCKFISH *Sebastes caurinus*   **Pl. 24**
Identification: Deep, stout body. Color varies: dark brown or
olive to pink or orange-red above, with patches of copper-pink and
sometimes yellow; whitish below. Usually 2 copper-orange bars
radiate backward from eye. Cheek sometimes yellowish. Fins
mostly coppery, often dusky. Often a pale stripe along lateral line
and vague bars behind head. To $22\frac{1}{2}$ in. (57 cm).
Range: Gulf of Alaska to cen. Baja. **Habitat:** Common in rocky
areas or rock-sand bottom in shallow water and to 600 ft. (183 m).
Remarks: An important sport fish in Calif. Color varies greatly.
Stripe along lateral line tends to be more noticeable in excited
individuals. Most specimens from s. Calif. are more reddish — they
may be a separate species (the Whitebelly Rockfish, *Sebastes
vexillaris*).
Similar species: See (1) Gopher Rockfish (p. 135) and (2) Kelp
(p. 134), (3) Grass (p. 147), and (4) Brown Rockfishes (p. 134) on
Pl. 26.

GREENSPOTTED ROCKFISH   **Pl. 25**
Sebastes chlorostictus
Identification: Many nearly *round, bright green spots* and 3-5
large whitish to pink blotches on back. Body yellowish pink. Fins
pinkish, with yellow on membranes. No scales on underside of
lower jaw. To $19\frac{3}{4}$ in. (50 cm).
Range: Copalis Head (Wash.) to cen. Baja. **Habitat:** Common on
soft bottom at 160-660 ft. (49-201 m).
Similar species: (1) Greenblotched (p. 148; Pl. 25) and (2) Pink
Rockfishes (p. 139) have irregular (not round) green marks on
back, scales on underside of lower jaw.

BLACK-AND-YELLOW ROCKFISH   **Pl. 24**
Sebastes chrysomelas
Identification: Mostly blackish or olive-brown, with about 5-6
large irregular *yellow areas on back;* paler below. A yellow patch
between dorsal fin spines 2-4. Faint dark stripes radiate from eye.
Lower pectoral fin rays fleshy. To $15\frac{1}{4}$ in. (39 cm).
Range: Eureka (n. Calif.) to cen. Baja. **Habitat:** Holes and crev-
ices in rocky areas. Intertidal and to 120 ft. (37 m), usually at less
than 60 ft. (18 m).
Remarks: Valued as a food fish but not caught in large numbers.
Caught on baited hook, usually near kelp beds or rocky areas.
Similar species: (1) Gopher Rockfish (p. 135; Pl. 24) has flesh-
colored (not yellow) pale areas on back. (2) China Rockfish (p. 145;
Pl. 23) has a broad yellow stripe along side. (3) Other rockfishes
with pale blotches on back (see Pl. 25) are mostly reddish or pink.

DUSKY ROCKFISH *Sebastes ciliatus*   **Pl. 26**
Identification: A *northern* rockfish. Gray-brown to bluish black
or greenish above; usually with *brown or red-brown flecks* on side

(absent in shallow-water specimens); light gray below. Lower jaw and pectoral and pelvic fins tinged with pink; fins otherwise mostly dusky. Head spines *weak*. Area between eyes bows outward (convex). A *knob* at tip of chin. Peritoneum black. To 16 in. (41 cm).
Range: Bering Sea to cen. B.C. **Habitat:** Usually off the bottom; near shore and to 900 ft. (274 m).
Remarks: Shallow-water specimens from the Aleutian Is. lack the red pigment and the flecks on the side; this "blue form" may be the true *ciliatus* and the species treated above may represent another, unnamed species.
Similar species: (1) Blue Rockfish (p. 144; Pl. 23) has a smaller mouth; usually anal fin more squared-off. (2) Black Rockfish (p. 143; Pl. 23) has a white peritoneum, no knob on chin, and often black specks on spinous dorsal fin. (3) Yellowtail Rockfish (p. 140; Pl. 26) has dusky yellow fins, a white peritoneum. (4) Olive Rockfish (p. 151; Pl. 26) has a white peritoneum and usually whitish blotches below dorsal fin; does not occur north of cen. Calif.

STARRY ROCKFISH *Sebastes constellatus* **Pl. 25**
Identification: *Red-orange* above, with 3–5 large *whitish* blotches on back; paler below. Small *white dots* cover most of body. To 18 in. (46 cm).
Range: San Francisco to s. Baja. **Habitat:** Usually on deep reefs at 80–900 ft. (24–274 m).
Remarks: Occasionally caught by sport fishermen. Highly esteemed for flavor.
Similar species: Other reddish rockfishes with pale areas on back (see Pl. 25) lack white dots on body.

DARKBLOTCHED ROCKFISH *Sebastes crameri* **Pl. 28**
Identification: Pinkish above; paler below. 4–5 irregular *dark saddles* on back (usually 3 below spinous dorsal fin, 1 under soft dorsal fin, and 1 on upper part of caudal peduncle); saddles indistinct in largest specimens. Fins red to orange; saddles extend onto base of dorsal fin. Body *deeper* than in similar species (see Pl. 28). To 22½ in. (57 cm).
Range: Bering Sea to near Santa Catalina I. (s. Calif.). **Habitat:** Soft bottom at 96–1800 ft. (29–549 m) but usually deeper than 250 ft. (76 m).
Similar species: See Pacific Ocean Perch (p. 133) and other species on Pl. 28.

CALICO ROCKFISH *Sebastes dallii* **Pl. 26**
Identification: A *small southern* rockfish. Broad *oblique bars on side,* interspersed with irregular brownish blotches. Background usually yellowish green. Brown to red-brown streaks and spots on caudal fin. To 10 in. (25 cm); usually less than 8 in. (20 cm).
Range: San Francisco to cen. Baja. Common in s. Calif.; rare

north of Santa Barbara (s. Calif.). **Habitat:** On or near soft bottom at 60–840 ft. (18–256 m).
Remarks: Often caught on baited hook; usually discarded because of small size.
Similar species: No other rockfish has this color pattern.

SPLITNOSE ROCKFISH *Sebastes diploproa*   **Pl. 28**
Identification: Nearly *solid pinkish red* except for belly, which is usually pale pink to white. *Toothed knob* projects at front of each upper jaw (with deep notch between jaws when viewed from above — hence the name "splitnose"). Eye *large* (diameter greater than snout length — about equal to length of 2nd spine in anal fin). Peritoneum black. To 18 in. (46 cm), usually about 1 ft. (30 cm).
Range: Se. Alaska to cen. Baja. **Habitat:** Common offshore; soft bottom at 300–1900 ft. (91–579 m). Young shallow, often at surface under drifting kelp.
Remarks: When trawled, scales usually rub off, leaving white pockets bordered by red.
Similar species: Aurora Rockfish (p. 134; Pl. 28) has smaller toothed knob on upper jaw, usually 6 soft rays in anal fin (usually 7–8 in Splitnose Rockfish), fewer gill rakers on first arch (24–28, not 32–37), and a smaller eye.

GREENSTRIPED ROCKFISH *Sebastes elongatus*   **Pl. 28**
Identification: An elongate rockfish. Pinkish, with *3–4 irregular* (often broken) *green stripes.* Also has green stripes on caudal fin membranes. To 15 in. (38 cm).
Range: Montague I. (Gulf of Alaska) to cen. Baja. **Habitat:** Widely distributed on rocky as well as soft bottom at 200–1320 ft. (61–402 m). Common.
Remarks: Occasionally caught on baited hook but usually trawled. Not a good food fish. Used by s. Calif. fishermen as bait for large Cowcods and Bocaccios.
Similar species: No other rockfish has green stripes on the body.

PUGET SOUND ROCKFISH   **Pl. 28**
Sebastes emphaeus
Identification: A *very small* northern rockfish. Reddish to copper-red, with dusky to greenish blotches on back and side. Pinkish to white below. Greenish bar behind eye and on lower side. Spinous dorsal fin greenish red to red. Caudal fin slightly reddish, but dusky in middle. Other fins mostly pinkish. To 7 in. (18 cm).
Range: Kenai Peninsula (Alaska) to n. Calif. **Habitat:** Rough bottom at 33–1200 ft. (10–366 m); observed by divers to occupy crevices and caves in areas of strong current.
Remarks: Rarely captured because of small size and rocky habitat.
Similar species: See Pygmy Rockfish (p. 152; Pl. 28).

SWORDSPINE ROCKFISH *Sebastes ensifer*   **Pl. 25**
Identification: Orange-red. Upper body and head mottled with
red or with purple tinged with greenish yellow. *3–5 pale areas* on
back but *no green spots*. Belly white. Fin rays mostly red, membranes yellowish. Scales on underside of lower jaw. Prominent
knob at tip of chin; chin projects beyond upper jaw. 2nd spine in
anal fin very long, nearly reaches tips of anal fin soft rays. To 1 ft.
(30 cm), usually less than 10 in. (25 cm).
Range: San Francisco to cen. Baja. **Habitat:** Deep water at 230–
1420 ft. (70–433 m).
Similar species: Resembles several other rockfishes on Pl. 25 but
is the only one of these with a prominent knob on the chin, which
projects slightly beyond upper jaw, *and* no green spots or short
wavy lines on the back.

WIDOW ROCKFISH *Sebastes entomelas*   **Pl. 26**
Identification: Dusky or brassy brown above, usually with a hint
of yellow. Whitish and often flushed with red below. Spinous dorsal fin tan. Other fins blackish; anal and pelvic fins sometimes tan
at base. Specimens under 10 in. (25 cm) paler, with vague orange
streaks. To 21 in. (53 cm).
Range: Se. Alaska to n. Baja. **Habitat:** Over rocky banks; adults
at about 80–1200 ft. (24–366 m). Young in shallow water. Often in
schools.
Remarks: Feeds mostly on small pelagic crustaceans and fishes.
Caught on hook and line, sometimes when trolling for salmon.
Similar species: (1) Bocaccio (p. 145; Pl. 24) has an upturned
mouth and a projecting chin. (2) Yellowtail Rockfish (p. 140;
Pl. 26) lacks red, has yellowish fins. (3) Blue (p. 144) and (4) Black
Rockfishes (p. 143) on Pl. 23 are blue-black (with no brown, yellow,
or red).

PINK ROCKFISH *Sebastes eos*   **Not shown**
Identification: Resembles Greenblotched Rockfish (Pl. 25). Pink,
with *olive-green vermiculations* (short wavy lines) on back and
head; white below. Usually 18 pectoral fin rays. Scales on underside of lower jaw. To 22 in. (56 cm).
Range: Monterey Bay to cen. Baja; possibly farther north.
Habitat: Deep water; rocky bottoms at 250–1200 ft. (76–366 m).
Similar species: (1) Very difficult to distinguish from Greenblotched Rockfish (p. 148; Pl. 25) except by technical features:
Greenblotched Rockfish usually has 17 (not usually 18) pectoral
fin rays; usually more gill rakers (29–34, not 26–31) on 1st arch
(first 4–7 are rudimentary and spiny in Pink Rockfish, but not in
Greenblotched Rockfish); and usually no spines on lower rear edge
of gill cover (1–2 spines in Pink Rockfish). (2) Greenspotted Rockfish (p. 136; Pl. 25) has round green spots (not vermiculations) on
back, upper gill rakers not rudimentary, and few or no scales on
lower jaw.

YELLOWTAIL ROCKFISH *Sebastes flavidus*   **Pl. 26**
Identification: Common. Mostly olive to greenish brown or dark
gray above; paler below. Often has *light areas* on upper back and
reddish-brown speckles on scales. Caudal fin *dirty yellow;* other
fins often tinged with yellow. Head spines *weak.* To 26 in. (66 cm).
Range: Kodiak I. to San Diego. Rare south of Pt. Conception.
Habitat: Wide-ranging, mostly *pelagic;* usually in schools. Near
surface to 900 ft. (274 m), usually at 80–150 ft. (24–46 m). Especially common over deep reefs.
Remarks: Often caught from Calif. party boats. Feeds mostly on
pelagic crustaceans and fishes.
Similar species: (1) Very difficult to distinguish from Olive
Rockfish (p. 151; Pl. 26). Olive Rockfish usually has 1 more soft ray
in anal fin (usually 9 rays, not 8—last ray double, counted as 1);
usually more prominent pale areas below the dorsal fin; and no
pink on the lower pectoral fin rays (sometimes pink in the
Yellowtail Rockfish). Olive Rockfish is rare north of Pt. Conception. (2) Widow Rockfish (p. 139; Pl. 26) usually has some red on
its belly, and rear edge of its anal fin is not vertical. (3) Kelp Bass
(p. 200; Pl. 29), which is unrelated, has 10–11 (not 13) spines in
dorsal fin, and no spines on rear cheek area.

BRONZESPOTTED ROCKFISH *Sebastes gilli*   **Pl. 25**
Identification: Large — commonly over 18 in. (45 cm). Reddish
orange, with *2 bright clear orange areas* below soft dorsal fin.
Roundish bronze to brown *spots* on back and upper side. Lateral
line in a narrow reddish zone. Head spines strong. Mouth *upturned*
and large. Brown bars radiate from eye. To 28 in. (71 cm).
Range: Monterey Bay to n. Baja. **Habitat:** Common in deep
water off s. Calif. at 246–1230 ft. (75–375 m).
Similar species: See other rockfishes on Pl. 25 — they have paler
white to pink (not orange) areas on back, and lack the strongly
upturned mouth.

CHILIPEPPER *Sebastes goodei*   **Pl. 24**
Identification: Mostly reddish pink above (young are light olive
on back); white below. Note the white lateral line in a *clear red or
pink zone* (less distinct in small specimens). Fins pinkish; soft dorsal and caudal fins dusky. Anal fin small. *Weak spines* on top
of head. Space between eyes broad, curves *outward* (convex).
Chin *projects.* Upper jaw ends below midpoint of eye. To 22 in.
(56 cm).
Range: Vancouver I. to s. Baja. **Habitat:** Frequents deep rocky
reefs as well as sand and mud bottom at 200–1080 ft. (61–329 m);
young in shallower waters.
Remarks: Important commercially in Calif.; sometimes caught
from party boats. Adults feed on krill, small squids, and fishes.
Similar species: (1) Pacific Ocean Perch (p. 133; Pl. 28) has
stronger head spines, black (not white) peritoneum, lateral line not
in a pink zone, usually has dark saddles on back, knob on tip of

chin. (2) In Bocaccio (p. 145; Pl. 24) mouth more upturned, upper jaw extends farther back (to rear of eye or beyond), and no clear red zone around lateral line. See (3) Redstripe (p. 147) and (4) Mexican Rockfishes (p. 142), also on Pl. 24.

ROSETHORN ROCKFISH *Sebastes helvomaculatus* **Pl. 25**
Identification: Pink mixed with greenish yellow above; white below. *4–5 white to pink blotches* (surrounded by pink or orange) on back. Fins pinkish, with some yellow-green. Dusky area on gill cover. Usually 16 pectoral fin rays. To 16 in. (41 cm); rare over 1 ft. (30 cm).
Range: Kodiak I. to San Diego; rare south of San Francisco.
Habitat: Soft bottom at 390–1800 ft. (119–549 m).
Similar species: (1) Most other rockfishes with white to pink blotches on upper back (Pl. 25) have more rays (usually 17–18) in pectoral fin and do not occur as far north. (2) Rosy Rockfish (p. 148) has purple on back, especially around the pale blotches; a thicker caudal peduncle; and weaker head spines. (3) Pinkrose Rockfish (p. 151) is a more uniform reddish pink and occurs south of San Pedro (s. Calif.).

SQUARESPOT ROCKFISH *Sebastes hopkinsi* **Pl. 26**
Identification: Small — usually under 10 in. (25 cm). Yellowish brown or dusky tan, with several *squarish dark brown blotches on back;* whitish below. Spines on top of head very *weak or absent.* To 11½ in. (29 cm).
Range: Farallon Is. (off San Francisco) to cen. Baja and Guadalupe I. (off n.-cen. Baja); rare north of Monterey Bay. **Habitat:** Shallow reefs at 60–600 ft. (18–183 m).
Remarks: Caught on baited hook.
Similar species: No other rockfish has the squarish blotches.

SHORTBELLY ROCKFISH *Sebastes jordani* **Pl. 24**
Identification: *Slender; small* — usually 8–10 in. (20–25 cm). Only rockfish with *anus far forward* — midway between pelvic fin base and anal fin (at least an eye diameter's distance before anal fin) rather than just before anal fin. Caudal fin *forked.* Chin projects *beyond* upper jaw. Spines on head weak. Olive-pink or dusky above; light pink on side; white below. To 12½ in. (32 cm).
Range: Vancouver I. to n. Baja. **Habitat:** Wide-ranging; sometimes in large schools well offshore and off bottom. Adults at about 300–930 ft. (91–283 m) but young shallower.
Remarks: Commonly caught in trawls, but not marketed because of small size. Adults feed on planktonic animals, mainly krill. The Shortbelly Rockfish is a very important prey species for predatory fishes and marine mammals.
Similar species: In the Chilipepper (p. 140; Pl. 24) anus is close to anal fin (within an eye diameter's distance from it), body is deeper, lateral line is in a pinkish red zone, and there are fewer pectoral fin rays (16–18, not 19–22).

FRECKLED ROCKFISH *Sebastes lentiginosus*   **Pl. 25**
Identification: *Small* — usually under 8 in. (20 cm). Back densely *freckled with dark green;* background pinkish, white below. 4–5 large pale blotches on back. Fins dusky pink; *dark streaks* on caudal fin. A toothed *knob* at front of each upper jaw. Scales on underside of lower jaw. To 9 in. (23 cm).
Range: Santa Catalina I. (s. Calif.) to n. Baja. **Habitat:** On bottom at about 130–550 ft. (40–168 m).
Similar species: Other species with pale blotches on upper back (see Pl. 25) lack toothed knob at front of each upper jaw: (1) In Honeycomb Rockfish (p. 151) scale edges are dark, creating a honeycomb pattern on side; (2) Greenblotched (p. 148) and (3) Pink Rockfishes (p. 139; not shown) have short wavy lines on upper back; (4) Greenspotted Rockfish (p. 136) has distinct green spots on upper back (not dense freckles or small irregular spots) and no dark streaks on caudal fin.

COWCOD *Sebastes levis*   **Pl. 27**
Identification: Large — often over 2 ft. (60 cm). Mostly pinkish red, with *4–5 narrow* (somewhat irregular) *bars. Eye small* (diameter is less than or no greater than distance from bottom of eye to upper jaw). In large specimens (shown) the dorsal fin membranes are *deeply notched* between spines, bars fainter, and body more red. Young have blackish speckles near the bars. One of the *largest* rockfishes — to 37 in. (94 cm), 28$\frac{1}{2}$ lb. (13 kg).
Range: Usal (Mendocino Co., cen. Calif.) to cen. Baja and Guadalupe I. (off n.-cen. Baja). **Habitat:** On bottom at moderate depths — to 1200 ft. (366 m). Adults common off s. Calif. on deep rocky banks at 500–800 ft. (152–244 m); young shallower.
Remarks: Also called the Cow Rockfish. Enthusiastically sought by fishermen because of its large size. Some caught commercially in trawls and on set lines.

MEXICAN ROCKFISH *Sebastes macdonaldi*   **Pl. 24**
Identification: Back *blackish red,* with a bright *red zone along lateral line;* reddish below. Membranes of pectoral fin black; dorsal and caudal fins blackish red; anal and pelvic fins reddish. Caudal fin slightly forked; caudal peduncle narrow. To 26 in. (66 cm).
Range: Pt. Sur (cen. Calif.) to s. Baja. and Gulf of Calif. **Habitat:** On bottom at 300–780 ft. (91–238 m).
Similar species: In Redstripe Rockfish (p. 147; Pl. 24) lateral line is in a clear *gray* zone *bordered by bright red;* membranes of pectoral fin reddish or slightly yellowish.

QUILLBACK ROCKFISH *Sebastes maliger*   **Pl. 23**
Identification: *Brown to blackish,* with large mottled *orange areas,* especially on back. Broad orange to yellow area near front of spinous dorsal fin, extends onto upper back. *Orange-brown spots* on pale orange breast. Pectoral and pelvic fins dark brown to

blackish. Dorsal fin spines very *long,* membrane between spines *deeply notched.* To 2 ft. (61 cm).
Range: Gulf of Alaska to Pt. Sur (cen. Calif.). **Habitat:** Among rocks, inshore and to 900 ft. (274 m); shallower in n. part of range.
Remarks: Valued as a sport fish.
Similar species: China Rockfish (p. 145; Pl. 23) usually has a continuous yellow stripe from spinous dorsal fin to caudal fin; yellowish white spots.

BLACK ROCKFISH *Sebastes melanops*   **Pl. 23**
Identification: *Black to blue-black,* mottled with gray; dirty white below. Some have lighter patches along back and gray stripe at midside. Black spots usually extend from back onto lower part of dorsal fin. Upper jaw reaches or extends *past rear* of eye. To 23¾ in. (60 cm), 10½ lb. (4.8 kg).
Range: Amchitka I. (Aleutian Is.) to San Miguel I. (s. Calif.)
Habitat: Wide-ranging, often in schools; lives both off and on bottom, near surface to 1200 ft. (366 m). Occurs near rocky reefs in shallow water and in open water over deep banks.
Remarks: Very common in party boat catches, and captured when trolling for salmon. Young important as food for other fishes, marine mammals, and birds.
Similar species: (1) Frequently confused with the Blue Rockfish (p. 144; Pl. 23) which has a smaller eye and mouth (upper jaw ends below middle of eye). (2) Dusky Rockfish (p. 136, Pl. 26) has a knob on chin, and usually some red or green on body. See (3) Yellowtail (p. 140) and Olive Rockfishes (p. 151) on Pl. 26.

SEMAPHORE ROCKFISH *Sebastes melanosema*   **Pl. 27**
Identification: A rare small rockfish. Small spines on side of snout (above upper jaw, below front of eye). Note *black membranes* on edge of spinous dorsal fin (and anal fin). Reddish, with lighter blotches; lateral line in a clear pinkish zone. Mouth dusky. 6 soft rays in anal fin and 11–12 soft rays in dorsal fin (last ray double, counted as 1). To 7¾ in. (20 cm).
Range: S. Calif. to cen. Baja. **Habitat:** Probably on craggy bottom, at 450–600 ft. (137–183 m).
Remarks: Recently discovered, few specimens known.
Similar species: Most other rockfishes lack small spines on side of snout, have more soft rays in dorsal fin, and lack black membranes on edge of spinous dorsal fin.

BLACKGILL ROCKFISH *Sebastes melanostomus*   **Pl. 27**
Identification: A dark red, deepwater rockfish with *black* on rear *edge of gill cover.* Black area on skin (in fold) above upper jaw. Inside of mouth mostly *black.* Back and snout sometimes dusky. Fins red, sometimes with dusky edge. To 2 ft. (61 cm).
Range: Wash. to cen. Baja. **Habitat:** Deep water; soft bottom at 720–2520 ft. (219–768 m) but young shallower.

Remarks: Scales usually rub off when caught in trawls. Sometimes captured in Sablefish traps.
Similar species: (1) Other mostly red rockfishes lack black on rear edge of gill cover. (2) Some individuals of Bank Rockfish (p. 149; Pl. 26) also have black on gill cover but membranes between most of their fin rays are black.

VERMILION ROCKFISH *Sebastes miniatus*   **Pl. 27**
Identification: A large rockfish. Reddish above; mottled with gray on side; reddish to orange below (smaller specimens more mottled). *Fins red,* but *frequently dark-edged* in small specimens. 3 orange stripes radiate from eye. Specimens over 18 in. (46 cm) have vague dark marks on head and back. Shallow-living specimens usually browner, deeper-living ones more reddish. Rear edge of anal fin oblique, slopes backward. To 2½ ft. (76 cm), 15 lb. (6.8 kg).
Range: Queen Charlotte Is. to cen. Baja. **Habitat:** Adults on shallow to deep rocky reefs (less common on deep ones); to 900 ft. (274 m). Young shallow.
Remarks: Caught on baited hook, mostly from boats; young sometimes taken from piers. Occasionally speared. An excellent food fish when fresh but doesn't keep well in freezer.
Similar species: (1) Canary Rockfish (p. 146; Pl. 27) has a dark spot at rear of spinous dorsal fin, in specimens up to 1 ft. (30 cm); lateral line in a broad gray zone; no scales on underside of lower jaw. (2) Small Yelloweye Rockfish (p. 148; Pl. 27) have 2 white side stripes; in large (plain-colored) specimens a rasplike ridge of spines is present above the eye and rear edge of anal fin is nearly vertical.

BLUE ROCKFISH *Sebastes mystinus*   **Pl. 23**
Identification: *Blue-black;* paler below. Fins blackish. No dark spots on dorsal fin. Upper jaw ends below *middle of eye.* Spines on top of head *virtually absent.* To 21 in. (53 cm). Young — to 5 in. (13 cm) — gray, with red streaks and black specks.
Range: Northern limit uncertain — at least Vancouver I. (possibly Aleutian Is.) to n. Baja. **Habitat:** One of the few schooling rockfishes. Lives off the bottom, generally over shallow reefs, also around kelp and over deep reefs. Near surface to about 1800 ft. (549 m).
Remarks: Often caught by sport fishermen. Sometimes schools with other rockfishes. Feeds mainly on krill. Young are important food for fishes and other marine vertebrates.
Similar species: (1) Black Rockfish (p. 143; Pl. 23) has a longer jaw, smaller eye, usually dark spots on dorsal fin, and more gray on body. (2) Dusky Rockfish (p. 136; Pl. 26) has a larger mouth (jaw extends to *rear* edge of eye) and a knob on the chin; deepwater population has brown or red flecks on side and some red on body or fins.

CHINA ROCKFISH *Sebastes nebulosus* **Pl. 23**
Identification: *Black to blue-black,* mottled or speckled with *yellowish white* (sometimes yellow tinged with blue). Usually a *broad yellowish stripe* slopes down from about 3rd or 4th spine in dorsal fin to midside, where it curves back and runs along lateral line to caudal fin. *Strong* head spines. To 17 in. (43 cm).
Range: Se. Alaska to Redondo Beach and San Miguel I. (s. Calif.).
Habitat: Inshore, on open coast among rocks and reefs, at 10–420 ft. (3–128 m). Territorial.
Remarks: Caught in small numbers by sport fishermen; highly esteemed as one of the tastiest rockfishes.
Similar species: See (1) Black-and-Yellow (p. 136; Pl. 24) and (2) Quillback Rockfishes (p. 142; Pl. 23).

TIGER ROCKFISH *Sebastes nigrocinctus* **Pl. 23**
Identification: Red or pink, with *5 black or dark red bars on body* (extending onto dorsal fin). Usually 4 dark bars radiate from eye (2 down and back, 1 up and back, and a smaller one toward mouth). Head spines strong. In young, anal and pelvic fins are black-tipped. To 2 ft. (61 cm).
Range: Se. Alaska to Pt. Buchon (cen. Calif.). **Habitat:** Solitary and territorial — defends a home crevice; among rocks at 180–900 ft. (55–274 m).
Similar species: (1) Treefish (p. 151; Pl. 23) also has black bars but on a *yellow to olive* background. (2) Redbanded (p. 135) and (3) Flag Rockfishes (p. 149), both on Pl. 23, have broad *red* bars on a whitish pink body.

SPECKLED ROCKFISH *Sebastes ovalis* **Pl. 26**
Identification: *Tan,* often tinged with pink; underparts usually whitish pink, sometimes yellowish. Side, back, and dorsal fin covered with *small round black spots.* Lower part of pectoral, pelvic, and anal fins tinged with pink or orange. No green. To 22 in. (56 cm).
Range: San Francisco to n. Baja.; rare north of Santa Barbara.
Habitat: Common on deep rocky areas in s. Calif. at 100–1200 ft. (30–366 m).
Similar species: Bank Rockfish (p. 149; Pl. 26) has black membranes between anal fin spines; some specimens have black specks on body and fins.

BOCACCIO *Sebastes paucispinis* **Pl. 24**
Identification: *Mouth large,* chin *projects,* upper jaw reaches or usually extends *beyond* rear of eye. Body somewhat compressed. Olive-brown to red above; silvery red or pink on side. Small specimens have brown spots on side. Profile slightly concave between snout and dorsal fin, with a noticeable *dip* above eye. Head spines *weak.* To 3 ft. (91 cm), about 15 lb. (6.8 kg).
Range: Kodiak I. to cen. Baja. **Habitat:** Wide-ranging; adults

live over rocky reefs but also common on open bottom, at about 90–1050 ft. (27–320 m). Young shallower.

Remarks: Reaches 30 years of age. Adults are voracious carnivores that feed mostly on fishes, including other rockfishes. Important commercially in Calif.; a popular sport fish throughout its range, but adults are not hooked very often. Large females contain over 2 million eggs. Young school and are caught more frequently, especially in rocky areas. Some individuals are melanistic (have abnormal black blotches) or plain bright red.

Similar species: Compare with other species on lower half of Pl. 24, especially the Silvergray Rockfish (p. 135).

CHAMELEON ROCKFISH *Sebastes phillipsi*   **Not shown**
Identification: Uniform *whitish pink* when first caught, turns to *crimson* upon death and exposure to air. No white blotches on upper back. Peritoneum *black*. First spine on side of snout (above upper jaw, below front of eye) has *several points*. Many gill rakers (36–39 on 1st arch). 1-2 small spines on lower rear edge of gill cover. To 17 in. (43 cm).
Range: Monterey Bay to Newport Beach (s. Calif.). **Habitat:** Usually deep reefs at 570–900 ft. (174–274 m); uncommon.
Similar species: Aurora Rockfish (p. 134; Pl. 28) also is uniform pinkish red but has fewer (24–28) gill rakers on 1st arch; first spine on side of snout has *only 1 point,* and no spines on lower rear edge of gill cover.

CANARY ROCKFISH *Sebastes pinniger*   **Pl. 27**
Identification: Usually *orange on a gray background*. Fins bright orange. In specimens under 14 in. (36 cm) rear of spinous dorsal fin is *dusky* (as shown). Lateral line usually in a plain *gray* zone (except in many large adults). To 2½ ft. (76 cm).
Range: Se. Alaska to n. Baja. **Habitat:** Rocky bottom at about 300–900 ft. (91–274 m); adults shallowest in northern part of range; young shallow throughout range.
Remarks: Eats small fishes and krill. Adults often caught on hook and line over deep reefs. Commonly trawled in northern areas.
Similar species: Vermilion Rockfish (p. 144; Pl. 27) is more reddish; lateral line not in a gray zone; scales present on underside of lower jaw. Usually found south of Pt. Conception (Canary Rockfish usually north of Pt. Conception).

NORTHERN ROCKFISH *Sebastes polyspinis*   **Not shown**
Identification: A *northern* species — the only rockfish east of the Aleutian Is. that normally has *14 spines in dorsal fin* (others have 13). Spines on top of head *weak* to virtually absent. Dark gray mottling on reddish background; orange flecks on body; belly white. 3 olive stripes radiate from eye. Dorsal fin reddish olive, edge blackish. Pectoral fin olive above, reddish orange below. Pelvic and

anal fins reddish orange, with red edges. To about 15 in. (38 cm).
Range: Bering Sea to Yakutat (Gulf of Alaska). **Habitat:** Soft
bottom at 240–1176 ft. (73–358 m).
Similar species: See Pacific Ocean Perch (p. 133; Pl. 28).

REDSTRIPE ROCKFISH *Sebastes proriger* **Pl. 24**
Identification: Light red. Upper back mottled with dusky olive;
side yellowish; whitish below. Lateral line in a *gray zone, bordered
by red*. Fins mostly reddish, frequently tinged with dusky or light
green. Lips *dusky*. Head spines *weak*. A toothed *knob* on chin. To
20 in. (51 cm).
Range: Bering Sea to at least Monterey Bay. **Habitat:** On bottom
at 40–900 ft. (12–274 m); shallowest in northern part of range.
Similar species: (1) Chilipepper (p. 140; Pl. 24) has lateral line in
a *red* zone, and more soft rays (8–9) in anal fin (Redstripe Rockfish
has 6–7 — last ray double, counted as 1). (2) Mexican Rockfish (p.
142; Pl. 24) is red and black, with lateral line in a bright *red* zone;
pectoral fin membranes black. (3) Adult Yelloweye Rockfish (p.
148; Pl. 27) are red-orange, with black and yellow blotches inside
mouth, yellow eye; small specimens have 1 or 2 white stripes on
side. (4) Harlequin Rockfish (p. 152; Pl. 27) has a mostly dusky
spinous dorsal fin and black blotches on body.

GRASS ROCKFISH *Sebastes rastrelliger* **Pl. 26**
Identification: A chunky, common, shallow-water rockfish. *Dark
green or olive* above; mottled with lighter gray or green on side;
whitish below. Fins dark. Lower pectoral fin rays pinkish in some
adults (no red or pink on body). Gill rakers on 1st arch *short* and
blunt (length nearly equals width). To 22 in. (56 cm).
Range: Yaquina Bay (Ore.) to Baja. **Habitat:** Common on rocky
bottom in tidepools and near shore, also in kelp and eelgrass beds;
to 150 ft. (46 m) but usually at less than 50 ft. (15 m).
Remarks: Most important rockfish to rocky shore and jetty fishermen. Good eating.
Similar species: Of all the dark-colored shallow-living rockfishes,
the Grass Rockfish is the chunkiest, with the thickest (deepest)
caudal peduncle. The dark color is distinctive, but the short,
stubby gill rakers are the clincher. Compare with (1) Brown (p.
134; Pl. 26), (2) Gopher (p. 135; Pl. 24), and (3) Black Rockfishes
(p. 143; Pl. 23).

YELLOWMOUTH ROCKFISH *Sebastes reedi* **Pl. 27**
Identification: Look for *yellow* and *black blotches inside* the
pinkish *mouth*. Jaws red. Body more or less red-orange; whitish
below. Specimens less than 16 in. (41 cm) usually red with black
mottling; larger specimens red, tinged with yellow-orange. 3–5
vague dusky saddles along back. Pink along lateral line. To 23 in.
(58 cm).
Range: Sitka (Alaska) to Crescent City (n. Calif.). **Habitat:**
Rough bottom at 462–1200 ft. (141–366 m).

Similar species: See (1) Redstripe (p. 147; Pl. 24) and (2) Aurora Rockfishes (p. 134; Pl. 28).

ROSY ROCKFISH *Sebastes rosaceus*   **Pl. 25**
Identification: *4-5 whitish blotches bordered by purple* on back. Reddish to purplish mottling on back, often with irregular patches of purple. Side red, with some yellow; whitish below. A vague purple bar across top of head behind eyes. Fins orange-red, fin membranes tinged with greenish yellow. *No* green spots or short wavy lines on upper back. To about 14 in. (36 cm), rarely over 11 in. (28 cm).
Range: Puget Sound to cen. Baja.; but doubtful north of Calif.
Habitat: On bottom at 50-420 ft. (15-128 m) but usually at 100-150 ft. (30-46 m).
Remarks: Caught fairly often by sport fishermen using small hooks.
Similar species: Similar to other rockfishes on Pl. 25 with large pale blotches but no green spots or wavy lines on upper back: (1) Often confused with Rosethorn Rockfish (p. 141), which normally has white blotches on the back surrounded by *red* (not purple) and usually 16 pectoral fin rays (usually 17 in Rosy Rockfish). (2) Pinkrose Rockfish (p. 151) is mostly plain red; caudal peduncle not as deep (depth less than eye diameter; usually greater than eye diameter in Rosy Rockfish). (3) Starry Rockfish (p. 137) is covered with white dots. (4) In Swordspine Rockfish (p. 139) underside of lower jaw is scaled (rough to touch; smooth in Rosy Rockfish).

GREENBLOTCHED ROCKFISH   **Pl. 25**
Sebastes rosenblatti
Identification: Pink, with large *pale blotches* on back and *olive green wavy lines* (not round spots) on back and head. Whitish below. Dorsal fin membranes olive-green at base. Scales sometimes bordered by greenish yellow. Scales on underside of lower jaw. Usually 17 pectoral fin rays. To 19 in. (48 cm).
Range: San Francisco to cen. Baja. **Habitat:** Rough bottom at 200-1300 ft. (61-396 m).
Similar species: (1) Pink Rockfish (p. 139; not shown) usually has 18 pectoral fin rays, 1-2 spines on lower rear edge of gill cover, and usually 30 or *more* gill rakers on 1st arch (instead of 30 or fewer in Greenblotched Rockfish). (2) Greenspotted Rockfish (p. 136; Pl. 25) has *roundish* green *spots* (not wormlike lines) on back and no scales on underside of lower jaw. (3) Freckled Rockfish (p. 142; Pl. 25) has a toothed knob at front of each upper jaw and dense green specks on back.

YELLOWEYE ROCKFISH *Sebastes ruberrimus*   **Pl. 27**
Identification: A large rockfish. Eye bright *yellow*. Head spines strong. Specimens over about 1 ft. (30 cm) have a *rasplike ridge of spines above eye.* Color changes with growth: specimens up to about 1 ft. (30 cm) are orange to reddish, with a *whitish stripe*

along lateral line (as shown) and a shorter *2nd stripe* below. Pale
bar at base of caudal fin; *black* on pectoral, anal, and caudal fins.
Larger individuals *lack* pale stripes (lower one disappears first) and
are more orange-yellow; fins pinkish, usually dark-edged. To 3 ft.
(91 cm).
Range: Gulf of Alaska to n. Baja. **Habitat:** Rocky reefs at 150–
1800 ft. (46–549 m).
Remarks: Also known as the Turkey-red Rockfish.
Similar species: Vermilion Rockfish (p. 144; Pl. 27) is orange,
with no whitish stripes on side and no rasplike ridge of spines
above eye.

FLAG ROCKFISH *Sebastes rubrivinctus*   **Pl. 23**
Identification: Pinkish white, with *broad red* or reddish-black
bars on body and caudal fin. Bars sometimes faint in individuals
over about 14 in. (36 cm); solid black in young. Bar at midbody
curves *away* from head. To 20 in. (51 cm).
Range: San Francisco to n. Baja. **Habitat:** Rocky areas at 100–
600 ft. (30–183 m).
Remarks: Reported to 25 in. (64 cm), but specimens over 20 in.
(51 cm) may have been the Redbanded Rockfish.
Similar species: In Redbanded Rockfish (p. 135; Pl. 23) bar behind head slants down and *back* toward pectoral fin (not just
down onto gill cover) and bar at midbody is vertical; usually 19
(not usually 17) pectoral fin rays, underside of lower jaw scaled.

DWARF-RED ROCKFISH *Sebastes rufinanus*   **Not shown**
Identification: A *small,* rare rockfish. Dusky red above; lighter
red below. Fins reddish. Lateral line pale; *few (30–33) lateral line
scales.* 37–38 gill rakers on 1st arch. 8 soft rays in anal fin (last ray
double, counted as 1). To $6\frac{3}{4}$ in. (17 cm).
Range: San Clemente I. (s. Calif.). **Habitat:** Probably deeper
than 600 ft. (183 m).
Remarks: Known from 2 small specimens killed in an underwater
explosion in 1970 and collected dead at surface. Expect slight differences in number of gill rakers, lateral line scales, and anal fin
soft rays in subsequent specimens.
Similar species: (1) Aurora Rockfish (p. 134; Pl. 28) is pinkish
red, with fewer (24–28) gill rakers, and 5–6 soft rays in anal fin (last
ray double). (2) Splitnose Rockfish (p. 138; Pl. 28) has prominent
knob at front of each upper jaw. (3) Chameleon Rockfish (p. 146;
not shown) has 6 soft rays in anal fin (last ray double), strong head
spines, and anterior lachrymal spine (at side of snout, above the
upper jaw) with several points. See (4) Redstripe (p. 147) and (5)
Mexican Rockfishes (p. 142) on Pl. 24, and (6) Yellowmouth Rockfish (p. 147) on Pl. 27.

BANK ROCKFISH *Sebastes rufus*   **Pl. 26**
Identification: Dusky light red to mostly gray; paler below.
Black spots on back and dorsal fin (in individuals from s. Calif. and

Baja). Lateral line in a narrow *pinkish* zone. Membranes of soft dorsal, anal, and pectoral fins *blackish*. Spines on top of head weak. To 20 in. (51 cm).
Range: Ft. Bragg (n. Calif.) to cen. Baja and Guadalupe I. (off n.-cen. Baja). **Habitat:** Offshore, on bottom at 102–810 ft. (31–247 m).
Remarks: Specimens caught off Morro Bay and Monterey Bay (cen. Calif.) on mud or sand bottom are more red (as shown) and lack conspicuous blackish spots on body; they are known locally as the Red-widow Rockfish and may represent a separate species.
Similar species: See Pl. 26: (1) Speckled Rockfish (p. 145) has smaller black spots on body and dorsal fin; body is orange-brown above, yellow-tan below. (2) Dusky Rockfish (p. 136) occurs farther north (Bering Sea to B.C.). (3) Squarespot Rockfish (p. 141) has squarish blotches along lateral line, no red. (4) Widow Rockfish (p. 139) lacks spots; no red. (5) See Yellowtail Rockfish (p. 140).

STRIPETAIL ROCKFISH   Pl. 28
Sebastes saxicola
Identification: *Green stripes on caudal fin* (but sometimes not distinct). Pinkish red or yellowish pink with traces of green; silvery to white on side and below. Faint dusky saddles along back. Fins yellowish pink. 1–2 spines on lower rear edge of gill cover. To 15¼ in. (39 cm) but rare over 1 ft. (30 cm).
Range: Se. Alaska to cen. Baja. **Habitat:** Mostly offshore on soft bottom at 150–1380 ft. (46–421 m). Common.
Remarks: Commonly caught in trawls but usually discarded because of small size. Rarely taken on baited hook in deep water.
Similar species: (1) Greenstriped Rockfish (p. 138; Pl. 28) has green stripes on body. (2) Halfbanded Rockfish (below; Pl. 28) has 2 large dusky blotches on side.

HALFBANDED ROCKFISH   Pl. 28
Sebastes semicinctus
Identification: Small — usually less than 8 in. (20 cm). Dusky pinkish above; more silvery below. *2 distinct blackish or blackish-red blotches* on side (1st one at midbody, 2nd one below soft dorsal fin). Brownish *streaks* and spots *on caudal fin;* brown spots on back and on dorsal fin; fins otherwise yellowish pink. 1–2 small spines on lower rear edge of gill cover. To 10 in. (25 cm).
Range: Pt. Pinos (Monterey Co., cen. Calif.) to cen. Baja.
Habitat: Common offshore on flat bottom at 192–1320 ft. (58–402 m).
Similar species: (1) Stripetail Rockfish (above; Pl. 28) has no large dark blotches on side. (2) A number of pink to red rockfishes (see Pls. 27–28) have dusky saddles or blotches on the back, but the one at midbody is generally not as prominent or as low down on side as in Halfbanded Rockfish (or there are more blotches on the midside).

OLIVE ROCKFISH *Sebastes serranoides*   **Pl. 26**
Identification: *Olive-brown* above; paler below. Fins olive, often with tinge of yellow. Usually has pale blotches at base of dorsal fin. Head spines virtually *absent.* To 2 ft. (61 cm).
Range: Redding Rock (n. Calif.) to cen. Baja. **Habitat:** Wide-ranging, from surface to 480 ft. (146 m) but usually at less than 100 ft. (30 m); sometimes well off bottom, in or near kelp or over rocky reefs.
Remarks: An important sport fish in s. Calif., particularly in Santa Barbara area.
Similar species: See (1) Yellowtail Rockfish (p. 140; Pl. 26). (2) Often confused with the Kelp Bass (p. 200; Pl. 29), which is unrelated but similar in shape and coloration; but Kelp Bass has no spines on rear cheek area and fewer spines (10–11, not 13) in dorsal fin.

TREEFISH *Sebastes serriceps*   **Pl. 23**
Identification: A distinctive rockfish with *5–6 black bars on side,* on a yellowish to olive (sometimes very dark) background. 2 oblique bars on head. Lips and chin usually pinkish in adults. Young have no pink on chin and lips, a more yellowish background, and white-edged fins. To 16 in. (41 cm).
Range: San Francisco to cen. Baja; fairly common in s. Calif., rare north of Santa Barbara. **Habitat:** Rocky areas, usually in crevices; to 150 ft. (46 m). Territorial.
Remarks: Occasionally caught on baited hook.
Similar species: (1) Tiger Rockfish (p. 145; Pl. 23) also has black bars, but on a red or pink background. (2) Other barred rockfishes are not olive or yellow.

PINKROSE ROCKFISH *Sebastes simulator*   **Pl. 25**
Identification: Reddish pink, occasionally with a dusky tinge and 3–4 pink blotches on back. Belly and breast white. *No green* blotches or wavy lines on upper back. To 1 ft. (30 cm).
Range: San Pedro (s. Calif.) to Guadalupe I. (off n.-cen. Baja). **Habitat:** On bottom at 325–960 ft. (99–293 m), usually at around 650 ft. (about 200 m). Uncommon.
Similar species: See Pl. 25: (1) No other rockfish with pale blotches on upper back is as uniformly pinkish red. (2) Rosethorn Rockfish (p. 141) is usually paler pink with a greenish yellow tinge, and typically has 16 (not usually 17) pectoral fin rays.

HONEYCOMB ROCKFISH *Sebastes umbrosus*   **Pl. 25**
Identification: A small rockfish. Dark olive border on each scale creates a *honeycomb* pattern on side. Pinkish yellow to light orange; back dusky, with *4–5 large whitish-pink patches;* pinkish to white below. Fins orange to pink; often dark olive between the fin rays. To 10½ in. (27 cm).
Range: Pt. Pinos (Monterey Co., cen. Calif.) to s.-cen. Baja; rare

north of Pt. Conception; common in s. Calif. **Habitat:** On or near bottom at 98–390 ft. (30–119 m) but usually shallower than 230 ft. (70 m).
Similar species: See Pl. 25: No other rockfish with 3–5 pale blotches on back has a honeycomb pattern on side.

HARLEQUIN ROCKFISH *Sebastes variegatus*   **Pl. 27**
Identification: A *northern* rockfish. Pinkish red, mottled with large dark patches on back and side. Lateral line in a pale clear zone. Spinous dorsal fin mostly black; anal and caudal fins black between rays. To 12½ in. (32 cm).
Range: Unimak Pass (Aleutian Is.) to Queen Charlotte Sound (B.C.). **Habitat:** On bottom at 230–1000 ft. (70–305 m).
Similar species: (1) In Redstripe Rockfish (p. 147; Pl. 24) clear zone along lateral line is bordered by red, and dorsal fin is not mostly black. (2) Sharpchin and (3) Pygmy Rockfishes (below; Pl. 28) have no clear zone along lateral line; dorsal fin not mostly black.

PYGMY ROCKFISH *Sebastes wilsoni*   **Pl. 28**
Identification: *Small* — usually less than 7 in. (18 cm). Light brown with red tint; silvery below. 4–5 dark saddles at base of dorsal fin. Usually a brownish red stripe below lateral line. To 8¼ in. (21 cm).
Range: Se. Alaska to Cortez Bank (s. Calif.) **Habitat:** At about 100–900 ft. (30–274 m).
Similar species: (1) Puget Sound Rockfish (p. 138; Pl. 28) lacks brownish red or orange stripe along lateral line, usually has 15 soft rays (not 13–14) in dorsal fin (last ray double, counted as 1). (2) In Shortbelly Rockfish (p. 141; Pl. 24) anus is located about midway between pelvic fin base and front of anal fin (not immediately in front of anal fin).

SHARPCHIN ROCKFISH   **Pl. 28**
Sebastes zacentrus
Identification: Pinkish, with about 5–6 vague dusky areas on back; yellowish red on side; white below. Usually 2 *dusky bars behind eye* that diverge and reach gill cover. To 13 in. (33 cm).
Range: Gulf of Alaska to San Diego. **Habitat:** Soft bottom at 300–1050 ft. (91–320 m).
Similar species: See Pl. 28: (1) Stripetail Rockfish (p. 150) has 2 sharp spines on side of snout (above upper jaw, below front of eye) and dark green stripes on caudal fin. (2) Halfbanded Rockfish (p. 150) has 2 large dark blotches on side (rear one sometimes absent), 2 small spines on lower rear edge of gill cover. (3) Pygmy Rockfish (above) is smaller, usually has 6 soft rays (not 7) in anal fin (last ray double, counted as 1).

SHORTSPINE THORNYHEAD   **Pl. 23**
Sebastolobus alascanus
Identification: *15 or more dorsal fin spines.* Pectoral fin *bilobed*

(as shown) *to square-cut* (not wedge-shaped), with *20–23 rays.*
Head very *spiny.* Mostly red or pink; often with some dusky areas
on body and fins; usually paler below. Gill chamber mostly pale.
Small specimens are paler, with more black on fins. To $29\frac{1}{2}$ in.
(75 cm).
Range: Bering Sea to n. Baja. **Habitat:** Very common on soft
bottom in deep water — at 84–5000 ft. (26–1524 m) or deeper but
usually below 300 ft. (91 m); shallower in n. part of range.
Remarks: Of some commercial importance — caught in trawls
and traps and on setlines. Also known as the Idiotfish, Channel
Rockcod, or by other common names.
Similar species: Longspine Thornyhead (below) is nearly identical, but usually has 15 (not usually 16) dorsal fin spines; 3rd spine
in dorsal fin longest (not shorter than 4th spine); gill chamber
mostly black.

LONGSPINE THORNYHEAD   **Not shown**
Sebastolobus altivelis
Identification: Similar to Shortspine Thornyhead — pectoral fin
bilobed to square-cut (not wedge-shaped) and head very spiny.
15–16 (usually 15) spines in dorsal fin, 3rd spine longest. Mostly
red, with some black on body and fins. Gill chamber mostly black.
To 15 in. (38 cm).
Range: Aleutian Is. to s. Baja. **Habitat:** Offshore on soft bottom
at 1000–5000 ft. (305–1524 m) or deeper.
Remarks: Juveniles — less than 2 in. (5.1 cm) long — are mostly
black and occur in midwater. Adults are caught in trawls and traps
and on setlines.
Similar species: See Shortspine Thornyhead (above).

Searobins: Family Triglidae

The *3 lower pectoral fin rays are free,* separated from each other
and from the rest of the pectoral fin, which is large. Head bony,
with spines and ridges. Spinous dorsal fin higher and shorter-based
than soft dorsal fin, usually separated from it. Usually brownish
above; pale below. Some species grow to 2–3 ft. (61–91 cm), most
are smaller. Searobins occur on the bottom in all temperate and
tropical seas at shallow to moderate depths — mostly above 590 ft.
(180 m). About 80 species, 2 in our area.

SPLITNOSE SEAROBIN *Bellator xenisma*   **Not shown**
Identification: Similar to Lumptail Searobin (see Pl. 34) with *3
separate* lower pectoral fin rays, but pectoral fin is shorter (does
not reach anal fin). *2 bony projections* on snout. Light brown, mottled with darker brown and black; white below. To 4 in. (10 cm).
Range: Gulf of Calif. to Colombia. 1 reportedly captured near
Channel Is. off Santa Barbara (s. Calif.). **Habitat:** Soft bottom at
198–309 ft. (60–94 m).
Similar species: See Lumptail Searobin (p.154).

LUMPTAIL SEAROBIN *Prionotus stephanophrys*   **Pl. 34**
Identification: Head bony. Pectoral fin long and *winglike,* with *3 separate* lower fin rays. Purplish brown above, with large blackish brown spots and blotches; pale below. To 15½ in. (39 cm).
Range: Columbia R. (Wash.) to Chile, but rare north of Baja.
Habitat: Sand or sandy-mud bottom at 48–360 ft. (15–110 m) but usually at 60–150 ft. (18–46 m).
Similar species: Splitnose Searobin (above) has a shorter pectoral fin and 2 bony projections on snout (none in Lumptail Searobin).

Sablefishes and Skilfishes: Family Anoplopomatidae

This family contains only the 2 species described below. The Skilfish is sometimes placed in its own family, the Erilepididae.

SABLEFISH *Anoplopoma fimbria*   **Pl. 34**
Identification: An elongate fish with *2 dorsal fins.* Anal fin similar to and opposite 2nd dorsal fin. Scales small, weakly ctenoid. Adults (shown) are blackish or greenish gray above; usually with slightly paler blotches or chainlike pattern on upper back; paler below. At 1–2 ft. (30–61 cm) often greenish, with faint stripes on back. Young under 6 in. (15 cm) are blue-black above; white below. Occasionally solid yellow, albino, or other unusual colors. To 40 in. (102 cm), over 126 lb. (57 kg); but usually less than 30 in. (76 cm) and 25 lb. (11 kg).
Range: Japan and Bering Sea to cen. Baja. **Habitat:** Wide-ranging, often migratory. Adults on mud bottom at moderate depths — from 1000–3000 ft. (305–914 m) to 6000 ft. (1829 m) or deeper. Young in shallow water.
Remarks: Known in Canada and among commercial fishermen as the Black Cod. An important commercial species caught in trawls and traps and on longlines. Mostly quick-frozen and marketed in the Orient.
Similar species: (1) Skilfish (below) has a deeper body, with dorsal fins closer together, 12–14 (not 17–30) spines in 1st dorsal fin. (2) True cods in our area (p. 97) have *3 dorsal* and *2 anal* fins. (3) Pacific Hake (p. 99) is silvery and has a long 2nd dorsal and anal fin (both notched at middle).

SKILFISH *Erilepis zonifer*   **Pl. 34**
Identification: Large, robust, basslike. *2 dorsal fins,* close together. 12–14 spines in 1st dorsal fin. No spines on head. 1 lateral line. Scales ctenoid, extend onto 2nd dorsal and anal fins. Largest specimens mostly black, with dirty white scale edges. Smaller specimens (shown) gray to blue or green, with large pale blotches; belly pale. Faint bars on fins. To 6 ft. (183 cm), 200 lb. (91 kg).
Range: Japan and Bering Sea to Monterey Bay. **Habitat:** Deep

water offshore; adults to 1440 ft. (439 m), but young shallow.
Remarks: Limited commercial value; trawled and taken on long-
lines.
Similar species: (1) In Sablefish (above) dorsal fins are widely
separated, body more elongate. (2) Most true basses (Pl. 29 and
Fig. 39, p. 198) occur south of the Skilfish's range. (3) Giant Sea
Bass (Pl. 29) has 9–10 (not 15–17) rays in soft dorsal fin and 8–9
(not 11–14) soft rays in anal fin.

Greenlings and Lingcods:
Family Hexagrammidae

A fairly small family of marine fishes that are related to rockfishes
and sculpins but lack a spiny head. Somewhat elongate, with 1
dorsal fin, usually divided by a notch into a nearly equal number
of spines and soft rays. Pelvic fins below pectoral fins. Anal fin
long. Most species have more than 1 lateral line (Fig. 34 opp. Pl.
22), and a skin flap (cirrus) above the eye. Scales small, usually
ctenoid (cycloid in Lingcod). *Color varies;* in some species sexes
differ. To 2 ft. (61 cm) or less, but the Lingcod reaches 5 ft.
(152 cm).

Greenlings and the Lingcod are limited to N. Pacific, usually
near shore. Some researchers place the Lingcod in a separate family (Ophiodontidae). The combfishes are sometimes included in
Family Hexagrammidae but we treat them as a separate family
(Zaniolepididae, p. 157). 8 species, 7 in our area.

KELP GREENLING *Hexagrammos decagrammus*   **Pl. 22**
Identification: Female *freckled all over* with small *reddish
brown to golden spots* on gray to brownish background; fins
mostly yellowish orange. Male gray to brownish olive, with *irregular blue spots* on front of body; each spot surrounded by ring of
small reddish brown spots. Inside of mouth yellowish. Often an
ocellus at end of soft dorsal fin. *5 lateral lines* (Fig. 34 opp. Pl. 22).
2 cirri (lateral view): 1st cirrus above eye; 2nd one tiny, midway
between eye and dorsal fin. Anal fin usually has 1 weak spine. To
21 in. (53 cm).
Range: Aleutian Is. to La Jolla (s. Calif.); rare in s. Calif., but
common northward. **Habitat:** Rocky inshore areas; common in
kelp beds, also on sand bottom; to 150 ft. (46 m).
Remarks: Prized as a sport fish; frequently caught by shore and
skiff fishermen and speared by divers.
Similar species: (1) Other greenlings are colored differently. (2)
Lingcod (p. 156) has a much larger mouth (upper jaw extends well
past eye), only 1 lateral line, no blue spots or freckles.

ROCK GREENLING *Hexagrammos lagocephalus*   **Pl. 22**
Identification: *5 lateral lines* (Fig. 34 opp. Pl. 22). A large *cirrus*
above eye (length nearly equal to eye diameter). *Color varies:* usu-

ally greenish to brown with darker mottling, but most large males usually have red blotches on side (as shown in specimen in foreground on Pl. 22). Inside of mouth usually bluish. Dark bars or blotches on fins. To 2 ft. (61 cm).
Range: Bering Sea to Pt. Conception; uncommon in s. Calif.
Habitat: Common in shallow rocky areas, especially on exposed coasts.
Remarks: Often caught by shore fishermen.
Similar species: (1) Masked Greenling (below) has no red; 4th lateral line short. (2) Other greenlings are colored differently.

MASKED GREENLING   Pl. 22
Hexagrammos octogrammus
Identification: A northern species. 5 lateral lines, but *4th line very short* (Fig. 34 opp. Pl. 22). A large *cirrus* above eye. Color varies: usually greenish brown, with darker saddles on back and mottling on side; lighter below. Dorsal and anal fins often black-edged; pelvic fin blackish. To 11 in. (28 cm).
Range: Sea of Okhotsk (USSR) to Banks I. (B.C.). **Habitat:** Shallow rocky areas.
Similar species: In Rock Greenling (above), 4th lateral line extends to area above anal fin for a total of 5 lines on the side.

WHITESPOTTED GREENLING   Pl. 22
Hexagrammos stelleri
Identification: Conspicuous *white spots* on body and head. 5 lateral lines, but 4th one very short (limited to breast area — see Masked Greenling in Fig. 34 opp. Pl. 22). 1st lateral line also short, inconspicuous — ends before middle of dorsal fin. A cirrus above the eye. Light brown to green, often tinged with red; dark bars or blotches. Anal fin yellowish; other fins with dark streaks or rows of dark spots. To 19 in. (48 cm).
Range: Japan to Puget Sound. **Habitat:** Inshore, near rocks, pilings, eelgrass beds; to about 150 ft. (46 m).
Similar species: (1) Masked Greenling (above) has no conspicuous white spots on head. (2) Other greenlings are colored differently, have 1 or 5 lateral lines on side.

LINGCOD *Ophiodon elongatus*   Pl. 22
Identification: Large, elongate. Dorsal fin long; spinous and soft-rayed parts nearly separated by a notch. Mouth *large,* upper jaw extends *past* eye. Teeth *large, caninelike.* 1 lateral line. Head unscaled; body covered with *small cycloid scales.* 3 spines in anal fin. A cirrus above eye. Gray to brown or green or bluish above, with darker and lighter spotting; paler below. Young blotched; caudal fin forked. To 5 ft. (152 cm), about 70 lb. (32 kg), but rarely more than 4 ft. (122 cm), 40 lb. (18 kg); females larger.
Range: Kodiak I. to n. Baja; possibly the Bering Sea. **Habitat:** Adults near rocks; inshore and to 1400 ft. (427 m). Young on sand or mud bottom of bays and inshore areas.

Remarks: Very important sport and commercial species. Prized by bottom-fishing sport and spear fishermen. Highly esteemed as food. Flesh sometimes greenish but not harmful; color disappears with cooking. A voracious predator; feeds mostly on other fishes. Spawns in shallow water in fall or early winter; male guards eggs. Sometimes placed in its own family (Ophiodontidae).
Similar species: (1) Other members of greenling family have distinctive color patterns. (2) Most sculpins (p. 158; Pls. 15–18) are much smaller, and nearly all are only partially scaled. (3) Another large sculpin, the Cabezon (p. 182; Pl. 16), lacks scales. (4) Sablefish (p. 154; Pl. 34) has 2 widely separated dorsal fins.

PAINTED GREENLING *Oxylebius pictus*   **Pl. 22**
Identification: 5–7 red or reddish brown *bars* on body, extending onto fins. 1 lateral line. 2 cirri (lateral view): 1st one above eye, 2nd one midway from eye to dorsal fin. 3–4 spines in anal fin. Snout pointed. Background color varies: usually grayish to brown, but occasionally quite dark; sometimes white-spotted. Throat usually dark-spotted. 3 dark bands radiate from eye (1 forward, 2 backward). Dark spots on caudal, pectoral, and pelvic fins. To 10 in. (25 cm) but usually less than 6 in. (15 cm).
Range: Kodiak I. to n.-cen. Baja; rare north of Wash. **Habitat:** Rocky areas; intertidal to 160 ft. (49 m).
Remarks: Commonly seen hovering motionless by divers; rarely caught on baited hook. Also known as the Convict Fish.
Similar species: (1) Other greenlings have 5 lateral lines, 1 or no spines in anal fin, and are colored differently. (2) Lingcod (p. 156; Pl. 22) has different shape, large mouth. (3) Barred rockfishes (Pl. 23) lack a pointed snout.

ATKA MACKEREL   **Pl. 22**
Pleurogrammus monopterygius
Identification: 5 lateral lines (as in Rock Greenling, Fig. 34 opp. Pl. 22). No cirri on head. *No notch* in dorsal fin. Caudal fin *forked.* Olive above; broad *dark bars* on side; paler below. To 19½ in. (50 cm).
Range: Sea of Japan to Bering Sea and to Redondo Beach (s. Calif.), but rare south of Alaska. **Habitat:** At 15–400 ft. (4.6–122 m).
Similar species: Other greenlings have a square-cut caudal fin, 1 or 2 cirri, and (except Painted Greenling) a deeply notched dorsal fin.

Combfishes: Family Zaniolepididae

This eastern N. Pacific group, with only 2 species, is sometimes included in the family Hexagrammidae (p. 155). Scales tiny, rough; skin sandpaperlike. 1 dorsal fin — longer spinous part separated from soft-rayed part by a deep notch; front spines elongate, free of connecting membrane for much of their length. 1 lateral line. Combfishes are cigar-shaped (nearly round in cross section) and grow to 1 ft. (30 cm) but commonly reach 6–8 in. (15–20 cm). Both species in our area.

SHORTSPINE COMBFISH *Zaniolepis frenata*   **Pl. 22**
Identification: Elongate, nearly round in cross section. *Skin sandpaperlike.* A cirrus above eye. 2nd spine in dorsal fin slightly longer than 3rd spine; front spines are separated by notches. Long anal fin, with 3 spines. Light tan with dark blotches; spots on fins more or less in oblique rows on yellowish background. Adult males darker. To 10 in. (25 cm).
Range: Southern Ore. to cen. Baja. **Habitat:** Mostly on mud bottom at 180–800 ft. (55–244 m).
Remarks: Occasionally caught on small baited hook. Often abundant in trawl catches, usually curls into a U when dumped on deck.
Similar species: (1) In Longspine Combfish (below) 2nd spine in dorsal fin is greatly elongate, cirrus above eye is very small when present. (2) Greenlings (above; Pl. 22) have 1 or no spines in anal fin; usually have several lateral lines. (3) Some sculpins (below) also have sandpaperlike skin and a similar shape, but soft-rayed part of their dorsal fin is longer than or equal to spinous part; no spines in anal fin; fewer soft rays (2–3, not 5) in pelvic fin.

LONGSPINE COMBFISH *Zaniolepis latipinnis*   **Pl. 22**
Identification: Similar to Shortspine Combfish in shape and skin texture, but *1st 3 spines in dorsal fin elongate,* 2nd spine much longer than 3rd. Cirrus above eye very small when present. Green to light yellowish brown, with dark spots. Fins have dark spots or bars and usually some red. Blackish stripe from snout tip to eye. To 1 ft. (30 cm).
Range: Vancouver I. to cen. Baja. **Habitat:** On bottom at 120–660 ft. (37–201 m).
Similar species: See Shortspine Combfish (above).

Sculpins: Family Cottidae

A large family of cold-water, mostly bottom-living fishes, which is split by some researchers into more than 1 family. Like rockfishes, greenlings, and other members of the Order Scorpaeniformes (p. 131), these fishes have a bony connection under the cheek (suborbital stay). Most sculpins have a stout, often nearly round body; a large head, usually with spines or knobs; and large *fanlike* pectoral fins. Some species are long and thin; a few are short and bubblelike. Most have 1–4 preopercular spines (at the front of the gill cover); a few have none.

Most sculpins are only *partially* scaled (see Fig. 19); some are unscaled or fully scaled. Scales are often modified into bony plates,

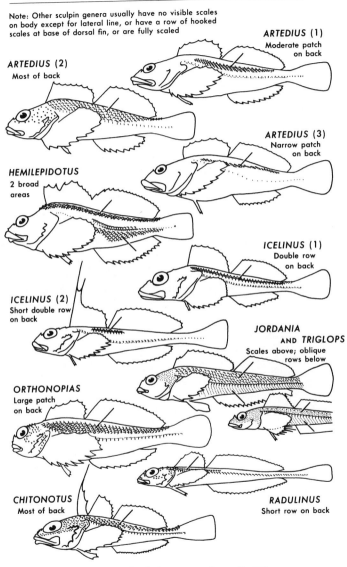

Note: Other sculpin genera usually have no visible scales on body except for lateral line, or have a row of hooked scales at base of dorsal fin, or are fully scaled

ARTEDIUS (1)
Moderate patch on back

ARTEDIUS (2)
Most of back

ARTEDIUS (3)
Narrow patch on back

HEMILEPIDOTUS
2 broad areas

ICELINUS (1)
Double row on back

ICELINUS (2)
Short double row on back

JORDANIA
AND **TRIGLOPS**
Scales above; oblique rows below

ORTHONOPIAS
Large patch on back

CHITONOTUS
Most of back

RADULINUS
Short row on back

Fig. 19 Sculpins — scale patterns

prickles, or spines, and they may be arranged in rows or scattered on the body. Almost all sculpins, including those with no body scales, have embedded scales or bony tubes buried along the lateral line. Dorsal fin long, with the spinous part usually *separated* from the soft-rayed part by a notch. Anal fin usually *long,* with no spines. Pelvic fins have 1 small spine that is covered by skin and closely attached to the 1st soft ray; 5 or fewer (most often 3) soft rays. 1 species in our area has no pelvic fins. Caudal fin usually rounded or square-cut. Males of some genera have a well-developed penislike appendage that is used for internal fertilization of the female; all species evidently lay eggs.

Most sculpins are drab — browns and greens predominate, and the color of many matches the algae among which they live. Most are small — under 5–6 in. (13–15 cm) — some reach about 1 ft. (30 cm). The Cabezon (our largest sculpin) grows to 39 in. (99 cm).

Sculpins are found in both marine and fresh water of N. America, Europe, and Asia; a few marine species occur in the S. Hemisphere. Most numerous in N. Pacific, particularly in shallow water and tidepools. Studies of some tidepool species have shown that they inhabit a "home pool" and if removed are able to find their way back. In our area most sculpins spawn in the winter and spring; the female commonly lays eggs among rocks, where they are guarded by the male. Except for the largest sculpins, most species eat small invertebrates. Though sculpins are often very common along our coast and can be seen darting around in tidepools, only a few are likely to be caught on hook and line. Only the Cabezon is fished commercially in our area. Sculpins are an important source of food for many other fishes. About 300 species (about 230 are marine); about 85 in our area.

At first glance, many sculpins look alike, and identification of species is difficult. A microscope may be needed to identify species of some genera, such as *Artedius, Oligocottus,* and *Clinocottus.* Important characters include differences in the number of pelvic fin rays; the number, location, and kind of scales; the shape of the upper preopercular spine, and the location of cirri (when present). *Note: If a genus contains more than 2 species from our area,* be sure to read the "genus characteristics" section first, located above the first species of that genus.

Plates

How to Use the Plates: The first step in identification is to locate an illustrated fish on a plate that closely matches your specimen. The first and most important feature to look at is the *general body shape* of your specimen. For example, it may be basslike, eel-like, cigar-shaped, oval, flattened (depressed), or slender-sided (compressed). Also note the size and shape of the mouth and snout. Next, examine the *placement* and *shape of the fins* (see rear endpapers). Does your specimen have a single or multiple dorsal fins; is there a tiny fleshy fin (adipose fin) on the back just before the caudal fin? Are the dorsal fin(s) and anal fin long (meaning long-based) or short; are they high or low? Remember that pectoral and pelvic fins (if present) come in pairs, even though only 1 of each pair can be seen from the side on the plates. Note the shape of the pectoral fins. Are the pelvic fins quite far back on the belly (abdominal) or farther forward (thoracic); are they united into a disk? Is the caudal fin square-cut, forked, rounded, or of a different shape? Third, you should determine if the *dorsal fin* and *anal fin* have *spines* or *only soft rays* (see rear endpapers); spines are usually hard, but soft rays are flexible, segmented, and usually branched. These characters should lead you to the correct plate. Next, note the diagnostic features highlighted by arrows on the plate, and compare them and the brief description on the legend page with your specimen. Select the illustrated specimen that most closely resembles yours. The legend page will direct you to the page on which that species is described in more detail. Compare the species account on that page with your specimen, and especially note the entries under the *Similar species* heading, where confusing look-alikes are discussed. See also **How to Use This Book** on p. 2.

SHORTCUT INDEX TO PLATES

PLATE 1

Hagfish, Lamprey, and Sharks (1)

PACIFIC HAGFISH *Eptatretus stoutii*   p. 11
Mouth suckerlike; surrounded by barbels. 10–14 porelike gill openings. No pectoral or pelvic fins. To 25 in. (64 cm).

Fig. 20
Mouth and
egg case

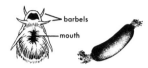

PACIFIC LAMPREY *Lampetra tridentata*   p. 12
Mouth suckerlike. 7 porelike gill openings. No pectoral or pelvic fins. To 30 in. (76 cm). See Fig. 21.

Fig. 21
Lampreys —
mouth parts

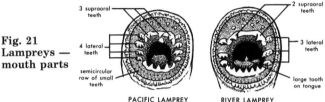

SEVENGILL SHARK *Notorynchus cepedianus*   p. 19
Our only shark with 7 gill slits. 1 dorsal fin. Scattered black spots. To 9 ft. (2.7 m).
SIXGILL SHARK *Hexanchus griseus*   p. 19
6 gill slits. 1 dorsal fin. To 15½ ft. (4.7 m).

Next 3 have 2 spineless dorsal fins, far back on body; catlike eyes; caudal fin nearly horizontal. (See also Fig. 7, p. 33.)

BROWN CAT SHARK *Apristurus brunneus*   p. 32
Snout long, flat. Brown to blackish. To 2¼ ft. (69 cm).
SWELL SHARK *Cephaloscyllium ventriosum*   p. 32
Spots and saddles. 1st dorsal fin larger than 2nd. Can inflate stomach. To 3¼ ft. (1 m).
FILETAIL CAT SHARK *Parmaturus xaniurus*   p. 33
Upper edge of caudal fin rough, with enlarged denticles. Fins dusky, sometimes white-edged; often white spots on body. To 2 ft. (61 cm).
HORN SHARK *Heterodontus francisci*   p. 24
Brownish, usually with black spots; young also have white spots. Snout short, blunt. Ridge above eye. 2 dorsal fins, each with a spine. To 3⅙ ft. (96 cm).
PACIFIC SLEEPER SHARK *Somniosus pacificus*   p. 22
2 small dorsal fins of about same size, without spines. No anal fin. 1st dorsal fin about midway between pectoral and pelvic fins. To at least 14$\frac{5}{12}$ ft. (4.4 m).

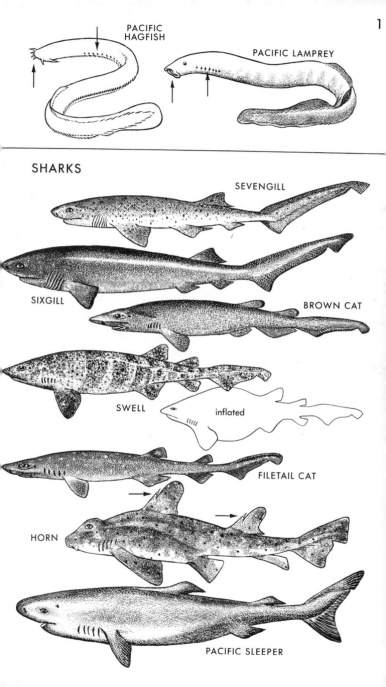

PACIFIC HAGFISH

PACIFIC LAMPREY

SHARKS

SEVENGILL

SIXGILL

BROWN CAT

SWELL

inflated

FILETAIL CAT

HORN

PACIFIC SLEEPER

PLATE 2

Sharks (2)

See also Pls. 1 and 3, Figs. 4 (p. 21) and 8 (p. 37).

SPINY DOGFISH *Squalus acanthias*   p. 23
Spine at front of each dorsal fin. No anal fin. Usually has white spots on side. To 5¼ ft. (1.6 m).

COMMON THRESHER *Alopias vulpinus*   p. 27
Caudal fin huge. To 20 ft. (6.1 m). See Fig. 22.

WHITE SHARK *Carcharodon carcharias*   p. 29
1st dorsal fin begins over rear of pectoral fin; 2nd dorsal fin over front of anal fin. Large caudal keel. Teeth triangular, serrated. To about 30 ft. (9.1 m).

SALMON SHARK *Lamna ditropis*   p. 30
2nd keel below rear of main caudal keel. 2nd dorsal fin opposite anal fin. To 10 ft. (3 m).

BASKING SHARK *Cetorhinus maximus*   p. 28
Gill slits huge. Caudal keel. To at least 40 ft. (12.2 m).

LEOPARD SHARK *Triakis semifasciata*   p. 35
Broad black bars, saddles, and spots. To 7 ft. (2.1 m).

BLUE SHARK *Prionace glauca*   p. 41
Dark blue above; white below. Snout long, narrow, and pointed. Pectoral fin long. To 12½ ft. (3.8 m).

Fig. 22 Thresher sharks (comparison)

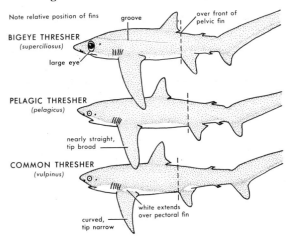

SHARKS

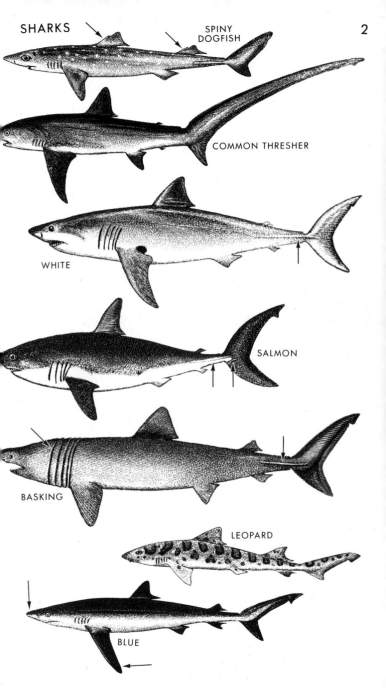

SPINY DOGFISH

COMMON THRESHER

WHITE

SALMON

BASKING

LEOPARD

BLUE

PLATE 3

2

Sharks (3), Angel Shark, Guitarfishes, Thornback

For rare sharks see Figs. 4 (p. 21) and 8 (p. 37).

SOUPFIN SHARK *Galeorhinus galeus* p. 34
Snout long, pointed. Anal fin nearly opposite and about same size as 2nd dorsal fin. Terminal lobe of caudal fin large, about $\frac{1}{2}$ length of upper lobe. To $6\frac{1}{2}$ ft. (2 m).
BROWN SMOOTHHOUND *Mustelus henlei* p. 35
Like Soupfin Shark but 2nd dorsal fin larger, terminal lobe of caudal fin smaller. To $3\frac{1}{12}$ ft. (94 cm). See Fig. 23.

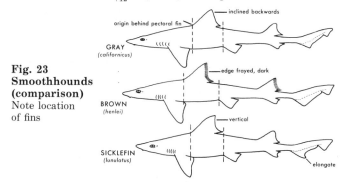

**Fig. 23
Smoothhounds
(comparison)**
Note location
of fins

SMOOTH HAMMERHEAD *Sphyrna zygaena* p. 43
Head shaped like a two-bladed ax. To 13 ft. (4 m). See Fig. 10 (p. 42).
PACIFIC ANGEL SHARK *Squatina californica* p. 44
Flattened body. Gill slits in notch behind head. Mouth at front. To 5 ft. (1.5 m).

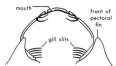

**Fig. 24
Angel Shark —
underside of head**

Last 3 are flattened; gill slits and mouth on undersurface. See also Pls. 4–5.

SHOVELNOSE GUITARFISH *Rhinobatos productus* p. 46
Snout long, pointed. 1 row of spines on back and tail. To $5\frac{1}{2}$ ft. (1.7 m).
BANDED GUITARFISH *Zapteryx exasperata* p. 46
Dark crossbars. Snout broadly pointed. 1 row of spines on back and tail. To 3 ft. (91 cm).
THORNBACK *Platyrhinoidis triseriata* p. 47
Snout rounded. 3 rows of spines on back and tail. To 3 ft. (91 cm).

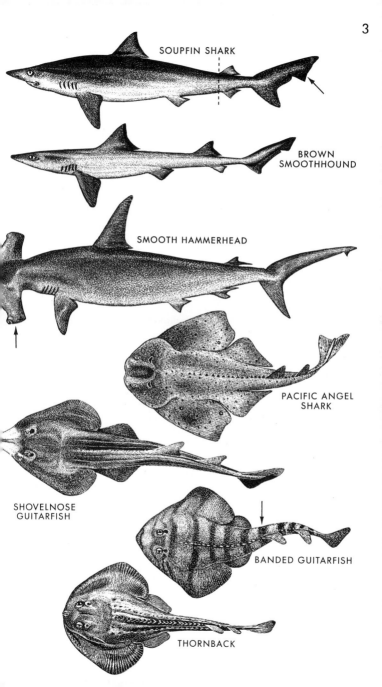

3

SOUPFIN SHARK

BROWN
SMOOTHHOUND

SMOOTH HAMMERHEAD

PACIFIC ANGEL
SHARK

SHOVELNOSE
GUITARFISH

BANDED GUITARFISH

THORNBACK

PLATE 4

Skates and Electric Ray

Additional rare species are treated in the text; see Fig. 11 (p. 48) for location of spines and body shape of skates.

LONGNOSE SKATE *Raja rhina*   p. 52
Snout long, acutely pointed. Front edge of disk curves inward (concave). Eyespots. To $4\frac{1}{2}$ ft. (137 cm).

BIG SKATE *Raja binoculata*   p. 51
Rear edge of pelvic fin weakly notched. Usually 1 spine at midback, 1 row toward rear. Eyespots. To 8 ft. (2.4 m).

STARRY SKATE *Raja stellulata*   p. 53
Snout short. Undersurface rough. 1 row of spines on back and tail. Eyespots. To $2\frac{1}{2}$ ft. (76 cm).

CALIFORNIA SKATE *Raja inornata*   p. 52
Snout acutely pointed. Sometimes eyespots. To $2\frac{1}{2}$ ft. (76 cm).

PACIFIC ELECTRIC RAY *Torpedo californica*   p. 53
Round, flabby; disk thick. Skin smooth. Tail short, stocky, with large caudal fin. To at least $4\frac{1}{2}$ ft. (137 cm).

SANDPAPER SKATE *Bathyraja kincaidii*   p. 50
Flat between eyes. Uppersurface rough. 1 row of spines on back and tail. Scapular spines. To 34 in. (86 cm).

BLACK SKATE *Bathyraja trachura*   p. 51
Snout short, broadly triangular. Both surfaces dark. No enlarged spines on disk (except alar spines of males). To 35 in. (89 cm).

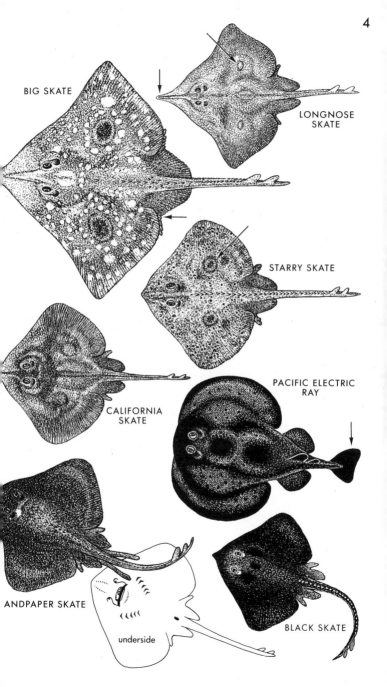

4

BIG SKATE

LONGNOSE SKATE

STARRY SKATE

CALIFORNIA SKATE

PACIFIC ELECTRIC RAY

ANDPAPER SKATE

underside

BLACK SKATE

PLATE 5

Stingrays, Manta, Butterfly Ray, Bat Ray

ROUND STINGRAY *Urolophus halleri*   p. 55
Disk nearly round. Tail stout, shorter than disk, with caudal fin and long sting. To 22 in. long. (56 cm).

DIAMOND STINGRAY *Dasyatis brevis*   p. 54
Disk diamond-shaped, angular in front (Fig. 25). Tail whiplike, longer than disk, with long sting. To 6 ft. (1.8 m) long.

Fig. 25 Stingrays (comparison)

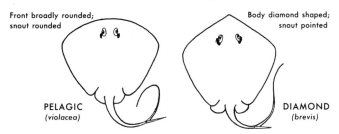

Front broadly rounded;
snout rounded

Body diamond shaped;
snout pointed

PELAGIC
(violacea)

DIAMOND
(brevis)

MANTA *Manta birostris*   p. 57
Large head with flaps and mouth at front edge (Fig. 26). Winglike disk edge. 1 dorsal fin at base of whiplike tail. To 22 ft. (6.7 m) wide.

CALIFORNIA BUTTERFLY RAY   p. 56
Gymnura marmorata
Disk diamond-shaped, twice as wide as it is long. Tail short, slender; small spine (rarely absent) at base. To 5 ft. (1.5 m) wide.

BAT RAY *Myliobatis californica*   p. 57
Head large, elevated. Tail whiplike. 1 dorsal fin at base of tail, followed by long spine. Teeth platelike. To 6 ft. (1.8 m) wide.

Fig. 26 Manta and mobula — underside of head

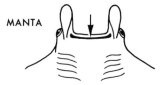

MANTA

MOBULA

Mouth at front edge;
head broad

Mouth on undersurface;
head narrow

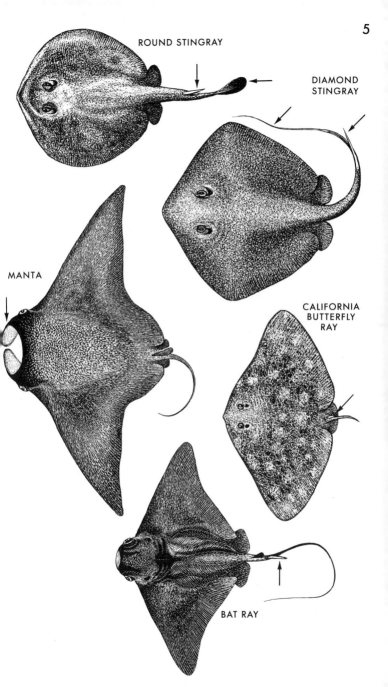

ROUND STINGRAY

DIAMOND STINGRAY

MANTA

CALIFORNIA BUTTERFLY RAY

BAT RAY

PLATE 6

Sturgeons, Eels, and Others

See Fig. 13 (p. 67) for deepsea eels.

WHITE STURGEON *Acipenser transmontanus*   p. 61
Rows of scutes; 38 or more in midside row. Barbels closer to snout tip than mouth. To about 10 ft. (3 m).

GREEN STURGEON *Acipenser medirostris*   p. 61
Rows of scutes: 30 or fewer in midside row; 1–2 scutes behind dorsal fin. Barbels usually nearer mouth than snout tip. To 7 ft. (2.1 m).

PACIFIC SNAKE EEL *Ophichthus triserialis*   p. 65
Dark-spotted. End of tail spikelike. To 44½ in. (113 cm).

YELLOW SNAKE EEL *Ophichthus zophochir*   p. 66
No spots. End of tail spikelike. To 34½ in. (88 cm).

CALIFORNIA MORAY *Gymnothorax mordax*   p. 64
No pectoral fin. Brown to green, mottled. To 5 ft. (152 cm).

CATALINA CONGER *Gnathophis catalinensis*   p. 64
Large pectoral fin; dorsal fin starts over pectoral fin. To 16½ in. (42 cm).

PACIFIC WORM EEL *Myrophis vafer*   p. 65
Dorsal fin starts far behind pectoral fin. Very elongate. To 18¼ in. (46 cm).

BONEFISH *Albula vulpes*   p. 62
Snout conical, fleshy. Mouth small. Caudal fin forked. To about 1½ ft. (46 cm).

MACHETE *Elops affinis*   p. 62
Silver. Mouth large. 1 dorsal fin. Pelvic fin abdominal. No adipose fin. Caudal fin forked. To 3 ft. (91 cm).

COMMON CARP *Cyprinus carpio*   p. 95
Scales large, smooth. Caudal fin forked. Barbel at corner of mouth. Probably to about 2 ft. (61 cm).

CHIHUIL *Bagre panamensis*   p. 96
Catfish shape. Adipose fin. Long barbels. Spine at front of dorsal and pectoral fins. To 20 in. (51 cm).

SPOTTED RATFISH *Hydrolagus colliei*   p. 59
Head and teeth rabbitlike. Tapered, silvery. Spine at front of 1st dorsal fin. To 38 in. (96 cm).

Fig. 27
Ratfish egg case

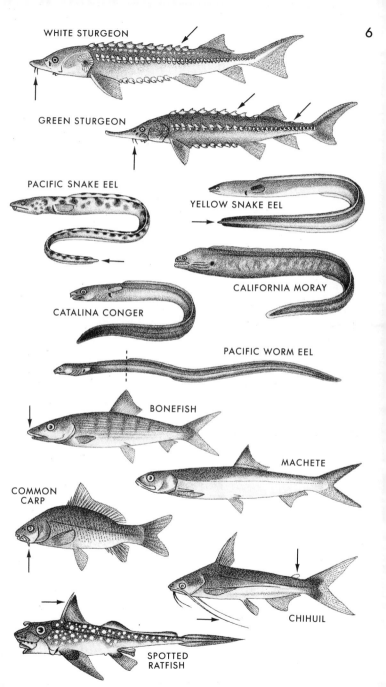

6

WHITE STURGEON

GREEN STURGEON

PACIFIC SNAKE EEL

YELLOW SNAKE EEL

CALIFORNIA MORAY

CATALINA CONGER

PACIFIC WORM EEL

BONEFISH

MACHETE

COMMON CARP

CHIHUIL

SPOTTED RATFISH

PLATE 7

Anchovies and Herrings

Silvery; no lateral line or adipose fin. Anchovies have a projecting snout and long jaw but herrings do not.

SLOUGH ANCHOVY *Anchoa delicatissima*　　　　　p. 74
23–26 anal fin rays. Small—to $3\frac{3}{4}$ in. (9.5 cm).

DEEPBODY ANCHOVY *Anchoa compressa*　　　　　p. 74
Body deeper than in other anchovies. 29 or more anal fin rays (other anchovies have 26 or fewer). To $6\frac{1}{2}$ in. (16 cm).

NORTHERN ANCHOVY *Engraulis mordax*　　　　　p. 74
Rounder than other anchovies, not strongly compressed. Anal fin starts below rear of dorsal fin. To 9 in. (23 cm).

PACIFIC ROUND HERRING *Etrumeus acuminatus*　　p. 73
No spots. No elongate dorsal fin ray. Pelvic fin after midbelly, not directly below dorsal fin. To 12 in. (30 cm).

FLATIRON HERRING *Harengula thrissina*　　　　　p. 72
Spot behind head. No elongate dorsal fin ray. To $7\frac{1}{4}$ in. (18 cm).

THREADFIN SHAD *Dorosoma petenense*　　　　　p. 71
Elongate, threadlike dorsal fin ray. Dark spot behind head. To 9 in. (23 cm).

PACIFIC SARDINE *Sardinops sagax*　　　　　p. 72
Dark spots. Gill cover striated. Weak scutes on belly. To $16\frac{1}{4}$ in. (41 cm).

PACIFIC HERRING *Clupea pallasii*　　　　　p. 71
No spots or elongate dorsal fin ray. Pelvic fin under dorsal fin. Weak scutes on belly (Fig. 28). To 18 in. (46 cm).

AMERICAN SHAD *Alosa sapidissima*　　　　　p. 71
Sharp-keeled scutes on belly (Fig. 28). Row of dark spots. To 30 in. (76 cm).

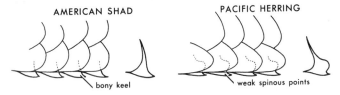

Fig. 28 Herrings — scutes

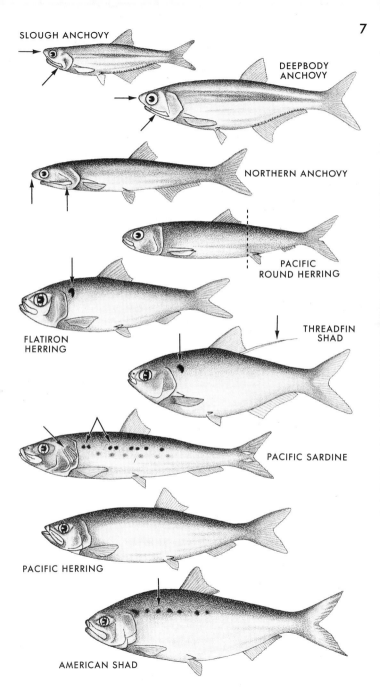

SLOUGH ANCHOVY

DEEPBODY ANCHOVY

NORTHERN ANCHOVY

PACIFIC ROUND HERRING

FLATIRON HERRING

THREADFIN SHAD

PACIFIC SARDINE

PACIFIC HERRING

AMERICAN SHAD

PLATE 8

Salmons, Trouts, and Dolly Varden

Silvery when in ocean; see Pl. 9 for spawning colors. Short dorsal fin at midbody; adipose fin present.

PINK SALMON *Oncorhynchus gorbuscha*   p. 76
Mostly oval black spots on back and all of caudal fin. To 30 in. (76 cm).

CHINOOK or KING SALMON   p. 77
Oncorhynchus tshawytscha
Irregular black spots on upper back and all of caudal fin. Large— to 58 in. (147 cm).

CHUM SALMON *Oncorhynchus keta*   p. 76
No large black spots. Lower fins white-tipped in adults. To 40 in. (102 cm).

SOCKEYE or RED SALMON *Oncorhynchus nerka*   p. 77
No large black spots. Fins not white-tipped. 28 or more gill rakers on 1st arch. To 33 in. (84 cm).

COHO or SILVER SALMON *Oncorhynchus kisutch*   p. 77
Black spots on back and upper half of caudal fin. Gums near teeth white. To 38½ in. (98 cm).

Last 3 have 12 or fewer anal fin rays (salmons have 14 or more).

RAINBOW TROUT or STEELHEAD *Salmo gairdnerii*   p. 78
Nearly fully spotted. Often a red lateral stripe. To 45 in. (114 cm), usually about 24 in. (61 cm).

CUTTHROAT TROUT *Salmo clarkii*   p. 78
Nearly fully spotted. Usually a red or orange "cutthroat" mark on lower jaw. To 30 in. (76 cm).

DOLLY VARDEN *Salvelinus malma*   p. 79
Cream-colored spots. No black spots. To about 36 in. (91 cm).

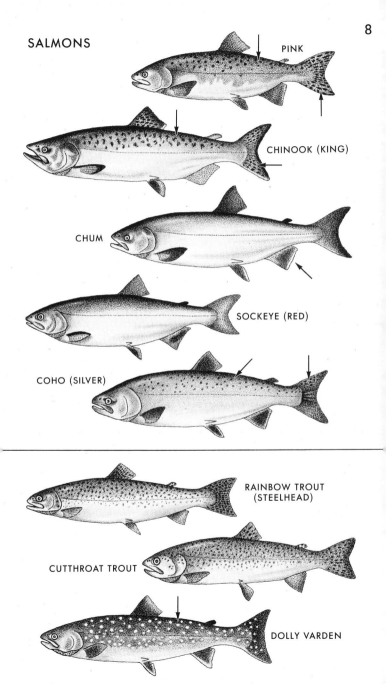

SALMONS

PINK

CHINOOK (KING)

CHUM

SOCKEYE (RED)

COHO (SILVER)

RAINBOW TROUT
(STEELHEAD)

CUTTHROAT TROUT

DOLLY VARDEN

PLATE 9

Spawning Salmons

See Pl. 8. Spawning colors vary with population.

PINK SALMON *Oncorhynchus gorbuscha*   p. 76
Spots on back. Spots and stripes on all of caudal fin. In males back humped, jaw hooked. Side reddish to yellow; female often more greenish. To 30 in. (76 cm).

CHINOOK or KING SALMON   p. 77
Oncorhynchus tshawytscha
Irregular spots on back and all of caudal fin. Often dark. Larger males blotchy dull red on side. To 58 in. (147 cm).

CHUM SALMON *Oncorhynchus keta*   p. 76
No black spots. Reddish or dusky bars or blotches on side. Tip of anal and pelvic fins usually white. To 40 in. (102 cm).

SOCKEYE or RED SALMON *Oncorhynchus nerka*   p. 77
Red with green head; lower jaw white. Some females with green or yellow blotches on side. To 33 in. (84 cm).

COHO or SILVER SALMON *Oncorhynchus kisutch*   p. 77
Black spots on back and upper part of caudal fin. Males bright red on side, belly often blackish; females bronze to pinkish red on side. To 38½ in. (98 cm).

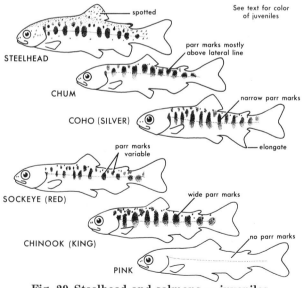

Fig. 29 **Steelhead and salmons — juveniles**

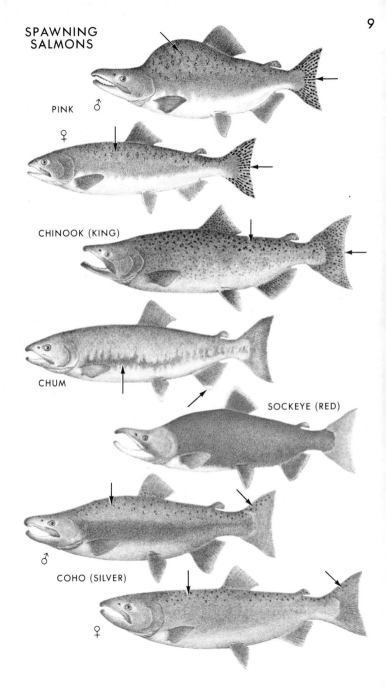

9

SPAWNING SALMONS

PINK ♂

♀

CHINOOK (KING)

CHUM

SOCKEYE (RED)

COHO (SILVER) ♂

♀

PLATE 10

Smelts, Argentine, Lizardfish

All have 1 dorsal fin and an adipose fin.

DELTA SMELT *Hypomesus transpacificus*   p. 81
Mouth small; no enlarged teeth. Pelvic fin starts under dorsal fin.
10–12 pectoral fin rays. To 4½ in. (11 cm).

NIGHT SMELT *Spirinchus starksi*   p. 82
Mouth large; teeth on tongue; no fangs on roof of mouth. To 9 in.
(23 cm).

LONGFIN SMELT *Spirinchus thaleichthys*   p. 82
Same as Night Smelt but pectoral fin large, often reaches front of
pelvic fin or beyond. Anal fin larger, rounder in adult males (as
shown at right). To 6 in. (15 cm).

WHITEBAIT SMELT *Allosmerus elongatus*   p. 80
Large canine on roof of mouth (Fig. 30). To 7 in. (18 cm).

EULACHON *Thaleichthys pacificus*   p. 82
Gill cover striated (Fig. 30). Only 4–6 gill rakers on upper limb of
1st arch. Caudal fin often speckled. To 10 in. (25 cm).

SURF SMELT *Hypomesus pretiosus*   p. 80
Mouth small; no enlarged teeth. Pelvic fin begins under dorsal fin.
14–17 pectoral fin rays. To about 10 in. (25 cm).

CAPELIN *Mallotus villosus*   p. 81
Adipose fin long-based, rectangular. 17–20 pectoral fin rays. Hairy
band at side and enlarged fins in adult males. To 8½ in. (22 cm).

RAINBOW SMELT *Osmerus mordax*   p. 82
Mouth large. 2 canines on roof of mouth; prominent teeth on
tongue. To 13 in. (33 cm).

EULACHON   WHITEBAIT SMELT

Fig. 30 Smelts (comparison)

PACIFIC ARGENTINE *Argentina sialis*   p. 83
Silvery. Mouth tiny, at tip of pointed snout. Eye large. To 8½ in.
(22 cm).

CALIFORNIA LIZARDFISH *Synodus lucioceps*   p. 91
Elongate. Snout triangular (from above). Mouth large, toothy. To
about 25 in. (64 cm).

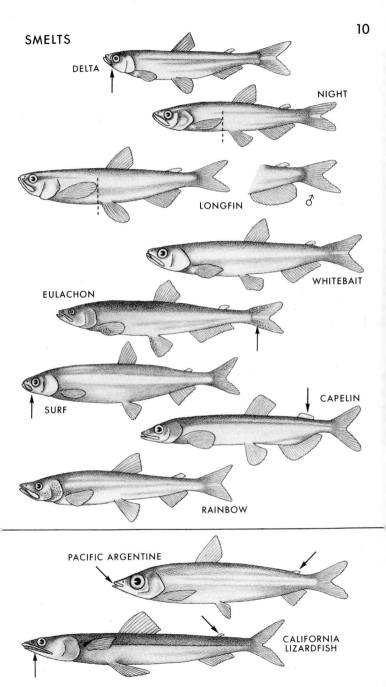

SMELTS

DELTA

NIGHT

LONGFIN

♂

WHITEBAIT

EULACHON

SURF

CAPELIN

RAINBOW

PACIFIC ARGENTINE

CALIFORNIA
LIZARDFISH

PLATE 11

Eelpouts and Cods

In eelpouts the long dorsal and anal fins join to form a pointed tail. Note tiny pelvic fin at throat in most species. Other eelpouts in our area are treated in the text.

BEARDED EELPOUT *Lyconema barbatum*　　　　　　p. 106
Cirri on lower jaw. Brown spots. To 6¾ in. (17 cm).

BLACK EELPOUT *Lycodes diapterus*　　　　　　　p. 105
Pectoral fin dark, indented. Pale marks on back. To 13 in. (33 cm).

SHORTFIN EELPOUT *Lycodes brevipes*　　　　　　p. 105
White bars on body. Pectoral fin rounded. Dorsal and anal fins black-edged. To 11¾ in. (30 cm).

BLACKBELLY EELPOUT *Lycodes pacificus*　　　　p. 105
Front of dorsal fin and belly black. Pectoral fin large, rounded. To 18 in. (46 cm).

PERSIMMON EELPOUT *Maynea californica*　　　　p. 106
No pelvic fin. Pectoral fin rounded. Rose-red or persimmon-colored; fins pale-edged. To 8¾ in. (22 cm).

BIGFIN EELPOUT *Lycodes cortezianus*　　　　　　p. 105
Pectoral fin large. Fins mostly black. To 19½ in. (49 cm).

small gill opening

Fig. 31 Midwater Eelpout *(Melanostigma pammelas)*

Next 3 species have 3 dorsal and 2 anal fins.

PACIFIC TOMCOD *Microgadus proximus*　　　　　p. 98
Small chin barbel. 1st anal fin begins slightly ahead of 2nd dorsal fin. Edges of fins usually dusky. To 12 in. (30 cm).

PACIFIC COD *Gadus macrocephalus*　　　　　　　p. 97
Chin barbel. 1st anal fin begins under 2nd dorsal fin. To 45 in. (114 cm).

WALLEYE POLLOCK *Theragra chalcogramma*　　　p. 98
Chin barbel tiny or absent. Lower jaw projects slightly. 1st anal fin begins under front of 2nd dorsal fin. To 36 in. (91 cm).

PACIFIC HAKE *Merluccius productus*　　　　　　p. 99
Mostly silvery. No chin barbel. Teeth sharp, strong. 2nd dorsal and anal fins notched (not separate). To 36 in. (91 cm).

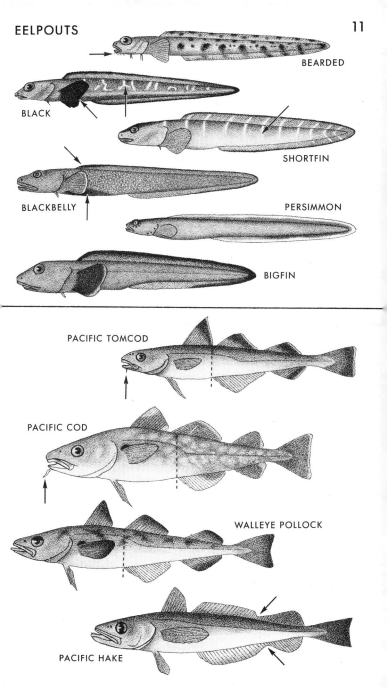

EELPOUTS

11

BEARDED

BLACK

SHORTFIN

BLACKBELLY

PERSIMMON

BIGFIN

PACIFIC TOMCOD

PACIFIC COD

WALLEYE POLLOCK

PACIFIC HAKE

PLATE 12

Flyingfishes, Halfbeaks, Silversides, Remoras, and Others

SHARPCHIN FLYINGFISH *Fodiator acutus*   p. 114
Pectoral fin long. Dorsal fin high, rounded. Snout length greater than eye diameter. Chin projects. To $9\frac{1}{2}$ in. (24 cm).

CALIFORNIA FLYINGFISH *Cypselurus californicus*   p. 113
Pectoral fin very long. Snout short. To 19 in. (48 cm).

CALIFORNIA HALFBEAK *Hyporhamphus rosae*   p. 115
Lower jaw long, red-tipped; upper jaw short. Pectoral fin short. To 6 in. (15 cm).

RIBBON HALFBEAK *Euleptorhamphus longirostris*   p. 114
Lower jaw long, upper jaw short. Pectoral fin long. To 18 in. (46 cm).

CALIFORNIA NEEDLEFISH *Strongylura exilis*   p. 116
Both jaws elongate. To 3 ft. (91 cm).

PACIFIC SAURY *Cololabis saira*   p. 116
5–6 finlets behind dorsal and anal fins. Snout short, pointed. To 14 in. (36 cm).

CALIFORNIA KILLIFISH *Fundulus parvipinnis*   p. 117
Mouth small. Dorsal fin at midbody. Caudal fin rounded. To $4\frac{1}{2}$ in. (11 cm).

Next 3 have 2 dorsal fins (1st small, spiny) and a small mouth.

CALIFORNIA GRUNION *Leuresthes tenuis*   p. 118
Anal fin begins directly below or just before 1st dorsal fin. Teeth tiny or absent. To $7\frac{1}{2}$ in. (19 cm).

JACKSMELT *Atherinopsis californiensis*   p. 118
Anal fin begins behind 1st dorsal fin. 10–12 scales between dorsal fins. Teeth simple, in rows. To $17\frac{1}{2}$ in. (44 cm).

TOPSMELT *Atherinops affinis*   p. 118
Anal fin begins under 1st dorsal fin. 5–8 scales between dorsal fins. Teeth forked, in 1 row. To $14\frac{1}{2}$ in. (37 cm).

Next 3 have a disk on the head. See text for other remoras.

REMORA *Remora remora*   p. 205
Disk smaller than in Whalesucker. Black or dark brown. To 34 in. (86 cm).

WHALESUCKER *Remora australis*   p. 204
Largest disk (nearly reaches midbody). To 30 in. (76 cm).

SHARKSUCKER *Echeneis naucrates*   p. 203
Dark side stripe, bordered by white. To 38 in. (97 cm).

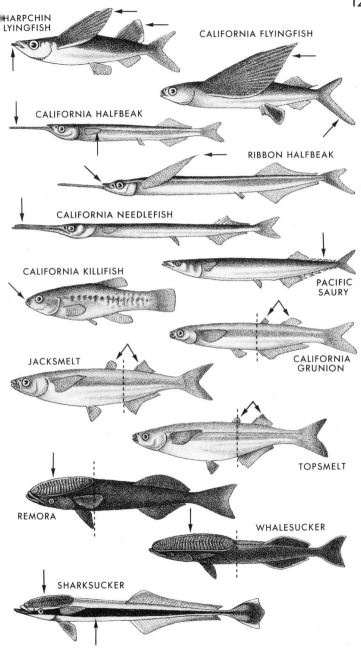

12

HARPCHIN LYINGFISH

CALIFORNIA FLYINGFISH

CALIFORNIA HALFBEAK

RIBBON HALFBEAK

CALIFORNIA NEEDLEFISH

CALIFORNIA KILLIFISH

PACIFIC SAURY

JACKSMELT

CALIFORNIA GRUNION

TOPSMELT

REMORA

WHALESUCKER

SHARKSUCKER

PLATE 13

Pipefishes and Others

First 3 have rings around their body and a tiny mouth.

SNUBNOSE PIPEFISH *Bryx arctus*   p. 130
Snout short. 18–23 dorsal fin rays. To $4\frac{3}{4}$ in. (12 cm).

BAY PIPEFISH *Syngnathus leptorhynchus*   p. 131
Snout long. 16–21 trunk (head to anus) rings. Only pipefish north of Calif. To 13 in. (33 cm).

BARRED PIPEFISH *Syngnathus auliscus*   p. 130
Snout moderate. 14–16 (usually 15) trunk rings, some white. 26–33 dorsal fin rays. To 7 in. (18 cm).

SLENDER SNIPEFISH *Macroramphosus gracilis*   p. 128
Tiny mouth at tip of tubular snout. Long 2nd spine in 1st dorsal fin. Mostly silvery, darker on back. To 6 in. (15 cm).

THREESPINE STICKLEBACK   p. 128
Gasterosteus aculeatus
Three isolated spines before soft dorsal fin. Thin plates on side. Caudal peduncle narrow, keeled. To 4 in. (10 cm).

PACIFIC SEAHORSE *Hippocampus ingens*   p. 129
Typical seahorse shape. Tail long, curled. To 1 ft. (30 cm).

TUBESNOUT *Aulorhynchus flavidus*   p. 128
About 25 isolated spines before soft dorsal fin. Snout long. Mouth small. To 7 in. (18 cm).

PACIFIC SANDFISH *Trichodon trichodon*   p. 238
Mouth upturned, lips fringed. 2 dorsal fins. No scales. To 1 ft. (30 cm).

SMOOTH STARGAZER *Kathetostoma averruncus*   p. 240
Large spine above pectoral fin. Eyes on top of head. Mouth nearly vertical. Pelvic fin at throat. To $12\frac{1}{4}$ in. (31 cm).

PACIFIC FAT SLEEPER *Dormitator latifrons*   p. 260
Head flat; stripes behind eye. 2 dorsal fins. Dark spot above pectoral fin. Caudal fin large, rounded. To 1 ft. (30 cm).

SPOTTED BATFISH *Zalieutes elater*   p. 112
Peculiar shape; flattened, prickly. Armlike pectoral fin. To 6 in. (15 cm).

ROUGHJAW FROGFISH *Antennarius avalonis*   p. 112
Globular; prickly. Small gill opening behind pectoral fin. Fleshy appendage ("lure") between eyes. To $13\frac{1}{2}$ in. (34 cm).

13

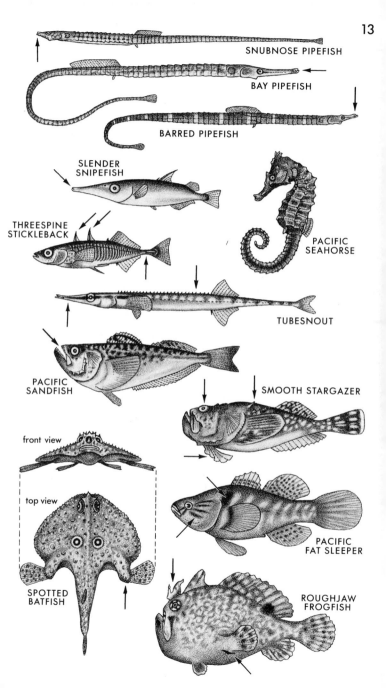

SNUBNOSE PIPEFISH

BAY PIPEFISH

BARRED PIPEFISH

SLENDER SNIPEFISH

THREESPINE STICKLEBACK

PACIFIC SEAHORSE

TUBESNOUT

PACIFIC SANDFISH

SMOOTH STARGAZER

front view

top view

SPOTTED BATFISH

PACIFIC FAT SLEEPER

ROUGHJAW FROGFISH

PLATE 14

Poachers (1)

Sizes of adults are from $3\frac{3}{4}$–$10\frac{1}{2}$ in. (9.5–27 cm).

1. **SMOOTH ALLIGATORFISH**   p. 186
   Anoplagonus inermis
   Our only poacher with 1 dorsal fin. Plates smooth.
2. **TUBENOSE POACHER** *Pallasina barbata*   p. 188
   Snout very long. Plates smooth.
3. **BLACKFIN STARSNOUT POACHER**   p. 187
   Bathyagonus nigripinnis
   Fins nearly solid black. 3 vertical spines at snout tip.
4. **SAWBACK POACHER** *Sarritor frenatus*   p. 189
   Long barbels. Snout spiny, projects.

Next 3 have a cluster of spines on a plate at snout tip.

5. **SPINYCHEEK STARSNOUT POACHER**   p. 187
   Bathyagonus infraspinatus
   Anal fin begins below rear of 1st dorsal fin.
6. **BIGEYE STARSNOUT POACHER**   p. 187
   Bathyagonus pentacanthus
   Eye large. 2 pairs of plates in front of pelvic fins.
7. **GRAY STARSNOUT POACHER**   p. 186
   Bathyagonus alascanus
   Anal fin begins below gap between dorsal fins.
8. **SMOOTHEYE POACHER** *Xeneretmus leiops*   p. 190
   3 vertical spines at snout tip. No scales on eye.

Next 4 species have 1 vertical spine at snout tip.

9. **PYGMY POACHER** *Odontopyxis trispinosa*   p. 188
   1 or 2 pits on upper rear of head.
10. **BLACKTIP POACHER** *Xeneretmus latifrons*   p. 189
    Dorsal fins dark-edged. Spiny scales on eye.
11. **STRIPEFIN POACHER** *Xeneretmus ritteri*   p. 190
    Base of 1st dorsal fin black.
12. **BLUESPOTTED POACHER**   p. 190
    Xeneretmus triacanthus
    Dorsal fins clear. 2 barbels at rear of upper jaw.

Last 3 have a long anal fin, which begins below 1st dorsal fin.

13. **WARTY POACHER** *Occella verrucosa*   p. 188
    Mouth upturned. Knobby plates on breast.
14. **PRICKLEBREAST POACHER**   p. 189
    Stellerina xyosterna
    Mouth upturned. Fine prickles on breast.
15. **NORTHERN SPEARNOSE POACHER**   p. 186
    Agonopsis vulsa
    2 spines at snout tip. Cirri on underside of head. Pelvic fin
    brown with white tip.

POACHERS

14

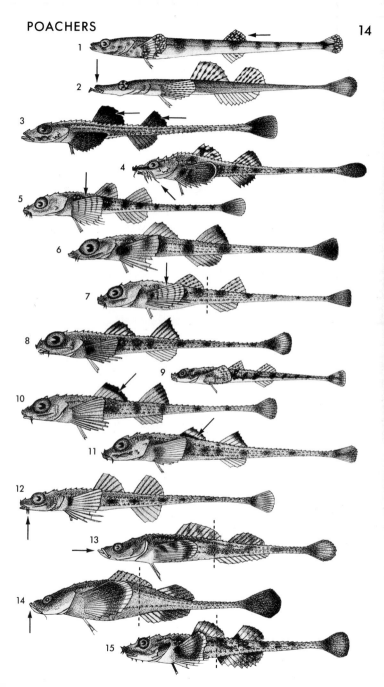

PLATE 15

Poachers (2), Sculpins (1)

ROCKHEAD *Bothragonus swanii* p. 187
Body plates smooth. Deep pit on top of head. Dark bars on brown
to orangish red background. To $3\frac{1}{2}$ in. (8.9 cm).

KELP POACHER *Agonomalus mozinoi* p. 185
Striking color. Peculiar shape. Fleshy skin flap on snout. To $3\frac{1}{2}$ in.
(8.9 cm).

FOURHORN POACHER *Hypsagonus quadricornis* p. 188
Cirrus on snout. Spine over eye. Profile slopes upward before
dorsal fin. To $3\frac{1}{2}$ in. (8.9 cm).

STURGEON POACHER *Agonus acipenserinus* p. 186
Mouth on underside of head. Cirri under snout and at mouth. To
1 ft. (30 cm).

LAVENDER SCULPIN *Leiocottus hirundo* p. 175
Spines at front of dorsal fin elongate. Unscaled. To 10 in. (25 cm).

GRUNT SCULPIN *Rhamphocottus richardsonii* p. 182
Body chunky. Striking color. Lower pectoral fin rays free. To
$3\frac{1}{4}$ in. (8.3 cm).

SILVERSPOTTED SCULPIN *Blepsias cirrhosus* p. 164
Cirri on lower jaw. Papillae cover body. 1st dorsal fin notched.
Body compressed, deep. 1 or more silvery white marks on side. To
$7\frac{1}{2}$ in. (19 cm).

SAILFIN SCULPIN *Nautichthys oculofasciatus* p. 176
1st dorsal fin very high. Dark bar through eye. Pit on top of head
behind eyes. Brown to gray. To 8 in. (20 cm).

CRESTED SCULPIN *Blepsias bilobus* p. 164
Cirri on lower jaw. Papillae cover body. 1st dorsal fin rounded.
Body compressed, deep. To 10 in. (25 cm).

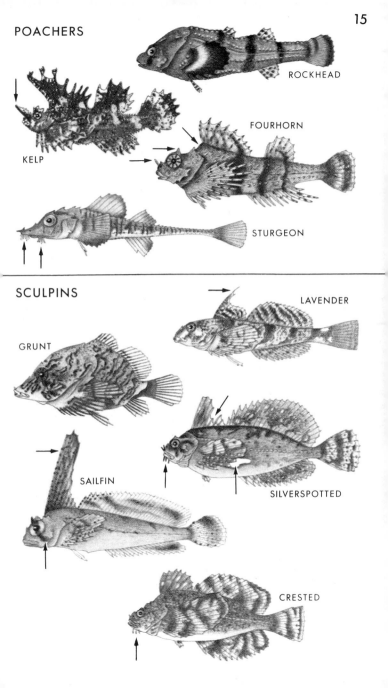

15

POACHERS

ROCKHEAD

KELP

FOURHORN

STURGEON

SCULPINS

LAVENDER

GRUNT

SAILFIN

SILVERSPOTTED

CRESTED

PLATE 16

Sculpins (2)

See Fig. 19 (p. 159) for scale patterns.

BLACKFIN SCULPIN *Malacocottus kincaidi* p. 175
No scales. Head large, knobby. Wide bars on caudal fin. To 8 in.
(20 cm).

ROUGHBACK SCULPIN *Chitonotus pugetensis* p. 164
1st dorsal fin notched; 1st spine long. Rough scales on back. To
9 in. (23 cm).

BIGMOUTH SCULPIN *Hemitripterus bolini* p. 171
Head spiny, flat. Mouth large. Dorsal fins well separated; dorsal fin
spines mostly free of skin. Large — to 27 in. (69 cm).

SPINYHEAD SCULPIN *Dasycottus setiger* p. 167
Vertical spines on large head. Skin loose. 1–2 rows of prickles at
base of dorsal fins. To 9 in. (23 cm).

PRICKLY SCULPIN *Cottus asper* p. 167
No scales or cirri. Usually 4 soft rays in pelvic fin. Upper
preopercular spine short. To 12 in. (30 cm).

PACIFIC STAGHORN SCULPIN p. 175
Leptocottus armatus
No scales. Upper preopercular spine antlerlike. Dark spot at rear
of 1st dorsal fin. Pectoral fin barred. Large — to 18 in. (46 cm).

BUFFALO SCULPIN *Enophrys bison* p. 168
Upper preopercular spine very long. Bony plates on lateral line.
8–10 anal fin rays. Large — to $14\frac{1}{2}$ in. (37 cm).

BULL SCULPIN *Enophrys taurina* p. 169
Similar to Buffalo Sculpin, but 6–7 anal fin rays. To $6\frac{3}{4}$ in. (17 cm).

GREAT SCULPIN p. 176
Myoxocephalus polyacanthocephalus
Upper preopercular spine long. Mouth large, upper jaw extends
past eye. Large — to 30 in. (76 cm). Wash. and north.

Next 3 species have a notch in 1st dorsal fin.

RED IRISH LORD *Hemilepidotus hemilepidotus* p. 170
2 scale bands (Fig. 19, p. 168), upper band 4–5 scale rows wide.
Large — to 20 in. (51 cm).

BROWN IRISH LORD *Hemilepidotus spinosus* p. 171
Similar to Red Irish Lord but upper scale band 6–8 scale rows
wide. To $11\frac{1}{4}$ in. (29 cm).

CABEZON *Scorpaenichthys marmoratus* p. 182
Skin flap on snout. 5 soft rays in pelvic fin. No scales. Common.
Large — to 39 in. (99 cm).

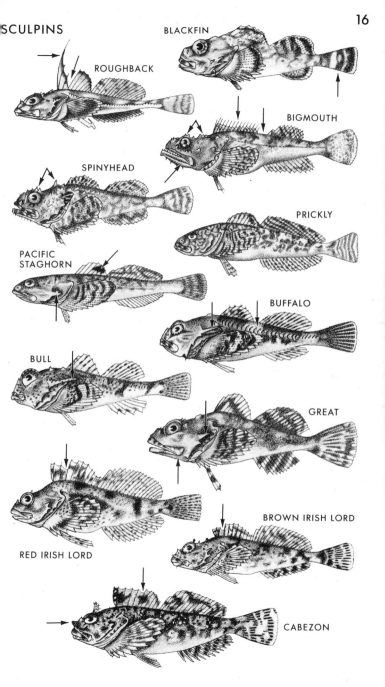

SCULPINS

16

ROUGHBACK

BLACKFIN

BIGMOUTH

SPINYHEAD

PRICKLY

PACIFIC STAGHORN

BUFFALO

BULL

GREAT

RED IRISH LORD

BROWN IRISH LORD

CABEZON

PLATE 17

Sculpins (3)

Except as noted, adult sizes are from 2$\frac{1}{2}$–8 in. (6.4–20 cm). See Fig. 19 (p. 159) for scale patterns.

ROSYLIP SCULPIN *Ascelichthys rhodorus*   p. 163
No pelvic fin. Slight notch in dorsal fin. No scales.

Next 5 (Clinocottus species) have no scales (Woolly Sculpin has prickles), anus about midway between anal fin and pelvic fin.

BALD SCULPIN *Clinocottus recalvus*   p. 167
Large cirri on head, but only on rear part of area between eyes.
WOOLLY SCULPIN *Clinocottus analis*   p. 166
Many cirri on head and upper back. Upper preopercular spine has 2–3 points.
MOSSHEAD SCULPIN *Clinocottus globiceps*   p. 166
Dense cirri on head (all of area between eyes) and lateral line. Head blunt. Upper preopercular spine single, blunt.
CALICO SCULPIN *Clinocottus embryum*   p. 166
Cirri only on lateral line and head. Upper preopercular spine single, blunt.
SHARPNOSE SCULPIN *Clinocottus acuticeps*   p. 165
Snout pointed. No scales on back. Dark bar on 1st dorsal fin.
SNUBNOSE SCULPIN *Orthonopias triacis*   p. 179
Head blunt. Head and back scaled. Anus well before anal fin.

Next 4 (Oligocottus species) have no scales.

TIDEPOOL SCULPIN *Oligocottus maculosus*   p. 178
1 forked preopercular spine. Front anal fin rays enlarged in males.
SADDLEBACK SCULPIN *Oligocottus rimensis*   p. 178
Head blunt. Skin prickly. Upper preopercular spine blunt, single.
FLUFFY SCULPIN *Oligocottus snyderi*   p. 178
Upper preopercular spine usually has 2 points. Comblike cirri on top of head. 1st anal fin ray enlarged in males.
ROSY SCULPIN *Oligocottus rubellio*   p. 178
Upper preopercular spine usually has 3 points.
LONGFIN SCULPIN *Jordania zonope*   p. 174
Anal fin long, starts far forward. Rows of fused scales below lateral line. Bars on cheek.
THORNBACK SCULPIN *Paricelinus hopliticus*   p. 179
Row of hooked spines on upper back. Lower pectoral fin rays mostly free of membrane.
ARMORHEAD SCULPIN *Gymnocanthus galeatus*   p. 169
Upper preopercular spine antlerlike. No scales on back. Large — to 14 in. (36 cm).
THORNY SCULPIN *Icelus spiniger*   p. 174
Row of thorny spines on back.
RIBBED SCULPIN *Triglops pingelii*   p. 184
Riblike folds of skin (edged with scales) on lower side. See also Roughspine Sculpin (Pl. 18).

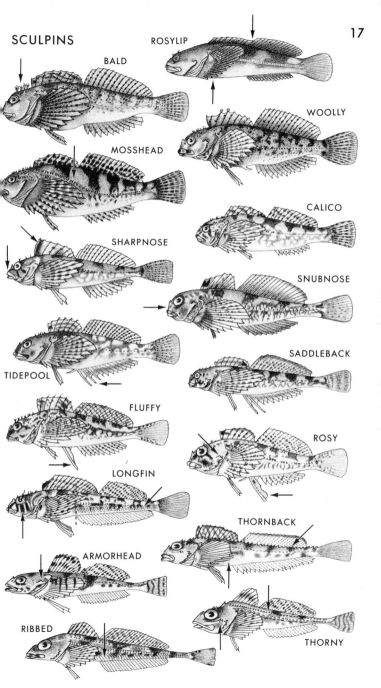

SCULPINS

17

ROSYLIP

BALD

MOSSHEAD

SHARPNOSE

TIDEPOOL

FLUFFY

LONGFIN

ARMORHEAD

RIBBED

WOOLLY

CALICO

SNUBNOSE

SADDLEBACK

ROSY

THORNBACK

THORNY

PLATE 18

Sculpins (4)

See Fig. 19 (p. 159) for scale patterns. Adult sizes are from 2½–5½ in. (6.4–14 cm) except as noted.

BONEHEAD SCULPIN *Artedius notospilotus*   p. 163
Narrow band of scales on back. Scales on head, none under eye. To 10 in. (25 cm).
SMOOTHHEAD SCULPIN *Artedius lateralis*   p. 162
Narrow band of scales on back; none on head. Fins barred.
CORALLINE SCULPIN *Artedius corallinus*   p. 161
Broad band of scales on back, ends below rear of 2nd dorsal fin. No scales on head.
ROUGHCHEEK SCULPIN *Artedius creaseri*   p. 162
Broad band of scales on back. Scales on top of head and snout.
SCALYHEAD SCULPIN *Artedius harringtoni*   p. 162
Broad band of scales on back. Scales on top of head, none on snout. Males have large pointed penis (not shown).
PIT-HEAD SCULPIN *Icelinus cavifrons*   p. 172
Pit on top of head behind eyes. Double row of scales on back. Upper preopercular spine antlerlike.
PADDED SCULPIN *Artedius fenestralis*   p. 162
Broad band of scales on back. Scales on top of head and below eye.
SOFT SCULPIN *Gilbertidia sigalutes*   p. 169
Only 1 dorsal fin. No scales. Skin loose.
TADPOLE SCULPIN *Psychrolutes paradoxus*   p. 180
Only 1 dorsal fin. Head smooth. Large black areas. No scales.

Next 3 (Icelinus species) have double row of scales on back, antlerlike preopercular spine.

SPOTFIN SCULPIN *Icelinus tenuis*   p. 173
1st 2 spines in dorsal fin elongate, 1st one usually longest. Males have dark spot on spinous dorsal fin.
THREADFIN SCULPIN *Icelinus filamentosus*   p. 173
1st 2 spines in dorsal fin elongate, about equal in length. To 10⅗ in. (27 cm).
NORTHERN SCULPIN *Icelinus borealis*   p. 172
Scale band extends onto caudal peduncle.
MANACLED SCULPIN *Synchirus gilli*   p. 183
Our only sculpin with pectoral fins joined at breast.
ROUGHSPINE SCULPIN *Triglops macellus*   p. 184
Elongate. Folds of skin (edged with scales) on lower side. Anal fin long. Lower pectoral fin rays long. To 8 in. (20 cm).
SLIM SCULPIN *Radulinus asprellus*   p. 181
Small scales in 1 row just above lateral line. Elongate. Anal fin long, with 21–25 rays. To 6 in. (15 cm).

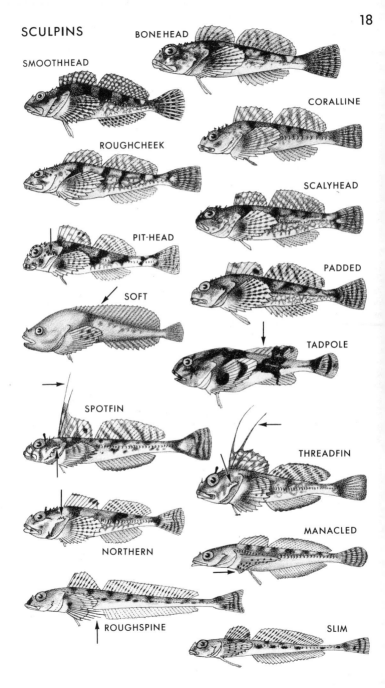

18

SCULPINS

BONEHEAD

SMOOTHHEAD

CORALLINE

ROUGHCHEEK

SCALYHEAD

PIT-HEAD

PADDED

SOFT

TADPOLE

SPOTFIN

THREADFIN

NORTHERN

MANACLED

ROUGHSPINE

SLIM

PLATE 19

Gobies (1)

Pelvic fins united into a cuplike sucking disk (Fig. 32 below).

CHEEKSPOT GOBY *Ilypnus gilberti* p. 263
Spot on gill cover. Black band on anal fin. To $2\frac{1}{2}$ in. (6.4 cm).

ARROW GOBY *Clevelandia ios* p. 261
Dorsal fins widely spaced, finely spotted. Jaw extends past eye. Males usually have black band on anal fin (rarely present in females). To $2\frac{1}{4}$ in. (5.7 cm).

SHADOW GOBY *Quietula y-cauda* p. 264
"Y" mark at base of caudal fin. Jaw extends past eye. To $2\frac{3}{4}$ in. (7 cm).

TIDEWATER GOBY *Eucyclogobius newberryi* p. 262
1st dorsal fin conspicuously clear at tip. 2nd dorsal and anal fins short and high. To $2\frac{1}{4}$ in. (5.7 cm).

BAY GOBY *Lepidogobius lepidus* p. 263
1st dorsal fin black at tip. Dorsal fins widely separated. To 4 in. (10 cm).

CHAMELEON GOBY *Tridentiger trigonocephalus* p. 264
Dark, then pale areas on pectoral fin base. Small spot at upper base of caudal fin. Stripes; often faint bars (see variations). To $4\frac{1}{2}$ in. (11 cm).

BLACKEYE GOBY *Coryphopterus nicholsii* p. 261
Eye and tip of 1st dorsal fin black. Disk black in breeding males. To 6 in. (15 cm).

LONGTAIL GOBY *Gobionellus longicaudus* p. 262
Caudal fin long, pointed. Oblong blotches on side. To 8 in. (20 cm).

LONGJAW MUDSUCKER *Gillichthys mirabilis* p. 262
Jaw moderately long in young, huge in adults. Anal fin short. To $8\frac{1}{4}$ in. (21 cm).

YELLOWFIN GOBY *Acanthogobius flavimanus* p. 261
Dorsal fins speckled. Zigzag bars on upper part of caudal fin. Color varies. To 1 ft. (30 cm).

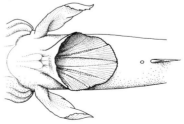

**Fig. 32
Gobies — disk**

GOBIES

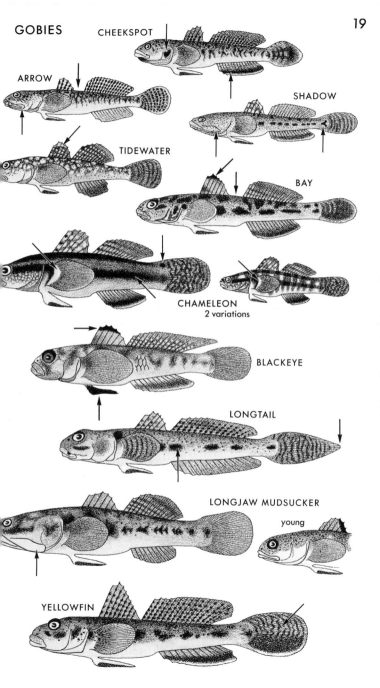

CHEEKSPOT

ARROW

SHADOW

TIDEWATER

BAY

CHAMELEON
2 variations

BLACKEYE

LONGTAIL

LONGJAW MUDSUCKER

young

YELLOWFIN

PLATE 20

Snailfishes (1), Gobies (2), Brotulas, Cusk-eels

First 4 (snailfishes) have a disk on breast (Fig. 33 opp. Pl. 21).

RINGTAIL SNAILFISH *Liparis rutteri*   p. 193
Gill opening small, above pectoral fin. Dorsal fin not lobed in front. Usually a white ring at base of caudal fin. To 6½ in. (16 cm).

SHOWY SNAILFISH *Liparis pulchellus*   p. 193
Plain-colored (specimen in rear) or with wavy stripes. Dorsal and anal fins join caudal fin for most of its length. To 10 in. (25 cm).

TIDEPOOL SNAILFISH *Liparis florae*   p. 192
Nearly separate lobe at front of dorsal fin. Skin loose. Plain-colored; brown, olive, or purplish. To 7¼ in. (18 cm).

BLACKTAIL SNAILFISH *Careproctus melanurus*   p. 191
Pinkish; black at rear. Disk small, about same size as eye. To 10¼ in. (26 cm).

Next 4 (gobies) have pelvic fins that join to form a cuplike disk (Fig. 32 opp. Pl. 19). 2 dorsal fins.

ZEBRA GOBY *Lythrypnus zebra*   p. 264
Numerous blue bars. To 2¼ in. (5.7 cm).

BLUEBANDED GOBY *Lythrypnus dalli*   p. 263
4–9 broad blue bars. High 1st dorsal fin. To 2½ in. (6.4 cm).

HALFBLIND GOBY *Lethops connectens*   p. 263
Eye tiny. Unscaled. Tan to pinkish. To 2½ in. (6.4 cm).

BLIND GOBY *Typhlogobius californiensis*   p. 265
Blind or eye tiny, remnant. Unscaled. Pinkish white. To 3¼ in. (8.3 cm).

RED BROTULA *Brosmophycis marginata*   p. 103
Separate caudal fin. Filamentous pelvic fin at breast. Mostly red or brownish red. To 18 in. (46 cm).

PURPLE BROTULA *Oligopus diagrammus*   p. 103
No separate caudal fin. Filamentous pelvic fin at breast. Slate gray or purplish black. To 8 in. (20 cm).

SPOTTED CUSK-EEL *Chilara taylori*   p. 102
No separate caudal fin. Pelvic fin at throat. Spotted. To 14 in. (36 cm).

BASKETWEAVE CUSK-EEL *Ophidion scrippsae*   p. 102
Similar to Spotted Cusk-eel, but no spots. Scales in crisscross pattern. To about 11 in. (28 cm).

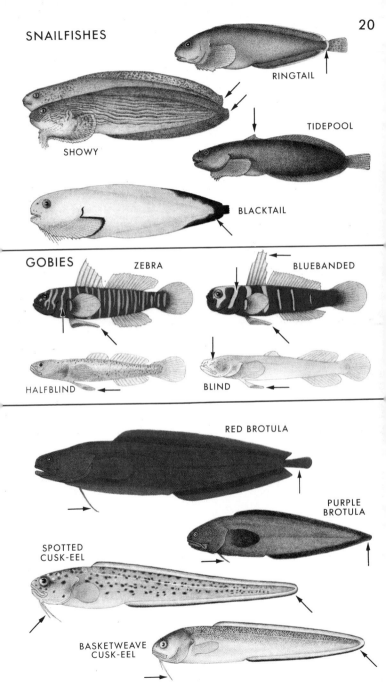

20

SNAILFISHES

RINGTAIL

SHOWY

TIDEPOOL

BLACKTAIL

GOBIES

ZEBRA

BLUEBANDED

HALFBLIND

BLIND

RED BROTULA

PURPLE BROTULA

SPOTTED CUSK-EEL

BASKETWEAVE CUSK-EEL

PLATE 21

Clingfishes, Snailfishes (2), Lumpfishes

In next 5 (clingfishes) note disk on breast (see Fig. 33 below). All are under 3 in. (7.6 cm) except Northern Clingfish.

LINED CLINGFISH *Gobiesox eugrammus*   p. 109
Cream-colored; orange or red marks.
NORTHERN CLINGFISH *Gobiesox maeandricus*   p. 109
Large disk. Gray to brown or red, often with chainlike pattern. Only clingfish over 3 in. (7.6 cm). To 6½ in. (16 cm).
CALIFORNIA CLINGFISH *Gobiesox rhessodon*   p. 109
Gray to brown with darker brown marks. Large fleshy pad in front of pectoral fin.
KELP CLINGFISH *Rimicola muscarum*   p. 110
Slender. Disk small. Dorsal and anal fins short.
SLENDER CLINGFISH *Rimicola eigenmanni*   p. 110
Similar to Kelp Clingfish, see text.

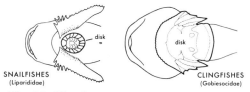

SNAILFISHES
(Liparididae)

CLINGFISHES
(Gobiesocidae)

Fig. 33 Clingfishes and snailfishes — disk

In next 5 (snailfishes) note small gill slit; long lower pectoral fin rays. Adults are under 7 in. (18 cm) except as noted.

SLIPSKIN SNAILFISH *Liparis fucensis*   p. 192
Color varies; often striped. Bars on caudal and pectoral fins.
SLIMY SNAILFISH *Liparis mucosus*   p. 193
Plain-colored or striped (as shown). Lobe at front of dorsal fin.
SPOTTED SNAILFISH *Liparis callyodon*   p. 191
Lobe at front of dorsal fin. Body and caudal fin spotted.
RIBBON SNAILFISH *Liparis cyclopus*   p. 192
Similar to Spotted Snailfish, but no lobe at front of dorsal fin.
MARBLED SNAILFISH *Liparis dennyi*   p. 192
Anal fin joins caudal fin for about ⅓ its length. Speckled. To 12 in. (30 cm).
PACIFIC SPINY LUMPSUCKER   p. 195
Eumicrotremus orbis
Globular. Cones on body. 2 dorsal fins. Small gill slit above pectoral fin. To 5 in. (13 cm).
SMOOTH LUMPSUCKER *Aptocyclus ventricosus*   p. 194
Globular. 1 dorsal fin, far back. Small gill slit above pectoral fin. To 10¾ in. (27 cm).

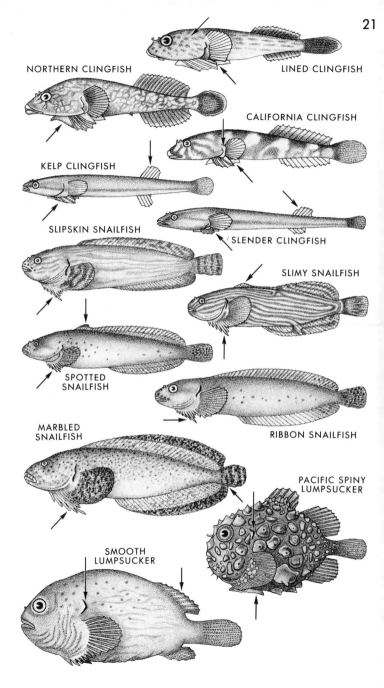

NORTHERN CLINGFISH

LINED CLINGFISH

CALIFORNIA CLINGFISH

KELP CLINGFISH

SLIPSKIN SNAILFISH

SLENDER CLINGFISH

SLIMY SNAILFISH

SPOTTED SNAILFISH

MARBLED SNAILFISH

RIBBON SNAILFISH

PACIFIC SPINY LUMPSUCKER

SMOOTH LUMPSUCKER

PLATE 22

Combfishes, Greenlings, Lingcod

SHORTSPINE COMBFISH *Zaniolepis frenata*   p. 158
Long cirrus above eye. Dorsal fin spines long. Skin rough. To 10 in. (25 cm).

LONGSPINE COMBFISH *Zaniolepis latipinnis*   p. 158
2nd spine in dorsal fin very long. No long cirrus above eye. Skin rough. To 12 in. (30 cm).

ATKA MACKEREL *Pleurogrammus monopterygius*   p. 157
5 lateral lines. Dorsal fin unnotched. Dark bars. Caudal fin forked. To 19½ in. (49 cm).

PAINTED GREENLING *Oxylebius pictus*   p. 157
Reddish bars. Some individuals very dark. Snout pointed. Only 1 lateral line. To 10 in. (25 cm).

WHITESPOTTED GREENLING   p. 156
Hexagrammos stelleri
Color varies; white spots on head and body. 5 lateral lines, 4th one short (as in Masked Greenling, Fig. 34). To 19 in. (48 cm).

MASKED GREENLING *Hexagrammos octogrammus*   p. 156
5 lateral lines, 4th one short (Fig. 34). Large cirrus above eye. Color varies. To 11 in. (28 cm).

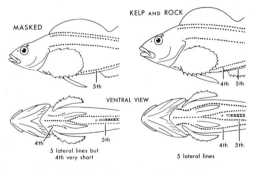

Fig. 34 Greenlings — lateral lines

ROCK GREENLING *Hexagrammos lagocephalus*   p. 155
Color varies (2 variations shown)—greenish to brown; red blotches in males. Large cirrus above eye. 5 lateral lines (Fig. 34). To 2 ft. (61 cm).

KELP GREENLING *Hexagrammos decagrammus*   p. 155
Males gray to brownish olive, with irregular blue spots at front. Females freckled reddish brown. 5 lateral lines (Fig. 34). To 21 in. (53 cm).

LINGCOD *Ophiodon elongatus*   p. 156
Large, elongate. Jaw long, teeth sharp. 1 lateral line. Scales tiny, cycloid. Young blotched; caudal fin forked. To 5 ft. (152 cm).

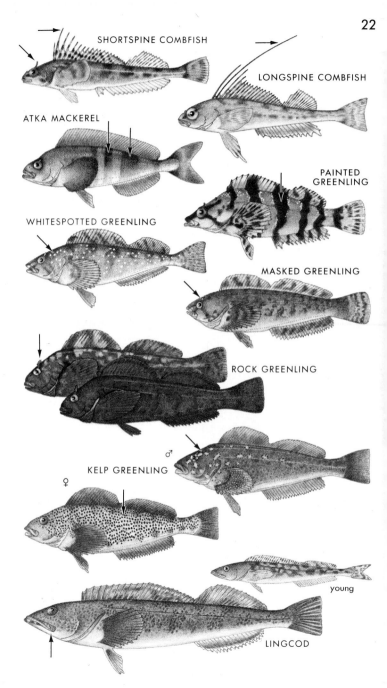

SHORTSPINE COMBFISH

LONGSPINE COMBFISH

ATKA MACKEREL

PAINTED GREENLING

WHITESPOTTED GREENLING

MASKED GREENLING

ROCK GREENLING

KELP GREENLING

♂

♀

young

LINGCOD

PLATE 23

Scorpionfishes, Rockfishes (1)

Note spines on rear cheek area.

CALIFORNIA SCORPIONFISH *Scorpaena guttata*   p. 132
Row of spines under eye. 12 dorsal fin spines. Body and fins spotted. To 17 in. (43 cm).

RAINBOW SCORPIONFISH *Scorpaenodes xyris*   p. 133
Row of spines below eye. 13 spines in dorsal fin. Spot on gill cover. To 6 in. (15 cm).

SHORTSPINE THORNYHEAD   p. 152
Sebastolobus alascanus
Pectoral fin bilobed, fleshy. Row of spines below eye. 15 or more spines in dorsal fin. To 29½ in. (75 cm).

TREEFISH *Sebastes serriceps*   p. 151
Black bars on yellowish to olive background (often quite dark); lips pinkish in adults. To 16 in. (41 cm).

FLAG ROCKFISH *Sebastes rubrivinctus*   p. 149
Broad bars — bar at front of dorsal fin vertical, extends onto gill cover; bar at midbody curves away from head. To 20 in. (51 cm).

TIGER ROCKFISH *Sebastes nigrocinctus*   p. 145
Black or dark red bars on pink or red body. In young, anal and pelvic fins black-tipped. To 24 in. (61 cm).

REDBANDED ROCKFISH *Sebastes babcocki*   p. 135
4 dark bars on body—1st one slants toward pectoral fin. To 25 in. (64 cm).

BLACK ROCKFISH *Sebastes melanops*   p. 143
Black to blue-black, with dirty white areas. Jaw extends to or past rear of eye. Often more spotted than specimen shown. To 23¾ in. (60 cm).

BLUE ROCKFISH *Sebastes mystinus*   p. 144
Similar to Black Rockfish but jaw does not extend past midpoint of eye. To 21 in. (53 cm).

CHINA ROCKFISH *Sebastes nebulosus*   p. 145
Black to blue-black, with yellow spots. Yellow stripe from dorsal fin to rear of body. To 17 in. (43 cm).

QUILLBACK ROCKFISH *Sebastes maliger*   p. 142
Brown to black, with large orange areas. Dorsal fin deeply notched between spines. To 24 in. (61 cm).

ROCKFISHES

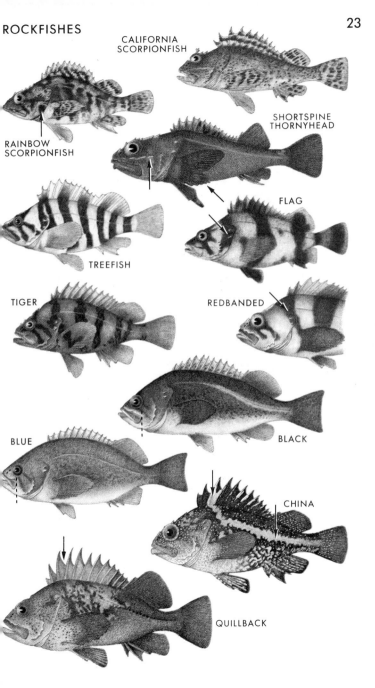

CALIFORNIA SCORPIONFISH

RAINBOW SCORPIONFISH

SHORTSPINE THORNYHEAD

FLAG

TREEFISH

TIGER

REDBANDED

BLUE

BLACK

CHINA

QUILLBACK

PLATE 24

Rockfishes (2)

Note spines on rear cheek area.

COPPER ROCKFISH *Sebastes caurinus*   p. 136
Often a pale stripe on rear of body. Color varies: brownish, olive, or reddish brown; often with yellow or pink patches. To $22\frac{1}{2}$ in. (57 cm).

BLACK-AND-YELLOW ROCKFISH   p. 136
Sebastes chrysomelas
Blackish or olive-brown; bright yellow areas. To $15\frac{1}{4}$ in. (39 cm).

GOPHER ROCKFISH *Sebastes carnatus*   p. 135
Brownish to olive; flesh-colored pale areas. To $15\frac{1}{2}$ in. (39 cm).

MEXICAN ROCKFISH *Sebastes macdonaldi*   p. 142
Black and red; lateral line in clear red zone. To 26 in. (66 cm).

In next 5 species lower jaw projects; head spines are weak.

REDSTRIPE ROCKFISH *Sebastes proriger*   p. 147
Red; lateral line in gray zone, bordered by red. Lips dusky. To 20 in. (51 cm).

SILVERGRAY ROCKFISH *Sebastes brevispinis*   p. 135
Silver gray above, white and pink below. Lips dusky. To 28 in. (71 cm).

SHORTBELLY ROCKFISH *Sebastes jordani*   p. 141
Anus at midbelly, not just before anal fin. Slender; small — to $12\frac{1}{2}$ in. (32 cm).

CHILIPEPPER *Sebastes goodei*   p. 140
Reddish pink; lateral line in clear pink zone (obscure in young). Caudal fin dusky. To 22 in. (56 cm).

BOCACCIO *Sebastes paucispinis*   p. 145
Mouth large, upturned; upper jaw extends to or past rear of eye. Brownish to red above; silvery red or pinkish below. Specimens under 1 ft. (30 cm) spotted. To 36 in. (91 cm).

OCKFISHES

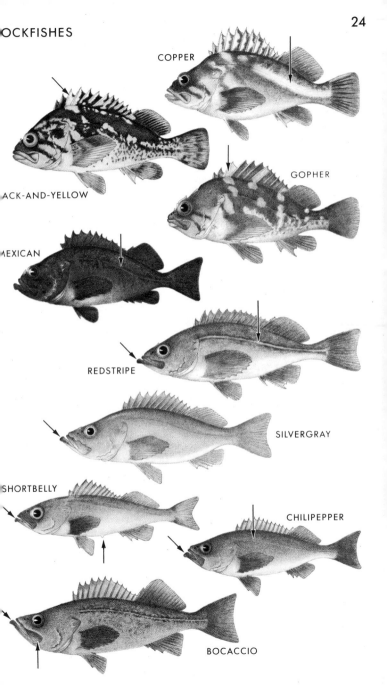

COPPER

ACK-AND-YELLOW

GOPHER

MEXICAN

REDSTRIPE

SILVERGRAY

SHORTBELLY

CHILIPEPPER

BOCACCIO

PLATE 25

Rockfishes (3)

Note glistening pale areas on back; spines on rear cheek area.

HONEYCOMB ROCKFISH *Sebastes umbrosus*　　　p. 151
Honeycomb pattern on side. To 10½ in. (27 cm).

ROSETHORN ROCKFISH *Sebastes helvomaculatus*　　p. 141
Pinkish to orangish, tinged with yellow or green. Faint dusky area
on gill cover. Pale areas bordered by pink. To 16 in. (41 cm).

ROSY ROCKFISH *Sebastes rosaceus*　　　p. 148
Back mottled with purple; purple surrounds white areas. Usually
has purple stripes on head. To 14 in. (36 cm).

STARRY ROCKFISH *Sebastes constellatus*　　　p. 137
Red to orange, with white specks. To 18 in. (46 cm).

GREENSPOTTED ROCKFISH　　　p. 136
Sebastes chlorostictus
Round green spots on back. No streaks on caudal fin. To 19¾ in.
(50 cm).

GREENBLOTCHED ROCKFISH　　　p. 148
Sebastes rosenblatti
Green wavy lines (not round spots) on back. To 19 in. (48 cm).

FRECKLED ROCKFISH *Sebastes lentiginosus*　　p. 142
Freckled with dark green. Toothed knob at tip of each upper jaw.
Dark streaks on caudal fin. Small — to 9 in. (23 cm).

SWORDSPINE ROCKFISH *Sebastes ensifer*　　　p. 139
Lower jaw projects, knob on chin. 2nd spine in anal fin long.
Orange-red, tinged with red or purple mixed with greenish yellow;
no green spots. To 12 in. (30 cm).

PINKROSE ROCKFISH *Sebastes simulator*　　　p. 151
Pinkish red above; white below. No green spots. To 12 in. (30 cm).

BRONZESPOTTED ROCKFISH *Sebastes gilli*　　　p. 140
2 orangish areas below soft dorsal fin; bronze or brown spots on
back. Bars radiate from eye. Mouth upturned. To 28 in. (71 cm).

ROCKFISHES

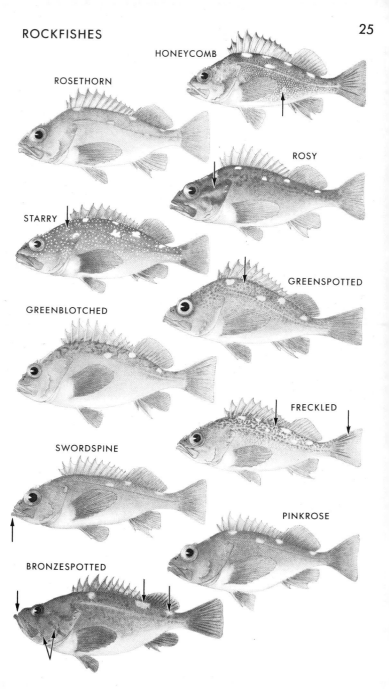

25

HONEYCOMB

ROSETHORN

ROSY

STARRY

GREENSPOTTED

GREENBLOTCHED

FRECKLED

SWORDSPINE

PINKROSE

BRONZESPOTTED

PLATE 26

Rockfishes (4)

Note spines on rear cheek area.

YELLOWTAIL ROCKFISH *Sebastes flavidus*   p. 140
Fins usually yellowish, especially caudal fin. Often pale areas on back. Head spines weak. Usually 8 soft rays in anal fin (last one double). Rare south of Pt. Conception. To 26 in. (66 cm).

WIDOW ROCKFISH *Sebastes entomelas*   p. 139
Dusky or brassy (often with hint of yellow); white or pinkish below. Most fin membranes dark. To 21 in. (61 cm).

OLIVE ROCKFISH *Sebastes serranoides*   p. 151
Like Yellowtail Rockfish but usually 9 soft rays in anal fin (last one double); fins less yellow. Rare north of Pt. Conception. To 24 in. (61 cm).

SQUARESPOT ROCKFISH *Sebastes hopkinsi*   p. 141
Several squarish dark brown blotches on brownish back. To 11½ in. (29 cm).

BANK ROCKFISH *Sebastes rufus*   p. 149
Lateral line in a clear pink zone. Fin membranes black. Dorsal fin speckled and body less red in specimens from s. Calif (not shown). To 20 in. (51 cm).

DUSKY ROCKFISH *Sebastes ciliatus*   p. 136
Color varies; brown or reddish brown flecks on side. Knob on chin. Head spines weak. To 16 in. (41 cm).

SPECKLED ROCKFISH *Sebastes ovalis*   p. 145
Tan (often tinged with pink); dark specks on much of body. To 22 in. (56 cm).

CALICO ROCKFISH *Sebastes dallii*   p. 137
Broad oblique bars. Streaks on caudal fin. To 10 in. (25 cm).

KELP ROCKFISH *Sebastes atrovirens*   p. 134
Olive-brown to gray-brown, mottled with darker brown; sometimes pinkish below. To 16¾ in. (42 cm).

BROWN ROCKFISH *Sebastes auriculatus*   p. 134
Dark brown patch on gill cover. Underparts often pinkish. To 21½ in. (55 cm).

GRASS ROCKFISH *Sebastes rastrelliger*   p. 147
Dark green or olive. Stubby gill rakers (nearly as wide as long). To 22 in. (56 cm).

ROCKFISHES

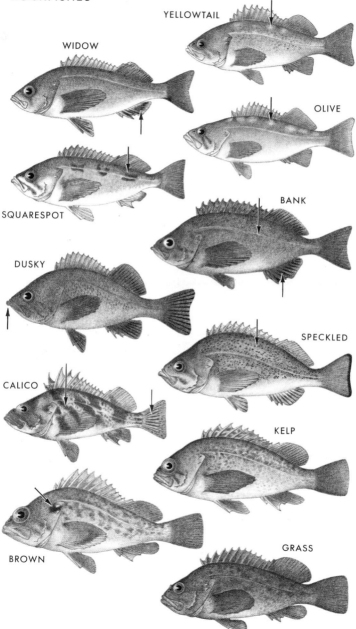

YELLOWTAIL

WIDOW

OLIVE

SQUARESPOT

BANK

DUSKY

SPECKLED

CALICO

KELP

BROWN

GRASS

PLATE 27

Rockfishes (5)

Note spines on rear cheek area.

SEMAPHORE ROCKFISH *Sebastes melanosema*　　p. 143
Orangish. Skin black at edge of dorsal fin. Small — to 7¾ in.
(20 cm).

BLACKGILL ROCKFISH *Sebastes melanostomus*　　p. 143
Rear edge of gill cover black. Black patches inside mouth. To 24 in.
(61 cm).

SHORTRAKER ROCKFISH *Sebastes borealis*　　p. 135
Pink or orange-pink, with vague bars. Pectoral and pelvic fins
sometimes dark-edged. Large — to 38 in. (96 cm).

YELLOWEYE ROCKFISH *Sebastes ruberrimus*　　p. 148
Color changes with growth: specimens under 1 ft. (30 cm) have 2
pale stripes on body; larger specimens have 1 stripe (as shown);
largest ones often lack stripe. Large — to 36 in. (91 cm).

ROUGHEYE ROCKFISH *Sebastes aleutianus*　　p. 133
Rasplike ridge just below front of eye. Red with dark blotches.
Fins usually have dusky edges. Large — to 38 in. (96 cm).

YELLOWMOUTH ROCKFISH *Sebastes reedi*　　p. 147
Yellow and black blotches inside mouth. Pink along lateral line.
Reddish above; paler below. Smaller specimens mottled. To 23 in.
(58 cm).

CANARY ROCKFISH *Sebastes pinniger*　　p. 146
Orange, with gray or dusky markings. Lateral line usually in a
clear gray zone. Rear of dorsal fin dark (as shown) in specimens
under 14 in. (36 cm). To 30 in. (76 cm).

VERMILION ROCKFISH *Sebastes miniatus*　　p. 144
Red to orange-red; fins often dark-edged. Orange stripes radiate
from eye. Small specimens more mottled. To 30 in. (76 cm).

HARLEQUIN ROCKFISH *Sebastes variegatus*　　p. 152
Dark blotches on back. Lateral line in a clear zone. Spinous dorsal
fin blackish. To 12½ in. (32 cm).

COWCOD *Sebastes levis*　　p. 142
Pinkish to yellowish red, with irregular bars. Large distance between eye and mouth. Large specimens (shown) have deep notches
between dorsal fin spines, redder body, fainter bars. Large — to
37 in. (94 cm).

ROCKFISHES

27

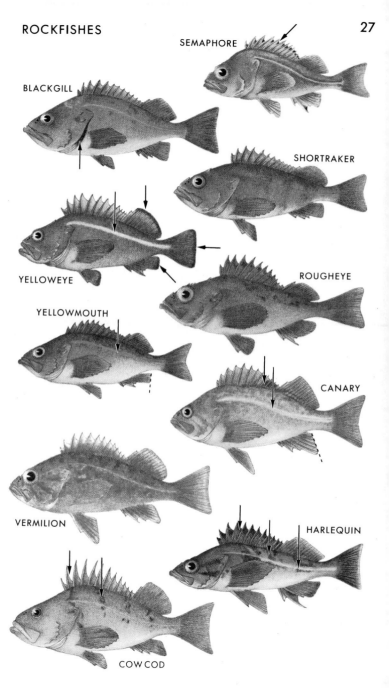

SEMAPHORE

BLACKGILL

SHORTRAKER

YELLOWEYE

ROUGHEYE

YELLOWMOUTH

CANARY

VERMILION

HARLEQUIN

COW COD

PLATE 28

Rockfishes (6)

Note spines on rear cheek area.

PYGMY ROCKFISH *Sebastes wilsoni*   p. 152
Dark saddles at base of dorsal fin. Small — to $8\frac{1}{4}$ in. (21 cm).

SHARPCHIN ROCKFISH *Sebastes zacentrus*   p. 152
Vague dusky areas on back. V-shaped mark behind eye. To 13 in. (33 cm).

DARKBLOTCHED ROCKFISH *Sebastes crameri*   p. 137
Large dark blotches on back. Body deep. To $22\frac{1}{2}$ in. (57 cm).

PACIFIC OCEAN PERCH *Sebastes alutus*   p. 133
Knob on chin. Head spines weak. Dark saddles at base of dorsal fin. To 20 in. (51 cm).

HALFBANDED ROCKFISH *Sebastes semicinctus*   p. 150
2 large dark areas on side. Streaks on caudal fin. To 10 in. (25 cm).

AURORA ROCKFISH *Sebastes aurora*   p. 134
Bright pinkish red to orange-red; whitish below. Inside of mouth red. To $15\frac{1}{2}$ in. (39 cm).

SPLITNOSE ROCKFISH *Sebastes diploproa*   p. 138
Similar to Aurora Rockfish but has a toothed knob at front of each upper jaw (when viewed from above). To 18 in. (46 cm).

STRIPETAIL ROCKFISH *Sebastes saxicola*   p. 150
Green streaks on caudal fin. Pinkish red to yellowish pink; whitish below. To $15\frac{1}{2}$ in. (39 cm).

PUGET SOUND ROCKFISH *Sebastes emphaeus*   p. 138
Small — to 7 in. (18 cm). Reddish to copper-red; often with a dark stripe on lower side.

GREENSTRIPED ROCKFISH *Sebastes elongatus*   p. 138
Green stripes on body. Green streaks on caudal fin. To 15 in. (38 cm).

ROCKFISHES

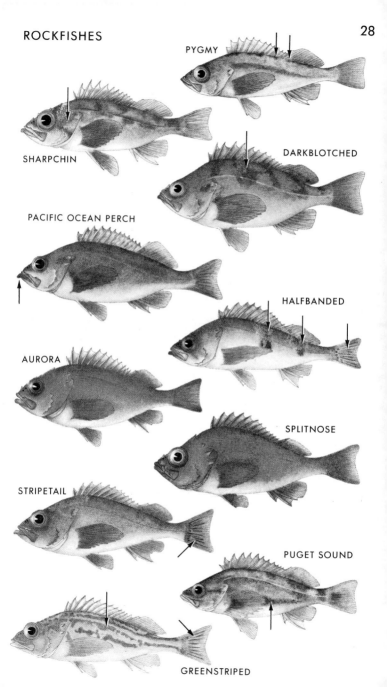

28

PYGMY

SHARPCHIN

DARKBLOTCHED

PACIFIC OCEAN PERCH

HALFBANDED

AURORA

SPLITNOSE

STRIPETAIL

PUGET SOUND

GREENSTRIPED

PLATE 29

Groupers and Basses

Rare basslike fishes are shown in Fig. 39 (p. 198).

GULF GROUPER *Mycteroperca jordani*   p. 199
Rear edge of anal fin nearly vertical. Caudal fin square-cut or slightly indented. Usually 17 pectoral fin rays. To 6½ ft. (198 cm).

BROOMTAIL GROUPER *Mycteroperca xenarcha*   p. 199
Rear edge of caudal fin sawtoothed. Color varies. To 4 ft. (122 cm).

STRIPED BASS *Morone saxatilis*   p. 196
Caudal fin forked. Greenish silver, with 6–9 dark stripes. To 4 ft. (122 cm).

GIANT SEA BASS *Stereolepis gigas*   p. 196
More spines than soft rays in dorsal fin. Adults dark — if spotted, spots fade at death. Juniors brownish to dusky, with large spots. Young — to about 6 in. (15 cm) — red with dark spots. Large — to $7\frac{5}{12}$ ft. (226 cm).

In last 3 the 1st 2 spines in dorsal fin are shorter — about ⅓ length of 3rd spine. No large spines on rear of cheek.

BARRED SAND BASS *Paralabrax nebulifer*   p. 201
3rd spine in dorsal fin longest. Dark bars and blotches on side. To 25½ in. (65 cm).

KELP BASS *Paralabrax clathratus*   p. 200
Mottled — usually pale spots on back. Dorsal fin spines 3–5 about equal in length. To 28½ in. (72 cm).

SPOTTED SAND BASS   p. 200
Paralabrax maculatofasciatus
Heavily spotted; also usually barred. To 22 in. (56 cm).

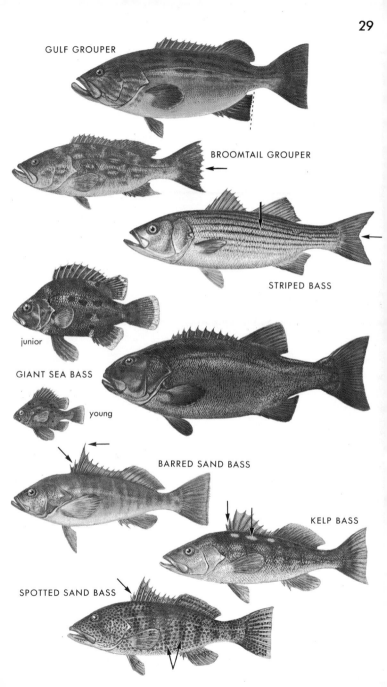

29

GULF GROUPER

BROOMTAIL GROUPER

STRIPED BASS

junior

GIANT SEA BASS

young

BARRED SAND BASS

KELP BASS

SPOTTED SAND BASS

PLATE 30

Wrasses, Damselfishes, Butterflyfishes, and Others

CALIFORNIA SHEEPHEAD *Semicossyphus pulcher*   p. 237
Distinctive color. White chin. Males dark at head and tail, reddish between. Females mostly pinkish. Young red with white streaks and dark spots. Front teeth protrude. To 3 ft. (91 cm).

SEÑORITA *Oxyjulis californica*   p. 236
Scales large. Cigar-shaped. Dark area at base of caudal fin. Back brownish, sides dirty yellow, belly pale. To 10 in. (25 cm).

ROCK WRASSE *Halichoeres semicinctus*   p. 236
Blackish or bluish black bar behind pectoral fin in males (usually absent in females); scattered dark scales on back. Scales large. Caudal fin square-cut. White side stripe in young (not shown). To 15 in. (38 cm).

BLACKSMITH *Chromis punctipinnis*   p. 233
Gray-blue to slate gray; black spots at rear of body and on soft dorsal and caudal fin. To 1 ft. (30 cm).

GARIBALDI *Hypsypops rubicundus*   p. 233
Orange or yellow-orange. Caudal fin notched, with rounded lobes. Young reddish orange with blue spots. To 14 in. (36 cm).

THREEBAND BUTTERFLYFISH   p. 225
Chaetodon humeralis
Bars on body and caudal fin. Strongly compressed. To 10 in. (25 cm).

SCYTHE BUTTERFLYFISH *Chaetodon falcifer*   p. 225
Distinctive scythe mark on side. No bars. Strongly compressed. To 6 in. (15 cm).

POPEYE CATALUFA *Pseudopriacanthus serrula*   p. 201
Crimson. Body oval. Eye large. To 13 in. (33 cm).

GUADALUPE CARDINALFISH *Apogon atricaudus*   p. 202
Bluish gray, olive, or purplish above; orange to rosy below. 2 dorsal fins. To 5 in. (13 cm).

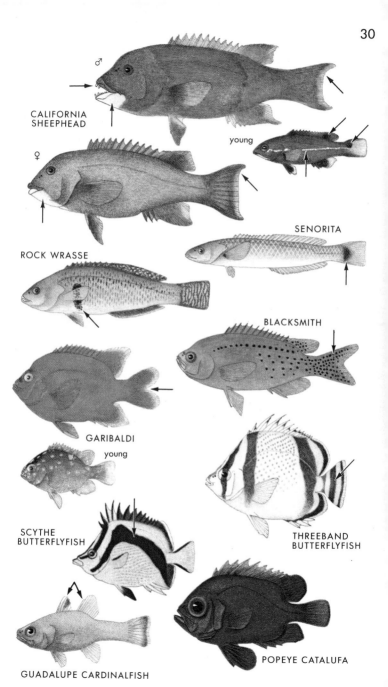

30

CALIFORNIA
SHEEPHEAD

♂

young

♀

ROCK WRASSE

SENORITA

BLACKSMITH

GARIBALDI

young

SCYTHE
BUTTERFLYFISH

THREEBAND
BUTTERFLYFISH

GUADALUPE CARDINALFISH

POPEYE CATALUFA

PLATE 31

Whitefish, Butterfish, Jacks, and Others

Rare jacks are shown in Fig. 40 (p. 207).

OCEAN WHITEFISH *Caulolatilus princeps*   p. 202
Dorsal fin long. Brilliant colors. To 40 in. (102 cm).

PACIFIC BUTTERFISH *Peprilus simillimus*   p. 280
Silvery. Front end blunt. Mouth small. Caudal fin deeply forked.
To 11 in. (28 cm).

PACIFIC BUMPER *Chloroscombrus orqueta*   p. 208
Pectoral fin long. Usually a dark spot on gill cover. Black on top of
caudal peduncle. Weak scutes before caudal fin. To 1 ft. (30 cm).

JACKMACKEREL *Trachurus symmetricus*   p. 211
Elongate. Spot on gill cover. Lateral line curved, with scutes along
entire length. To 32 in. (81 cm).

MEXICAN SCAD *Decapterus scombrinus*   p. 208
Elongate. Pectoral fin short. 1 finlet, behind dorsal and anal fins.
Usually a spot on gill cover and an orange or reddish side stripe.
Strong scutes on rear of lateral line. To $18\frac{1}{4}$ in. (46 cm).

GREEN JACK *Caranx caballus*   p. 206
Pectoral fin long. Usually a spot on gill cover. Strong scutes on rear
of lateral line. To 15 in. (38 cm).

GAFFTOPSAIL POMPANO *Trachinotus rhodopus*   p. 210
Body deep, compressed. Narrow bars on side. Spinous dorsal fin
low. 2nd dorsal and anal fins high, with a pointed lobe at front. To
2 ft. (61 cm).

PACIFIC MOONFISH *Selene peruviana*   p. 209
Strongly compressed. Forehead high, humped. To $11\frac{1}{4}$ in. (29 cm).

YELLOWTAIL *Seriola lalandi*   p. 209
Yellow side stripe. Spinous dorsal fin low. Anal fin begins well behind front of 2nd dorsal fin. No scutes on lateral line. To 5 ft.
(152 cm).

PILOTFISH *Naucrates ductor*   p. 208
Dark bars cross body. Spinous dorsal fin low. To 2 ft. (61 cm).

ROOSTERFISH *Nematistius pectoralis*   p. 211
Spines at front of dorsal fin long, threadlike. 2 curved stripes. To
4 ft. (122 cm).

31

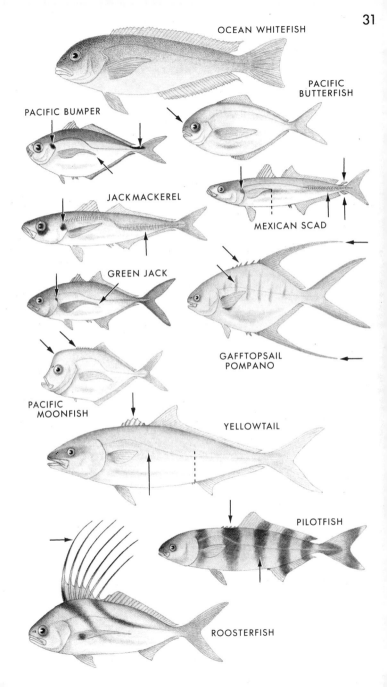

PLATE 32

Mackerels, Tunas, Billfishes

Rare mackerels and tunas are shown in Fig. 41 (p. 270). Note finlets in mackerels and tunas.

PACIFIC MACKEREL *Scomber japonicus*   p. 273
Dorsal fins widely separated. About 30 wavy oblique bars on back. Small — to 25 in. (64 cm).

PACIFIC BONITO *Sarda chiliensis*   p. 272
Oblique stripes on body. 7–9 finlets behind dorsal and anal fins. To 40 in. (102 cm).

SKIPJACK TUNA *Euthynnus pelamis*   p. 272
4–5 stripes on belly, none on back. To 40 in. (102 cm).

ALBACORE *Thunnus alalunga*   p. 274
Pectoral fin very long. Finlets not yellow. To $4\frac{1}{2}$ ft. (137 cm).

BLUEFIN TUNA *Thunnus thynnus*   p. 275
Upper back blue. No dark stripes. White spots and lines on belly. All of liver striated (see text). To $6\frac{1}{6}$ ft. (188 cm).

YELLOWFIN TUNA *Thunnus albacares*   p. 274
Pectoral fin long, reaches area below 2nd dorsal fin. Fins yellowish. 2nd dorsal and anal fins high in large adults. To $6\frac{1}{3}$ ft. (193 cm).

STRIPED MARLIN *Tetrapturus audax*   p. 278
Upper jaw spearlike. 1st dorsal fin long-based; 2nd dorsal fin small, far back. 2 keels at base of caudal fin. Light blue bars on side. To $13\frac{5}{12}$ ft. (4.1 m).

SWORDFISH *Xiphias gladius*   p. 275
Upper jaw spearlike, but flattened. 1st dorsal fin short-based; 2nd dorsal fin tiny, far back. 1 keel at base of caudal fin. Pectoral fin low on side, no pelvic fin. Large — to 15 ft. (4.6 m).

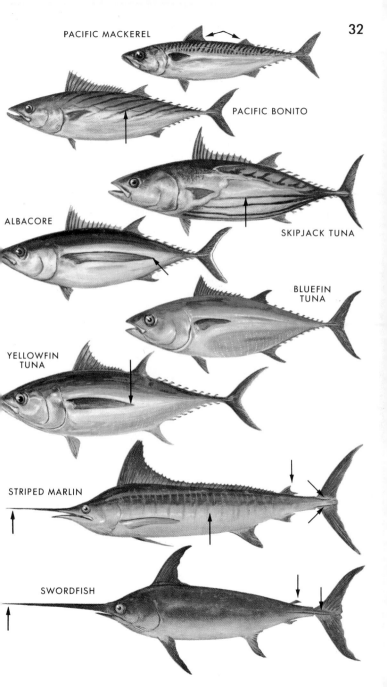

PACIFIC MACKEREL

32

PACIFIC BONITO

ALBACORE

SKIPJACK TUNA

BLUEFIN TUNA

YELLOWFIN TUNA

STRIPED MARLIN

SWORDFISH

PLATE 33

Croakers

Mostly silvery, basslike. Snout projects, except in first 2.

QUEENFISH *Seriphus politus*   p. 221
Our only croaker with a wide gap between dorsal fins. 2nd dorsal
fin base about as long as anal fin base. To 12 in. (30 cm).

WHITE SEABASS *Atractoscion nobilis*   p. 219
Black spot at base of pectoral fin. Young have dark bars on side.
Large — to 5 ft. (152 cm).

CALIFORNIA CORBINA *Menticirrhus undulatus*   p. 220
Short chin barbel. Pectoral fin large, fanlike. Belly flat. To 28 in.
(71 cm).

YELLOWFIN CROAKER *Umbrina roncador*   p. 222
Short chin barbel. Wavy dark stripes on back and side. Fins mostly
yellow. To 20 in. (51 cm).

WHITE CROAKER *Genyonemus lineatus*   p. 220
Usually more spines (12–16) in 1st dorsal fin than in other
croakers. Anal fin with 2 spines, 10–12 soft rays. Usually a small
black spot at upper base of pectoral fin. To $16\frac{1}{4}$ in. (41 cm).

SPOTFIN CROAKER *Roncador stearnsii*   p. 221
Black spot at base of pectoral fin. No chin barbel. 1st 2 spines (not
just 2nd spine) in anal fin strong. To 27 in. (69 cm).

BLACK CROAKER *Cheilotrema saturnum*   p. 219
Our only croaker with black on rear of gill cover. Young striped.
To 15 in. (38 cm).

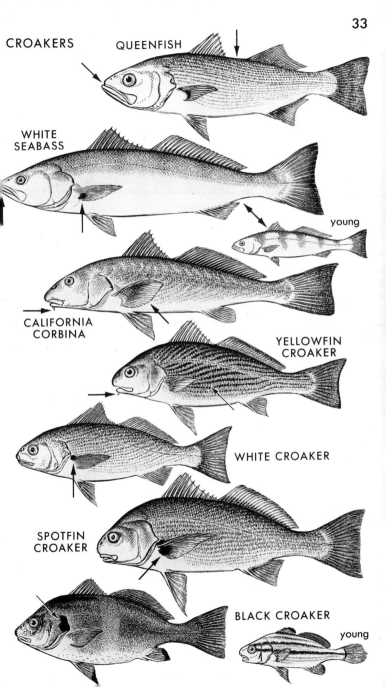

CROAKERS

QUEENFISH

WHITE SEABASS

young

CALIFORNIA CORBINA

YELLOWFIN CROAKER

WHITE CROAKER

SPOTFIN CROAKER

BLACK CROAKER

young

PLATE 34

Mojarra, Midshipmen, Sablefish, and Others

PACIFIC FLAGFIN MOJARRA p. 216
Eucinostomus gracilis
Perchlike; silvery. Caudal fin forked. Mouth very protrusible. Tip of 1st dorsal fin dark (clear in Silver Mojarra — see text). To $8\frac{1}{4}$ in. (21 cm).

LUMPTAIL SEAROBIN *Prionotus stephanophrys* p. 154
Head bony, ridged. Pectoral fin winglike, lower 3 rays free. To $15\frac{1}{2}$ in. (39 cm).

SPECKLEFIN MIDSHIPMAN *Porichthys myriaster* p. 107
Rows of tiny light organs. 2 spines in tiny 1st dorsal fin. Pelvic fin under head. Pectoral fins spotted. See photophore arrangement in Fig. 35. To 20 in. (51 cm).

PLAINFIN MIDSHIPMAN *Porichthys notatus* p. 108
Similar to Specklefin Midshipman but no spots on pectoral fin. See Fig. 35. To 15 in. (38 cm).

**Fig. 35
Midshipmen —
photophores on
underside of head**

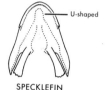

PLAINFIN SPECKLEFIN

OPALEYE *Girella nigricans* p. 223
Eye blue-green; body olive-green or gray-green, usually with 2 pale spots below dorsal fin. To 26 in. (66 cm).

ZEBRAPERCH *Hermosilla azurea* p. 224
Oval. Bright blue spot on gill cover; about 12 faint bars on side. To $17\frac{1}{2}$ in. (44 cm).

HALFMOON *Medialuna californiensis* p. 224
Mouth small. Bluish; darker above, sometimes with faint bars on side. Usually dark on upper rear of gill cover. To 19 in. (48 cm).

SABLEFISH *Anoplopoma fimbria* p. 154
Elongate. 2 dorsal fins. Scales small, weakly ctenoid. To 40 in. (102 cm).

SKILFISH *Erilepis zonifer* p. 154
12–14 spines in 1st dorsal fin. Scales ctenoid. Mostly black, with dirty white areas; young greenish with white blotches. To 6 ft. (183 cm).

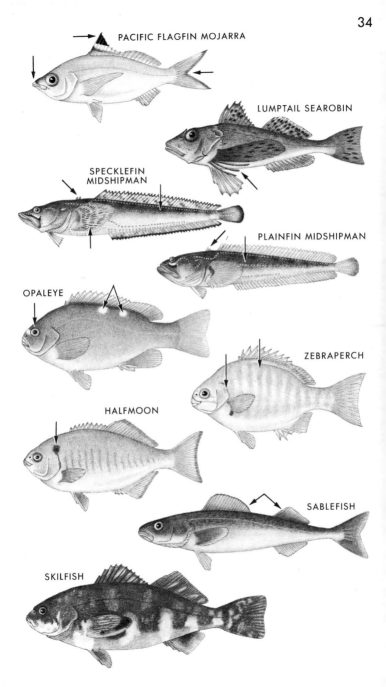

34

PACIFIC FLAGFIN MOJARRA

LUMPTAIL SEAROBIN

SPECKLEFIN MIDSHIPMAN

PLAINFIN MIDSHIPMAN

OPALEYE

ZEBRAPERCH

HALFMOON

SABLEFISH

SKILFISH

PLATE 35

Barracuda, Goatfish, and Others

STRIPED MULLET *Mugil cephalus*   p. 234
2 dorsal fins — 1st with 4 spines. Mostly silvery; chunky. Faint stripes on side. Mouth small. Fleshy translucent area around eye. To 3 ft. (91 cm).

CALIFORNIA BARRACUDA *Sphyraena argentea*   p. 235
2 widely separated dorsal fins. Mouth large, toothy. Snout long. Dark along lateral line. To 4 ft. (122 cm).

BLUE BOBO *Polydactylus approximans*   p. 235
Lower pectoral fin rays long, separate. 2 dorsal fins. Caudal fin deeply forked. Snout projects. To 14 in. (36 cm).

MEXICAN GOATFISH *Mulloidichthys dentatus*   p. 222
2 long chin barbels (often folded back). 2 dorsal fins. Red to yellow side stripe, with blue borders. To $12\frac{1}{4}$ in. (31 cm).

SALEMA *Xenistius californiensis*   p. 217
6–8 orange-brown stripes on side, darker in young. Dorsal fin deeply notched or fully divided into 2 fins (as shown). To 10 in. (25 cm).

SARGO *Anisotremus davidsonii*   p. 217
Mostly silvery, with dark bar on back. Mouth fairly small. Young (not shown) have 2 stripes. To $17\frac{1}{2}$ in. (44 cm).

PACIFIC SPADEFISH *Chaetodipterus zonatus*   p. 224
Nearly circular. Dark bars (faint in large silvery adults). To $25\frac{1}{2}$ in. (65 cm).

PACIFIC PORGY *Calamus brachysomus*   p. 218
Body deep. Mouth low on head. Rear teeth molarlike. Mostly silver, can change to blotched pattern. To 2 ft. (61 cm).

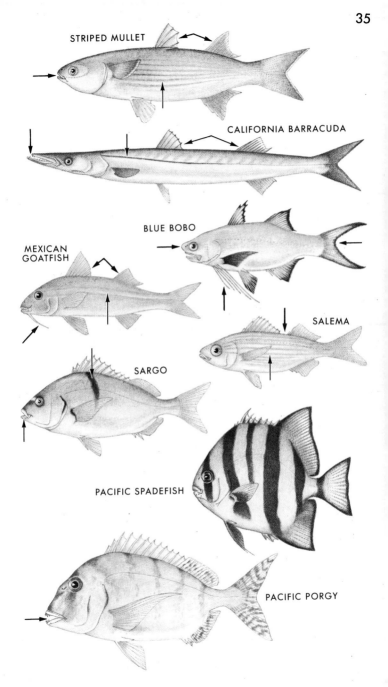

STRIPED MULLET

CALIFORNIA BARRACUDA

BLUE BOBO

MEXICAN GOATFISH

SALEMA

SARGO

PACIFIC SPADEFISH

PACIFIC PORGY

PLATE 36

Surfperches (1)

DWARF SURFPERCH *Micrometrus minimus*   p. 231
Black triangle at base of pectoral fin. Irregular dark stripe, crossed by barlike dark blotches. Usually a dark patch on dorsal fin. To $6\frac{1}{4}$ in. (16 cm).

REEF SURFPERCH *Micrometrus aurora*   p. 231
Black-edged scales on lower side. Black triangle at base of pectoral fin. To 7 in. (18 cm).

SHINER SURFPERCH *Cymatogaster aggregata*   p. 228
Silvery. 3 yellow bars (present in males only in winter — males darker in summer). Often a dark spot above lip (as shown). Horizontal rows of dark spots on side. Slight indentation above eye. To 7 in. (18 cm).

RAINBOW SURFPERCH *Hypsurus caryi*   p. 230
Colorful bars, stripes, blotches. Blackish area on soft dorsal and anal fins. Belly flat. Usually a dark spot at rear of upper jaw. To 12 in. (30 cm).

STRIPED SURFPERCH *Embiotoca lateralis*   p. 229
Orange and blue stripes. Blue spots on head and gill cover. Upper lip dark. To 15 in. (38 cm).

BLACK SURFPERCH *Embiotoca jacksoni*   p. 229
Patch of enlarged scales below pectoral fin. About 9 bars on side. Color varies; lips often orangish, with dark "moustache." To $15\frac{1}{2}$ in. (39 cm).

BARRED SURFPERCH *Amphistichus argenteus*   p. 226
Bars and spots on side. Caudal fin not red (see Redtail Surfperch on Pl. 37). To 17 in. (43 cm).

KELP SURFPERCH *Brachyistius frenatus*   p. 227
Lower jaw juts forward; mouth upturned. Slight indentation above eye. Rosy to coppery brown, often blue-spotted. Dorsal fin spines long. Usually a pale stripe on upper side. To $8\frac{1}{2}$ in. (22 cm).

RUBBERLIP SURFPERCH *Rhacochilus toxotes*   p. 232
Lips thick, whitish; lower lip with 2 lobes. Usually silvery to brassy, sometimes quite dark; usually with 1 or 2 faint bars in adults. Largest surfperch — to $18\frac{1}{2}$ in. (47 cm).

SURFPERCHES

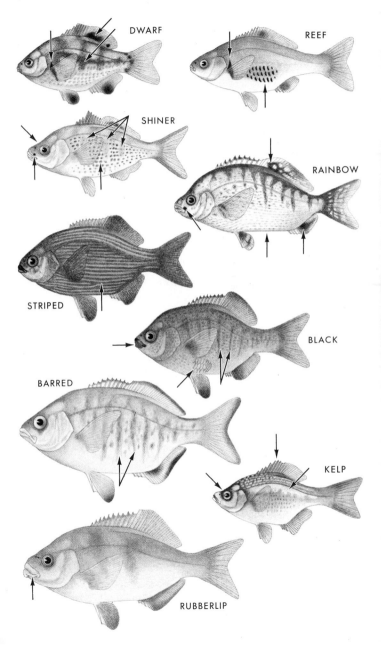

DWARF

REEF

SHINER

RAINBOW

STRIPED

BLACK

BARRED

KELP

RUBBERLIP

PLATE 37

Surfperches (2)

PILE SURFPERCH *Damalichthys vacca*   p. 228
Soft dorsal fin high, pointed at front. Usually a broad bar at
midside. Often a dark spot below eye (as shown). Scales on lower
side dusky. Caudal fin deeply forked. To 17½ in. (44 cm).

WHITE SURFPERCH *Phanerodon furcatus*   p. 232
Silvery. Thin dark line below dorsal fin. Often yellow at base of
lower fins. Caudal fin deeply forked. To 12½ in. (32 cm).

SPOTFIN SURFPERCH *Hyperprosopon anale*   p. 229
Silvery. Mouth oblique. Black spot on dorsal and anal fins; other
fins mostly clear. To 8 in. (20 cm).

SHARPNOSE SURFPERCH *Phanerodon atripes*   p. 231
Olive to sooty gray, with a reddish cast. Caudal fin deeply forked.
Anal and pelvic fins usually dark-edged. To 11½ in. (29 cm).

SILVER SURFPERCH *Hyperprosopon ellipticum*   p. 230
Silvery. Mouth oblique. No black on pelvic fin. Caudal fin usually
pinkish. Usually an orange spot on anal fin. To 10½ in. (27 cm).

WALLEYE SURFPERCH *Hyperprosopon argenteum*   p. 230
Silvery. Striking black tip on pelvic fin, especially in breeding
males. Mouth oblique. Eye large. Caudal fin usually black-edged.
To 12 in. (30 cm).

PINK SURFPERCH *Zalembius rosaceus*   p. 232
Pinkish silver. 2 dark spots below dorsal fin. Upper ray in caudal
fin often elongate in males (shown). To 8 in. (20 cm).

REDTAIL SURFPERCH *Amphistichus rhodoterus*   p. 227
Fins red, especially caudal fin. Bars on side. Longest dorsal fin
spines longer than soft rays. To 16 in. (41 cm).

CALICO SURFPERCH *Amphistichus koelzi*   p. 227
Most fins red. Vague bars on side. Dorsal fin spines no longer than
soft rays. To 12 in. (30 cm).

SURFPERCHES

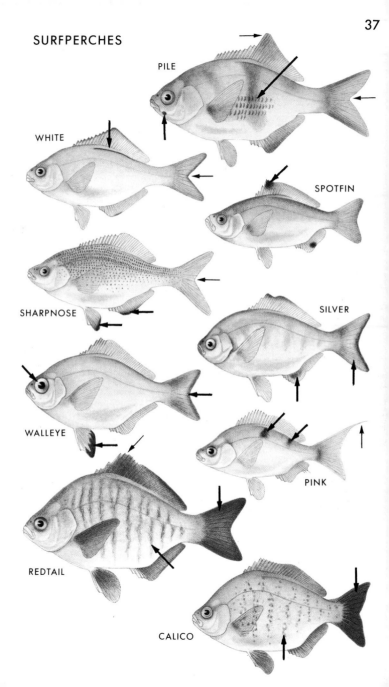

PILE

WHITE

SPOTFIN

SHARPNOSE

SILVER

WALLEYE

PINK

REDTAIL

CALICO

PLATE 38

Kelpfishes, Fringeheads

Some kelpfishes are extremely variable in color.

DEEPWATER KELPFISH *Cryptotrema corallinum*   p. 242
Pectoral fin long. Dark blotches on side. Red streaks. To 5 in.
(13 cm).

ISLAND KELPFISH *Alloclinus holderi*   p. 241
Pectoral fin long. No ocellus on dorsal fin. Soft rays in dorsal fin
evenly spaced. Middle rays in caudal fin branched. To 4 in.
(10 cm).

SPOTTED KELPFISH *Gibbonsia elegans*   p. 242
Dorsal fin high in front. Soft rays more widely spaced at rear of
dorsal fin. Ocelli often present on body. Color matches background (2 variations shown). To 6¼ in. (16 cm).

CREVICE KELPFISH *Gibbonsia montereyensis*   p. 243
Reddish to brown or lavender. Pectoral fin does not reach anal fin.
Soft rays at rear of dorsal fin more widely spaced than preceding
ones. No ocellus on dorsal fin. To 4½ in. (11 cm).

REEF FINSPOT *Paraclinus integripinnis*   p. 245
Dorsal fin all spines — no soft rays. Large ocellus toward rear of
dorsal fin. To 2½ in. (6.4 cm).

STRIPED KELPFISH *Gibbonsia metzi*   p. 243
Pectoral fin short, does not reach front of anal fin. Dorsal fin high
in front. Soft rays at rear of dorsal fin equally spaced. To 9½ in.
(24 cm).

GIANT KELPFISH *Heterostichus rostratus*   p. 243
Snout long. Caudal fin forked. No ocellus on dorsal fin. Color
matches habitat (2 variations shown). To 2 ft. (61 cm).

SARCASTIC FRINGEHEAD *Neoclinus blanchardi*   p. 244
Jaws huge (especially in males). 2 ocelli near front of dorsal fin.
Cirri above eye. To 1 ft. (30 cm).

YELLOWFIN FRINGEHEAD *Neoclinus stephensae*   p. 244
Jaws large, but shorter than in our other fringeheads. Branched
cirri above eye. No ocellus on dorsal fin. To 4 in. (10 cm).

ONESPOT FRINGEHEAD *Neoclinus uninotatus*   p. 244
Jaws large. Cirri above eye. Ocellus between 1st 2 spines in dorsal
fin. To 9¾ in. (25 cm).

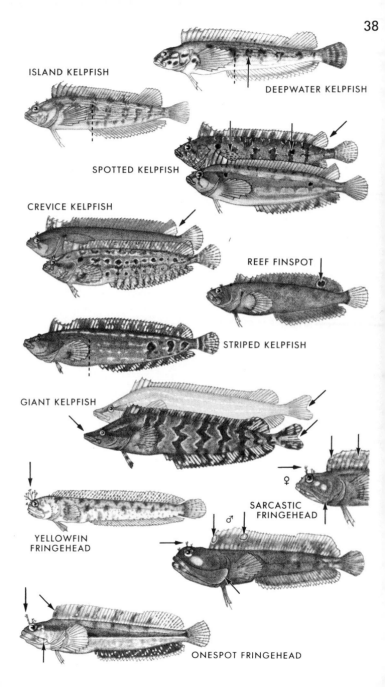

38

ISLAND KELPFISH

DEEPWATER KELPFISH

SPOTTED KELPFISH

CREVICE KELPFISH

REEF FINSPOT

STRIPED KELPFISH

GIANT KELPFISH

♀

SARCASTIC FRINGEHEAD

♂

YELLOWFIN FRINGEHEAD

ONESPOT FRINGEHEAD

PLATE 39

Pikeblenny, Blennies, Gunnels

ORANGETHROAT PIKEBLENNY p. 245
Chaenopsis alepidota
Elongate, unscaled. Mouth large. Throat often orange. Sexes differ in color (see text). To 6 in. (15 cm).

Blennies: Note blunt head, location of pelvic fins. No scales.

BAY BLENNY *Hypsoblennius gentilis* p. 246
Skin flap (cirrus) above eye serrated. Throat sometimes reddish. To 5¾ in. (15 cm).

ROCKPOOL BLENNY *Hypsoblennius gilberti* p. 247
Skin flap above eye divided into filaments. Lateral line extends to area above middle of anal fin. Head profile notched behind eye. To 6¾ in. (17 cm).

MUSSEL BLENNY *Hypsoblennius jenkinsi* p. 247
Skin flap above eye branched at tip. Lateral line stops above front of anal fin. Usually a curved bar behind eye. To 5 in. (13 cm).

Gunnels: Elongate. Long dorsal fin (spines only). Color varies. See Pls. 40–41 for look-alikes (pricklebacks).

LONGFIN GUNNEL *Pholis clemensi* p. 255
Anal fin long — longer than ½ body. About 15 pale saddles with dark spots at base of dorsal fin. Pelvic fin tiny. To 5 in. (13 cm).

KELP GUNNEL *Ulvicola sanctaerosae* p. 257
No pectoral or pelvic fins. Color usually uniform. To 11¼ in. (29 cm).

PENPOINT GUNNEL *Apodichthys flavidus* p. 255
1st spine in anal fin strong, pointed, grooved. Dark bar below eye. No pelvic fin. Pectoral fin large. To 18 in. (46 cm).

RED GUNNEL *Pholis schultzi* p. 256
Pale area bordered by dark bars below eye. Pelvic fin tiny. Anal fin often barred. Reddish to brownish. To 5 in. (13 cm).

ROCKWEED GUNNEL *Xererpes fucorum* p. 257
No pelvic fin. Pectoral fin tiny. Bright green to reddish or brownish; sometimes dark spots on side. To 9 in. (23 cm).

CRESCENT GUNNEL *Pholis laeta* p. 256
Crescent-shaped marks at base of dorsal fin. Pectoral fin large. Pelvic fin tiny. Bar below eye. To 10 in. (25 cm).

SADDLEBACK GUNNEL *Pholis ornata* p. 256
Dark U- or V-shaped marks at base of dorsal fin. Pectoral fin large. Pelvic fin tiny. Bar below eye. To 12 in. (30 cm).

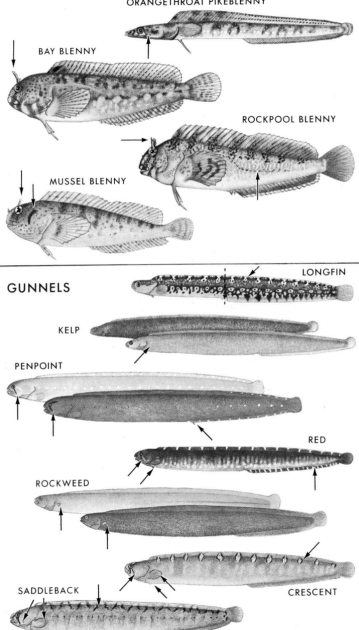

ORANGETHROAT PIKEBLENNY

BAY BLENNY

ROCKPOOL BLENNY

MUSSEL BLENNY

GUNNELS

LONGFIN

KELP

PENPOINT

RED

ROCKWEED

CRESCENT

SADDLEBACK

PLATE 40

Pricklebacks (1), Wolf-eel

MONKEYFACE PRICKLEBACK   p. 249
Cebidichthys violaceus
Dark streaks radiate from eye. Pectoral fin large. No pelvic fin.
Soft rays in last $\frac{1}{2}$ of dorsal fin. To $2\frac{1}{2}$ ft. (76 cm).

Rest of pricklebacks have only spines (no soft rays) in dorsal fin.

BLACK PRICKLEBACK *Xiphister atropurpureus*   p. 253
2–3 dark bars with white edges radiate from eye. Usually a white
bar at base of caudal fin. Pectoral fin tiny. No pelvic fin. To 1 ft.
(30 cm).

ROCK PRICKLEBACK *Xiphister mucosus*   p. 253
2–3 black-edged bars radiate from eye. Pectoral fin tiny. No pelvic
fin. To 23 in. (58 cm).

RIBBON PRICKLEBACK *Phytichthys chirus*   p. 251
Alternating light and dark streaks radiate back from eye. Pectoral
fin small. No pelvic fin. To 8 in. (20 cm).

SIXSPOT PRICKLEBACK *Kasatkia* species   p. 250
5–6 ocelli on dorsal fin. Caudal fin white-edged. Dark stripe
through eye. Pectoral fin large. Pelvic fin consists of only 1 spine,
or absent. To $5\frac{1}{2}$ in. (14 cm).

MASKED PRICKLEBACK *Stichaeopsis* species   p. 252
Dark stripe from snout through eye to area above pectoral
fin. Pectoral fin large. Pelvic fin present. Chocolate-colored. To
$12\frac{3}{4}$ in. (32 cm).

CRISSCROSS PRICKLEBACK   p. 252
Plagiogrammus hopkinsii
Platelike divisions on side. Pelvic fin large. To $7\frac{3}{4}$ in. (20 cm).

WOLF-EEL *Anarrhichthys ocellatus*   p. 257
Eel-like. Canine teeth in front; molars behind. No pelvic fin or
lateral line. Large — to $6\frac{2}{3}$ ft. (203 cm). Young striped; often
orangish.

PRICKLEBACKS

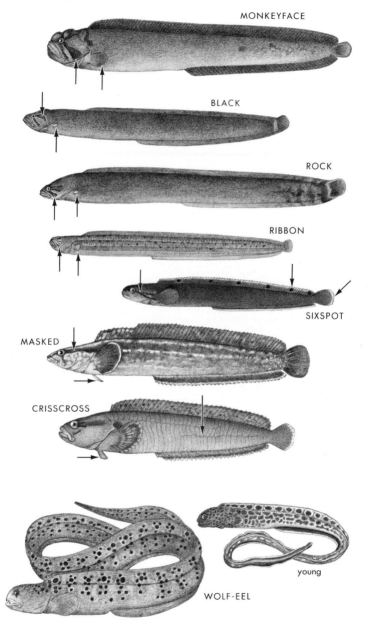

MONKEYFACE

BLACK

ROCK

RIBBON

SIXSPOT

MASKED

CRISSCROSS

WOLF-EEL

young

PLATE 41

Pricklebacks (2)

Note long dorsal and anal fins; small rounded caudal fin.

Y-PRICKLEBACK *Allolumpenus hypochromus*   p. 248
Spots on lower side form Y's. About 5 spots at base of dorsal fin.
To 3 in. (7.6 cm).

DAUBED SHANNY *Lumpenus maculatus*   p. 251
Snout overhangs mouth. Pectoral fin large; lower rays free of
membrane at tip. Dark spots on side. To $7\frac{1}{8}$ in. (18 cm).

STOUT EELBLENNY *Anisarchus medius*   p. 248
Diagonal bars on dorsal fin. Pectoral fin large. To $5\frac{1}{2}$ in. (14 cm).

SNAKE PRICKLEBACK *Lumpenus sagitta*   p. 251
Elongate. Greenish to brown streaks on side. Caudal fin barred. To
20 in. (51 cm).

LONGSNOUT PRICKLEBACK   p. 251
Lumpenella longirostris
Snout overhangs mouth. Dorsal fin spines stiff, tips free. To $12\frac{1}{4}$ in.
(31 cm).

PEARLY PRICKLEBACK *Bryozoichthys majorius*   p. 249
Long branched cirri above eye and on spines at front of dorsal fin;
few cirri on rear of head. To 12 in. (30 cm).

MOSSHEAD WARBONNET *Chirolophis nugator*   p. 250
Cirri on top of head. Males have about 12–13 ocelli on dorsal fin;
females (not shown) usually have bars, not ocelli. Dark bars on
cheek. To at least 6 in. (15 cm).

DECORATED WARBONNET *Chirolophis decoratus*   p. 250
Cirri on top of head and on spines at front of dorsal fin. Fins
barred. To $16\frac{1}{2}$ in. (42 cm).

BLUEBARRED PRICKLEBACK   p. 252
Plectobranchus evides
Pelvic fin long. Pectoral fin angular. Blue bars on side. 2–3 black
spots or ocelli on rear of dorsal fin. To $5\frac{1}{4}$ in. (13 cm).

WHITEBARRED PRICKLEBACK   p. 252
Poroclinus rothrocki
About 10–12 white bars with dark brown or blackish borders on
upper back. To 10 in. (25 cm).

SLENDER COCKSCOMB *Anoplarchus insignis*   p. 248
Fleshy crest on head. No pelvic fin. 40–46 rays in anal fin. To $4\frac{3}{4}$ in.
(12 cm).

HIGH COCKSCOMB *Anoplarchus purpurescens*   p. 249
Similar to Slender Cockscomb but with 41 or fewer rays in anal fin.
To $7\frac{3}{4}$ in. (20 cm).

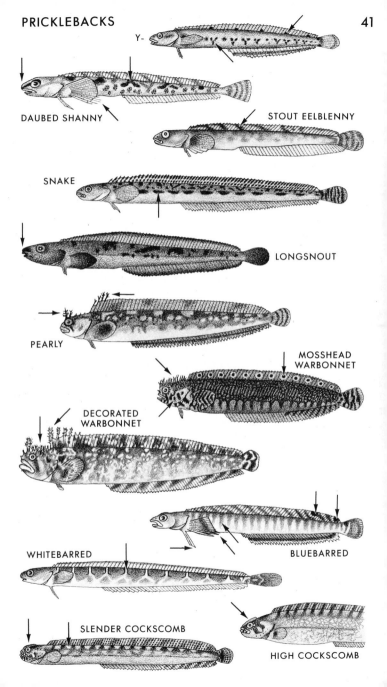

Y-

DAUBED SHANNY

STOUT EELBLENNY

SNAKE

LONGSNOUT

PEARLY

MOSSHEAD WARBONNET

DECORATED WARBONNET

WHITEBARRED

BLUEBARRED

SLENDER COCKSCOMB

HIGH COCKSCOMB

PLATE 42

Wrymouths, Ronquils, and Others

GIANT WRYMOUTH *Delolepis gigantea*   p. 254
Dorsal and anal fins join rounded caudal fin. Mouth upturned. No pelvic fin. Scaled. Spotted. To 46 in. (117 cm).

DWARF WRYMOUTH *Lyconectes aleutensis*   p. 254
Similar to Giant Wrymouth but without scales; mostly plain red or pink. Long nasal tube in front of eye. To 12 in. (30 cm).

GRAVELDIVER *Scytalina cerdale*   p. 259
Dorsal and anal fins begin at midbody and join caudal fin. No pelvic fin. No scales. To 6 in. (15 cm).

PACIFIC SAND LANCE *Ammodytes hexapterus*   p. 259
Lower jaw projects. Lateral line high on back. Fold of skin along belly. Caudal fin small, forked. To 8 in. (20 cm).

QUILLFISH *Ptilichthys goodei*   p. 258
Long, slender. Row of short hooked spines from head to front of soft dorsal fin. Tail threadlike. To $13\frac{1}{2}$ in. (34 cm).

PROWFISH *Zaprora silenus*   p. 258
Head blunt, with large white-ringed pores. No pelvic fin. Caudal fin large. To $34\frac{1}{2}$ in. (88 cm).

SMALLMOUTH RONQUIL *Bathymaster leurolepis*   p. 239
Mouth smaller than in other ronquils. Faint bars on side. To $8\frac{1}{4}$ in. (21 cm).

STRIPEFIN RONQUIL *Rathbunella hypoplecta*   p. 239
Yellow and blue stripes on anal fin. Pectoral fin does not reach front of anal fin. (See text for additional ronquils.) To $6\frac{1}{2}$ in. (16 cm).

NORTHERN RONQUIL *Ronquilus jordani*   p. 240
1st 20–30 rays in dorsal fin unbranched. Scales nearly smooth, embedded. Dark between eyes and before dorsal fin. To 7 in. (18 cm).

ALASKAN RONQUIL *Bathymaster caeruleofasciatus*   p. 238
Bluish green bars on side. Dark spot on gill cover in young (shown). Scales ctenoid, no scales on cheek. To 12 in. (30 cm).

SEARCHER *Bathymaster signatus*   p. 239
Dark patch at front of dorsal fin. Scales ctenoid. To 12 in. (30 cm).

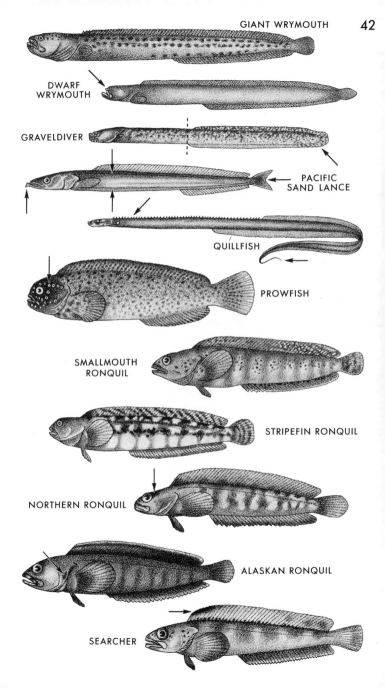

GIANT WRYMOUTH

42

DWARF WRYMOUTH

GRAVELDIVER

PACIFIC SAND LANCE

QUILLFISH

PROWFISH

SMALLMOUTH RONQUIL

STRIPEFIN RONQUIL

NORTHERN RONQUIL

ALASKAN RONQUIL

SEARCHER

PLATE 43

Flatfishes (1)

Eyes usually on left side, except in last 2 species.

CALIFORNIA TONGUEFISH *Symphurus atricauda*   p. 294
Teardrop shape. Caudal fin pointed, joined to dorsal and anal fins.
Mouth small, twisted to eyed side. To 8¼ in. (21 cm).
PACIFIC SANDDAB *Citharichthys sordidus*   p. 284
Pectoral fin on eyed side shorter than length of head. Bony ridge
above lower eye. To 16 in. (41 cm).
SPECKLED SANDDAB *Citharichthys stigmaeus*   p. 284
Brown or tan, with black speckles and spots. Pectoral fin on eyed
side shorter than length of head. Small — to 6¾ in. (17 cm).
LONGFIN SANDDAB *Citharichthys xanthostigma*   p. 285
Pectoral fin on eyed side very long. To 10 in. (25 cm).
FANTAIL SOLE *Xystreurys liolepis*   p. 286
Mouth small. Pectoral fin on eyed side longer than length of head.
Lateral line arched over pectoral fin. To 21 in. (53 cm).
BIGMOUTH SOLE *Hippoglossina stomata*   p. 285
Mouth large. Lateral line arched over pectoral fin. Dark blotches
on back. Often with bluish speckles. To 15¾ in. (40 cm).

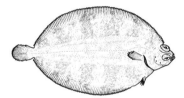

Fig. 36 Deepsea Sole (*Embassichthys bathybius*)

In next 2 species, eyes can be on either side (see variations).

STARRY FLOUNDER *Platichthys stellatus*   p. 291
Black and yellow bands on dorsal, anal, and caudal fins. Rough
scaly plates on eyed side. To 3 ft. (91 cm).
CALIFORNIA HALIBUT *Paralichthys californicus*   p. 285
Lateral line arched over pectoral fin. Caudal fin slightly indented
at top and bottom, not evenly rounded. Mouth large. To 5 ft.
(152 cm).

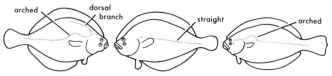

Fig. 37 Flatfishes — lateral line

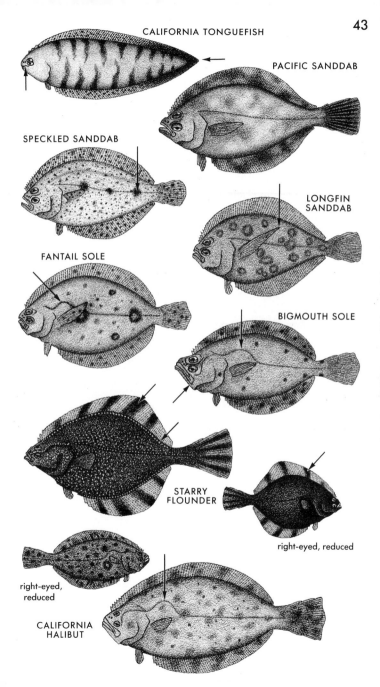

CALIFORNIA TONGUEFISH

PACIFIC SANDDAB

SPECKLED SANDDAB

LONGFIN SANDDAB

FANTAIL SOLE

BIGMOUTH SOLE

STARRY FLOUNDER

right-eyed, reduced

right-eyed, reduced

CALIFORNIA HALIBUT

PLATE 44

Flatfishes (2)

Eyes on right side. Note dorsal branch of lateral line. First 5 species oval to diamond-shaped, with long branch to lateral line.

DIAMOND TURBOT *Hypsopsetta guttulata* p. 289
Often blue-spotted; yellow around mouth on blind side. To 18 in. (46 cm).

C-O TURBOT *Pleuronichthys coenosus* p. 292
Spot on caudal fin preceded by a curved dark bar (forms upside-down "C O" when viewed from above). Usually a dark spot at midside. To 14 in. (36 cm).

SPOTTED TURBOT *Pleuronichthys ritteri* p. 293
Usually 1–2 large dark spots at midside, and 2 other spots at end of dorsal and anal fins. About first 6 rays in dorsal fin on blind side (Fig. 38). To $11\frac{1}{2}$ in. (29 cm).

about 9 rays on blind side; 1st ray at level of mouth

CURLFIN TURBOT

4–6 rays on blind side; 1st ray above level of mouth

HORNYHEAD, SPOTTED, AND C-O TURBOT

Fig. 38 Turbots — dorsal fin rays on blind side

HORNYHEAD TURBOT *Pleuronichthys verticalis* p. 293
First 4–6 rays in dorsal fin on blind side (Fig. 38). Ridge between eyes, with a spine at each end. To $14\frac{1}{2}$ in. (37 cm).

CURLFIN TURBOT *Pleuronichthys decurrens* p. 292
First 9–12 rays in dorsal fin on blind side (Fig. 38). Ridge between eyes, with a spine at each end. To $14\frac{1}{2}$ in. (37 cm).

ENGLISH SOLE *Parophrys vetulus* p. 291
Snout pointed. Smooth scales on front half of body, rough ones on rear half. Upper eye visible from blind side. To $22\frac{1}{2}$ in. (57 cm).

In next 4 species dorsal branch of lateral line is short.

HYBRID SOLE p. 291
Parophrys vetulus x *Platichthys stellatus*
Rough scales on both sides of body. Dark bars on dorsal and anal fins. To 18 in. (46 cm).

ROCK SOLE *Lepidopsetta bilineata* p. 289
Lateral line arched over pectoral fin. Rough scales on eyed side. Usually mottled. To $23\frac{1}{2}$ in. (60 cm).

BUTTER SOLE *Isopsetta isolepis* p. 289
Lateral line slightly arched over pectoral fin. Edges of dorsal and anal fins yellowish. Rough scales on eyed side. To $21\frac{3}{4}$ in. (55 cm).

SAND SOLE *Psettichthys melanostictus* p. 293
Rays at front of dorsal fin free of membrane. Mouth large; jaw extends to middle of eye. To $24\frac{3}{4}$ in. (63 cm).

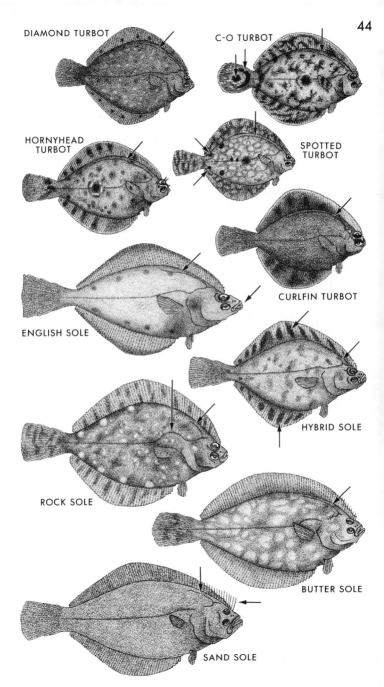

DIAMOND TURBOT

C-O TURBOT

44

HORNYHEAD TURBOT

SPOTTED TURBOT

CURLFIN TURBOT

ENGLISH SOLE

HYBRID SOLE

ROCK SOLE

BUTTER SOLE

SAND SOLE

PLATE 45

Flatfishes (3)

Eyes usually on right side. No dorsal branch to lateral line.

REX SOLE *Glyptocephalus zachirus*   p. 288
Body very flat (strongly compressed). Mouth small. Pectoral fin
long. Fins dark-edged. To 23¼ in. (59 cm).

SLENDER SOLE *Lyopsetta exilis*   p. 290
Slender. Jaw extends below eye. Scales large, easily lost. To 13¾ in.
(35 cm).

DOVER SOLE *Microstomus pacificus*   p. 290
Slim, flaccid, slimy. Mouth small. Lateral line nearly straight. To
2½ ft. (76 cm).

YELLOWFIN SOLE *Limanda aspera*   p. 290
Yellowish, usually spotted. Dorsal and anal fins yellow with dark
bars. Fins scaled. Rough scales on both sides of body. Lateral line
arched over pectoral fin. B.C. northward. To 17½ in. (44 cm).

FLATHEAD SOLE *Hippoglossoides elassodon*   p. 288
Thin, very flat. Often blotched. Pores under lower eye. Jaw long,
extends below eye. Teeth white, in 1 row on upper jaw. To 1½ ft.
(46 cm).

PETRALE SOLE *Eopsetta jordani*   p. 287
Jaw ends below middle of eye. 2 rows of teeth on upper jaw. Faint
blotches on dorsal and anal fins. To 27½ in. (70 cm).

ARROWTOOTH FLOUNDER *Atheresthes stomias*   p. 286
Mouth large. Teeth large, in 2 rows on upper jaw. Eye large.
Caudal fin slightly indented. Blind side mostly white. To 2¾ ft.
(84 cm).

GREENLAND HALIBUT   p. 294
Reinhardtius hippoglossoides
Dark; blind side mostly dusky. Eyes far apart. Mouth large. 1 row
of large teeth on each jaw. Caudal fin slightly indented. To 3 ft.
(91 cm).

PACIFIC HALIBUT *Hippoglossus stenolepis*   p. 288
Jaw ends below middle of eye. Lateral line arched over pectoral fin.
Caudal fin slightly indented. Large — to 8¾ ft. (267 cm).

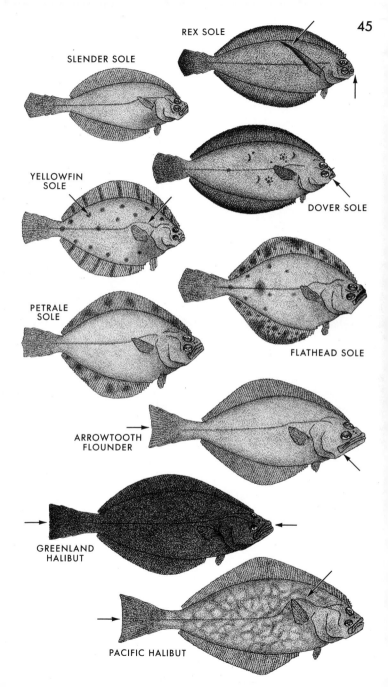

45

REX SOLE

SLENDER SOLE

YELLOWFIN SOLE

DOVER SOLE

PETRALE SOLE

FLATHEAD SOLE

ARROWTOOTH FLOUNDER

GREENLAND HALIBUT

PACIFIC HALIBUT

PLATE 46
Deepsea and Oceanic Fishes (1)

RAGFISH *Icosteus aenigmaticus* p. 283
Limp. Eye small. Dorsal and anal fins long; no pelvic fin (except in young). Caudal fin forked. Young have a much deeper body, round caudal fin. To about 7 ft. (2.1 m).

MEDUSAFISH *Icichthys lockingtoni* p. 280
Limp. Gray to dusky brown, fins darker. Dorsal and anal fins long. Caudal fin round. Young pinkish, unscaled. To 16 in. (41 cm).

In next 4 species note gill slit, tiny mouth, fin location. See also Fig. 44 (p. 297).

OCEAN SUNFISH *Mola mola* p. 300
Rear end looks "cut off." Large — to 10 ft. (3.1 m).

BLACK DURGON *Melichthys niger* p. 296
Black, with a pale white to bluish band at base of dorsal and anal fins. To 20 in. (51 cm).

REDTAIL TRIGGERFISH *Xanthichthys mento* p. 296
Caudal fin red in males (shown), yellowish in females. 5–8 blue stripes on cheek. To 10 in. (25 cm).

OCEANIC PUFFER *Lagocephalus lagocephalus* p. 298
Back dark blue; side silvery, dark-spotted; belly white. Mouth small. To 2 ft. (61 cm).

CRESTFISH *Lophotus lacepede* p. 120
Silvery, fins crimson. Forehead points forward. Caudal and anal fins tiny. To at least 40 in. (102 cm).

OARFISH *Regalecus glesne* p. 122
Silvery, with black blotches and streaks. Dorsal fin red, high in front. Pelvic fin rodlike. To 35 ft. (11 m).

KING-OF-THE-SALMON *Trachipterus altivelis* p. 121
Elongate. Fins crimson. Dorsal fin high in front. Mouth small. Caudal fin small, upturned. Young blotched. To 6 ft. (1.8 m).

OPAH *Lampris guttatus* p. 119
Oval. Fins and jaws scarlet. Bluish silver, with white spots. To at least $4\frac{1}{2}$ ft. (137 cm).

DOLPHIN or DOLPHINFISH *Coryphaena hippurus* p. 212
Brilliant yellowish green, iridescent; sometimes barred. Dorsal fin long. Males have a high forehead (as shown). To $6\frac{3}{4}$ ft. (2.1 m).

LOUVAR *Luvarus imperialis* p. 279
Pectoral and caudal fins red. Front end blunt. Mouth tiny. Eye low on head, with groove in front. Has a caudal keel. To $6\frac{1}{6}$ ft. (1.9 m).

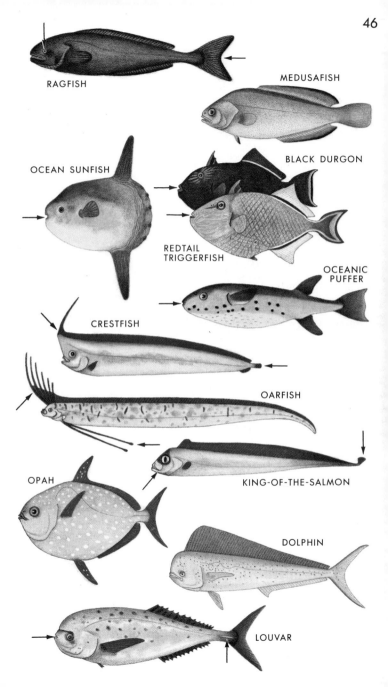

RAGFISH

MEDUSAFISH

OCEAN SUNFISH

BLACK DURGON

REDTAIL
TRIGGERFISH

OCEANIC
PUFFER

CRESTFISH

OARFISH

KING-OF-THE-SALMON

OPAH

DOLPHIN

LOUVAR

PLATE 47

Deepsea and Oceanic Fishes (2)

WHIPTAIL RIBBONFISH *Desmodema lorum*   p. 121
Silvery, fins mostly red. Extremely elongate. Tiny caudal fin at
end of long tail. No anal fin. To $3\frac{3}{4}$ ft. (112 cm).

TAPERTAIL RIBBONFISH *Trachipterus fukuzakii*   p. 121
Similar to Whiptail Ribbonfish but rear of body more straplike.
To $4\frac{2}{3}$ ft. (143 cm).

RAZORBACK SCABBARDFISH *Assurger anzac*   p. 266
Elongate, straplike. Pelvic fin tiny. Caudal fin small, forked. To
about $7\frac{3}{4}$ ft. (237 cm).

PACIFIC SCABBARDFISH *Lepidopus xantusi*   p. 266
Similar to Razorback Scabbardfish but body deeper, area between
eyes concave. Adults blackish; young — to 1 ft. (30 cm) — silvery.
To 3 ft. (91 cm).

SCALLOPED RIBBONFISH *Zu cristatus*   p. 122
Silvery, with vague bars. Most fins red, caudal fin mostly black.
Young shown; changes radically with growth (see text). To 41 in.
(111 cm).

PACIFIC CUTLASSFISH *Trichiurus nitens*   p. 267
Tapers to hairlike filament. No pelvic fin. To 44 in. (112 cm).

SMALLEYE SQUARETAIL *Tetragonurus cuvieri*   p. 282
2 spiny keels before caudal fin. Peculiar scales arranged in curved
rows (partly illustrated). To 15 in. (38 cm).

DAGGERTOOTH *Anotopterus pharao*   p. 92
No dorsal fin. Adipose fin tiny. Chin projects. To about 5 ft.
(1.5 m).

LONGNOSE LANCETFISH *Alepisaurus ferox*   p. 92
Long, slender. Dorsal fin sail-like. Adipose fin small. To $6\frac{5}{6}$ ft.
(208 cm).

SNAKE MACKEREL *Gempylus serpens*   p. 268
Straplike, blackish. Teeth large. 5–7 dorsal and anal finlets.
Caudal fin forked. To 5 ft. (152 cm).

ESCOLAR *Lepidocybium flavobrunneum*   p. 268
Lateral line wavy. Dark brown. 4–6 dorsal and anal finlets.
Reaches 6 ft. (1.8 m) or more.

OILFISH *Ruvettus pretiosus*   p. 269
Tunalike. Brown to black. Skin rough. Spinous dorsal fin low,
black. 2 dorsal and anal finlets. To $6\frac{2}{3}$ ft. (2 m).

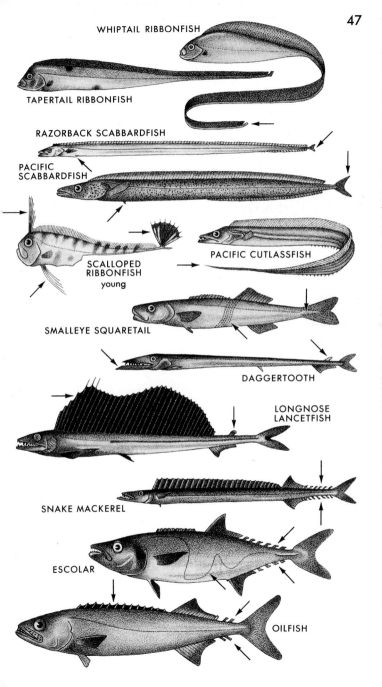

47

WHIPTAIL RIBBONFISH

TAPERTAIL RIBBONFISH

RAZORBACK SCABBARDFISH

PACIFIC
SCABBARDFISH

SCALLOPED
RIBBONFISH
young

PACIFIC CUTLASSFISH

SMALLEYE SQUARETAIL

DAGGERTOOTH

LONGNOSE
LANCETFISH

SNAKE MACKEREL

ESCOLAR

OILFISH

PLATE 48

Deepsea and Oceanic Fishes (3)

NORTHERN LAMPFISH *Stenobrachius leucopsarus*　　p. 94
Head blunt. Has tiny light organs and an adipose fin. To 5 in.
(13 cm). (See lanternfishes, p. 94.)

SILVER HATCHETFISH *Argyropelecus lychnus*　　p. 85
Hatchet-shaped. Mouth points upward. Large light organs. (See
hatchetfishes, p. 85.) To $2\frac{1}{3}$ in. (5.9 cm).

PACIFIC FANFISH *Pteraclis aesticola*　　p. 213
Peculiar shape. Silvery. Dorsal and anal fins huge, black. To 2 ft.
(61 cm).

PACIFIC POMFRET *Brama japonica*　　p. 213
Compressed. Head blunt. Dorsal, anal, and pectoral fins long.
Caudal fin large, forked. To 2 ft. (61 cm).

OXEYE OREO *Allocyttus folletti*　　p. 126
Eye large. Mouth protrusible. Granular scales at front of body.
Young oval, dark-spotted (Fig. 18, p. 127). To 15 in. (38 cm).

MIRROR DORY *Zenopsis nebulosa*　　p. 127
Note scutes at base of dorsal and anal fins; also on belly. Dorsal
fin spines elongate, especially in young. Mostly silver. To 19 in.
(48 cm).

PELAGIC ARMORHEAD *Pentaceros richardsoni*　　p. 225
Head bones striated. Usually 4 anal fin spines. Bluish brown to
gray; young have dark wavy lines. To 21 in. (53 cm).

PACIFIC FLATNOSE *Antimora microlepis*　　p. 100
Snout pointed, flattened. 1st ray in dorsal fin elongate. Small chin
barbel. Blackish. Anal fin notched. To $29\frac{1}{2}$ in. (75 cm).

SHOULDERSPOT GRENADIER　　p. 101
Coelorinchus scaphopsis
Tapered tail. Snout pointed. Spiny ridge below eye. 1st dorsal fin
short; 2nd dorsal and anal fins long. Spot above pectoral fin.
To $13\frac{1}{3}$ in. (34 cm). (See grenadiers, p. 100.)

PACIFIC GRENADIER *Coryphaenoides acrolepis*　　p. 101
Similar to Shoulderspot Grenadier but no spiny ridge below eye,
no spot, 2nd dorsal fin ray spiny. To $34\frac{1}{4}$ in. (87 cm). (See
grenadiers, p. 100.)

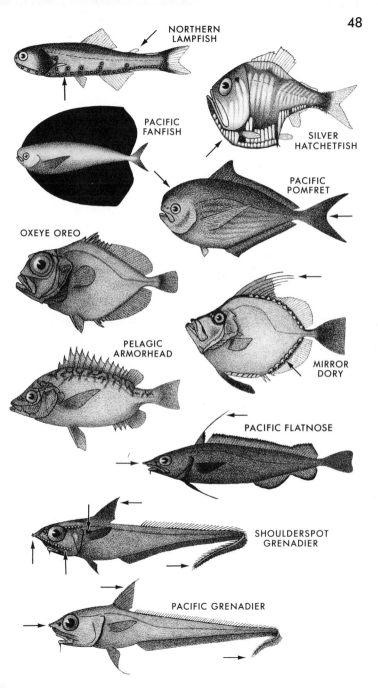

48

NORTHERN LAMPFISH

PACIFIC FANFISH

SILVER HATCHETFISH

PACIFIC POMFRET

OXEYE OREO

MIRROR DORY

PELAGIC ARMORHEAD

PACIFIC FLATNOSE

SHOULDERSPOT GRENADIER

PACIFIC GRENADIER

PACIFIC HOOKEAR SCULPIN   **Not shown**
Artediellus pacificus
Identification: A northern *unscaled* sculpin. 3 soft rays in pelvic
fin. Upper preopercular spine strongly *curved and hooked upward.*
Cirri above eye and on top of head; 1 cirrus also at rear of upper
jaw. 1st dorsal fin is high in males, lower in females. 3 wide dark
areas on back, whitish below. Side and top of head dark, with light
spots or wavy lines. Dorsal, caudal, and pectoral fins barred. To at
least $2\frac{1}{4}$ in. (5.7 cm).
Range: Bering Sea to se. Alaska. **Habitat:** Little known; mud and
sand bottom at 50–450 ft. (15–137 m).
Similar species: No other *scaleless* sculpins in our area have
such a strongly hooked upper preopercular spine.

Artedius species

Genus characteristics: The next 7 sculpins (*Artedius* species)
are small and have a band of scales on the back (see 3 variations in
Fig. 19, p. 159). Upper preopercular spine short, with 1 or more
points. 3 soft rays in pelvic fin. Anus immediately in front of anal
fin. Found in tidepools and inshore rocky areas.
Similar genera: (1) In Snubnose Sculpin (*Orthonopias,* p. 179)
anus is not just in front of anal fin (usually closer to pelvic fin base
than to front of anal fin). (2) *Hemilepidotus* species (p. 170; Fig.
19) have scales below lateral line. No scales in (3) *Clinocottus* species (p. 165) or (4) Cabezon (*Scorpaenichthys marmoratus,* p. 182).
(5) *Oligocottus* species (p. 177) lack scales except for minute
prickly scales on back in Saddleback Sculpin. (6) In *Icelinus* species (p. 171) the upper preopercular spine is antlerlike.

CORALLINE SCULPIN   **Pl. 18**
Artedius corallinus
Identification: No scales on head. Broad band of scales on back
(see *Artedius* 1 in Fig. 19, p. 159) — 39–49 oblique rows, with 10–18
scales in longest row; 3–10 scales between top (upper end) of pectoral fin base and lateral line. 15–16 rays in 2nd dorsal fin. 12–13 anal
fin rays. Grayish to brownish, mottled with red, purplish red, or
lavender. Blackish saddles with green borders along back. Golden-
red streak below lateral line. Roundish gray spots (with yellow
centers) on side, merging into gray below. Chin brownish, spotted
with yellow. To $5\frac{1}{2}$ in. (14 cm).
Range: Orcas I. (Wash.) to n.-cen. Baja.; fairly common in Calif.,
rarer northward. **Habitat:** Rocky areas; intertidal and to 70 ft.
(21 m).
Similar species: (1) Most like the Smoothhead Sculpin (p. 162).
(2) See also similar species under Thorny Sculpin, *Icelus spiniger*
(p. 174).

ROUGHCHEEK SCULPIN   Pl. 18
Artedius creaseri
Identification: Conspicuous *scales on top of head,* on snout, and below eye; but no scales on eye or barely visible ones. Nearly *fully scaled* between dorsal fin base and lateral line (see *Artedius* 2 in Fig. 19, p. 159). Upper preopercular spine single. Cirrus above front of eye. 12–14 rays in 2nd dorsal fin. 9–11 anal fin rays. Olive-green to light brown, with about 5 dark bars on back. To 3 in. (7.6 cm). **Range:** Carmel Bay (cen. Calif.) to cen. Baja. **Habitat:** Intertidal and to 90 ft. (27 m); rare.
Similar species: Most like the more northern Puget Sound Sculpin (p. 163) but it has visible scales on eye and 15–16 (rarely 14 or 17) rays in 2nd dorsal fin.

PADDED SCULPIN *Artedius fenestralis*   Pl. 18
Identification: Scales *on head* and cheek, and usually below *front* of eye. Nearly *fully scaled* between dorsal fin base and lateral line (*Artedius* 2 in Fig. 19, p. 159). Scales extend onto top of caudal peduncle. No cirrus above front of eye. 16–18 (usually 17) rays in 2nd dorsal fin. 12–14 anal fin rays. Usually pale orange or yellowish to greenish, with dark saddles on back; paler below. To 5½ in. (14 cm).
Range: Aleutian Is. to Diablo Cove (s. Calif.); apparently more common in n. part of range, abundant off B.C. **Habitat:** Intertidal and to 180 ft. (55 m).
Similar species: See Bonehead Sculpin (p. 163).

SCALYHEAD SCULPIN *Artedius harringtoni*   Pl. 18
Identification: Scales *on head,* sometimes on cheek, but not on snout. Broad band of scales on back (see *Artedius* 1 in Fig. 19, p. 159) — *38–51 oblique rows* of scales, with 9–16 scales in longest row. Cirrus above front of eye; head cirri more developed in males, smaller in females and young. 15–18 (usually 17) rays in 2nd dorsal fin. 10–14 (usually 13–14) anal fin rays. The only species of *Artedius* in which genital papilla of mature males is markedly enlarged to form a penis that terminates in a slender tapered tip. Color varies: brownish to olive above, with 5–7 dark saddles on back. Lower side has prominent roundish pale areas, merging onto white belly. Underside of head orange in adults. Red bars radiate from eye. Red spot near tip of 1st 2 spines in dorsal fin. Dorsal, caudal, and pectoral fins have brown spots arranged in bands. Anal and pelvic fins white to pink or red in females, dusky in males. To 4 in. (10 cm).
Range: Kodiak I. to s. Calif. **Habitat:** Intertidal and especially subtidal rocky areas, around pilings; to 70 ft. (21 m).

SMOOTHHEAD SCULPIN *Artedius lateralis*   Pl. 18
Identification: Profile of head steep (not rounded) in front. *No scales* on head. A *narrow band* of scales on back (*Artedius* 3 in Fig. 19, p. 159) — *18–29 oblique rows,* 3–11 scales in longest row.

No scales between top of pectoral fin base and lateral line. 15–18 rays in 2nd dorsal fin. 12–14 anal fin rays. Greenish to brown above, with about 6 dark saddles on back; cream to light green below. Pale spots on underside of head and body. Fins (except pelvic fin) barred. To 5½ in. (14 cm).

Range: Kodiak I. to n. Baja. **Habitat:** Intertidal and to 43 ft. (13 m); common intertidally.

Similar species: Coralline Sculpin (p. 161) has more scale rows on back and scales between top of pectoral fin base and lateral line.

PUGET SOUND SCULPIN *Artedius meanyi*   **Not shown**
Identification: *Nearly fully scaled* between dorsal fin base and lateral line (*Artedius* 2 in Fig. 19, p. 159). Head (including snout) scaled; visible scales on *upper part of eye.* Long slender cirrus above front of eye, 3–4 cirri (from 1 base) directly above eye. Upper preopercular spine has 2 points. 15–16 (rarely 14 or 17) rays in 2nd dorsal fin. 11–12 (rarely 10 or 13) soft rays in anal fin. Greenish to cream, with dark saddles on back and dusky smudges on underparts. Dorsal, caudal, and pectoral fins streaked with brown. Breeding males have dusky dorsal, anal (except first 2 rays — clear), and pelvic fins. Small — to 2⅓ in. (5.9 cm).

Range: Fillmore I. (se. Alaska) to Arena Cove (n. Calif.). **Habitat:** Intertidal and subtidal, on rocks or vertical rock faces at 5–269 ft. (1.5–82 m); rare.

Similar species: The more southern Roughcheek Sculpin (p. 162) has no scales on the eye; usually has fewer rays (12–14, not 14–17) in 2nd dorsal fin.

BONEHEAD SCULPIN *Artedius notospilotus*   **Pl. 18**
Identification: Scales on top of head and sometimes on cheek, but not below front of eye. A *narrow band* of scales on back (*Artedius* 3 in Fig. 19, p. 159). Upper part of caudal peduncle lacks scales or has scattered ones (not in rows). No cirrus above front of eye; larger specimens have a spiny lump at upper rear of eye. 14–16 (usually 15) rays in 2nd dorsal fin. 11–13 anal fin rays. Green to gray above, with dark saddles on back. Lower side mottled with roundish white spots, merging to white below. Rear of head often reddish. Black spot usually between 1st and 2nd spines in dorsal fin, also a spot at rear of fin. To 10 in. (25 cm).

Range: Puget Sound to n. Baja. **Habitat:** Intertidal and to 170 ft. (52 m); uncommon.

Similar species: Padded Sculpin (p. 162) has scales below front of eye, and scales (in rows) on upper part of caudal peduncle.

ROSYLIP SCULPIN *Ascelichthys rhodorus*   **Pl. 17**
Identification: The *only sculpin* in our area with *no pelvic fins. No scales.* 1 preopercular spine, hooked upward. Branched cirrus above eye. Dark olive-brown above; paler below. Lips and edge of 1st dorsal fin sometimes red. Other fins dark, but can have lighter edges. To about 6 in. (15 cm).

Range: Sitka (Alaska) to Pillar Pt. (cen. Calif.). **Habitat:** Tide-pools and rocky inshore areas on exposed coast. A very common tidepool species in some areas.
Similar species: All other sculpins in our area have pelvic fins.

CRESTED SCULPIN *Blepsias bilobus*   **Pl. 15**
Identification: Deep, compressed body. Most of body covered with *papillae,* each supported by a minute spine embedded on a platelike scale. *Cirri* on chin. 1st dorsal fin evenly rounded (not notched). 2nd dorsal fin and anal fin large, opposite each other. 15–17 pectoral fin rays. 3 soft rays in pelvic fin. Brown to olive-green above, with faint blotches on back; paler below. Pectoral fin has dark bars; other fins have dusky blotches. To 10 in. (25 cm).
Range: N. Sea of Japan to Bering Sea and to n. B.C. Rare; apparently more common in the nw. Pacific. **Habitat:** Near shore; details poorly known.
Similar species: (1) Silverspotted Sculpin (below) has white or silver marks on side, 11–13 pectoral fin rays, notch in 1st dorsal fin. (2) The 3 *Nautichthys* species in our area (p. 176) have similar papillae, but body is more elongate; no cirri on chin.

SILVERSPOTTED SCULPIN *Blepsias cirrhosus*   **Pl. 15**
Identification: Similar to Crested Sculpin (above) with a com-pressed body, covered with papillae, and long *cirri* on chin, but 1st dorsal fin is *notched.* Anal and 2nd dorsal fins large, opposite each other. 3 soft rays in pelvic fin. *11–13* pectoral fin rays. Brownish to greenish above, with dark patches on back; coppery red or yellow below. Reddish behind head. Dark bars radiate from eye. *White or silver marks* on side near pectoral fin. Fins brown to black, with large clear areas. Inside of mouth bluish. To 7½ in. (19 cm).
Range: Sea of Japan to Bering Sea and to San Simeon (cen. Calif.). **Habitat:** Often among algae; intertidal and to 120 ft. (37 m), more common subtidally.
Similar species: See Crested Sculpin (above).

ROUGHBACK SCULPIN *Chitonotus pugetensis*   **Pl. 16**
Identification: 1st dorsal fin deeply *notched between 3rd and 4th spines;* 1st spine very *long.* 3 (rarely 2) soft rays in pelvic fin. Rough scales on back and top of head (see *Chitonotus* in Fig. 19, p. 159). Note the *antlerlike* upper preopercular spine. Brown to gray-ish green above, with dark blotches and saddles on back; white to gray below. 1st dorsal fin black-edged; other fins often have dark bars. Often a red blotch on side in breeding season; some breeding males have a dark head and fins. To 9 in. (23 cm).
Range: Northern B.C. (and probably se. Alaska) to s. Baja. **Habitat:** Relatively common on sand bottom, also on mud bottom; intertidal and to 466 ft. (142 m).
Remarks: Aquarium observations suggest that this sculpin, like some others, is nocturnal and spends much of the time buried in the bottom with only part of its head sticking out.

Similar species: (1) *Icelinus* species (p. 171) have only 2 soft rays in pelvic fin, no notch between 3rd and 4th spines in dorsal fin, no scales on head. (2) The 2 *Gymnocanthus* species (pp. 169, 170) and (3) Pacific Staghorn Sculpin, *Leptocottus armatus* (p. 175), have no scales on back. (4) *Enophrys* species (p. 168) have platelike scales along lateral line.

Clinocottus species

Genus characteristics: The next 5 sculpins (*Clinocottus* species) have no scales — except for 1 species (Woolly Sculpin), which has minute prickles on the back. Upper preopercular spine short, with 1 or more points. Cirri often well developed on head. 3 soft rays in pelvic fin. Anus about *midway* between anal fin and pelvic fin bases or closer to pelvic fin bases (*not* just in front of anal fin). Anal fin usually begins below 2nd dorsal fin. Within this genus, note the head shape, number and location of cirri on head, and number of points on the upper preopercular spine. **Similar genera:** (1) In *Oligocottus* species (p. 177) the anus is located near or *just in front* of anal fin, and anal fin usually begins below 1st dorsal fin. (2) *Artedius* species (p. 161; Fig. 19) have scales in distinct rows on back. (3) Prickly Sculpin (*Cottus asper*, p. 167) has no cirri on its head or body. **Note:** Two other similar genera (3 species) occur in the Aleutian Is.: (1) Spineless Sculpin, *Phallocottus obtusus*, has a highly arched lateral line; a small, thin upper preopercular spine; 22 or more anal fin rays. (2) Kelp Sculpin, *Sigmistes caulias*, and (3) Arched Sculpin, *Sigmistes smithi*, have a highly arched lateral line, anus located *well ahead* of the anal fin, and 14–20 anal fin rays. Kelp Sculpin has 19–21 rays in 2nd dorsal fin and Arched Sculpin has 24–26 rays.

SHARPNOSE SCULPIN   Pl. 17
Clinocottus acuticeps
Identification: A small, *unscaled* sculpin with a pointed snout. The only *Clinocottus* species in which the inner pelvic fin ray is *attached* by a broad flap of skin to the belly. 1–2 cirri at rear of upper jaw. Usually has a well-developed cirrus on eye. No cirri between dorsal fin base and lateral line. Males have a thick penis-like structure that curves forward. Brownish to green on back and side; cream to white below. Silver to white on cheek. About 6 dark saddles (with light blotches between them) on back. Fins spotted or barred with light and dark (except pelvic fins, which are clear). To 2½ in. (6.4 cm).
Range: Bering Sea to Big Sur R. (cen. Calif.). **Habitat:** Common in rocky intertidal and subtidal areas, but also over sand and in eelgrass and seaweeds. Often found in waters of low salinity.
Similar species: In other *Clinocottus* species (below) the inner pelvic fin ray is not broadly attached to belly.

WOOLLY SCULPIN *Clinocottus analis* **Pl. 17**
Identification: *Numerous cirri* and minute prickles *on back.* 1-2 cirri at rear of upper jaw; *many cirri* on top of *head.* Upper preopercular spine has 2-3 points. Grayish green to olive-brown, flecked or spotted with white, yellow, and pink. Dark saddles on back. Pale below (yellow, greenish, or white), sometimes with dark specks. To 7 in. (18 cm) but usually much smaller.
Range: Cape Mendocino (n. Calif.) to cen. Baja. **Habitat:** Common in s. and cen. Calif. tidepools; to 60 ft. (18 m). Often among intertidal algae.
Similar species: See Mosshead Sculpin (below) and Bald Sculpin (p. 167).

CALICO SCULPIN *Clinocottus embryum* **Pl. 17**
Identification: A small, uncommon sculpin with *no cirri, prickles, or scales* between dorsal fin base and lateral line. No cirri above base of pectoral fin except on lateral line. Cirri on top of head, but none at rear of upper jaw. Upper preopercular spine single. *Small fleshy tubercle* at middle of upper lip (visible from above). Olive-green to pink or red or maroon above; mottled below lateral line, pale below. Brownish green saddles on back. Lips usually black at front. Dark bar across cheek. Fins usually have light and dark bars (except pelvic fin, which has dusky mottling). To $2\frac{3}{4}$ in. (7 cm).
Range: Bering Sea to n. Baja. **Habitat:** Intertidal rocky areas, most often in middle intertidal zone.
Similar species: Sharpnose Sculpin (p. 165) has 1-2 cirri at rear of upper jaw, inner pelvic fin ray attached by broad flap of skin to belly.

MOSSHEAD SCULPIN *Clinocottus globiceps* **Pl. 17**
Identification: A blunt-headed sculpin with *many cirri on top of its head,* covering the *entire* area between the eyes. Dense multiple cirri on front part of lateral line. No cirri on rear of upper jaw. No cirri, scales, or prickles between dorsal fin base and lateral line. Small patch of cirri between top of pectoral fin base and lateral line. Upper preopercular spine single, blunt. Reddish brown to olive-green above, with about 5 dark bars on back; tan to pale yellow or brown below. Fins barred or spotted with brown or olive. To $7\frac{1}{2}$ in. (19 cm).
Range: Kodiak I. to Gaviota (s. Calif.). **Habitat:** Common in tidepools and shallow rocky areas, often in strong surf. Sometimes seen resting on rocks out of water, but usually found under rocks or among seaweed.
Similar species: (1) Bald Sculpin (p. 167) has cirri only on rear half of space between eyes, but small specimens — less than $1\frac{1}{2}$ in. (3.8 cm) — of Mosshead and Bald Sculpins cannot be distinguished without great difficulty. If caught *north* of San Francisco, specimen is probably a Mosshead Sculpin; if caught *south* of Santa Cruz (cen. Calif.), it is probably a Bald Sculpin.

BALD SCULPIN *Clinocottus recalvus* **Pl. 17**
Identification: Blunt-headed, with *long cirri on head* — but covering only *rear half* of area between eyes. No cirri, scales, or prickles between dorsal fin base and lateral line. Small patch of cirri between top of pectoral fin base and lateral line. No cirri at rear of upper jaw. Upper preopercular spine single, blunt. Brown, mottled with white above; olive-green to brown below. Faint saddles (usually white-edged) on back. Often 2 pinkish spots on upper part of caudal peduncle. Some lavender or pink on head. Fins barred or spotted with brown and white. Young can be bright green. To about 5 in. (13 cm).
Range: Brookings (s. Ore.) to cen. Baja. **Habitat:** Common in tidepools and shallow rocky areas.
Similar species: See Mosshead Sculpin (p. 166).

PRICKLY SCULPIN *Cottus asper* **Pl. 16**
Identification: *No scales,* but sometimes partially or completely covered with rough *prickles. 4* (rarely 3) *soft rays* in pelvic fin. Upper preopercular spine short, curved. *No cirri* on head or body. Mottled black or brown, becoming white to yellowish below. 3 vague dark saddles below 2nd dorsal fin. Dorsal, anal, caudal, and pectoral fins usually have dark bars. Black blotch usually on rear part of 1st dorsal fin. Spawning males much darker overall. To 1 ft. (30 cm) but usually less than 5 in. (13 cm).
Range: Se. Alaska to Ventura R. (s. Calif.). **Habitat:** Fresh water, but sometimes in salt water near river mouths.
Remarks: Large individuals are reported to be excellent eating as well as good bait fishes.
Similar species: The combination of *4* pelvic fin soft rays, a *small* upper preopercular spine, and *no cirri* distinguishes this sculpin. **Note:** The freshwater Coastrange Sculpin, *Cottus aleuticus,* is occasionally found in estuaries. It is similar to the Prickly Sculpin but has a smooth body (or prickles are restricted to the area behind the pectoral fin), and all 4 nostrils are tubular (only front nostril of each pair is tubular in Prickly Sculpin). To about $5\frac{3}{4}$ in. (15 cm). Bering Sea and Aleutian Is. to San Luis Obispo Co. (cen. Calif.).

SPINYHEAD SCULPIN *Dasycottus setiger* **Pl. 16**
Identification: *Upright spines* on large head; large spine above eye and another spine on side, halfway between eye and dorsal fin. *Skin* flabby, *loose;* with prickly papillae *in 1 or 2* broken *rows below* dorsal fin. Large and small *cirri* scattered on body and head, including on snout and *lower jaw.* Upper preopercular spine short, stout. 3 soft rays in pelvic fin. Grayish, usually with brown spots or patches on back and side and dark saddles on back; brown to white below. Fins with black specks and dark bars. To 9 in. (23 cm).
Range: Japan to Bering Sea and to Wash. **Habitat:** Soft bottom at 60–400 ft. (18–122 m).

Similar species: (1) Bigmouth Sculpin (p. 171) has body covered
with small papillae, a flatter head, and dorsal fin spines free of
membrane at tips.

Enophrys species

Genus characteristics: The next 2 species (plus 2 more mentioned in Note below) have 3 (rarely 2) soft rays in pelvic fin; no
scales, except for the large lateral plates along the upper back; a
very long upper preopercular spine; and a blunt head with sculptured bony ridges. **Similar genera:** (1) *Hemilepidotus* species (p.
170; Fig. 19) have scale rows above *and below* lateral line. (2)
Gymnocanthus species (pp. 169, 170) have small, rough, platelike
scales on the head and peculiar T-shaped scales behind the pectoral fin. (3) The 3 *Myoxocephalus* species in our area (p. 176) lack
plates on the upper back. (4) The Cabezon (*Scorpaenichthys
marmoratus,* p. 182) has no scales and a short upper preopercular
spine. (5) See Flabby Sculpin, *Zesticelus profundorum* (p. 184).
Note: 2 additional rare *Enophrys* species are found in our area.
Both have a long upper preopercular spine, but with barbs on its
upper surface; and the total of the 2nd dorsal fin rays plus the anal
fin rays equals 21 or more. Habitat and depth poorly known. (1)
Antlered Sculpin, *Enophrys diceraus,* has 13–15 (average 14) rays
in 2nd dorsal fin, 11–13 (average 12) anal fin rays, and a long upper
preopercular spine (length equals distance from rear of eye to or
beyond large spine on top of head). To 6½ in. (16 cm). Bering Sea
to se. Alaska. (2) Leister Sculpin, *Enophrys lucasi,* has 13–14 (average 13) rays in 2nd dorsal fin, 9–11 (average 11) anal fin rays, and a
shorter upper preopercular spine (usually much shorter than the
distance from the rear of the eye to the large spine on top of head).
To 8 in. (20 cm). Bering Sea to B.C.

BUFFALO SCULPIN *Enophrys bison*   **Pl. 16**
Identification: One of the larger sculpins. Note the extremely
long upper preopercular spine. Lowermost preopercular spine
points downward. Lateral line scales *large,* platelike, *high* on back;
rest of body *unscaled.* Head bony, with prominent ridges. 9–13
(usually 12) rays in 2nd dorsal fin. 8–10 (usually 9) anal fin rays.
Greenish to blackish brown above; pale below. Usually 3 wide dark
areas on back. Pelvic fin clear. Other fins have dark blotches, spots,
or bars (fewer on anal fin); some individuals have orange on caudal
fin. To 14½ in. (37 cm).
Range: Kodiak I. to Monterey Bay. **Habitat:** Common in inshore
rocky and sandy areas; to 65 ft. (20 m).
Remarks: Feeds heavily on algae. Spawns in late winter and early
spring in low intertidal areas. Male guards egg cluster and fans
eggs with his pectoral fins.
Similar species: Bull Sculpin (below) usually has fewer rays in
its dorsal and anal fins.

BULL SCULPIN *Enophrys taurina*   **Pl. 16**
Identification: Closely resembles the Buffalo Sculpin (above), but with fewer fin rays: 8–10 (avg. 9) rays in 2nd dorsal fin; 6–7 (usually 7) anal fin rays. Olive-brown above, with blackish spots and vague lighter mottling; whitish below. Usually 3 dark bars on back. Dorsal, caudal, and pectoral fins marbled or spotted with olive-brown. Pelvic fin clear. Anal fin somewhat dusky. To $6\frac{3}{4}$ in. (17 cm).
Range: Off San Francisco to Santa Catalina I. (s. Calif.). **Habitat:** On bottom at 36–840 ft. (11–256 m).
Similar species: See Buffalo Sculpin (p. 168).

SMOOTHCHEEK SCULPIN *Eurymen gyrinus*   **Not shown**
Identification: A rare northern sculpin with *no preopercular spines.* Body somewhat flattened. *No scales* or papillae. Cirri on lower jaw, other parts of head, and on gill cover. 3 soft rays in pelvic fin. Spinous and soft-rayed portions of dorsal fin joined, with only a slight notch (if any) between them. 25 or more pectoral fin rays. Color varies with habitat: red, yellow, or gray, with dark bars or mottling under dorsal fin and on caudal fin. To just under 6 in. (15 cm).
Range: Japan to Bering Sea and to Kodiak I. **Habitat:** Virtually unknown; collected at 46–413 ft. (14–126 m).
Similar species: (1) Soft Sculpin (below) and (2) *Psychrolutes* species (p. 180) also have no scales or preopercular spines, but they are shaped more like a bubble or a tadpole and have no cirri on the lower jaw.

SOFT SCULPIN *Gilbertidia sigalutes*   **Pl. 18**
Identification: Small, *tadpole-shaped* body, with soft flesh, loose skin. *No scales,* but often has papillae on body. *No preopercular spines.* Dorsal fin *not divided* into 2 fins; front of fin buried, but tips of spines visible. 17 or fewer pectoral fin rays. 3 soft rays in pelvic fin. Pink to gray or brown; fins lighter. Pectoral fin sometimes orange. Vague dark spots or marks on body and fins. Eye orange. To $3\frac{1}{4}$ in. (8.3 cm).
Range: Bering Sea to s. Puget Sound. **Habitat:** Rocky areas and among sponges, also on soft bottom; near shore and to 738 ft. (225 m).
Remarks: Possibly more than 1 species is involved.
Similar species: (1) *Psychrolutes* species (p. 180) and (2) Smoothcheek Sculpin (above) have 19 or more pectoral fin rays.

ARMORHEAD SCULPIN *Gymnocanthus galeatus*   **Pl. 17**
Identification: Rather elongate. *No scales, except* for modified *T-shaped* ones behind pectoral fin and small, rough, platelike scales on top of head (often not well developed in young) that sometimes extend down onto gill cover and cheek. Upper pre-

opercular spine *antlerlike* (with barbs on upper surface). 3 soft rays in pelvic fin. Brown to tan above; paler below. Parts of head darker. 4 pale areas below dorsal fins. Fins with oblique bars. To about 14 in. (36 cm).

Range: Bering Sea to Wales I. (cen. B.C.). **Habitat:** Soft bottom, near shore and to 548 ft. (167 m). Apparently most common below 165 ft. (50 m).

Similar species: (1) Roughback Sculpin (p. 164) and (2) *Icelinus* species (p. 171) have a similar antlerlike upper preopercular spine, but they have scales on the back. (3) Pacific Staghorn Sculpin (p. 175) also has a similar upper preopercular spine but head is smooth; *4* soft rays in pelvic fin. (4) *Enophrys* species (p. 168) have a row of enlarged plates on the lateral line. **Note:** Threaded Sculpin, *Gymnocanthus pistilliger,* closely resembles the Armorhead Sculpin, but may be distinguished from it by comparing the total fin ray count of both dorsal fins, both pectoral fins, and the anal fin. If the *total is 81 or more,* it is an Armorhead Sculpin; if *80 or fewer,* it is a Threaded Sculpin. To 9 in. (23 cm). Japan to Bering Sea and to se. Alaska. Near shore and to 328 ft. (100 m).

Hemilepidotus species

Genus characteristics: The Irish Lords (*Hemilepidotus* species) are our only sculpins with a broad band of scales on the back *and also below* the lateral line (see *Hemilepidotus* in Fig. 19, p. 159). Normally *4* soft rays in pelvic fin. They are large-headed, robust sculpins. 4 short, simple preopercular spines. 1st dorsal fin notched between spines 3–4 (sometimes 4–5), 4th spine longer than 3rd. **Similar genera:** No other genus has similar scale bands.

RED IRISH LORD *Hemilepidotus hemilepidotus* **Pl. 16**
Identification: *Large.* 1st dorsal fin notched between 3rd and 4th spines. Scales on body in 2 main bands (*Hemilepidotus* in Fig. 19, p. 159): band on back is 4–5 scale rows wide (with much smaller scales above); 2nd band *below* lateral line, about 10 scale rows wide. Reddish, with brown, white, and black mottling above; whitish below. Usually 4 dark saddles on back. To 20 in. (51 cm) but rarely over 1 ft. (30 cm).

Range: Kamchatka (USSR) to Monterey Bay; common in Alaska, rare in Calif. **Habitat:** Usually near shore in rocky areas; intertidal and to 158 ft. (48 m).

Remarks: Most common species of this genus. Often caught on baited hook; good eating.

Similar species: (1) Brown Irish Lord (p. 171) has a wider scale band on back, 6–8 scales (not 4–5) scales wide. (2) Yellow Irish Lord (below) also has band 4–5 scales wide, but cirrus on upper jaw is slimmer (width equals *less than* $\frac{1}{2}$ its length; *more* than $\frac{1}{2}$ its length in Red Irish Lord). **Note:** A rare 4th species, the Longfin Irish Lord, *H. zapus,* is similar to the Red Irish Lord and Yellow

Irish Lord but has fewer (58 or less, not 59 or more) lateral line
pores and is much smaller — about 5 in. (13 cm). Bering Sea and
Aleutian Is. at 200–351 ft. (61–107 m).

YELLOW IRISH LORD *Hemilepidotus jordani*   **Not shown**
Identification: Resembles the Red Irish Lord in shape, scale pattern, and other features, but cirrus on rear of upper jaw is slimmer
(width equals *less* than ½ its length). Yellow-tan to dark brown,
with 4 vague bars on back; mottling on side. Most fins barred,
pelvic fin pale, but in breeding males anal, pelvic, and pectoral
fins are black. To 16 in. (41 cm).
Range: Kamchatka (USSR) to Sitka (Alaska). **Habitat:** Subtidal
and to 360 ft. (110 m).
Remarks: Fished commercially in the Bering Sea.
Similar species: Sea Red Irish Lord (above).

BROWN IRISH LORD *Hemilepidotus spinosus*   **Pl. 16**
Identification: Similar to Red Irish Lord but scale band on back
is wider (6–8 scale rows wide, with much smaller scales above) and
2nd band — below lateral line — is narrower (usually 4–5 scale
rows wide). Brownish, often tinged with red above. Dark saddles
on back. Fins mottled and barred with dusky. To 11¼ in. (29 cm).
Range: Puffin Bay (se. Alaska) to Santa Barbara I. (s. Calif.)
Habitat: Intertidal and to 318 ft. (97 m). Usually subtidal areas of
exposed coast.
Similar species: See Red Irish Lord (p. 170).

BIGMOUTH SCULPIN *Hemitripterus bolini*   **Pl. 16**
Identification: A *large* northern sculpin. Note the large flattened
head, with *blunt spines* and *knobby ridges. Mouth very large,*
lower jaw projects. Upper preopercular spine short, stout. Most of
body covered with prickles or papillae. Wide gap between dorsal
fins. No notch in 1st dorsal fin; 11–15 spines, spine tips free of
membrane. 3 soft rays in pelvic fin. Gray to brown above, with
vague saddles on back; paler below. Fins have dark bars or stripes.
To 27 in. (69 cm).
Range: Bering Sea to n. B.C. **Habitat:** Offshore at 402–708 ft.
(122–216 m). Often common.
Similar species: (1) See Spinyhead Sculpin (p. 167). (2) *Blepsias*
species (p. 164) and (3) *Nautichthys* species (p. 176) have similar
papillae but they have a compressed body. **Note:** Another *Hemitripterus* species, *H. villosus* (not shown), has been recorded from
Japan to the Bering Sea and Kodiak I. It has a deep notch and
more spines (16–19) in the 1st dorsal fin.

Icelinus species

Genus characteristics: The next 7 sculpins (*Icelinus* species)
have a *double row* of scales on the back (see 2 variations in Fig. 19,
p. 159). They also have prominent lateral line scales, an *antlerlike*

upper preopercular spine, and *only* 2 soft rays in pelvic fin. To identify species within this genus, note especially *where the double row* of scales *begins and ends.* **Similar genera:** (1) Our other sculpins usually have 3 or more soft rays in the pelvic fin. (2) Some *Artedius, Chitonotus, Enophrys,* and *Zesticlus* species can have 2 soft rays in the pelvic fin, but their scale patterns differ, or they lack scales, or the upper preopercular spine is not antlerlike. (3) Thorny Sculpin, *Icelus spiniger* (p. 174), has 3 soft rays in pelvic fin, a row of thorny spines at base of dorsal fin, and a hooked upper preopercular spine. **Note:** An undescribed rare species of *Icelinus* is known from off La Jolla (s. Calif.). It most closely resembles the deep-bodied species of *Artedius* and is currently under study.

NORTHERN SCULPIN *Icelinus borealis*   **Pl. 18**
Identification: Double row of scales on back begins under *1st or 2nd* dorsal fin *spine* and extends onto caudal peduncle (*Icelinus* 1 in Fig. 19, p. 159). Cirrus in front of eye, at base of nasal spine. 1 pore on tip of chin. Brown to gray above, with dark saddles on back; pale below. Brown bars or spots on head and fins (except anal fin). 2 dark patches on edge of 1st dorsal fin. To 4 in. (10 cm). **Range:** Bering Sea to s. Puget Sound. **Habitat:** Soft or shell bottom at 30–700 ft. (9.1–213 m) or deeper.

DUSKY SCULPIN *Icelinus burchami*   **Not shown**
Identification: Similar to Northern Sculpin (above), but with larger head pores and a shorter upper preopercular spine. Double row of scales on back begins under *5th or 6th* dorsal fin *spine* and ends under rear of 2nd dorsal fin. Pelvic fin tiny, extends at most $\frac{1}{3}$ of distance to front of anal fin. No scales behind upper base of pectoral fin. No distinct spines in area behind upper rear of eye (bumps may be present). Color in life unknown — probably brownish to blackish, with pale spots and irregular dark blotches on body and pale spots on dorsal and anal fins. To 5 in. (13 cm). **Range:** Behm Canal (se. Alaska) to La Jolla (s. Calif.). **Habitat:** Rare; offshore at about 200–1860 ft. (61–567 m). Most common near dropoffs; captured in prawn traps.
Similar species: See Northern Sculpin (above).

PIT-HEAD SCULPIN *Icelinus cavifrons*   **Pl. 18**
Identification: Similar to Dusky Sculpin (above). Double row of scales on back does *not* extend beyond rear of 2nd dorsal fin. 2 distinct spines in area behind upper rear of eye. Top of head with a shallow *depression* or pit (about the size of eye pupil). 12–15 rays in 2nd dorsal fin. Olive to red above, with darker patches; lower side with pale blotches. Base of pectoral fin black. To $3\frac{1}{2}$ in. (8.9 cm).
Range: Monterey Bay to Guadalupe I. (off n.-cen. Baja). **Habitat:** Sand bottom at 36–300 ft. (11–91 m). Uncommon.
Similar species: See Northern and Dusky Sculpins (above).

THREADFIN SCULPIN *Icelinus filamentosus*   **Pl. 18**
Identification: Largest sculpin in this genus. 1st 2 spines in dorsal fin usually greatly *elongate,* threadlike (sometimes broken). Double row of scales on back begins under *3rd or 4th* dorsal fin *spine* and ends under rear of 2nd dorsal fin. 2-6 scales behind upper base of pectoral fin. No distinct spines in area behind upper rear of eye (bumps may be present). No depression on top of head. Pelvic fin extends ⅓ or more of distance to front of anal fin. Brown to green above, with dark saddles on back; yellowish tan to light brown below. Males sometimes marked with orange. To $10\frac{3}{5}$ in. (27 cm).
Range: Northern B.C. to Cortez Bank (s. Calif.). **Habitat:** Common on sand and mud bottom at 60-1224 ft. (18-373 m).
Similar species: (1) In Spotfin Sculpin (below) 1st 2 dorsal fin spines also are greatly elongate, but 1st one usually longer (not both equal or 2nd spine longer); double row of scales short (ends *before* middle of 2nd dorsal fin); 2 distinct spines behind upper rear of eye. (2) See Lavender Sculpin (p. 175).

FRINGED SCULPIN *Icelinus fimbriatus*   **Not shown**
Identification: Double row of scales on back extends onto caudal peduncle. 2 pores on chin. Pelvic fin short — extends at most about ⅓ of distance to anal fin. Several cirri at rear of upper jaw; cirrus at nasal spine has an expanded, fringed tip. Pale olive brown, speckled with small irregular yellowish-green spots; silvery white belly. 5 dark bars on back. Dorsal, caudal, and pectoral fins yellowish green, barred with brown. To $7\frac{1}{2}$ in. (19 cm).
Range: B.C. to San Diego. **Habitat:** On soft bottom at 164-869 ft. (50-265 m).
Similar species: See Yellowchin Sculpin (below).

YELLOWCHIN SCULPIN   **Not shown**
Icelinus quadriseriatus
Identification: Double row of scales begins under *4th or 5th* dorsal fin *spine* and extends onto caudal peduncle. 1 pore on chin, no cirrus at base of nasal spine. Pale olive green with brownish wavy lines. 3 broad blackish bars on back. Dorsal fin barred with brown; black spot between first 2 rays in dorsal fin. Pectoral fin and caudal fin barred near tip. Anal and pelvic fins pale in females, blackish in males. Males have an orange-yellow chin and black gill membranes. To $3\frac{1}{2}$ in. (8.9 cm).
Range: Off Sonoma Co. (cen. Calif.) to s. Baja. **Habitat:** On soft bottom at 20-660 ft. (6.1-201 m); common off s. Calif.
Similar species: See Fringed Sculpin (above).

SPOTFIN SCULPIN *Icelinus tenuis*   **Pl. 18**
Identification: Similar to Threadfin Sculpin (above) — *1st 2 dorsal fin spines greatly elongate,* filamentous (sometimes broken); *1st spine longer than 2nd.* Double row of scales on back is short — begins *under middle of 1st* dorsal fin and ends *under front*

of 2nd dorsal fin (*Icelinus* 2 in Fig. 19, p. 159). 2 distinct spines behind upper rear of eye. Top of head more or less concave. 16–18 rays in 2nd dorsal fin. Light brown with orangish blotches above; white below. Dark saddles on back; dusky blotches on lower side. Silvery in front of pectoral fin; yellow on fin. Males have dark spot on 1st dorsal fin. To $5\frac{1}{2}$ in. (14 cm).

Range: Queen Charlotte Is. to cen. Baja; Alaska (?). **Habitat:** Sand bottom at about 108–1224 ft. (33–373 m).

Similar species: (1) See Threadfin Sculpin (p. 173). (2) See Lavender Sculpin (p. 175).

THORNY SCULPIN *Icelus spiniger*   **Pl. 17**
Identification: A single row of large platelike scales (each with a *thornlike spine*) on upper back from head to caudal fin. Lateral line scales large, with a spinous ridge at middle of each scale. Upper preopercular spine short, strong, with 2 points. Strong head spines. 3 soft rays in pelvic fin. Brownish above; pale below. Dark patches on back. To $7\frac{1}{2}$ in. (19 cm).

Range: Bering Sea to n. B.C. **Habitat:** On bottom at 102–981 ft. (31–299 m).

Similar species: (1) *Icelinus* species (p. 171; Fig. 19, p. 159) have a *double* row of scales on back, 2 soft rays in pelvic fin. (2) Other similar sculpins (such as *Artedius* species — p. 161; Fig. 19) have a wider scale band on the back. (3) Poachers (p. 185; Pls. 14–15) have body covered by fused plates. **Note:** Other poorly known species of this genus have been reported from Alaska and the Bering Sea, but are not treated in this guide.

LONGFIN SCULPIN *Jordania zonope*   **Pl. 17**
Identification: Slender, elongate. 1st dorsal fin long, with 17–18 spines. Anal fin long, with 23–24 rays; begins below *1st* dorsal fin. 5 (sometimes 4) *soft rays* in pelvic fin. Scales cover most of body above lateral line; scales below lateral line are in *fused oblique rows* (see *Jordania* in Fig. 19, p. 159). Upper preopercular spine tiny, usually not curved; lower preopercular spine strong, curved upward, sharp. Olive-green, marked with red. *3 dark bars* on cheek below eye. 6–8 dark saddles on back; large dark blotches on side. Caudal fin bright orange; pelvic fin dusky. To 6 in. (15 cm).

Range: Baranof I. (se. Alaska) to Diablo Canyon (cen. Calif.). **Habitat:** Rocky areas and kelp; intertidal and to 126 ft. (38 m). Frequently hangs vertically on rock faces.

Similar species: (1) *Triglops* species (p. 183; Fig. 19) have a similar body shape and oblique scale rows below the lateral line, but they have *only 3* soft rays in pelvic fin and *no bars* below the eye. (2) *Gymnocanthus* species (p. 169, 170) and (3) *Radulinus* species (p. 181; Fig. 19) have *only 3* soft rays in pelvic fin and *no* rows of oblique *scales below* lateral line. (4) Thornback Sculpin, *Paricelinus hopliticus* (p. 179), and (5) Thorny Sculpin, *Icelus spiniger* (above), have strong spines on scales on upper back.

LAVENDER SCULPIN *Leiocottus hirundo* **Pl. 15**
Identification: *No scales.* Upper preopercular spine has 2 points. 1st 2 spines in dorsal fin *elongate.* 3 soft rays in pelvic fin. Anus *midway* between pelvic fin base and front of anal fin (not just in front of anal fin). Some cirri on front of lateral line, on preopercle, rear of upper jaw, and at base of nasal spine. Mostly brownish or olive-green, with blue shading and reddish brown mottling. 3–4 brownish or reddish bars on side. Orangish brown below, often with pale spots. To 10 in. (25 cm).
Range: Gaviota Pier (s. Calif.) to n. Baja. **Habitat:** Inshore and to 120 ft. (37 m).
Similar species: Might be confused with other *scaleless* sculpins such as (1) *Clinocottus* (p. 165) and (2) *Oligocottus* species (p. 177), but their first 2 dorsal fin spines are *not* elongate. (3) Other sculpins with elongate dorsal fin spines have scales, prickles, or papillae on the body.

PACIFIC STAGHORN SCULPIN **Pl. 16**
Leptocottus armatus
Identification: A large, common sculpin with *no scales.* Upper preopercular spine long, *antlerlike.* 4 *soft rays* in pelvic fin. Tan to greenish brown or grayish above; yellowish to white below. Dorsal, caudal, and pectoral fins whitish yellow, with dark bars. Dark spot at rear of 1st dorsal fin. To 1½ ft. (46 cm).
Range: S. Bering Sea to n.-cen. Baja. **Habitat:** Common near shore, especially in bays and estuaries; sometimes enters lower reaches of coastal streams; most frequently on sand bottom; to 300 ft. (91 m).
Remarks: One of the few sculpins commonly caught on baited hook. Eaten by cormorants, sea lions, and other predators.
Similar species: Some other sculpins have an antlerlike upper preopercular spine — see (1) Roughback Sculpin (p. 164), (2) some *Gymnocanthus* species (pp. 169, 170), (3) *Icelinus* species (p. 171), and (4) *Enophrys* species (p. 168) — but they have 2–3 (not 4) soft rays in pelvic fin and scales in various patterns.

BLACKFIN SCULPIN *Malacocottus kincaidi* **Pl. 16**
Identification: Flabby; skin loose, nearly smooth, but with scattered prickles. 3 soft rays in pelvic fin. Upper preopercular spine short, stout, sharp. Head *knobby, large,* quite deep. Dorsal fins separated by a notch. Gray to light brown, with dark brown blotches and small light spots; bluish to black or brown below. Fins (except pelvic fin) usually white-edged, with 1 or more dark bars; in breeding season white edges turn golden. To 8 in. (20 cm).
Range: Off Bird I. (Alaska) to s. Puget Sound; also Japan.
Habitat: Usually on soft bottom at 89–902 ft. (27–275 m).
Similar species: (1) *Enophrys* species (p. 168) have enlarged lateral line scales. (2) Spinyhead Sculpin (p. 167) has well-developed spines on the head. (3) Bigmouth Sculpin (p. 171) has a wide flat-

tened head and papillae on the body. (4) *Myoxocephalus* species (below) have accessory pores above and below the lateral line pores (single row in *Malacocottus*). **Note:** A 2nd species of *Malacocottus, M. zonurus,* has been reported from within the range of the Blackfin Sculpin. It is said to differ in having an outward-directed spine at the base of the upper preopercular spine. Both species of *Malacocottus* are poorly known and might be the same species, but some small specimens have a more rounded head, suggesting that another small undescribed species occurs in our area.

GREAT SCULPIN   Pl. 16
Myoxocephalus polyacanthocephalus
Identification: One of our *largest* sculpins. Few scales, embedded in fleshy papillae; prominent on head and sometimes above lateral line. *Head wide; mouth large,* jaw extends to rear of eye or beyond. Upper preopercular spine *very long,* single. Lateral line pores paralleled by a row of pores both above and below. Olive with dark saddles above; paler below. Fins with bars or rows of dark spots. To at least 2½ ft. (76 cm).
Range: Japan to Bering Sea and to s. Puget Sound. **Habitat:** Sand and mud bottom; intertidal and to 800 ft. (244 m).
Remarks: A common sculpin, often collected near shore. Often confused with other rare species of the same genus (see Note below).
Similar species: *Enophrys* species (p. 168) have large plates along lateral line, shorter upper jaw (not reaching past eye), and no accessory pores next to lateral line. **Note:** 2 other rare species of this genus are known from our area (and at least 1 more in the Aleutian Is.): (1) 1 species was only recently discovered and is currently being described; (2) Plain Sculpin, *Myoxocephalus jaok,* is known from the Bering Sea to se. Alaska in shallow water. It differs from the Great Sculpin in having a more slender body, a much narrower head (when viewed from below), and a U-shaped (not rounded) mouth. To 1½ ft. (46 cm).

Nautichthys species

Genus characteristics: The next 3 sculpins (*Nautichthys* species) have 3 soft rays in pelvic fin, prickles covering much of body, small upper preopercular spine, head with knobs and ridges, and a diagonal stripe through the eye. **Similar genera:** (1) *Blepsias* species (p. 164) and (2) *Hemitripterus* species (p. 171) have similar prickly skin but have conspicuous cirri on the lower jaw.

SAILFIN SCULPIN *Nautichthys oculofasciatus*   **Pl. 15**
Identification: *1st dorsal fin high.* 2nd dorsal fin long (27–30 rays). 16–21 (usually 19) anal fin rays. 13–14 pectoral fin rays. *Black diagonal bar across cheek, through eye,* and onto cirrus

above eye. Brown to gray above; pale brown to cream below. Usually black blotches on body. Fins (except pelvic fin) with dark bars. Dorsal fin sometimes flecked with red. To 8 in. (20 cm).
Range: Kodiak I. to San Miguel I. (s. Calif.); possibly Japan and Bering Sea; common from Puget Sound northward. **Habitat:** Mostly on rocky bottom and often in areas with algae; inshore and to 360 ft. (110 m).
Remarks: This sculpin does well in captivity and is a popular display fish in public aquariums.
Similar species: (1) Smallsail and (2) Eyeshade Sculpins (below) have a much smaller 1st dorsal fin and fewer rays in the 2nd dorsal fin.

EYESHADE SCULPIN *Nautichthys pribilovius*   **Not shown**
Identification: Similar to Sailfin Sculpin (above), but 1st dorsal fin not high and sail-like. 2nd dorsal fin longer, with 22–26 (avg. 23) rays. 15–20 (usually 16–17) anal fin rays. *Rounded* spines on top of head. Mottled light olive with 1 dark bar below 1st dorsal fin, 3–4 bars below 2nd dorsal fin. 1st dorsal fin dusky, pelvic fin pale, other fins speckled. To about 2½ in. (6.4 cm).
Range: Japan to Bering Sea and to Stephens Passage (se. Alaska). **Habitat:** Little known; reported from 6½–413 ft. (2–126 m); usually found deeper than the other 2 species in this genus. Uncommon.
Similar species: (1) See Sailfin Sculpin (above). (2) See Smallsail Sculpin (below).

SMALLSAIL SCULPIN *Nautichthys robustus*   **Not shown**
Identification: Similar to Sailfin Sculpin (above), but 1st dorsal fin low. *Black bar across cheek,* through eye, and onto cirrus above eye. 19–21 (usually 20) rays in 2nd dorsal fin. 14–15 anal fin rays. *Pointed* spines on head. Pale brown with dark saddles on back; lighter below. Dark bar at base of caudal fin. Fins speckled and spotted. To 2½ in. (6.4 cm).
Range: Attu I. (Alaska) to n. Wash. **Habitat:** Sand and rock bottom and shallow exposed areas; near shore and to 240 ft. (73 m).
Remarks: Also known as the Shortmast Sculpin.
Similar species: See other *Nautichthys* species (above).

Oligocottus species

Genus characteristics: The next 4 sculpins (*Oligocottus* species) have *no scales* (except Saddleback Sculpin, which has minute prickles covering most of the body). Upper preopercular spine short, with 1 or more points. 3 soft rays in pelvic fin. Anus usually directly in front of anal fin. Common tidepool species. Within this genus, note whether body prickles are present; number of points on the upper preopercular spine; and number and location of cirri on head, when present. **Similar genera:** *Clinocottus* species (p.

165) are very similar but the anus is farther *forward* — closer to the pelvic fin base than to front of anal fin, or about midway between.

TIDEPOOL SCULPIN *Oligocottus maculosus*   **Pl. 17**
Identification: *Smooth — no prickles or scales.* Single preopercular spine, forked at tip (rarely with 3 points). Few cirri on top of head, no cirri between dorsal fin base and lateral line, no cirri on nasal spine. In males 1st 3–4 rays in anal fin large, swollen. Green to red above, with irregular dark saddles on back; white or cream tinged with green or blue below. To $3\frac{1}{2}$ in. (8.9 cm).
Range: Sea of Okhotsk (USSR) and Bering Sea to Los Angeles Co., but records west of the Gulf of Alaska doubtful. **Habitat:** Common in tidepools; prefers sheltered areas in intertidal zone. In areas with rough surf it inhabits the higher, more sheltered places. **Remarks:** A study revealed that individuals of this species can find their home tidepool even when displaced up to 335 ft. (102 m) and for a period of 6 months.

SADDLEBACK SCULPIN *Oligocottus rimensis*   **Pl. 17**
Identification: Mouth small; head blunt. Body covered with minute *prickles*. Single upper preopercular spine is blunt, often hooked upward. Cirri sparse on head, present on nasal spine, absent on body above lateral line. Olive-green to reddish brown above, with 5 irregular saddles on back; tan to greenish below. Mottled on side. Fin rays greenish; fins barred with red (except pelvic fin clear). To $2\frac{1}{2}$ in. (6.4 cm).
Range: Alaska to n. Baja. **Habitat:** Rocky areas and in kelp. Uncommon; usually taken from lower tidepools (farthest from shore). **Similar species:** Other *Oligocottus* species lack prickly skin.

ROSY SCULPIN *Oligocottus rubellio*   **Pl. 17**
Identification: Body *smooth,* with *no* prickles or scales. Single cirrus on nasal spine, 1–4 cirri at rear of upper jaw. Tufts of cirri on head, along base of dorsal fins, and on lateral line. Upper preopercular spine has 2–4 (usually 3) points. Reddish brown to pink or lavender above; greenish to brown below. 4–5 dark saddles on back; pale spots on side. Dark bars radiate from eye. To 4 in. (10 cm).
Range: Ft. Bragg (n. Calif.) to n. Baja. **Habitat:** Intertidal and subtidal. Uncommon.
Similar species: See Fluffy Sculpin (below).

FLUFFY SCULPIN *Oligocottus snyderi*   **Pl. 17**
Identification: *Body smooth,* with *no* prickles or scales. Single cirrus at nasal spine; tufts of cirri on head, along base of dorsal fins, and on lateral line. No cirri on upper jaw or below eye. Upper preopercular spine usually has 2 points (sometimes 3). In males 1st ray in anal fin is *enlarged* and 1st 2–3 rays are *separate* from rest of fin. *Color extremely variable:* green to reddish brown to pink;

side spotted and mottled; belly often bluish. White spots usually present on underside of head. Usually 4-6 dark saddles on back. Fins banded (except pelvic fin clear). To $3\frac{1}{2}$ in. (8.9 cm).
Range: Sitka (Alaska) to n. Baja. **Habitat:** Shallow rocky areas. Common in tidepools; often in algae.
Similar species: Rosy Sculpin (above) has cirri at rear of upper jaw and below eye.

SNUBNOSE SCULPIN *Orthonopias triacis*   **Pl. 17**
Identification: Head *blunt. Dense scales* on top of head and over most of back (see *Orthonopias* in Fig. 19, p. 159). *Anus far forward* (in adults, closer to pelvic fin base than to anal fin; in young, midway between those fins). Upper preopercular spine small but sharp, usually with 2 or more points. 3 soft rays in pelvic fin. Green to reddish brown or orange above, with dark and light mottling; white below. About 5 saddles on back. Black spot at front of 1st dorsal fin. To 4 in. (10 cm).
Range: Monterey Bay to n. Baja. **Habitat:** Intertidal rocky areas and to about 100 ft. (30 m).
Similar species: (1) In *Artedius* species (p. 161) anus is just in front of anal fin. (2) *Clinocottus* species (p. 165) and (3) *Oligocottus* species (p. 177) have no regular scales on upper back (though prickles — highly modified scales — may be present).

THORNBACK SCULPIN *Paricelinus hopliticus*   **Pl. 17**
Identification: A slender, elongate sculpin. *1 row of scales* (each with a prominent *hooked spine*) at base of dorsal fins. Most of body scaled — each scale has a small spine. Preopercular spines short and slightly curved. Hooked spines below eye. Anal fin longer-based than 2nd dorsal fin. Mostly olive-green; grayish below. 4-6 poorly defined brownish bars on back. 7-8 dusky purplish blotches on side. Yellow-brown flecks along lateral line, with series of blue spots below it. 1st dorsal fin barred with brown. 2nd dorsal, caudal, and upper part of pectoral fins mostly clear but with brown rays. Pelvic fin yellow toward edge. To $7\frac{3}{4}$ in. (20 cm).
Range: Hecate Str. (B.C.) to nw. of Cortez Bank (s. Calif.).
Habitat: Mostly on rocky bottom; near shore and to 600 ft. (183 m) but usually at depths below about 250 ft. (76 m). Rare.
Similar species: (1) Longfin Sculpin, *Jordania zonope* (p. 174), and (2) *Triglops* species (p. 183) lack hooked spines at base of dorsal fins, have oblique rows of scales below lateral line (Fig. 19). (3) Thorny Sculpin, *Icelus spiniger* (p. 174), has fewer anal fin rays (fewer than 20, not more than 20 as in Thornback Sculpin) and no scales below lateral line. (4) In poachers (p. 185; Pls. 14–15) body is encased in fused plates.

PORED SCULPIN *Porocottus bradfordi*   **Not shown**
Identification: *No scales.* Upper preopercular spine small and

slightly curved, ends in a single point. 3 pairs of cirri on head. 3 soft rays in pelvic fin. 12–14 pectoral fin rays. Many small pores on top and side of head. Lateral line paralleled above and below by *many smaller pores* scattered among larger pores. Males often have tubercles or serrations on inner pelvic fin rays. Dusky above; pale below. 4 dark bars on back. 1st dorsal fin dusky, other fins barred or blotched. To about $2\frac{3}{4}$ in. (7 cm).

Range: Bering Sea to Kodiak I.; 1 record from se. Alaska (?).
Habitat: Tidepools. Reported to be abundant, but little known.
Similar species: (1) *Clinocottus* species (p. 165) and (2) *Oligocottus* species (p. 177) lack the numerous pores on head and along lateral line. (3) *Myoxocephalus* species (p. 176) have 16 or more pectoral fin rays.

TADPOLE SCULPIN *Psychrolutes paradoxus* **Pl. 18**
Identification: Small, *tadpolelike,* with a large smooth head. Minute prickles in 2 rows on belly; otherwise unscaled. Stout papillae on head, body, and at bases of some fins, but flesh soft. *No cirri. No preopercular spines.* Front part of dorsal fin buried in skin. 3 soft rays in pelvic fin. 19–23 (avg. 20–21) pectoral fin rays. Brown to gray above; white below. Barred and mottled, with large black areas. Pectoral fin orange to pinkish or yellow, with dark bar. To $2\frac{1}{2}$ in. (6.4 cm).

Range: Northern Sea of Japan (?); Sea of Okhotsk (USSR) and Bering Sea to s. Puget Sound. **Habitat:** Soft bottom and possibly rocky bottom at 30–720 ft. (9.1–219 m); also reported near shore.
Similar species: (1) Blob Sculpin (below) also has no preopercular spines but grows larger, usually has 24–25 pectoral fin rays, and adults have no prickles on body. (2) Soft Sculpin (p. 169) has similar shape and also lacks preopercular spines but has 17 or fewer pectoral fin rays. (3) See Smoothcheek Sculpin (p. 169). **Note:** One or more possibly undescribed globe-shaped sculpins are known from very small specimens collected in midwater off Ore. Their pelvic fins are recessed into individual pockets in the skin, with only the tips exposed. To about $1\frac{1}{4}$ in. (3.2 cm).

BLOB SCULPIN *Psychrolutes phrictus* **Not shown**
Identification: A strange, *large,* flabby, *globular* sculpin. Skin *loose,* with prickles in young — to 2 in. (5.1 cm) — but none in larger specimens. Scattered cirri on head and body. *No preopercular spines.* Front of dorsal fin buried under skin. 22–26 (avg. 24–25) pectoral fin rays. Gray to black above, with vague mottling on head; paler below. Face whitish in large specimens. To about $27\frac{1}{2}$ in. (70 cm), 21 lb. (9.5 kg).

Range: Bering Sea to off San Diego. **Habitat:** *Very deep;* 2753–9186 ft. (839–2800 m).
Remarks: First captured in late 1960s off Calif. One specimen from very deep water had a plastic bag in its stomach. Feeds on sea pens, crabs, and mollusks.
Similar species: See Tadpole Sculpin (above).

Radulinus species

Genus characteristics: The next 4 sculpins (*Radulinus* species) are long and slender. Scales present on head and sometimes on cheek and snout; large spiny lateral line scales, 1–4 rows of smaller scales above lateral line (see *Radulinus* in Fig. 19, p. 159). Lateral line fairly straight (not arched). Upper preopercular spine small. 3 soft rays in pelvic fin. Within this genus, note the length of the snout and nasal spine and the number of dorsal and anal fin rays.

Similar genera: (1) Longfin Sculpin, *Jordania zonope* (p. 174), and (2) *Triglops* species (p. 183) have folds of fused scales *below* the lateral line (Fig. 19). (3) Manacled Sculpin, *Synchirus gilli* (p. 183), has pectoral fins *joined* at breast. (4) Thorny Sculpin, *Icelus spiniger* (p. 174), and (5) Thornback Sculpin, *Paricelinus hopliticus* (p. 179), have strong hooked spines near base of dorsal fin. (6) Poachers (p. 185; Pls. 14–15) have body enclosed by fused bony plates.

SLIM SCULPIN *Radulinus asprellus*   **Pl. 18**
Identification: *Slender,* slightly flattened. *1 row* of small scales above lateral line — from eye to below middle of 2nd dorsal fin (*Radulinus* in Fig. 19, p. 159). Nasal spine long and slender, needle-like. Snout short (length equal to or less than eye diameter). Anal fin long (21–25 rays). 20–23 rays in 2nd dorsal fin. Brown to green above, with 3–4 faint saddles on back; dark blotches below lateral line. Dark spot at rear of 1st dorsal fin. To 6 in. (15 cm).
Range: Kodiak I. to n. Baja. **Habitat:** Soft bottom at 60–930 ft. (18–283 m).
Similar species: (1) Darter Sculpin (below) has a short nasal spine and a longer snout (snout length greater than eye diameter); (2) Spinynose Sculpin (below) and (3) Smoothgum Sculpin (p. 182) have fewer anal fin rays (18 or fewer, not 21–25).

DARTER SCULPIN *Radulinus boleoides*   **Not shown**
Identification: Similar to Slim Sculpin (above). Snout length greater than eye diameter. Nasal spine short, stout. 20–22 rays in 2nd dorsal fin. 21–23 anal fin rays. Olive-gray to gray above; silvery or white below. 3–4 brown bars on back, small dark blotches below lateral line. To 5½ in. (14 cm).
Range: Langara I. (B.C.) to Santa Catalina I. (s. Calif.). **Habitat:** At 50–480 ft. (15–146 m). Rare.
Similar species: See other *Radulinus* species, especially Slim Sculpin (above).

SPINYNOSE SCULPIN *Radulinus taylori*   **Not shown**
Identification: Similar to Slim Sculpin (above), but body a little deeper. Snout length equal to or less than eye diameter. Nasal spine short, stout. 15–16 rays in 2nd dorsal fin. 15–16 anal fin rays. Olive-brown above, with 4 dark saddles on back; paler below. Brown bars on caudal and pectoral fins. To about 3 in. (7.6 cm).

Range: Se. Alaska to Str. of Georgia (Wash.). **Habitat:** Fairly common on shell bottom near rocks, usually at 20–60 ft. (6.1–18 m) or deeper.
Remarks: Sometimes placed in the genus *Asemichthys.*
Similar species: (1) See other *Radulinus* species, especially Smoothgum Sculpin (below).

SMOOTHGUM SCULPIN *Radulinus vinculus*   **Not shown**
Identification: Similar to Slim Sculpin (p. 181), but body a little deeper. Snout length equal to or less than eye diameter. Nasal spine short, stout. 17 rays in 2nd dorsal fin. 18 anal fin rays. Light brown, with 4 dark bars or saddles on back and 1 at base of caudal fin. Dorsal and pectoral fins faintly barred. To $2\frac{1}{2}$ in. (6.4 cm).
Range: Cen. Calif. to Diablo Cove (s. Calif.). **Habitat:** 70–90 ft. (21–27 m). Rare.
Remarks: Few specimens known; expect slightly different number of rays in 2nd dorsal and anal fins.
Similar species: (1) See other *Radulinus* species, especially Spinynose Sculpin (p. 181).

GRUNT SCULPIN *Rhamphocottus richardsonii*   **Pl. 15**
Identification: *Striking,* with a short *stocky body. Lower pectoral fin rays free* of membrane. Most of body covered with prickles. Body and head yellowish to tan, streaked with dark brown. Belly cream to yellow or pale red. *Bright red* at base of caudal fin. Fin rays mostly reddish, membranes mostly clear. Black spots on 1st dorsal fin and near base of 2nd dorsal fin. To $3\frac{1}{4}$ in. (8.3 cm).
Range: Japan to Alaska and at least to Santa Monica Bay (s. Calif.). **Habitat:** Tidepools and rocky areas but also on sand bottom; intertidal and to 540 ft. (165 m).
Remarks: A peculiar species that virtually jumps and crawls around on the bottom. Feeds on crustaceans. Eyes operate independently. Produces gruntlike sounds when removed from water. A popular public aquarium species. Aquarium observations show that during the spawning season the female chases the male until he is trapped in a cavern among rocks; she keeps him trapped until her eggs are laid.

CABEZON *Scorpaenichthys marmoratus*   **Pl. 16**
Identification: *Common* — often caught by fishermen. Large — usually over 18 in. (46 cm). *Unscaled.* Upper preopercular spine stout, slightly curved. A large branched cirrus above eye. A *skin flap on snout. 5 soft rays* in pelvic fin. Brown, reddish, or greenish above; whitish or greenish below. To 39 in. (99 cm); 15 lb. (6.8 kg.) at $28\frac{1}{2}$ in. (72 cm) but reported to 25 lb. (11 kg).
Range: Sitka (Alaska) to cen. Baja. **Habitat:** Intertidal and to 250 ft. (76 cm).
Remarks: Commonly caught by sport fishermen (from shore, boats, or piers) and by scuba divers. One of the few sculpins in our

area that is of some commercial importance. Flesh is good eating, but *eggs are poisonous* and will make humans violently ill. Flesh is often bluish-green but turns white when cooked. Aggregates for spawning. Feeds mostly on crustaceans and mollusks, including abalones.

Similar species: Other sculpins are smaller, usually have fewer soft rays in the pelvic fin, or scales. (1) *Hemilepidotus* species (p. 170) have a similar shape but have scales above lateral line (Fig. 19). (2) See Lingcod (a large member of the greenling family — p. 156).

MANACLED SCULPIN *Synchirus gilli*   **Pl. 18**
Identification: Our only sculpin in which *pectoral fins are joined* across the breast. Sometimes has 1 row of scales near base of dorsal fin. 3 soft rays in pelvic fin. Single preopercular spine — strong, with 2 points. Body slender. Color varies with habitat: green to yellowish brown above; paler below. About 7 pale blotches on back. Usually has dark spots on rays of dorsal, caudal, and pectoral fins. To $2\frac{3}{4}$ in. (7 cm).
Range: Sitka (Alaska) to San Miguel I. (s. Calif.). **Habitat:** In bays, tidepools, and among kelp. Can cling to bottom or pilings with its pectoral and pelvic fins. Formerly thought to be rare, but relatively common in some areas, especially in kelp.
Similar species: (1) Other slim, elongate sculpins are similar, but they all have *separate* pectoral fins (not joined across breast). (2) Gobies (p. 260; Pl. 19) have separate pectoral fins and their pelvic fins are united into a disk.

Triglops species

Genus characteristics: The next 2 sculpins plus the 3 rare Alaskan species described below (all *Triglops* species) are slender and elongate, with rough fused scales in *oblique folds* below the lateral line (Fig. 19, p. 159). Scales sometimes present on head and back. Upper preopercular spine small and blunt or slightly curved. 3 soft rays in pelvic fin. **Similar genera:** (1) Other elongate narrow-bodied sculpins lack the folds below the lateral line, except the Longfin Sculpin, *Jordania zonope* (p. 174; Fig. 19), but Longfin Sculpin has 4-5 soft rays in pelvic fin. **Note:** In addition to the 2 species of *Triglops* with separate accounts below, 3 other rare species occur from Alaska northward: (1) Scissortail Sculpin, *T. forficata,* usually has a forked caudal fin, small bony tubercles at base of dorsal fin; folds of skin across breast poorly developed or absent; 27-32 soft rays in dorsal fin, and 27-32 (usually 29 or more) anal fin rays. To about 10 in. (25 cm). Bering Sea to the Gulf of Alaska at 226-433 ft. (69-132 m). (2) Another rare Alaskan sculpin, *T. metopias,* has small bony tubercles at base of dorsal fin, prominent folds across breast, no scales on maxillary or lower part of gill cover (not prickly), fewer than 28 soft rays in dorsal and anal fins; eye diameter goes into head length about $3\frac{1}{2}$ times. To about 6 in. (15 cm). Bering Sea to Auke Bay (Alaska) at 226–433 ft. (69–132 m). (3) Spectacled Sculpin, *T. scepticus,* has small bony tubercles at base of dorsal fin; skin folds across breast usually prominent; maxillary and lower portion of gill cover have small prickly scales; eye large (diameter goes into head length about $2\frac{1}{2}$ times). To about $6\frac{1}{4}$ in. (16 cm). Bering Sea to se. Alaska at 259–827 ft. (79–252 m).

ROUGHSPINE SCULPIN   Pl. 18
Triglops macellus
Identification: Slender, elongate, with *oblique folds of skin on lower side,* edged with tiny rough scales (see *Triglops* in Fig. 19, p. 159). Tiny scales on back; *no* small bony tubercles near base of dorsal fin. 15–17 (avg. 16) pectoral fin rays — tips of lower rays free of membrane. Olive-green to light brown above; white below. Throat silvery. About 5 dark saddles on back. To 8 in. (20 cm). **Range:** Bering Sea to Wash. **Habitat:** Flat bottom at about 60–300 ft. (18–91 m).
Similar species: Other *Triglops* species have small bony tubercles near base of dorsal fin.

RIBBED SCULPIN *Triglops pingelii*   Pl. 17
Identification: Elongate, slender; similar to Roughspine Sculpin (above) in body shape and presence of *scaled folds of skin below the lateral line* (*Triglops* in Fig. 19, p. 159). Riblike folds of skin usually readily apparent across breast. Small bony tubercles at base of dorsal fin. Upper jaw and lower part of gill cover lack scales (not prickly). Fewer than 28 soft rays in dorsal and anal fins. 16–19 (usually 18) pectoral fin rays. Eye small (diameter goes into head length about $3\frac{1}{2}$ times). Olive-brown above; white below. About 5 dark saddles on back. Irregular dark areas or blackish stripe below lateral line. To 8 in. (20 cm).
Range: Japan to Bering Sea and to Wash.; also in N. Atlantic. **Habitat:** Widespread; on bottom, usually at 60–300 ft. (18–91 m). **Similar species:** (1) See Roughspine Sculpin (above). (2) *Triglops metopias* (see Note under genus characteristics, p. 183) has thicker and more numerous skin folds below the lateral line (about *twice* as many folds as lateral line plates, not roughly the same number of each).

FLABBY SCULPIN   Not shown
Zesticelus profundorum
Identification: A small, rare deepwater sculpin. Most like a tiny Buffalo Sculpin (p. 168). *No scales* or cirri or papillae. Upper preopercular spine long and slightly curved, with a single point. 2–3 soft rays in pelvic fin. *Large pores* below eye and on preopercle. Dorsal fins well separated. No plates or scales on lateral line — just pores. Light brown above; slightly darker below. Mouth and gill chamber dusky. Fins blackish. To about $2\frac{1}{2}$ in. (6.4 cm).

Range: Bering Sea to n. Baja. **Habitat:** Deep water at 289–8465 ft. (88–2580 m). Rare; wide-ranging, but few specimens known.
Similar species: Our other sculpins *lack* prominent *pores* on the head.

Poachers: Family Agonidae

Most poachers are elongate. Their scales are modified into large *fused bony plates,* arranged in rows and usually bearing spines. Usually 2 dorsal fins — 1st one of spines (sometimes absent); 2nd one soft-rayed. Pectoral fins fanlike, with lower rays elongate in some species. Pelvic fins below pectoral fins, with 1 spine and only *2 soft rays.* Anal fin roughly opposite 2nd dorsal fin, with only soft rays. Pelvic fins and sometimes anal fin usually larger in males than in females. Most poachers are brownish above; paler below. Most are 6 in. (15 cm) or less, some reach 1 ft. (30 cm). Not normally caught on hook and line but might be encountered as a stomach content; usually captured in trawls.

Poachers occur in the N. Pacific and N. Atlantic; 1 species is found in the S. Hemisphere, off the tip of S. America. They live on the bottom. A few occur in shallow water but most are found on soft bottom at moderate depths; some at depths up to about 4200 ft. (1280 m). Most feed on crustaceans. About 50 species, 21 in our area.

KELP POACHER *Agonomalus mozinoi* **Pl. 15**
Identification: Immediately recognizable by the *striking red and brown coloration.* Has a long skin flap on snout. 1st dorsal fin high. Rows of spines on side. To 3½ in. (8.9 cm).
Range: Dixon Entrance (B.C.) to San Simeon (cen. Calif.).
Habitat: Shallow rocky areas and to 35 ft. (11 m).
Remarks: Crawls over bottom and climbs rock faces with its pectoral fins. Body often covered with small sponges and seaweed, which provide camouflage.
Similar species: Fourhorn Poacher (p. 188) has no red; its lower pectoral fin rays are free of membrane for much of their length.

SOUTHERN SPEARNOSE POACHER **Not shown**
Agonopsis sterletus
Identification: Similar to Northern Spearnose Poacher (Pl. 14), with 2 forward-pointing spines at snout tip, but no cirri present under snout and pelvic fin *white.* Brown to blackish, with about 7 dark bars on side; paler below. Fins banded or clear. To 5¾ in. (15 cm).
Range: San Simeon (cen. Calif.) to cen. Baja. **Habitat:** Soft bottom at about 138–300 ft. (42–91 m).
Similar species: (1) See Northern Spearnose Poacher (p. 186) and (2) Pygmy Poacher (p. 188).

NORTHERN SPEARNOSE POACHER   Pl. 14
Agonopsis vulsa

Identification: Snout pointed, wtih 2 forward-pointing spines at tip. A pit at rear of head. Gill membranes attached to throat (not joined to each other). Anal fin begins below 1st dorsal fin. Brown above; whitish below. 6 or more dark bars on side. Pelvic fin dark *brown with white tip.* To 8 in. (20 cm).

Range: Se. Alaska to Pt. Loma (s. Calif.). **Habitat:** On bottom at 60–534 ft. (18–163 m).

Remarks: Formerly had the scientific name *Agonopsis emmelane.*
Similar species: (1) Southern Spearnose Poacher (p. 185) has white pelvic fins and 6–8 (not 8–11) spines in 1st dorsal fin. See (2) Sawback (p. 189) and (3) Pygmy Poachers (p. 188).

STURGEON POACHER *Agonus acipenserinus*   Pl. 15

Identification: A large poacher. *Mouth on underside of head,* points down; *cluster of cirri* at corners of mouth and under snout. Head and eye larger than in most poachers. Gray to brown above; yellowish to orange below. Usually has dark bars on side; bony plates often dark-edged. To 1 ft. (30 cm).

Range: Bering Sea to Eureka (n. Calif.). **Habitat:** Common on soft bottom at 60–180 ft. (18–55 m).

Similar species: (1) In other poachers mouth is at front or at least points mostly forward (not down); no clusters of *long* cirri present. (2) Sawback Poacher (p. 189) has long cirri on cheek, fewer (not a dense cluster) under its snout.

SMOOTH ALLIGATORFISH *Anoplagonus inermis*   Pl. 14

Identification: Only poacher in our area with *only 1 dorsal fin* (not 2). Body plates *smooth.* Brown above; brownish gray below. 2 pale areas on dusky caudal fin. To 6 in. (15 cm).

Range: Bering Sea to B.C. and to Pt. Arena (n. Calif.). **Habitat:** On bottom, often among rocks; at 25–334 ft. (7.6–102 m).

GRAY STARSNOUT POACHER   Pl. 14
Bathyagonus alascanus

Identification: A *cluster of 5 spines* (3 vertical, 2 lateral — appearing as a half-star or whorl when viewed from front) on a movable *plate* at extreme tip of snout. Anal fin begins *below gap* between dorsal fins. 35–39 plates in top row on body. A row of plates in front of pelvic fins. Brown to greenish gray above, with 5–6 dark saddles on back; paler below. Pectoral fin *barred.* Dorsal fins spotted. To 5 in. (13 cm).

Range: Bering Sea to n. Calif. **Habitat:** Rocky areas at 60–828 ft. (18–252 m).

Similar species: 3 other *Bathyagonus* species in our area have the "starsnout" (cluster of spines at the extreme tip of snout): (1) In Spinycheek Starsnout Poacher (below) anal fin begins below *rear* of 1st dorsal fin; spine usually present below rear of eye.

(2) In Bigeye Starsnout Poacher (below) eye is larger; 41–44 plates in top row on body. (3) In Blackfin Starsnout Poacher (below) fins are black. (4) Other poachers can have spines on a movable plate or fixed spines at tip of snout, but the spines are not arranged in a cluster of 3 vertical and 2 lateral ones.

SPINYCHEEK STARSNOUT POACHER   Pl. 14
Bathyagonus infraspinatus
Identification: A *cluster of spines* on *plate* at tip of snout as in Gray Starsnout Poacher (above). Spines on *cheek* and side of snout. Anal fin begins below *rear* of 1st dorsal fin. 35–39 plates in top row on body. 1 row or 1 pair of plates in front of pelvic fins. 2 cirri at rear of upper jaw. Olive to brown above; dark blotches on side; paler below. Narrow *bars* on pectoral fin. To 4¾ in. (12 cm).
Range: Bering Sea to Eureka (n. Calif.). **Habitat:** On bottom at 60–600 ft. (18–183 m).
Similar species: See Gray Starsnout Poacher (above).

BLACKFIN STARSNOUT POACHER   Pl. 14
Bathyagonus nigripinnis
Identification: Our only poacher in which *all fins* are *entirely black* or bluish black. Lower jaw projects beyond upper jaw. Eye large. Brown; underside of head bluish. To 8½ in. (21 cm).
Range: Commander Is. (USSR) to Eureka (n. Calif.). **Habitat:** Soft bottom at 300–4092 ft. (91–1247 m).
Remarks: Also known as the Blackfin Poacher.
Similar species: See Gray Starsnout Poacher (p. 186).

BIGEYE STARSNOUT POACHER   Pl. 14
Bathyagonus pentacanthus
Identification: A cluster of spines on snout as in preceding 2 poachers. Eye *large*. Anal fin begins below rear of 1st dorsal fin or below gap between dorsal fins. Body *elongate,* slender. 2 pairs of plates just in front of pelvic fins. Lower pectoral fin rays usually elongate. Olive-brown above, with 5–6 dark blotches on back; paler below. Dusky areas on fins (except on anal and pelvic fins, which are mostly pale); caudal fin often quite dark. To 9¼ in. (23 cm).
Range: Bering Sea to s. Calif. **Habitat:** Soft bottom at 360–1230 ft. (110–375 m).
Remarks: Also known as the Bigeye Poacher.
Similar species: See Gray Starsnout Poacher (p. 186).

ROCKHEAD   Pl. 15
Bothragonus swanii
Identification: A deep-bodied poacher, with *large smooth plates.* Dorsal and anal fins small — with 5 or fewer rays in each fin. Note the deep *pit on top of the head.* Dark brown to bluish bars on brown to orangish red or red background. Most fins spotted; often white on pectoral fin. To 3½ in. (8.9 cm).

Range: Kodiak I. to Lion Rock (cen. Calif.). **Habitat:** Intertidal and to 60 ft. (18 m).
Similar species: Fourhorn Poacher (below) has much larger dorsal and anal fins, spines on body plates, and only a shallow depression on top of head.

FOURHORN POACHER *Hypsagonus quadricornis*   **Pl. 15**
Identification: A deep-bodied poacher. A *cirrus* at tip of snout. A spine above the eye. 9–11 spines in 1st dorsal fin. Lower pectoral fin rays *free* of membrane. Brown, with yellow and darker brown marks. Broad *dark bars on body*. To $3\frac{1}{2}$ in. (8.9 cm).
Range: Sea of Okhotsk (USSR) and Bering Sea to Puget Sound. **Habitat:** On bottom at 160–730 ft. (49–223 m).
Remarks: Frequently covered by featherlike polyps (small hydroid animals).
Similar species: (1) Kelp Poacher (p. 185) differs in color. (2) See Rockhead (above).

WARTY POACHER *Occella verrucosa*   **Pl. 14**
Identification: Head flattened; spines weak when present. Mouth upturned. Anal fin *long* (usually with 10–12 rays), begins below 1st dorsal fin. 15 or fewer pectoral fin rays. Breast covered with *knobby plates*. Gray or brown above; pale below. Males have a long orange and black pelvic fin. To 8 in. (20 cm).
Range: Shelikof Str. (Alaska) to off Pt. Montara (cen. Calif.). **Habitat:** Soft bottom at 60–900 ft. (18–274 m).
Similar species: Pricklebreast Poacher (p. 189) also has an upturned mouth and similar body shape, but usually has 8–9 anal fin rays, 18–19 pectoral fin rays, and small prickles on the breast.
Note: The Pixie Poacher, *Occella impi*, has recently been described from a $\frac{3}{4}$-in. (2-cm) juvenile specimen from Graham I. (B.C.). It has 18 pectoral fin rays; 9 dorsal and anal fin rays.

PYGMY POACHER *Odontopyxis trispinosa*   **Pl. 14**
Identification: 1 vertical spine (and sometimes 2 lateral ones) on plate at extreme tip of snout (also 2 nasal spines at middle of snout). A heart-shaped or double pit at rear of head. No barbels, except on rear of upper jaw. Gray to olive above, with 6 or more dark blotches on side; a little paler below. Small — to $3\frac{3}{4}$ in. (9.5 cm).
Range: Se. Alaska to cen. Baja. **Habitat:** Soft bottom at 30–1224 ft. (9–373 m).
Similar species: (1) Northern (p. 186) and (2) Southern (p. 185) Spearnose Poachers also have a pit at rear of head, but they have 2 *forward-pointing* spines at tip of snout and barbels at corner of mouth. (3) See Blacktip Poacher (p. 189).

TUBENOSE POACHER *Pallasina barbata*   **Pl. 14**
Identification: A long slender poacher, easily identified by its

long snout and *smooth* body plates. Lower jaw projects, has a barbel at tip. Gray to brown above, often with dark spots; paler below. Dorsal and pectoral fins spotted. To about $5\frac{2}{3}$ in. (14 cm).
Range: Japan to Bering Sea and to Bodega Bay (cen. Calif.).
Habitat: Often in eelgrass or seaweed. Intertidal and to 180 ft. (55 m), possibly to 420 ft. (128 m).
Similar species: Smooth Alligatorfish (p. 186) also has smooth body plates, but *only 1* dorsal fin, shorter snout.

SAWBACK POACHER *Sarritor frenatus*   **Pl. 14**
Identification: A *northern* poacher. *Spiny projecting snout* overhangs mouth. Several *long barbels* at rear of mouth; usually 2 cirri under tip of snout. Strong spines behind upper rear of eye. Body fairly deep at front of pectoral fin, but tapers toward the rear. Brownish above; paler below. Usually faint blotches on head and back. Caudal and pectoral fins mostly dusky. Other fins blotched or mostly clear. To $10\frac{1}{2}$ in. (27 cm).
Range: Bering Sea to se. Alaska. **Habitat:** Soft bottom at about 60–510 ft. (18–155 m).
Similar species: (1) In Sturgeon Poacher (p. 186) mouth points down (not forward); clumps of cirri in front of mouth. (2) Northern (p. 186) and (3) Southern (p. 185) Spearnose Poachers have a pit at rear of head, 9–12 rays (not 8 or fewer) in anal fin, 2 spines at extreme tip of snout, and gill membranes joined to side of throat (not to each other). **Note:** Longnose Poacher, *Sarritor leptorhynchus,* occurs in deep water — at 820–984 ft. (250–300 m) — from the Bering Sea to the Gulf of Alaska. It closely resembles the Sawback Poacher in shape and fin ray counts, but snout is shorter, blunter; eye smaller; and body less deep at pectoral fin. To 10 in. (25 cm).

PRICKLEBREAST POACHER   **Pl. 14**
Stellerina xyosterna
Identification: Mouth upturned. Many small *prickles* (not large bony plates) on breast. 18–19 pectoral fin rays. 8 or fewer anal fin rays. Anal fin begins below 1st dorsal fin. Body deep (less so in young). Olive-brown above; pale below. Often has dark spots on back. Caudal fin and rear of anal fin black; large black area on pectoral fin. To $6\frac{1}{2}$ in. (16 cm).
Range: Queen Charlotte Is. to n.-cen. Baja. **Habitat:** Mud or sand bottom at 15–246 ft. (4.6–75 m).
Similar species: See Warty Poacher (p. 188).

BLACKTIP POACHER *Xeneretmus latifrons*   **Pl. 14**
Identification: *1 vertical spine* at tip of snout, usually bordered by 2 small lateral spines. Dorsal fins *black at edge.* 1–3 barbels at rear of upper jaw. 14–15 pectoral fin rays. *Row of spiny scales across eye.* Brown or tan above; pale below. About 5 dark blotches on side. To $7\frac{1}{2}$ in. (19 cm).

Range: Burrard Inlet (B.C.) to n. Baja. **Habitat:** Soft bottom at 60–1312 ft. (18–400 m).
Similar species: (1) Smootheye Poacher (below) has a dark blotch on front of 1st dorsal fin and no spiny scales on eye. (2) In Stripefin Poacher (below) 1st dorsal fin is black at base; 16–17 pectoral fin rays. (3) Bluespotted Poacher (below) usually has 13 pectoral fin rays. (4) Pygmy Poacher (p. 188) lacks barbel on upper jaw and has a pit at rear of head.

SMOOTHEYE POACHER *Xeneretmus leiops*   **Pl. 14**
Identification: 1 vertical spine at tip of snout, often bordered by 2 tiny lateral spines. 1st dorsal fin has a *black blotch* at front. No spiny scales on eye. 1 barbel at rear of upper jaw. Dusky olive above; paler below. Snout tip black; black blotch below eye. To 9½ in. (24 cm).
Range: Southern B.C. to Santa Catalina I. (s. Calif.). **Habitat:** On bottom at 122–1308 ft. (37–399 m).
Similar species: Blacktip Poacher (above) has a row of spiny scales across the eye.

STRIPEFIN POACHER *Xeneretmus ritteri*   **Pl. 14**
Identification: 1 vertical spine at tip of snout, bordered by 2 small lateral spines. 2 barbels at rear of upper jaw. 16–17 pectoral fin rays. Dark brown above; pale below. Faint blotches on side. Dorsal fins usually dark-edged 1st one *black* at *base*. To 6¼ in. (16 cm).
Range: Malibu (s. Calif.) to cen. Baja; isolated population in n. Gulf of Calif. **Habitat:** Soft bottom at 600–1200 ft. (183–366 m).
Similar species: (1) In Blacktip (p. 189) and (2) Bluespotted Poachers (below) 1st dorsal fin is not black at base; 15 or fewer pectoral fin rays.

BLUESPOTTED POACHER   **Pl. 14**
Xeneretmus triacanthus
Identification: 1 vertical spine at tip of snout, with 2 small lateral spines. Dorsal fins clear (not black at edge). Often bright *blue spots* behind head. *2 barbels* at rear of upper jaw. 3–4 bony plates below eye. Anal fin short (with 5–7 rays), directly *opposite* 2nd dorsal fin. Usually 13 pectoral fin rays. Olive-brown above; paler below. About 6 dark blotches on side. To 7 in. (18 cm).
Range: Kwatna Inlet (B.C.) to n.-cen. Baja. **Habitat:** Soft bottom at 240–1200 ft. (73–366 m).
Similar species: See (1) Blacktip (p. 189) and (2) Stripefin Poachers (above).

Snailfishes: Family Liparididae

In most snailfishes the pelvic fins are modified into a *sucking disk* — see Fig. 33 opp. Pl. 21 — with which these fishes can cling to rocks (disk is absent in some deepsea species). Snailfishes are elongate, with a more or less continuous dorsal fin and a long anal fin — often both fins are joined to the caudal fin. Skin soft and loose, with jellylike tissue underneath. *No* scales or plates on body, but prickles are present in a few species. Most snailfishes are under 6 in. (15 cm), 1 grows to about 2 ft. (61 cm). Most species vary in color — in some both a striped and a plain-colored pattern are common.

Most snailfishes are found in cold waters of the N. Hemisphere (including the Arctic) and in the Antarctic. A few species occur in deep water in the tropics, 1 in the Red Sea. Some are found in tidepools; most occur offshore on soft bottom at moderate depths, but some are found in *extremely* deep water — at depths up to 24,894 ft. (7588 m). A few deep-living species are pelagic. About 150 species; at least 10 genera and about 50 species in our area, but many of these are found only in the deep sea. We include below the inshore species and those which occur at depths less than about 656 ft. (200 m) for a total of 13 species. The shallow-water species are in need of further study, particularly in northern areas such as the Gulf of Alaska, Aleutian Is., and Bering Sea.

Snailfish species are hard to identify; researchers rely on technical features such as fin ray counts, pore patterns, location and size of the gill slit, gill rakers, color of the lining inside the body cavity (peritoneum), and the shape of the teeth (magnification needed).

BLACKTAIL SNAILFISH *Careproctus melanurus*   **Pl. 20**
Identification: *Disk very small* (about same size as eye diameter); located on the *throat,* directly under the eye. Gill slit *completely above* pectoral fin. Pinkish; rear of dorsal and anal fins and caudal fin black. Inside of mouth black. To 10¼ in. (26 cm).
Range: Bering Sea to off San Diego. **Habitat:** Mud bottom at about 300–5250 ft. (91–1600 m).
Remarks: Sometimes caught in bottom trawls and Sablefish traps.
Similar species: Prickly Snailfish (p. 194) is also mostly pale, but it has prickly skin and no disk.

SPOTTED SNAILFISH *Liparis callyodon*   **Pl. 21**
Identification: A *northern* snailfish. Front rays of dorsal fin form a bluntly pointed *lobe.* Dorsal and anal fins extend nearly onto caudal fin. 29–31 pectoral fin rays, lower rays elongate. Gill slit above pectoral fin or extends down in front of the uppermost ray. Color varies: olive-brown or olive to purplish above; paler below. Usually has small dark spots on side. To 5 in. (13 cm).
Range: Bering Sea to Ore. **Habitat:** Tidepools and other intertidal areas.
Similar species: 3 other snailfishes have a lobe at front of dorsal fin: (1) Tidepool Snailfish (p. 192) has no small black spots on side, anus slightly closer to anal fin than to disk (anus much nearer disk in the Spotted Snailfish). (2) Slimy Snailfish (p. 193) lacks spots on side. (3) Lobefin Snailfish (p. 194) has 33–37 pectoral fin rays.

RIBBON SNAILFISH *Liparis cyclopus*   **Pl. 21**
Identification: Dorsal fin *unnotched* (no lobe at front). Dorsal
and anal fins extend barely (if at all) onto caudal fin. Lower pectoral fin rays elongate. Gill slit extends down to area in front of upper
6–8 pectoral fin rays. Dark (mostly olive) above; paler below.
Sometimes has about 4 pale stripes on side. Often has olive-brown
speckles on body and fins. To 4½ in. (11 cm).
Range: Bering Sea to Ore. **Habitat:** Near shore and to 600 ft.
(183 m).
Similar species: In Slipskin Snailfish (below) gill slit extends
farther down (to area in front of pectoral fin rays 12–16).

MARBLED SNAILFISH *Liparis dennyi*   **Pl. 21**
Identification: Dorsal and anal fins extend onto about *first ⅓* of
caudal fin. Gill slit *large,* extends down in front of 10–18 pectoral
fin rays. Slight notch at most in dorsal fin — no noticeable lobe at
front. Lower pectoral fin rays elongate. Color varies: plain,
streaked, spotted, or marbled. Background color usually olive. To
1 ft. (30 cm).
Range: Gulf of Alaska to Wash.; Aleutian Is. (?). **Habitat:** Fairly
common at 240–730 ft. (73–223 m).
Similar species: Other snailfishes treated here have a lobe at
front of dorsal fin, or a smaller gill slit, or dorsal and anal fins that
do not join to the caudal fin. **Note:** The Dusky Snailfish, *Liparis
gibbus,* has no lobe on the dorsal fin, fewer dorsal fin rays (37–40,
not 40–44), a large gill slit that extends down in front of about 8–16
(usually about 14) pectoral fin rays. Mostly plain-colored, often
reddish pink to yellowish. To at least 20½ in. (52 cm). Found in the
extreme N. Atlantic, Arctic, and to se. Alaska at depths up to
1200 ft. (366 m).

TIDEPOOL SNAILFISH *Liparis florae*   **Pl. 20**
Identification: A common tidepool snailfish. Front rays of dorsal
fin form a bluntly pointed, nearly separate *lobe.* Dorsal and anal
fins extend only slightly onto caudal fin. Lower pectoral fin rays
elongate. Gill slit extends down in front of 3–5 pectoral fin rays.
Color varies: brown, olive, or purplish; sometimes yellowish or various shades of greenish brown to red-brown. Fins usually about
same color as body. To about 7¼ in. (18 cm).
Range: Kodiak I. to Pt. Conception. **Habitat:** Inshore, in tidepools on exposed coast.
Similar species: (1) Spotted Snailfish (p. 191) also has lobe at
front of dorsal fin, but has spots on side. See (2) Lobefin (p. 194)
and (3) Slimy Snailfishes (p. 193).

SLIPSKIN SNAILFISH *Liparis fucensis*   **Pl. 21**
Identification: Gill slit extends down in front of 12–16 pectoral
fin rays. Dorsal and anal fins extend *only slightly* onto caudal fin.
Dorsal fin sometimes slightly notched. Lower pectoral fin rays

elongate. Color varies: olive-brown to dark brown, faint mottling
or bands on side and fins; paler below. Rarely striped. To 7 in.
(18 cm).
Range: Aleutian Is. to near San Simeon (cen. Calif.). **Habitat:**
Near shore and to 1272 ft. (388 m).
Similar species: (1) In Ribbon Snailfish (p. 192) gill slit extends
down in front of only a few pectoral fin rays. (2) Marbled Snailfish
(p. 192) has more anal fin rays (30–34, not 27–29).

SLIMY SNAILFISH *Liparis mucosus*   **Pl. 21**
Identification: Dorsal fin has a lobe at front. Dorsal and anal fins
do not extend noticeably onto caudal fin. Lower pectoral fin rays
elongate. Gill slit extends down in front of upper pectoral fin rays.
Color varies: brownish to red, often with dark stripes. To nearly
5 in. (13 cm).
Range: Sitka (Alaska) to s. B.C. and to Baja. **Habitat:** Intertidal
and to 50 ft. (15 m); usually not in tidepools.
Similar species: (1) See under Spotted Snailfish (p. 191).
(2) Tidepool Snailfish (p. 192) has a higher lobe at front of dorsal
fin, is thinner and almost always plain-colored. It also has more
anal fin rays (31–33, not 22–25).

SHOWY SNAILFISH *Liparis pulchellus*   **Pl. 20**
Identification: Elongate. Dorsal fin *unnotched* in front. Dorsal
and anal fins extend onto caudal fin for *most of its length*. Lower
pectoral fin rays elongate. Gill slit ends just above pectoral fin or
extends down in front of 1–7 rays. Color varies: light to dark brown
above; paler below. Usually has wavy lines, sometimes spotted or
plain-colored. Dorsal and anal fins darker at edge. To 10 in.
(25 cm).
Range: USSR to Bering Sea and to Monterey Bay. **Habitat:** Soft
bottom at about 30–600 ft. (9.1–183 m).
Similar species: Our other inshore snailfishes have a more distinct caudal fin (dorsal and anal fins not joined to it for most of its
length).

RINGTAIL SNAILFISH *Liparis rutteri*   **Pl. 20**
Identification: Gill slit *small,* rarely extends past 1st pectoral fin
ray. Disk large, usually more than $\frac{1}{2}$ of head length (snout tip to
gill slit). Dorsal fin *not lobed* at front. Usually a *white ring* at base
of caudal fin. Blackish to brown; sometimes with black wavy
streaks or spots on side. Caudal fin usually has dark specks. To just
over $6\frac{1}{2}$ in. (16 cm).
Range: Bering Sea to San Francisco. **Habitat:** Intertidal and to
240 ft. (73 m).
Similar species: Can be confused with other snailfishes with no
lobe on dorsal fin; but they lack the white ring at base of caudal fin
and/or have a gill slit that extends farther down. **Note:** A similar
species is known (but not yet named or formally described) from

the mouth of the Columbia River, Ore./Wash. It has about 60–80 fingerlike appendages (pyloric caeca) overlying the stomach (Ringtail Snailfish has about 20–25).

PRICKLY SNAILFISH *Paraliparis deani*   **Not shown**
Identification: *No disk.* Lower rays of pectoral fin nearly *free* of membrane. Gill slit extends down in front of 10–13 pectoral fin rays. Pale, usually whitish. To 4 in. (10 cm).
Range: Se. Alaska to n. Calif. **Habitat:** Apparently on bottom; shallower in Alaska and B.C., at 180–1644 ft. (55–501 m), but deeper off Calif., at 2333–3306 ft. (711–1008 m).
Remarks: Caught in bottom trawls; habits poorly known.
Similar species: (1) Other shallow-living snailfishes in our area have a disk. (2) See Blacktail Snailfish (p. 191). **Note:** Other *Paraliparis* species occur in deep water off our coast, but rarely at depths less than 656 ft. (200 m). They lack a disk, and have elongate lower pectoral fin rays, a tapered body, and a small caudal fin.

LOBEFIN SNAILFISH *Polypera greeni*   **Not shown**
Identification: Dorsal fin has a *prominent lobe* at front. Gill slit extends down no farther than 4th ray in pectoral fin. Dorsal and anal fins extend *only slightly* onto caudal fin. Skin loose. Brownish to blackish; blotched cream to light brown on belly. To about 12¼ in. (31 cm).
Range: Bering Sea to Wash. **Habitat:** Virtually unknown.
Similar species: (1) Tidepool (p. 192) and (2) Spotted Snailfishes (p. 191) also have a prominent lobe at front of dorsal fin, but they have *tricuspid* — not simple — teeth (magnification needed). They also have fewer anal fin rays (27 or fewer; 30 or more in Lobefin Snailfish).

Lumpfishes: Family Cyclopteridae

Close relatives of the snailfishes (above), with a similar disk on the breast. Lumpfishes are more globular than snailfishes. They usually have 2 short dorsal fins — 1st one of spines, 2nd one soft-rayed (1st fin absent in some species). Many are covered with large *conical plates,* or tubercles. The *gill slit* is *small* (above the pectoral fin). Drab, mostly brown or gray. To 2 ft. (61 cm).
   Lumpfishes live only in cold marine waters of the N. Hemisphere, mostly in shallow water on the bottom, and usually in rocky areas. They can cling to rocks and other objects with their disk. The females lay their eggs in a spongy mass that sticks to rocks and seaweed. In some species the male guards the eggs. About 25 species, 2 in our area.

SMOOTH LUMPSUCKER *Aptocyclus ventricosus*   **Pl. 21**
Identification: More or less *globular.* Skin smooth, with no conical plates or scales. *1 short dorsal fin far back,* opposite a simi-

larly-shaped anal fin — neither fin joined to caudal fin. *Disk large.*
Brownish to gray, with dark spots on upper back and head. To
10¾ in. (27 cm).
Range: Japan to Bering Sea and to B.C. **Habitat:** On bottom; to
738 ft. (225 m).
Similar species: (1) See Pacific Spiny Lumpsucker (below).
(2) Similar to globe-shaped sculpins (*Psychrolutes* species, p. 180),
but they lack a disk and have a longer gill slit.

PACIFIC SPINY LUMPSUCKER   Pl. 21
Eumicrotremus orbis
Identification: *Globular.* Large *conical bony plates* on most of
body. 2 widely separated dorsal fins. Disk very *large,* covers all of
breast. Green to brown above; light brown or purplish below.
Bony plates usually orangish in males, greenish in females. To 5 in.
(13 cm).
Range: Kuril Is. (north of Japan) to Bering Sea and to Puget
Sound. **Habitat:** Common inshore on bottom, to 480 ft. (146 m).
Can be seen at low tide attached to rocks.
Similar species: Smooth Lumpsucker (above) has only 1 dorsal
fin and no bony plates on body.

Order Perciformes

This huge order includes all the typical spiny-rayed fishes and
their relatives. It is the largest order of vertebrates, with about
7500 species. Most species have fin spines; the dorsal fin typically
has both spines and soft rays. Pelvic fins are normally present and
usually thoracic, and most commonly have 1 spine and 5 soft rays.
The upper jaw is bordered mostly or entirely by the premaxillary
bone. No bony connection (suborbital stay) from below eye to
front of gill cover as in the Order Scorpaeniformes (p. 131).
    Perciform fishes are the dominant group in marine seas, particu-
larly in shallow water, although important subgroups can be
found throughout the world in fresh water, the deep sea, and oceanic waters. About 20 suborders are recognized, but the limits of
the order and some suborders are uncertain and change as new
studies become available. Except for the families in the 2 orders
described near the end of this book, all the families treated from
here on belong to this order. **Note:** In our area 2 species of swal-
lowers (Family Chiasmodontidae) occur in very deep midwaters
and are otherwise not discussed in this guide.

Temperate Basses:
Family Percichthyidae

Basslike, usually with 1 main spine on the gill cover and a forked
caudal fin. Researchers use anatomical features to separate them

from the true basses (Family Serranidae, p. 197). Temperate basses occur in both fresh water and marine seas of most continents and in all shallow warm oceans. Perhaps 40 species, 3 in our area.

PELAGIC BASSLET   Fig. 39, p. 198
Howella brodiei

Identification: Small, *black,* basslike. *2 separate dorsal fins.* Gill cover spiny. Pectoral fin long. Scales ctenoid. To at least 3 in. (7.6 cm).
Range: Cen. Calif. to Chile. **Habitat:** Open ocean; spends day in midwater at about 1000–6000 ft. (305–1829 m), migrates near surface at night.
Remarks: Unlikely to be seen except by researchers using midwater trawls.
Similar species: Guadalupe Cardinalfish (p. 202; Pl. 30) has same shape and 2 dorsal fins, but is a different color.

STRIPED BASS *Morone saxatilis*   Pl. 29
Identification: Well-known, basslike. 6–9 *black stripes* on side — each stripe covers a scale row and often is slightly irregular. Caudal fin *forked.* Usually greenish above, silvery on side; white below. In e. Pacific to 4 ft. (122 cm), 90 lb. (41 kg), but usually less than 10 lb. (4.5 kg.); in Atlantic to 6 ft. (183 cm), 125 lb. (57 kg).
Range: Barkley Sound (B.C.) to n. Baja. Also in nw. Atlantic. Introduced into some large freshwater lakes elsewhere. **Habitat:** Somewhat migratory, moves along coast. Common in bays, moves into rivers in spring to spawn in fresh water.
Remarks: There were no Striped Bass on the Pacific Coast of N. America until the late 1800s. In 1879 and 1882, 2 shipments (totaling 432 specimens) were transported by train from the eastern U.S. and were released near San Francisco. 10 years later the Striped Bass was widely distributed on our coast. It is an important sport fish and is sometimes fished commercially. Some researchers place it in the genus *Roccus.*
Similar species: Other striped, basslike species are a different color.

GIANT SEA BASS *Stereolepis gigas*   Pl. 29
Identification: Very *large.* Adults gray or dark brown (as shown); paler below. Midsize specimens ("juniors") brownish; young (also shown on Pl.) reddish or reddish with white blotches. Except in young, there are large brown to blackish spots on side, but in adults these fade almost immediately after fish is removed from the water. Caudal fin slightly indented in adults. 2 spines on gill cover. Fewer soft rays in dorsal fin (10–11, not 12 or more) than in any grouper or true sea bass (next family). To $7\frac{5}{12}$ ft. (226 cm), over 500 lb. (227 kg).
Range: Humboldt Bay to Gulf of Calif.; rare north of s. Calif. **Habitat:** On rock bottom; near shore, outside kelp beds, and along drop-offs; 18–150 ft. (5.5–46 m). Large specimens usually deeper

than 100 ft. (30 m), small ones occur over sand and in kelp beds — mostly at 40–70 ft. (12–21 m).
Remarks: Also known as the Black Sea Bass. An important sport fish, but populations reduced in our area by overfishing. Aggregates for spawning in summer. Lives to at least age 70.

Sea Basses and Groupers: Family Serranidae

Generally robust fishes, usually with the well-known bass shape. Spinous dorsal fin is joined to soft dorsal fin, with or without a prominent notch. The mouth generally is large — lower jaw often projects beyond upper jaw. Rear part of the upper jaw (maxillary) fully *exposed,* not tucked under a shelf or sheathed by skin. Jaw teeth are sharp, frequently canine. Cheek and gill cover scaled. Body scales usually ctenoid (sometimes cycloid). Caudal fin usually rounded or square-cut, rarely deeply forked. Pelvic fins usually below pectoral fins. Usually 3 anal fin spines. Rear edge of preopercle often serrate (sawtoothed). Typically have 2–3 flattened spines on gill cover. Most are between about 2 in. (5.1 cm) and 1 ft. (30 cm), but some grow much larger.

Sea basses and groupers are most common in tropical seas, less so in temperate waters, and are absent from the Arctic and Antarctic. A few species live in fresh water. Many sit on the bottom or roam near the bottom. Some change radically in body shape as they grow. Many can change color rapidly. They are carnivores, and feed mostly on other fishes and crustaceans. Most are hermaphroditic, and individuals of some species are both male and female at the same time! Others mature as females first and become males when they grow larger. A large family with about 375 species, 10 in our area. Rare species of this and 2 other families are shown (in outline form) in Fig. 39 (p. 198).

SPOTTED CABRILLA *Epinephelus analogus* **Fig. 39, p. 198**
Identification: Reddish brown, with *brown spots* on body and fins. Vague broad, dusky reddish bars on side. Spinous dorsal fin about same height as soft dorsal fin, with *no notch* between. Caudal fin rounded. To about $34\frac{1}{4}$ in. (87 cm), 28 lb. (13 kg).
Range: San Pedro (s. Calif.) to Peru, including Galapagos Is. Common in Gulf of Calif.; very rare north of Baja. **Habitat:** Adults on rocky bottom; inshore and to 210 ft. (64 m).
Similar species: In Spotted Sand Bass (p. 200), edge of caudal fin is straight or slightly indented (not rounded), and 3rd spine in dorsal fin is about twice as long as 2nd spine.

SNOWY GROUPER *Epinephelus niveatus* **Fig. 39, p. 198**
Identification: Our only grouper with round *white spots* on body; background reddish brown. In Pacific to $31\frac{1}{2}$ in. (80 cm); in Atlantic to nearly 4 ft. (122 cm).

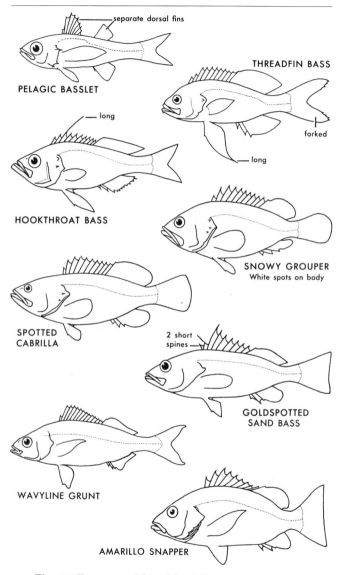

separate dorsal fins

PELAGIC BASSLET

THREADFIN BASS

forked

long

HOOKTHROAT BASS

long

SNOWY GROUPER
White spots on body

SPOTTED
CABRILLA

2 short
spines

GOLDSPOTTED
SAND BASS

WAVYLINE GRUNT

AMARILLO SNAPPER

Fig. 39 Basses and basslike fishes — rare species

Range: Warm waters of Atlantic and e. Pacific; San Luis Obispo Co. (cen. Calif.) to Peru but rare north of Baja. **Habitat:** Near shore and to 426 ft. (130 m); in Atlantic at depths up to 1500 ft. (457 m).

HOOKTHROAT BASS *Hemanthias signifer*   **Fig. 39**
Identification: A strong spine at throat (at front of *isthmus* — see ventral view, bottom right, front endpapers). Third spine in dorsal fin elongate. Caudal fin forked. 18–19 pectoral fin rays. Striking rose-red, with yellow spots on lower side. Yellow streak extends from below eye to gill cover; yellow specks on gill cover. Fins red, marked with yellow. To about 15 in. (38 cm).
Range: Playa del Rey (s. Calif.) to Peru; rare. **Habitat:** Little known; 75–1000 ft. (23–305 m).
Similar species: Threadfin Bass (p. 201) has elongate pelvic fin, scales on rear of upper jaw; 3rd spine in dorsal fin only slightly longer than 2nd.

GULF GROUPER *Mycteroperca jordani*   **Pl. 29**
Identification: Mostly plain, with a *square-cut or slightly indented caudal fin* (rear edge smooth, not sawtoothed). Rear of anal fin *vertical*. Normally 17 pectoral fin rays. *2 color patterns:* plain brown or gray (usually large adults); or with dark gray oblong blotches on upper back and fins, and dark streaks on head (as shown). In aquariums individuals have been observed to change quickly from 1 pattern to the other. Most fins white-edged. To 6½ ft. (198 cm), 117½ lb. (53 kg), but reported to weigh up to 200 lb. (91 kg).
Range: La Jolla (s. Calif.) to Mazatlan (Mex.). **Habitat:** Rock and sand bottom, near shore. Deeper in summer, shallower in winter.
Similar species: (1) Broomtail Grouper (below) is another mostly plain-colored large grouper with a big mouth, but rear edge of its caudal fin is notched (sawtoothed). Also has more gill rakers on the 1st arch (29–33, not 21–26) and anal fin of different shape. (2) Barred Sand Bass (p. 201) usually is barred, but can be nearly plain-colored; has fewer soft rays in anal fin (9 or fewer, not 10–11) and a long 3rd spine in dorsal fin.

BROOMTAIL GROUPER *Mycteroperca xenarcha*   **Pl. 29**
Identification: A large grouper. Rear edge of caudal fin *sawtoothed.* Rear of soft dorsal fin high and pointed in large specimens. 29–33 gill rakers on 1st gill arch. Mostly plain brown or gray, but often mottled and streaked with darker brown and gray-green. Young have a dark blotch on top of caudal peduncle. To about 4 ft. (122 cm), 97 lb. (44 kg), but reported to 200 lb. (91 kg).
Range: San Francisco Bay to Peru, including Galapagos Is.; rare north of s. Calif. **Habitat:** Inshore and to 70 ft. (21 m).
Similar species: See Gulf Grouper (above).

GOLDSPOTTED SAND BASS   Fig. 39, p. 198
Paralabrax auroguttatus

Identification: First 2 spines in dorsal fin short, 3rd one longest (as in the next 3 species). Olive, with bright *golden oblong spots.* Pectoral fin pale yellow, semitransparent. Usually has a pale streak along lateral line. Gill chamber lining orange. To 28 in. (71 cm).

Range: S. Calif. to Baja and Gulf of Calif. **Habitat:** Sand bottom near rocks; to 350 ft. (107 m).

Similar species: See Spotted Sand Bass (below).

KELP BASS   Pl. 29
Paralabrax clathratus

Identification: Pale blotches on back. 10–11 dorsal fin spines; 1st 2 spines shorter than next 3 spines; 3rd spine *not* noticeably longer than the 4th. Olive or brown above; cream below. Fins have a yellowish tinge. In breeding males chin and lower jaw dusky orange. To about $28\frac{1}{2}$ in. (72 cm), $14\frac{1}{2}$ lb. (6.6 kg).

Range: Columbia River (Wash.) to s. Baja, rare north of s. Calif. **Habitat:** Usually in or near kelp beds, shallow water and to about 150 ft. (46 m) but mostly at 8–70 ft. (2.4–21 m). Found throughout water column; larger specimens usually occur deeper.

Remarks: An important sport fish, widespread and abundant from s. Calif. south. Caught by trolling, on baited hook, and by spearfishing. Good eating. Does not migrate; can be depleted by overfishing in an area.

Similar species: Sometimes confused with (1) Yellowtail Rockfish (p. 140; Pl. 26) and (2) Olive Rockfish (p. 151; Pl. 26), but rockfishes have strong spines on rear of cheek. (3) In sand basses (above and below) the 3rd spine in the dorsal fin is noticeably longer than the 4th.

SPOTTED SAND BASS   Pl. 29
Paralabrax maculatofasciatus

Identification: Brownish to olive above; paler below, with round *blackish spots* on body and fins. Also has broad *faint bars* on back and side. Young have dark stripes. Rear of anal fin rounded. Caudal fin square-cut. First 2 spines in dorsal fin short, 3rd spine longest — about twice length of 2nd spine. To 22 in. (56 cm).

Range: Monterey to Mazatlan (Mex.), including Gulf of Calif.; recorded as far north as San Francisco in late 1800s. **Habitat:** Usually on sand or mud bottom near rocks and eelgrass; inshore and to about 200 ft. (61 m).

Remarks: An important sport fish, commonly caught in bays and near harbor entrances.

Similar species: (1) Spotted Cabrilla (p. 197) also has dark spots, but has more soft rays (16–18, not 13–14) in dorsal fin, and its 2nd and 3rd dorsal fin spines are nearly equal in length. (2) Goldspotted Sand Bass (above) has *golden* spots.

BARRED SAND BASS   **Pl. 29**
Paralabrax nebulifer
Identification: Gray to greenish brown above, with faint to dark bars on blotches on side; pale below. No small round dark spots on body but often has gold-brown spots on head. Caudal fin square-cut. Rear of anal fin rounded. First 2 spines in dorsal fin short, 3rd spine longest — about twice length of 2nd spine. To 25½ in. (65 cm), about 8 lb. (36 kg).
Range: Santa Cruz (cen. Calif.) to s. Baja. **Habitat:** Usually on sand bottom among or near rocks; shallow areas and to about 600 ft. (183 m), but usually at less than 100 ft. (30 m).
Remarks: An important sport fish; sometimes common in s. Calif.
Similar species: See (1) Kelp Bass (p. 200) and (2) Spotted Sand Bass (above).

THREADFIN BASS   **Fig. 39, p. 198**
Pronotogrammus multifasciatus
Identification: Small, with a *long pelvic fin* and a *forked* caudal fin. Reddish orange, with darker reticulations; caudal fin yellow. To about 10¼ in. (26 cm).
Range: Los Angeles Co. (s. Calif.) to n. Peru. **Habitat:** Rough bottom, deep reefs at about 131–673 ft. (40–205 m).
Remarks: Feeds on small planktonic crustaceans. Habits little known. Observed from diving saucer to be common at Cape San Lucas (s. Baja). Formerly thought to be *Holanthias gordensis.*

Bigeyes: Family Priacanthidae

Compressed fishes with *very large eyes* and small *rough scales. Mouth oblique,* lower jaw projects. Spinous dorsal fin joined to soft dorsal fin. Most bigeyes are bright red. To about 1 ft. (30 cm), 1 species to 2 ft. (61 cm).

Bigeyes are bottom-dwelling fishes of warm seas. Most occur at moderate depths. Those in shallow water are active at night, spend the day in caves or crevices. About 12 species, 1 in our area.

POPEYE CATALUFA   **Pl. 30**
Pseudopriacanthus serrula
Identification: Body *crimson;* fins often black-edged, dorsal fin spines white-tipped. Compressed, with an elongate oval body and a *large eye.* Pelvic fins attached to belly by a broad membrane. To 13 in. (33 cm).
Range: Malibu (s. Calif.) to Peru, including Galapagos Is.
Habitat: Rough bottom at 30–198 ft. (9.1–60 m). Nocturnal.
Remarks: Some researchers include this species in the genus *Pristigenys.*

Cardinalfishes: Family Apogonidae

Small fishes, usually with *2 separate dorsal fins.* Eye large. Only *2 anal fin spines* in most species. Scales mostly ctenoid, sometimes cycloid, rarely absent. Many are red with dark markings. To 7-8 in. (18–20 cm), most less than 4 in. (10 cm).

Cardinalfishes occur mostly in tropical and subtropical waters of the world. Most are reef-dwelling or shallow marine species. Some live in brackish or even fresh water. Many are mouthbrooders — in some species the males carry the eggs, in others the females do; or both sexes may incubate the eggs. Most cardinalfishes are active at night and secretive during the day. They are often quite abundant, commonly found in small schools near hiding places. Some species live between sea urchin spines, or in holes and other sheltered places. Perhaps 200 species, 1 in our area.

GUADALUPE CARDINALFISH   Pl. 30
Apogon atricaudus
Identification: Small, with a large eye, *2 dorsal fins,* and 2 anal fin spines. Note the long caudal peduncle. Bluish gray, olive, or purplish above; red-orange to rosy below. Much of 1st dorsal fin black in smaller specimens. To 5 in. (13 cm).
Range: San Clemente I. (s. Calif.) to Gulf of Calif. and offshore islands of e. Pacific. **Habitat:** Rocky areas at 30–60 ft. (9.1–18 m).
Remarks: Sometimes identified as *Apogon guadalupensis.*
Similar species: Pelagic Basslet (p. 196; Fig. 39, p. 198) has same body shape and 2 dorsal fins, but is a black, deep-living species.

Tilefishes: Family Malacanthidae

This family contains 2 groups that are sometimes recognized as separate families — tilefishes and sand tilefishes. Only tilefishes are found in our area. They are elongate, with a long continuous dorsal fin (6–8 spines, 13–27 soft rays) preceded by a ridge. Anal fin moderately long, with only 1 or 2 spines, 13–24 soft rays. Caudal fin square-cut to lunate (see rear endpapers). Lips usually fleshy. Scales ctenoid on body, mostly cycloid on head. Moderate sized — the largest species grow to about $2\frac{1}{2}$ ft. (76 cm), most are 1-2 ft. (30–61 cm).

Tilefishes are found in temperate and tropical waters of the Atlantic, Pacific, and Indian Oceans. Some species occur in shallow water but most are outer continental shelf fishes found at moderate depths — 65–1969 ft. (20–600 m) but usually deeper than 165 ft. (50 m). About 31 species in the family, 1 or 2 in our area.

OCEAN WHITEFISH *Caulolatilus princeps*   Pl. 31
Identification: Elongate, with a small mouth. Dorsal and anal fins *long;* 8–9 dorsal fin spines, 1–2 anal fin spines, many soft rays

in both fins. Pelvic fins thoracic. Yellowish brown above; whitish
below. Fins have yellow or yellowish green edge. Pectoral fin has
yellow streak at center. Blue stripe near edge of dorsal and anal
fins. To 40 in. (102 cm).
Range: Vancouver I. to Peru, including Galapagos Is.; rare north
of cen. Calif. **Habitat:** Mostly offshore rocky reefs and banks, especially around islands; usually at 33–300 ft. (10–91 m).
Similar species: (1) In Dolphin (p. 212; Pl. 46) dorsal fin extends
farther forward onto head. (2) Some wrasses (top 3 species on
Pl. 30) have a similar shape, but they have protruding teeth, 3
spines in anal fin, different color. **Note:** A close relative of the
Ocean Whitefish, *Caulolatilus hubbsi,* might reach our area. It
has a more rounded head, larger jaws (that end short of or just
reach area below front of eye — in Ocean Whitefish jaws usually
reach area below pupil), and no scales just behind the eye (present
in Ocean Whitefish). Color in life not described. To about 15 in.
(38 cm). Gulf of Calif. to Peru and near e. Pacific islands at about
59–135 ft. (18–41 m); apparently an old record from s. Calif.

Remoras: Family Echeneididae

In these unusual fishes the spinous 1st dorsal fin is highly modified
to form a *sucking disk* on top of the head, which is used to cling to
other marine animals. The *number of ridges* across the disk, called
laminae (which are actually modified dorsal fin spines that are
divided into 2 halves and bent outwards in opposite directions), is
useful for identifying species. Body elongate, more or less cylindrical. Scales cycloid. Anal fin opposite soft dorsal fin. Lower jaw
projects beyond upper jaw. To 3–4 ft. (91–122 cm) but most under
2 ft. (61 cm).

Remoras are found worldwide in warm seas. Some species cling
to only certain types of hosts, and are said to be *host-specific;* for
example, the Whalesucker attaches itself to whales or porpoises.
Some remoras use marlins or other billfishes as hosts. Most
remoras usually associate with sharks, but some may attach themselves to sea turtles, manta rays, other large fishes, and even boats.
Some species are free-swimming (unattached) some of the time.

Remoras are thought to eat scraps left by their hosts and pelagic
food that they catch on their own. Parasites are important in the
diet of some species — particularly as young, some eat parasitic
copepods, which they remove from the host's body, and from the
inside of the host's gill chamber or mouth. Remoras are most likely
to be found on the boat deck after capture of their host, especially
after capture of billfishes and sharks. Some can be found inside the
host's gill chamber. They are rarely caught on baited hook. 8 species, 7 in our area.

SHARKSUCKER *Echeneis naucrates*   **Pl. 12**
Identification: Gray to brown. Usually has a *dark side stripe*

with a white border. 20–28 disk laminae. 31–42 dorsal fin rays, 30–38 anal fin rays, 21–24 pectoral fin rays. Dorsal, anal, and caudal fins white-edged. To 38 in. (97 cm).
Range: Worldwide in warm seas; s. Calif. south. **Habitat:** Sometimes free-swimming; not host-specific — attaches itself to large fishes (especially sharks and rays) and to sea turtles, also to ships, buoys, wharfs, and other floating objects. Often enters shallow coastal waters.
Remarks: Sometimes attaches itself to bathers; occasionally caught on baited hook.
Similar species: Slender Suckerfish (below) is the only other remora in our area with a dark side stripe. It has a smaller disk, with only 9–11 laminae.

SLENDER SUCKERFISH   Not shown
Phtheirichthys lineatus
Identification: *Slender.* Usually has a *black side stripe with a white border.* Disk *small,* with only 9–11 laminae. 30–40 dorsal fin rays; 29–38 anal fin rays; 17–21 pectoral fin rays. Fins white-edged. Usually to about 17 in. (43 cm), but reported to 2½ ft. (76 cm).
Range: Worldwide in warm seas; s. Calif. south. **Habitat:** Oceanic. Not strongly host-specific — most frequently on barracudas but also found on other fishes, on sea turtles, or free-swimming (not attached to anything). Clings to body of host; also found inside gill chamber.
Similar species: See Sharksucker (above).

WHALESUCKER *Remora australis*   Pl. 12
Identification: *Largest disk* — covers about ½ *of body* (excluding caudal fin); 24–28 laminae. Bluish to gray or brown, usually lighter *above.* Dorsal and anal fins white-edged. To 2½ ft. (76 cm).
Range: Worldwide in warm seas; Vancouver I. to Chile. **Habitat:** Oceanic, mostly in warm seas. Host-specific — clings to marine mammals.
Similar species: (1) Spearfish Remora (below) also has a large disk that extends past the pectoral fin, but it has only 14–17 disk laminae. (2) Other unstriped remoras in our area have a smaller disk (20 or fewer laminae), and cling to different hosts.

SPEARFISH REMORA *Remora brachyptera*   Not shown
Identification: Light brown to gray above; darker below. No side stripe. Disk *small;* 14–17 laminae. 27–34 dorsal fin rays; 25–30 anal fin rays; 23–27 pectoral fin rays. Rarely exceeds 10 in. (25 cm).
Range: Worldwide in warm seas; from s. Calif. south. **Habitat:** On body and inside gill chamber of billfishes and swordfishes; rarely on any other fishes.
Remarks: Also known as the Gray Marlinsucker.
Similar species: Two other unstriped remoras in our area have a small disk: (1) Remora (p. 205) has 21–25 anal fin rays, 26–30 pec-

toral fin rays. (2) White Suckerfish (below) has only 16–22 dorsal fin rays.

MARLINSUCKER *Remora osteochir* **Not shown**
Identification: Brown, with a *very long disk* that extends beyond tip of pectoral fin; disk length about twice its width; 17–20 laminae. 21–27 dorsal fin rays; 20–26 anal fin rays; 20–23 pectoral fin rays. To about 15 in. (38 cm).
Range: Worldwide in warm seas; s. Calif. to Peru. **Habitat:** Oceanic. Strongly host-specific on billfishes, may occasionally cling to other large fishes. On body and inside gill chamber of host.
Similar species: (1) Whalesucker (p. 204) also has a long disk, but it has more (24–28) laminae. (2) Other unstriped remoras in our area have a shorter disk that does not reach tip of pectoral fin.

REMORA *Remora remora* **Pl. 12**
Identification: *Black or dark brown.* Disk *small;* 16–20 laminae. 21–27 dorsal fin rays; 21–25 anal fin rays; 26–30 pectoral fin rays. To 34 in. (86 cm).
Range: Worldwide in warm seas; San Francisco to Chile.
Habitat: Oceanic. Usually on sharks, also attaches itself to other large fishes, sea turtles, and even ships. Sometimes free-swimming.
Remarks: Parasitic copepods taken from the host's body and gill chamber are an important part of this remora's diet. Occasionally caught on baited hook.
Similar species: (1) Marlinsucker (above) has a longer disk (extends past tip of pectoral fin); uses billfishes as hosts. (2) Spearfish Remora (p. 204) has different fin ray counts; other hosts. (3) White Suckerfish (below) has a short, wide disk with only 12–14 laminae, only 16–21 pectoral fin rays; uses manta rays and sharks as hosts.

WHITE SUCKERFISH *Remorina albescens* **Not shown**
Identification: *Grayish to brownish,* no side stripe. Disk *wide and short* — length about $1\frac{1}{2}$ times its width; only 12–14 laminae. 16–22 dorsal fin rays; 20–26 anal fin rays; 16–21 pectoral fin rays. Small — to about 9 in. (23 cm).
Range: Worldwide in warm seas; off San Francisco to Chile, but rare north of Baja. **Habitat:** Host-specific on manta rays, occasionally on sharks. Often inside host's gill chamber and mouth.
Similar species: (1) Spearfish Remora (p. 204) has 27–34 dorsal fin rays; uses billfishes and swordfishes as hosts. (2) Other unstriped remoras have more disk laminae.

Jacks, Amberjacks, and Pompanos: Family Carangidae

Most are silvery, streamlined, fast-swimming fishes. Body shape varies widely, from elongate or torpedo-shaped to deep-bodied and strongly compressed. They usually can be identified by their deeply forked caudal fin, narrow caudal peduncle, and by the *2 detached spines* preceding the anal fin (spines are covered by skin in large adults of some species). Lateral line arched in front and straight behind; in many species the straight part, especially before the caudal fin, is covered by a row of pointed *scutes* (plates formed of modified scales). 3–9 spines in the dorsal fin. Spinous dorsal and soft dorsal fins are separate in adults; spinous dorsal fin low in most species (sometimes covered by skin in adults of some species). Soft dorsal and anal fins usually highest near front, lobed. Usually *no* finlets (detached rays that form tiny flaglike fins at end of soft dorsal and anal fins — see Family Scombridae, p. 269) but some species have 1 finlet, one species has 2. Scales small, usually cycloid (ctenoid in Pilotfish, needlelike in some others outside our area).

Most adults in this family are green, blue, or blackish above; silver to white or yellow-gold on the side and belly; some are barred or striped. The young of many species have bars on the body, often differ from adults in body shape, and have long threadlike fin rays. (Young of many species associate with jellyfish or floating objects.) Adults of most species are 1–3 ft. (30–91 cm).

Jacks and their relatives occur around the world, mostly in warm seas. A few species sometimes enter fresh water, but all apparently spawn in the sea. Most school. Many are sport fishes, and most are important as food fishes. In certain areas, large individuals of some species in this family may contain ciguatera toxin, which can cause a type of severe food poisoning. About 200 species, 12 in our area, but several of them are very rare north of Baja. The more common jacks and their relatives are shown on Pl. 31 and the rarer species are shown in Fig. 40.

GREEN JACK *Caranx caballus* Pl. 31

Identification: Pectoral fin *long. Well-developed scutes* before caudal fin. Breast completely scaled. Usually a spot on rear of gill cover. To 15 in. (38 cm).
Range: Santa Cruz I. (s. Calif.) to Peru, including Galapagos Is.
Habitat: Shallow; inshore to offshore, pelagic. In schools.
Similar species: 2 other jacks have a *long* pectoral fin and often a dark spot on the gill cover: (1) Pacific Crevalle Jack (below) has a blunter snout, a deeper body, a largely unscaled breast (except for a small central patch of scales just in front of pelvic fins — whole breast area fully scaled in the Green Jack), a larger mouth (upper jaw extends to area below rear of eye), and a *dark blotch* on the pectoral fin. (2) Pacific Bumper (p. 208) has weak scutes before caudal fin, a deeper body, and a dark blotch on top of caudal peduncle. (3) See also Mexican Scad (p. 208).

PACIFIC CREVALLE JACK Fig. 40, p. 207
Caranx caninus
Identification: Deeper-bodied than the Green Jack, with a steep,

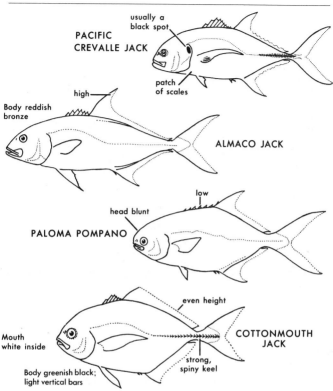

Fig. 40 Jacks (Carangidae) — rare species

rounded head (in profile); but otherwise similar in having *strong* scutes, and usually a *dark spot* on upper rear of gill cover. A black blotch on front part of pectoral fin. Breast unscaled, except for a small patch of scales in front of pelvic fins. Upper jaw extends to area below rear of eye. To at least 2½ ft. (76 cm), probably larger.
Range: Warm waters of e. Pacific; San Diego southward.
Habitat: Inshore; shallow, but larger individuals live deeper. Also in brackish water. Usually in fast-moving schools; large adults sometimes solitary.
Remarks: Feeds mostly on other fishes, also on shrimps and other invertebrates. Often makes a grunting sound when captured. Not especially desirable as a food fish. May be the same species as the Atlantic Crevalle Jack, *Caranx hippos.*
Similar species: See Green Jack (p. 206).

PACIFIC BUMPER *Chloroscombrus orqueta* **Pl. 31**
Identification: Pectoral fin *long,* extends well past front of anal
fin. A dark *blotch* on top of caudal peduncle. Often a dusky blotch
on rear of gill cover. *Weak* scutes on *rear part* of lateral line, near
caudal fin. Soft dorsal and anal fins *long;* 25–30 soft rays in anal
fin. In profile, lower part of body *sags* more than dorsal contour
bows out. Dark bluish above; silvery below. Most fins yellowish.
Dorsal and anal fins have dusky edges. To 1 ft. (30 cm), but usually
less than 8½ in. (22 cm).
Range: San Pedro (s. Calif.) to Peru. **Habitat:** Usually shallow
inshore areas, including brackish water. In schools.
Remarks: Often makes a grunting noise when caught. One of the
smaller jacks in our area.
Similar species: (1) In other jacks with a dark spot on the gill
cover, body is less deep, and scutes before caudal fin are more
prominent. See (2) Green Jack (p. 206), (3) Pacific Crevalle Jack
(p. 206), and (4) Mexican Scad (below).

MEXICAN SCAD *Decapterus scombrinus* **Pl. 31**
Identification: *Elongate.* Spinous dorsal fin *higher* than soft dorsal fin. Pectoral fin *short* — ends well before anal fin. 1 isolated
finlet after dorsal and anal fins. Scutes well developed on straight
part of lateral line (at rear). Greenish or bluish above; yellowish
below. Often has an orangish or reddish side stripe. Fins mostly
dirty yellow. A small dark spot on upper rear of gill cover. To
18¼ in. (46 cm).
Range: Pacific Grove (cen. Calif.) to Galapagos Is.
Habitat: Surface to 78 ft. (24 m). In schools.
Similar species: Often confused with the Jackmackerel (p. 211),
but it has scutes *all along* the lateral line, an accessory lateral line
branch (hard to see) that extends from the head to below the spinous dorsal fin, and its range extends farther north. The Mexican
Scad is firmer and rounder — experts can separate these two species by "feel."

PILOTFISH *Naucrates ductor* **Pl. 31**
Identification: Blackish silver to bluish; with 5-7 *dark bars* that
completely cross the body (in adults). A groove across upper and
lower part of caudal peduncle; a low keel on side of caudal peduncle. Snout rounded. *No scutes* on lateral line. Scales *ctenoid*
(rough). Spinous dorsal fin low. Caudal fin banded, lobes white-
tipped. Also has a temporary color variation (apparently when fish
is excited): bars disappear and background turns silvery white,
with 3 broad blue patches on back. To 2 ft. (61 cm), but usually
less than 1 ft. (30 cm) in our area.
Range: All warm seas; Vancouver I. to Galapagos Is. Uncommon
in our area. **Habitat:** Oceanic, surface or near surface. Usually
around floating or moving objects; young usually associate with
jellyfishes and drifting seaweeds.

Remarks: Pilotfishes congregate around large fishes and ships. The name Pilotfish comes from legendary tales of this species leading lost swimmers, ships, or whales to safety. Often displayed in public aquariums.
Similar species: (1) Atka Mackerel (p. 157; Pl. 22) has a long dorsal fin and a large round pectoral fin. (2) Young of some other jacks have dark bars, but these are lost with growth — disregard color and *use other features* to identify barred specimens under about 4–5 in. (10–13 cm). (Body proportions and fin shape also change with growth, making identification difficult.)

PACIFIC MOONFISH *Selene peruviana*   **Pl. 31**
Identification: The high, *steeply sloping forehead* distinguishes this *strongly compressed* species. Pectoral fin *long,* extends past front of anal fin. Pelvic fin tiny. Spinous dorsal fin *low.* Lateral line strongly arched over pectoral fin; scutes weak. Scales easily rubbed off. Silvery. Often has a faint dark spot on upper rear of gill cover. Young — to about 2 in. (5.1 cm) — have a dark spot on the side. To 11¼ in. (29 cm).
Range: Redondo Beach (s. Calif.) to Peru, but usually rare north of Baja. **Habitat:** Usually inshore, in schools.

YELLOWTAIL *Seriola lalandi*   **Pl. 31**
Identification: A large silvery fish, with *yellowish fins* and a *yellow* to dusky *side stripe.* A darker, slightly oblique stripe extends from snout through eye. Spinous dorsal fin *low.* Anal fin begins well *behind* front of soft dorsal fin. Pectoral fin short, ends below spinous dorsal fin. *No scutes* on lateral line. A cross-groove on upper and lower part of caudal peduncle. To 5 ft. (152 cm), 80 lb. (36 kg), but usually 10–20 lb. (4.5–9.1 kg).
Range: B.C. to Chile; nearly worldwide in subtropical waters (see Remarks below). Adults occur farther north in summer and fall. **Habitat:** Common around offshore islands; also coastal; off kelp beds and rocky areas; near surface in summer and fall. To 228 ft. (69 m). Usually in schools.
Remarks: A common large sport fish in s. Calif. and Baja; caught mostly on live bait or by trolling, also by spearfishing. Fished commercially. Excellent eating when fresh or smoked (most cooks remove the oily dark flesh along midside). As in many jack species, young under 5 in. (13 cm) have dark bars on side. Eats fishes, squids, pelagic crabs, and other invertebrates. The e. Pacific population of yellowtails is sometimes treated as a separate subspecies, *S. lalandi dorsalis,* or even as a separate species, *S. dorsalis.*
Similar species: Almaco Jack (below) has a reddish bronze body and dark fins.

ALMACO JACK *Seriola rivoliana*   **Fig. 40, p. 207**
Identification: A *large* jack, with a *low* spinous dorsal fin, *no finlets,* a *short* pectoral fin, and *no scutes.* Pelvic fin longer than

pectoral fin. Anal fin begins well behind front of soft dorsal fin. Soft dorsal fin very high at front. A cross-groove on upper and lower part of caudal peduncle. Usually *metallic bronze* or brown, olive, or sometimes bluish green. Often a dark stripe through eye to upper back. Sometimes an amber stripe extends from eye along the body. Fins mostly dusky, but variable — some have pale areas. Young — under about $7\frac{3}{4}$ in. (20 cm) — have bars. To at least 59 in. (150 cm), 126 lb. (57 kg).

Range: Worldwide in warm tropical seas. Oceanside (s. Calif.) to Peru, including Galapagos Is. **Habitat:** Pelagic, also near bottom; offshore and inshore. Young are pelagic, usually found under floating objects offshore.

Remarks: Sometimes captured on baited hook on bottom or by trolling. Good eating. The e. Pacific population is thought by some researchers to be a separate species, *S. colburni,* with the common name Pacific Amberjack.

Similar species: (1) See Yellowtail (p. 209). (2) Other similar jacks have no cross-grooves before the caudal fin and most of them have scutes on the lateral line.

PALOMA POMPANO *Trachinotus paitensis*   **Fig. 40, p. 207**
Identification: Note the blunt head, with a *rounded snout* and a *small mouth* (lower jaw does not project beyond upper jaw). Spinous dorsal fin very *low.* No finlets. Pectoral fin *short.* Dorsal and anal fin bases about same length. *No cross-groove* on upper and lower part of caudal peduncle. *No scutes* on lateral line. No distinctive markings. Metallic bluish or greenish above; silvery on side; white below. Fins more or less blackish, highest part of dorsal fin black. To 20 in. (51 cm).

Range: Redondo Beach (s. Calif.) to Peru, including Galapagos Is.; rare north of Baja. **Habitat:** Usually in shallow inshore sandy areas.

Remarks: Excellent eating.

Similar species: (1) Other similar jacks and pompanos have a *long* pectoral fin, a *high* spinous dorsal fin, *scutes* on the lateral line, a more *pointed* snout, or distinctive color markings. (2) Gafftopsail Pompano (below) usually has bars on body and higher lobes on dorsal and anal fins.

GAFFTOPSAIL POMPANO *Trachinotus rhodopus*   **Pl. 31**
Identification: Deep-bodied, compressed. Easily identified by the narrow yellowish *bars* on the side and the *elongate lobe* at the front of the soft dorsal and anal fins. Snout *blunt.* No scutes on lateral line. Spinous dorsal fin *low;* pectoral fin short. Silvery, with dusky to yellowish bars on side. Fins yellow to reddish, usually darker at edge. To 2 ft. (61 cm).

Range: Zuma Beach (s. Calif.) to Peru, including Galapagos Is.; rare north of s. Baja. **Habitat:** Inshore sandy areas, also around reefs and rocky areas.

Similar species: Paloma Pompano (above) has a similar shape but rays at front of its soft dorsal and anal fins are only *slightly* elongate; *no bars* on side.

JACKMACKEREL *Trachurus symmetricus*   **Pl. 31**
Identification: A common northern jack. Spinous dorsal fin slightly higher than soft dorsal fin. Pectoral fin ends before front of anal fin. *Scutes on all of lateral line* — scutes at front are smaller. Lateral line dips strongly at end of pectoral fin. In some large individuals, last few rays at rear of soft dorsal and anal fins are almost entirely separate from rest of fin — like finlets. Metallic blue to olive-green above; silvery below. *Dark spot* on upper rear of gill cover. Top of head and area near eye quite dark. Fins mostly clear, but caudal fin yellowish to reddish. To 32 in. (81 cm).
Range: Se. Alaska to s. Baja; reported from Acapulco (Mex.) and Galapagos Is. **Habitat:** Surface to at least 600 ft. (183 m); often offshore. Pelagic, often in large schools. Young frequently school near kelp and under piers.
Remarks: Often caught on baited hook from piers and boats, also while salmon trolling. Commercially fished along our coast; canned. Feeds on crustaceans, other pelagic organisms, small fishes. Large individuals often move inshore and north in the summer.
Similar species: See under Mexican Scad (p. 208).

COTTONMOUTH JACK *Uraspis secunda*   **Fig. 40, p. 207**
Identification: A *dark,* oval jack. Spinous dorsal fin low. Pectoral fin long, more so in adults. 2 detached spines before anal fin (as in other jacks) are often buried or absent in individuals larger than about 6 in. (15 cm). No scales on breast. Scutes present on straight part of lateral line (at rear). No dark spot on rear of gill cover. Tongue, roof, and floor of *mouth white* (hence the name); sides and rear of mouth black. Body and head blackish. 6–8 narrow pale bars in young — absent in specimens over about 1 ft. (30 cm). To about $18\frac{1}{2}$ in. (47 cm), but usually less than $14\frac{1}{2}$ in. (37 cm).
Range: Warm waters of Atlantic and Pacific; Santa Catalina I. (s. Calif.) to Costa Rica; rare north of Baja. **Habitat:** Apparently mostly oceanic and pelagic, sometimes near bottom; often near islands. Solitary or in small schools.
Similar species: Other jacks *lack* the *white and black* areas inside the mouth.

Roosterfishes: Family Nematistiidae

ROOSTERFISH *Nematistius pectoralis*   **Pl. 31**
Identification: A large, jacklike fish. Easily recognized by the "comb" of elongate, *threadlike dorsal fin spines.* Spines dark at tips, yellow in middle, dusky at base. *2 dark curved stripes* on

body. Back slightly dusky, iridescent; silvery below. To about 4 ft. (122 cm), 100 lb. (45 kg); usually under 3 ft. (91 cm).

Range: San Clemente (s. Calif.) to Peru, including Galapagos Is.; rare north of Baja. **Habitat:** Shallow inshore areas; frequents sandy shores along beaches. Young sometimes in tidepools.

Remarks: Only 1 species in the family; some researchers place it in the previous family (Carangidae, p. 205). A good sport fish — good eating and a scrappy fighter on light tackle.

Dolphins or Dolphinfishes: Family Coryphaenidae

There are 2 species of dolphins and both apparently occur worldwide in tropical and subtropical seas, but only 1 reaches our area. These colorful, iridescent fishes have a long compressed body and a deeply *forked* caudal fin. Dorsal and anal fins *long,* with no sharp spines; dorsal fin begins on head, ends just before caudal fin. Scales *tiny,* cycloid. The species in our area is larger; it grows to $6\frac{3}{4}$ ft. (207 cm). These oceanic fishes are sometimes called dolphinfishes to distinguish them from dolphins (porpoises).

DOLPHIN *Coryphaena hippurus*   **Pl. 46**
Identification: Dorsal fin *long,* begins on head. Caudal fin forked. Body compressed. Lateral line wavy above pectoral fin. Forehead high and rounded in males (shown); less steep in females. Brilliant *yellowish green, with iridescent tints* and blue to green spots. Silvery on side, often with a golden sheen. Occasionally displays bars when excited. Most fins dark; anal fin often has a pale edge. Color changes rapidly at death — becomes purplish or gray and dull greenish yellow. Young — under about 6 in. (15 cm) — have dark bars on body, black pelvic fin, and white tips on caudal fin. To $6\frac{3}{4}$ ft. (207 cm) or larger, commonly to $3\frac{1}{4}$ ft. (99 cm); weighs up to 87 lb. (39 kg) or more.

Range: Worldwide in warmer seas; Grays Harbor (Wash.) to Chile, including Galapagos Is.; rare north of s. Calif. **Habitat:** Usually near surface in open ocean, sometimes inshore. Common near objects, will follow boats.

Remarks: A fast swimmer — said to reach 40 mph (64 km/hr). Prized as a sport fish — caught mainly by trolling and with floating lines behind boats. Good eating (the source of *mahi mahi* served in restaurants). Uncommon in our area, usually in small schools offshore in warm-water years and late summer. Feeds on other fishes, crustaceans, and squids.

Pomfrets: Family Bramidae

A small family of oceanic deepsea fishes. Head *blunt,* rounded. Body deep, somewhat compressed. Dorsal and anal fins are long, usually highest in front; rays at front often quite elongate. Pectoral fin long. Caudal fin forked. Mouth oblique, fairly large, with teeth in bands. Scales moderate to large, usually extend *well onto* dorsal and anal fins. (*Scale size* is useful for identification — scales in midlateral row are counted at the midside from the gill opening to the end of scales on the caudal fin.) Most species are black, bluish black, or silvery. To about 39 in. (1 m), but most species are smaller.

Pomfrets occur in temperate and tropical waters of all oceans, usually near the surface in open ocean. Some species probably school. They eat mostly fishes and squids. Rarely seen except by researchers, but sometimes caught by salmon and Albacore trollers, and on longlines. About 20 species (some poorly known), 5 in our area.

PACIFIC POMFRET *Brama japonica*   **Pl. 48**
Identification: Nearly *oval, blunt-headed,* compressed. *Silvery black,* with pectoral, pelvic, and caudal fins paler at edge. Dorsal and anal fins black-edged. Caudal fin large, *forked.* Unscaled area on snout. Scales on body moderate in size; smaller scales extend well onto dorsal and anal fins. Front of dorsal and anal fins *high* in adults, rounded in young. To 2 ft. (61 cm), perhaps larger.
Range: Throughout N. Pacific — Japan to Bering Sea and south to Peru. **Habitat:** Oceanic, near surface; rarely taken inshore. Often abundant.
Similar species: (1) In Sickle Pomfret (p. 214) dorsal and anal fins are higher at front, scales on caudal peduncle are *abruptly larger* than those at base of caudal fin (scale size increases gradually in Pacific Pomfret). (2) See Pacific Fanfish (below). (3) Some jacks (Pl. 31 and Fig. 40, p. 207) are similar, but they are not silvery black; usually have 2 detached anal fin spines before the rest of the anal fin, and tiny scales. (4) Pacific Butterfish (p. 280; Pl. 31) lacks pelvic fins, has tiny scales. **Note:** 2 additional rare pomfrets occur in our area: (1) Bigtooth Pomfret, *Brama orcini,* is nearly identical to Pacific Pomfret but has *larger scales* (fewer than 60 in midlateral row; over 75 in Pacific Pomfret). In large adults pectoral fin is set higher on body and its base is more horizontal; upper lobe of caudal fin longer than lower lobe. To at least 13¾ in. (35 cm). Mid-Pacific and Indian Ocean to s. Calif. (2) In Rough Pomfret, *Taractes asper,* area between eyes is *flat* to concave (not arched and rounded). Scales *large;* about 40–45 scales in midlateral row. To at least 19¾ in. (50 cm). Known from scattered records from all oceans, including from Alaska to s. Calif.

PACIFIC FANFISH   **Pl. 48**
Pteraclis aesticola
Identification: Note the *huge, blackish fanlike dorsal and anal fins,* which can be folded into a scaly sheath at base of each fin.

Pelvic fin small. Silvery body. Eye orange-red. To about 2 ft. (61 cm).
Range: Probably throughout n. and se. Pacific; rare off Calif.
Habitat: Oceanic; poorly known. Young probably shallow, adults deep. Sometimes caught in bottom trawls.
Remarks: Very rare — most likely to be seen as stomach content of large predatory fishes, such as tunas.
Similar species: (1) Young of other pomfrets in our area have large dorsal and anal fins, but no scaled sheath along the base. (2) Veilfin (below) is more oval, and has a larger pelvic fin.

SICKLE POMFRET   **Not shown**
Taractichthys steindachneri
Identification: Similar to other pomfrets, but with *larger scales* (38 or fewer in midlateral row). Scales just before caudal fin *abruptly larger* than those on caudal fin. Scales rough in young, smooth in adults. Scales extend onto dorsal and anal fins. No lateral line in adults. Area between eye *rounded outward* (convex). Fins do not fit into a groove. Front of dorsal and anal fins high, *sickle-shaped* (except in young). Pectoral fin long. Caudal fin deeply forked. To 3 ft. (91 cm).
Range: Warmer waters of Pacific and Indian Oceans; from about Pt. Conception south. Rare in our area. **Habitat:** Oceanic; may range widely in water column. Little known.
Remarks: Frequently caught on tuna longlines by Japanese; marketed in Japan.
Similar species: See under Pacific Pomfret (p. 213).

Veilfins: Family Caristiidae

A poorly known family of deepsea fishes. Dorsal fin *high,* anal fin large. Pelvic fins long. Dorsal, anal, and pelvic fins can be folded into a *deep groove* (scaly sheath) at base of fins. Scales thin, cycloid. Bones weak — specimens usually are damaged during capture. Adults brownish; young pale, with well-marked bars. To about 12½ in. (32 cm). Veilfins occur in deep midwaters; adults sometimes are caught in bottom trawls. About 6 species, 1 in our area.

VEILFIN *Caristius macropus*   **Not shown**
Identification: Most like the Pacific Fanfish (Pl. 48), with a sail-like dorsal fin and large anal and pelvic fins, but body more oval, head blunt. *Fins black;* body paler — probably brownish or pinkish brown, possibly silver in life. To 12½ in. (32 cm).
Range: N. Pacific and other oceans. **Habitat:** Little known; normally deep. Adults occasionally are caught in bottom trawls at about 1000–2000 ft. (305–610 m).
Similar species: See Pacific Fanfish (p. 213).

Snappers: Family Lutjanidae

Only stragglers from this tropical family reach our area. They are perchlike or basslike. Usually 1 continuous dorsal fin, 1st half spinous. Snout and area around eye unscaled; ctenoid scales cover most of head and body. Caudal fin square-cut to forked. Rear of upper jaw fits into a *groove* (and is partially hidden) when mouth is closed. Jaw teeth sharp, conical, usually in a few rows; no molars. Color varies: mostly yellow, red, and blue; often striped, barred, or blotched. Most are about 1–2 ft. (30–61 cm).

Snappers occur worldwide in tropical seas, mostly in shallow inshore areas and on reefs. About 230 species. Two species rarely reach our area, although other e. Pacific snappers might also be encountered in warm-water years.

AMARILLO SNAPPER   **Fig. 39, p. 198**
Lutjanus argentiventris
Identification: Basslike. Body *rose-red* at front, lighter (*mostly yellow*) at rear; often mostly golden overall. Back sometimes bronze-brown. Caudal fin yellow. *Blue spots or streak under eye* and usually a dark streak through eye (often absent in large individuals). Rear of upper jaw fits into a groove when mouth is closed. To at least 2 ft. (61 cm).
Range: Oceanside (s. Calif.) to Peru, including Galapagos Is. Rare north of Baja. **Habitat:** Inshore, shallow.
Similar species: (1) Colorado Snapper (below) is mostly reddish, caudal fin not yellow. In (2) true basses (p. 197; Pl. 29 and Fig. 39, p. 198) and (3) rockfishes (p. 132; Pls. 23–28) rear of the upper jaw is fully *exposed,* not concealed in a groove when mouth is closed. Rockfishes also have spines on the rear cheek area. (4) Pacific Porgy (p. 218; Pl. 35) has *molarlike* teeth in rear of jaws. (5) Grunts (p. 216; Pl. 35) have scales between the mouth and eye (absent in our snappers).

COLORADO SNAPPER *Lutjanus colorado*   **Not shown**
Identification: Same shape as Amarillo Snapper (Fig. 39), but body mostly *red,* caudal fin *not* yellow. Sometimes a blue streak under eye. Young barred. Pectoral fin longer (reaches past anus). To 3 ft. (91 cm).
Range: Estero Bay (San Luis Obispo Co., cen. Calif.) to Panama; rare north of Baja. **Habitat:** Inshore.
Similar species: See Amarillo Snapper (above).

Mojarras: Family Gerreidae

These are small fishes, with a compressed oblong body, *forked* caudal fin, and *pointed* snout. 1 dorsal fin, with a spinous and soft-

rayed part. Dorsal and anal fins fold into a groove formed by
scaled sheath at base. Pectoral fin pointed, fairly long. Pelvic fins
on breast, below or slightly behind front of pectoral fin, with a
fleshy skin flap at base. Mouth small and *very protrusible* —
points downward when extended. Chin concave in profile.
Mojarras are mostly silver; some are barred or striped, often with
black and yellow. Most are under 8 in. (20 cm); a few species reach
15 in. (38 cm).

Mojarras occur in shallow tropical and warm temperate coastal
seas off N. and S. America, and in the w. Pacific and Indian
Oceans. They are common inshore, frequently on sand or mud
bottom. Most species are marine; a few enter brackish or fresh
water. About 40 species, 2 rarely in our area.

SPOTFIN MOJARRA   Not shown
Eucinostomus argenteus
Identification: Similar to Pacific Flagfin Mojarra (Pl. 34) but
dorsal fin is dusky, with no distinct spot at tip. Greenish on back;
silvery below. To 8 in. (20 cm).
Range: Anaheim Bay (s. Calif.) to Peru. **Habitat:** Bays and
shallow inshore areas, often along sand beaches.
Similar species: See Pacific Flagfin Mojarra (below).

PACIFIC FLAGFIN MOJARRA   Pl. 34
Eucinostomus gracilis
Identification: Silvery, compressed, with a *forked* caudal fin and
a very *protrusible mouth* (open mouth to observe). Spinous dorsal
fin *dark at tip,* silver in middle, dark near base. Body greenish
above; silvery below. To $8\frac{1}{4}$ in. (21 cm).
Range: Anaheim Bay (s. Calif.) to Peru; rare north of Baja.
Habitat: Bays and shallow inshore areas.
Similar species: (1) In Spotfin Mojarra (above) spinous dorsal
fin is dusky, not black-tipped. (2) In Surfperches (p. 226; Pls. 36–
37) mouth is not as protrusible; 2nd and 3rd spines in dorsal fin are
shorter.

Grunts: Family Haemulidae

A large, mostly tropical family of basslike fishes that are hard to
characterize. Usually 1 dorsal fin, with a spinous and a soft-rayed
part. Caudal fin square-cut to indented. Area between mouth and
eye *scaled.* Mouth fairly small, with thick lips; *no* long canines or
molars. No large spines on rear cheek area. Upper jaw fits into a
groove when mouth is closed. Family name comes from grunting
sounds these fishes make by rubbing tooth plates in throat together. Solid-colored to barred, striped, or spotted. Most species
grow to about 1 ft. (30 cm).

Grunts occur worldwide in shallow warm seas. Most are marine, but a few occur in brackish or fresh water. Some researchers call this family Pomadasyidae or Pristipomatidae. About 175 species, 3 in our area.

SARGO *Anisotremus davidsonii*   Pl. 35

Identification: Note the *dark bar* on the back, just before mid-body (occasionally absent). Young have 2 stripes on body, no bar. Mouth fairly small. Dorsal fin long, notched; with 11–12 spines, 14–16 soft rays. Back gray; most of body silvery, except for dark bar on side and dark patch at base of pectoral fin. Gill cover dark-edged. Albino or golden specimens are seen occasionally. To 17½ in. (44 cm), but reported to 23 in. (58 cm).
Range: Santa Cruz (cen. Calif.) to s. Baja; isolated population in Gulf of Calif. Rare north of Pt. Conception. **Habitat:** Over rocky or rock-sand bottom, often near kelp beds. To 130 ft. (40 m), but usually shallower than 25 ft. (7.6 m). Usually in schools.
Remarks: Good eating. Caught on baited hook from shore or boats. Feeds on crustaceans, mollusks, and bryozoans.
Similar species: Often confused with surfperches (p. 226; Pls. 36–37), especially (1) Pile Surfperch (p. 228; Pl. 37) and (2) Rubberlip Surfperch (p. 232; Pl. 36); but surfperches usually have *more than 20* soft rays in anal fin (Sargo has 9–11), a sheath of scales at the base of the dorsal fin, a different-shaped dorsal fin, and *smooth* scales (scales rough in Sargo).

WAVYLINE GRUNT   Fig. 39, p. 198
Microlepidotus inornatus

Identification: Basslike. 7–9 *orange-brown stripes* on a bluish gray background; stripes on upper back *wavy*. Mouth fairly small. No deep notch in dorsal fin. Scaled sheath at base of dorsal and anal fins. To about 1 ft. (30 cm).
Range: Baja to Mazatlan (Mex.); stragglers reach s. Calif.
Habitat: Reefs and rocky areas. In large schools during the day.
Similar species: See Salema (below).

SALEMA *Xenistius californiensis*   Pl. 35

Identification: 6–8 *orange-brown to yellowish stripes* (darker in young). Body iridescent blue to greenish silver above; silvery below. Mouth small. Eye large. Dorsal fin in 2 distinct parts, not joined to each other. To 10 in. (25 cm) but usually 6 in. (15 cm) or less.
Range: Monterey Bay to Peru; common in s. Calif. but rare north of Pt. Conception. **Habitat:** Among rocks and high up in kelp beds at 4–35 ft. (1.2–11 m). Usually in schools.
Similar species: Wavyline Grunt (above) has *wavy* orangish stripes, a continuous dorsal fin, and rarely reaches our area.

Porgies: Family Sparidae

Deep-bodied, compressed, perchlike fishes with a small mouth that is located low on the head. Forehead often steep (in profile). Snout unscaled. Scales on body cycloid or weakly ctenoid (see rear endpapers). 1 dorsal fin. Pectoral fin long, pointed. Fleshy skin flap at base of pelvic fins. Caudal fin usually forked. Porgies usually have canine teeth or incisors but also have strong *molars* at middle and rear of jaws. Most species are plain — silver to reddish or very dark; some are striped (especially when young) or spotted. Usually 1 ft. (30 cm) or less; a few reach 2 ft. (61 cm), and 1 off S. Africa grows to 4 ft. (122 cm).

Porgies are bottom-dwelling fishes of tropical and temperate seas. A few species occur in cold water and some occasionally enter brackish or fresh water. Many are important as food fishes. About 100 species, 1 in our area.

PACIFIC PORGY *Calamus brachysomus*   **Pl. 35**
Identification: Deep-bodied. Mouth set *low* on the head. *Rear teeth molarlike.* 1 dorsal fin, with 12–13 spines, 11–13 soft rays. No scales between mouth and eye. Mostly silver; brownish or greenish on back and side. Faint brownish bars and mottling on body and fins, especially on caudal fin. Can change color pattern rapidly to dark irregular blotches. To about 2 ft. (61 cm), but usually under 16 in. (41 cm).
Range: Oceanside (s. Calif.) to Peru; rare north of Baja. **Habitat:** Sandy areas. To 225 ft. (69 m) but usually at 10–60 ft. (3–18 m).
Similar species: Our other perchlike fishes usually have a larger mouth with *no molarlike teeth,* a less deep body, shorter pectoral fin, and scales between mouth and eye.

Croakers: Family Sciaenidae

These elongate, usually silvery fishes have a long dorsal fin — usually divided by a notch into a spinous part with 7–16 (usually 9–11) spines, and a soft-rayed part with 1 spine and many soft rays. (The spinous and soft-rayed parts are separate in some species.) Usually 2 anal fin spines. Pelvic fins thoracic, just behind and below the pectoral fins. Caudal fin often pointed or rounded, or square-cut to slightly indented, but not deeply forked; fin usually longer in young. Lateral line extends to *rear edge* of caudal fin. Mouth at front end, or on underside of head in bottom-feeding species. Scales cycloid or ctenoid. Muscular, modified air bladder enables most croakers to produce drumming sounds. Most adults are silvery to dark brown, often with a yellowish belly. Some have dark spots, stripes, or blotches on body or fins. Young sometimes have a radically different color pattern.

Croakers are common shore fishes of tropical and warm temperate seas, with fewer species in cold waters. Many species live in estuaries; some are found in fresh water. Most occur in shallow water, some at depths up to 1969 ft. (600 m) or more. Croakers have large calcareous "earstones" in their inner ear canals; these were considered good luck charms by early Europeans and were used by American Indians in jewelry and for other ornamental purposes. About 250 species, 8 in our area.

WHITE SEABASS *Atractoscion nobilis*   Pl. 33
Identification: A large croaker. Lower jaw *projects slightly* beyond upper jaw. No enlarged canine teeth. *No chin barbel. Raised ridge* down center of belly. Young — up to about 2 ft. (61 cm) — have 3–6 dusky bars on side and dusky yellow fins. Adults gray-blue to coppery above; whitish or silvery below. Small dark specks on body; black spot at base (on inner side) of pectoral fin. To 5 ft. (152 cm), about 90 lb. (41 kg).
Range: Juneau (Alaska) to s. Baja and n. Gulf of Calif.; rare north of n. Calif. **Habitat:** Usually in schools over rocky bottom and in kelp beds. Also in surf zone. To about 400 ft. (122 m). Young in bays and along sand beaches.
Remarks: An important sport and commercial species. Spawns Mar.–Aug., often near kelp beds. Feeds on fishes and squids.
Similar species: (1) Shortfin Corvina (p. 220) has 1 or 2 large canine teeth on each side of upper jaw. (2) Queenfish (p. 221) has a wide *gap* between the dorsal fins and many more soft rays in anal fin (21–23, not 8–10).

BLACK CROAKER *Cheilotrema saturnum*   Pl. 33
Identification: Our only croaker with *black on upper rear of gill cover.* Upper jaw projects beyond lower jaw. Head profile quite steep; body deep. *No chin barbel.* Dusky to purplish or blackish, with coppery patches above; silvery with dark specks below. Usually a vague pale bar at midbody. Fins dusky. Young (shown) have stripes on upper $\frac{2}{3}$ of body but older fish usually have broad bars. Color also depends on habitat and time of day — striped when over sand, light tan in clear open water; mostly dark brown to blackish, with pale spots, at night or when in caves. To 15 in. (38 cm), $1\frac{1}{2}$ lb. (0.7 kg).
Range: Pt. Conception to n.-cen. Baja and upper Gulf of Calif. **Habitat:** Near sand bottom, often in caves and crevices of exposed coast and open bays. To 150 ft. (46 m) but adults usually at 10–50 ft. (3–15 m).
Remarks: Active mostly at night; feeds on small crustaceans, especially crabs. Common, but seldom caught on hook and line. Often speared. Cannot be sold (protected under Calif. law).
Similar species: (1) Our other croakers *lack* the prominent black patch on the gill cover. Striped young Black Croakers resemble

and sometimes school with young (2) Salemas and (3) Sargos (p. 217) — see Pl. 35.

SHORTFIN CORVINA *Cynoscion parvipinnis* **Not shown**
Identification: Mostly silver. *Lower jaw projects* beyond upper jaw. *No black spot* at base of pectoral fin. *No chin barbel.* Pectoral fin short, does not reach tip of pelvic fin (when pelvic fin is depressed against body). 1 or 2 large canine teeth on each side of upper jaw. Caudal fin slightly indented. Blue-gray above; silvery below. Inside of mouth yellow-orange. To 20 in. (51 cm).
Range: Huntington Beach (s. Calif.) to Mazatlan (Mex.), including Gulf of Calif.; rare north of Baja. **Habitat:** Shallow inshore sandy areas.
Similar species: (1) Black Croaker (p. 219) has a *black spot* at base of pectoral fin. (2) White Seabass (p. 219) has *no* canine teeth in upper jaw. (3) Other croakers have bars or stripes, or have a black spot on the gill cover, a chin barbel, a projecting snout, or 2 separate dorsal fins.

WHITE CROAKER *Genyonemus lineatus* **Pl. 33**
Identification: 12–16 spines in 1st dorsal fin (11 or fewer in our other croakers). Snout projects slightly beyond mouth. Upper jaw extends forward beyond lower jaw. Some individuals have inconspicuous barbels on chin, but no single large barbel. Usually a *small black spot* at top of pectoral fin base. Silvery above, sometimes brassy with dark specks; lighter below. Indistinct wavy lines along scale rows. Fins white to yellowish; caudal fin usually dark-edged. To $16\frac{1}{4}$ in. (41 cm), but usually less than 1 ft. (30 cm).
Range: Barkley Sound (B.C.) to s. Baja; rare north of Calif.
Habitat: Inshore, usually shallower than 100 ft. (30 m); to 600 ft. (183 m). In schools.
Remarks: This species and the White Seabass are the *only* croakers normally found *north* of cen. Calif. An important sport fish commonly caught from piers and boats; commercial catch sold in fresh-fish markets.
Similar species: Similar to other croakers with a projecting snout but (1) California Corbina (below) has a single chin barbel; (2) Yellowfin Croaker (p. 222) has a single chin barbel and dark wavy lines on its body; and (3) Spotfin Croaker (p. 221) has a *large* black area at base of pectoral fin. (4) See Black Croaker (p. 219).

CALIFORNIA CORBINA *Menticirrhus undulatus* **Pl. 33**
Identification: Large, elongate — more *slender* than other croakers. A short, stiff chin *barbel.* Belly markedly *flattened.* Snout blunt, *projects* beyond mouth. Pectoral fin large, *fanlike.* Deep gray to steel blue on back; white below. Sometimes has alternating light and dark oblique streaks. Pectoral fin black. To at least 28 in. (71 cm), about $8\frac{1}{2}$ lb. (3.9 kg); but usually weighs 3–4 lb. (1.4–1.8 kg).

Range: Pt. Conception to Gulf of Calif. **Habitat:** Along sandy shores and in bays; usually in sandy surf of exposed outer coast. To 45 ft. (14 m). Usually in small groups; larger fish are more solitary.
Remarks: An important sport fish for surf and pier fishermen. Illegal to take with nets or to sell in Calif. Adults eat mostly sand crabs, also small crustaceans and marine worms. No air bladder (unlike in most croakers) — unable to make croaking sounds.
Similar species: Yellowfin Croaker (p. 222) also has a chin barbel but it has a deeper body, small spines on rear cheek area, and 2 anal fin spines (only 1 weak spine in California Corbina).

SPOTFIN CROAKER *Roncador stearnsii*   **Pl. 33**
Identification: Recognizable by the large *black spot at base of pectoral fin*. Snout *blunt, projects* beyond mouth. *No chin barbel.* First 2 spines (not just 2nd one) in anal fin strong. Small spines on rear cheek area (preopercle). Bluish gray to metallic gray above; brassy on side, silver to white below. Occasionally golden. Breeding males have golden pectoral and pelvic fins; females have blackish streaks on belly. To 27 in. (69 cm), 10½ lb. (4.8 kg).
Range: Pt. Conception to s. Baja; not common north of Los Angeles. **Habitat:** Sandy shores and bays, mostly in shallow surf zone, but also to 50 ft. (15 m). Often near rocks and entrances to bays. Usually in small groups, but aggregates for spawning.
Remarks: An excellent sport fish, caught in surf and off piers. Adults feed on invertebrates, such as marine worms, clams, crabs, and small crustaceans.
Similar species: (1) White Croaker (p. 220) has a small dark spot at upper base of pectoral fin; 12–16 (not 9–10) spines in 1st dorsal fin. (2) White Seabass (p. 219) is more elongate and its snout does not project beyond the mouth.

QUEENFISH *Seriphus politus*   **Pl. 33**
Identification: Our only croaker with a *wide gap* between spinous and soft-rayed dorsal fins. Soft dorsal and anal fins about *equal* in length; 21–23 soft rays in anal fin. Mouth large, slightly oblique; snout does *not* project beyond mouth. No chin barbel. Bluish or tan above; becoming silver below. Fins often yellowish. To 1 ft. (30 cm).
Range: Yaquina Bay (Ore.) to s.-cen. Baja. Common in Calif. **Habitat:** Inshore, often over sand bottom; common in bays and tidal sloughs, around pilings. Reported at depths up to 70 ft. (21 m), usually at 4–27 ft. (1.2–8.2 m). In schools. Moves into deeper water at night.
Remarks: Often used as a bait fish, but has limited value as a food fish. Feeds mostly on crustaceans and small fishes. Frequently caught on baited hook; occasionally fished commercially.
Similar species: (1) Most like the White Seabass (p. 219), but it has 8–10 anal fin soft rays. (2) Other croakers have little or no gap

between spinous and soft-rayed parts of dorsal fin; shorter anal fin
(with fewer than 15 rays).

YELLOWFIN CROAKER *Umbrina roncador*   **Pl. 33**
Identification: Short *chin barbel.* Snout projects beyond mouth.
2 strong anal fin spines. Metallic gray or green or bluish above;
white below. Dark brownish yellow oblique stripes on back and
side (along scale rows). Fins mostly yellow, dorsal fin darker. To
20 in. (51 cm), 3.9 lb. (1.8 kg).
Range: Pt. Conception to Gulf of Calif.; old records from as far
north as San Francisco. **Habitat:** Shallow sandy areas, often in
surf, bays, and tidal sloughs; to 25 ft. (7.6 m).
Remarks: Often caught by surf fishermen. In Calif. a sport fish
only—protected by law (cannot be bought, sold, or caught with
nets). Feeds on small fishes and invertebrates.
Similar species: California Corbina (p. 220) also has a chin
barbel, but its body is more elongate and stripes on back (when
present) are not oblique; only 1 (weak) spine in anal fin.

Goatfishes: Family Mullidae

Elongate, chunky fishes, with a pair of *long barbels under the
chin.* The barbels can be concealed in a groove on the throat. 2
dorsal fins — spinous dorsal fin (with 6–8 spines) well *separated*
from soft-rayed dorsal fin (with 1 spine, usually 8 soft rays). Caudal fin forked. Mouth fairly small, on lower part of head. Teeth
small, conical. Scales large, weakly ctenoid. Many species are red,
orange, or yellowish to brown. Usually striped. Fins usually striped
or barred. Young often light tan or blue. Usually under 1 ft.
(30 cm); a few approach 2 ft. (61 cm).
   Goatfishes occur in all warm seas, mostly in the tropics. A few
species live in temperate waters. These fishes are found near shore,
normally on sand or mud bottom where they feed, using their
barbels to probe for small invertebrates. Many are important as
food fishes. About 55–60 species, 2 rarely in our area.

MEXICAN GOATFISH *Mulloidichthys dentatus*   **Pl. 35**
Identification: Easily identified by the pair of *long barbels under
the chin* (but these may be folded back and hard to see). *2 dorsal
fins,* 1st one with 7 spines. Caudal fin forked. Scales large. Yellowish silver or pink to rose; a darker red or yellow *side stripe,* usually
bordered with blue. Fins mostly yellow. To 12¼ in. (31 cm).
Range: Long Beach (s. Calif.) to Peru, including Galapagos Is.;
rare north of s. Baja. **Habitat:** Rocky inshore areas and to 125 ft.
(38 m). Often in small schools. Young pelagic.
Similar species: In our area no other fishes have a pair of long
barbels under the chin. **Note:** Bigscale Goatfish, *Pseudupeneus
grandisquamis,* normally occurs from Baja to Chile, but 1 speci-

men was caught at the artificially warm outfall at the San Onofre (s. Calif.) nuclear power plant in 1979. It is like the Mexican Goatfish but it is nearly solid rosy red and has 3 (not 6) rows of scales between the dorsal fins. To about 12 in. (30 cm).

Sea Chubs: Family Kyphosidae

This family includes 3 subfamilies: the rudderfishes (Kyphosinae), nibblers (Girellinae), and halfmoons (Scorpidinae); some researchers treat them as separate families. These fishes have a small mouth and a blunt head, an indented caudal fin, a somewhat oval body, and a more or less continuous dorsal fin. Cutting (incisorlike) *teeth, usually in 1 main row;* each tooth has a round tip and a *long* curved base. Main row of teeth bordered by small pointed teeth. Scales small, ctenoid; extend onto most fins. Sea chubs are usually drab, with yellowish or bluish stripes; some are spotted. A few reach 3 ft. (91 cm), most grow to 2 ft. (61 cm) or less.

Rudderfishes occur in all warm seas, nibblers only in the Pacific, and halfmoons in the Pacific and Indian Oceans. Usually occur in schools in inshore waters, particularly around rocks or reefs. Many species are herbivorous (feed on algae). About 30 species; 3 in our area, 2 more as stragglers.

OPALEYE *Girella nigricans*   **Pl. 34**
Identification: *Oval; olive-green* or gray-green, usually with *2 pale spots* below dorsal fin (some specimens over 1 ft. — 30 cm — lack the pale spots). Eye *blue-green.* Often a white bar across snout (as shown). Caudal fin square-cut. Young are blue above, silvery below. To 26 in. (66 cm).
Range: San Francisco to s. Baja; common in s. Calif. **Habitat:** Near or over rocks and in kelp. Intertidal and to about 100 ft. (30 m). Young pelagic.
Remarks: Feeds mostly on seaweed, occasionally eats invertebrates. Dense schools form in spring in kelp beds. Caught on small baited hook, also by spearfishing.
Similar species: (1) In Halfmoon (p. 224), body is same shape but bluish, with *no* pale spots below dorsal fin. (2) Zebraperch (p. 224) has *blue spot* on gill cover. (3) In surfperches (p. 226; Pls. 36–37) rear of upper jaw is exposed (does not slide under a shelf when mouth is closed). They also have 15 or more soft rays in anal fin and cycloid scales. **Note:** 2 tropical sea chubs have been taken in the artificially warmed waters off the Encina Power Plant in San Diego — far outside their normal range: (1) Blue-bronze Sea Chub, *Kyphosus analogus,* is metallic blue, with about 10 bronze streaks along side. To $17\frac{3}{4}$ in. (45 cm). Normally occurs from s. Baja to Peru. (2) Bluestriped Sea Chub, *Sector ocyurus,* is olive, with blue and golden spots and stripes. To about 18 in. (46 cm). Normally occurs from cen. Baja south.

ZEBRAPERCH *Hermosilla azurea* **Pl. 34**
Identification: Note the *oval* body and the bright *blue spot on the gill cover,* behind the eye. Brown to blackish or greenish or silver-gray above; whitish below. About a dozen *faint bars* on side. To 17½ in. (44 cm).
Range: Monterey Bay to Gulf of Calif.; rare north of s. Calif.
Habitat: Shallow inshore areas and to 25 ft. (7.6 m).
Remarks: Also known as the Zebra Perch.
Similar species: See under Opaleye (p. 223).

HALFMOON *Medialuna californiensis* **Pl. 34**
Identification: *Oval,* with a *small mouth.* Caudal fin slightly indented. Soft dorsal and anal fins nearly fully covered by a thick sheath of scales. Dark blue above; light blue to whitish below. Fins dark. Upper rear of gill cover usually *dusky.* Young are blue above, silvery below; pelagic. To 19 in. (48 cm).
Range: Vancouver I. to Gulf of Calif.; rare north of Pt. Conception. **Habitat:** Often in rocky areas and in kelp; inshore and to 130 ft. (40 m).
Remarks: Feeds on seaweed, also on small invertebrates. Can be caught on small baited hook; also speared.
Similar species: See under Opaleye (p. 223).

Spadefishes: Family Ephippidae

Nearly circular, deep-bodied, compressed fishes. Usually one or more dorsal fin spines are elongate. Front of soft dorsal and anal fins becomes elongate in large specimens of some species. Mouth small. Most spadefishes have bars crossing the body. Most are under 1½ ft. (46 cm), some grow to 3 ft. (91 cm). Spadefishes occur in all tropical marine seas but are rare in temperate waters. Generally shallow; often in small schools. About 14 species, 1 in our area.

PACIFIC SPADEFISH *Chaetodipterus zonatus* **Pl. 35**
Identification: Note the *nearly circular* body outline and the *small mouth.* Young—under 3 in. (7.6 cm)—are quite dark. Medium-sized specimens have *5–6 dark bars,* but bars fade and body becomes more silver in largest specimens or when over sand. To 25½ in. (65 cm).
Range: San Diego to n. Peru; rare in s. Calif. **Habitat:** Inshore and to 150 ft. (46 m); usually in small schools.
Similar species: Threeband Butterflyfish (p. 225) has fewer bars and its spinous dorsal fin is a different shape.

Butterflyfishes: Family Chaetodontidae

Colorful, *discus-shaped, compressed* fishes with a small protrusible mouth and *comblike or brushlike teeth* in a narrow band on the jaws. Scales ctenoid, extend well onto dorsal and anal fins.

Color varies — some are barred or striped; yellow and brown or black predominate. They rarely exceed 8 in. (20 cm).

These common reef fishes are found in all warm seas. Most species occur inshore in coral or rocky habitats. Butterflyfishes eat small invertebrates, including coral polyps; some browse on algae. Young of some species are cleaners (pick parasites from other fishes). About 115 species, 2 rarely reach s. Calif.

SCYTHE BUTTERFLYFISH *Chaetodon falcifer*   **Pl. 30**
Identification: A strongly compressed, discus-shaped fish. Snout pointed, mouth small. A dark *scythe-shaped mark on side;* black bar extends through eye. Purplish gray and yellowish above; pale yellow below. To 6 in. (15 cm).
Range: Santa Catalina I. (s. Calif.) to Galapagos Is. **Habitat:** One of the deeper-living species of the family at 40–492 ft. (12–150 m).
Similar species: See Threeband Butterflyfish (below).

THREEBAND BUTTERFLYFISH   **Pl. 30**
Chaetodon humeralis
Identification: Similar to Scythe Butterflyfish but with vertical *bars* on body and *caudal fin,* another bar through eye. Bars black to brownish or orangish. Background silvery white to yellowish brown. To 10 in. (25 cm).
Range: San Diego to Peru, including Galapagos Is. **Habitat:** Tidepools and rocky inshore areas. To 180 ft. (55 m); common at 10–40 ft. (3–12 m). Usually in pairs.
Remarks: Known from San Diego over 100 years ago; no recent records north of Baja.
Similar species: (1) See Scythe Butterflyfish (above). (2) See Pacific Spadefish (p. 224; Pl. 35).

Armorheads: Family Pentacerotidae

A small family of medium-sized compressed fishes. Head bones rough, exposed (not skin-covered). *2–5 spines in anal fin.* Dorsal fin continuous, with a long spinous part. Caudal fin square-cut to slightly indented. Mouth fairly small, with small teeth. Most grow to 1–2 ft. (30–61 cm). Armorheads occur offshore in the Atlantic, Pacific, and Indian Oceans. About 12 species; 2 species in the N. Pacific, 1 in our area.

PELAGIC ARMORHEAD *Pentaceros richardsoni*   **Pl. 48**
Identification: Note the *exposed, striated head bones.* Usually has *4 anal fin spines.* Spinous part of dorsal fin much longer than soft-rayed part, can be folded into a groove. Bluish brown or gray; belly paler. Often orange on pelvic and anal fin spines; head sometimes pinkish. Large adults plain; small specimens often have *dark wavy lines* or spots. To 21 in. (53 cm).

Range: Cold waters of Pacific and Indian Oceans; Japan to Alaska and to cen. Calif. **Habitat:** Offshore; surface to 1320 ft. (402 m). Sometimes seen feeding at the surface at night; may school.

Similar species: In our area no other species has rough, exposed head bones; only a few other species have 4 spines in the anal fin.

Surfperches: Family Embiotocidae

These perchlike, compressed, elliptical to oblong fishes are common in our area. Dorsal fin continuous (unnotched), usually with 9–11 spines, 19–28 soft rays. Anal fin with 3 spines and about 15–35 soft rays. Caudal fin forked. Scales cycloid. Most surfperches are brightly colored: silver to barred or striped; in some species color varies (especially during breeding season); or adults and young differ. To 4–18 in. (10–46 cm) but most are under 10 in. (25 cm).

Surfperches are found only in the N. Pacific; 2 species occur off Japan and Korea, the rest are found in our area. Most occur inshore — many live in the surf zone, others in kelp and tidepools; 1 lives in fresh water. Surfperches are often caught by fishermen and some species are fished commercially.

Fertilization is internal in these fishes, aided by the thickened front part of the male's anal fin. Surfperches are viviparous; most species bear as few as 3–10 live young per litter. Young (embryos) are nurtured in the female prior to birth and are quite *large* as newborns. Some young males are sexually active right after birth. Researchers are not in agreement on the common names for species in this family; we use the last name "surfperch" for all species of the family, but mention alternate names under Remarks. 21 species; 18 in the sea in our area, 1 in Calif. confined to fresh water.

BARRED SURFPERCH *Amphistichus argenteus*   **Pl. 36**
Identification: A large surfperch with about 8–10 *rust-colored bars* on side (bars sometimes irregular, usually with spots between them). Longest dorsal fin spines are about $\frac{3}{4}$ the length of the soft rays. Background usually silvery, sometimes whitish, occasionally brassy olive; back tinged with blue or gray. No red on fins. Occasionally nearly uniform-colored, without bars. Breeding adults darker. To 17 in. (43 cm), $4\frac{1}{2}$ lb. (2 kg); usually about 1 ft. (30 cm), 1 lb. (0.4 kg).
Range: Bodega Bay (n. Calif.) to n.-cen. Baja. Abundant in s. Calif. **Habitat:** Mostly in surf of sand beaches, but reported from trawl catches at depths up to 240 ft. (73 m); also near rocks, pilings, and other sources of cover and food. Usually in small groups.
Remarks: A common surf species of sandy open coast; also caught from piers and skiffs. Sand crabs are preferred food, also feeds on clams and other invertebrates. Young — about $1\frac{3}{4}$ in. (4.4 cm) — born mid-March to July after a 5-month gestation;

number of young depends on age and size of female (litter size 4–113, averages 33).
Similar species: (1) Calico Surfperch (below) and (2) Redtail Surfperch (below) are also barred, but they have a *reddish caudal fin*. (3) Black Surfperch (p. 229) has a patch of *enlarged scales* below the pectoral fin and 20–22 (not 25–28) pectoral fin rays. (4) Zebraperch (p. 224; Pl. 34) has a blue spot on the gill cover, longer dorsal fin spines, and 11 soft rays (not 21–27) in dorsal fin.

CALICO SURFPERCH *Amphistichus koelzi*   **Pl. 37**
Identification: Deep-bodied. Fins usually *reddish;* caudal fin *dusky.* Narrow *rows* of reddish to brownish spots (mixed with red and black flecks) form faint *bars* on side; bars are *offset* (not continuous) at lateral line. Middle dorsal fin spines and soft rays about equal in length. Mostly silvery blue or brassy to olive above; paler below. Often tinged with red. To 1 ft. (30 cm), usually under 1 lb. (0.4 kg).
Range: Near Cape Flattery (Wash.) to n. Baja; rare north of Calif.
Habitat: Usually sand beaches in surf; to 30 ft. (9.1 m).
Remarks: Not especially abundant, but fairly common in sport catches from surf and piers south of San Francisco.
Similar species: (1) Redtail Surfperch (below) has similar color pattern, but middle dorsal fin spines are *longer* than soft rays. (2) Barred Surfperch (above) has no red on fins.

REDTAIL SURFPERCH *Amphistichus rhodoterus*   **Pl. 37**
Identification: All fins (especially caudal fin) usually *reddish.* 8–11 reddish to *brownish bars* on side. Silvery (sometimes brassy) overall, with a pale olive tinge above. Longest dorsal fin spines *much longer* than soft rays. To 16 in. (41 cm).
Range: Vancouver I. to Monterey Bay. **Habitat:** Sand beaches in surf on exposed coast, sometimes in bays and backwaters; to 24 ft. (7.3 m).
Remarks: An important sport fish — the most common surfperch caught in the surf from cen. Calif. northward.
Similar species: (1) Calico Surfperch (above) also has bars and red fins, but its dorsal fin spines and soft rays are about equal in length. (2) Barred Surfperch (p. 226) lacks red on fins.

KELP SURFPERCH *Brachyistius frenatus*   **Pl. 36**
Identification: Note the *upturned snout* and *oblique mouth.* Head profile slightly *concave* at eye. Dorsal fin short (a long gap between end of dorsal fin and caudal fin). Longest dorsal fin spines about equal in length to soft rays. Upper base of pectoral fin usually peppered with black specks, but with no large black triangle. Often an irregular pale stripe at midside. Brassy or golden brown, nearly matching color of kelp. Darker above, sometimes with blue spots or streaks; paler and often somewhat reddish below. Fins

mostly plain, sometimes with a rosy tint. Anal fin often darker at front. To $8\frac{1}{2}$ in. (22 cm).
Range: Northern B.C. to cen. Baja, including Guadalupe I. (off n.-cen. Baja). **Habitat:** Among giant kelp, usually up in kelp canopy; to about 100 ft. (30 m).
Remarks: Rarely far from kelp (hence its name). Feeds on small crustaceans, especially ones that live on kelp. Also a cleaner — picks external parasites from other fishes. Usually in large aggregations in summer.
Similar species: See (1) Dwarf and (2) Reef Surfperches (p. 231).

SHINER SURFPERCH *Cymatogaster aggregata*   **Pl. 36**
Identification: Silvery, usually with rows of dark spots (on scales), forming *black stripes* on side. These broken stripes are usually crossed by *3 yellow bars*. Males usually have *yellow bars only* in winter, and are darker overall in summer. Often a dark spot above lip (as shown). Head profile slightly concave at eye. Small — can reach 7 in. (18 cm), but usually 4–5 in. (10–13 cm).
Range: Wrangell (se. Alaska) to n.-cen. Baja. **Habitat:** Usually shallow water — around eelgrass beds, piers, and pilings — common in bays and quiet backwaters, also in calm areas of exposed coast. Enters brackish and fresh waters. Lives at depths up to 480 ft. (146 m). Usually in loose schools or aggregations.
Remarks: Also known as the Shiner Perch. Most abundant surfperch throughout most of its range. Easily caught, especially from piers; often caught by children using small hooks. Feeds mostly on small crustaceans. Usually mates in summer; young born the following spring and summer; a 6-in. (15-cm) female contains about 20 embryos, each about $1\frac{1}{2}$ in. (3.8 cm) long. **Note:** Specimens from the n. Channel Is. (s. Calif.) — with a more slender body and slightly larger eye — have been called the Island Surfperch (*C. gracilis*), but some researchers now believe they are only a population of the Shiner Surfperch.
Similar species: (1) Dwarf and (2) Reef Surfperches (p. 231) have a triangular black blotch at base of the pectoral fin. (3) Dark breeding male Shiner Surfperches (with no yellow bars) might be confused with the deeper-bodied Black Surfperch (p. 229), but that surfperch has a patch of *enlarged scales* below the pectoral fin.

PILE SURFPERCH *Damalichthys vacca*   **Pl. 37**
Identification: A large surfperch. Rays at front of soft dorsal fin *long* — about *twice as long* as dorsal fin spines. Caudal fin *deeply forked*. Blackish, gray, or brownish above; silvery below. Usually a broad dark bar at midside (darker in young). Some specimens are almost entirely silver; breeding males can be quite dark. Often a dark spot below eye. To $17\frac{1}{2}$ in. (44 cm).
Range: Wrangell (se. Alaska) to Guadalupe I. (off n.-cen. Baja). **Habitat:** Rocky shores; often around kelp, pilings, and underwater structures. Inshore and to 150 ft. (46 m).

Remarks: Also known as the Pileperch; sometimes placed in the genus *Rhacochilus*. Feeds on hard-shelled mollusks, crabs, and barnacles.
Similar species: (1) See Rubberlip Surfperch (p. 232). (2) See Sargo (p. 217; Pl. 35).

BLACK SURFPERCH *Embiotoca jacksoni*   **Pl. 36**
Identification: Look for the patch of *enlarged scales* between the pectoral and pelvic fins. Usually 9 dark brown or blackish *bars* on side. Longest dorsal fin spines shorter than soft rays. Lips *thick,* usually reddish brown to orange or yellow. Often has a dark "mustache." Background color varies: blackish or orangish brown or reddish brown. Often has blue specks on scales. Pelvic fin often orange to reddish; anal fin sometimes has blue and gold stripes. To 15½ in. (39 cm), 1½ lb. (0.7 kg); usually less than 1 ft. (30 cm).
Range: Ft. Bragg (n. Calif.) to cen. Baja, including Guadalupe I. (off n.-cen. Baja). **Habitat:** Chiefly rocky areas near kelp; occasionally over sand bottom of coastal bays and around piers and pilings; rarely in surf. Intertidal and to 150 ft. (46 m), but usually at about 20 ft. (6.1 m). Usually in small groups.
Remarks: Also known as the Blackperch or Butterlips. Most young born in spring or summer; newborn about 2 in. (5.1 cm).
Similar species: Some other surfperches can be quite dark during breeding season, but they *lack* the patch of *enlarged scales* below the pectoral fin.

STRIPED SURFPERCH *Embiotoca lateralis*   **Pl. 36**
Identification: A colorful surfperch with reddish *orange and blue stripes* (curved above lateral line, horizontal below it). Brilliant *blue streaks and spots* on head and gill cover. Middle dorsal fin spines about one-half the length of the soft rays. Upper lip often black (as shown). To 15 in. (38 cm).
Range: Wrangell (se. Alaska) to n. Baja. **Habitat:** Rocky coasts and kelp beds, occasionally in sandy surf near rocks; to 70 ft. (21 m).
Remarks: Also known as the Striped Seaperch. Important in rocky shore sport catch, also fished commercially. Often speared by divers.
Similar species: Rainbow Surfperch (p. 230) has bars on back and fewer soft rays (21–23, not 29–33) in anal fin.

SPOTFIN SURFPERCH *Hyperprosopon anale*   **Pl. 37**
Identification: A small surfperch with a *dark spot* on the *dorsal and anal fins;* other fins clear. Longest dorsal fin spines longer than soft rays. Dusky above; silvery below. To 8 in. (20 cm), but usually 5–6 in. (13–15 cm).
Range: Seal Rock (Ore.) to cen. Baja. **Habitat:** In surf on sand beaches and over sand at depths up to 300 ft. (91 m).

Remarks: Rarely caught from surf and piers by sport fishermen.
Similar species: (1) Walleye Surfperch (below) has black-tipped
pelvic fin. (2) Silver Surfperch (below) has 29–35 soft rays (not
21–26) in anal fin; usually a pinkish caudal fin.

WALLEYE SURFPERCH *Hyperprosopon argenteum*   **Pl. 37**
Identification: Note the striking *black tip* on the *pelvic fin* (especially in breeding males). Mouth oblique. *Eye very large* (diameter
equals about $\frac{1}{3}$ of head length). Body strongly *compressed.* Silvery
to bluish above; usually with faint dusky pinkish bars that fade
quickly after death. Anal and caudal fins often dark-edged. Breeding males darker, with a more angular anal fin. Breeding females
have a dark anal fin. To 1 ft. (30 cm).
Range: Vancouver I. to cen. Baja, including Guadalupe I. (off
n.-cen. Baja). Very abundant in s. Calif. **Habitat:** In surf on sand
beaches and over sand near rocks, often around piers; to 60 ft.
(18 m). Often in dense schools.
Remarks: An important commercial and sport fish; one of the
most common species caught by pier fishermen. Feeds on small
crustaceans. Usually bears 5–12 young; newborn about $1\frac{1}{2}$ in.
(3.8 cm).
Similar species: Silver Surfperch (below) lacks black tip on pelvic fin.

SILVER SURFPERCH *Hyperprosopon ellipticum*   **Pl. 37**
Identification: Body *compressed. Eye large.* Pelvic fin *not* black-
tipped. Longest dorsal fin spines slightly longer than soft rays. Silver-gray to greenish above, sometimes with faint dusky bars on
side; silvery below. *Caudal fin* usually *pinkish.* Occasionally a
black to orange *spot* (as shown) on anal fin. Dorsal and caudal fins
often dark-edged. To $10\frac{1}{2}$ in. (27 cm), but usually much smaller.
Range: Southern B.C. to n. Baja. **Habitat:** Inshore, in surf and
sandy areas; also around rocks and piers. At depths up to 360 ft.
(110 m).
Remarks: Frequently caught, but not of much importance as a
sport fish because of its small size.
Similar species: Walleye Surfperch (above) has *black-tipped*
pelvic fin.

RAINBOW SURFPERCH *Hypsurus caryi*   **Pl. 36**
Identification: A colorful surfperch with *orange and blue horizontal stripes* on body and *orangish bars* on back. *Blue streaks
and spots on head.* Fins usually tinged with orange; a blackish
blotch on soft dorsal and anal fins. Pelvic fin sometimes barred.
Usually a *dark spot* at rear of upper jaw (as shown). Belly characteristically *flat* and long, turns upward sharply (in profile) at anal
fin. Anal fin short and far back, with 3 spines, 20–24 soft rays.
Longest dorsal fin spines shorter than soft rays. To 1 ft. (30 cm).
Range: Cape Mendocino (n. Calif.) to n. Baja. **Habitat:** Rocky

shores, often at edges of kelp beds, occasionally over sand but not in surf. In depths up to 130 ft. (40 m).
Remarks: Also known as the Rainbow Seaperch. Not especially abundant; caught mostly by rocky shore fishermen. Aggregates in the fall.
Similar species: Striped Surfperch (p. 229) *lacks bars* and has more soft rays (29–33) in anal fin.

REEF SURFPERCH *Micrometrus aurora*   **Pl. 36**
Identification: A small surfperch, with a *black triangular blotch* at base of pectoral fin. *Scales* between anal and pectoral fins *black-edged.* Bluish to greenish above; shading to silvery below. Usually an orange-gold side stripe (from pectoral fin almost to caudal fin). To about 7 in. (18 cm).
Range: Tomales Bay (n. Calif.) to n.-cen. Baja. **Habitat:** Usually shallow rocky areas; in tidepools and at depths up to 20 ft. (6.1 m).
Remarks: Also known as the Reefperch. Feeds on algae, also on small invertebrates.
Similar species: See Dwarf Surfperch (below).

DWARF SURFPERCH *Micrometrus minimus*   **Pl. 36**
Identification: Small — usually less than 3 in. (7.6 cm). A *black triangle* at base of *pectoral fin.* Longest dorsal fin spines slightly longer than or same length as soft rays. Silvery blue or greenish to olive on back; greenish shading to silvery below. An *irregular dark stripe* on side, crossed by *barlike dark blotches.* Dorsal, anal, and pelvic fins usually have a *black blotch* (as shown). To $6\frac{1}{4}$ in. (16 cm).
Range: Bodega Bay (n. Calif.) to cen. Baja. **Habitat:** Rocky inshore areas and to 30 ft. (9.1 m); often among seaweed.
Remarks: Also known as the Dwarfperch. Feeds on algae and small invertebrates. Occasionally caught on small baited hook.
Similar species: Reef Surfperch (above) has 16–19 (not 12–16) soft rays in dorsal fin, no dark stripe on side.

SHARPNOSE SURFPERCH *Phanerodon atripes*   **Pl. 37**
Identification: Caudal fin *deeply forked.* Body usually has a *reddish tint* (caused by a reddish-brown spot at base of each scale; spots form reddish streaks along scale rows). Scales often have blue edges. Usually mostly silvery, dusky olive on back. Pelvic fin usually *blackish* at *tip.* Anal fin often has a dark spot at front. Caudal fin clear. Dorsal fin spines increase in size toward the rear — last spine shorter than rays at front of soft-rayed part. Snout somewhat pointed (hence the name). To $11\frac{1}{2}$ in. (29 cm).
Range: Bodega Bay (n. Calif.) to cen. Baja. A rare species, common only in Monterey Bay; formerly more abundant throughout Calif. **Habitat:** Inshore and offshore, to 750 ft. (229 m).
Remarks: Also known as the Sharpnose Seaperch. Seldom caught by fishermen.

Similar species: White Surfperch (below) lacks reddish tint, has a *pale* pelvic fin, and a *black line* at base of dorsal fin.

WHITE SURFPERCH *Phanerodon furcatus*   **Pl. 37**
Identification: Note the *black line at base of dorsal fin.* Dorsal fin spines longer toward the rear. Caudal fin deeply *forked.* Silvery to bluish or pale olive above; shading to silvery below. Body sometimes has a yellowish or rosy tinge. Fins usually yellowish, with dusky edge on caudal fin. Sometimes a black spot on front edge of anal fin. To 12½ in. (32 cm).
Range: Vancouver I. to n. Baja. **Habitat:** Varies — often near piers, docks, in bays and sandy areas, but usually in quiet water and offshore areas near rocks. To 140 ft. (43 m).
Remarks: Also known as the White Seaperch. Fished commercially in Calif.
Similar species: Sharpnose Surfperch (above) has *blackish* anal and pelvic fins; reddish body.

RUBBERLIP SURFPERCH   **Pl. 36**
Rhacochilus toxotes
Identification: A large surfperch, with *very thick lips* (at least twice as thick as those of any other surfperch); *lips white or pink.* Rays at front of soft dorsal fin slightly longer than dorsal fin spines. Color varies: usually silvery olive, fading to brassy below. Sometimes a blackish, bluish, or purplish tint on back, often quite dark overall. Adults have 1 or 2 dusky bars on side; young — to 6 in. (15 cm) — are mostly pinkish, with a dark bar at midside. Pectoral fin yellowish or orangish; pelvic fin (and sometimes anal fin) often blackish. To 18½ in. (47 cm) — *the largest surfperch.*
Range: Mendocino Co. (n. Calif.) to cen. Baja, including Guadalupe I. (off n.-cen. Baja). **Habitat:** Usually rocky areas, also in kelp and near jetties and pilings; in depths up to 150 ft. (46 m). Often in schools.
Remarks: Also known as the Rubberlip Seaperch. Important both in sport and commercial catch — one of the more sought-after surfperches.
Similar species: (1) In Pile Surfperch (p. 228), rays at front of soft dorsal fin are *much* longer than dorsal fin spines; lips are thinner. (2) See Sargo (p. 217; Pl. 35).

PINK SURFPERCH *Zalembius rosaceus*   **Pl. 37**
Identification: A small, *rosy*-colored surfperch — the only one with *2 brown to black spots below dorsal fin.* Middle dorsal fin spines longer than dorsal fin soft rays. In males (shown) upper lobe of caudal fin is long. To 8 in. (20 cm).
Range: Sonoma Co. (n. Calif.) to cen. Baja. An isolated population lives in the Gulf of Calif. **Habitat:** Offshore, at 30–750 ft. (9.1–229 m). Usually found in deeper water than other surfperches.
Remarks: Also known as the Pink Seaperch. Caught in trawls.

Damselfishes: Family Pomacentridae

A large family of small, shallow-water marine fishes that have a round to oval, compressed body. Usually only *1 nostril on each side* (most fishes have 2 on each side). Mouth small, with small teeth. Lateral line usually *ends below soft dorsal fin*. Scales ctenoid in most species, usually extend onto dorsal and anal fins. Dorsal fin continuous — spinous part longer-based than soft-rayed part. *2 anal fin spines* (3 in most perchlike species in our area). Many species are drab, others are colorful. Often the young are more brightly colored.

Some damselfishes are cleaners (pick parasites off other fishes). Most are under 6 in. (15 cm); a few grow to about 1 ft. (30 cm). Damselfishes occur in all tropical seas; a few reach temperate waters. Most species live on coral or rocky reefs. Some tropical damselfishes (anemonefishes) live in association with anemones. About 300 species, 2 in our area.

BLACKSMITH *Chromis punctipinnis*   **Pl. 30**
Identification: The only perchlike fish in our area that is *gray-blue to slate, with black spots* on rear half of body and on soft dorsal and caudal fins. Breeding males have a dark bar through the eye. Males guarding eggs may be quite pale. Young — up to about 2 in. (5.1 cm) — are purplish at front, yellow-orange at rear, with blue edges on dorsal, anal, and caudal fins. Mouth small. Lateral line ends below soft dorsal fin. To 1 ft. (30 cm), but usually smaller.
Range: Monterey Bay to cen. Baja; rare north of Pt. Conception, common in s. Calif. **Habitat:** Near bottom over or near rocks, especially over steep banks, also in kelp beds. To 150 ft. (46 m) and probably deeper. Young school in open ocean.
Remarks: Small adults will eat parasites from fishes that present themselves to be cleaned. Can be caught on a small baited hook; good eating. At night Blacksmiths retire to rocky holes.

GARIBALDI *Hypsypops rubicundus*   **Pl. 30**
Identification: Adults are *bright orange* or yellow-orange. Eye *green*. Young (shown) are reddish orange to brick red, with iridescent *blue spots* and blotches — these disappear gradually; may be present in individuals up to 6 in. (15 cm). Caudal fin notched, with rounded lobes. To 14 in. (36 cm).
Range: Monterey Bay to s. Baja and Guadalupe I. (off n.-cen. Baja); rare north of Pt. Conception. **Habitat:** Over rocky bottom in clear water; often near crevices and small caves, occasionally in kelp. Adults defend a home territory. Inshore and to 95 ft. (29 m).
Remarks: In Calif. it is illegal to spear or retain this species (if caught, release alive). Disturbed specimens will emit thumping sounds that can be heard by a diver. Normally propels itself with its pectoral fins. Feeds mostly on attached invertebrates. Male

clears a sheltered nest site; female deposits eggs, which male guards.

Mullets: Family Mugilidae

Thick-bodied, *torpedo-shaped* fishes that are rounder (in cross-section) in front, slightly compressed at rear. Head usually flat. *2 widely-spaced dorsal fins;* 1st with *4 spines* (first 3 spines clumped at base). Lateral line barely visible or absent. Mouth usually at front; small, *corners turn downward* (when viewed from front). Eye often partly covered with fatty tissue (adipose eyelid). Pectoral fin high on side. Most mullets are blue, green, or olive on back; silvery on side and belly. Many have dark horizontal streaks. To 3 ft. (91 cm).

Mullets are found in all tropical and temperate seas, but most species occur in the n. Indian and w. Pacific Oceans. Common in brackish water, but also in the sea and in fresh water. Most have a gizzardlike stomach and a long intestine; they feed on algae and detritus, usually taking mouthfuls from the bottom. Most species school. Some mullets are important as food and are even raised in ponds in some areas. About 100 species, 1 in our area.

STRIPED MULLET *Mugil cephalus*　　　　　　　　　**Pl. 35**
Identification: *2 widely-spaced dorsal fins;* 1st one with *4 weak spines.* Torpedo-shaped. Head broad, flat between eyes. Mouth small. Olive-green on back, with faint dark stripes on side (along scale rows); silvery below. To 3 ft. (91 cm).
Range: Found in all warm seas; San Francisco Bay to Chile and Galapagos Is. Rare north of s. Calif. **Habitat:** Coastal, including estuaries and fresh water, in sea at depths up to 400 ft. (122 m). Usually in schools over sand or mud bottom.
Remarks: Often seen leaping out of water. A rare catch with small baited hook. In our area spawning is thought to occur well offshore in winter.
Similar species: (1) Similar to silversides (p. 117; specimens 8–10 on Pl. 12) in fin placement, but our silversides are smaller and have 5 or more spines in 1st dorsal fin, usually a silver side stripe, a more compressed head, 21 or more (not 7–9) soft rays in anal fin. (2) In our area other species with 2 dorsal fins have *more than 4 spines* in the 1st dorsal fin.

Barracudas: Family Sphyraenidae

Elongate pikelike fishes, with a large mouth, a protruding lower jaw, and *formidable teeth.* Body cylindrical. Scales small, cycloid. *2 widely-spaced dorsal fins,* 1st usually with 5 spines. Pelvic fins abdominal. Caudal fin forked. Lateral line prominent. Mostly silvery, often with faint diagonal bars; upper back blue, green, or gray. Some grow to 6 ft. (183 cm), with unconfirmed records to twice that size; others are small, not exceeding 2 ft. (61 cm).

Barracudas occur worldwide in warm seas. They are usually seen in small schools near the surface, but large adults are often solitary. All species are predators. Usually good eating, but occasionally contain ciguatera toxin, which causes food poisoning. About 20 species, 1 in our area.

CALIFORNIA BARRACUDA *Sphyraena argentea*   **Pl. 35**
Identification: A northern barracuda. *2 small, widely-spaced dorsal fins;* 1st one usually with *5 spines.* Snout long; mouth large, with strong jaws and *large teeth.* Brownish or bluish above, with bluish reflections; silvery below. Some have faint oblique bars on back (as shown). Caudal fin usually yellowish. To about 4 ft. (122 cm), 18 lb. (8.2 kg).
Range: Kodiak I. to s. Baja; rare north of Pt. Conception.
Habitat: Usually near shore or near surface, also to 60 ft. (18 m). Often in small schools. On our coast moves north in summer, south in autumn. Young enter bays.
Remarks: Also known as the Pacific Barracuda. Eats mostly other fishes. An important s. Calif. sport fish, also caught commercially with gill nets. Unlike some barracudas, our species is apparently not dangerous to divers.
Similar species: In our area, other species with 2 dorsal fins do *not* have such a long snout or strong teeth.

Threadfins: Family Polynemidae

In threadfins the *lower pectoral fin rays* (which are usually long and *threadlike*) form a *separate* section of the fin. The snout is *long, conical,* and *fleshy,* and it *overhangs* the mouth, which is on the lower surface of the head. *2 widely-spaced dorsal fins,* 1st one with 7–8 spines. Caudal fin *deeply forked.* Eye surrounded by fatty tissue. Lateral line nearly straight, continues to *rear* of caudal fin. Scales weakly ctenoid. Threadfins are usually dull silver or brownish; some are striped. Their fins are usually dusky. To about 2 ft. (61 cm), but 1 species (outside our area) grows to 6 ft. (183 cm). Threadfins occur inshore in all warm seas; often on mud bottom, particularly near river mouths. About 35 species, 2 in our area.

BLUE BOBO *Polydactylus approximans*   **Pl. 35**
Identification: Note the *lower 5–6 pectoral fin rays,* which are threadlike and *free* (separate) from each other. *2 dorsal fins,* 1st one usually with 8 spines. Snout *conical,* projects beyond mouth. Bluish silver above; yellowish below. To 14 in. (36 cm).
Range: Monterey Bay to Peru and Galapagos Is.; rare north of Baja. **Habitat:** Inshore on mud bottom. Young pelagic.
Similar species: Yellow Bobo (below) has 8–9 (not 5–6) separate lower pectoral fin rays.

YELLOW BOBO *Polydactylus opercularis*   **Not shown**
Identification: Similar to Blue Bobo (above; Pl. 35), but with *more* (8–9) threadlike rays in lower, separate part of pectoral fin. Greenish brown above; yellow below. To 15¾ in. (40 cm).
Range: Los Angeles Harbor to Peru; rare north of Baja. **Habitat:** Inshore on mud bottom.

Wrasses: Family Labridae

A large family of marine tropical fishes of varied sizes and shapes. Most wrasses are *bucktoothed,* with curved or forward-pointing *canine teeth* protruding from front of mouth. Scales cycloid, often quite *large.* 1 long dorsal fin, with fairly weak spines at front. Wrasses usually swim with only their pectoral fins. They are often brightly colored. Most species are small — under 3–6 in. (7.6–15 cm) — but some are quite large and 1 (outside our area) reaches nearly 10 ft. (3 m).

Wrasses are found worldwide in the tropics, with a few occurring in warm temperate waters. Smaller species bury themselves in sand at night. Young usually differ from adults in color. Usually males are larger and colored differently than females. In many species, an individual fish functions first as a female but changes sex in later life. About 400 species, 3 in our area.

ROCK WRASSE *Halichoeres semicinctus*   **Pl. 30**
Identification: Look for *large, forward-pointing teeth* in front part of mouth. Scales *large.* Greenish above; yellow below. *Males* (shown) have a blue-black to *black bar* behind base of yellow pectoral fin; other fins mostly orange. Some females have many faint bars. Often wavy blue lines radiate from red eye. Young are orangish brown, with 2 white stripes (narrow one along upper back, wide one on side) and 2 dark spots on dorsal fin; spots disappear when fish is 4–6 in. (10–15 cm) long. Very small young are bright green. Dark flecks on back, especially in young. Body moderately compressed. Caudal fin square-cut. To 15 in. (38 cm).
Range: Pt. Conception to Guadalupe I. (off n.-cen. Baja) and Gulf of Calif. **Habitat:** Close to rocks near patches of sand; tidepools and to 78 ft. (24 m).
Remarks: When disturbed will dart into sand. Sleeps at night buried in sand, with head protruding. During the day forages on small invertebrates. Occasionally caught on small baited hook. Each individual functions first as a female but changes to a male at length of about 1 ft. (30 cm).

SEÑORITA *Oxyjulis californica*   **Pl. 30**
Identification: Cigar-shaped. Mostly *dirty yellow.* Orangish or brownish above; paler below, with a *large black area at base of*

caudal fin. Very small young — about 1 in. (2.5 cm) — are nearly transparent, with a large black spot on dorsal and anal fins. Mouth small; small teeth protrude. Scales cycloid, large. To 10 in. (25 cm).
Range: Salt Pt. (n. Calif.) to s.-cen. Baja; common in s. Calif. **Habitat:** In kelp and other seaweeds and over rocks; usually shallower than 75 ft. (23 m) but caught at depths up to 240 ft. (73 m). Often in small groups, frequently well off bottom.
Remarks: Forages widely; usually seen well off the bottom, high up in kelp canopy or in open water around rocks. When disturbed often burrows in bottom sediment. Sleeps at night buried in sand, with head protruding. Eats a variety of small invertebrates, also picks parasites from other fishes that come to be cleaned. No sex reversal. Occasionally caught on small baited hook, but mostly considered a bait-stealing nuisance.

CALIFORNIA SHEEPHEAD *Semicossyphus pulcher*   **Pl. 30**
Identification: Easily identified by color (3 patterns shown). Males have a *white chin,* blackish head, red eye; midsection usually red or pinkish to dusky red; rear of body blackish. Over sand males can be light pink. Females also have a *white chin,* but rest of body brownish red to rose, sometimes very dark or with irregular bars. Young (shown) are red-orange, usually with at least 1 *white stripe* at midside and with large *black spots* on fins and caudal peduncle. Large males have a fleshy lump on forehead. Stout canine teeth in front of mouth; somewhat *bucktoothed.* To 3 ft. (91 cm), 36¼ lb. (16 kg).
Range: Monterey Bay to Guadalupe I. (off n.-cen. Baja) and Gulf of Calif., uncommon north of Pt. Conception. **Habitat:** Prefers rocky bottom, particularly in kelp beds; to 180 ft. (55 m) but usually at 10–100 ft. (3–30 m).
Remarks: Populations off s. Calif. have declined because of fishing pressure and reduction of kelp beds; large males are now rare. Because of their size they are sought after by spear fishermen. They pick at baits and are sometimes caught on baited hook. Considered good eating. Diet of this wrasse varies: often feeds on hard-shelled organisms such as sea urchins, mollusks, lobsters, and crabs, which it crushes with tooth-plates in rear of mouth. Can pry food from rocks with canine teeth. Lives to over 50 years of age. As in the Rock Wrasse (p. 236), each individual functions first as a female but changes to a male at a length of about 1 ft. (30 cm). Formerly placed in the genus *Pimelometopon.*

Sandfishes: Family Trichodontidae

A small family of N. Pacific marine fishes with an upturned, *fringed mouth.* Body deeper at front, compressed; *no scales. 2 dorsal fins.* To about 1 ft. (30 cm). Sandfishes live on or partially buried in mud or sand bottom. 2 species, 1 or both in our area.

PACIFIC SANDFISH *Trichodon trichodon*   **Pl. 13**
Identification: *Mouth upturned, lips fringed. 2 dorsal fins.* Body compressed, unscaled. Pectoral fin large. Caudal fin forked. Spines on cheek. Dusky above; shading to silvery below. Irregular dark patches along on back. Dark streaks on spinous dorsal fin. To 1 ft. (30 cm).
Range: Kamchatka (USSR) to Bering Sea and to San Francisco.
Habitat: Inshore and to 180 ft. (55 m), usually buried in mud or sand bottom with mouth protruding.
Remarks: Usually captured in trawls; may be seen as stomach content of predatory fishes; some have even been caught by hand in shallow water. In Alaska harbor seals feed on them. Eggs of this fish are laid in a gelatinous mass that is attached to rocks.
Similar species: Smooth Stargazer (p. 240; Pl. 13) has only 1 dorsal fin, a chunky body, rounded caudal fin, and pelvic fins located at the throat. **Note:** Sailfin Sandfish, *Arctoscopus japonicus,* has a higher 1st dorsal fin (nearly twice height of 2nd dorsal fin) and a wider gap between its dorsal fins. Japan to the Bering Sea; and to Alaska (?).

Ronquils: Family Bathymasteridae

A small family of elongate, cold-water fishes. Dorsal and anal fins long, both composed almost entirely of soft rays (some species have a few weak spines at front). Caudal and pectoral fins rounded. Pelvic fins thoracic. Lateral line straight, *high up* on side. To about 1 ft. (30 cm), but most are smaller.
   Ronquils occur only in the N. Pacific. They live on the bottom, usually in rocky areas near shore (except Searcher, p. 239). Rarely captured, except by researchers; can be observed by divers. This family is under study and some undescribed species exist. About 8 species, all in our area, including some that have not yet been formally named and described.

ALASKAN RONQUIL   **Pl. 42**
Bathymaster caeruleofasciatus
Identification: Dorsal and anal fins long. Caudal fin rounded. Scales ctenoid; no scales on cheek. Upper jaw extends to or past rear of eye. 17–19 pectoral fin rays. Vivid bluish green bars on side, on a drab bluish black background (when out of water bars turn dull dark blue). Smaller specimens have a reddish tinge; young are paler, with a *dark spot* (as shown) on the gill cover. To about 1 ft. (30 cm).
Range: Bering Sea to Queen Charlotte Is. **Habitat:** Rocky areas, will retreat into a hole or crevice. Depths poorly known, perhaps to 100 ft. (30 m).
Similar species: (1) Smallmouth Ronquil (below) has much *smoother* scales and a smaller mouth. (2) Northern Ronquil (p.

240) has shorter jaw (not extending past rear of eye) and a *higher* dorsal fin (noticeably higher than $\frac{1}{2}$ body depth). See (3) Searcher and (4) Stripefin Ronquil (below).

SMALLMOUTH RONQUIL *Bathymaster leurolepis*   **Pl. 42**
Identification: Similar to other ronquils, but *mouth is small* (upper jaw does not extend past *middle of eye*). Scales on body ctenoid, but nearly smooth and embedded. Color varies: reddish brown, with 9–14 bluish black bars on side. Fins dusky; dorsal fin usually flecked with white, anal fin often white-edged. Red dots often present at base of anal fin rays. No obvious color differences between male and female. To about $8\frac{1}{4}$ in. (21 cm).
Range: Japan to Gulf of Alaska. **Habitat:** Tidepools and shallow inshore areas.
Similar species: (1) Stripefin Ronquil (below) also has a small mouth, but its anal fin has a yellow stripe bordered by blue. (2) Other ronquils have a larger mouth (upper jaw extends past middle of eye).

SEARCHER *Bathymaster signatus*   **Pl. 42**
Identification: Note the conspicuous *black patch at front of dorsal fin*. Head fleshy, unscaled, with many small pores. Nearly all dorsal fin rays are branched. Scales ctenoid. Light olive-brown to brown above; paler below. Often has darker brown patches on upper back, yellow and orange streaks on underparts. Some dusky pigment on fins. Eye blue. To 1 ft. (30 cm).
Range: East Siberian Sea and Bering Sea to Queen Charlotte Is. **Habitat:** Details poorly known; adults offshore on soft bottom at about 200–500 ft. (61–152 m).
Similar species: (1) Other ronquils lack the black patch at the front of the dorsal fin (except Northern Ronquil males). (2) Northern Ronquil (p. 240) has embedded scales on the cheek, nearly smooth scales on the body.

STRIPEFIN RONQUIL *Rathbunella hypoplecta*   **Pl. 42**
Identification: Same shape as other ronquils, but pectoral fin *does not* extend to front of anal fin. A bright yellow stripe on anal fin, bordered by blue stripes; outer edge of fin dark in males and white in females. Dark brown to purplish, with lighter areas. Usually has dark brown blotches, sometimes forming vague bars on back. To at least $6\frac{1}{2}$ in. (16 cm).
Range: Near San Francisco to n. Baja. **Habitat:** Rocks and sand on exposed coast at about 20–300 ft. (6.1–91 m).
Remarks: Feeds on invertebrates. Male guards eggs. Rarely captured on small baited hook, occasionally caught in trawls. Also known as the Smooth Ronquil, but other ronquils are smoother. Some researchers refer to this species (in part) as the Rough Ronquil (*R. alleni*); we treat it here as the same species as the Stripefin Ronquil.

Similar species: See Smallmouth Ronquil (p. 239). **Note:** 2 other *Rathbunella* species may occur in our area and are being studied by researchers. They have not yet been formally named and are not described further in this guide. (1) Fanged Ronquil closely resembles the Stripefin Ronquil, and its anal fin has the same color pattern, but it has 1 fanglike tooth about halfway back on each side of lower jaw. (2) Deepwater Ronquil has 2 alternating red and blue *bars* (not horizontal stripes) on membrane between each pair of anal fin rays.

NORTHERN RONQUIL *Ronquilus jordani*   **Pl. 42**
Identification: Shape and fin placement same as in preceding ronquils. First 20–30 rays in dorsal fin are *unbranched.* Scales weakly ctenoid, almost smooth to touch. Tiny embedded scales on cheek. Males orange above, with vague dark bars on side; olive-green below. Females olive-green above; paler below. Rear of head and fins dark. To about 7 in. (18 cm).
Range: Bering Sea to Monterey Bay. **Habitat:** On bottom, usually among rocks at 10–540 ft. (3–165 m); shallowest in northern part of range.
Similar species: (1) Searcher (p. 239) has no scales on cheek and rough scales on side. (2) In Stripefin Ronquil (above) and (3) Smallmouth Ronquil (p. 239), pectoral fin does not reach front of anal fin (extends past front of anal fin in Northern Ronquil); mouth smaller. (4) Alaskan Ronquil (p. 238) has rougher scales on side, dorsal fin not as high (height about equal to or less than $\frac{1}{2}$ body depth; higher than $\frac{1}{2}$ body depth in Northern Ronquil).

Stargazers: Family Uranoscopidae

In these fishes the eyes are on *top* of the head (hence the family name). Head broad, thick. Mouth nearly vertical, with *fringed lips.* A large venomous *spine* is present (sometimes buried) *above base of pectoral fin.* Pelvic fins located at *throat.* Most species have a small spinous dorsal fin (with 3–5 spines) but our stargazers do not. 12–15 rays in soft dorsal fin. Anal fin with no spines, 12–17 soft rays. Pectoral fin large, with 13–24 rays. Caudal fin square-cut to rounded. Stargazers are drab — dark above; paler below. Some species are spotted. Most are about 1 ft. (30 cm), some grow to $1\frac{1}{2}$ ft. (46 cm). Stargazers occur in shallow to very deep waters in all tropical and temperate seas. About 24 species, 1 in our area.

SMOOTH STARGAZER *Kathetostoma averruncus*   **Pl. 13**
Identification: Eyes on *top* of head. Head and body thick. Mouth nearly *vertical;* short, fringelike papillae on lips. Note the *large spine* above the base of the pectoral fin. 1 dorsal fin, far back on body. Pelvic fin at *throat. No scales.* White spots or blotches on a black or gray background; pale below. Dorsal, caudal, and pectoral

fins have white spots. Caudal and pectoral fins white-edged. To
12$\frac{1}{4}$ in. (31 cm).
Range: Piedras Blancas Pt. (cen. Calif.) to Peru; rare north of cen.
Baja. **Habitat:** On bottom at 42–1260 ft. (13–384 m).
Remarks: Feeds mostly on other fishes. Usually trawled; occasionally caught on hook and line. Young are pelagic and are sometimes seen as stomach content of large predatory fishes, such as
tunas. Spine above pectoral fin probably slightly venomous.
Similar species: Pacific Sandfish (p. 238; Pl. 13) also has an upturned mouth, but it has 2 dorsal fins, a more compressed body, no
large spine above pectoral fin.

Kelpfishes, Fringeheads, and Other Clinids: Family Clinidae

Small elongate fishes, with a long dorsal fin extending from the
rear of the head almost to the caudal fin. Usually all fin rays are
unbranched. Most have more spines than soft rays in the dorsal
fin; fin sometimes highest in front or at both ends. Pelvic fins thoracic, with *fewer than 5* soft rays (usually 1 hidden spine and 3 soft
rays). Our species have 2 anal fin spines. Usually *scaled* — unlike
the pikeblennies (Family Chaenopsidae, p. 245) and the combtooth
blennies (Family Blenniidae, p. 246), which are unscaled. Teeth
small and conical; no long canines. Most species are small — many
are under 3 in. (7.6 cm).
  Clinids occur inshore in all temperate and tropical seas. Most of
them are carnivores. They are difficult to see, blending well with
their surroundings. Most live on the bottom. They can be captured
by scuba divers using small handnets, and make good marine
aquarium fishes. Some species give birth to live young. Researchers
disagree on classification: fringeheads and some other species are
sometimes placed in a separate family (Labrisomidae). In our area,
2 subgroups are common: kelpfishes and fringeheads. About 300
species, 11 in our area.

ISLAND KELPFISH *Alloclinus holderi*   **Pl. 38**
Identification: Pectoral fin long — reaches *past* front of anal fin.
No ocelli in dorsal fin. No pronounced notch or dip at front of
dorsal fin. First 2–3 spines in dorsal fin are soft and flexible, rest
sharp and stiff. Middle rays of caudal fin *branched.* A few unbranched cirri on head. Reddish stripes and 6–7 irregular dark bars
on side. Orangish or red splotches on head. Dorsal fin red-orange,
with a greenish area at front. Anal fin somewhat olive. Dorsal and
anal fins usually have light edges. Other fins mostly orangish or
yellowish. To 4 in. (10 cm).
Range: Santa Cruz I. (s. Calif.) to cen. Baja. **Habitat:** Rocky
areas; subtidal and to 162 ft. (49 m).
Similar species: In Deepwater Kelpfish (below) lateral line is

high on side and dips at front of soft dorsal fin (in Island Kelpfish, lateral line dips at midbody, *well in front* of the soft dorsal fin). Deepwater Kelpfish also has dark spots and streaks in front of the pectoral fin.

DEEPWATER KELPFISH *Cryptotrema corallinum*   **Pl. 38**
Identification: Similar to Island Kelpfish but lateral line is high on the side for about ⅔ of body length (dips around midbody in Island Kelpfish). Color varies: dusky olive above, with streaks of red on upper back; shading to yellow streaks below. About 6 dusky blotches on side. Head has red (and sometimes blue) streaks and spots on a pale background. Caudal fin has red bars. Dorsal fin has rows of red spots. Spot or streaks in front of pectoral fin. Other fins mostly dark in males, pale in females. To 5 in. (13 cm).
Range: Santa Cruz I. (s. Calif.) to Baja. **Habitat:** Rocky bottom at 78–300 ft. (24–91 m).
Remarks: Also known as the Deepwater Blenny.
Similar species: See Island Kelpfish (above).

Gibbonsia species

Genus characteristics: The next 4 kelpfishes (*Gibbonsia* species) are very similar and difficult to identify. Color varies widely — usually matches habitat. Dorsal fin higher at front *and* rear (soft-rayed part *elevated*). Within this genus, note the number and location of eyespots (ocelli) when present, the spacing between soft rays in dorsal fin, and whether scales are present on the caudal fin (magnification needed).

SPOTTED KELPFISH *Gibbonsia elegans*   **Pl. 38**
Identification: Color varies widely (2 variations shown on Pl. 38): green to brown or tan or reddish — often blotched or streaked. 1–3 (often 2) ocelli on back (if 2, 1 near front, 1 toward rear). Soft rays *more widely spaced* toward rear of dorsal fin. Scales extend *well onto* caudal fin. To 6¼ in. (16 cm).
Range: Piedras Blancas Pt. (cen. Calif.) to s. Baja, including Guadalupe I. (off n.-cen. Baja). **Habitat:** Subtidal rocky areas and to 185 ft. (56 m); usually in seaweed.
Remarks: Rarely caught on baited hook. Can be captured by hand. Females lay white eggs in seaweed, male guards egg mass.
Similar species: Easily confused with next 3 kelpfishes: (1) Scarlet Kelpfish is usually red to reddish brown, usually with 1 ocellus above the pectoral fin and *several* toward rear of body; scales at the base of the caudal fin but *not* farther out on the fin. (2) Striped Kelpfish usually *lacks* ocelli on body, has *equal* spacing between dorsal fin soft rays (rear rays not farther apart). (3) Crevice Kelpfish has *no scales* at base of or on caudal fin, shortest pectoral fin (ends well in front of anal fin); usually occurs north of Pt.

Conception. (4) Giant Kelpfish (below) has a *forked* caudal fin. (5) In Island (p. 241) and (6) Deepwater Kelpfishes (p. 242) dorsal fin is *not* strongly peaked in front.

SCARLET KELPFISH *Gibbonsia erythra*   **Not shown**
Identification: Usually red to reddish brown, often with several ocelli on back. Dorsal fin soft rays *more widely spaced* at rear. Scales present at base of caudal fin but none farther out on caudal fin (magnification needed). To 6 in. (15 cm).
Range: Santa Cruz I. (s. Calif.) to n. Baja. **Habitat:** Rocky bottom at 48–120 ft. (15–37 m); details poorly known.
Similar species: See other species of this genus, especially the Spotted Kelpfish (p. 242).

STRIPED KELPFISH *Gibbonsia metzi*   **Pl. 38**
Identification: Usually *no ocelli* on body. Reddish to light brown, with stripes or darker mottling; color matches seaweed nearby. Dorsal fin soft rays *equally spaced* throughout fin. Pectoral fin *shorter* than in most other kelpfishes (clearly ends before front of anal fin). To 9½ in. (24 cm).
Range: Vancouver I. to cen. Baja. **Habitat:** Among seaweed, especially in tidepools and kelp. To 30 ft. (9.1 m).
Similar species: (1) See other kelpfishes of this genus (compared under Spotted Kelpfish, p. 242). (2) Giant Kelpfish (below) has a forked caudal fin.

CREVICE KELPFISH *Gibbonsia montereyensis*   **Pl. 38**
Identification: Usually reddish to brown or lavender; plaincolored to spotted or striped. Dorsal fin soft rays *more widely spaced* at rear of fin. *No scales* at base of or farther out on the caudal fin. To 4½ in. (11 cm).
Range: B.C. to n. Baja; usually north of Pt. Conception. **Habitat:** Inshore rocky areas in algae; usually on exposed coast. To 70 ft. (21 m).
Similar species: (1) See other kelpfishes of this genus (compared under Spotted Kelpfish, p. 242).

GIANT KELPFISH *Heterostichus rostratus*   **Pl. 38**
Identification: Our only kelpfish with a *forked caudal fin* and a total of 32 or more anal fin spines plus soft rays. Dorsal fin peaked at front and rear. Pectoral fin short, ends before anal fin. Snout pointed. Color matches habitat (2 variations shown): light brown to green and purple; often with lighter mottling, silver stripes, or irregular bars. To 2 ft. (61 cm).
Range: B.C. (?); Calif. to s. Baja, including Guadalupe I. (off n.-cen. Baja). **Habitat:** Among rocks with large seaweed, often in kelp. Subtidal and to 132 ft. (40 m).
Remarks: Occasionally caught on baited hook or speared. Fairly good eating, but can have an iodine flavor. Usually seen resting

among algae, often with body at an angle — well camouflaged. Feeds on small crustaceans, mollusks, and small fishes. Female attaches pink to greenish eggs to seaweed, male guards them. Young — to $2\frac{1}{2}$ in. (7.6 cm) — in schools; adults solitary.
Similar species: No other kelpfish has a *forked* caudal fin.

SARCASTIC FRINGEHEAD *Neoclinus blanchardi*   **Pl. 38**
Identification: *Our largest fringehead.* Note the *huge jaw* (extends well past eye; *larger* in males). *2 ocelli* on *spinous dorsal fin;* 1st one between spines 1-2, 2nd one between spines 5-9. Cirri above eye unbranched; shorter than eye diameter. Dorsal fin nearly uniform in height, with more spines than soft rays. Brown to gray (but males can be almost all black); often with red tinge, green or pale blotches. Usually pale spots or patch on cheek. Rear of jaw yellow in males. Ocelli usually metallic blue, surrounded by a golden ring. To 1 ft. (30 cm).
Range: San Francisco to cen. Baja. **Habitat:** Usually on exposed coast, on sand or hard mud bottom below low tide; rarer in bays; at 10-200 ft. (3-61 m). Usually found *inside objects,* especially mollusk shells, clam burrows, and bottles.
Remarks: Female deposits eggs in clam burrows or under rocks; male guards them. Divers often see the menacing head of a fringehead protruding from a burrow; fringeheads will even "charge" and snap at divers.
Similar species: (1) Onespot Fringehead (below) also has a huge jaw, but no ocellus at *middle* of spinous dorsal fin. (2) Yellowfin Fringehead (below) has a smaller jaw and no ocelli in dorsal fin.

YELLOWFIN FRINGEHEAD *Neoclinus stephensae*   **Pl. 38**
Identification: Jaw shorter than in other fringeheads (but still extends well past eye). 3 pairs of large *branched cirri* above eye. *No ocelli* on spinous dorsal fin. Dorsal fin nearly uniform in height; with more spines than soft rays. Color varies, matches habitat: dark, mottled gray to olive, sometimes red-orange. Often has purplish bars on side; sometimes blue spots on underparts. Caudal fin yellow and head purplish in many specimens. To 4 in. (10 cm).
Range: Monterey Bay to cen. Baja. **Habitat:** Usually in empty shells and holes; in rocks and bays near jetties; 10-90 ft. (3-27 m).
Similar species: (1) The other 2 fringeheads (above and below) in our area have 1 or 2 *ocelli* on the dorsal fin. (2) Most of our kelpfishes (pp. 241-243) have a dip or *notch* in the dorsal fin, and the soft-rayed part of the dorsal fin is usually *higher* than the spinous part; small cirri usually present on top of head. (3) Blennies (p. 246) have deeper bodies, with no scales.

ONESPOT FRINGEHEAD *Neoclinus uninotatus*   **Pl. 38**
Identification: *Huge jaw* (somewhat larger in males), extends well past eye. One *large ocellus* (eyespot) between dorsal fin *spines 1-2.* Dorsal fin nearly uniform in height. A few cirri above eye; one

at front *large* (longer than eye diameter), *forked* at tip. Usually light to dark brown, with black specks and mottling; sometimes with red specks. To 9¾ in. (25 cm).
Range: Bodega Bay (n. Calif.) to n. Baja. **Habitat:** Usually on bottom along coast and in bays; 10–90 ft. (3–27 m). Lives inside objects, including bottles, cans, tires, etc.
Remarks: Like the Sarcastic Fringehead, this species is strongly territorial and will "charge" and snap at divers or other intruders. Occasionally caught on baited hook. Easily seen around piers where "homes" are available in soda bottles, cans, and other refuse. Rarely seen outside of its protected home. Female lays orangish egg mass on objects. Both sexes guard the eggs; male circulates water over them, both sexes keep them free of foreign objects.
Similar species: (1) Sarcastic Fringehead (p. 244) also has a large jaw and an ocellus between dorsal fin spines 1–2, but it has a *second* ocellus (near middle of spinous dorsal fin). (2) See Yellowfin Fringehead (p. 244).

REEF FINSPOT *Paraclinus integripinnis*   **Pl. 38**
Identification: *No soft rays* in dorsal fin — just thin, *stiff spines* (run finger over top of fin). A dip between 3rd and 4th spines in dorsal fin; a large *ocellus* (eyespot) at about spine 25. Moderately large *scales* on body. Color varies radically: brown or black to white (or with all 3 colors), often mottled with red, pink, or cream. To 2½ in. (6.4 cm).
Range: Serena Cove (Santa Barbara Co., s. Calif.) to s. Baja.
Habitat: Tidepools and rocky areas; to 50 ft. (15 m).
Similar species: The position of the ocellus, scaled body, and the lack of soft rays in the dorsal fin readily distinguish this species from kelpfishes, blennies, and other look-alikes.

Pikeblennies: Family Chaenopsidae

A small family of *elongate* blennies with no scales or lateral line (a few pores may be present at front). Dorsal fin extends from rear of head to caudal fin; dorsal fin unnotched, with about twice as many spines as soft rays. Pelvic fins with 1 spine and 3 soft rays. To about 6 in. (15 cm).

Pikeblennies live in abandoned tubes of marine worms on sand bottom in tropical to warm-temperate waters, mostly in the New World. Some researchers include this family in the previous family (Clinidae, p. 241). About 50 species, 1 in our area.

ORANGETHROAT PIKEBLENNY   **Pl. 39**
Chaenopsis alepidota
Identification: *Elongate.* No scales. Mouth *large,* jaw extends well past eye. Dorsal fin long, with no notch; higher at front in

males (shown). First ⅓ of dorsal fin has soft flexible spines, remainder soft rays. Color varies: olive-green to brownish with dark blotches on side; throat often orange; pearly dots on side and at base of dorsal and anal fins. Fins mostly clear in females, mostly black in males. Often an ocellus between first 2 spines in dorsal fin. Gill membranes dusky, darker in males. To 6 in. (15 cm).
Range: Anacapa Is. (s. Calif.) to Banderas Bay (Mex.), including Gulf of Calif. **Habitat:** Sandy areas, in worm tubes; to 35 ft. (11 m).
Remarks: Rarely caught on small baited hook.
Similar species: In (1) pricklebacks (p. 247; Pls. 40–41) the dorsal fin is composed only of spines — no soft rays. In (2) eelpouts (p. 103; Pl. 11) pelvic fins are tiny, when present; dorsal fin begins farther back. (3) Most other elongate fishes in our area, such as gunnels (p. 255; Pl. 39), have a smaller mouth and a blunter head. (4) Our shallow-water eels (p. 63; Pl. 6) have no pelvic fins.

Combtooth Blennies: Family Blenniidae

Small, unscaled fishes with a blunt head. Fleshy cirri (skin flaps) usually present above eye. Eye located high on side of head. Mouth set low on head, usually horizontal or tilted downward. Common name for this family comes from the close-set row of incisorlike teeth in each jaw — resembling a comb. Some species also have a large canine tooth at rear of lower jaw (or both jaws). Pelvic fins with 1 hidden spine and 2–4 soft rays (3 rays in our species); fins begin in front of the pectoral fins. Dorsal fin long, usually unnotched, with nearly the same number of spines as soft rays; spines flexible. Caudal fin rays usually branched. Anal fin has 1–2 weak visible spines, which support a bulbous swelling in males of some species. They are drab in color, often mottled or irregularly banded. To about 7 in. (18 cm), but most species are under 3 in. (7.6 cm).

Combtooth blennies are common bottom-living fishes that occur in very shallow water in all tropical seas; a few species live in temperate waters. Some are found in estuaries or in fresh water. They are often very abundant in tidepools, on pilings, among oyster and clam beds, and in other shore habitats. They can be caught on a tiny baited hook or may be seen as stomach content of inshore predatory fishes. About 300 species, 3 in our area.

BAY BLENNY *Hypsoblennius gentilis*   **Pl. 39**
Identification: Head blunt; mouth on underside of head. Dorsal fin *long,* with flexible spines in front half, soft rays in rear half. *No scales.* An *unbranched cirrus* above the eye, with a *sawtoothed rear edge.* Head profile slopes evenly, *no notch* behind eye. 11–12 pectoral fin rays. Brown and green, with reddish spots. Throat sometimes reddish. Usually a dark spot between 1st and 2nd spines

in dorsal fin (as shown). Dusky areas at base of dorsal fin. To 5¾ in. (15 cm).
Range: Monterey Bay to Gulf of Calif. **Habitat:** Usually in bays and estuaries; to 80 ft. (24 m).
Similar species: (1) In Rockpool Blenny (below) cirrus above eye is divided into several filaments; 13–15 pectoral fin rays; and head profile is *notched* behind eye. (2) In Mussel Blenny (below) cirrus above eye is divided *at tip;* 12–15 pectoral fin rays. (3) Kelpfishes (p. 241; Pl. 38) and (4) fringeheads (p. 244; Pl. 38) have scales on the body.

ROCKPOOL BLENNY *Hypsoblennius gilberti*   **Pl. 39**
Identification: Similar to Bay Blenny, but cirrus above eye is divided into several *filaments*. Profile of head *notched* behind eye. Lateral line ends over *middle* of anal fin (usually ends before anal fin in our other 2 blennies). Color varies: usually olive to gray. Often has dark streaks below eye; dark saddles at base of dorsal fin. To 6¾ in. (17 cm).
Range: Pt. Conception to s. Baja. **Habitat:** Usually in intertidal and subtidal rocky areas; to 60 ft. (18 m).
Remarks: Also known as the Notchbrow Blenny. Egg cluster guarded by male.
Similar species: See Bay Blenny (above).

MUSSEL BLENNY   **Pl. 39**
Hypsoblennius jenkinsi
Identification: Skin flap (cirrus) above eye divided into *filaments at tip*. Lateral line ends above or before front of anal fin. No notch or dip in head profile (behind eye). Mottled brown, often tinged with red. Usually a prominent *dark crescent* behind the eye; dark bars at base of dorsal fin. Fins mottled. To about 5 in. (13 cm).
Range: Coal Oil Pt. (Santa Barbara Co., s. Calif.) to Mexico, including Gulf of Calif. **Habitat:** Usually in holes and crevices — often in burrows of boring clams or tubes of marine worms, also in mussel beds. Mostly sedentary and territorial. Subtidal and to 70 ft. (21 m).
Similar species: See Bay Blenny (p. 246).

Pricklebacks: Family Stichaeidae

A cold-water, mostly N. Pacific family that is well represented in our area. Pricklebacks are long, compressed, and somewhat eel-like. Mouth small, often oblique. Dorsal fin long, sometimes joined to caudal fin. These fishes are called pricklebacks because *all* rays in the dorsal fin are *spinous* in most species; some have soft rays at rear of fin. Anal fin long, with 1–5 small spines; begins at or before midbody and extends to (and often joins) the caudal fin. Pelvic fins (when present) are small and thoracic, with 1 spine and 2–4 soft rays. Scales tiny, often buried or absent on part of body. Most species are small — under 10 in. (25 cm).

Pricklebacks occur in the N. Hemisphere in cold marine waters. Most species live inshore. Pricklebacks are similar to gunnels (p. 255; Pl. 39), but gunnels have a *shorter* anal fin (distance from snout tip to front of anal fin greater than length of anal fin). About 60 species, 23 in our area.

Y-PRICKLEBACK *Allolumpenus hypochromus*   **Pl. 41**
Identification: About 5 dark spots on lower part of dorsal fin. *Large* pectoral fin, about as long as head. Pelvic fin present. *Spots on lower side form Y's.* About 45–50 dorsal fin spines, no soft rays. Anal fin has 1 spine and about 30 soft rays. Pair of large canines at front of jaw, separated by smaller teeth. Color in life not recorded. To about 3 in. (7.6 cm).
Range: Southern B.C. to Calif. at about 122 ft. (37 m). **Habitat:** Details unknown.
Similar species: Other pricklebacks lack the Y-shaped marks on the side.

STOUT EELBLENNY *Anisarchus medius*   **Pl. 41**
Identification: Rather plain — brownish yellow. Oblique dusky reddish *bars* on dorsal fin. Caudal fin banded. Pelvic fin present. Dorsal *and* anal fins *join caudal fin.* Anal fin increases slightly in height toward the *rear.* About 60 dorsal fin spines, no soft rays. To $5\frac{1}{2}$ in. (14 cm).
Range: N. Atlantic and N. Pacific; Japan to Bering Sea and se. Alaska. **Habitat:** Soft bottom at about 50–400 ft. (15–122 m), but few depth records from N. Pacific.
Similar species: See Arctic Shanny (p. 253).

SLENDER COCKSCOMB *Anoplarchus insignis*   **Pl. 41**
Identification: A *fleshy crest* on top of head. *No pelvic fins.* Width of gap between gill slits (under head) usually equals about $\frac{1}{2}$ eye diameter or less. Usually 40 or more soft rays in anal fin. Color varies: usually dark brown to black or mottled with dark and light; sometimes red. Usually has dark and light bars on cheek and saddles on back. To $4\frac{3}{4}$ in. (12 cm).
Range: Aleutian Is. to Arena Cove (Mendocino Co., n. Calif.). **Habitat:** Prefers subtidal areas among rocks; to about 100 ft. (30 m).
Similar species: (1) In High Cockscomb (below), gap between gill slits (under head) is *wider* (usually about $\frac{3}{4}$ of eye diameter); and usually 41 or fewer soft rays in anal fin. (2) Often confused with young Monkeyface Pricklebacks (p. 249), but they have soft rays in rear half of dorsal fin (dorsal fin all spines in cockscombs and most pricklebacks), and their gill slits are *joined* at the throat. In (3) Black and (4) Rock Pricklebacks (p. 253) pectoral fin is *much* smaller (about same size as eye). (5) Gunnels (p. 255; Pl. 39)

that might be confused with cockcombs have a *shorter* anal fin —
less than $\frac{1}{2}$ body length (about $\frac{2}{3}$ body length in cockscombs).

HIGH COCKSCOMB *Anoplarchus purpurescens*   **Pl. 41**
Identification: Similar to the Slender Cockscomb, with a *fleshy
crest* on top of head and *no pelvic fins*. Gap between gill slits (on
underside of head) is usually wider — more than $\frac{3}{4}$ of eye diameter. Color varies: blackish or purple to brown, often with darker
and lighter mottling. Usually 2 dark streaks on cheek. Males sometimes have orangish fins. To $7\frac{3}{4}$ in. (20 cm).
Range: Pribilof Is. (Alaska) to Santa Rosa I. (s. Calif.). **Habitat:**
Usually intertidal, under rocks; to 100 ft. (30 m).
Similar species: See Slender Cockscomb (p. 248).

PEARLY PRICKLEBACK *Bryozoichthys marjorius*   **Pl. 41**
Identification: A large northern prickleback, not found south of
B.C. *Long cirri above the eye,* smaller cirri on head and *on spines*
at front of dorsal fin. *No* ocelli on dorsal fin. Mottled with dark and
light pigment (but color in life not recorded). Dark saddles on
back. Black bar below eye. 2–4 curved bars on caudal fin. Anal fin
with dark stripe down center. To 1 ft. (30 cm).
Range: Aleutian Is. to southern B.C. **Habitat:** Poorly known;
trawled on bottom at about 600–1017 ft. (183–310 m).
Similar species: (1) Decorated and (2) Mosshead Warbonnets (p.
250) also have cirri on head and usually on 1 or more spines at
front of dorsal fin; but those pricklebacks have *many* cirri behind
the eye (only a few cirri in Pearly Prickleback). Mosshead
Warbonnet has about 12 black ocelli or bars on the dorsal fin. (3)
See Note under Decorated Warbonnet (p. 250).

MONKEYFACE PRICKLEBACK   **Pl. 40**
Cebidichthys violaceus
Identification: Large. Dorsal fin consists of about *half spines and
half soft rays*. Adults have lumpy ridge on top of head. *No pelvic
fins.* One lateral line, at base of dorsal fin. 2 dark streaks radiate
downward from eye. Gill membranes are not attached to the
throat but are joined to each other across throat. Usually uniform
black, olive, or gray, except for black streaks at eye. Some specimens have 1 or more orange spots on body and orange at edge of
fins. To $2\frac{1}{2}$ ft. (76 cm).
Range: Southern Ore. to n.-cen. Baja; rare south of Pt. Conception. **Habitat:** Common inshore, in tidepools or shallow rocky
areas, also to 80 ft. (24 m).
Remarks: Some researchers place this species in a separate family
(Cebidichthyidae) and call it the Monkeyface-eel. It feeds mostly
on crustaceans and algae. Good eating — commonly caught by
"poke-poling," a method using a long bamboo pole with a very
short wire leader (less than 1 ft. — 30 cm — long) and baited hook.

The pole is poked in cracks and around or under rocks of surge channels and tidepools.

Similar species: (1) Other pricklebacks have *spines* (not soft rays) in rear half of dorsal fin, and many of them have pelvic fins. (2) See Black Prickleback (p. 253). **Note:** Two unnamed pricklebacks occur in our area. Both have *dorsal fin soft rays* as in Monkeyface Prickleback, but they have *several* (not just 1) lateral lines on the side. (1) 1st species has about *20* dorsal fin soft rays, *5* lateral lines on side, (including one on each side of ventral midline), no pelvic fins. Mostly olive brown to rosy, with median white stripe from chin across forehead. Pacific Grove (cen. Calif.) to n. Baja. To about $7\frac{1}{8}$ in. (18 cm). (2) 2nd species has about 16 dorsal fin soft rays, *3* lateral lines on side, *no* lateral line near ventral midline, *tiny* remnant pelvic fin spines. Color unrecorded. Farallon Is. (off San Francisco) to Pt. Loma (s. Calif.). Rare. To about $3\frac{1}{4}$ in. (8.2 cm).

DECORATED WARBONNET *Chirolophis decoratus*　　**Pl. 41**
Identification: A large cirrus in front of eye, and dense *cirri on head and spines at front of dorsal fin.* Pelvic fin present. Brownish, with paler areas. Broad dark bars on most fins. To $16\frac{1}{2}$ in. (42 cm). **Range:** Bering Sea and Aleutian Is. to Humboldt Bay. **Habitat:** Usually among seaweed on rocky bottom; subtidal and to 300 ft. (91 m).
Similar species: (1) Mosshead Warbonnet (below) has shorter cirri (and all cirri of about the same length) on top of head; males have about 12 black *ocelli* in dorsal fin. (2) Pearly Prickleback (p. 249) also has cirri on head and on spines at front of dorsal fin, but has only a few small cirri *before* the dorsal fin. **Note:** The poorly known Matcheek Warbonnet, *C. tarsodes,* has large cirri on top of its head and on the spines at front of its dorsal fin, but it also has a *dense* growth of matted *cirri on cheek* and side of head. To about $7\frac{1}{2}$ in. (19 cm). Bering Sea and Queen Charlotte Is., in shallow subtidal rocky areas.

MOSSHEAD WARBONNET *Chirolophis nugator*　　**Pl. 41**
Identification: Numerous *cirri on top of head,* all about same length. About *12 ocelli* (sometimes short bars instead) on dorsal fin. Pelvic fin present. Brown or reddish brown; usually with pale areas along belly. Dark streak below eye; usually several dark blotches on cheek. To at least 6 in. (15 cm).
Range: Aleutian Is. to San Miguel I. (s. Calif.). **Habitat:** Usually in subtidal rocky areas, also to 264 ft. (80 m). Sometimes hides in crevices and tubeworm holes, with only head protruding.
Similar species: See (1) Decorated Warbonnet (above) and (2) Pearly Prickleback (p. 249).

SIXSPOT PRICKLEBACK *Kasatkia* species　　**Pl. 40**
Identification: *5-6 ocelli* (eyespots) *on dorsal fin.* Pectoral fin

large. No pelvic fins (or if present, consisting only of 1 small spine). Reddish brown; caudal fin *white-edged*. A *dark stripe* extends through eye and across cheek. To about 5½ in. (14 cm).
Range: Mendocino (n. Calif.) to Diablo Cove (cen. Calif.).
Habitat: Inshore and to 85 ft. (26 m). Rare.
Remarks: Not yet given a formal species name.
Similar species: Arctic Shanny (p. 253) also has 5–6 ocelli on the dorsal fin, but it has pelvic fins and dark bars below the eye.

LONGSNOUT PRICKLEBACK   Pl. 41
Lumpenella longirostris
Identification: Dorsal fin spines *stiffer* than in other pricklebacks; spines free at tips. *Head scaled. Snout overhangs mouth.* Usually 3–5 anal fin spines. Mostly olive to brown or blackish blue, usually with darker blotches on upper back. Fins blackish at edge. To 12¼ in. (31 cm).
Range: Kodiak I. to Burrard Inlet (B.C.). **Habitat:** Offshore at 300–462 ft. (91–141 m).
Similar species: (1) Daubed Shanny (below) also has long snout, but *no* scales on most of head, *longer* pelvic fin, and *elongate* lower pectoral fin rays. (2) Snake Prickleback (below) has a more elongate body, bars on caudal fin, and only 1 spine in anal fin.

DAUBED SHANNY *Lumpenus maculatus*   Pl. 41
Identification: Snout *overhangs* mouth, as in Longsnout Prickleback. Pectoral fin *large* (about as long as head); lower rays *elongate* (*free* of membrane at tips). Pelvic fin long. Cheek unscaled. Yellowish, with *dark spots* on back and side; paler below. Oblique dark curved bars on dorsal fin. About 4 dark curved bars on caudal fin. To 7⅛ in. (18 cm) in N. Pacific.
Range: Arctic Alaska and Bering Sea to Puget Sound; also in N. Atlantic. **Habitat:** Sand bottom; in our area at about 180–200 ft. (55–61 m).
Similar species: See under Longsnout Prickleback (above).

SNAKE PRICKLEBACK *Lumpenus sagitta*   Pl. 41
Identification: *Elongate;* head length equals nearly ¹⁄₁₀ of total length. Cheeks unscaled. 1 spine in anal fin. Light green above; cream below. Greenish to brown *streaks on side*. Dark spots at base of dorsal fin rays and near edge of fin. About 5 narrow irregular bars on caudal fin. To 20 in. (51 cm).
Range: Sea of Japan and Bering Sea to Humboldt Bay. **Habitat:** Varies — shallow bays and offshore, to about 680 ft. (207 m).
Remarks: One of the few pricklebacks sometimes caught on baited hook.
Similar species: See under Longsnout Prickleback (above).

RIBBON PRICKLEBACK *Phytichthys chirus*   Pl. 40
Identification: *No pelvic fins. Small* pectoral fin, as long as or longer than eye diameter. *4 lateral lines;* one on belly stops at anal

fin. Several alternating *light and dark streaks* radiate down and back from eye. Olive-green to olive-brown above; yellow to green below, usually with small spots on side. To 8 in. (20 cm).
Range: Bering Sea to s. Calif. **Habitat:** Under rocks in intertidal areas and to about 40 ft. (12 m).
Similar species: (1) In Black Prickleback (p. 253) dorsal fin starts *well* behind pectoral fin; 2–3 white-edged dark bars radiate from eye. (2) Rock Prickleback (p. 253) has a *smaller* pectoral fin (*shorter* than eye diameter); only 1 spine (not 2–3) in anal fin. (3) Similar gunnels (p. 255; Pl. 39) have a shorter anal fin (begins *after* midbody).

CRISSCROSS PRICKLEBACK   Pl. 40
Plagiogrammus hopkinsii
Identification: Lateral line *branched,* forming *platelike divisions on side.* Pectoral fin large. Pelvic fin present. Nearly uniform *blackish to dusky brown,* with dusky fins and a dark *stripe* behind eye. To 7¾ in. (20 cm).
Range: Pacific Grove (cen. Calif.) to San Nicolas I. (s. Calif.). **Habitat:** Intertidal rocky areas and to 70 ft. (21 m).
Similar species: (1) Our other pricklebacks *lack* the obvious *platelike divisions* formed by the lateral line. (2) See Masked Prickleback (below).

BLUEBARRED PRICKLEBACK   Pl. 41
Plectobranchus evides
Identification: *2–3 spots or ocelli on rear of dorsal fin.* Pectoral fin large, *lower rays elongate.* Pelvic fin *long* (for a prickleback). Dusky olive above; paler below. About 25 bluish bars on body. Oblique dark bars on dorsal fin. Anal fin dusky or with dark stripe (as shown); pale edge. A dark band on caudal and pectoral fins. To 5¼ in. (13 cm).
Range: B.C. to San Diego. **Habitat:** Mud or sand bottom at 276–900 ft. (84–274 m).
Similar species: See Arctic Shanny (p. 253).

WHITEBARRED PRICKLEBACK   Pl. 41
Poroclinus rothrocki
Identification: About *10–12 white bars* on back, edged with black. Pectoral fin large, rounded. Pelvic fin present. Caudal fin long (for a prickleback). Light brown above; pale below. No dark oblique bars or spots on fins. To 10 in. (25 cm).
Range: Bering Sea to San Diego. **Habitat:** At 150–420 ft. (46–128 m).
Similar species: See Bluebarred Prickleback (above).

MASKED PRICKLEBACK *Stichaeopsis* species   Pl. 40
Identification: Mostly *chocolate-colored,* with a *dark stripe* from snout through eye to area above pectoral fin. Lighter below, with light and dark streaks. Cheek and pale areas on body are cream-

colored. Fins mostly dark. Pectoral fin large, white-edged. Pelvic fin present. To 12¾ in. (32 cm).
Range: Monterey Bay to San Miguel I. (s. Calif.). **Habitat:** Intertidal rocky areas and to 70 ft. (21 m).
Remarks: Not yet given a formal species name.
Similar species: See Crisscross Prickleback (p. 252).

ARCTIC SHANNY *Stichaeus punctatus*   **Not shown**
Identification: Similar to the Stout Eelblenny (Pl. 41) in body shape, size, and shape of pectoral and pelvic fins. Dorsal fin has *5–6 dark spots or ocelli,* the last 2 toward the rear, as in Bluebarred Prickleback. Lateral line ends around midbody. Brown to bright scarlet above; paler below. Dark mottling on side; short dark bars on lower side. Fins banded. To 8½ in. (22 cm).
Range: Widespread in cold waters of the N. Atlantic, Arctic, and N. Pacific; south to B.C. **Habitat:** Subtidal rocky to sandy areas.
Similar species: (1) Stout Eelblenny (p. 248) has oblique bars (*not* dark *spots*) on dorsal fin. (2) Daubed Shanny (p. 251) and (3) Bluebarred Prickleback (p. 252) have *elongate* lower pectoral fin rays. (4) Y-Prickleback (p. 248) has Y-shaped marks on sides. (5) Sixspot Prickleback (p. 250) has *no* pelvic fins (or fins consisting of only 1 small spine); a *stripe* through eye across cheek.

BLACK PRICKLEBACK *Xiphister atropurpureus*   **Pl. 40**
Identification: A common, shallow-water prickleback. *2 dark bars with white edges* radiate down and back from eye. *No* pelvic fins. Pectoral fin *tiny* (smaller than eye diameter). 4 lateral lines on front part of body (as in Ribbon Prickleback, but less pronounced). Color varies: blackish or dark brown to reddish brown; often with a pale bar at base of caudal fin. To 1 ft. (30 cm).
Range: Kodiak I. to n. Baja. **Habitat:** Under rocks, in gravel areas; intertidal and to 25 ft. (7.6 m).
Similar species: (1) In Rock Prickleback (below), dusky bars radiating from eye are *black-edged.* (2) Monkeyface Prickleback (p. 249) has a *much larger* pectoral fin; soft rays (not spines) in rear half of dorsal fin. (3) Crisscross Prickleback (p. 252) has rectangular platelike divisions on side, formed by branches of lateral line. (4) In Ribbon Prickleback (p. 251), length of pectoral fin equals or exceeds eye diameter; several alternating dark and light streaks radiate from eye. (5) See Note under Monkeyface Prickleback (p. 249).

ROCK PRICKLEBACK *Xiphister mucosus*   **Pl. 40**
Identification: Very similar to Black Prickleback but the 2 dusky *bars* radiating down and back from eye are bordered by *black* (not white). Color varies: greenish black to gray or brown. Smaller specimens have faint, broad dusky bars on rear of body (as shown). To about 23 in. (58 cm).
Range: Port San Juan (se. Alaska) to Pt. Arguello (Santa Barbara

Co., s. Calif.). **Habitat:** Rocky areas; intertidal and to 60 ft. (18 m), mostly on exposed coast.
Remarks: Feeds mostly on algae. As in the Black Prickleback, female lays eggs in a cluster under a rock; male guards the egg mass by wrapping his body around it.
Similar species: See under Black Prickleback (p. 253).

Wrymouths: Family Cryptacanthodidae

Elongate fishes, with a long dorsal fin composed *only of* stiff spines. Wrymouths resemble pricklebacks (above) and are sometimes included in that family (Stichaeidae). Anal fin long, with 2 spines and many soft rays. Dorsal and anal fins *join* the caudal fin. *No* pelvic fins. Head broad, flat; eyes set *high* on head. Mouth points *upward,* lower jaw projects. Pits on side of head and lower jaw. To 1-4 ft. (30-122 cm). Wrymouths are found only in the N. Atlantic and N. Pacific. About 4 species, 2 in our area.

GIANT WRYMOUTH *Delolepis gigantea*   **Pl. 42**
Identification: Elongate. Dorsal and anal fins long, join caudal fin. *No* pelvic fins. Head *broad,* flat on top. Mouth oblique, lower jaw projects; upper jaw extends past eye (with mouth closed). *Exposed scales* on rear of body, buried ones on front of body. Pale brown, with rows of dark blotches; tinged with yellow and violet. To at least 46 in. (117 cm).
Range: Bering Sea to Humboldt Bay. **Habitat:** Soft bottom, at 20-420 ft. (6.1-128 m).
Similar species: (1) Dwarf Wrymouth (below) has *no* scales; body red or pink. (2) Most pricklebacks (preceding family) which lack pelvic fins (Pl. 40) have a smaller pectoral fin, a compressed (not flattened) head, and are a different color. (3) In Graveldiver (p. 259; Pl. 42) dorsal fin begins farther back, opposite or just behind front of anal fin.

DWARF WRYMOUTH *Lyconectes aleutensis*   **Pl. 42**
Identification: Elongate, *unscaled.* Dorsal and anal fins long, join base of caudal fin. *No* pelvic fins. Head *broad,* flat on top. Mouth nearly *vertical.* Eyes point mostly *upward.* A long *tube* extends from nostril, in front of eye. Pink or red, mostly uniform in color. To 1 ft. (30 cm).
Range: Bering Sea to Eureka (n. Calif.). **Habitat:** Not well known — apparently lives partly buried in bottom at 150-1150 ft. (46-350 m).
Similar species: (1) See Giant Wrymouth (above). (2) Gunnels (below; Pl. 39) have a shorter anal fin and a more compressed head. (3) Pricklebacks (p. 247; Pls. 40-41) have a compressed head and (usually) smaller pectoral fins; they are a different color. (4) See Graveldiver (p. 259).

Gunnels: Family Pholididae

Colorful, eel-like fishes with a long compressed body. The dorsal fin is *very* long (extends from head to caudal fin) and is composed of flexible spines (no soft rays). Dorsal and anal fins *join* caudal fin. Pelvic fins *tiny or absent;* when present, usually consist of 1 spine and only 1 soft ray. Scales tiny, cycloid; usually inconspicuous and covered with thick mucus. Lateral line absent. Most gunnels are under 1 ft. (30 cm); the largest one grows to about 1½ ft. (46 cm).

Gunnels are shallow marine fishes of the N. Pacific and N. Atlantic. They usually hide under rocks and in crevices near algae. These fishes are very similar to pricklebacks (previous family, p. 247), but pricklebacks usually have a longer anal fin (in nearly all species, anal fin base is longer than distance from tip of snout to front of anal fin). Most pricklebacks have at least 1 lateral line. About 15 species, 7 in our area.

PENPOINT GUNNEL *Apodichthys flavidus*   **Pl. 39**
Identification: A *single grooved spine* at front of the anal fin (shaped like a *penpoint*). *No* pelvic fins. Pectoral fin large. Color varies with habitat and diet; can be green to brown or red. Row of dark and/or light spots at midside. A *dark streak* extends down from eye; often a 2nd streak radiates from upper rear of eye. Often a silvery bar (with orange or black border) extends from mouth through eye to rear of head. To 1½ ft. (46 cm).
Range: Kodiak I. to Santa Barbara I. (s. Calif.). **Habitat:** In algae; intertidal areas, especially in tidepools.
Similar species: (1) Rockweed Gunnel (p. 257) has *no* grooved spine at front of anal fin; a *smaller* pectoral fin (length nearly equals eye diameter). (2) Kelp Gunnel (p. 257) has *no* pectoral *or* pelvic fins. (3) Other gunnels have tiny pelvic fins. (4) See pricklebacks (p. 247; Pls. 40–41).

LONGFIN GUNNEL *Pholis clemensi*   **Pl. 39**
Identification: Anal fin *longer* than in any other gunnel in our area — length exceeds ½ body length (as in pricklebacks). About *15 pale saddles* (often with dark specks inside) at base of dorsal fin. Large pectoral fin. *Tiny* pelvic fin. No lateral line. Color varies: usually magenta and silver; some pale specimens also encountered. To about 5 in. (13 cm).
Range: Alaska to Arena Cove (Mendocino Co., n. Calif.).
Habitat: Rocky areas at 24–210 ft. (7.3–64 m).
Remarks: Sometimes placed in the genus *Allopholis*.
Similar species: (1) Most likely to be confused with pricklebacks (p. 247; Pls. 40–41) because of its long anal fin, but they have a lateral line and the most similar pricklebacks have no pelvic fins. (2) See Red Gunnel (p. 256).

CRESCENT GUNNEL *Pholis laeta*   **Pl. 39**
Identification: A series of black, *crescent-shaped* to nearly circular marks at base of dorsal fin, enclosing a yellow or orange
space. Pectoral fin *large.* Pelvic fin *tiny.* Yellowish green, slightly
mottled on side. Sometimes a green spot on gill cover. Anal fin and
often caudal fin orange. 1 or more streaks radiate from eye. To
10 in. (25 cm).
Range: Bering Sea and Aleutian Is. to Crescent City (n. Calif.).
Habitat: Tidepools and to 240 ft. (73 m).
Remarks: Sometimes placed in the genus *Allopholis.*
Similar species: (1) Often confused with the Saddleback Gunnel
(below), but in that species the marks at base of dorsal fin are
V-shaped or *U-shaped.* When the markings are obscure the 2
species are difficult to separate, but pectoral fin is *shorter* in the
Crescent Gunnel (fin length goes into head length 2.4–3 times, not
1.8–2.3 times). (2) In the Longfin Gunnel (p. 255) the anal fin is
longer — starts before midbody. (3) Cockscombs (2 species at bottom of Pl. 41) and (4) pricklebacks with dark marks along base of
dorsal fin (Pls. 40–41) have a longer anal fin (starts before midbody) and a longer pelvic fin or no pelvic fins.

SADDLEBACK GUNNEL *Pholis ornata*   **Pl. 39**
Identification: Note the distinctive *U-shaped or V-shaped black
marks* at base of dorsal fin. Pectoral fin *large.* Pelvic fin *tiny.* Color
varies: olive-green to brown; yellow, orange, or red below. Dusky
bars on side. Dark streak below eye. Caudal, anal, and pectoral fins
orange in some specimens; anal fin can also be light green with
white bars. To 1 ft. (30 cm).
Range: Vancouver I. to Carmel Beach (cen. Calif.). **Habitat:** Mud
bottom among eelgrass and seaweed; inshore and to 120 ft. (37 m).
Remarks: Feeds on small mollusks and crustaceans. Both sexes
guard egg mass.
Similar species: See under Crescent Gunnel (above).

RED GUNNEL *Pholis schultzi*   **Pl. 39**
Identification: A small gunnel with a *tiny* pelvic fin. Two dark
bars radiate down and back from eye; area between bars *pale;* also
pale before first bar. Body usually *reddish,* sometimes brownish.
Weak bars and often green mottling on side. Sometimes has small
black spots along undersurface. Dorsal and anal fins often have
alternating light and dark bars (as shown). To 5 in. (13 cm).
Range: Queen Charlotte Is. to Diablo Cove (cen. Calif.). **Habitat:**
Intertidal and subtidal, in exposed surge areas (tidal surge channels) and to 60 ft. (18 m).
Remarks: Sometimes placed in the genus *Allopholis.*
Similar species: (1) In Longfin Gunnel (p. 255), anal fin starts
before midbody, has more rays (50 or more, not 44 or fewer). (2)
Penpoint Gunnel (p. 255), (3) Rockweed Gunnel (p. 257), and (4)

similar-looking shallow-water pricklebacks (Pl. 40) have *no* pelvic fins.

KELP GUNNEL *Ulvicola sanctaerosae*   **Pl. 39**
Identification: The *only* gunnel in our area with *no pectoral or pelvic fins.* Usually solid yellowish brown, but often tan to red-brown, depending on color of kelp where it occurs. To $11\frac{1}{4}$ in. (29 cm).
Range: Pacific Grove (cen. Calif.) to n. Baja, including Guadalupe I. (off n.-cen. Baja). **Habitat:** Rests on kelp, usually high up in kelp canopy; at depths to about 40 ft. (12 m).
Remarks: Usually hard to see against its kelp background but kelp harvesting by special barges reveals it to be common (Kelp Gunnels fall out on deck). Feeds on small crustaceans in the kelp canopy. Vestiges of pectoral fins sometimes present (dissection needed). Sometimes placed in the genus *Apodichthys*.
Similar species: No other gunnel lacks *both* the pelvic and pectoral fins.

ROCKWEED GUNNEL *Xererpes fucorum*   **Pl. 39**
Identification: Color mostly *uniform;* varies from bright green to reddish or brown, depending on color of algae patches where it lives (2 variations shown). Usually a small *dark streak* below eye. Sometimes dark spots in a row at midside. Pectoral fin *tiny.* No pelvic fins. To 9 in. (23 cm).
Range: Banks I. (B.C.) to n.-cen. Baja. **Habitat:** Common among algae in tidepools and inshore areas; to 30 ft. (9.1 m).
Remarks: Feeds on crustaceans and mollusks. Sometimes placed in the genus *Apodichthys*.
Similar species: (1) Penpoint Gunnel (p. 255) has a large grooved *anal fin spine* and usually a silvery or dark streak below the eye. (2) Kelp Gunnel (above) has *no* pectoral fins.

Wolffishes: Family Anarhichadidae

Large, elongate compressed fishes. The dorsal fin is long and contains only flexible spines (no soft rays). Our species is eel-like, with a body that tapers to a point at the rear. No pelvic fins. Strong *canine teeth* at front of mouth; *molars at rear.* These fishes are large — 2 species exceed 6 ft. (183 cm), maximum recorded length 9 ft. (274 cm).

Wolffishes inhabit cold waters of the N. Pacific and N. Atlantic. Most species live on rocky bottoms at moderate depths — 50–500 ft. (15–152 m). They feed on hard-shelled organisms, especially mollusks. Some wolffishes are of commercial importance as a source of food. 9 species, 1 in our area.

WOLF-EEL *Anarrhichthys ocellatus*   **Pl. 40**
Identification: An *eel-like* fish with stout *canine* teeth at front of

mouth; *molars* at rear. *No pelvic fins or lateral line.* Dorsal fin long, with flexible spines — no soft rays. Mostly gray to brown, sometimes greenish. Round dark spots with pale rings on body and fins. Larger specimens more mottled. Young often orangish (as shown), with dark areas merging into stripes at rear of body. To at least 6⅔ ft. (203 cm).

Range: Sea of Japan and Aleutian Is. to Imperial Beach (s. Calif.).
Habitat: Adults live on bottom, usually among rocks in subtidal areas; often in dens; to 740 ft. (226 m).
Remarks: Eats hard-shelled invertebrates and also fishes. Large specimens reportedly can be vicious and can inflict a painful bite. Eggs are laid in rocky protected areas and are guarded by both sexes. Flesh reported to be good eating. Sometimes caught on hook and line.
Similar species: True eels (Anguilliformes, p. 63) in our area have a smaller gill opening and soft rays in the dorsal fin.

Quillfishes: Family Ptilichthyidae

QUILLFISH *Ptilichthys goodei*   **Pl. 42**
Identification: Extremely *elongate*. Front part of dorsal fin is a long row of short *hooked spines*. Caudal fin *filamentous. No scales or lateral line.* Mouth small, lower jaw projects. No pelvic fins. Color varies: amber green, yellowish, or orange, sometimes with 2 maroon stripes on body. To 13½ in. (34 cm).
Range: Kuril Is. (USSR) to Bering Sea and to cen. Ore. **Habitat:** Little known. At surface at night; evidently on bottom during the day, at depths up to 263 ft. (80 m). Apparently buries itself in mud or sand.
Remarks: Only 1 species in the family. Most likely to be encountered as stomach content of other fishes.
Similar species: Spiny Eel (p. 69; Fig. 14, p. 70) has a projecting snout.

Prowfishes: Family Zaproridae

PROWFISH *Zaprora silenus*   **Pl. 42**
Identification: Stout and compressed, with a blunt front end, an oblique mouth, and a large caudal fin. *No* pelvic fins. Dorsal fin long, composed *only of* flexible *spines*. Large *pores* on head, ringed with white or blue. *No* lateral line. Scales small, ctenoid. Color varies: gray to dark green or brown above; paler below. Dark spots and mottling; often yellow spots on side. Yellow or orange on side of head and inside mouth. Fins often dark-edged. To 34½ in. (88 cm).
Range: Japan to Gulf of Alaska and to Monterey Bay. **Habitat:** Adults live near bottom at 96–1170 ft. (29–357 m) but usually shallower than 600 ft. (183 m).

Remarks: Only 1 species in the family. Young are pelagic, usually associate with jellyfishes. Adults are rarely caught on hook and line, occasionally trawled.

Graveldivers: Family Scytalinidae

GRAVELDIVER *Scytalina cerdale*   **Pl. 42**
Identification: Elongate, *eel-like,* compressed. Dorsal and anal fins begin at *midbody, join* caudal fin. Eye small, set nearly on top of broad head. *No* scales or pelvic fins. Pale pink, violet, or reddish brown to yellowish, with darker mottling. To 6 in. (15 cm).
Range: Bering Sea to Diablo Cove (cen. Calif.). **Habitat:** Rocky areas; burrows in loose gravel and sand or among broken shells on the bottom; also in tidepools and off beaches. To 25 ft. (7.6 m).
Remarks: Only 1 species in the family. Rarely seen except by researchers. Occasionally specimens are dug from sand by clam diggers.
Similar species: In (1) pricklebacks (p. 247; Plates 40–41), (2) wrymouths (p. 254; Pl. 42), (3) gunnels (p. 255; Pl. 39), and (4) other look-alikes, the dorsal fin begins *farther forward,* much closer to the head.

Sand Lances: Family Ammodytidae

A small family of *elongate* fishes with a *pointed* snout, a long dorsal fin *without* spines, *no* pelvic fins, and a *forked* caudal fin. Scales small, cycloid. Lateral line *high* on back. Fleshy ridge on each side, near midbelly.
  Sand lances occur in the N. Pacific, N. Atlantic, and Indian Oceans; inshore and offshore. They often bury themselves in sand. Some species form large schools and are important as food for other fishes. About 12 species, 1 in our area.

PACIFIC SAND LANCE   **Pl. 42**
Ammodytes hexapterus
Identification: Elongate. Lateral line *high on back.* Fold of skin *along* each side of *belly.* Lower jaw *projects.* Caudal fin *forked.* Metallic blue or green above; silvery below. To 8 in. (20 cm) in our area, but reaches 10½ in. (27 cm) in the Bering Sea.
Range: Sea of Japan to Arctic Alaska, the Bering Sea, and to Balboa I. (s. Calif.). **Habitat:** Varies — can occur in large schools near surface in inshore or offshore waters; also buries itself in sand. Intertidal and to 156 ft. (47 m) when inshore; stays near surface over deep water offshore.
Remarks: Important as food for predatory fishes, sea birds, and marine mammals. Most likely to be seen as stomach content, or on sand beaches (wiggling in sand at low tide).

Sleepers: Family Eleotridae

Sleepers resemble gobies (next family) in most features. The body is usually stocky and the head fairly flat and blunt. 2 dorsal fins — 1st one of flexible spines, 2nd one with 1 spine and 7–10 soft rays. Anal fin has 1 weak spine, 7–10 soft rays. The pelvic fins are separate (*not* united into a cuplike disk as in most gobies). The inner pelvic fin ray is usually the longest. Scales cycloid or ctenoid. Most sleepers are dark-colored, often with mottling. Usually 4–12 in. (10–30 cm).

Sleepers are mostly tropical and subtropical fishes, both bottom-living and free-swimming. Most species occur in fresh or brackish water, but some live in the sea; usually on mud bottom. The family name is sometimes spelled Eleotrididae. About 150 species; 1 just reaches our area.

PACIFIC FAT SLEEPER *Dormitator latifrons*   **Pl. 13**
Identification: Stocky. Head broad, nearly flat between the eyes. 2 dorsal fins — 1st one with 7–8 spines, 2nd one with 1 weak spine and (usually) 8 soft rays. Pelvic fins not united into a disk. A *dark spot* above pectoral fin. Dark olive-brown, with faint darker areas. *Dark bars* radiate from the eye. Dorsal and anal fins usually spotted. To 1 ft. (30 cm), but reported to 2 ft. (61 cm).
Range: Palos Verdes (s. Calif.) to Ecuador; rare north of Baja.
Habitat: Shallow inshore areas; typically in fresh water but moves freely into the sea.
Similar species: (1) In our gobies (below; Pl. 19) the pelvic fins are *united* into a cuplike *disk*. (2) Sculpins (p. 158; Pls. 15–18) have a longer 2nd dorsal fin, and most species have few or no scales on the body.

Gobies: Family Gobiidae

A large family of small, bottom-dwelling fishes with pelvic fins *usually fully united* to form a *suction cup* or *disk* (see Fig. 32 opp. Pl. 19). Eyes near top of head, usually close together. Usually 2 dorsal fins — 1st one spinous, 2nd one with 1 or no spines and 9–25 soft rays. Lateral line not evident. Gobies are often brightly colored; many species are capable of rapid changes in color and pattern. Most are small — under 4 in. (10 cm) — in fact, this family contains the smallest fishes, with adults under $\frac{1}{2}$ in. (1.3 cm). Our largest goby is $9\frac{3}{4}$ in. (25 cm).

Gobies are abundant in the tropics, less so in temperate waters. They are found in shallow to moderate depths in salt and brackish water; some spend their entire lives in fresh water. Most live on soft bottom or near reefs. Gobies are among the most common small fishes around tropical reefs. An estimated 2000 species (including about 1000 not formally described); 14 in our area (including 2 species introduced from Asia).

YELLOWFIN GOBY   Pl. 19
Acanthogobius flavimanus

Identification: Brownish, with conspicuous dots on the dorsal fins. Often has 5 or more indefinite dark patches on side; pattern may change quickly. Upper part of caudal fin *barred.* Scales large, clearly visible, 55–65 along side. Our largest goby — to $9\frac{3}{4}$ in. (25 cm); reaches up to 1 ft. (30 cm) in Japan.
Range: Expanding; native to Japan, China, and Korea — now well established in San Francisco Bay and other cen. and s. Calif. bays. **Habitat:** Bays and estuaries, sometimes ascends rivers.
Remarks: First observed in the Sacramento River Delta in 1963. Presumed to have been transported to e. Pacific in a ship's ballast or with live seed oysters. Considered a delicacy in Japan, usually sold there alive.
Similar species: (1) Bay Goby (p. 263) has fewer bars on caudal fin, *bigger gap* between dorsal fins, and *black-tipped* 1st dorsal fin. (2) In Tidewater Goby (p. 262), 1st dorsal fin is *clear at tip.* (3) See Cheekspot Goby (p. 263).

ARROW GOBY *Clevelandia ios*   Pl. 19
Identification: *Wide gap* between dorsal fins. Mouth *large,* jaw extends well *beyond eye.* Anal fin long. Pale olive or tan to gray, speckled with black; some individuals have white spots on side and head. Dorsal fin with dotted stripes. Males usually have a black stripe on the anal fin; stripe rarely present in females. To $2\frac{1}{4}$ in. (5.7 cm).
Range: Rivers Inlet (B.C.) to n.-cen. Baja. **Habitat:** Sand and mud bottom; marine to fresh water. Common in estuaries, lagoons, and tidal sloughs.
Remarks: Unlike other gobies, this species does not build a nest or care for its young. Eggs are spewed over a considerable area; peak spawn Mar.–June. Uses burrows for shelter, and can be collected at low tide by digging.
Similar species: (1) Cheekspot Goby (p. 263) has a shorter upper jaw (not extending past eye), and a *dark spot* on gill cover. (2) Young Arrow Gobies (not shown) may be confused with 3 other long-jawed gobies — see under Longjaw Mudsucker (p. 262).

BLACKEYE GOBY *Coryphopterus nicholsii*   Pl. 19
Identification: Eye and tip of 1st dorsal fin *black.* Scales conspicuously *large* (as in sample patch shown on side of body). A fleshy ridge extends from area between eyes to dorsal fin. Pectoral fin reaches front of anal fin. Usually very pale tan, with some brown or greenish speckling. A small blue spot below the eye. Pelvic *disk black* (as shown) in breeding males. To 6 in. (15 cm).
Range: Northern B.C. to cen. Baja. **Habitat:** Quiet water. Usu-

ally in sandy areas near rocks; retreats to rocks or holes when approached. Intertidal and to 348 ft. (106 m).

Remarks: Nesting occurs from April–Oct.; male cleans spawning site under rock, then attracts female by rising from bottom to display his black pelvic disk. After female lays eggs, male guards nest. Young occasionally found offshore among plankton.

Similar species: (1) In Bay Goby (p. 263) pectoral fin ends well before anal fin. (2) In other similar-colored gobies the upper jaw extends past the eye. (3) See Chameleon Goby (p. 264).

TIDEWATER GOBY *Eucyclogobius newberryi*   **Pl. 19**
Identification: Edge of 1st dorsal fin conspicuously *clear.* 2nd dorsal and anal fins opposite each other, with a short base, long rays. Mouth large, oblique; upper jaw extends nearly to rear edge of eye. Eyes widely spaced. Nearly transparent when alive. Body brownish, upper surface mottled. Dorsal and anal fins dusky, often spotted or barred. To $2\frac{1}{4}$ in. (5.7 cm).
Range: Del Norte Co. (n. Calif.) to Del Mar (s. Calif.). **Habitat:** Coastal lagoons and brackish bays at mouth of freshwater streams.
Similar species: (1) In Longjaw Mudsucker (below) mouth is horizontal rather than oblique; rays in anal fin are shorter than those in 2nd dorsal fin. (2) See comparisons of young (not shown) under Longjaw Mudsucker.

LONGJAW MUDSUCKER *Gillichthys mirabilis*   **Pl. 19**
Identification: In adults *upper jaw is huge,* reaching almost to gill opening. (In young of 1 in. — (2.5 cm) — upper jaw reaches rear edge of eye, as shown.) Head flattened, broad. Eyes far apart, small. Pectoral fin rounded, broad. Anal fin short. Brownish to bluish black, mottled on back and side; yellowish below. Young sometimes have about 8 bars on body and dark blotch (as shown) on rear of 1st dorsal fin. To $8\frac{1}{4}$ in. (21 cm).
Range: Tomales Bay (n. Calif.) to Gulf of Calif. **Habitat:** Tidal flats, bays, coastal sloughs; prefers mud bottom in shallow water.
Remarks: Can live out of water for 6–8 days if kept moist. Used as bait — can be caught in traps. Spawns from Jan.–July. Female lays several thousand club-shaped eggs in nest built by male. Eggs are guarded by male during 10–12 day incubation.
Similar species: Young Longjaw Mudsuckers (with jaw not yet fully enlarged) are often confused with other long-jawed gobies: (1) Tidewater Goby (above) has an oblique (not horizontal) mouth. (2) Shadow Goby (p. 264) has 15 (not 10–11) rays in anal fin; eyes close together. (3) In Arrow Goby (p. 261), eyes are close together; dorsal fins are widely separated. (4) Bay Goby (p. 263) has a black-tipped 1st dorsal fin.

LONGTAIL GOBY *Gobionellus longicaudus*   **Pl. 19**
Identification: Our only goby with a long *pointed* caudal fin. Mouth on underside of head. Large dark spot above pectoral fin

base. Brown spot at rear of upper lip. A conspicuous stripe on cheek. About 5 *oblong blotches* on side. Body yellow-tan above; paler below. Dorsal, caudal, and pectoral fins spotted or barred. Anal and pelvic fins (disk) clear. To 8 in. (20 cm).
Range: San Diego Bay to Panama. **Habitat:** Lagoons and river mouths.
Remarks: Last reported from Calif. about 100 years ago.

CHEEKSPOT GOBY *Ilypnus gilberti*   **Pl. 19**
Identification: A small goby with a conspicuous *black blotch on the gill cover* (or "cheek," hence the name). Anal fin with a black stripe (in both sexes). Upper jaw short, ends below eye. Small gap between dorsal fins. Light tan overall; chin and throat usually blackish (as shown). Chainlike pattern of fine dots on side. To $2\frac{1}{2}$ in. (6.4 cm).
Range: Tomales Bay (n. Calif.) to s. Baja; also Gulf of Calif.
Habitat: Mudflats and shallow bays.
Similar species: In (1) Arrow Goby (p. 261) and (2) Shadow Goby (p. 264), upper jaw extends well past eye. (3) Yellowfin Goby (p. 261) has 7–8 spines in 1st dorsal fin (4–6 in Cheekspot Goby).

BAY GOBY *Lepidogobius lepidus*   **Pl. 19**
Identification: Note the *black edge* on the 1st dorsal fin. *Wide gap* between dorsal fins. Scales *minute,* hard to see. Jaw short, ends below eye. Tan or pale olive to reddish brown, sometimes with elongate blotches on side. To 4 in. (10 cm).
Range: Welcome Harbour (n. B.C.) to cen. Baja. **Habitat:** Mostly on mud bottom; intertidal and to 660 ft. (201 m).
Similar species: (1) Yellowfin Goby (p. 261) has large scales, no dark edge on 1st dorsal fin, little or no gap between dorsal fins. In (2) Shadow Goby (p. 264) and (3) Longjaw Mudsucker (p. 262), the jaw extends *past* the eye.

HALFBLIND GOBY *Lethops connectens*   **Pl. 20**
Identification: Mostly *tan to pinkish,* with a *tiny eye.* 1st dorsal fin low, with 6 spines. Mouth large, jaw extends past rear of eye. *No scales.* To $2\frac{1}{2}$ in. (6.4 cm).
Range: Carmel (cen. Calif.) to n. Baja. **Habitat:** Adults are secretive, hide among rocks and kelp holdfasts. Young are often in schools in kelp canopy.
Remarks: Also known as the Kelp Goby.
Similar species: Blind Goby (p. 265) is blind or nearly blind and has *only 2* spines in 1st dorsal fin.

BLUEBANDED GOBY *Lythrypnus dalli*   **Pl. 20**
Identification: Brightly colored — red, *with 4-9* iridescent *blue bars;* bars narrower at rear of body. 1st dorsal fin high, especially in males. To $2\frac{1}{2}$ in. (6.4 cm).
Range: Morro Bay (cen. Calif.) to Guadalupe I. (off n.-cen. Baja) and Gulf of Calif. **Habitat:** Usually in open rocky areas but re-

treats to crevices or holes or hides among spines of sea urchins when threatened. Territorial; sits on exposed rock surfaces near a hole or crevice. Intertidal and to 250 ft. (76 m).
Remarks: Often found with the Zebra Goby, but Bluebanded Goby prefers more exposed rocky areas and is seen more often. Eats mostly small crustaceans. Female deposits oblong eggs in empty shells; male guards them.
Similar species: Zebra Goby (below) has more blue bands.

ZEBRA GOBY *Lythrypnus zebra* **Pl. 20**
Identification: Similar to Bluebanded Goby but has more (13–18) *iridescent blue bars,* with short narrow bars between. 1st dorsal fin high in males. To $2\frac{1}{4}$ in. (5.7 cm).
Range: Carmel Bay (cen. Calif.) to Clarión I. (Mex.). **Habitat:** Rocky areas, often in caves and crevices. Intertidal and to 318 ft. (97 m).
Remarks: A small specimen from deep water was brilliant orange with chocolate bars. This goby is often collected for home aquariums.
Similar species: Bluebanded Goby (above) has only 4–9 bars on body.

SHADOW GOBY *Quietula y-cauda* **Pl. 19**
Identification: Distinctive sideways *"Y" mark* at base of caudal fin. Upper jaw *long,* extends past eye. Anal fin long, usually with 15 rays. *Eyes close together.* Color varies: can be light or dark above; pale below. Dark blotches on side; small dark specks on head and body. Mature males have a black stripe on anal fin. To $2\frac{3}{4}$ in. (7 cm).
Range: Morro Bay (cen. Calif.) to Gulf of Calif. **Habitat:** Mud flats of lagoons and river mouths. Sometimes in worm or shrimp burrows.
Remarks: Sometimes collected with Cheekspot and Arrow Gobies.
Similar species: (1) Bay Goby (p. 263) has shorter jaw, black-tipped 1st dorsal fin. (2) See under Longjaw Mudsucker (p. 262).

CHAMELEON GOBY *Tridentiger trigonocephalus* **Pl. 19**
Identification: A fat goby with a wide, flat head. Pectoral fin has a dark bar near base, followed by a *pale* curved bar. Usually a *black spot* at upper base of caudal fin. Usually has 2 stripes from head to caudal fin, sometimes connected on side by 6–7 bars that may look somewhat marbled (see variations). Occasionally black overall. Small light spots on side of head. To $4\frac{1}{2}$ in. (11 cm).
Range: San Francisco Bay and Los Angeles Harbor (but expect range to expand). Native to China, Siberia, and Japan.
Habitat: Oyster shells and crevices among barnacles and other fouling organisms. Salt, brackish, and fresh water.
Remarks: Can *change color rapidly* from striped to barred pattern, like a chameleon (2 variations shown). An Asian species that appeared in Calif. in 1960, presumably from ship's ballast.

BLIND GOBY *Typhlogobius californiensis*   **Pl. 20**
Identification: Nearly blind — *eye very small,* functional only in young. *Pale to bright pink. Unscaled* — skin loose and smooth. Head large, with flabby cheeks. To 3¼ in. (8.3 cm).
Range: San Simeon Pt. (cen. Calif.) to s. Baja. **Habitat:** Usually under rocks in shallow water or surf; sandy areas among rocks in kelp beds, and holes in rocks. Intertidal and to 50 ft. (15 m).
Remarks: Usually spends most of its life inside a ghost shrimp's burrow, which it shares with its host. Also survives well in captivity.
Similar species: Halfblind Goby (p. 263) is mostly tan and has more spines (6, not 2) in 1st dorsal fin.

Cutlassfishes and Scabbardfishes: Family Trichiuridae

Oceanic, often deepwater fishes, with an elongate, ribbonlike, compressed body. Most have a large, *well-toothed* mouth, a pointed snout, and a projecting lower jaw. Rear of body tapers to a point *or* ends in a small caudal fin. Dorsal fin long, sometimes with a notch between spinous and soft-rayed parts. Spines are flexible and difficult to distinguish from soft rays; spines and soft rays are usually about equal in height. Pelvic fins *tiny* (with 1 scalelike spine and 1 rudimentary ray) *or absent. No scales.* Lateral line usually well-marked (absent in some species). Generally silvery, slightly darker on back; usually no blotches or other marks. Most species are 3–4 ft. (91–122 cm).

Cutlassfishes and scabbardfishes are found in all warm seas, mostly in deep water. They are voracious predators. Occasionally captured in trawls or on hook and line; also seen washed ashore or as stomach content of large oceanic fishes and marine mammals. They are often *damaged* during capture and are difficult to identify when crucial features are lost. (For example, a damaged dorsal fin can make it hard, if not impossible, to determine if a notch was present.) Experts depend on x-ray examination to aid in counting fin rays. About 20 species, 6 in our area.

BLACK SCABBARDFISH   **Not shown**
Aphanopus carbo
Identification: Body shape and *small forked caudal* fin similar to Pacific Scabbardfish (Pl. 47). A few large teeth. Spinous and soft-rayed parts of dorsal fin about equal in length, separated by a *notch;* total of dorsal fin spines plus soft rays equals about 90–95. 2 spines and about 55 soft rays in anal fin; 2nd spine in anal fin larger, *strong,* flattened. Forehead flat; no bony crest at midline. Copper-colored, with metallic reflections; turns dull black shortly after capture (whitish when stripped of skin during trawl capture). To about 3¾ ft. (114 cm).

Range: Atlantic Ocean; rare in Pacific and Indian Oceans; B.C. to Calif. **Habitat:** Pelagic; open ocean, but also near bottom (occasionally captured in bottom trawls). Wide-ranging in water column, probably in shallower water at night; most common at depths of 590–2133 ft. (180–650 m). (Our specimens were collected at about 1620–2340 ft. — 494–713 m — but expect shallower captures.)
Similar species: (1) See Pacific Scabbardfish (below). (2) Frostfish (below) has 1–2 *weak* spines at front of anal fin.

RAZORBACK SCABBARDFISH   Pl. 47
Assurger anzac
Identification: *Very elongate,* ribbonlike — body over 20 times as long as it is deep. Bony crest extends from snout to front of dorsal fin. Caudal fin *small, forked.* Dorsal and anal fins *low. No* notch in dorsal fin; total of dorsal fin spines plus soft rays equals about 115–120. Anal fin partly buried (in adults), with only about 15–20 visible rays. Silvery overall. Some individuals have black on head and between spines at front of dorsal fin. To about 7¾ ft. (237 cm).
Range: Nearly worldwide in tropical and temperate seas; Pt. Dume (s. Calif.) to Chile. **Habitat:** Pelagic in deep water; shallowest capture in N. Pacific at about 492 ft. (150 m).
Remarks: Very rare — occasionally hooked, captured in nets, or found washed ashore.
Similar species: (1) Lined Cutlassfish (p. 267) also is very elongate, but it has a higher dorsal fin, with a deep notch between the spinous and soft-rayed parts. (2) Other cutlassfishes have a deeper body.

FROSTFISH *Benthodesmus elongatus*   Not shown
Identification: Similar to Pacific Scabbardfish (Pl. 47), with an elongate compressed body that ends in a small *forked caudal fin.* Notch in dorsal fin between spinous and soft-rayed parts; spinous part *about half* as long as soft-rayed part. Total of dorsal fin spines plus soft rays equals about 140–145. No bony crest from snout to front of dorsal fin. Silvery overall; slightly darker above. Black on front of dorsal fin. To about 4 ft. (122 cm).
Range: Caribbean Sea and warmer waters of N. Atlantic; Juan de Fuca Str. and off Calif. Rare in our area. **Habitat:** Mostly deep water; pelagic.
Remarks: Occasionally trawled at about 985–1310 ft. (300–400 m). A few captured in shallower waters on hook and line; some also found floundering in surf.
Similar species: See Pacific Scabbardfish (below).

PACIFIC SCABBARDFISH   Pl. 47
Lepidopus xantusi
Identification: *Elongate,* compressed; body tapers to a slender caudal peduncle followed by a *small forked caudal fin.* Area be-

tween eyes slightly concave. A low crest just in front of dorsal fin. Body about 15 times as long as it is deep. *No notch* in dorsal fin; total of dorsal fin spines plus soft rays equals about 80. Adults blackish, young silvery. To about 3 ft. (91 cm).
Range: Eureka (n. Calif.) to Mazatlan (Mexico). **Habitat:** Young — to 1 ft. (30 cm) — apparently near the surface, adults deeper.
Remarks: Occasionally trawled or caught on hook and line near bottom, at depths up to 1650 ft. (503 m). Some wash ashore or are found in stomach of tunas.
Similar species: (1) Frostfish (above) has a notch in the dorsal fin, black on front of dorsal fin. (2) Razorback Scabbardfish (p. 266) has a longer body; crest extends from *snout tip* to front of dorsal fin — area between eyes is convex. (3) Black Scabbardfish (p. 265) has a notch in dorsal fin; total of dorsal fin spines and soft rays equals about 95.

PACIFIC CUTLASSFISH *Trichiurus nitens*   **Pl. 47**
Identification: Silvery-brown, elongate; body tapers to a *hairlike filament* (*no caudal fin*). Anal fin (in adults) a row of buried or nearly buried spinules. To 44 in. (112 cm).
Range: Worldwide in warmer seas; San Pedro (s. Calif.) to Peru.
Habitat: Mostly oceanic, at moderate depths but sometimes near shore; at 18–1260 ft. (5.5–384 m).
Remarks: Usually captured in nets. In some other areas sought as food.
Similar species: Other members of this family have a small, forked caudal fin.

LINED CUTLASSFISH   **Not shown**
Diplospinus multistriatus
Identification: Body extremely elongate; ends in a *forked caudal fin*. *No* lateral line. Spinous and soft-rayed parts of dorsal fin separated by a deep notch; spinous part about twice as long as soft-rayed part. Total of dorsal fin spines and soft rays equals about 70–75. No finlets behind soft dorsal or anal fins. Pelvic fin present but tiny (proportionally longer in young). Color of live adults unknown — probably silvery overall, darker on back and toward the rear. Many short *dark lines* on the side. Specimens reported are small — under 1 ft. (30 cm); this species may grow to about 3 ft. (91 cm).
Range: Worldwide in tropical and temperate seas; small specimens collected off s. Calif. Rare. **Habitat:** Deep midwater; details poorly known. Young occur shallower.
Remarks: Some researchers include this species in the next family (Gempylidae).
Similar species: (1) Other members of this family (Trichiuridae) have a prominent lateral line. (2) Our snake mackerels (next family; p. 268) have finlets behind the dorsal and anal fins.

Snake Mackerels, Escolars, Oilfishes: Family Gempylidae

These oceanic fishes are related to mackerels and tunas (p. 269). They are speedy oceanic predators of tropical and temperate seas. Body compressed and long or somewhat tunalike. Mouth large, with strong jaw teeth; teeth at front often fanglike. Spinous part of dorsal fin usually separated from soft-rayed part. Anal fin similar to and usually opposite soft-rayed dorsal fin; both fins usually followed by *finlets* (tiny flaglike fins). Pelvic fins usually small, often reduced to 1 spine and a few or no soft rays. *Caudal fin strongly forked.* No keel before caudal fin (on caudal peduncle) except in Escolar (below). 1-2 lateral lines, often wavy. Scales small or virtually absent; modified (prickly) in some. Most species are solid brown, often silvery on the lower side; fins usually darker. Moderate to large — most are 3-6 ft. (91-183 cm). These fishes occur in all warm seas; some species live in deep water. Occasionally caught on hook and line. About 12 species (depending on classification used), 3 in our area.

SNAKE MACKEREL *Gempylus serpens*　　　　**Pl. 47**
Identification: *Dark brown to blackish; straplike.* Caudal fin forked. Head long and pointed, with a pointed snout and large mouth. Huge daggerlike teeth on roof of mouth. *2 lateral lines* (1 on side and 1 at base of spinous dorsal fin). Spinous dorsal fin long (with about 25-30 spines); connected to (or slightly separated from) soft dorsal fin, which is followed by *5-7 finlets.* Anal fin opposite soft dorsal fin, with 1-2 small spines at front; followed by *6-7 finlets.* Pelvic fin tiny. Scales mostly absent. Silvery brown to blackish; fins dark. To 5 ft. (152 cm).
Range: Worldwide in warm seas; San Pedro (s. Calif.) to Chile.
Habitat: To at least 3300 ft. (1006 m), but usually seen at surface.
Remarks: Sometimes caught by tuna fishermen; small specimens found in stomach of tunas and marlins.
Similar species: (1) In Escolar (below), (2) Oilfish (p. 269), and (3) Jacks (p. 205; Pl. 31), body is deeper, less elongate. (4) Cutlassfishes and scabbardfishes (preceding family, p. 265) with a forked caudal fin have *no* finlets and only 1 (or no) lateral line. (5) Longnose Lancetfish (p. 92; Pl. 47) has a sail-like dorsal fin (sometimes damaged during capture) and an adipose fin.

ESCOLAR *Lepidocybium flavobrunneum*　　　　**Pl. 47**
Identification: Robust; dark brown to blackish. *Lateral line wavy,* dips to *belly* at tip of pectoral fin. Scales smooth; tiny scales surround large scales in a mosaic pattern. Look for low *keel* on the caudal peduncle, flanked by *2 smaller keels.* 1st dorsal fin low, with 8-9 short spines. 2nd dorsal fin has 16-18 soft rays, followed

by *4-6 finlets.* Anal fin similar to 2nd dorsal fin, with 4-6 finlets. To 6 ft. (183 cm) or longer.
Range: Worldwide in tropical and temperate seas; s. Calif. to Peru. **Habitat:** Pelagic in oceanic waters; to 660 ft. (201 m) or deeper.
Similar species: (1) Oilfish (below) has a nearly *straight* lateral line; only 2-3 dorsal finlets. (2) Jacks (p. 205; Pl. 31) with finlets have 2 detached spines before the anal fin; 1st dorsal fin shorter-based than 2nd dorsal fin; scutes usually present on lateral line. (3) In similar-looking tunas and their relatives (Pl. 32), lateral line is not wavy; color less uniform.

OILFISH *Ruvettus pretiosus*   **Pl. 47**
Identification: Resembles the Escolar in body shape and fin placement. Usually 2 dorsal and 2 anal *finlets. No keels* on caudal peduncle. Lateral line (often obscure) nearly straight — slants to midside, then continues straight to base of caudal fin. Skin *scratchy* — most scales are prickly. A rigid scaled *keel on belly.* Brown to dark brown. To $6\frac{2}{3}$ ft. (203 cm), about 100 lb. (45 kg); reported to 10 ft. (305 cm), 200 lbs. (90 kg).
Range: All warm seas; Encinitas (s. Calif.) to Peru. **Habitat:** Pelagic, mostly over continental shelf, to 650 ft. (198 m) and deeper.
Similar species: Escolar (above) has more finlets; lateral line *dips to belly* just behind tip of pectoral fin; keels on the caudal peduncle.

Mackerels and Tunas: Family Scombridae

Fast-moving, schooling pelagic fishes with a sleek, streamlined, cigar-shaped body. Snout pointed. 2 dorsal fins. 5-10 finlets follow the 2nd dorsal and anal fins. 1-3 keels on the caudal peduncle. Some species are fully scaled; others have scales only on narow "corselet" on head (see Fig. 41) and along front part of lateral line. Most species are silvery, with iridescent blue and green tints. Adults can be 1-14 ft. (0.3-4.3 m), weigh up to 1800 lb. (816 kg).

This family includes the true mackerels, Spanish mackerels, bonitos, and true tunas. These fishes occur worldwide in temperate and tropical seas, both inshore and offshore. Many species migrate long distances. Some support major commercial fisheries. About 47 species, 14 in our area. The more common species are shown on Pl. 32; the rarer ones in Fig. 41 (p. 270).

SLENDER TUNA *Allothunnus fallai*   **Fig. 41, p. 270**
Identification: *No* distinctive dark marks; *more gill rakers* (about 75) on the 1st arch than in other family members. Bluish above; silvery below. To 38 in. (96 cm).
Range: Usually in warm seas of S. Hemisphere; 1 record from Los

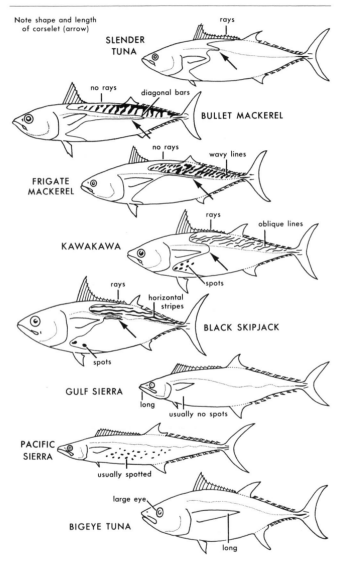

Note shape and length of corselet (arrow)

SLENDER TUNA — rays

BULLET MACKEREL — no rays, diagonal bars

FRIGATE MACKEREL — no rays, wavy lines

KAWAKAWA — rays, oblique lines, spots

BLACK SKIPJACK — rays, horizontal stripes, spots

GULF SIERRA — long, usually no spots

PACIFIC SIERRA — usually spotted

BIGEYE TUNA — large eye, long

Fig. 41 Mackerels and tunas — rare species

Angeles-Long Beach Harbor. **Habitat:** Oceanic; little known.
Similar species: The 4 true tunas in our area (*Thunnus* species, pp. 274–275) have small scales on *all* parts of the body (not just corselet) and fewer gill rakers.

BULLET MACKEREL *Auxis rochei*   **Fig. 41, p. 270**
Identification: A *wide gap* between dorsal fins; 1st fin high and short. Corselet prominent, extends far back along lateral line. 15 or more *diagonal bars* on back. Usually 8 dorsal finlets, 7 anal finlets. A large, single-pointed skin flap on the belly, between the pelvic fins. A strong keel on caudal peduncle, followed by 2 smaller ones. Head deep purple to almost black; back bluish; silvery to white below. Pectoral and pelvic fins purple (inner side black). To 20 in. (51 cm).
Range: Worldwide in warm seas; Redondo Beach (s. Calif.) to Peru. **Habitat:** Epipelagic. Adults mostly inshore and around islands. In schools.
Similar species: (1) Frigate Mackerel (below) has thin *wavy* lines on back; corselet becomes narrower at rear (5 or fewer scales wide below front of 2nd dorsal fin, not 6–20 scales wide). (2) Pacific Mackerel (p. 273) lacks corselet of enlarged scales and has only 2 small keels on the caudal peduncle. (3) In our area the other family members have little or no gap between dorsal fins.

FRIGATE MACKEREL *Auxis thazard*   **Fig. 41, p. 270**
Identification: Very similar to the Bullet Mackerel (above). A *wide gap* between the dorsal fins. Corselet prominent but becomes narrower toward the rear. 15 or more narrow, oblique to nearly horizontal *wavy lines* on back. A large, single-pointed skin flap between the pelvic fins. A strong keel on caudal peduncle, followed by 2 smaller keels. Usually 8 dorsal finlets, 7 anal finlets. Color about the same as in Bullet Mackerel. To about 20 in. (51 cm).
Range: Worldwide in warm seas; Santa Catalina I. (s. Calif.) to Peru. **Habitat:** Epipelagic; in schools.
Similar species: (1) See under Bullet Mackerel (above). (2) In Pacific Mackerel (p. 273), the wavy lines on the back extend *onto the head;* scales cover entire body (no corselet).

KAWAKAWA *Euthynnus affinis*   **Fig. 41, p. 270**
Identification: A small tuna. Slightly *wavy oblique stripes* on back (stripes fade quickly at death). Stripes begin where corselet ends — see Fig. 41 (p. 270). *Dark spots below pectoral fin* (sometimes obscure). No stripes on belly. Dorsal fins separated by a small notch. 8–10 dorsal finlets, 6–7 anal finlets. Double-pointed skin flap between the pelvic fins. Dark blue above; silvery white below. To about 3 ft. (91 cm).
Range: Warm waters of Indian Ocean and w. and cen. Pacific; stragglers occasionally reach s. Calif. **Habitat:** Epipelagic. Usually coastal, enters estuaries.

Remarks: Also known as the Wavyback Skipjack.
Similar species: (1) Black Skipjack (below) has *horizontal* stripes on back. (2) Skipjack Tuna (below) has stripes *on belly* and *no* dark spots below pectoral fin.

BLACK SKIPJACK *Euthynnus lineatus*   **Fig. 41, p. 270**
Identification: Similar to Kawakawa except stripes on back are mostly *horizontal* (stripes fade quickly at death). *Dark spots below pectoral fin* (sometimes obscure). Some have faint stripes on belly. Usually 8 dorsal finlets, 7 anal finlets. Double-pointed skin flap between the pelvic fins. Dark blue above; silvery below. To about $3\frac{1}{4}$ ft. (99 cm), 12 lb. (5.4 kg).
Range: San Simeon (cen. Calif.) to Colombia and the Galapagos Is.; rare north of Baja. **Habitat:** Epipelagic; usually coastal.
Similar species: Kawakawa (above) has *oblique* stripes on back.

SKIPJACK TUNA *Euthynnus pelamis*   **Pl. 32**
Identification: A small tuna — usually under 2 ft. (61 cm). *4–6 stripes on lower side* and belly. Corselet present (scales only on front of body). *No stripes on back.* 53–63 gill rakers on 1st arch. 7–9 dorsal finlets, 7–8 anal finlets. Double-pointed skin flap between the pelvic fins. No black spots below pectoral fin. Bluish to violet above; shading to silvery below. To 40 in. (102 cm), 50 lb. (23 kg).
Range: All temperate and tropical seas; Vancouver I. to Peru. **Habitat:** Inshore and offshore, in large schools.
Remarks: Important commercially in some areas; occasionally caught by sport fishermen in the fall in s. Calif. Some researchers place the Skipjack Tuna in the genus *Katsuwonus*.
Similar species: (1) Black Skipjack (above) and (2) Kawakawa (p. 271) have stripes on back and black spots below the pectoral fin. (3) Our true tunas (*Thunnus* species, pp. 274–275) have scales on *all* of the body (no corselet); fewer gill rakers.

PACIFIC BONITO *Sarda chiliensis*   **Pl. 32**
Identification: *Slightly oblique stripes* on back. Dorsal fins not widely separated. 7–9 dorsal finlets, 6–7 anal finlets. Body *fully* scaled, scales in corselet are larger. Upper jaw extends to rear of eye or beyond. A double-pointed skin flap between the pelvic fins. Greenish blue above; shading to silvery below. To 40 in. (102 cm), 12 lb. (5.4 kg).
Range: 2 populations: northern one (ours) occurs from Alaska to s. Baja and the Revillagigedo Is. (off Mexico); southern population off Peru and Chile (see Remarks below). Rare north of Calif.
Habitat: Usually near shore, in schools.
Remarks: Feeds on fishes and squid. In s. Calif. spawns from Jan.–May. Excellent sport fish. Most of e. Pacific commercial catch comes from Baja, where it is canned. Northern population is recognized as the subspecies *S. chiliensis lineolata;* the southern population as *S. chiliensis chiliensis*.

Similar species: (1) Slender Tuna (p. 269; Fig. 41) lacks dark marks on back. (2) In our area most other family members have a shorter jaw (which ends before rear of eye).

PACIFIC or CHUB MACKEREL *Scomber japonicus* **Pl. 32**
Identification: *Dorsal fins widely separated;* 8–10 spines in 1st dorsal fin. Usually 5 dorsal and 5 anal finlets. A small, single-pointed skin flap between the pelvic fins. Body *fully scaled;* no corselet. About 30 irregular, *nearly vertical bars* along back, extending onto head. Greenish or bluish above; shading to silvery below, usually with *dusky spots* on lower side. To 25 in. (64 cm), $6\frac{1}{3}$ lb. (2.9 kg); but usually no bigger than 16–18 in. (41–46 cm), $1\frac{1}{2}$–$2\frac{1}{2}$ lb. (0.7–1.1 kg).
Range: Worldwide in temperate and subtropical seas; Alaska to Mexico; most abundant between Monterey Bay and s. Baja.
Habitat: Pelagic; usually inshore. In schools.
Remarks: A very important commercial species — sold fresh, canned, smoked, and used as bait. Known as the Pacific Mackerel (especially in Calif.) and as the Chub Mackerel. Some researchers place it in the genus *Pneumatophorus.*
Similar species: (1) Frigate and (2) Bullet Mackerels (p. 271; Fig. 41) have 7–9 dorsal and anal finlets, a prominent corselet, no scales on rear of body, a strong keel and 2 weak keels on caudal peduncle. (3) Other mackerels and tunas lack the wide gap between the dorsal fins.

GULF SIERRA *Scomberomorus concolor* **Fig. 41, p. 270**
Identification: Body compressed and fully scaled; no corselet. Usually 8–9 dorsal and anal finlets. A double-pointed skin flap between the pelvic fins. 15 or more gill rakers on lower part of 1st arch. Blue above; silvery below. Males have no streaks or spots; females (not shown) sometimes have 2 alternating rows of brown spots on side. To $28\frac{1}{2}$ in. (72 cm).
Range: Monterey Bay to Mexico; abundant in Monterey Bay 1870–1880, then disappeared. Abundant in n. part of Gulf of Calif.; stragglers reach s. Calif. **Habitat:** Usually inshore; pelagic, often in schools.
Remarks: Also known as the Monterey Spanish Mackerel.
Similar species: Pacific Sierra (below) has only 10–12 gill rakers on lower part of 1st arch; several rows of golden spots along side in both sexes.

PACIFIC SIERRA *Scomberomorus sierra* **Fig. 41, p. 270**
Identification: Similar to Gulf Sierra, but with fewer (10–12) gill rakers on lower limb of 1st arch. 5–6 rows of small golden spots on side. Silver-blue above; silvery below. 1st dorsal fin yellowish, but dusky at front and tip; 2nd dorsal fin silvery. Caudal fin dusky. To 32 in. (81 cm).
Range: La Jolla (s. Calif.) to Peru and Galapagos Is.; rare north of Baja. **Habitat:** Pelagic, near surface; usually near shore.

Remarks: Also known as the Sierra.
Similar species: Gulf Sierra (p. 273) usually lacks orange-yellow spots on side and has 15–20 gill rakers on lower limb of 1st gill arch.

ALBACORE *Thunnus alalunga*   **Pl. 32**
Identification: Pectoral fin *extremely long* — extends well *beyond* front of anal fin except in specimens under about 1 ft. (30 cm). Usually 7–9 dorsal finlets, 7–8 anal finlets. *Liver striated* on ventral surface. 25–31 gill rakers on 1st arch. Dark blue above; shading to silvery white below. 1st dorsal fin deep yellow, 2nd dorsal and anal fins light yellow. Anal finlets dark. Caudal fin white-edged. To about $4\frac{1}{2}$ ft. (137 cm), 96 lb. (43 kg); on our coast to 76 lb. (34 kg).
Range: Worldwide in temperate seas; rare in tropics; Alaska to Revillagigedo Is. (Mex.). **Habitat:** Open seas and clear water; seldom close to shore.
Remarks: Migrates across the Pacific in 1 year. Probably spawns in mid-Pacific. A very important commercial and sport species — Pacific Coast fishing season June–Sept.
Similar species: In (1) Bigeye and (2) Yellowfin Tunas (below), pectoral fin is moderately long, but does not reach front of anal fin in adults; no white edge on caudal fin. (3) Other family members have a short pectoral fin at all sizes.

YELLOWFIN TUNA *Thunnus albacares*   **Pl. 32**
Identification: *Fins* tinged with *yellow; finlets bright yellow, black-edged.* Dark blue above; grading to silvery gray below. Yellow stripe in some specimens. Young usually have white bars and spots on belly (usually absent in adults). 2nd dorsal and anal fins often greatly *elongate* in large adults. Pectoral fin *long* but does not extend past front of anal fin. *No* striations on liver. 27–34 gill rakers on 1st arch. To $6\frac{1}{3}$ ft. (193 cm), 450 lb. (204 kg); but rarely more than 125 lb. (57 kg) in our area.
Range: Widely distributed in temperate and tropical waters of Atlantic, Pacific, and Indian Oceans; Pt. Conception to Peru. **Habitat:** Open sea; in schools.
Remarks: Infrequently caught as a sport fish in s. Calif. in summer and fall; fished commercially farther south.
Similar species: (1) Bigeye Tuna (below) also has a long pectoral fin, but it has striations on the liver, and its 2nd dorsal and anal fins are never elongate. (2) Albacore (above) has an even longer pectoral fin; no yellow on anal finlets, white edge on caudal fin.

BIGEYE TUNA *Thunnus obesus*   **Fig. 41, p. 270**
Identification: Pectoral fin *long* — extends past front of 2nd dorsal fin. Usually 8–10 dorsal finlets, 7–10 anal finlets. Ventral surface of *liver striated.* 23–31 gill rakers on 1st arch. Caudal fin not white-edged. Dark metallic blue above; whitish below. Often a blue stripe on side. 1st dorsal fin deep yellow, 2nd dorsal and anal

fins light yellow. Finlets yellow, black-edged. To about 8 ft. (244 cm) but usually less than 6 ft. (183 cm); to 435 lb. (197 kg). **Range:** Worldwide in warmer seas; Iron Springs (cen. Wash.) to Peru and Galapagos Is. **Habitat:** Pelagic and oceanic; surface to about 820 ft. (250 m).
Similar species: (1) In Albacore (p. 274) pectoral fin is even longer — usually reaches well past *front of anal fin;* caudal fin white-edged. (2) In Yellowfin Tuna (above) liver is not striated, 2nd dorsal and anal fins are elongate in adults. (3) In Bluefin Tuna (below) pectoral fin is short.

BLUEFIN TUNA *Thunnus thynnus*   **Pl. 32**
Identification: Our only large tuna (*Thunnus* species) with a *short* pectoral fin — fin ends below 1st dorsal fin. Back dark bluish to blackish; *no yellow.* Silvery white below — belly usually marked with white spots and lines. 1st dorsal fin bluish or yellow, 2nd dorsal fin reddish brown. Finlets dusky yellow, black-edged. Ventral surface of liver *striated.* 32–43 gill rakers on 1st arch. To $6\frac{1}{6}$ ft. (188 cm), 297 lb. (135 kg); in our area most weigh 10–45 lb. (4.5–20 kg).
Range: Shelikof Strait (Alaska) to s. Baja, but most common south of Los Angeles. **Habitat:** Open seas; inshore and offshore.
Remarks: An important commercial and sport species.
Similar species: (1) Other large, true tunas in our area have *longer* pectoral fins. (2) Most likely to be confused with Yellowfin Tuna (p. 274) when yellow pigment has faded after death; use presence of striations on liver to distinguish Bluefin Tuna (no striations in Yellowfin Tuna).

Swordfishes: Family Xiphiidae

SWORDFISH *Xiphias gladius*   **Pl. 32; Fig. 42, p. 277**
Identification: In this well-known species the upper jaw is shaped like a long *flattened sword* or bill. Pectoral fin set low on body. *No pelvic fins.* Adults have no scales. 1st dorsal fin high, with a short base. In young both parts of the dorsal fin and anal fin are connected, but midsection becomes covered by skin when individuals reach 1 ft. (30 cm) — resulting in 2 dorsal and 2 anal fins (as in Fig. 42). One strong *keel* on caudal peduncle. Very dark — usually black or brownish black above; shading to light brown below. To 15 ft. (457 cm), 1182 lb. (536 kg).
Range: Worldwide, in tropical and temperate seas; from Ore. southward. **Habitat:** Offshore; shallow to moderately deep, wide-ranging in water column. Migratory, usually not in schools.
Remarks: Only 1 species in the family. An excellent sport and food fish. In our area fishing season May–Dec.; most catches Aug.–Oct. Eats other fishes, pelagic crustaceans, and squids; reportedly uses sword to kill prey.

Similar species: Billfishes (next family) have pelvic fins, 2 (not 1) keels on the caudal peduncle, a rounder bill, and compressed body (nearly round in Swordfish).

Billfishes: Family Istiophoridae

This family of marlins, sailfishes, and spearfishes is well known and sought after by sport fishermen. As in swordfishes, the upper jaw extends into a *sword* or bill, but the sword is round in cross-section. Body elongate, moderately compressed. 2 dorsal fins — first one much larger than the 2nd; first fin usually highest in front (sail-like in all young billfishes). 2 anal fins — first one largest. 1st dorsal and anal fins can be folded into a groove at base. Caudal fin is boomerang-shaped (lunate), with a pair of keels on either side at the base. Pelvic fins rodlike, located below the pectoral fins. Scales embedded, narrow and pointed. Females grow larger than males. Billfishes are blue above; silvery white below. Some species have dark spots or bars on body and spots on first dorsal fin. They are large — to about 6–12 ft. (183–366 cm).

Billfishes occur in all tropical seas, with a few species entering temperate waters (especially when following schools of prey fishes). They are among the largest and fastest swimming fishes; many migrate long distances. They can change depths quickly, but are usually found near the surface. They eat other fishes, squids, and crustaceans; they often regurgitate their stomach contents when hooked. Often found near floating objects that attract prey. All billfishes are fished commercially to some extent, especially by the Japanese. Usually 10 species are recognized (some with subspecies); 1 common species and 4 rare ones in our area. All species in our area are compared in Fig. 42 and 1 species (a marlin) is shown in color on Pl. 32.

SAILFISH *Istiophorus platypterus*   **Fig. 42, p. 277**
Identification: Easily recognized by the *fan-shaped dorsal fin,* with the longest rays (highest part) near the middle. Dark blue above; silvery below. Dorsal fin dark blue with darker spots. To $10\frac{3}{4}$ ft. (328 cm), 182 lb. (83 kg).
Range: Generally worldwide in warm seas; San Diego to Chile.
Habitat: Oceanic; near surface.
Remarks: Currently only 1 sailfish species is recognized, but there are different populations. At night young frequently will come to a light at surface. Bill thought to be used in capturing prey; cases of attacks on boats are recorded.
Similar species: In other fishes in our area with a fan-shaped dorsal fin the upper jaw is not drawn out into a long sword or bill.

BLACK MARLIN *Makaira indica*   **Fig. 42, p. 277**
Identification: *Pectoral fin* rigid in position (cannot be folded against body); points downward and outward. Forehead steep. 1st

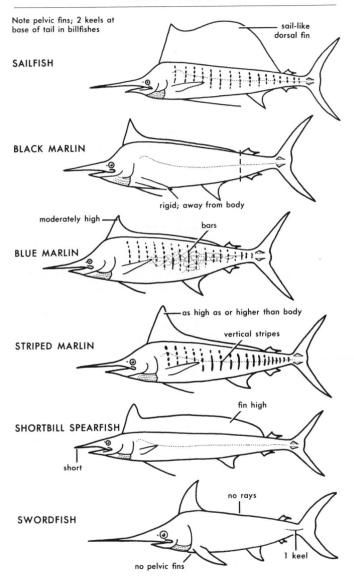

Note pelvic fins; 2 keels at base of tail in billfishes

sail-like dorsal fin

SAILFISH

BLACK MARLIN

rigid; away from body

moderately high

bars

BLUE MARLIN

as high as or higher than body

vertical stripes

STRIPED MARLIN

fin high

SHORTBILL SPEARFISH

short

no rays

SWORDFISH

no pelvic fins

1 keel

Fig. 42 Swordfish and billfishes

dorsal fin bluish black, other fins brownish black. Upper back blackish blue, side silvery white. *No spots* or bars on side. To 14¾ ft. (4.5 m), 1560 lb. (708 kg).
Range: Pacific and Indian Oceans, with a few captures in the Atlantic; rarely s. Calif. Highly migratory. **Habitat:** Oceanic; usually near surface.
Similar species: In other billfishes, pectoral fin is movable; most of them have spots on the side (see Fig. 42).

BLUE MARLIN *Makaira nigricans*   **Fig. 42, p. 277**
Identification: A *large* marlin — common to about 11 ft. (3.4 m). Body (at front of anal fin) *round* in cross-section. Forehead steep. Height of front part of dorsal fin less than body depth. Pectoral fin movable, except in very large specimens. Lateral line branched, in a chainlike pattern (hard to see in large specimens; shown in Fig. 42). Dark blue to brownish above; silvery white below. About *15 bars on side* (bars are vertical rows of pale blue spots). To 14⅔ ft. (about 4.5 m), 1805 lb. (819 kg).
Range: Warm waters of Atlantic and Pacific; rarely s. Calif. Migrates widely.
Habitat: Oceanic: near surface.
Remarks: Usually 2 subspecies are recognized: the Atlantic Blue Marlin (*M. nigricans nigricans*) and the Pacific Blue Marlin (*M. nigricans mazara*). Atlantic specimens are smaller, have a more branched lateral line, and more flexible pectoral fins.
Similar species: In Striped Marlin (below) body is more compressed (not round in cross-section) at front of anal fin; front part of 1st dorsal fin as high as or higher than body depth. Like other marlins (except the Blue Marlin) it has a relatively straight (unbranched) lateral line.

SHORTBILL SPEARFISH   **Fig. 42, p. 277**
Tetrapturus angustirostris
Identification: Upper jaw *short,* lower jaw more than ⅔ length of upper jaw. 1st dorsal fin *elevated* (*high*) for most of its length. Forehead slopes gently upward (not steep). Dark blue above; brownish silvery white on side; silvery white below. No bars or spots on body. 1st dorsal fin blue-black; other fins brown-black. To at least 8 ft. (2.4 m), 114 lb. (52 kg).
Range: Warm waters of Pacific; some strays reported from the Atlantic. Off Cape Mendocino (cen. Calif.) to Chile; rare north of Mexico. **Habitat:** Oceanic; near surface. Usually does not enter coastal waters.
Similar species: In other billfishes in our area the upper jaw is about twice as long as the lower one; 1st dorsal fin is higher at front, very low toward the rear (except much higher in Sailfish).

STRIPED MARLIN   **Pl. 32; Fig. 42, p. 277**
Tetrapturus audax
Identification: Dorsal fin very *high in front* (as high as or higher

than depth of body) then slopes quickly toward the rear. Bill long. Dark blue above; silvery white below. 15–25 light *blue bars* (or vertical rows of spots) on side. Pectoral fin movable. To 13$\frac{5}{12}$ ft. (4.1 m), 692 lb. (314 kg).
Range: Pacific and Indian Oceans; Pt. Conception southward. A stray caught off Oregon. **Habitat:** Oceanic; near surface. Offshore — usually not in coastal waters, but often common around oceanic islands.
Remarks: Feeds on other fishes, squids, pelagic crabs, and shrimps. An important sport fish, usually caught in summer and fall off s. Calif. In Calif., billfishes can be caught *only by hook and line;* commercial fishing prohibited.
Similar species: In Blue Marlin (p. 278), body is less compressed (rounder in cross-section just before anal fin), lateral line is branched, and 1st dorsal fin is lower.

Louvars: Family Luvaridae

LOUVAR *Luvarus imperialis*   **Pl. 46**
Identification: A large, peculiar, *striking* tunalike fish. The boomerang-shaped (lunate) caudal fin is preceded by a *keel*. Head blunt, with a *tiny mouth.* Eye set *low* on head. 1 dorsal fin, opposite the anal fin. Pelvic fin small, below pectoral fin. *Body pinkish* (turns silvery when dead). Dark spots on side. *Fins red.* Pectoral fin often yellowish; dorsal fin dark between rays. In young specimens, eye, dorsal and anal fins, and spots proportionately larger; dorsal and anal fins darker. To 6$\frac{1}{6}$ ft. (1.9 m), 305 lb. (138 kg).
Range: Worldwide. Newport (Ore.) to Chile in e. Pacific; most from Monterey Bay south. **Habitat:** Oceanic; near surface or in deep water.
Remarks: Only 1 species in the family. Eats mostly jellyfishes and other gelatinous planktonic animals — intestine long, modified to digest them. A weak-boned, delicate fish; most likely to be seen cast ashore or injured at surface.

Butterfishes: Family Stromateidae

Most are silvery, with a rounded head. Body compressed, somewhat oval. Mouth small. Dorsal and anal fins are long, similar in shape and size, and usually higher at front; each fin usually has 3 small, flattened spines. Pectoral fins long and pointed. Pelvic fins absent in adults (except in 1 species outside our area); present in young of some species. Caudal fin forked. Scales tiny, cycloid, easily rubbed off. Eye surrounded by fatty tissue. Gray to blue or green above; iridescent silver below. Like their relatives, the medusafishes (p. 280), flotsamfishes (p. 281), and squaretails (p. 282), butterfishes have a modified pharynx (muscular pouch on each side) lined with peculiar teeth. To about 1 ft. (30 cm).

Butterfishes are found nearly worldwide in temperate and tropical seas. Pelagic, often in large schools, usually near the coast. Young are found under floating objects. Where abundant, butterfishes support commercial fisheries. About 12–15 species, 1 in our area.

PACIFIC BUTTERFISH *Peprilus simillimus* **Pl. 31**
Identification: Body silvery and compressed; head blunt. Mouth small. Dorsal and anal fins long, opposite each other. *No* pelvic fins. Caudal fin *deeply forked.* Iridescent greenish or bluish above; silvery below. Fins dusky. To 11 in. (28 cm).
Range: Queen Charlotte Sound (B.C.) to cen. Baja and Gulf of Calif. **Habitat:** Common on sand bottom of exposed coast at 30–300 ft. (9.1–91 m).
Remarks: Also called the Pacific Pompano, but not a true pompano (Family Carangidae, p. 205). Popular in fresh-fish markets for fine flavor. Periodically abundant in Calif.
Similar species: (1) Resembles some jacks (Pl. 31 and Fig. 40, p. 207), but jacks and their relatives *have* pelvic fins and usually 2 strong spines in front of the anal fin. (2) Surfperches (p. 226; Pls. 36–37) have pelvic fins and prominent dorsal fin spines.

Medusafishes: Family Centrolophidae

Somewhat elongate, compressed fishes. Dorsal fin long and low, with 3–9 spines (3 in our species). 3 anal fin spines. Pelvic fins can be folded into a groove at base. Head unscaled, body covered with small cycloid scales (except in 1 species outside our area). Most medusafishes are dark green to gray or brownish, with vague stripes or irregular bars. Eye often golden. They have unique toothed pharyngeal sacs, as in the butterfishes (p. 279), flotsamfishes (p. 281), and squaretails (p. 282). Most medusafishes are small — usually under 5 in. (13 cm); largest species reach about 39 in. (100 cm).

Medusafishes occur in all temperate and subtropical seas. Young medusafishes live near jellyfishes and can be found inside the jellyfish "bell." (Presumably, young medusafishes are immune to the stinging cells of jellyfishes and move inside them for protection from predators.) The young also eat jellyfishes, especially the tentacles and gonads. About 20–25 species, 1 in our area.

MEDUSAFISH *Icichthys lockingtoni* **Pl. 46**
Identification: Body *limp or spongy, compressed.* Dorsal and anal fins long and low. 3 weak dorsal fin spines. Pelvic fins present. Caudal fin rounded. Adults have small cycloid scales and are gray to dusky brown, with blackish fins. Young have a deeper body, no scales, and are nearly transparent, pinkish. To 16 in. (41 cm).
Range: Japan and Gulf of Alaska to cen. Baja. **Habitat:** Near

surface and to at least 300 ft. (91 m). Young abundant offshore, often among jellyfishes.

Remarks: Most likely to be seen as stomach content of predatory fishes, but occasionally washed ashore. Captured by researchers using nets near the surface.

Similar species: (1) Ragfish (p. 283; Pl. 46) has *no* pelvic fins (in adult), a smaller eye, and no dorsal fin spines; its young are scaled and have spines on lateral line. (2) Blackrag (below) has 2 dorsal fins. (3) Pacific Butterfish (p. 280) is more oval, lacks pelvic fins, and has a deeply forked caudal fin.

Flotsamfishes: Family Nomeidae

These slender to deep-boiled fishes are related to butterfishes (p. 279) and medusafishes (p. 280). Body compressed. 2 dorsal fins; 1st one with about 10 slender spines that fold into a shallow groove at the base of the fin. Anal fin with 1–3 spines preceding the soft rays. Pectoral fins proportionately longer in larger specimens, winglike. Pelvic fins small in adults, very long in young (Fig. 43); fins fold into a groove at base. Caudal fin forked. Lateral line high, follows contour of body. Scales cycloid or weakly ctenoid, rub off easily. Color varies: usually bluish; some species are blotched or striped. Most species are small — usually under 4 in. (10 cm); largest to about 39 in. (1 m).

Flotsamfishes are found in all tropical and temperate seas; mostly oceanic, rarely inshore. Adults live deep; young near surface, often among jellyfishes. Frequently in schools. Flotsamfishes feed on zooplankton and jellyfishes. They are sometimes included in the Family Stromateidae (p. 279). About 15–20 species, 2 in our area.

BLACKRAG *Psenes pellucidus* Fig. 43, p. 282

Identification: A soft, *flabby* fish with 2 dorsal fins. 1st dorsal fin has about 10 spines; folds into a groove. Body rather slender in adults, deeper in young. Head blunt. Knifelike teeth in lower jaw. Scales tiny. Fins longer in young (see Fig. 43). Adults dark brown to blackish; young pale, with irregular mottling. To 20 in. (51 cm).

Range: Tropical and temperate waters of all oceans; rarely s. Calif. **Habitat:** Young fairly common in surface waters of high seas, usually under objects. Adults in deep water, possibly near bottom.

Remarks: Also known as the Bluefin Driftfish.

Similar species: (1) Ragfish (p. 283) and (2) Medusafish (p. 280) have *only 1* dorsal fin. **Note:** (1) Longfin Cigarfish, *Cubiceps paradoxus,* has been caught once in our area. This species has a more elongate body than the Blackrag, with an extremely long winglike pectoral fin in large specimens. To 27½ in. (70 cm). Atlantic and Pacific; rare. (2) Another rare species, *Psenes sio,* occurs off Baja

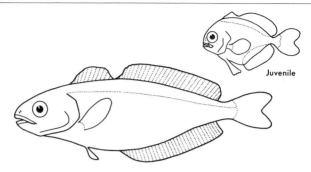

Fig. 43 Blackrag

and in the e. Pacific and might be found off s. Calif. in warm-water
years. It resembles the Blackrag but has fewer dorsal fin rays (23–
25, not 27–35) and fewer anal fin rays (23–24, not 36–31). To about
$9\frac{1}{2}$ in. (24 cm).

Squaretails: Family Tetragonuridae

Elongate, rounded fishes, with an unusual (somewhat puckered)
mouth. Shovel-like lower jaw slides inside the upper jaw. The caudal peduncle is deep, *squarish* in cross-section, with modified
scales forming 2 *keels* on each side. The body *scales* are peculiar, in
regular *curved rows,* with fine ridges on each scale. 2 dorsal fins;
1st one folds into a groove. Inner ray of pelvic fin is attached to
belly by membrane; fins fold into a depression. These fishes are
nearly solid *dark brown.* To 1–2 ft. (30–61 cm).
   Squaretails are oceanic fishes of tropical to temperate seas. They
eat salps and jellyfishes with their modified mouth, but the details
of their feeding habits are poorly known. Squaretails are sometimes placed in the Family Stromateidae (p. 279). 3 species, 1 in
our area.

SMALLEYE SQUARETAIL *Tetragonurus cuvieri*   **Pl. 47**
Identification: An elongate, cylindrical, *dark brown* fish. *2 spiny
keels at base of caudal fin.* Note the peculiar scooplike mouth.
Spinous dorsal fin low; soft dorsal fin higher and nearly opposite
anal fin. *Scales firmly attached, in curved rows.* To 15 in. (38 cm)
in ne. Pacific; larger off New Zealand (to $24\frac{1}{2}$ in. — 62 cm).
Range: Atlantic and Pacific; Aleutian Is. to Baja. **Habitat:** Oceanic, usually near surface; possibly near bottom. Perhaps in
schools.
Remarks: Eats jellyfishes and salps. Most likely to be found as

stomach content of predatory fishes such as Albacores. Young occur near the surface, usually among jellyfishes or inside large salps.

Ragfishes: Family Icosteidae

RAGFISH *Icosteus aenigmaticus*   **Pl. 46**
Identification: Body *limp* (like a rag, hence the name); eye *small.* Dorsal and anal fins long, composed only of soft rays. Young and adults differ markedly: Young — to about 16 in. (41 cm) — have a deeper body, a rounded caudal fin, pelvic fins, a spiny lateral line, and are brown and yellow with darker blotches. Adults (shown) have a less deep body, a *slightly forked* caudal fin, no pelvic fins, and are *chocolate brown. Large* — to about 7 ft. (213 cm).
Range: N. Pacific, including mid-Pacific; Japan to se. Alaska and to Pt. Loma (s. Calif.). **Habitat:** Offshore; at 60–1200 ft. (18–366 m).
Remarks: Only 1 species in the family. Eats fishes and squids. Fed on by sperm whales. Occasionally captured in trawls.

Order Pleuronectiformes

These fishes, known as flatfishes, are unique in that *both eyes are on the same side* of the body. (In the larvae of these fishes, one eye is on each side, but one eye eventually migrates to the other side as the fish grows.) A flatfish is called right-eyed if its eyes are on the right side, and left-eyed if its eyes are on the left side. In a few species, the pair of eyes can be on either side, but in most species the eyes are characteristically on one side or the other.

Flatfishes lie on the bottom and often bury themselves in the bottom sediment with just the eyes exposed. The dark pigment is usually restricted to the eyed side, which faces up; the other side, which is in contact with the bottom, is usually pale and is called the blind side. Many flatfish groups, including halibuts, soles, flounders, and turbots, are of commercial importance as food fishes. Adults vary in size from about 6 in. (15 cm) to 10 ft. (305 cm); most are about 1–2 ft. (30–61 cm).

Flatfishes are found nearly worldwide; most are marine and many occur in cold waters. Most occur in shallow water, but some live in the deep sea. About 600 species, usually grouped into 6 families. 3 families in our area.

Lefteye Flounders: Family Bothidae

In these flatfishes the *eyes* and *dark color* are typically on the *left side* of the body (except in 2 species in our area). Blind side usually white. Lateral line single, with no dorsal branch (Fig. 37 opp. Pl. 43), but sometimes forked above the upper eye. In some species the eyes are farther apart in males than in females, and the pectoral fin is sometimes longer in males. Eyed side usually brown, often with darker blotches or ringlike ocelli. Many species can change color to match the bottom. Most are about 1 ft. (30 cm), but some grow much larger.

Lefteye flounders occur worldwide in tropical and temperate seas. They live on the bottom, where they often bury themselves in the sediment, with only their eyes exposed. They are carnivores, and feed mostly on small crustaceans and fishes. Many lefteye flounders are important as food fishes. About 220 species, 7 in our area.

GULF SANDDAB *Citharichthys fragilis* **Not shown**
Identification: Eyes and color on *left* side. A *bony ridge* above lower eye. Left pectoral fin *shorter* than head length. Lateral line *straight.* Eyed side brown, mottled with darker brown. Blind side whitish. To about 5½ in. (14 cm).
Range: Manhattan Beach (s. Calif.) to Gulf of Calif.; uncommon in our area. **Habitat:** Sand bottom at 60–1138 ft. (18–347 m).
Similar species: See under Pacific Sanddab (below).

PACIFIC SANDDAB *Citharichthys sordidus* **Pl. 43**
Identification: Eyes and color on *left* side. Left pectoral fin *shorter* than head length. Lateral line straight. Diameter of lower eye greater than snout length. A *bony ridge* above lower eye. Eyed side light brown, mottled with dark brown; sometimes with yellow and orange spots. Blind side whitish or light tan. To 16 in. (41 cm).
Range: Bering Sea to s. Baja. **Habitat:** Sand bottom, at 30–1800 ft. (9.1–549 m); young sometimes occur shallower.
Remarks: A fairly common species. A popular food fish, particularly in Calif.
Similar species: (1) Gulf Sanddab (above) is smaller and has more gill rakers (16–21, not 12–16) on the lower part of the 1st arch); fewer scales (46–51, not 61–70) in the lateral line. (2) Longfin Sanddab (p. 285) has a *very long* left pectoral fin — longer than head length (tip of snout to rear edge of gill cover). (3) In Speckled Sanddab (below) left pectoral fin is short — extends to or ends just short of the rear of the stomach cavity (in fresh-caught specimens, this cavity is visible through the side of the fish as a dark shadow). The area between the eyes is narrower and not concave; diameter of lower eye is nearly equal to snout length; maximum length only 6¾ in. (17 cm).

SPECKLED SANDDAB *Citharichthys stigmaeus* **Pl. 43**
Identification: A small, *speckled,* left-eyed flatfish. Diameter of lower eye *nearly* equals snout length. Left pectoral fin *shorter* than head length; fin extends to or ends just short of rear of stomach cavity. Lateral line straight. 8–10 gill rakers on lower limb of 1st

arch. Eyed side brown or tan with black speckles and spots. Blind side white. To about $6\frac{3}{4}$ in. (17 cm), but rarely over 5 in. (13 cm).
Range: Se. Alaska to s. Baja. **Habitat:** Sand bottom, near shore to 1200 ft. (366 m) but usually shallower than 300 ft. (91 m).
Remarks: Common, but of little commercial importance because of its small size. Eaten by fishes, marine mammals, and sea birds.
Similar species: (1) Gulf Sanddab (p. 284) has 16–21 gill rakers on lower part of 1st arch. (2) Pacific Sanddab (above) lacks the dense spotting, is larger, and has a *longer* left pectoral fin (when folded forward, fin reaches about to middle of eye — fin barely reaches or falls short of eye in Speckled Sanddab). (3) In Longfin Sanddab (below) left pectoral fin is longer than head length.

LONGFIN SANDDAB *Citharichthys xanthostigma*   **Pl. 43**
Identification: *Left-eyed,* with a *very long* blackish *pectoral fin* on the left side (nearly twice length of caudal fin and longer than head length — as measured from tip of snout to rear of gill cover). Lateral line straight. Eyed side usually nearly uniform dark brown, with rust-orange and white speckles. Blind side whitish. To 10 in. (25 cm).
Range: Monterey Bay to Costa Rica; common off s. Calif., rare north of Santa Barbara (s. Calif.). **Habitat:** On bottom at 8–660 ft. (2.4–201 m).
Similar species: (1) Other sanddabs and most left-eyed flatfishes have a shorter pectoral fin (not longer than head lenth). (2) See under Speckled Sanddab (above) and (3) Pacific Sanddab (p. 284).

BIGMOUTH SOLE *Hippoglossina stomata*   **Pl. 43**
Identification: Left-eyed, with a *large mouth.* Body thin. Lateral line *arched* over pectoral fin. Caudal fin rounded. Eyed side brown with bluish speckles and dark blotches. Blind side whitish. To about $15\frac{3}{4}$ in. (40 cm).
Range: Monterey Bay to Gulf of Calif. **Habitat:** On bottom at 100–450 ft. (30–137 m).
Similar species: (1) California Halibut (below) is much larger — to 5 ft. (152 cm) — and has a different shaped caudal fin and longer jaw teeth. (2) Other left-eyed flatfishes have a smaller mouth (with shorter jaws).

CALIFORNIA HALIBUT *Paralichthys californicus*   **Pl. 43**
Identification: Large — frequently over 2 ft. (61 cm). Both eyes may be on *either side* (not just the left side as in most lefteye flounders). Lateral line *arched* over pectoral fin. Caudal fin slightly indented above and below, not evenly rounded. *Mouth large,* jaw extends beyond rear of lower eye; numerous *sharp teeth.* Eyed side mostly uniform dark brown to black, but often mottled with light and dark. Blind side usually white. To 5 ft. (152 cm), 72 lb. (33 kg).
Range: Quillayute R. (n. Wash.) to s. Baja. **Habitat:** Varies —

mostly on sand bottom. Common beyond surf line, also in bays
and estuaries. Near shore and to 600 ft. (183 m).
Remarks: Eats fishes and squids; often feeds well off the bottom.
An important sport and commercial species. Sport fishermen usually catch it with live bait or metal lures.
Similar species: (1) Bigmouth Sole (above) is never right-eyed,
has an *evenly* rounded caudal fin, lacks prominent jaw teeth, and
does not exceed 16 in. (41 cm). (2) Pacific Halibut (p. 288; Pl. 45) is
nearly always right-eyed, and jaw only reaches front edge of eye.
(3) Greenland Halibut (p. 294) has *dark pigment* on *both sides* of
body. (3) Arrowtooth Flounder (below) is nearly always right-
eyed, has a *straight* lateral line.

FANTAIL SOLE *Xystreurys liolepis*   **Pl. 43**
Identification: Usually left-eyed, but frequently right-eyed. Lateral line *arched* over pectoral fin. Mouth small; jaw does not extend beyond rear of lower eye. Left pectoral fin *longer* than head.
Eyed side nearly uniform brown; often with 2 ocelli (1 near pectoral fin, 2nd one far back on body). Blind side white. To 21 in.
(53 cm).
Range: Monterey Bay to Gulf of Calif.   **Habitat:** Sandy-mud
bottom at 15–260 ft. (4.6–79 m). Usually buried in bottom.
Remarks: Rarely caught by sport fishermen. Feeds almost exclusively on crustaceans.
Similar species: (1) Bigmouth Sole (p. 285) has a *larger* mouth
and a shorter pectoral fin. (2) Longfin Sanddab (p. 285) has a
straight lateral line. (3) Most right-eyed flatfishes have *shorter*
pectoral fins; many have a dorsal branch to the lateral line and/or
a straight lateral line.

Righteye Flounders:
Family Pleuronectidae

In these flatfishes the *eyes* and *dark color* are characteristically on
the *right side*. In many species the lateral line has a dorsal branch
near the front that runs along the base of the dorsal fin (Fig. 37
opp. Pl. 43); the lateral line is straight in some, arched over the
pectoral fin in others. Most righteye flounders are light brown on
the eyed side. Usually under 2 ft. (61 cm); a few reach 4–6 ft. (122–
183 cm); the largest grow to 8¾ ft. (267 cm). Most of these
flounders live in cold seas; a few occur in the tropics or in brackish
and fresh water. About 100 species, 22 in our area.

ARROWTOOTH FLOUNDER *Atheresthes stomias*   **Pl. 45**
Identification: Right-eyed. Mouth *large,* jaw extends to or beyond rear of eye. Upper eye set *high* on head (at midline), even
visible from blind side. Caudal fin slightly *indented.* Teeth prominent, *arrow-shaped,* in *2 rows* on upper jaw. Lateral line nearly

straight. Eyed side brown; scales slightly darker at edges. Blind side mostly white, with fine dark specks. To $2\frac{3}{4}$ ft. (84 cm).
Range: Chukchi Sea (?) and Bering Sea to coast off San Pedro (s. Calif.). Common offshore from Alaska to B.C. **Habitat:** Soft bottom, at 60–2400 ft. (18–731 m).
Remarks: Usually caught in trawls. Quality of flesh poor, not marketed as human food; used for mink food.
Similar species: (1) Greenland Halibut (p. 294; Pl. 45) is mostly dusky on the *blind* side. (2) In California Halibut (p. 285; Pl. 43) lateral line is *arched* over the pectoral fin; caudal fin is rounded at middle, not indented. (3) Bigmouth Sole (p. 285; Pl. 43) has eyes on *left* side.

ROUGHSCALE SOLE *Clidoderma asperrimum*   **Not shown**
Identification: Irregular rows of *rough scaly plates* (tubercles) on eyed side. No scales on blind side. Eyed side brown; blind side *gray*. To $21\frac{1}{2}$ in. (55 cm).
Range: N. Pacific; Japan to s. Ore.; common off Japan but rare in the ne. Pacific. **Habitat:** Mud bottom; in our area at about 1100 ft. (335 m).
Similar species: Starry Flounder (p. 291; Pl. 43) also has tubercles on the eyed side, but it has alternating light and dark radiating *bars* on dorsal, anal, and caudal fins.

DEEPSEA SOLE   **Fig. 36 opp. Pl. 43**
Embassichthys bathybius
Identification: A deep-living, *slimy,* flabby flatfish. Right-eyed. Mouth small. Caudal fin small. Lateral line nearly straight. Usually dusky gray, often mottled with blue; dusky blotches usually run inward from edge of body. Blind side dusky. To $18\frac{1}{2}$ in. (47 cm).
Range: Japan to Gulf of Alaska and to Mexican border.
Habitat: Mud bottom at 1050–4700 ft. (320–1433 m).
Similar species: (1) Other flatfishes are less flabby and have a different shape, or more of an arch in lateral line, a larger mouth, or an indented caudal fin. (2) Roughscale Sole (above) is also found in deep water but it has rough tubercles on the eyed side.

PETRALE SOLE *Eopsetta jordani*   **Pl. 45**
Identification: Right-eyed. Mouth large — jaw extends below *middle* of eye. 2 rows of small teeth on upper jaw. Eyed side brown. Blind side white, sometimes with traces of pink. Dorsal and anal fins have faint dark blotches. To $27\frac{1}{2}$ in. (70 cm).
Range: Bering Sea to n. Baja. **Habitat:** Sand bottom at 60–1500 ft. (18–457 m).
Remarks: An important food fish. Sold fresh or as frozen filets, common in markets.
Similar species: (1) Flathead Sole (p. 288) has large teeth in 1 row on the upper jaw and its caudal fin membranes are usually

clear (usually brownish in Petrale Sole). (2) In Arrowtooth Flounder (p. 286) caudal fin is indented at middle. (3) In Sand Sole (p. 293; Pl. 44) rays at front of dorsal fin are *free* of membrane.

REX SOLE *Glyptocephalus zachirus*   **Pl. 45**
Identification: *Small-mouthed,* right-eyed, *slender,* with a *long pectoral fin* on eyed side (longer than head or caudal fin). Head rounded in front. Lateral line nearly straight. Eyed side light brown. Blind side white to dusky. Fins dark-edged; pectoral fin mostly black. To $23\frac{1}{4}$ in. (59 cm).
Range: Bering Sea to n. Baja. **Habitat:** Sand or mud bottom at 60–2100 ft. (18–640 m); more abundant below 200 ft. (61 m).
Remarks: Slow-growing; lives up to 24 years. Not usually caught by sport fishermen. An important food fish, trawled commercially.
Similar species: (1) Our other right-eyed flatfishes have a *shorter* pectoral fin; many have a larger mouth, an indented caudal fin (rounded in Rex Sole), an arched lateral line, or a dorsal branch to the lateral line. (2) Longfin Sanddab (p. 285) has a long pectoral fin, but it is left-eyed.

FLATHEAD SOLE *Hippoglossoides elassodon*   **Pl. 45**
Identification: *Thin,* right-eyed. Look for small *pores* below lower eye. Teeth long, white, in *1 row* on upper jaw. Lateral line nearly straight (not strongly arched over pectoral fin). Eyed side brown, sometimes blotched with dusky brown. Blind side white. Dorsal and anal fins have dark blotches. To $1\frac{1}{2}$ ft. (46 cm).
Range: Sea of Japan to Bering Sea and to Pt. Reyes (cen. Calif.).
Habitat: Soft bottom at 20–1800 ft. (6.1–549 m); adults usually below 600 ft. (183 m).
Similar species: In Petrale Sole (p. 287) caudal fin membranes are usually brownish (usually clear in Flathead Sole); 2 rows of teeth on upper jaw.

PACIFIC HALIBUT *Hippoglossus stenolepis*   **Pl. 45**
Identification: The *largest* flatfish in our area — commonly over $2\frac{1}{2}$ ft. (76 cm). Almost always right-eyed. Caudal fin slightly *indented,* more so in larger specimens. Lateral line *arched* over pectoral fin. Jaw does not extend past middle of eye. Scales on both sides small, cycloid. Eyed side dark brown to blackish, often with marbling or spots. Blind side usually white. Females to $8\frac{3}{4}$ ft. (267 cm), about 500 lb. (227 kg), but reported to 800 lb. (363 kg); males smaller; average size caught by fishermen probably 5–10 lb. (2.3–4.5 kg).
Range: Sea of Japan to Bering Sea and to Santa Rosa I. (s. Calif.). Wide-ranging, often migratory. **Habitat:** On a variety of bottom types. Young near shore, adults deeper — to about 3600 ft. (1097 m).
Remarks: An important commercial and sport fish in northern

waters. Fished commercially by long-lining. Commercial stocks declined in 1920s but increased with regulation.
Similar species: (1) California Halibut (p. 285) has a larger mouth, is usually left-eyed, caudal fin rounded at middle (not indented). (2) Greenland Halibut (p. 294) has dark pigment on *blind* side, rough (ctenoid) scales, a larger mouth, little or no arch in lateral line.

DIAMOND TURBOT *Hypsopsetta guttulata*   Pl. 44
Identification: Right-eyed. Dorsal and anal fins highest at middle, giving body a *diamond-shaped* outline. Note the *long* dorsal branch of lateral line. Mouth small. Eyed side *dark gray or greenish,* often with bright blue spots. Blind side white, with bright yellow around mouth. To $1\frac{1}{2}$ ft. (46 cm).
Range: Cape Mendocino (n. Calif.) to s. Baja; isolated population in Gulf of Calif. **Habitat:** Mud or sand bottom, often in bays and sloughs; at 5–150 ft. (1.5–46 m).
Similar species: (1) In other turbots in our area (*Pleuronichthys* species — Pl. 44), 4 or more rays at front of dorsal fin extend down on the *blind* side (see Fig. 38 opp. Pl. 44). (2) In other flatfishes the dorsal lateral line branch is absent or much shorter.

BUTTER SOLE *Isopsetta isolepis*   Pl. 44
Identification: Right-eyed. *Dorsal and anal fins yellow at edge.* Ctenoid scales on eyed side; scales extend onto fin rays. Dorsal lateral line branch extends below first one-third of dorsal fin. Main lateral line has a low arch over pectoral fin. Eyed side brown, with darker and lighter mottling, sometimes vaguely spotted with yellow or green. Blind side white. To $21\frac{3}{4}$ in. (55 cm), but usually under 1 ft. (30 cm).
Range: Bering Sea to Ventura (s. Calif.). **Habitat:** Common in shallow water, occasionally as deep as 1200 ft. (366 m).
Remarks: A tasty species, sometimes marketed. Also used for mink food. More than 1 million lb. (454 mt) have been harvested commercially in Canada in 1 year.
Similar species: (1) English Sole (p. 291) has cycloid scales on the front part of the eyed side, *no* scales on the fin rays. (2) In Rock Sole (below) lateral line is more strongly arched over the pectoral fin, with a shorter dorsal branch.

ROCK SOLE *Lepidopsetta bilineata*   Pl. 44
Identification: Right-eyed. Our only flatfish with *both* an *abrupt arch* in lateral line over pectoral fin *and* a *dorsal* lateral line *branch* (Fig. 37 opp. Pl. 43). Ctenoid scales on eyed side. Eyed side light to dark brown or gray, with darker mottling; sometimes mottled with yellow and red. Blind side whitish, sometimes yellowish toward the rear. To $23\frac{1}{2}$ in. (60 cm).
Range: Sea of Japan and Bering Sea to Tanner Bank (off s. Calif.). **Habitat:** Shallow water and to about 1200 ft. (366 m), usu-

ally shallower than 600 ft. (183 m). On more pebbly bottom than most other flatfishes.
Remarks: A tasty food fish; in some years commercial catch reaches 6–7 million lb. (2722–3175 mt) in Canada.
Similar species: Butter Sole (p. 289) has only a *slight* arch in lateral line over pectoral fin, longer dorsal branch.

YELLOWFIN SOLE *Limanda aspera*   Pl. 45
Identification: A right-eyed, northern species. Lateral line *arched* over pectoral fin, with *no* dorsal branch. Dorsal and anal fins *covered with scales.* Ctenoid scales on *both sides* of body. Eyed side brown, with darker mottling. Blind side white. Dorsal and anal fins *yellowish,* with faint dark bars, and a narrow black line at base of each fin. To about $17\frac{1}{2}$ in. (44 cm).
Range: Korea to Bering Sea and to Barkley Sound (B.C.). Common in the Bering Sea, but rare in our area. **Habitat:** Shallow, usually at less than 300 ft. (91 m), maximum about 600 ft. (183 m).
Similar species: (1) Butter Sole (p. 289), (2) Hybrid Sole (p. 291), and (3) Rock Sole (p. 289) have a dorsal lateral line branch (Fig. 37 opp. Pl. 43).

SLENDER SOLE *Lyopsetta exilis*   Pl. 45
Identification: A small, *slender,* right-eyed species. Mouth medium-sized; jaw ends roughly below middle of lower eye. Upper eye at midline, visible from blind side. Scales *large,* rub off easily; *ctenoid* on *both sides* of body. Lateral line nearly straight. Eyed side light brown; scales often darker at edges. Blind side white to orange-yellow. Fins slightly dusky, dorsal and anal fins often pale at edges. To about $13\frac{3}{4}$ in. (35 cm).
Range: Se. Alaska to cen. Baja. **Habitat:** Moderate depths; 250–1680 ft. (76–512 m).
Similar species: (1) Dover Sole (below) has a much smaller mouth, more flaccid body, dusky blind side. (2) Rex Sole (p. 288) has a smaller mouth and a *long,* dusky pectoral fin. (3) Sanddabs (pp. 284–285; Pl. 43) are usually *left-eyed,* with the upper eye set lower — that eye completely on the eyed side (*not* visible from blind side).

DOVER SOLE *Microstomus pacificus*   Pl. 45
Identification: *Slender,* right-eyed. Gill slit usually does not extend above base of pectoral fin. *Slimy, flaccid; slippery* to handle. Mouth *small,* jaw ends below front of lower eye. Lateral line nearly straight, *not* strongly arched over pectoral fin. Eyed side brown, fins dusky. Blind side light to dark gray, sometimes with reddish blotches. To $2\frac{1}{2}$ ft. (76 cm).
Range: Bering Sea to cen. Baja. **Habitat:** Mud bottom at 60–3000 ft. (18–914 m). Moves into deep water in winter.
Remarks: Important commercially — trawled, marketed as filets. Rarely caught by sport fishermen.

Similar species: (1) Slender Sole (p. 290) has a larger mouth (jaw ends roughly below middle of lower eye); gill slit extends above base of pectoral fin. (2) Rex Sole (p. 288) has a *long,* dusky pectoral fin. (3) Deepsea Sole (p. 287; Fig. 36 opp. Pl. 43) also occurs in deep water; it has a deeper body and is usually blotched.

ENGLISH SOLE *Parophrys vetulus*   **Pl. 44**
Identification: Right-eyed; snout *pointed.* Upper eye set high (at midline) — *visible from the blind side.* Mouth looks *twisted* when viewed from the front. A dorsal branch to lateral line; main lateral line nearly straight. Scales cycloid (smooth) on front half of body, ctenoid (rough) on rear half. Caudal fin nearly square-cut (not rounded), slightly pointed at middle. Eyed side brown. Blind side white to pale yellow, tinged with reddish brown. To 22½ in. (57 cm).
Range: Bering Sea to cen. Baja.   **Habitat:** To 1800 ft. (549 m); young intertidal.
Remarks: Important commercially. Called the Lemon Sole in some areas because it sometimes has a lemon odor. Apparently interbreeds with the Starry Flounder (below); the resulting hybrid is known as the Hybrid Sole (below).
Similar species: Other flatfishes have a larger mouth, and/or an abrupt arch in the lateral line, or a rounded caudal fin.

HYBRID SOLE   **Pl. 44**
Parophrys vetulus x *Platichthys stellatus*
Identification: Right-eyed. Dorsal lateral line branch short; main lateral line nearly straight. Ctenoid scales on *both* sides of body; those on blind side are mixed with cycloid scales. Eyed side brown with lighter and darker areas. Blind side white. Dorsal and anal fins have faint dark bars. To 1½ ft. (46 cm).
Range: Bering Sea to San Francisco. Rare, most frequent in Puget Sound. **Habitat:** Soft bottom; to about 2165 ft. (660 m).
Remarks: This form is thought by most researchers to be a hybrid resulting from a cross between the English Sole and Starry Flounder. If it proves to be a separate species and not a hybrid, it will have the scientific name *Inopsetta ischyra*. Also called the Forkline Sole.
Similar species: (1) English Sole (*P. vetulus,* above) has a *longer* dorsal lateral line branch, a more *pointed* snout, and *no* bars on the dorsal and anal fins. (2) Starry Flounder (*P. stellatus,* below) has star-shaped *tubercles* on body, bars on *caudal* fin, and more vivid light and dark bars on the fins. (3) Yellowfin Sole (p. 290; Pl. 45) lacks a dorsal lateral line branch.

STARRY FLOUNDER *Platichthys stellatus*   **Pl. 43**
Identification: Can be *right-eyed or left-eyed.* Prominent *oblique dark bars* alternate with *yellowish to orange bars* on dorsal, anal, and caudal fins. No dorsal branch to lateral line. Rough, *star-*

shaped tubercles (modified scales) are scattered on eyed side. Eyed side mostly brown to nearly black. Blind side white, sometimes with darker blotches. To 3 ft. (91 cm), 20 lb. (9.1 kg).
Range: Japan to Bering Sea and Arctic Alaska, and to Santa Barbara (s. Calif.). **Habitat:** Mostly near shore, often in estuaries. To 900 ft. (274 m). Common.
Remarks: In our area (Gulf of Alaska to waters off Calif.) about 60–70% have eyes on left side, but from w. Alaska to Japan nearly all are left-eyed. An important sport fish. Marketed in moderate quantities, but not highly regarded as a food fish. Apparently hybridizes with the English Sole (*P. vetulus*), and the resulting form is known as the Hybrid Sole (above).
Similar species: (1) Hybrid Sole (p. 291) has a short, forked dorsal branch to lateral line, *paler* bars on the dorsal and anal fins, *no* bars on the caudal fin, and *no* tubercles on eyed side. (2) See Roughscale Sole (p. 287).

C-O TURBOT *Pleuronichthys coenosus* **Pl. 44**
Identification: Deep-bodied, oval; *right-eyed.* A dark *spot* on caudal fin preceded by a curved dark bar (upside down, the marks look like "C-O" — hence the common name). Eyed side *dark brown to blackish,* often with a conspicuous dark spot at midside. Blind side white. A long dorsal branch to lateral line; no abrupt arch over pectoral fin. Scales cycloid, embedded. First 5–6 rays in dorsal fin are on *blind* side (Fig. 38 opp. Pl. 44). To 14 in. (36 cm).
Range: Se. Alaska to n. Baja. **Habitat:** On flat bottom but also in rocky areas, common in shallow water; to 1150 ft. (350 m).
Remarks: Also known as the C-O Sole.
Similar species: (1) Spotted Turbot (p. 293) also may have a dark spot at the midside but usually also has 1–2 spots far back on body, at base of dorsal and anal fins; no C-O mark on caudal fin. (2) Other flatfishes with a dorsal branch to lateral line (Pl. 44) lack the "C-O" mark on the caudal fin.

CURLFIN TURBOT *Pleuronichthys decurrens* **Pl. 44**
Identification: Deep-bodied, oval; right-eyed. A long dorsal branch to lateral line; no abrupt arch over pectoral fin. Dorsal and anal fin rays longest at middle of fins, giving body a diamond-shaped outline. 1st *9–12 rays* in dorsal fin are on *blind* side, lowermost ray about *in line with mouth* (Fig. 38 opp. Pl. 44). Scales cycloid, embedded. Bony *ridge between eyes,* with a tubercle or spine at each end. Eyed side brown to blackish or reddish brown, often mottled. Blind side white. Fins dark. To 14½ in. (37 cm).
Range: Prince William Sound (Alaska) to n.-cen. Baja. **Habitat:** A common soft-bottom species, at about 25–1746 ft. (7.6–532 m).
Remarks: Also known as the Curlfin Sole. Fished commercially in Calif., usually for mink food.
Similar species: (1) In Spotted and (2) Hornyhead Turbots (below), only 1st 4–6 rays in dorsal fin are on the blind side

(Fig. 38). See (3) C-O Turbot (above) and (4) Diamond Turbot (p. 289).

SPOTTED TURBOT *Pleuronichthys ritteri*   **Pl. 44**
Identification: Small; oval; right-eyed. Usually has at least 1 dark spot at midside (sometimes 2) and 2 other dark spots, at rear of dorsal and anal fins. A long dorsal branch to lateral line; no abrupt arch over pectoral fin. About first *6 rays* in dorsal fin are on the *blind side* (Fig. 38 opp. Pl. 44). Eyed side brown to gray-brown with light speckles. Blind side white. To $11\frac{1}{2}$ in. (29 cm).
Range: Morro Bay (cen. Calif.) to s. Baja. **Habitat:** Common inshore and to 150 ft (46 m).
Similar species: (1) Hornyhead Turbot (below) has sharp *spine* at rear of bony ridge between eyes. (2) Curlfin Turbot (above) has *more* dorsal fin rays (9–12) on the blind side, 1st ray in line with mouth (Fig. 38).

HORNYHEAD TURBOT   **Pl. 44**
Pleuronichthys verticalis
Identification: Oval; small-mouthed; right-eyed. First *4–6 rays* in dorsal fin on *blind* side. A long dorsal branch to lateral line; no abrupt arch over pectoral fin. *Ridge between eyes* with a *spine at rear* (and usually another spine at front); spine at rear sharp, points toward the rear. No teeth in lower jaw on right (eyed) side. Eyed side dark brown or yellowish brown with gray blotches, often marbled. Blind side white. To $14\frac{1}{2}$ in. (37 cm).
Range: Pt. Reyes (cen. Calif.) to s. Baja; isolated population in n. Gulf of Calif. **Habitat:** Soft bottom at 30–660 ft. (9.1–201 m).
Similar species: (1) Spotted Turbot (above) has 1 row of tiny teeth in lower jaw on eyed side, no sharp spine at rear of ridge between eyes. (2) Curlfin Turbot (p. 292) has 9–12 dorsal fin rays on blind side (Fig. 38 opp. Pl. 44). (3) C-O Turbot (p. 292) has teeth in lower jaw on eyed side, no sharp spine at the rear of the ridge between the eyes; usually has C-O mark on caudal fin.

SAND SOLE *Psettichthys melanostictus*   **Pl. 44**
Identification: Right-eyed. Note the *threadlike rays* at *front of dorsal fin* (rays mostly free of membrane). Mouth large; jaw ends below middle of eye. A dorsal branch to lateral line; no abrupt arch over pectoral fin. Color on eyed side varies: gray to brown or greenish, with black speckles. Blind side white. To $24\frac{3}{4}$ in. (63 cm).
Range: Bering Sea to Redondo Beach (s. Calif.). **Habitat:** Near shore and to 600 ft. (183 m).
Remarks: Common; often caught on hook and line, especially from shore.
Similar species: Sometimes confused with small specimens of the California Halibut (p. 285), but they have more of an arch in the lateral line over the pectoral fin; rays at front of dorsal fin are not threadlike.

GREENLAND HALIBUT   **Pl. 45**
Reinhardtius hippoglossoides
Identification: Large; right-eyed. Caudal fin slightly *indented.*
Eyed side blackish or dark brown. Blind side *dusky,* with pale
areas. Mouth large; jaw extends below eye. *1 row* of large teeth in
each jaw. *Eyes far apart;* upper eye set high (touches dorsal midline — visible from the blind side). To about 3 ft. (91 cm).
Range: N. Atlantic and N. Pacific; Sea of Japan to Bering Sea and
to n. Baja; rare south of Alaska. **Habitat:** Usually deep-living;
reported at 48–2100 ft. (15–640 m).
Remarks: A northern commercial species, marketed as the Greenland Turbot.
Similar species: See Pl. 45 — (1) Arrowtooth Flounder (p. 286)
also has an indented caudal fin and a large mouth, but its blind
side is white; jaw teeth arrow-shaped, in *2 rows.* (2) Pacific Halibut
(p. 288) has a *high arch* in lateral line over the pectoral fin; blind
side white.

Tonguefishes: Family Cynoglossidae

Left-eyed, *teardrop-shaped* flatfishes with a *pointed caudal fin*
that is *joined* to the *dorsal and anal fins.* Mouth *small, curved,*
twisted to eyed side; snout projects beyond mouth. *Eyes small,*
close together or even touching. No lateral line in many species. *No*
pectoral fins. Pelvic fin present only on eyed side. Brownish, sometimes with bars across body; blind side paler. Small — most species
are under 1 ft. (30 cm).

Tonguefishes occur mainly in tropical seas at shallow to moderate depths; but some species occur quite deep. About 140 species, 1
in our area. **Note:** Several species of soles of the tropical Family
Soleidae occur off Baja, and stragglers might reach s. Calif. in
warm-water years. They resemble tonguefishes in having a small
twisted mouth and small eyes, but they are *right*-eyed and have a
separate caudal fin, a deeper body, and no groove on the cheek
(between the eyes and the gill opening).

CALIFORNIA TONGUEFISH   **Pl. 43**
Symphurus atricauda
Identification: Teardrop-shaped; slippery. Caudal fin *pointed,*
fully *joined* to dorsal and anal fins. Mouth small, twisted to eyed
side. Eyes *tiny,* on left side. *No pectoral fins.* No pelvic fin on blind
side. No lateral line. Eyed side brown to gray, with dark bars or
mottling. Blind side white. To $8\frac{1}{4}$ in. (21 cm).
Range: Yaquina Bay (Ore.) to Panama; rare north of Pt. Conception. **Habitat:** Mud or sandy-mud bottom at 5–660 ft. (1.5–201 m).
Remarks: Common in s. Calif., but rarely seen. Sometimes caught
by fishermen using very small hooks.

Order Tetraodontiformes

Most of these fishes are armored with a bony shield, bony plates, spines, or prickles; some are naked (unscaled). All of them have a *small gill slit,* just in front of the pectoral fin. 2nd dorsal fin opposite the anal fin. Most are found near shore in tropical or subtropical waters, but a few are pelagic, or ascend rivers in the tropics. A few other species live in temperate waters. Some species are eaten, but in subtropical and tropical areas many are highly toxic and constitute a public health problem. Death (from "puffer poisoning") can result from eating the skin, flesh, or internal organs of these fishes. 8-10 families (depending on classification used); 5 families in our area. About 320 species; 12 in our area. (3 species are shown on Pl. 46, 11 species are compared in Fig. 44.)

Triggerfishes and Filefishes: Family Balistidae

Deep-bodied, compressed fishes with a spinous dorsal fin composed of 2–3 spines, followed by a long soft dorsal fin, opposite a long anal fin. Mouth *small;* with sturdy incisorlike jaw teeth. Gill opening a small slit in front of pectoral fin. Pelvic fins absent or fused to form a small spinous knob. Also known as "leatherjackets" — skin thick, leathery, covered with rough scales.

Triggerfishes have 3 dorsal fin spines; in filefishes the 1st spine is farther forward, the 2nd spine is rudimentary, and the 3rd spine is absent. The 1st spine in both groups can be locked in an upright position by a "trigger" mechanism; this rigid spine can cause injury to predators attempting to swallow triggerfishes and filefishes. Many species are brightly colored. Most are small — under 1 ft. (30 cm). They occur in all warm seas. Young and adults of many species are pelagic. About 120 species; 3 triggerfishes occur rarely in our area.

FINESCALE TRIGGERFISH   **Fig. 44, p. 297**
Balistes polylepis
Identification: Note the characteristic triggerfish shape. Small gill slit in front of pectoral fin. 3 spines in 1st dorsal fin, all fully visible. *Brownish* with blue speckles on head. To $2\frac{1}{2}$ ft. (76 cm).
Range: Crescent City (n. Calif.) to Chile; rare north of Baja.
Habitat: Adults on bottom, near shore and to 1680 ft. (512 m); young pelagic.
Similar species: (1) Black Durgon (p. 296) is black. (2) Redtail Triggerfish (p. 296) is a different color and has *only 2* visible dorsal fin spines.

BLACK DURGON   Pl. 46; Fig. 44, p. 297
Melichthys niger
Identification: Our only *black* triggerfish. A *white to bluish line*
at base of dorsal and anal fins. 2 visible dorsal fin spines; 3rd spine
tiny, virtually absent in large adults. To 20 in. (51 cm).
Range: Probably worldwide in warm seas; San Diego to Colombia. **Habitat:** Oceanic, near the surface, usually around islands.
Remarks: Records from San Diego date back to the middle 1800s;
not known north of Mexico since then.

REDTAIL TRIGGERFISH   Pl. 46; Fig. 44, p. 297
Xanthichthys mento
Identification: 5-8 *grooves on cheek*. 2 visible dorsal fin spines.
Dark pigment between scales. Color varies in both sexes. Males
(shown) are yellowish, and have *blue spots* on body, a bluish head
or blue streaks in grooves on head, and a red caudal fin. Females
have a bluish head, a bluish green body, and a yellowish caudal fin.
To 10 in. (25 cm).
Range: Warm waters of e. Pacific; also Hawaii, Japan, and Easter
I.; Ventura (s. Calif.) southward. **Habitat:** Oceanic, surface-living;
usually found around oceanic islands.
Similar species: (1) Black Durgon (above) is black. (2) Finescale
Triggerfish (p. 295) lacks the grooves on the cheek and has *3* visible
dorsal fin spines.

Trunkfishes and Boxfishes:
Family Ostraciidae

Peculiar fishes with the body encased in a *"box" or trunklike bony
carapace* with openings for the mouth, nostrils, gill slits, fins,
anus, and tail. *No* dorsal fin spines, but often a body spine on the
upper back. Soft dorsal fin small, far back on body, slightly in
front of anal fin. No pelvic fins. Largest species reach about 2 ft.
(61 cm); most are smaller.
  Most trunkfishes and boxfishes are found in tropical and subtropical seas; a few wide-ranging species reach temperate waters.
The fishes in this family are slow swimmers, and depend on their
armor (rather than speed) for protection. Most live on the bottom
in shallow water; a few are oceanic. About 25 species, 1 boxfish in
our area.

SPINY BOXFISH *Ostracion diaphanum*   Fig. 44, p. 297
Identification: Body enclosed in a *bony box* formed of more or
less *hexagonal* plates. Light brown. To 10 in. (25 cm).
Range: Tropical waters of Pacific and Indian Ocean; Santa Barbara (s. Calif.) to Peru; rare on our coast. **Habitat:** Oceanic; at or
near surface.
Remarks: Eaten by tunas and other large oceanic predators. In
our area usually found cast up on beach.

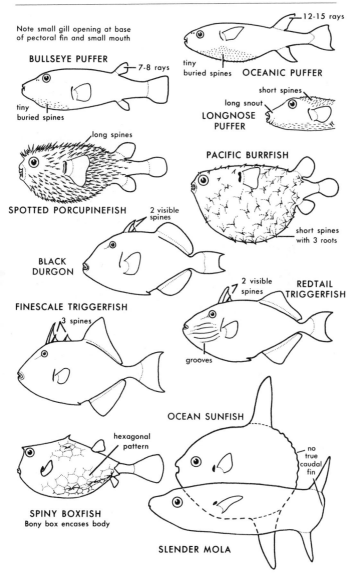

Note small gill opening at base of pectoral fin and small mouth

BULLSEYE PUFFER

7-8 rays

tiny buried spines

12-15 rays

tiny buried spines

OCEANIC PUFFER

short spines

long snout

LONGNOSE PUFFER

long spines

SPOTTED PORCUPINEFISH

PACIFIC BURRFISH

short spines with 3 roots

2 visible spines

BLACK DURGON

FINESCALE TRIGGERFISH

2 visible spines

REDTAIL TRIGGERFISH

grooves

3 spines

OCEAN SUNFISH

no true caudal fin

hexagonal pattern

SPINY BOXFISH
Bony box encases body

SLENDER MOLA

Fig. 44 Tetraodontiform fishes

Similar species: Puffers (next family) are not enclosed in a body box.

Puffers: Family Tetraodontidae

Peculiar, torpedo-shaped fishes which can inflate themselves like balloons by swallowing water or air (evidently to discourage predators from attacking them). Skin tough and prickly. Each jaw has a beaklike *bony plate* (composed of 2 powerful teeth). Gill slit *small,* just before pectoral fin. *No* pelvic fins. Short dorsal and anal fins far back on body, opposite each other. Often spotted or barred. Most species are about 1 ft. (30 cm).

The flesh and viscera of puffers can be very toxic, causing a type of food poisoning (known as puffer poisoning) that can be fatal to humans. The lethal nerve toxin is *not* destroyed by cooking, but species in the ne. Pacific are not known to be toxic. Puffers occur in warm waters of all oceans; some enter brackish or fresh water. About 120 species, 3 in our area.

OCEANIC PUFFER   Pl. 46; Fig. 44, p. 297
Lagocephalus lagocephalus
Identification: Note the characteristic puffer shape. Tiny buried spines on throat and belly. Back dark blue; side silver with *black spots;* belly white. Mouth small, with projecting beak of 4 teeth (2 above, 2 below). No pelvic fins. To 2 ft. (61 cm).
Range: Worldwide in warm seas; Mendocino Co. (n. Calif.) southward. **Habitat:** Oceanic; near surface; the most oceanic puffer.
Remarks: In our area usually found cast up on beach.
Similar species: (1) Bullseye Puffer (below) has a dark brown back, covered with darker spots and mottling. (2) Longnose Puffer (p. 299) has a longer snout and short spines on upper back. (3) Porcupinefishes (next family, p. 299) have a single tooth plate in each jaw.

BULLSEYE PUFFER *Sphoeroides annulatus*   Fig. 44, p. 297
Identification: Note the typical puffer shape and fin placement. Brown above, with round dark spots and mottling on back and side; white below. Area between eyes flat, not concave. Body mostly smooth, with tiny buried spines on throat and belly. 7–8 rays in dorsal fin. To 15 in. (38 cm).
Range: San Diego to Peru; rare in Calif. **Habitat:** Near shore.
Similar species: (1) Longnose Puffer (below) has short spines on the back, behind the eyes (this area smooth in Bullseye Puffer), and eyes set closer together and higher so that there is a slight *depression* between them. (2) Oceanic Puffer (above) has 12–15 dorsal fin rays and a shorter snout; is a different color. (3) Our porcupinefishes (next family) have longer spines on the body and their beaklike tooth plates are solid — not divided at the middle.

LONGNOSE PUFFER *Sphoeroides lobatus*   **Fig. 44, p. 297**
Identification: Closely resembles the Bullseye Puffer but has *short spines* on the upper back, behind the eyes. Eyes are set higher, area between them is slightly concave; gap between eyes roughly equals the diameter of 1 eye. Snout long — 4 or more times as long as the distance between the eyes. Dusky above; a series of dusky areas along lower side; belly white. To 10 in. (25 cm).
Range: Redondo Beach (s. Calif.) to Peru; rare in Calif. **Habitat:** Little known; apparently mostly coastal.
Similar species: In Bullseye Puffer (above) eyes are set wider apart (gap nearly equals 2 times the eye diameter); area between eyes is flat; no spines are present on the upper back behind the eyes.

Porcupinefishes: Family Diodontidae

These peculiar, blunt-headed, torpedo-shaped fishes are easily identified by the *elongate spines or quills* (highly modified scales) on the body (Fig. 44, p. 297). Spines are fixed in some species; movable in others. Gill slit is located just in front of the pectoral fin. These fishes resemble puffers (preceding family) in having a beaklike tooth plate in each jaw, but in porcupinefishes the plate is solid — there is *no median groove* dividing each plate. The peculiar beaklike mouth is used to crush hard-shelled invertebrates, such as mollusks.

Like puffers, porcupinefishes also inflate themselves when disturbed — presenting an intimidating large spiny ball to a potential predator. Background usually pale, with darker brown to black spots, bars, blotches, or reticulations. Most of these fishes are small — about 1 ft. (30 cm) — some grow to 3 ft. (91 cm).

Porcupinefishes occur in all warm seas. Most species live on the bottom in inshore waters, but others live at moderate depths and some are pelagic. Like puffers, they can be very poisonous and should not be eaten. In many parts of the world, porcupinefishes are dried while their bodies are inflated, and sold as curios. About 20 species, 3 rarely reach our area.

PACIFIC BURRFISH   **Fig. 44, p. 297**
Chilomycterus affinis
Identification: Easily identified by the numerous *fixed spines* on the body. Bluish with dark spots above; whitish below. To about 20 in. (51 cm).
Range: Warm waters of Pacific; San Pedro (s. Calif.) to Galapagos Is. and Peru. **Habitat:** Coral or rocky areas in shallow water.
Remarks: Usually found washed up on beaches.

Similar species: (1) Balloonfish and (2) Spotted Porcupinefish (below) have more spines, which are longer and *movable.* (2) In puffers (preceding family), each beaklike tooth plate is *divided by a* median *groove* (not divided in Pacific Burrfish or in other porcupinefishes).

BALLOONFISH *Diodon holocanthus*　　　　**Not shown**
Identification: Very similar to Spotted Porcupinefish (Fig. 44), with long movable spines covering the body. A broad dark bar passes through the eye; usually 4 large dark saddles are present on back. Rest of body brownish yellow with dark brown spots. To about 1½ ft. (46 cm).
Range: Worldwide in tropical seas; rarely s. Calif. **Habitat:** Usually shallow inshore areas.
Similar species: Spotted Porcupinefish (below) lacks the dark bar through the eye and the dark saddles on the upper back; it has spotted fins and shorter spines on the body.

SPOTTED PORCUPINEFISH　　　　**Fig. 44, p. 297**
Diodon hystrix
Identification: Body covered with long movable spines. *No dark bar* through the eye. Light brown to whitish, often with greenish tints; belly white. Dark spots on body and fins. To about 3 ft. (91 cm), but usually about 1 ft. (30 cm).
Range: Worldwide in warm seas; San Diego to Chile. **Habitat:** Shallow water and to about 165 ft. (50 m).
Similar species: (1) See Balloonfish (above). (2) Pacific Burrfish (p. 299) has shorter, *fixed* spines on the body.

Molas: Family Molidae

Strange, large oceanic fishes with an unusual shape. Rear of body appears to be cut-off — caudal fin reduced to a leathery flap with a scalloped rear edge. Gill slit *tiny,* located just in front of pectoral fin. Mouth small; teeth united and beaklike. 1 dorsal fin opposite the anal fin, far back. No pelvic fins. Skin rough, leathery. Young — under 2 in. (5.1 cm) — have spines on the body. Molas are gray above; silvery gray-brown on side; paler or dusky below. 3 species in the family; 2 reach at least 10 ft. (305 cm), 3rd one grows to about 2½ ft. (76 cm); largest specimen estimated at 3300 lb. (about 1500 kg).

Molas eat jellyfishes, but are also known to feed on other fishes and algae. They are pelagic fishes found worldwide in tropical to temperate seas. 2 species in our area.

OCEAN SUNFISH *Mola mola*　　　　**Pl. 46; Fig. 44, p. 297**
Identification: Note the strange shape: body nearly oval, with a blunt rear end. Mouth tiny. 1 dorsal fin far back, opposite anal fin.

Gill slit small, in front of pectoral fin. Gray to silvery. Huge — at least to 10 ft. (305 cm), possibly to 13 ft. (396 cm); can weigh over 3000 lb. (1361 kg), but in our area rarely weighs over 100 lb. (45 kg). **Range:** Worldwide in tropical and temperate seas; B.C. to S. America in e. Pacific. **Habitat:** Oceanic, at surface.
Remarks: Often seen "basking" at surface; sometimes jumps out of water. Flaps its dorsal and anal fins from side to side for propulsion. Occasionally caught on hook and line, also speared, gaffed, or netted. Usually heavily infested with parasites, but some people consider this fish good eating.
Similar species: Slender Mola (below) is more elongate (body more than twice as long as it is deep) and its mouth is in a vertical slit that cannot be closed.

SLENDER MOLA *Ranzania laevis*   **Fig. 44, p. 297**
Identification: Similar to Ocean Sunfish but more slender (depth of body changes with growth — about 2 times as long as it is deep in large specimens). Mouth small, inside a vertical slit that *cannot* be closed. Dusky on back, silvery on side; usually with white streaks below the eye. To 2 ft. (46 cm).
Range: Tropical Pacific; San Luis Obispo Co. (cen. Calif.) to Chile; rare north of Mexico. **Habitat:** Oceanic; at surface.
Similar species: Not likely to be confused with any other fish except the Ocean Sunfish (above).

Glossary
Selected References
Index

Glossary

Some of the terms below have broader (or alternate) meanings, but they are defined here as they apply specifically to fishes. For anatomical features that are illustrated in this book, a cross-reference is given (in **boldface**) after the definition:

(F) = on the front endpapers
(R) = on the rear endpapers
(Fig.) = in a text figure (line drawings are numbered in sequence throughout the text)

Abdomen: The belly or lower surface of a fish, especially between the pelvic fins and the anus.

Abdominal: Refers to the location of the pelvic fins on the belly. **(R)**

Adipose eyelid: Fatty, translucent tissue that partially covers the eyeball in some fishes.

Adipose fin: A small fleshy fin with no rays or spines; located on the back (just before the caudal fin) in some fishes. **(F)**

Alar spines: A group of spines near the disk edge in some male skates. (See also **malar spines**.)

Anadromous: Moving from the sea into fresh water to spawn, as in salmons and shads.

Anal fin: A median fin located on the undersurface, usually just behind the anus; rarely notched or subdivided. **(F)**

Anterior: Front; located toward the front.

Anus: The rear external opening of the digestive tract; the vent. **(F)**

Axil: The inner base of a pectoral fin; the "armpit."

Bar: A vertical band of color. (Compare with **stripe.**)

Barbel: An elongate projection (usually fleshy and whiskerlike) found on the lower surface of the head or near the mouth in some fishes.

Base of fin: The part of a fin that is attached to the body.

Bathypelagic: In the deep sea — deeper than about 1200 ft. (366 m); refers to the habitat of deepsea fishes.

Benthic: Living on or near the bottom or in close association with the bottom.

Blind side: The light-colored underside, which lacks eyes, in flatfishes.

Branchiostegal rays: Raylike bony supports for the gill membranes, located at the throat.

Breast: The chest area; usually in front of the pelvic fins. **(F)**

Canine: A pointed, conical tooth, which is usually larger than the surrounding teeth.

Cartilaginous: Made of cartilage. Cartilage is the translucent material that makes up the skeleton of young fishes, which persists in adults of some species (notably sharks and rays) but is largely converted to bone in most fishes.

Caudal fin: A median fin at the rear of body; the "tail fin." **(F, R)**

Caudal peduncle: The narrower part of the body just before the caudal fin; usually refers to the part of a fish between the rear of anal fin and the base of the caudal fin. **(F)**

Cirrus (*pl.* cirri): A small, thin flap of skin; a fleshy appendage that can be located anywhere on the fish (on the eyeball, on a nostril, on top of the head, along the lateral line, etc.).

Clasper: A fleshy modified part of the pelvic fins in male sharks and their relatives; used in transfer of sperm. **(F)**

Compressed: Flattened from side to side.

Concave: Bowed or curved inward.

Continuous: Unbroken; usually refers to a dorsal fin in which the spinous part is joined to the soft-rayed part, with no gap or notch between the two. **(R)**

Convex: Bowed or curved outward.

Copepods: A group of tiny crustaceans. Some are free-swimming; others are parasitic on fishes.

Corselet: A scaled area on the front of the body in certain tunalike fishes. **(Fig. 41)**

Crescent-shaped: Shaped like a quarter moon; used to describe the shape of the caudal fin (see **lunate**), or pigmented patches on a fish's body.

Crustaceans: A large class of arthropods, usually covered with a horny shell (such as shrimps and crabs).

Ctenoid: A type of scale; the rear (exposed) edge of each scale is toothed, making the scale rough to touch. **(R)**

Cusp: The main point of a tooth (compare with **cusplet**); used here for shark teeth. **(Fig. 3)**

Cusplet: A small projection on a tooth; used here in reference to shark teeth. **(Fig. 3)**

Cycloid: Another type of scale, with a smooth rear edge; which makes the scale smooth to touch. **(R)**

Denticles: Small teeth; usually refers to prickles (modified scales) on some fishes, especially sharks and rays.

Disk: (1) The flat, nearly round body of skates and rays, formed by pectoral fins that are fully attached to the body. **(F)**
(2) An adhesive (clinging) organ in some fishes, such as clingfishes, snailfishes, and remoras. **(Figs. 32–33)**

Dorsal: Above; on top.

Dorsal fin: A median, rayed fin on the back, often notched or subdivided; sometimes fully divided into 2 separate fins. **(F, R)**

Echinoderms: A group (phylum) of marine invertebrates, including starfishes and sea urchins.

Embedded: Used to describe scales that are buried or wholly covered by skin.

Epipelagic: At or near the surface; usually in the open ocean.

Eyed side: In flatfishes, the dark-colored side, on which both eyes are located.

Eyespot: See **ocellus.**

Filamentous: Threadlike; usually refers to elongated fin rays or barbels.

Finlet: A small rayed fin, usually in a series, and often following the main dorsal or anal fin (as in tunas and mackerels).

Forked: Usually applied to a caudal fin with a distinct upper and lower lobe, separated by a deep notch. **(R)**

Fusiform: Cigar-shaped; tapering at both ends (usually refers to body shape).

Gas bladder: An air sac found in many fishes, which is located under the spinal column, above the gut cavity; also called the swim bladder by some researchers.

Genital papilla: A small, fleshy swelling or projection near the anus in some fishes; sometimes developed into a penis-like structure.

Gills: The respiratory organs in fishes; including the highly vascularized filaments that are used to extract oxygen from the water. **(R)**

Gill arch: The bony support to which the gill filaments and gill rakers are attached. **(R)**

Gill chamber: The cavity where the gills are located.

Gill cover: A bony flap that covers the outside of the gill chamber. **(F)**

Gill openings: The openings at the rear of the head, from the gill chamber to the outside (most fishes have 1 on each side); called gill slits in sharks and rays. **(F)**

Gill rakers: Bony, toothlike projections from the front edge of the gill arch, opposite the gill filaments; often used as water filters to trap food items between the gill arches. **(R)**

Gill slits: The slitlike gill openings (5–7 on each side) in sharks and rays. **(F)**

Habitat: The place where a fish (or other kind of animal) normally lives.

Head length: The length as measured from the tip of the snout to the rear edge of the gill cover.

Herbivorous: Vegetarian, feeding on plants; among fishes, those that feed on algae.

Hermaphrodite: Having both male and female organs in one body.

Heterocercal: A type of caudal fin in which the vertebral column extends into the upper lobe, which is usually larger. **(R)**

Incised: Cut away or notched (such as the fin membranes between the spines).

Incisors: Front teeth that are flattened to form a cutting edge.

Indented: Usually refers to the shape of the rear of the caudal fin; with a slight notch at the middle. **(R)**

Interorbital: Between the eyes (orbits).

Intertidal: Between high-water mark and low-water mark; also refers to fishes living in this area, especially tidepool fishes.

Isthmus: A narrow extension of the throat between the gill chambers.

Jugular: In the throat area; usually refers to location of the pelvic fins.

Juvenile: Young of a species; usually a miniature version of the adult.

Keel: A horizontal (shelflike) fleshy or bony ridge; often located at the base of the caudal fin. **(F)**

Labial groove: A groove or furrow at the corner of the mouth in sharks. **(Fig. 9)**

Larva (*pl.* larvae): Newborn; the developmental stage of a fish before it becomes a juvenile.

Lateral: Side; on the side.

Lateral line: A row of porelike openings on head and body; usually applied to the series of pores or pored scales along the side of the fish's body. **(F)**

Leptocephalus: A ribbonlike pelagic larva of eels and some primitive fishes. **(Fig. 12)**

Light organ: A light-producing structure — see **photophore.**

Lunate: Crescent-shaped; usually refers to the shape of the caudal fin. **(R)**

Malar spines: A group of spines near the front of the disk in some male skates (see also **alar spines**).

Maxillary: A bone in the upper jaw, comprising most of the upper jaw or only the rear part of the upper jaw.

Median fin: One of the unpaired fins located on the midline (on the median plane, which divides the body vertically into two halves) — the dorsal, anal, and caudal fins.

Molar: A flat-topped tooth used for crushing food.

Naked: Smooth or unscaled.

Nictitating eyelid: A membrane of skin that can be extended over the eye in some sharks and bony fishes. **(Fig. 5)**

Nocturnal: Active at night.

Nostril: A nasal opening (fishes usually have 2 on each side). **(F)**

Notched: Indented; especially refers to a fin in which some rays (at the middle) are shorter.

Ocellus (*pl.* **ocelli**): An eyelike, pigmented spot; usually dark, bordered by a ring of pale pigment.

Opercle: The thin bone forming most of the gill cover.

Orbit: The bony eye socket.

Orbital: Related to the eye. (See also **interorbital, suborbital.**)

Ovary: Female reproductive gland.

Oviparous: Egg-laying. The eggs develop into embryos after being laid by the female.

Ovoviviparous: Another type of embryonic development, in which the fertilized eggs complete all or nearly all of their development inside the female's body before they hatch. (Compare with **viviparous.)**

Papilla (*pl.* **papillae**): A small fleshy knob or projection.

Pectoral fin: One of a pair of fins (one on each side) that are attached to the shoulder girdle, behind the head. **(F)**

Peduncle: See **caudal peduncle.**

Pelagic: Found in open water; in the water column, usually near the surface.

Pelvic fin: One of a pair of fins on the lower surface of the body, usually located below the pectoral fins. **(F, R)**

Peritoneum: The membrane lining the abdominal cavity.

Photophore: A dotlike light-producing organ.

Plankton: Small plants (called phytoplankton) and animals (called zooplankton) that are mostly free-floating in the ocean currents.

Pore: A tiny opening in the skin; usually involved with sensory perception in fishes.

Posterior: Rear, behind; toward the rear.

Precaudal pit: In sharks, a horizontal notch just in front of the caudal fin (which may be on the upper or lower part of the caudal peduncle). **(F)**

Preopercle (*adj.,* **preopercular**): A cheek bone, at the front of the gill cover (which often bears spines, as in sculpins). **(F)**

Protrusible: Refers to the mouth; having jaws that can be protruded (thrust forward and out).

Reticulate: Color markings in a chainlike pattern or network.

Rostral: Pertaining to the snout; a beaklike extension or plate at the tip of the snout.

Scapular spine: A spine on the disk of some skates, on each side of midline, on back. **(F)**

Scute: A bony projection, often a modified scale.

Serrate: Sawlike; usually refers to a sawtoothed edge.

Snout: The part of head in front of the eyes. **(F)**

Soft dorsal fin: A median fin on the back, composed entirely of soft fin rays, or having one stiff spine at the front. **(F, R)**

Soft ray: A flexible, jointed (segmented) fin ray; often branched. **(R)**

Spine: (1) A bony projection, usually on the head. (2) A single hard, unbranched ray in a fin — a spinous ray. **(R)**

Spinous ray: A hard spine (fin ray), with no segments or branches. **(R)**

Spiracle: The opening (behind the eye) of a separate duct or canal that leads to the gill chamber in sharks, skates, and rays, and certain primitive fishes. (Not the gill opening.) **(F)**

Sting: The long spine on the tail of some skates and rays.

Striations: Small ridges or lines, found on the gill cover or head bones of some fishes.

Stripe: A horizontal band of color. (Compare with **bar**.)

Suborbital: Below the eyes.

Subspecies: A geographic subgroup within one species; when designated, the subspecies name follows the species name.

Subtidal: Just below the low-water mark; also refers to fishes living in this area.

Tail: The area of the body behind the anus in most fishes (not just the tail fin).

Terminal lobe: The rear part of the upper lobe of the caudal fin in sharks. **(F)**

Territorial: Defending a home (such as a burrow or reef crevice) or a particular area.

Testis (*pl.* testes): Male reproductive gland.

Thoracic: In the breast area (refers to pelvic fin location). **(R)**

Truncate: Having a sqaure-cut rear edge (refers to the shape of the caudal fin). **(R)**

Tubercles: Small (often cone-shaped) projections.

Vent: The combined external opening of the digestive, urinary, and reproductive tubes. **(F)**

Ventral: On the lower surface; on the belly.

Vermiculations: A color pattern of short, wavy (often wormlike) lines or spots.

Viviparous: Giving birth to live young. The young are nourished by a placentalike structure in the mother before their birth. (Compare with **ovoviviparous** and **oviparous**.)

Vomerine: Pertaining to the vomer — usually a median bone in the front of the roof of the mouth; often used to describe location of teeth on this bone.

Selected References

The information used to prepare a Field Guide like this one is drawn primarily from technical papers. We do not cite them here because of the nature of this book and space limitations. Listed below are general books and articles that provide additional information and serve as sources for the technical literature.

Pacific Coast Marine Fishes

Clemens, W.A., and G.V. Wilby. 1961. *Fishes of the Pacific Coast of Canada*. Fisheries Research Board (Canada) Bulletin 68. 2nd ed.

Fitch, John E., and Robert J. Lavenberg. 1968. *Deep-water Teleostean Fishes of California*. California Natural History Guides, vol. 25. Berkeley: Univ. of California Press.

―――. 1971. *Marine Food and Game Fishes of California*. California Natural History Guides, vol. 28. Berkeley: Univ. of California Press.

―――. 1975. *Tidepool and Nearshore Fishes of California*. California Natural History Guides, vol. 38. Berkeley: Univ. of California Press.

Hart, J.L. 1973. *Pacific Fishes of Canada*. Fisheries Research Board (Canada) Bulletin 180.

Hubbs, Carl L., W. I. Follett, and Lillian J. Dempster. 1979. *List of the Fishes of California*. Occasional Papers of the California Academy of Sciences, no. 133.

Miller, Daniel J., and Robert N. Lea. 1972. *Guide to the Coastal Marine Fishes of California*. Calif. Dept. of Fish & Game, Fish Bulletin 157. (1976 edition includes an addendum.)

Quast, Jay C., and Elizabeth L. Hall. 1972. *List of Fishes of Alaska and Adjacent Waters with a Guide to some of their Literature*. Washington, D.C.: U.S. Dept. of Commerce, NOAA Technical Report NMFS SSRF-658.

Squire, James L., Jr., and Susan E. Smith. 1977. *Anglers' Guide to the United States Pacific Coast*. Washington, D.C.: U.S. Dept. of Commerce, NOAA, National Marine Fisheries Service.

Thomson, Donald A., Lloyd T. Finley, and Alex N. Kerstitch.

1979. *Reef Fishes of the Sea of Cortez*. New York: John Wiley & Sons.

Walford, Lionel A. 1974. *Marine Game Fishes of the Pacific Coast from Alaska to the Equator*. Reprint. Neptune City, N.J.: T.F.H. Publications.

General Books on Ichthyology

Bond, Carl E. 1979. *The Biology of Fishes*. Philadelphia: W. B. Saunders Co.

Herald, Earl S. 1962. *Living Fishes of the World*. Rev. ed. New York: Doubleday & Co.

———. 1972. *Fishes of North America*. New York: Doubleday and Co.

Lagler, Karl F., John E. Bardach, Robert R. Miller, and Dora R. Passino. 1977. *Ichthyology*. 2nd ed. New York: John Wiley & Sons.

Marshall, N.B. 1966. *The Life of Fishes*. New York: Universe Books.

Migdalski, Edward C., and George S. Fichter. 1976. *The Fresh & Salt Water Fishes of the World*. New York: Alfred A. Knopf.

Nelson, Joseph S. 1976. *Fishes of the World*. New York: John Wiley & Sons.

Norman, J.R., and P.H. Greenwood. 1963. *A History of Fishes*. 2nd ed. New York: Hill and Wang.

Robins, C. Richard, *et al.* (eds). 1980. *A List of Common and Scientific Names of Fishes from the United States and Canada*. 4th ed. American Fisheries Society, Special Publication 12.

Wheeler, Alwyne C. 1975. *Fishes of the World: An Illustrated Dictionary*. New York: Macmillan Publishing Co.

Fish Photography

Emery, Alan R., and Richard Winterbottom. 1980. A technique for fish specimen photography in the field. *Canadian Journal of Zoology,* vol. 58, no. 11:2158–2162.

Randall, John E. 1961. A technique for fish photography. *Copeia,* no. 2 (1961):241–242.

Index

The common and scientific names of all fishes discussed in this *Field Guide* are listed in the Index below. Alternate or obsolete names are followed by an equals sign (=) and the current preferred name for the species. Numbers in **boldface** type after common names refer to the plates on which species are illustrated. Pages where additional illustrations of species (whole specimens) appear in the text are listed in *italics*. The *see under* cross-references usually follow 2 types of entries: those for extralimital species and species that serve as representatives for certain deepsea families.

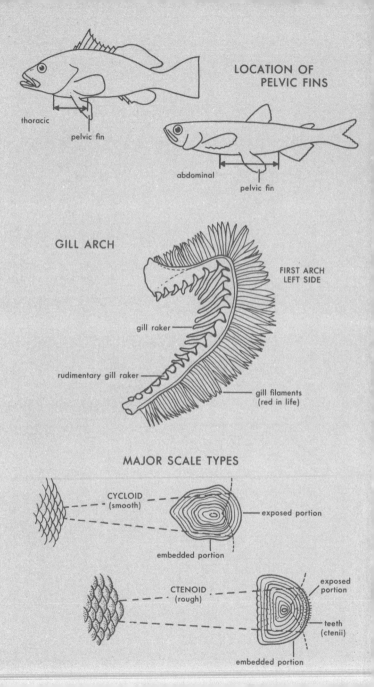

LOCATION OF PELVIC FINS

thoracic

pelvic fin

abdominal

pelvic fin

GILL ARCH

FIRST ARCH
LEFT SIDE

gill raker

rudimentary gill raker

gill filaments
(red in life)

MAJOR SCALE TYPES

CYCLOID
(smooth)

exposed portion

embedded portion

CTENOID
(rough)

exposed
portion

teeth
(ctenii)

embedded portion